Collins

Scotland

Touring
Guide

Published by Collins
An imprint of HarperCollins*Publishers*
77-85 Fulham Palace Road
London W6 8JB

www.collins.co.uk
www.collinsbartholomew.com

First published 1998
New edition 2000, 2002, 2004, 2006
Text © HarperCollins*Publishers* Limited 2006
Maps © Collins Bartholomew Limited 2006

The Publisher would like to thank everyone who has helped in the provision of
information for this publication, particularly VisitScotland, staff of the Area Tourist Boards
and Tourist Information Centres throughout Scotland, Historic Scotland, the National
Trust for Scotland, Forest Enterprise, the Royal Society for the Protection of Birds, Scottish
Natural Heritage, and all of the visitor attractions which provided information.

The Publisher welcomes comments from readers. Please write to:
Touring Guide/Map Scotland, HarperCollins Reference, HarperCollins Publishers, Westerhill
Road, Bishopbriggs, Glasgow, G64 2QT or email touring@harpercollins.co.uk

Printed and bound in Great Britain by Clays Ltd, St Ives plc.
ISBN-13 978-0-00-721797-7
ISBN-10 0-00-721797-8
SJ12055

Front cover : The A93 between Braemar and Blairgowrie
Back Cover : Post box on the Isle of Skye
Credit : © Paul Tomkins, VisitScotland/Scottish Viewpoint

CONTENTS

INTRODUCTION

HOW TO USE THIS GUIDE

This new edition of the *Touring Guide Scotland* features over 1700 visitor attractions and is one of the most comprehensive gazetteers of places to visit and things to do in Scotland.

Attractions are listed alphabetically within regions, according to the name of the attraction. The location is only given when it is part of the attraction name, eg Alloa Tower. The exceptions to this are attractions in Aberdeen, Dundee, Edinburgh, Glasgow, Inverness and Perth – as there are so many attractions close together, they are listed under the name of the city, to make planning a day out easier.

Each attraction is numbered (eg **56**) and the numbers appear on the location maps (see pages 12–25). The number is also used for reference in the index (see pages 374–384). Attractions are indexed within subject areas. Each attraction also has a map reference (eg **2 E4**) to help you pinpoint the location of each attraction on the maps. The first number (**2**) refers to the location map, the letter and number (**E4**) refer to the grid square in which the attraction is located.

Many of the properties listed in this guide are owned or managed by charities or statutory bodies. We have indicated where an attraction is under the care of Historic Scotland (HS), The National Trust for Scotland (NTS), Forest Enterprise (FE) and the Royal Society for the Protection of Birds (RSPB).

The following information is given on each attraction: address/location; how to get to the attraction by public transport (if relevant); opening times; admission charge (if free, stated thus, otherwise, based on the adult admission price – up to £3 indicated by £, £3–£5 indicated by ££, £5 and over indicated by £££); facilities such as refreshments and parking; followed by a brief description of what the attraction has to offer. We assume that guided tours (where available) are in English. If they are provided in other languages, or if translated material is available, this is stated.

For disabled visitors, we have used three categories to describe access: *wheelchair access* (most or all of the site is accessible, no more than one step, no rough terrain, but not all the footpaths may be suitable); *wheelchair access with assistance* (two or more steps, but not as many as a flight); *limited wheelchair access* (easy access to part of the site, but the rest may not be possible because of stairs, rough ground). Where no access is indicated this is because it is strenuous or dangerous. We assume that all attractions welcome guide dogs. Where dogs are not admitted, this is mentioned in the text. Special facilities for deaf and blind visitors are mentioned.

Visitor attraction opening and closing times, and other details, often change. It is always advisable to check with the visitor attraction in advance. Telephone numbers and, where available, websites are listed for each attraction.

SCOTLAND BY REGION

We have split Scotland into eight regions and a brief description of each is given below. For further information on the areas highlighted, contact the relevant Area Tourist Board (see page 9).

South of Scotland

The **Scottish Borders** is an area of tranquil villages and textile towns, with a soft rolling landscape and a rugged coastline. Visitors can enjoy a wide range of attractions, from craft workshops to magnificent historic houses and the great Border abbeys. The beautiful natural surroundings of **Dumfries and Galloway** – lochs and craggy hills, rugged cliffs and long sandy beaches, are ideal for fishing, golfing, birdwatching, walking and cycling, and there are a large number of beautiful gardens. **Ayrshire and Arran** offer all the contrasts of mainland and island life. The island of Arran, easily reached by ferry, has been a playground for generations of outdoor enthusiasts. On the mainland visitors can explore the area's industrial history, numerous golf courses and enjoy the heritage of Robert Burns, Scotland's most famous poet.

Edinburgh and Lothians
Edinburgh, Scotland's capital, needs little introduction. Edinburgh Castle dominates the skyline and, from the castle, the Royal Mile sweeps down through the medieval Old Town. As well as hosting the largest arts festival in the world, Edinburgh offers a wide range of galleries, theatres and museums. The surrounding **Lothians** ring Edinburgh with country houses and ruined castles and offer space for outdoor activities as well as a variety of nature and heritage-based attractions.

Greater Glasgow and Clyde Valley
Glasgow is Scotland's largest city and one of Europe's great cultural destinations, with over 20 museums and galleries. It is the UK's biggest retail centre outside London, with the top names in fashion and design. The **Clyde Valley** is a complete contrast, with dramatic ruined castles, industrial heritage and country parks.

West Highlands and Islands, Loch Lomond, Stirling and Trossachs
From the islands of Coll and Tiree, lying in the Hebridean Sea to the west, to the green slopes of the Ochil Hills east of Stirling, this area of Scotland straddles Highland and Lowland and encompasses Scotland's first national park, Loch Lomond and the Trossachs National Park. Peaceful glens, shapely peaks and clear lochs contrast vividly with the gentle hills and historic towns of the lowlands.

Perthshire, Angus and Dundee, and the Kingdom of Fife
Perthshire, located just 80 miles (129km) north of Edinburgh and Glasgow, is an ideal holiday destination. The area has mountains, lochs and castles, as well as fine theatres, museums and restaurants. **Angus and Dundee** make a good touring base, with mountainous glens, rugged coastline, pleasant beaches and plenty to see and do. The ancient **Kingdom of Fife** has plenty of character. The attractive East Neuk fishing villages nestle amongst the natural harbours of the coastline, and St Andrews is the location of the oldest university in Scotland, and, of course, the home of golf.

Aberdeen and Grampian Highlands – Scotland's Castle and Whisky Country
This quiet corner of Scotland is rich in historic castles, royal connections and whisky distilleries. The **North East Coast** has more than 100 miles (160km) of unspoilt coastline and the **Grampian Highlands** contain more mountain tops over 4000 feet (1219m) than anywhere else in Scotland. Follow the Castle Trail or take the Royal Road along the beautiful Dee Valley and visit Balmoral Castle.

The Highlands of Scotland
One of the last wildernesses in Europe and the location of Scotland's newest national park, Cairngorms National Park. From the soaring crags of Glen Coe to the wide rolling moors of Caithness, from the old pinewoods of upper Speyside to the spectacular Cuillin mountains of Skye, the north and west offer unmatched scenic splendour. **The Highlands of Scotland** are rich in places to visit, with castles, battlefields and forts to remind you of a turbulent past, while distilleries, woollen mills and other crafts contribute to today's diverse Highland economy.

The Outer Islands
The Outer Islands are for those looking for a totally different experience. **Orkney** is made up of 70 islands, rich in historical and archaeological remains. Here you will find villages, burial chambers and standing stones built before the great pyramids of Egypt. **Shetland**, a cluster of islands set between Scotland and Scandinavia, shares something of the character of both, while guarding a rich local identity. Magnificent seascapes and fine seabird colonies are among the many features of these untamed islands. The **Outer Hebrides,** a 130-mile long chain of islands lying to the north west of Scotland, offer a unique experience. The combinations of land, sea and loch produced landscapes which have been designated areas of outstanding scenic value.

TRANSPORT AND ACCOMMODATION

Driving

Many visitors choose to see Scotland by road – distances are short and roads are generally uncrowded. The motorways and trunk roads are fast and efficient, with plenty of services en route. If you are not in a hurry, follow one of the many designated routes and trails. National Tourist Routes (see page 7) take the visitor off the motorways and main trunk roads along attractive routes. There are also varied special interest trails – from the Malt Whisky Trail in Speyside to the Castle Trail in Aberdeenshire. Contact Scotland's National Booking and Information Centre (see page 9) for further information.

Comprehensive touring and leisure information can be found on the companion *Touring Map Scotland*.

As you travel around Scotland look out for the tourist signposting – distinctive brown

signs bearing the thistle symbol. These signs will direct you to a wide variety of things to do and places to visit. They are also used to indicate the National Tourist Routes and the tourist trails mentioned above.

In common with the rest of the UK, all driving in Scotland is on the left and overtaking is permissible only on the right. Particular care is needed at roundabouts (priority is given to traffic from the right, and you should go round the roundabout in a clockwise direction) and on single track roads, where passing places must be used to overtake.

Speed limits are as follows: dual carriageways 70mph (112kph); single carriageways 60mph (96kph); built-up areas (unless otherwise signposted) 30mph (48kph). The maximum speed limit for camper vans and caravans is 50mph (80kph).

Parking is restricted on yellow lines. Many towns have a system of metered or 'pay and display' parking. Car parks can be found in most cities, towns and villages. Look out for the P symbol.

Although there are no tolls on Scottish roads, three bridges do have a toll charge – the Forth, Tay and Erskine bridges.

All filling stations provide LRP (lead replacement petrol), unleaded petrol and diesel. In remote areas distances between stations may be greater and opening hours shorter.

It is compulsory to wear seatbelts at all times. Small children and babies must be restrained with an appropriate child seat or carrier.

Public Transport

There is a good internal rail network in Scotland. Multi-journey tickets and discount cards allow you to save on fares. Local bus companies in Scotland offer explorer tickets and discount cards. Postbuses (normally minibuses) take passengers on rural routes throughout Scotland. Ferries to and around the islands are regular and reliable; most ferries carry vehicles, although some travelling to smaller islands convey only passengers.

Contact Scotland's National Booking and Information Centre (see page 9), or call in to any Tourist Information Centre for information. Alternatively, contact the following travel companies direct:

Airlines

British Airways
Telephone (0870) 8509850
www.ba.com

bmi
Telephone (0870) 6070555
www.flybmi.com

bmi baby
Telephone (0870) 2642229
www.bmibaby.com

Eastern Airways
Telephone (0905) 8210905
www.easternairways.com

easyJet
Telephone (0905) 8210905
www.easyjet.com

Flybe
Telephone (01392) 268500
www.flybe.com

flyglobespan
www.flyglobespan.com

Jet 2
Telephone (0871) 2261737
www.jet2.com

Ryanair
Telephone (0871) 2460000
www.ryanair.com

ScotAirways
Telephone (0870) 6060707
www.scotairways.com

National Public Transport Timetable
For all bus, coach and rail enquiries
Telephone (0870) 6082608
www.traveline.org.uk

Bus companies
National Express
Telephone (08705) 808080
www.nationalexpress.com

Scottish Citylink
Telephone (08705) 505050
www.citylink.co.uk

Ferry companies
Caledonian MacBrayne
(west coast of Scotland and Firth of Clyde)
Telephone (08705) 650000
www.calmac.co.uk

Corran
(Ardgour and Nether Lochaber)
Telephone (01397) 709000
www.lochabertransport.org.uk/
corranferry.html

John o'Groats Ferries
(John o'Groats and Orkney)
Telephone (01955) 611353
www.jogferry.co.uk

Skye Ferry
(Glenelg and Kylerhea)
Telephone (01599) 511302
www.skyeferry.co.uk

Northlink Ferries
(Aberdeen, Scrabster, Orkney and Shetland)
Telephone (0845) 6000449
www.northlinkferries.co.uk

Orkney Ferries Ltd
(Orkney mainland and islands)
Telephone (01856) 872044
www.orkneyferries.co.uk

Pentland Ferries
(Gills Bay and Orkney)
Telephone (01856) 831226
www.pentlandferries.com

ASP Seascot (Islay and Jura)
Telephone (01496) 840681
www.juradevelopment.co.uk/ ferry

Shetland Islands Council
(Inter-island services)
Telephone (01595) 693434
www.shetland.gov.uk

Western Ferries
(Gourock and Dunoon)
Telephone (01369) 704452
www.western-ferries.co.uk

6° West
(Gairloch and Portree)
www.overtheseatoskye.com
Telephone (01445) 712777

Rail companies
National Rail Enquiries
Telephone (0845) 7484950
www.nationalrail.co.uk

GNER
Telephone (08457) 225225
www.gner.co.uk

First ScotRail
Telephone (08457) 550033
www.firstscotrail.com

Virgin Trains
Telephone (08457) 222333
www.virgintrains.co.uk

Where to stay
There is an extensive choice of bed and breakfast (B&B) accommodation in Scotland, and somewhere to stay for all budgets – hotels, guest houses, youth hostels, lodges, caravan and camping parks and self-catering accommodation. VisitScotland produces four accommodation guides, revised annually, covering all types of accommodation and including VisitScotland's star system – the more stars, the better the quality.

Information for visitors with mobility difficulties

VisitScotland operates an inspection scheme to assess accommodation with disabled provision. These form three categories of accessibility – unassisted wheelchair access, assisted wheelchair access, access for those with mobility difficulties. Many establishments will be able to cater for those with a sensory impairment but please do check with the proprietor before booking.

Capability Scotland
Advice Service
11 Ellersly Road
Edinburgh EH12 6HY
Telephone 0131 313 5510
Textphone 0131 346 2529
www.capability-scotland.org.uk

Radar
Information Department
12 City Forum, 250 City Road
London
EC1V 8AF
Telephone 020 7250 3222
www.radar.org.uk

Tourism For All
The Hawkins Suite
Enham Place
Enham Alamein
Andover, SP11 6JS
Telephone 0845 1249971
www.tourismforall.org.uk

NATIONAL TOURIST ROUTES

Scotland has 12 National Tourist Routes designed to provide an alternative to the main trunk roads and motorways. Varying in length and as diverse as the Scottish landscape itself, these routes also offer a variety of things to see and do on the way to your chosen destination. They are all well signposted and easy to follow.

Angus Coastal Route *(58 miles/93km)*

Begins in Dundee, with its fascinating industrial heritage and maritime traditions, and takes you north towards Aberdeen. Along the way you will discover a spectacular coastline with picturesque seaside resorts, sandy beaches, championship golf courses, nature reserves, country parks and a fertile countryside reaching inland through the Mearns and the Vale of Strathmore to the scenic splendour of the Angus Glens and the Grampians.

Argyll Coastal Route *(149 miles/238km)*

From Tarbet on the bonny banks of Loch Lomond, climb steadily to a famous beauty spot called, aptly, Rest-and-be-Thankful. Descend to Inveraray and continue to follow the shores of Loch Fyne to Lochgilphead. Turning north, pass the lovely Crinan Canal and proceed to the bustling holiday town of Oban. Here there is an exceptionally fine view across the Firth of Lorn and the Sound of Mull to the Inner Hebrides. From Oban, cross the impressive Connel Bridge and journey on up through Ballachulish to Fort William at the foot of Ben Nevis.

Borders Historic Route *(95 miles/152km)*

Travelling in either direction between the great northern English city of Carlisle and Scotland's capital, Edinburgh, savour the area which has been at the heart of Scotland's history and culture for centuries and a major inspiration for Sir Walter Scott's romantic novels. Follow in the footsteps of the Reivers by crossing the border between England and Scotland at Scots Dyke and explore Royal Burghs, historic houses and visitor centres. Borders hospitality, local goods, crafts and culture make this journey a memorable start or finish to your visit to Scotland.

Clyde Valley Route *(42 miles/67km)*

Turn off the M74 at Abington (or Hamilton from the opposite direction) to follow the

River Clyde through an area of contrasting landscapes, rich in historical interest. Attractions include the World Heritage village of New Lanark, the model industrial community brainchild of philanthropist, Robert Owen, founded by his father-in-law David Dale. Visit the magnificently restored Chatelherault, near Hamilton, the David Livingstone Centre at Blantyre or the cluster of fascinating museums around the market town of Biggar. Or take advantage of the extensive watersport facilities, theme park and nature trails at Strathclyde Country Park.

Deeside Tourist Route *(107 miles/171km)*
From Perth all the way to Aberdeen. The area around Blairgowrie has long been associated with soft fruit growing, and Blairgowrie itself is a popular touring base. Thereafter, the Highland landscape takes over as the route climbs to 2182 feet (665m) on Britain's highest main road. Enjoy spectacular views in every direction as you pass through the Glenshee Ski Centre before descending to Braemar. In Royal Deeside drive past Balmoral Castle, summer residence of the Royal Family. Continue through the delightful villages of Ballater, Aboyne and Banchory before finally reaching Aberdeen.

Fife Coastal Route *(85 miles/136km)*
Between the Firths of Forth and Tay lies the historic Kingdom of Fife. Best known is St Andrews, home of golf and seat of Scotland's oldest university. Just south of St Andrews are the picturesque villages of the East Neuk with their distinctive pantiled roofs and unspoilt beaches. More golden sands can be enjoyed at Burntisland and Aberdour. Dunfermline is the country's ancient capital, the Westminster of the North and final resting place of Robert the Bruce. Don't miss Deep Sea World at North Queensferry, or Culross, an outstanding example of a 16th-century town.

Forth Valley Route *(39 miles/62km)*
This short route from Edinburgh to Stirling takes in the attractive old burgh of South Queensferry, dominated by the mighty Forth Bridges. Nearby are Dalmeny House and the elegant Hopetoun House, one of Scotland's finest mansions. Alternatively, take a trip on the Union Canal from Ratho or delve into the Lothians' clay mining heritage. Visit the bustling town of Falkirk, with its impressive Callendar House, or take a nostalgic ride on the Bo'ness and Kinneil Steam Railway.

Galloway Tourist Route *(96 miles/154km)*
This route, stretching from Gretna to Ayr, links the Robert Burns attractions in both Dumfries and Ayr. En route, it gives you an introduction to the Galloway Forest Park and the industrial heritage of the Doon Valley. Look out for the Old Blacksmith's Shop at Gretna Green, the award-winning Robert Burns Centre and Bridge House Museum in Dumfries, or the Carsphairn Heritage Centre. Enjoy the peace and tranquility of colourful Threave Garden, or ponder over the bloody history of Threave Castle, ancient stronghold of the Black Douglas. The Galloway Tourist Route connects with the Solway Coast Heritage Trail at Dalbeattie, providing an opportunity to visit the castles, abbeys, gardens and harbours further west.

Highland Tourist Route *(118 miles/189km)*
From Aberdeen to Inverness, passing the Grampian Transport Museum at Alford. Continue through the lovely valley of Upper Donside and on up the heather-clad slopes of the Lecht to Tomintoul in the fringes of the Cairngorms, at the heart of whisky country. Take a guided tour round one of the many distilleries and continue on through Grantown-on-Spey, a popular salmon fishing centre, to Inverness, capital of the Highlands.

Moray Firth Route *(80 miles/128km)*
A semi-circular route around three of the most beautiful inlets on the east coast of Britain – the Beauly, Cromarty and Dornoch Firths – north from Inverness into the heart of the northern Highlands. On the way you can enjoy wonderful scenery (the Struie

viewpoint over the Dornoch Firth will take your breath away), seals and clan history at Foulis Ferry, salmon leaping at Shin Falls, whisky being made at Glen Ord and Highland wine at Moniack Castle. Walk to the Fyrish Monument, visit Beauly Priory or learn about the archaeology of the north at Ferrycroft, Lairg.

North and West Highlands Route *(140 miles/224km)*
This route boasts some of the wildest and magnificent scenery in Europe – wild mountains and lochs, foaming salmon rivers, rugged coastlines with mighty sea cliffs and secluded sandy bays, isolated crofts and large farms, small fishing villages and bustling towns. Starting at the thriving fishing village of Ullapool, the route winds its way north through magnificent mountain country to Durness in the north west corner of Scotland. From Durness, the route heads east through gradually softening scenery to John o'Groats, taking you from one end of Scotland's north coast to the other.

Perthshire Tourist Route *(45 miles/72km)*
Beginning north of Dunblane and ending at Ballinluig near Pitlochry. An attractive alternative to the main A9, the route runs through fertile, rolling farmland before arriving at the pleasant hillside town of Crieff. Beyond Crieff the cultivated landscape changes dramatically and gives way to the rugged splendour of the Sma' Glen, associated with Bonnie Prince Charlie. Descend to Aberfeldy and skirt the River Tay on the A827, rejoining the A9 near Pitlochry.

TOURIST INFORMATION
Every one of Scotland's 123 tourist information centres has qualified, friendly and knowledgeable staff able to answer your questions and give expert advice on:
    Events, activities, routes, what to see and do, places of local interest
    Local and national accommodation booking
    Tickets for local and national events, excursions, tours and travel
    Purchase of maps, guide books, Scottish literature and books for holiday reading
    Films, souvenirs, gifts, local crafts, bureau de change

For further information on any aspect of your visit to Scotland, contact Scotland's National Booking and Information Centre on (0845) 22 55 121 (within the UK); +44 (0) 1506 832121 (outwith the UK); email info@visitscotland.com or visit www.visitscotland.com

visitscotland.com
PO Box 121
Livingston
EH54 8AF

* A £3 booking fee applies to telephone bookings of accommodation

Visitor Attraction Quality Assurance
VisitScotland operates an inspection scheme for visitor attractions. The scheme provides an assurance that the condition and standard of the facilities and services have been assessed, alongside the all important warmth of welcome, efficiency and friendliness of service, level of cleanliness and standard of the overall visitor services. The grades are indicated by one to five stars. Look out for the stars when planning your day out.

Association of Scottish Visitor Attractions (ASVA)
As you travel round Scotland, you may see the ASVA symbol displayed at visitor attractions. Over 500 key visitor attractions are members. All are committed to providing a quality service and are always striving to ensure that the highest standards are maintained.

Argyll's Lodging
Castle Wynd
Stirling FK8 1EG
Telephone (01786) 475152
www.asva.co.uk

Welcome Host
When you visit an attraction in Scotland, you may see the Welcome Host badge being worn by staff who have taken part in the Welcome Host training programme, and who have given a personal commitment to providing quality service during your visit.

Other Useful Contacts

British Waterways Scotland
Canal House, Applecross Street
Glasgow G4 9SP
Telephone 0141 332 6936
www.scottishcanals.co.uk

Forestry Commission
Silvan House
231 Corstorphine Road
Edinburgh EH12 7AT
Telephone 0131 334 0303
www.forestry.gov.uk

Historic Houses Association
2 Chester Street
London SW1X 7BB
Telephone 0207 259 5688
www.hha.org.uk

Historic Scotland
Longmore House, Salisbury Place
Edinburgh EH9 1SH
Telephone 0131 668 8600
www.historic-scotland.gov.uk

Landmark Trust
Shottesbrooke, Maidenhead
Berkshire SL6 3SW
Telephone (01628) 825925
www.landmarktrust.org.uk

National Cycle Network
Sustrans Scotland
16a Randolph Crescent
Edinburgh EH3 7TT
Telephone 0131 539 8122
www.sustrans.org.uk

The National Trust for Scotland
Wemyss House
28 Charlotte Square
Edinburgh EH2 4ET
Telephone 0131 243 9300
www.nts.org.uk

Royal Society for the
Protection of Birds
Dunedin House
25 Ravelston Terrace
Edinburgh EH4 3TP
Telephone 0131 311 6500
www.rspb.org.uk/scotland

Scotland's Gardens Scheme
22 Rutland Square
Edinburgh EH1 2BB
Telephone 0131 229 1870
www.gardensofscotland.org

Scotland's Churches Scheme
Dunedin, Holehouse Road
Eaglesham, Glasgow G76 0JF
Telephone (01355) 302416
www.churchnet.org.uk/scotchurch

Scottish Natural Heritage
12 Hope Terrace
Edinburgh EH9 2AS
Telephone 0131 447 4784
www.snh.org.uk

Scottish Tourist Guides Association
Old Town Jail, St John Street
Stirling FK8 1EA
Telephone (01786) 447784
www.stga.co.uk

Scottish Wildlife Trust
Cramond House
Cramond Glebe Road
Edinburgh EH4 6NS
Telephone 0131 312 7765
www.swt.org.uk

Scottish Youth Hostels Association
7 Glebe Crescent
Stirling FK8 2JA
Telephone (01786) 891400
www.syha.org.uk

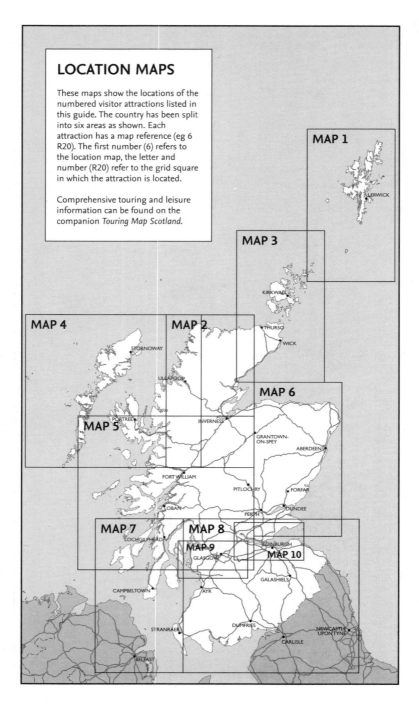

LOCATION MAPS

These maps show the locations of the numbered visitor attractions listed in this guide. The country has been split into six areas as shown. Each attraction has a map reference (eg 6 R20). The first number (6) refers to the location map, the letter and number (R20) refer to the grid square in which the attraction is located.

Comprehensive touring and leisure information can be found on the companion *Touring Map Scotland*.

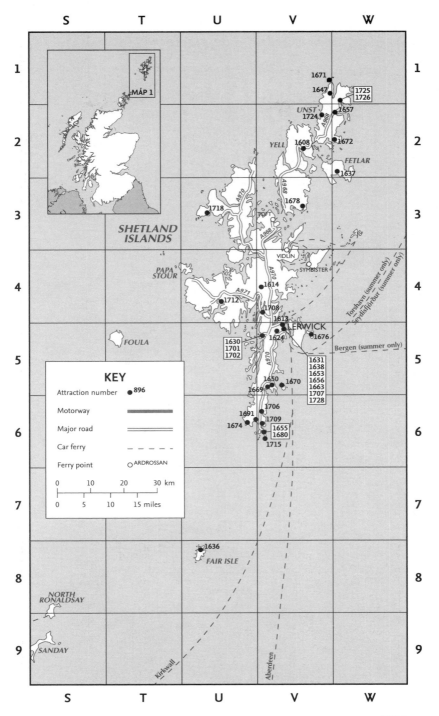

KEY

Attraction number ● 896

Motorway

Major road

Car ferry

Ferry point ○ ARDROSSAN

0   10   20   30 km
0   5   10   15 miles

MAP 1   13

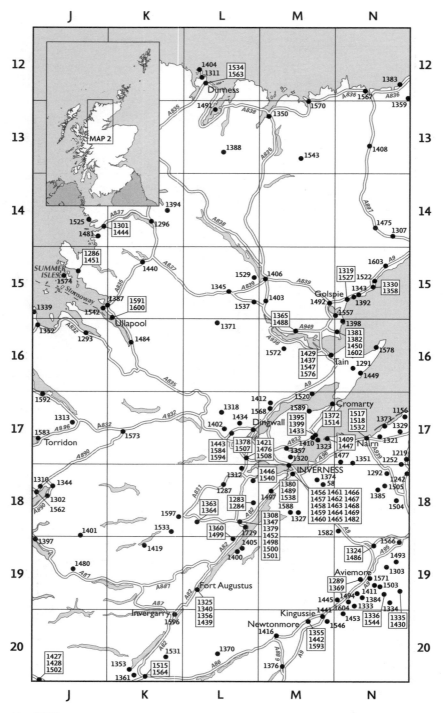

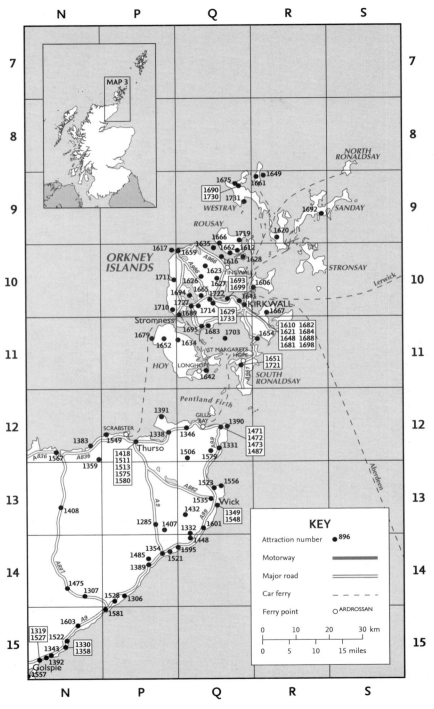

N P Q R S

MAP 3

ORKNEY ISLANDS

NORTH RONALDSAY

WESTRAY

SANDAY

ROUSAY

STRONSAY

Lerwick

TINGWALL

KIRKWALL

Stromness

St MARGARETS HOPE

HOY

LONGHOPE

SOUTH RONALDSAY

Pentland Firth

GILLS BAY

SCRABSTER

Thurso

Wick

Aberdeen

Golspie

1675 1649
1661
1690 1731
1730
1692

1719
1666 1620
1635 1662 1612
1617 1616 1628
1659 A966
1623
1711 1626 1627 1606
1665 1693
1694 1722 1699
1710 1727 1722 1641
1714 1667
1689 1629 1610 1682
1695 1733 1621 1684
1679 1683 1703 1648 1688
1652 1634 1654 1681 1698
1642 1651
1721

1391
1390
1383 1338 1346 1471
1549 1472
1567 A836 1331 1473
1359 A836 1506 1579 1487
1418
1511 1523 1556
1513 1535
1575 1432 Wick
1580 1285 1349
1408 1407 1601 1548
1332
1448
1354 1595
1485 1521
1389
1475
1307
1528 1306
1581
1603 A9
1319
1527 1522
1343 1330
1392 1358
1557

KEY

Attraction number   ● 896

Motorway

Major road

Car ferry   - - -

Ferry point   ○ ARDROSSAN

0 10 20 30 km

0 5 10 15 miles

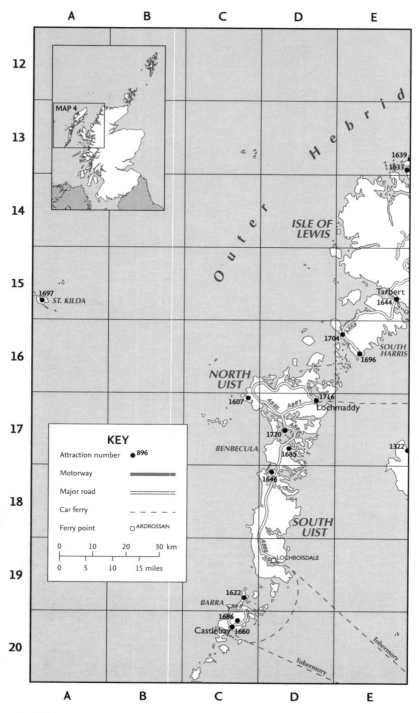

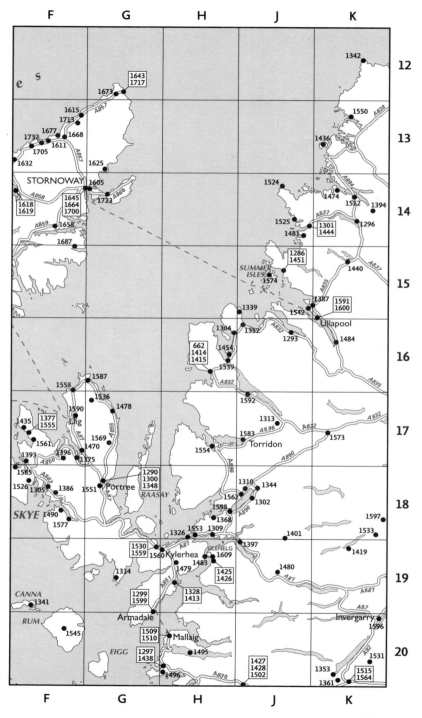

MAP 4   17

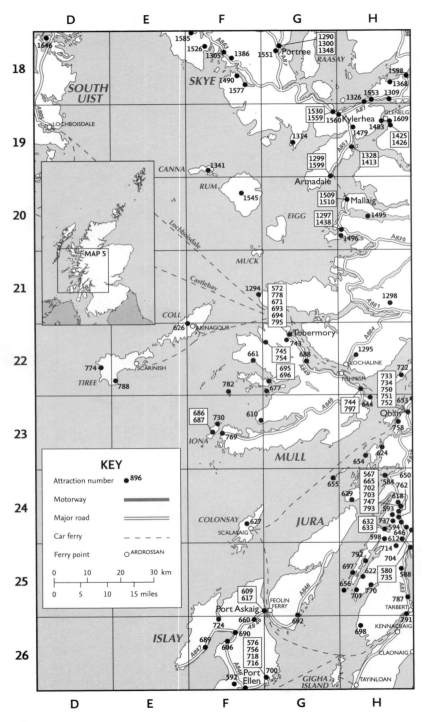

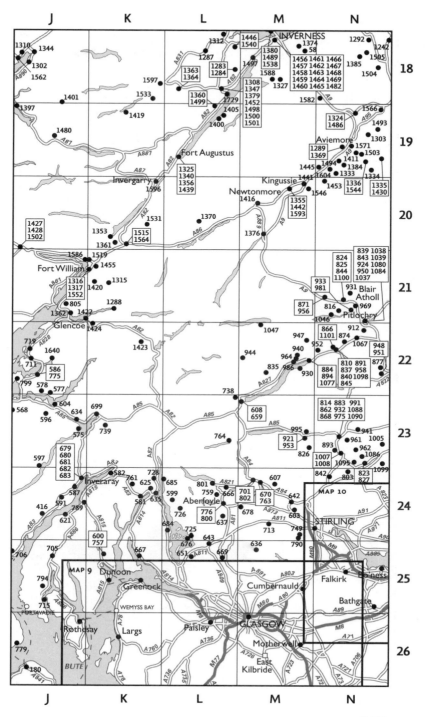

MAP 5   19

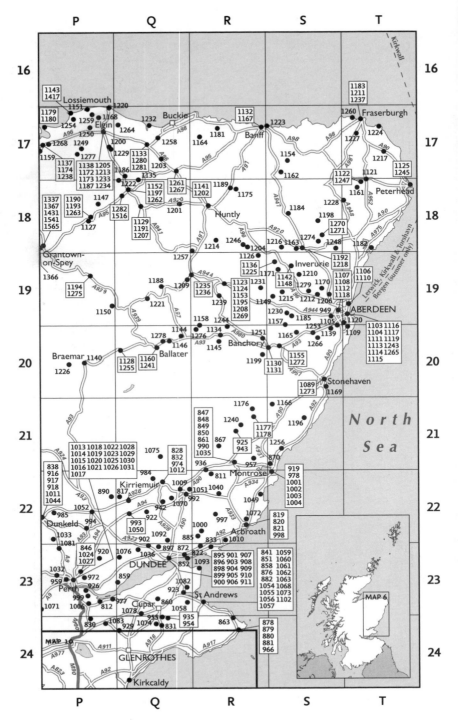

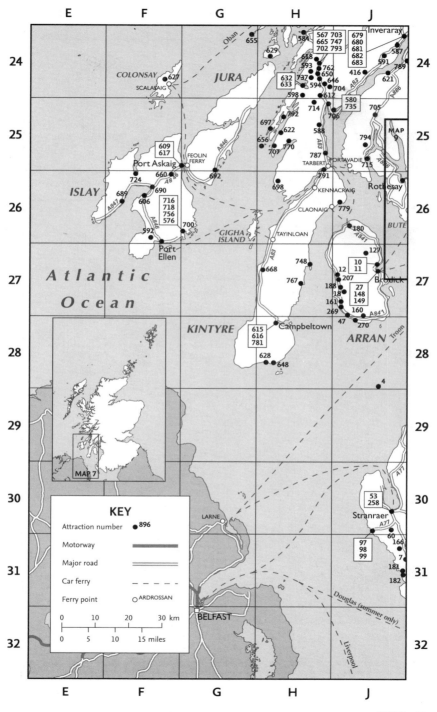

E F G H J

24

Oban
655
629
COLONSAY 627
SCALASAIG
JURA 584
567 703
665 747
702 793
618
593
762
737 650 646
632 594 704
633 612
598 580
714 735
792 706
706
697 622
588
656 787
707 770 TARBERT PORTAVADIE
791
698 KENNACRAIG
CLAONAIG 779
TAYINLOAN
GIGHA
ISLAND
668 748
767
188
18
161
269
47

679
680
681
682
683
Inveraray
587
591 589
416 621
705
MAP
9
794
715
Rothesay

BUTE

180
127
10
11
12 207
27
148
149
160
270 A841
Troon
ARRAN

609
617
FEOLIN
FERRY
Port Askaig
660 692
724
690
689 A847
606
716
718 700
592 756
576
Port
Ellen

ISLAY

Atlantic
Ocean

KINTYRE
615
616
781 Campbeltown
628 648

MAP 7

KEY
Attraction number ● 896
Motorway
Major road
Car ferry
Ferry point ○ ARDROSSAN
0   10   20   30 km
0   5   10   15 miles

LARNE

4

53
258
Stranraer
A77
60
166
97 7
98
99 181
182

BELFAST

Douglas (summer only)
Liverpool

24

25

26

27

28

29

30

31

32

MAP 7   21

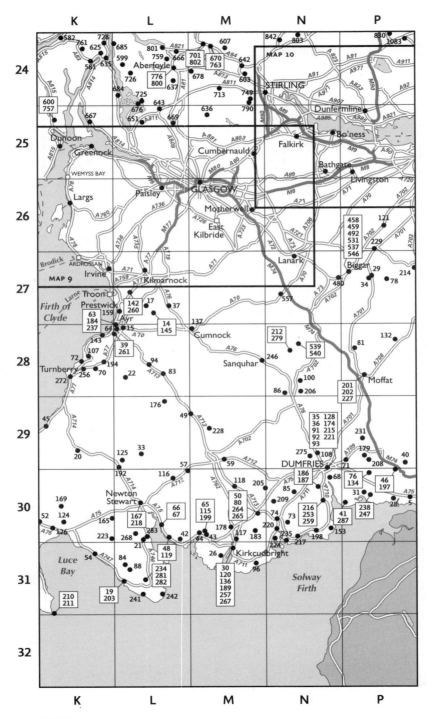

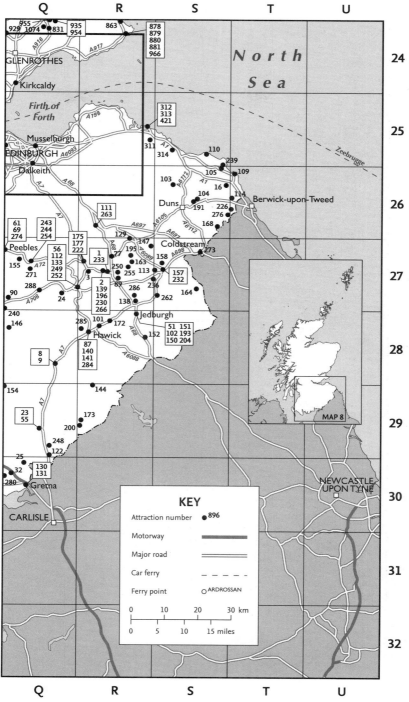

Q   R   S   T   U

955
929 1074 831   935   863   878
954   879
880
A916   881
A917   966

North

GLENROTHES   Sea   24

Kirkcaldy

Firth of   312
Forth   A198   313   25
421

Musselburgh   A7
EDINBURGH   A6093   311   110
Dalkeith   314   105   239
A7   109
103   16
A6112   104   114
A7   Duns   191   226   Berwick-upon-Tweed   26
276
111   168
263
61   243   175   129   Coldstream
69   244   177   147   A697   273
274   254   222   56   1   195   273   27
Peebles   112   233   77   158
155   A72   133   250   163   157
271   249   288   255   113   232
252   3   89   286   236   164   27
90   2   138   262
139   Jedburgh
240   196   101   172   51 151
146   230   285   152   102 193
266   Hawick   150 204   28
87
8   140
9   141
284

154   144

23   173
55   29
200

248
122
25
32   130
280   131   NEWCASTLE
Gretna   UPON TYNE   30

CARLISLE

KEY   31

Attraction number   ●896

Motorway

Major road   32

Car ferry

Ferry point   ○ARDROSSAN

0   10   20   30 km

0   5   10   15 miles

Q   R   S   T   U

MAP 8   23

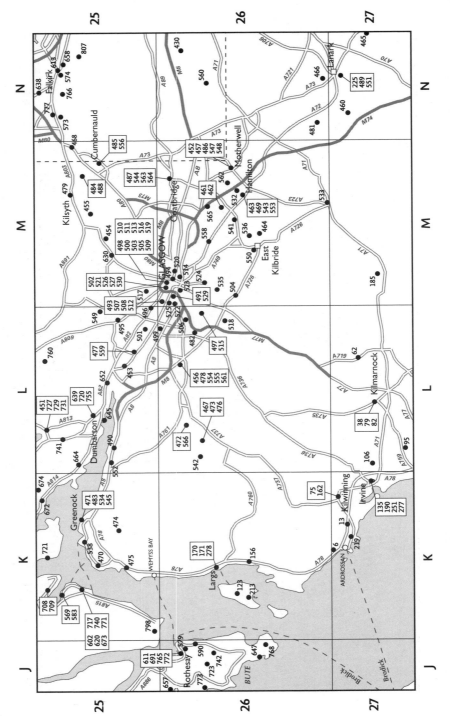

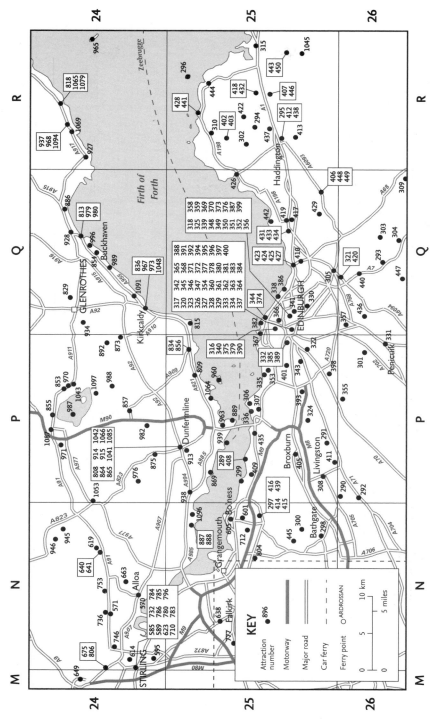

KEY

● 896 Attraction number

━━━ Motorway

━━━ Major road

--- Car ferry

○ ARDROSSAN Ferry point

0   5   10 km
0   5   miles

MAP 10 - EDINBURGH   25

SOUTH OF SCOTLAND

100 AKER WOOD VISITOR CENTRE   1   8 R27

Annay Road, Melrose. On the B6361 between Melrose and Newstead. Buses to Melrose then 5 minute walk. Open all year, Mon–Sat 0900–1730, Sun 1000–1700. Free. Coffee shop with outside seating. WC. Wheelchair access. Disabled WC. Car and coach parking. Telephone (01896) 823717. www.1stforfencing.com

Visitor centre with a well-stocked garden centre, gift shop and coffee shop with wonderful views overlooking Melrose Abbey and the Eildon Hills. Secure children's play area and woodland walk.

THE ABBEY MILL   2   8 R27

Annay Road, Melrose. Close to Melrose Abbey. Bus service to Melrose. Open all year, Mon–Fri 0900–1730. Free. Gift shop. Tearoom. WC. Limited wheelchair access. Car and coach parking. Telephone (01896) 822138. www.ewm.co.uk

The original corn mill, known as Abbey Mill, was built during the early Middle Ages and probably belonged to the abbey up until the reformation. Today the building houses a fine selection of Scottish knitwear.

ABBOTSFORD   3   8 R27

Abbotsford, Melrose, Roxburghshire. On the B6360 between Selkirk and Melrose, 2 miles (3km) from Melrose. Bus from Galashiels or Melrose to within 0.25 mile (0.5km). Open Mar–Oct, Mon–Sat 0930–1700; Jun–Sep, Sun 0930–1700; Mar–May and Oct, Sun 1400–1700. Charge ££. Group concessions. Guided tours for groups (French available). Gift shop. Tearoom and picnic area. Garden, woodland walk, walled garden. WC. Limited wheelchair access via private entrance. Disabled WC. Car and coach parking. Telephone (01896) 752043. www.scottsabbotsford.co.uk

Built by Sir Walter Scott, the 19th century novelist, in 1812 on the site of Cartley Hole farmhouse. He lived here until he died in 1832. Features Scott's collection of historical relics, including armour, weapons, Rob Roy's gun and Montrose's sword; library with over 9000 rare volumes; chapel.

AILSA CRAIG   4   7 J28

Island in the Firth of Clyde, 10 miles (17km) west of Girvan. To arrange a visit telephone the Lighthouse Attendant on (01465) 713219.

A granite island rock, 1114 feet (339.5m) high with a circumference of 2 miles (3km). The rock itself was used to make some of the finest curling stones and the island has a gannetry and colonies of guillemots and other sea birds.

ANNAN MUSEUM   5   8 P30

Bank Street, Annan. Open Mar–Dec, Mon–Sat and Bank Holiday Mondays 1100–1600. Free. Explanatory displays. WC. Wheelchair access. Disabled WC. Car parking. Telephone (01461) 201384. www.annan.org.uk

Museum with a regular programme of local history, archeology, photographic and arts and craft exhibitions.

ARDROSSAN CASTLE   6   9 K27

Ardrossan, on a hill overlooking Ardrossan Bay. Access at all reasonable times. Free.

Mid 12th-century castle. Fine views of Arran and Ailsa Craig. Destroyed by Cromwell and only part of the north tower and two arched cellars remain.

ARDWELL GARDENS   7   7 J31

Ardwell Estate, Ardwell, Stranraer, Wigtownshire. On the A716, 10 miles (16km) south of Stranraer. Nearest railway station Stranraer, bus from Stranraer. Open Mar–Sep, daily 1000–1700. Charge £. Guided tours by arrangement. Plant sales. Picnic area. WC. Limited wheelchair access. Disabled WC. Car and coach parking. Telephone (01776) 860227.

Gardens surrounding an 18th-century country house (not open to the public) with the formal layout around the house blending into the informality of woods and shrubberies. Daffodils, azaleas, camellias, rhododendrons. Walled garden and herbaceous borders. Walks and fine views over Luce Bay. Plants for sale and pick-your-own fruit.

JOHNNIE ARMSTRONG GALLERY   8   8 Q28

Henderson's Knowe, Teviothead, By Hawick. 9 miles (14.5km) south of Hawick on A7. On Carlisle–Edinburgh bus route. Open all year, Wed–Mon 0900–1800. Free. Explanatory displays. Gift shop. Wheelchair access. Car parking. Telephone (01450) 850237. www.thecelticgoldsmith.com

Located in an historic smithy, the gallery specialises in the design, production and sale of high quality gold and silver jewellery in celtic, Scottish and Viking styles. There is also a small but regularly changing display of historic artefacts, covering many aspects of Scottish history but in particular the Border reivers of the 16th century.

JOHNNIE ARMSTRONG OF GILNOCKIE MEMORIAL   9   8 Q28

Carlanrig, Teviothead. Take the A7 south from Hawick for 9 miles (14.5km) then turn right on to unclassified road. Memorial is 100 yards (91m) south on left next to churchyard. Access at all times. Free. Information plaque. Wheelchair access via nearby field gate. Car parking.

A stone marker marks the mass grave of Laird of Gilnockie and his men, hanged without trial by King James V of Scotland in 1530.

ARRAN AROMATICS VISITOR CENTRE   10   7 J27

The Home Farm, Brodick, Isle of Arran. 1 mile (1.5km) from Brodick on road north to Lochranza. Ferry and bus terminal in Brodick. Open Apr–May daily, 0930–1700; Jun–Sep daily, 0930–1730; Oct–Nov, Tue–Sun 0930–1700; Dec, Tue–Sun 0930–1630; Jan–Mar, Tue–Sat 1000–1630. Free. Explanatory displays. Gift shop. Restaurant and tearoom. WC. Wheelchair access. Disabled WC. Car parking. Telephone (01770) 302595. www.arranaromatics.com

Visitors can watch the production of natural soaps and body care products. Set in a courtyard next to a cheese factory and seafood restaurant.

ARRAN BREWERY   11   7 J27

Arran Brewery, Cladach, Brodick. 1 mile (1.5km) north of Brodick. Ferry from Ardrossan to Brodick. Bus from pier stops close to brewery. Open all year, Mon–Sat 1000–1700, Sun 1230–1700. Telephone for winter hours. Nominal charge per adult (including sample). Children free. Concessions by arrangement. Explanatory displays and self-guided tour. Guided tours by arrangement. Gift shop. Refreshments nearby (open Apr–Oct only). Wheelchair access. Car and coach parking. Telephone (01770) 302353. www.arranbrewery.com

Arran's first and only commercial craft brewery, producing three different real ales (plus two seasonal beers) using traditional methods. Visitors may see the beer fermenting and watch the bottling when in progress. Displays explain the story of brewing; questions about the process are welcomed.

AUCHAGALLON STONE CIRCLE   12   7 J27

HS. Isle of Arran. 4 miles (6.5km) north of Blackwaterfoot on the Isle of Arran. By ferry from Ardrossan to Brodick. Bus from Brodick to Blackwaterfoot. Access at all reasonable times. Free. Telephone (0131) 5507603. www.historic-scotland.gov.uk

A Bronze Age burial cairn surrounded by a circle of 15 standing stones.

AUCHENHAKVIE LEISURE CENTRE   13   9 K27

Saltcoats Road, Stevenston, Ayrshire. Open all year except Christmas to New Year. Mon 1000–1900, Tue 0900–2000, Wed 1000–1800, Thu 1000–2100, Fri 0900–2100, Sat 1000–1700, Sun 0900–1230. Charges dependant on activity. Group booking advised. Vending machines for tea, coffee and soft drinks. WC. Car and coach parking. Telephone (01294) 605126.

Twenty-five metre pool, split-level ice rink, hi-tech fitness salon, health suite and studio fitness centre.

AYR GORGE WOODLANDS   14   8 L27

At Failford, south of A758 Ayr–Mauchline road. Access at all times. Free. Viewing platform. Car parking.

Gorge woodland, semi-natural, dominated by oak and some coniferous plantation. Situated by the River Ayr. Historic sandstone steps and extensive network of well-maintained footpaths.

AYR RACECOURSE   15   8 L28

2 Whitletts Road, Ayr. Close to Ayr town centre, 5 minutes from A77. Well signposted from all directions. Rail and bus service to Ayr. Charges vary. Beer garden and champagne bar. Children's play areas. WC. Wheelchair access. Disabled WC. Car and coach parking. Telephone (01292) 264179. www.ayr-racecourse.co.uk

The racecourse hosts both Flat and National Hunt fixtures, usually holding at least 25 days racing every year, including the Scottish Grand National (Apr) and the Ayr Gold Cup (Sep)

AYTON CASTLE   16   8 S26

Ayton, Eyemouth, Berwickshire. 7 miles (11km) north of Berwick on A1. Nearest railway station Berwick-upon-Tweed. Open May–Sep, Wed and Sun only 1400–1700. Other times by appointment. Charge £. Under 15s free. Guided tours. WC. Wheelchair access with assistance. Disabled WC. Car and coach parking. Telephone (01890) 781212.

Historic castle, built in 1846 and an important example of the Victorian architectural tradition. Ayton Castle has been restored in recent years and is lived in as a family home.

BACHELORS' CLUB   17   8 L27

NTS. Sandgate Street, Tarbolton, South Ayrshire. A77 south of Kilmarnock and off A76 at Mauchline. Bus from Ayr. Open Apr–Sep, Fri–Tue 1300–1700, weekends in Oct 1330–1730. Charge ££. Group concessions. Explanatory displays. Limited wheelchair access. Car parking. Telephone (01292) 541940. www.nts.org.uk

Robert Burns and his friends founded a debating society here in 1780. Period furnishings.

BALMICHAEL VISITOR CENTRE   18   7 J27

Shiskine, Isle of Arran. 7 miles (11km) from Brodick on B880. Bus service from Blackwaterfoot or Brodick. Open Apr–Oct, Mon–Sat 1000–1700, Sun 1200–1700;

Nov–Mar, Wed–Sat 1000–1700, Sun 1200–1700. Free. Charge for activities. Group concessions. Gift shop. Tearoom and picnic area. WC. Wheelchair access. Disabled WC. Car and coach parking. Telephone (01770) 860430. www.thebalmichaelcentre.co.uk

Converted farm buildings and courtyard including ice cream parlour and jewellery/craft shop, working pottery, antique and tapestry shops. Adventure playground and indoor play barn. Off-road quad biking for all ages. Scenic tours of Arran by helicopter. Heritage area with working mill wheel.

BARSALLOCH FORT 19   8 L31

HS. Off A747, 7.5 miles (12km) west north-west of Whithorn, Wigtownshire. Nearest railway station Stranraer, bus from Stranraer or Newton Stewart to Whithorn. Above Barsalloch Point, 0.75 mile (1km) west of Monreith. Car parking. Telephone (01387) 770244. www.historic-scotland.gov.uk

Remains of an Iron Age hill fort on the edge of a raised beach bluff. Defended by a deep ditch in horseshoe form.

BARWINNOCK HERBS 20   8 K29

Barrhill, Ayrshire. 12 miles (19km) north west of Newton Stewart, turning right off B7027 near Loch Maberry. Open Apr–Oct, daily 1000–1700. Free. Guided tours for groups by prior arrangement. Explanatory displays. Picnic area. Plant sales. Wheelchair access with assistance. Car and coach parking. Telephone (01465) 821338. www.barwinnock.com

A garden and nursery with a fascinating collection of culinary, medicinal and aromatic herbs. Also Rural Life exhibition describing herbs for healing and flavour, and the local countryside, its natural materials and wildlife.

BLADNOCH DISTILLERY 21   8 L30

Bladnoch, Wigtown, Dumfries and Galloway. 1 mile (1.5km) south west of Wigtown on A746. Open all year, Mon–Fri 0900–1700, plus Jul–Aug, Sat 1100–17.00 and Sun 12.00–17.00. Charge £. Under 18's free of charge. Guided tours. Explanatory displays. Gift shop. Picnic areas. WC. Riverside walks adapted for wheelchairs. Limited wheelchair access. Car and coach parking. Telephone (01988) 402605. www.bladnoch.co.uk

Scotland's most southerly distillery and visitor centre. The distillery is an attractive old stone/slate building dating from 1817 set in a charming location adjacent to the River Bladnoch with fishing and camping nearby.

BLAIRQUHAN 22   8 L28

Blairquhan Estate Office, Maybole, Ayrshire. 14 miles (22.5km) south east of Ayr. Bus service from Maybole (7 miles/11km) and Ayr. Open most Sun May–Sep 1400–1700 (telephone to confirm dates). Gardens open 1400–1800. Charge £££. Group concessions in advance. Guided tours available (also in French). Explanatory displays. Gift shop. Tearoom. Garden. WC. Limited wheelchair access. Disabled WC. Car and coach parking. Telephone (01655) 770239. www.blairquhan.co.uk

Four families have lived at Blairquhan. The first tower-house was built in 1346. The new house was designed and built by the Scottish architect William Burn between 1821 and 1824. Walled garden with original glasshouse. Pinetum. Sir James Hunter Blair's Collection of Scottish Colourists.

BORDER FINE ARTS GALLERY 23   8 Q29

Market Place, Langholm, Dumfriesshire. 20 miles (32km) north of Carlisle, 7 miles (11km) from the Border. Nearest railway station Carlisle. On main A7 Edinburgh bus route. Open all year, Mon–Fri 0900–1700, Sat 1000–1600. Free. Explanatory displays. Gift shop. Wheelchair access. Car parking. Telephone (01387) 383033.

Border Fine Arts have been producing high quality ceramic figurines for over twenty-five years and have many collectors throughout the world. Visitors can see an extensive display of current sculptures which collectors find enthralling.

BOWHILL HOUSE AND COUNTRY PARK   24   8 Q27

Bowhill, Selkirk. 3 miles (5km) west of Selkirk on A708. Nearest bus at Selkirk. Park open Easter-Aug, daily (except Fri) 1200–1700; house and park open Jul 1300-1630. Also open all year for educational groups by appointment. Charge £££. Free to wheelchair users. Group concessions. Guided tours. Explanatory displays. Gift shop. Licensed restaurant, tearoom and picnic area. Garden. WC. Personal guided tours for blind visitors. Wheelchair access. Disabled WC. Car and coach parking. Telephone (01750) 22204.

For many generations Bowhill has been the Border home of the Scotts of Buccleuch. Inside the house, begun in 1812, there is an outstanding collection of pictures, including works by Van Dyck, Reynolds, Gainsborough, Canaletto, Guardi, Claude Lorraine, Raeburn. There is also a selection of the world-famous Buccleuch collection of portrait miniatures. Also porcelain and furniture, much of which was made in the famous workshop of André Boulle in Paris. Restored Victorian kitchen. In the grounds are an adventure woodland play area, loch, river and woodland walks. Audio-visual presentation, theatre and visitor centre. The popular visitor attraction featuring the life and work of James Hogg, the Ettrick Shepherd, is now installed at Bowhill. Accompanying the story of James Hogg are memorabilia, books, paintings and Ann Carrick's exquisite costume figures.

BRIDGE END NURSERIES   25   8 Q30

Gretna Green, Dumfries and Galloway. 1.5 miles (2.5km) north of Gretna Green. Nearest railway station Gretna Green, bus from Dumfries or Carlisle. Open all year, daily 0930–1700. Free. Guided tours. Explanatory displays. Self-service refreshments available. WC. Wheelchair access with assistance. Car parking. Telephone (01461) 800612. www.bridgendnurseries.co.uk

A unique cottage garden nursery specialising in rare and unusual varieties of hardy perennials. Mature plants can be seen in all their glory in the herbaceous borders and also in the stock beds. The proprietors are well known and respected exhibitors at major flower shows, having won a host of gold medal awards. Friendly advice and assistance is always available.

BRIGHOUSE BAY TREKKING CENTRE   26   8 M31

Brighouse Bay, Borgue, Kirkcudbright. 6 miles (10km) south west of Kirkcudbright off the B727 Borgue road. Open Easter–Oct, telephone to confirm times. Charge £££. Gift shop. Bistro, licensed lounge, take-away food and picnic area. Childrens play area, swimming pool, golf course. WC. Disabled riders telephone in advance. Wheelchair access. Disabled WC. Car and coach parking. Telephone (01557) 870267. www.brighouse-bay.co.uk

Approved by the British Horse Society, the Trekking Centre offers riding for all abilities. Hard hats are provided. Riding is within the 1200 acre (486ha) holiday/farm complex. Also holiday park.

BRODICK CASTLE   27   7 J27

NTS. Isle of Arran, Bute. 2 miles (3km) north of Brodick. By ferry from Ardrossan to Brodick, by bus from Brodick. Open easter–Oct, daily 1100–1630 (closes 15.30 in Oct). Charge £££. Group concessions. Guided tours by arrangement. Explanatory displays. Guidebook in French and German. Text in eight languages. Gift shop. Restaurant with terrace overlooking sea, picnic area. WC. Braille information sheet. Limited wheelchair access (wheelchairs available). Disabled WC. Car and coach parking. Telephone (01770) 302202. www.nts.org.uk

Mainly Victorian castle, but original parts date from the 13th century. Fine collections of furniture, paintings, porcelain and silver collected by the Dukes of Hamilton. Beautiful walled garden, and woodland garden with famous rhododendron collection. The castle occupies a fine site overlooking Brodick Bay, on the slopes of Goatfell (2866 feet/873m). Nature trail and other walks in country park.

BROOM FISHERIES   28   8 P30

The Lodge, Broom Farm Estate, Newbie, Annan, Dumfries and Galloway. Off B724, 2 miles (3km) west of Annan. Nearest railway station at Annan. Open all year, daily 0830–dusk; Oct–Jan closed Tue only. Charge £££. Mid-week OAP concession on first two fish ticket. Tackle and flies for sale. Fishing lodge with refreshments available. WC. Limited wheelchair access. Disabled WC. Car and coach parking. Telephone (01461) 700209. www.broomfisheries.co.uk

Four fly only lochs, well stock with rainbow, brown and golden trout, set in beautiful surroundings. Prolific natural aquatic life forms make these waters ideal for nymph and dry fly fishing. Additional 50 peg coarse water, roach, tench, perch, bream, carp, chub, ghost carp. Easy access from car park.

BROUGHTON GALLERY   29   8 P27

Broughton, Biggar, Lanarkshire. On the A701 just north of Broughton village. Bus from Peebles or Biggar. Open Apr–Sep and mid Nov–Christmas, Thu–Tue 1030–1800. Free. Gift shop. WC. Wheelchair access with assistance. Access for small coaches only. Car parking. Telephone (01899) 830234.

Sells paintings and crafts by living British artists and makers in Tower House, designed in 1937 by Sir Basil Spence.

BROUGHTON HOUSE AND GARDEN   30   8 M31

NTS. 12 High Street, Kirkcudbright. Off A711/A755. By bus from Dumfries and Castle Douglas. Open easter–Jun and Sep–Oct, daily 1200–1700; Jul–Aug, daily 1000–1700. Charge £££. Group concessions. Explanatory displays (information sheets in French and German). Small shop. WC. Limited wheelchair access. Car parking. Telephone (01557) 330437. www.nts.org.uk

Eighteenth-century town house, home and studio (1901-33) of artist E. A. Hornel, one of the Glasgow Boys. Permanent exhibition of his work. Extensive collection of Scottish books including Burns' works. Attractive Japanese-style garden, added by Hornel, leading down to River Dee estuary.

BROW WELL   31   8 P30

On B725, 1 mile (1.5km) west of Ruthwell. Access at all times. Free.

Ancient mineral well visited by Robert Burns in July 1796, when at Brow sea bathing under his doctor's orders.

ROBERT THE BRUCE'S CAVE   32   8 Q30

Cove Lodge, Kirkpatrick Fleming, Dumfries and Galloway. 3 miles (5km) north of Gretna Green, 10 miles (16km) south of Lockerbie. Nearest railway at Gretna, bus stop in Kirkpatrick Fleming then 0.25 mile (0.5km) walk. Open all year, daily; Apr–Sep 0900–2100; Oct–Mar 0900–1700. Charge £. Guided tours. Explanatory displays. Gift shop. Picnic area. Family wash rooms and baby changing area. Wheelchair access with assistance. Disabled WC. Car and coach parking. Telephone (01461) 800285. www.brucescave.co.uk

Situated in an 80-acre (32ha) estate high above the River Kirtle, the cave is reputed to be where Robert the Bruce hid for 3 moths in 1313. Watching a spider try and retry to spin its web, he found inspiration – going on to beat the English at the Battle of Bannockburn in 1314. Scenic area with abundant wildlife.

BRUCE'S STONE   33   8 L29

North side of Loch Trool, unclassified road off A714, 13 miles (21km) north of Newton Stewart. Access at all times. Free.

A massive granite memorial to Robert the Bruce's first victory over the English, which led to his subsequent success at Bannockburn. Fine views of Loch Trool and the hills of Galloway. Start of hill climb to the Merrick (2764 feet/842.5m), the highest hill in southern Scotland.

JOHN BUCHAN CENTRE   34   8 P27

Broughton, Biggar, Lanarkshire. On the A703, 6 miles (9.5km) east of Biggar and 28 miles (45km) from Edinburgh. Bus service from Edinburgh. Open Easter and May–Sep, daily 1400–1700. Charge £. Explanatory displays. Second-hand books for sale. Bookshop. WC. Wheelchair access with assistance. Car and coach parking. Telephone (01899) 221050.

The Centre tells the story of John Buchan, 1st Lord Tweedsmuir, author of *The Thirty Nine Steps* and also lawyer, politician, soldier, historian, and Governor-General of Canada. Broughton village was his mother's birthplace, and a much-loved holiday home.

ROBERT BURNS CENTRE   35   8 N29

Mill Road, Dumfries. Situated on the west bank of the River Nith. 15 minute walk from Dumfries railway station, five minute walk from Whitesands bus station. Open Apr–Sep, Mon–Sat 1000–2000, Sun 1400–1700; Oct–Mar, Tue–Sat 1000–1300 and 1400–1700. Free. Charge £ (for audio-visual presentation only). Group concessions by advance booking. Explanatory displays. Leaflet guides in European languages, Russian and Japanese. Gift shop. Café. WC. Induction loop. Wheelchair access. Disabled WC. Car and coach parking. Telephone (01387) 264808. www.dumgal.gov.uk/museums

Award-winning centre illustrates the connection between Robert Burns, Scotland's national poet, and the town of Dumfries. Situated in the town's 18th-century watermill, the centre tells of Burns' last years spent in the busy streets and lively atmosphere of Dumfries in the 1790s. Film theatre shows feature films in the evening.

BURNS HOUSE   36   8 N29

Burns Street, Dumfries. Five minute walk from Dumfries town centre. Dumfries railway station 15 minutes walk, Loreburn Centre bus stance two minute walk. Open Apr–Sep, Mon–Sat 1000–1700, Sun 1400–1700; Oct–Mar, Tue–Sat 1000–1300 and 1400–1700. Free. Explanatory displays. Gift shop. Leaflets in European languages and Japanese. Wheelchair access with assistance. Car parking. Telephone (01387) 255297. www.dumgal.gov.uk/museums

It was in this ordinary sandstone house that Robert Burns, Scotland's national poet, spent the last years of his brilliant life. Now a place of pilgrimage for Burns enthusiasts around the world. The house retains much of its 18th-century character and contains many relics of the poet. Visitors can see the chair in which he wrote his last poems and many original letters and manuscripts. The famous Kilmarnock and Edinburgh editions of his work are also on display.

BURNS HOUSE MUSEUM   37   8 L27

Castle Street, Mauchline, Ayrshire. 11 miles (18km) from Ayr and Kilmarnock. Nearest railway and bus stations Ayr and Kilmarnock, bus stop close to museum. Open all year Tue–Sat 11.00–17.00. Free. Guided tours by appointment. Explanatory displays. Gift shop. Garden available for picnics. WC. Limited wheelchair access. Disabled WC. Car and coach parking. Telephone (01290) 550045.

A museum with a gallery devoted to Burns memorabilia. On the upper floor is the room Burns took for Jean Armour in 1788. Furnished in the style of the period. Visitors can also see a large collection of Mauchline boxware and an exhibition devoted to curling and curling stones. Nearby is Mauchline churchyard in which are buried four of Burns' daughters and a number of his friends and contemporaries.

BURNS MONUMENT   38   9 L27

Kay Park, Kilmarnock. 0.5 mile (1km) from centre of Kilmarnock. View from outside only.

Victorian red sandstone monument with statue of Burns by W. G. Stevenson. Set in an attractive park with boating, pitch and putt, and children's play area.

BURNS NATIONAL HERITAGE PARK   39   8 L28

Murdochs Lone, Alloway, Ayr. 2 miles (3km) south of Ayr on B7024. Nearest railway station Ayr. Bus service to Alloway from Ayr. Open all year except Christmas and New Year. Tam o'Shanter Experience Apr–Sep 1000–1730; Oct–Mar 1000–1700. Burns Cottage Apr–Sep 1000–1730; Oct–Mar Mon–Sat 1000–1700.. Charge ££. Group concessions. Explanatory displays . Gift shop. Restaurant, tearoom and picnic area. Gardens and children's play area. WC. Wheelchair access. Disabled WC. Car and coach parking. Telephone (01292) 443700. www.burnsheritagepark.com

The Burns National Heritage Park was established in 1995. It embraces Burns' Cottage, Museum, Monument, Auld Brig o' Doon and Alloway Kirk together with the Tam o' Shanter Experience. The old and new are linked in time by a 5-minute walk which transports the visitor from 1759 (when Burns was born) to the exciting, humorous and action-filled Tam o' Shanter Experience (see 261).

BURNSWARK HILL   40   8 P29

By unclassified road, 1.5 miles (2.5km) north of B725, Ecclefechan to Middlebie road. Access at all reasonable times. Free.

A native hill fort (circa 6th century BC) with extensive earthworks, flanked by a Roman artillery range. Thought to have been a series of Roman practice siege works, best seen from the hilltop. The excavated ditches and ramparts of Birrens Fort are nearby.

CAERLAVEROCK CASTLE   41   8 P30

HS. Glencaple, Dumfries. Off the B725, 9 miles (14.5km) south of Dumfries. Bus from Dumfries to Shearington. Open Apr–Sep, daily 0930–1830; Oct–Mar, Mon–Sat 0930–1630, Sun 1400–1630. Charge £. Group concessions. Explanatory displays and visitor centre. Gift shop. Tearoom and picnic area. Children's park and nature trail to old castle. WC. Limited wheelchair access. Disabled WC. Car and coach parking. Telephone (01387) 770244. www.historic-scotland.gov.uk

One of the finest castles in Scotland – its remarkable features are the twin-towered gatehouse and the Nithsdale Lodging, a splendid Renaissance range dating from 1638.

CAIRN HOLY CHAMBERED CAIRNS   42   8 L30

HS. 6.5 miles (10.5km) south east of Creetown, Kirkcudbrightshire. Nearest railway station Dumfries, buses from Dumfries, Newton Stewart or Stranraer. Car parking. Telephone (0131) 5507603. www.historic-scotland.gov.uk

Two remarkably complete Neolithic burial cairns situated on a hill giving good views over Wigtown Bay.

CALLY GARDENS   43   8 M30

Gatehouse-of-Fleet, Castle Douglas, Dumfries and Galloway. Off A75 taking the road to Gatehouse-of-Fleet, turn off towards Cally Palace Hotel. Nearest railway station Dumfries, bus service from Dumfries. Car parking. Coach parking nearby. Open Easter–Sep, Tue–Fri 1400–1730, Sat–Sun 1000–1730. Charge £. Children under 13 free. Group concessions. Gift shop. WC. Wheelchair access. Disabled WC. Telephone 01557 815029 for information. www.callygardens.co.uk

A specialist nursery in an 18th-century walled garden. There is a unique collection of over 3,500 varieties, mainly perennials, planted out in 32 large borders. Plants for sale.

CARDONESS CASTLE   44   8 M30

HS. Gatehouse-of-Fleet, Kirkcudbrightshire. 1 mile (2km) south west of Gatehouse-of-Fleet on A75. Situated on main bus route from Stranraer to Dumfries. Open Apr–Sep, daily 0930–1830; Oct–Mar, Sat and Sun 0930–1630. Charge £. Group concessions. Explanatory displays. Gift shop. Picnic area. Blind visitors may touch carvings. Car and coach parking. Telephone (01557) 814427. www.historic-scotland.gov.uk

The well-preserved ruin of a 15th-century tower house, the ancient home of the McCullochs of Galloway. Four storeys with a vaulted basement. Features include the original stairway, stone benches and elaborate fireplaces.

CARLETON CASTLE   45   8 K29

Off A77, 6 miles (9.5km) south of Girvan. Access at all reasonable times. Free.

One in a link of Kennedy watchtowers along the coast. Now a ruin, it was famed in a ballad as the seat of a baron who got rid of seven wives by pushing them over the cliff, but who was himself disposed of by May Culean, his eighth wife.

THOMAS CARLYLE'S BIRTHPLACE   46   8 P30

NTS. The Arched House, Ecclefechan, Lockerbie. On A74 in Ecclefechan, 5.5 miles (9km) south east of Lockerbie. Bus from Lockerbie. Open May–Sep, Thur–Mon 1300–1700. Charge ££. Group concessions. Explanatory displays. WC. Car and coach parking. Telephone (01576) 300666. www.nts.org.uk

Birthplace of writer Thomas Carlyle (born 1795). Furnished to reflect domestic life in his time, with an important collection of family portraits and belongings.

CARN BAN   47   7 J27

HS. 3.5 miles (5.5km) north east of Lagg on the west side of Arran. By ferry from Ardrossan to Brodick, bus from Brodick to Corriecravie. Access at all reasonable times. Free. Telephone (0131) 5507603. www.historic-scotland.gov.uk

One of the most famous Neolithic long cairns of south west Scotland.

CARSLUITH CASTLE   48   8 L30

HS. 3.5 miles south of Creetown on A75. Nearest railway station Dumfries, buses from Dumfries, Newton Stewart or Stranraer. Access at all reasonable times. Free. Car parking. Telephone (0131) 5507603. www.historic-scotland.gov.uk

The delightful and well-preserved ruin of a 16th-century tower house with 18th-century ranges of outhouses still in use by the farmer. One of its owners was the last abbot of Sweetheart Abbey.

CARSPHAIRN HERITAGE CENTRE   49   8 M29

Carsphairn. On A713, 25 miles (40km) south of Ayr and 25 miles (40km) north of Castle Douglas. Limited bus service from Castle Douglas and Ayr. Open Easter–May and early Oct, Sat 1030–1700, Sun and bank holidays 1400–1700; Jun–Sep, Mon–Sat (except Wed) 1030–1700, Sun 1400–1700. Free. Explanatory displays. Gift shop. Picnic area. Garden. WC. Wheelchair access. Disabled WC. Car and coach parking. Telephone (01644) 460653. www.carsphairnheritage.co.uk

Carsphairn Heritage Centre houses a permanent display on the parish together with a temporary annual exhibition, featuring local history. There is also a reference section which pays particular attention to family history records relevant to the area and a small display of locally made articles for sale together with other relevant mementos of the area.

CASTLE DOUGLAS ART GALLERY   50   8 M30

Market Street, Castle Douglas, Dumfries and Galloway. Adjacent to Castle Douglas library at the east end of the town. Nearest railway station Dumfries, bus to Castle Douglas. Open Mar–Dec, Mon–Sat 1100–1600; telephone to confirm. Free. Wheelchair access. Telephone (01557) 331643. www.dumgal.gov.uk/museums

First opened in 1938, having been gifted to the town by Mrs Ethel Bristowe, a talented artist in her own right. The gallery now forms an excellent venue for an annual programme of temporary exhibitions between Easter and Christmas, ranging from fine art and craft to photography.

CASTLE JAIL   51   8 R28

Castle Gate, Jedburgh, Roxburghshire. Short walk from town centre up the Castlegate. Nearest railway station Edinburgh; bus from Edinburgh. Open late Mar–Oct, Mon–Sat 1000–1645, Sun 1300–1600. Open on bank holidays. Last entry 30 minutes before closing time. Charge £. Children and Scottish Borders residents admitted free. Group concessions. Guided tours if pre-booked. Explanatory displays. Gift shop. Picnic area, drinks available. Children's play area. WC. Limited wheelchair access. Disabled WC. Car and coach parking. Telephone (01835) 863254.

Jedburgh Castle, which was built in 1824, is one of the few remaining examples of a Howard Reform prison. It stands on the site of the old Jedburgh Castle, which was razed to the ground in the mid 1400s. It takes its architectural appearance from the earlier castle.

CASTLE KENNEDY GARDENS   52   8 K30

Stair Estates, Rephad, Stranraer, Dumfries and Galloway. 4 miles (6.5km) east of Stranraer on A75. Open Apr–Sep, daily 1000–1700. Charge ££. Group concessions. Gift shop. Tearoom. WC. Limited wheelchair access. Disabled WC. Car and coach parking. Telephone 01776 702024/01581 400225. www.castlekennedygardens.co.uk

Situated on a peninsula between two lochs, the gardens around the old castle were first laid out in the early 18th century. Noted for their rhododendrons and azaleas and a walled kitchen garden with fine herbaceous borders, the gardens contain many avenues and walks amid beautiful scenery.

CASTLE OF ST JOHN   53   7 J30

Charlotte Street, Stranraer, Wigtownshire. In Stranraer centre. Nearest railway station Stranraer, bus from Glasgow or ferry from Belfast. Open Easter–mid Sep, Mon–Sat 1000–1300 and 1400–1700. Free. Explanatory displays. Gift shop. Telephone (01776) 705088.

Medieval tower house built circa 1500. An exhibition tells the castle's story, highlighting its use by Government troops during the suppression of the Covenanters, and its Victorian use as a prison. Family activities.

CHAPEL FINIAN   54   8 K31

HS. 5 miles (8km) north west of Port William on the A747, Wigtownshire. Nearest railway station Stranraer, then bus to Port William. Access at all reasonable times. Free. Telephone (0131) 5507603. www.historic-scotland.gov.uk

The foundation remains of a small chapel or oratory, probably dating from the 10th or 11th century, in an enclosure about 50 feet (15m) wide.

CLAN ARMSTRONG MUSEUM   55   8 Q29

Lodge Walk, Castleholm, Langholm, Dumfries and Galloway. Off the A7 in Langholm, north of Carlisle. Regular bus service from Edinburgh to Carlisle passes on A7. Open Easter–mid Oct, Tue–Wed and Fri–Sun, 1400–1700. Charge £. Clan Armstrong Trust members free on production of card. Group concessions. Guided tours. Explanatory displays. Gift shop. Picnic area nearby. Garden. Wheelchair access. Car and coach parking. Telephone (01387) 381610.

The world's largest Armstrong Museum, containing the most extensive Armstrong archives and displaying the history of this formidable Borders' family from the reiving days of the 15th and 16th centuries to the present.

ROBERT CLAPPERTON'S DAYLIGHT PHOTOGRAPHIC STUDIO   56   8 Q27

The Studio, 28 Scotts Place, Selkirk. 15 minute walk from Selkirk market place. Open May–Aug, Fri–Sun 1400–1600. Telephone for other times. Charge £. Group concessions. Guided tours. Explanatory displays. Wheelchair access. Telephone (01750) 20523. www.scottishbordercamera.org.uk

One of the oldest surviving daylight photographic studios in the UK. The studio is set up as a working museum and photographic archive, in the building originally used by Robert Clapperton in 1867. Photographic equipment, cameras and prints. Demonstrations of black and white print processing in the original dark room can be arranged. Archive photographs and postcards for sale.

CLATTERINGSHAWS VISITOR CENTRE   57   8 L30

FE. New Galloway, Castle Douglas. Open daily Apr–Sep, 1000–1700; Oct, 1030–1630. Free. Explanatory displays. Gift shop. Tearoom and picnic area. WC. Wheelchair access. Disabled WC. Car and coach parking. Telephone (01644) 420285. www.forestry.gov.uk

Situated in Galloway Forest Park. Forest wildlife exhibition. Guided walks. Fishing (by permit). Waymarked walks and cycle trails.

CLOG AND SHOE WORKSHOP   59   8 M29

Balmaclellan, Dumfries and Galloway. 13 miles (21km) north of Castle Douglas in Balmaclellan. Bus service from Castle Douglas or Dalmellington. Open Easter–Oct, Mon–Fri 1000–1700. Workshop available to view all year round, but telephone in advance out of season. Free. Guided tours by appointment (charge £12). Explanatory displays. Gift shop. Wheelchair access. Disabled WC. Car parking. Telephone (01644) 420465. www.clogandshoe.com

Rural workshop where visitors can watch ongoing work which includes the making of modern and traditional clogs, boots, sandals, baby footwear, bags and purses. Footwear can be made to measure.

COLFIN SMOKEHOUSE   60   7 J30

Colfin Creamery, Portpatrick, Stranraer. 2 miles (3km) from Portpatrick on A77 at Colfin. Bus service from Stranraer passes close within 200 yards (200m). Open all year, Mon–Sat 0900–1700, Sun 1000–1500, closed Christmas and New Year. Free. Guided tours. Explanatory displays. Gift shop. WC. Wheelchair access. Disabled WC. Car and coach parking. Telephone (01776) 820622.

Visitors can observe the salmon smoking process in detail and purchase the product.

CORNICE MUSEUM OF ORNAMENTAL PLASTERWORK   61   8 Q27

Innerleithen Road, Peebles. Near Peebles town centre, opposite the Park Hotel. Nearest railway station Edinburgh, bus service with stop close to museum. Open all year, Mon–Thu 1030–1200 and 1400–1600, Fri 1030–1200 and 1400–1530; closed weekends and holiday periods such as Easter, 2 weeks in summer and 2 weeks at Christmas, telephone to check. Admission by donation. Guided tours. Explanatory displays. Some items for sale. WC. Wheelchair access with assistance. Car and coach parking. Telephone (01721) 720212.

The museum is a plasterer's casting workshop virtually unchanged since the turn of the century and illustrates the main methods of creating ornamental plasterwork in Scotland at that time. It also displays probably the largest surviving collection of 'masters' in Scotland.

COWANS LAW TROUT FISHING AND COUNTRY SPORTS   62   9 L27

Hemphill Road, Moscow, Galston, Ayrshire. From A77 take A719 to Moscow, signposted. Nearest railway and bus station Kilmarnock. Special transport from local hotels. Open summer months, daily 0800–dusk; winter months, daily 1000–1600. Charge £££. Group concessions. Restaurant and clubhouse. WC. Staff have sign language. Limited wheelchair access. Car and coach parking. Telephone (01560) 700666. www.countrysports-scotland.com

A 4 acre (1.7ha) trout loch set in the heart of Ayrshire's farming country. Also clay shooting, archery and air rifle range. Families and beginners welcome.

CRAFT DAFT   63   8 L28

2 Cow Wynd, Alloway Street, Ayr. In Ayr town centre, diagonally opposite Hourstons department store. Railway and bus station in Ayr. Open all year, Mon, Wed, Fri and Sat 1000–1730, Tue and Thu 1000–2100, Sun 1200–1730. ££ plus cost of chosen piece (from 99p–£33). Group concessions. Explanatory displays. Gift shop. Refreshments available. WC. Wheelchair access. Disabled WC. Car parking. Telephone (01292) 280844.

A drop-in craft studio. Visitors can try ceramic paining, silk painting, the potters' wheel and pyrography. Suitable for all ages and abilities. Parties welcome.

CRAIGIE ESTATE   64   8 L28

On the outskirts of Ayr. Nearest railway station Ayr, then a few minutes walk. Open all year, daily 1000–1700. Free. Guided tours. Explanatory displays. Shop with plant sales. Tearoom and picnic area. WC. Wheelchair access. Disabled WC. Car and coach parking. Telephone (01292) 263275.

Craigie Estate, situated on the banks of the River Ayr, provides a range of attractions, including woodland walks, the River Ayr walkway, formal gardens and Craigie Horticultural Centre, with tropical and temperate houses.

CREAM O' GALLOWAY   65   8 M30

Rainton, Gatehouse-of-Fleet, Castle Douglas, Dumfries and Galloway. 4 miles (6.5km) south of Gatehouse-of-Fleet off A75. Open daily, Apr–Aug 1000–1800, Sep–Oct 1000–1700, Sep 1000–1700; Nov weekends only 1000–1600. Free. Adventure playground £ (over 60s and under 5s free). Guided tours, weekends and daily during holidays "Farm and Creamery Tour" and the "Ice Cream Experience". Explanatory displays. Gift shop selling souvenirs, local crafts, preserves and art. Tearoom and picnic area. Designated dog walk. WC. Limited wheelchair access. Disabled WC. Car and coach parking. Telephone (01557) 814040. www.creamogalloway.co.uk

Cream o' Galloway is a small farm-based ice cream manufacturer specialising in traditional quality ice cream and frozen yoghurt with unusual flavours. There is a farm shop and a viewing gallery where visitors can watch the manufacturing process. Also 4 miles (6.5km) of nature trails, 2 of which are wheelchair and buggy accessible, cycle hire, garden, guided walks and events, extensive adventure playground (with 3 D maze), treasure hunt and nature quizzes.

CREETOWN GEM ROCK MUSEUM   66   8 L30

Chain Road, Creetown, Newton Stewart. 7 miles (11km) east of Newton Stewart on A75. Bus service from Dumfries or Stranraer. Open Mar–Easter, daily 1000–1600; Easter–Sep, daily 0930–1730; Oct–Nov, daily 1000–1600; Dec and Feb, weekends only 1000–1600; closed Christmas and Jan . Charge ££. Tickets valid 2 weeks. Group concessions. Guided tours. Explanatory displays. Gift shop. Tearoom. WC. Wheelchair access. Disabled WC. Car and coach parking. Telephone 0845 456 0245. www.gemrock.net

The museum houses one of the finest collections of privately owned gemstones, crystals, minerals and fossils in Europe. Visitors can witness the spectacular Crystal Cave and a 15-minute audio-visual programme 'Fire in the stones'. Geology and gemology quizzes.

CREETOWN HERITAGE MUSEUM   67   8 L30

91 St John Street, Creetown, Newton Stewart. On the main village street. On Dumfries to Stranraer bus route, local services from Newton Stewart. Open Easter–May and Sep–mid Oct, Sun–Tue and Thu–Fri 1100–1600; Jun–Aug, daily 1100–1600, except Sat. Small admission charge. Group concessions by prior arrangement. Guided tours by prior arrangement. Explanatory displays. Children's activities available. WC. Wheelchair access. Disabled WC. Car and coach parking. www.creetown-heritage-museum.com

Creetown is portrayed from its origin as an 18th-century fishing hamlet, through the growth and decline of its famous granite quarries, to the present day. Displays include a large collection of old photographs, war-time memorabilia, village shop, information on local nature reserve, work of local artists, wood-carver and sculptor.

THE CRICHTON   68   8 N30

Bankend Road, Dumfries. 1.5 miles (2.5km) south of Dumfries centre. Nearest railway station Dumfries, local bus service. Open at all reasonable times. Free. Garden or project tours for special interest groups by arrangement. Range of leaflets available. Restaurant and bar. Disabled WC. Car and coach parking. Telephone (01387) 247544. www.crichton.co.uk

The Crichton is on the site of the former Crichton Royal (psychiatric) Hospital. It covers 100 acres (62.5km) of conservation parkland and gardens within which are many fine sandstone buildings, including the outstanding cathedral-style Crichton Memorial Church dating from 1897. The estate has been substantially redeveloped as the UK's first multi university and college campus and a business park, but it also operates effectively as a major public park. The project has received five major national awards across the field of planning, architecture, landscape quality and property and economic regeneration, and has much to offer visitors from a wide range of interests.

CROSS KIRK   69   8 Q27

HS. In Cross road, Peebles. Open at all reasonable times (key from custodian in nearby house). Free. Limited wheelchair access. Telephone (0131) 5507603. www.historic-scotland.gov.uk

The remains of a Trinitarian friary founded in the late 13th century. Consists of nave, west tower and foundations of domestic buildings.

CROSSRAGUEL ABBEY   70   8 K28

HS. Maybole, Ayrshire. On the A77, 2 miles (3km) south west of Maybole. Nearest railway station Maybole, bus service via Maybole from Ayr to Girvan. Open Apr–Sep, daily 0930–1830. Charge £. Group concessions. Picnic area. WC. Wheelchair access. Car and coach parking. Telephone (01655) 883113. www.historic-scotland.gov.uk

A Cluniac monastery built in 1244 by the Earl of Carrick. Inhabited by Benedictine monks until the end of the 16th century. Extensive and remarkably complete remains of high quality, including the church, cloister, chapter house and much of the domestic premises.

CRUCK COTTAGE   71   8 P29

Torthorwald, left off A709. Key from Manor Country House Hotel, Torthorwald (arrangements are posted on the cottage). Car parking.

An example of an early 19th-century thatched cottage, restored using traditional skills and local materials.

CULZEAN CASTLE AND COUNTRY PARK   72   8 K28

NTS. Maybole. On A719, 12 miles (19km) south of Ayr. Bus from Ayr. Open Apr–Oct, daily 1030–1700; park open all year, daily 0930–sunset. Charge £££. Group concessions. Guided tours of castle by arrangement; guided walks by rangers in park. Explanatory displays. Information sheets in six languages, guidebook in French and German. Gift shop. Two restaurants and several snack-bars and picnic areas. Gardens, plant sales, adventure playground. WC. Induction loop and basic language audio tape tour. Braille guidebooks and tactile models. Wheelchair access (wheelchairs and batricars available). Disabled WC. Car and coach parking. Telephone (01655) 884455. www.nts.org.uk

High on a cliff above the Firth of Clyde, Robert Adam's Culzean Castle is one of the most romantic in Scotland. Designed at the end of the 18th century, the elegant interior includes the spectacular Oval Staircase and the Circular Saloon. Fascinating associated buildings in the 563 acre (227ha) country park include the Fountain Court and the Camellia House. Swan pond, deer park, woodland and beach walks.

DALBEATTIE FOREST 73   8 N30

FE. 9 miles (14.5km) west of Dumfries. Free access at all times. Forest walks
including Red Squirrel Interpretation Trail. Wheelchair access. Car parking.
Telephone (01387) 247745. www.forestry.gov.uk

Dalbeattie Forest cloaks the granite outcrops that surround the town itself. Its
name means 'valley of the birches' and even today these trees are common
throughout. At the heart of the forest lies the Plantain Loch, a tranquil retreat
where birds and dragonflies can be viewed from the boardwalk. Mountain biking
for all abilities, from quiet roads to technical single track.

DALBEATTIE MUSEUM 74   8 N30

1 Southwick Road, Dalbeattie. On A711 13 miles (21km) west of Dumfries. Local bus
service. Open Jun–Sep, Mon–Sat 1100–1600, Sun 1400–1600. Charge £. Children free
if accompanied by adult. Guided tours. Explanatory displays. Gift shop. Play material
for children. WC. Limited wheelchair access (stairs to first floor). Car and coach
parking. Telephone (01556) 610437.

Victorian and Edwardian household memorabilia. Most items can be handled by
visitors, from a machine for crushing seashells and the first wooden electrical
washing machine to a blow billiards game. A museum with a difference.

DALGARVEN MILL AND COUNTRY LIFE MUSEUM 75   9 K27

Dalgarven, Dalry Road, Kilwinning, Ayrshire. On the A737 between Dalry and
Kilwinning. Bus from Dalry or Kilwinning (or express bus from Glasgow). Open
Easter–Oct, Tue–Sun 1000–1700; Sep–Mar, Tue–Fri 1000–1600, Sat–Sun 1000–1700.
Charge ££. Group concessions and guided tours available by prior arrangement.
Explanatory displays. Antiques shop. Gift shop. Coffee shop. Riverside walk and wild
flower meadow. WC. Limited wheelchair access. Disabled WC. Car and coach
parking. Telephone (01294) 552448. www.dalgarvenmill.org.uk

A 17th-century restored water mill, set in a secluded hollow, housing an
exhibition of traditional flour production. In the adjoining granary there is a
museum of Ayrshire country life, with collections of farming and domestic
memorabilia and local costume, including some good examples of Ayrshire
whitework. Room reconstructions of 1880 lifestyle.

DALTON POTTERY ART CAFÉ 76   8 P30

Meikle Dyke, Dalton, Dumfries and Galloway. Signposted on the B725, 1 mile (2km)
towards Dalton from Carrutherstown (off A75 between Dumfries and Annan). Bus
from Dumfries. Open all year, Mon–Fri 1000–1700, Sat–Sun 1000–1700 (closed 23
Dec–4 Jan). Free. Guided tours by prior arrangement. Explanatory displays. Gift
shop. Tearoom and picnic area. Adventure play park. WC. Wheelchair access.
Disabled WC. Car parking. Telephone (01387) 840236. www.daltonpottery.co.uk

A working pottery where visitors can see porcelain and raku ceramics being
made and decorated. The pottery produces a wide selection of clocks, vases,
bowls and cat and fish themed ceramics. Visitors can also choose from a range of
glazed pots to decorate themselves and take home, or try out the potters' wheel.

TOM DAVIDSON GALLERY 77   8 R27

High Street, Earlston, Berwickshire. On the A68, 14 miles (22km) north of Jedburgh,
38 miles (61km) south of Edinburgh. Bus from Edinburgh, Jedburgh, Galashiels or
Berwick-upon-Tweed. Open all year, including bank holidays, Mon–Sat. Free.

Explanatory displays. Gift shop. Wheelchair access with assistance. Car and coach parking. Telephone (01896) 848898. www.tomdavidson.co.uk

A gallery featuring mostly landscape paintings, etchings and linocuts. Davidson is known as one of Scotland's leading exponents of the linocut and he can be seen at work either cutting or printing the block. Time is given to explain the process to visitors.

DAWYCK BOTANIC GARDEN 78   8 P27

Stobo, Peeblesshire. On the B712, 8 miles (13km) south west of Peebles. Bus from Peebles. Open daily, Apr–Sep 1000–1800; Mar and Oct closes 1700; Feb and Nov closes 1600. Charge ££. Group concessions. Guided tours by arrangement. Explanatory displays. Gift shop. Tearoom and picnic area. WC. Limited wheelchair access. Disabled WC. Car and coach parking. Telephone (01721) 760254. www.rbge.org.uk

A specialist garden of the Royal Botanic Garden, Edinburgh (see 379). A historic arboretum with landscaped walks. The mature trees include the unique Dawyck Beech. There are also many varieties of flowering trees, shrubs and herbaceous plants. Visitors can explore Heron Wood and the world's first Cryptogamic Sanctuary and Reserve to see non-flowering plants. Other notable features include the Swiss Bridge, stonework and terracing created by Italian craftsmen in the 1820s.

DEAN CASTLE AND COUNTRY PARK 79   9 L27

Dean Road, Kilmarnock. On A77. Nearest railway station Kilmarnock (15 minute walk), bus service from Kilmarnock. Park open all year, daily from dawn to dusk. Castle open all year, daily 1200–1700; closed Christmas and New Year. Free. Guided tours. Explanatory displays. Gift shop. Restaurant and picnic areas. WC. Limited wheelchair access. Disabled WC. Car and coach parking. Telephone (01563) 554708.

A magnificent collection of buildings dating from the 1350s. For 400 years Dean Castle was the stronghold of the Boyds of Kilmarnock, and today important collections of arms and armour, musical instruments and tapestries are on display in public rooms. The country park comprises 200 acres (81ha) of mixed woodland. Ranger service and programme of events.

DESIGNS GALLERY AND CAFÉ 80   8 M30

179 King Street, Castle Douglas, Dumfries and Galloway. On the A75, 18 miles (29km) west of Dumfries. Bus from Dumfries. Open all year (except Christmas and New Year), Mon–Sat 0930–1730. Free. Shop and exhibition gallery. Café/restaurant. Garden. WC. Limited wheelchair access. Disabled WC. Telephone (01556) 504552. www.designsgallery.co.uk

A focal point for arts and crafts in south west Scotland. Changing exhibitions of high quality crafts. Adjacent shop sells cards, prints, ceramics, knitwear, studio glass and jewellery.

DEVIL'S BEEF TUB 81   8 P28

A701, 6 miles (9.5km) north of Moffat. Access at all times. Free. Car parking.

A huge, spectacular hollow among the hills, at the head of Annandale. In the swirling mists of this out-of-the-way retreat, Border reivers hid cattle lifted in their raids. Can be seen from the road.

DICK INSTITUTE 82   9 L27

Elmbank Avenue, Kilmarnock. Nearest railway station Kilmarnock (ten minute walk). Open all year, Tue–Sat 1100–1700. Free. Explanatory displays. Craft shop selling contemporary works predominantely from local makers. WC. Wheelchair access. Disabled WC. Car and coach parking. Telephone (01563) 554343. www.east-ayrshire. gov.uk/comser/arts_museums/main.asp

Temporary and permanent exhibitions over two floors of this grand Victorian building. Fine art, social and natural history collections are upstairs whilst galleries downstairs house temporary exhibitions of international, national and regional visual arts and crafts.

DOON VALLEY MUSEUM   83   8 L28

Carthcartston, Dalmellington. Nearest railway station Ayr, bus from Ayr. Open all year, Thur–Sat 1100–1700. Free. Explanatory displays. WC. Wheelchair access. Car parking. Telephone (01292) 550633.

Local history museum with a fine collection of photographs and maps illustrating the Doon Valley over the centuries. Also local history displays combined with changing art exhibitions.

DRUCHTAG MOTTE   84   8 L31

HS. At the north end of Mochrum village on the A747, 2 miles (3km) north of Port William, Wigtownshire. Nearest railway station Stranraer, bus from Newton Stewart or Stranraer to Mochrum or Port William. Access at all reasonable times. Free. Telephone (0131) 5507603. www.historic-scotland.gov.uk

A well-preserved Norman motte castle.

DRUMCOLTRAN TOWER   85   8 N30

HS. Off A711, 8 miles (13km) south west of Dumfries. The tower can be found among farm buildings. Nearest railway station Dumfries, bus services from Dumfries, Stranraer, Dalbeattie then walk. Open at all reasonable times (apply to keyholder). Free. Car parking. Telephone (0131) 5507603. www.historic-scotland.gov.uk

A well-preserved mid 16th-century tower house. Simple and severe.

DRUMLANRIG CASTLE   86   8 N28

Thornhill, Dumfries and Galloway. Off A76, 4 miles (6.5km) north of Thornhill (16 miles/25.5km from M74, junction 14). Nearest railway station at Dumfries (18 miles/29km). Nearest bus stop 1.5 mile (2.5km). Open May–Aug, Mon–Sat 1200–1600, Sun 1200–1600. Charge £££. Group concessions. Guided tours. Gift shop. Licensed restaurant. WC. Wheelchair access. Disabled WC. Car and coach parking. Telephone (01848) 331555. www.drumlanrig.com

Dumfriesshire home of the Duke of Buccleuch and Queensberry, built between 1679 and 1691 by William Douglas, 1st Duke of Queensberry. Includes works by Rembrandt, Holbein and Leonardo. Associations with Bonnie Prince Charlie, Robert Bruce and Mary, Queen of Scots. French furniture, 300-year-old silver chandelier and cabinets made for Louis XIV's Versailles. Douglas family exhibition room. Extensive gardens now being restored to original 18th-century plans. Woodland walks. Craft centre. Children's adventure playground. Visitor centre with live wildlife TV. Ranger service. Cycle museum and cycle hire. Mountain bike trails. Working forge. Plant centre.

DRUMLANRIG'S TOWER   87   8 R28

1 Towerknowe, Hawick. In the centre of Hawick, off the High Street. Bus from Edinburgh or Carlisle. Open Mar–Sep, Mon–Sat 1000–1700, Sun 1200–1500; Oct Mon–Sat 1000–1700. Charge £. Group concessions. Guided tours by arrangement. Explanatory displays in visitor centre (touch screen audio-visual). Gift shop. Baby

changing and feeding facilities. WC. Wheelchair access. Disabled WC. Car parking. Telephone (01450) 377615. www.scotborders.gov.uk/museums

This 15th-century fortified tower house, stronghold of the Douglases, tells the story of Hawick and Scotland using period sets, costumed figures and audio-visuals. Themes include Border Reivers and Hawick's renowned knitwear industry.

DRUMTRODDAN CUP AND RING MARKS   88 · 8 L31

HS. On the B705, 2 miles (3km) north east of Port William, Wigtownshire. Nearest railway station Stranraer, bus services from Dumfries, Stranraer and Dalbeattie then walk. Access at all reasonable times. Free. Telephone 0131 550 7603. www.historic-scotland.gov.uk

A group of Bronze Age cup and ring markings in bedrock. An alignment of three stones stands 400 yards (365m) south.

DRYBURGH ABBEY   89 · 8 R27

HS. Dryburgh, St Boswells, Melrose. Near St Boswells on the B6404, 8 miles (13km) south east of Melrose. Bus service from Newtown to St Boswells, alight at College Stop, then 20 minute walk. Open Apr–Sep, daily 0930–1830; Oct–Mar, daily 0930–1630. Charge £. Group concessions. Explanatory displays. Gift shop. Picnic area. WC. Wheelchair access. Car and coach parking. Telephone (01835) 822381. www.historic-scotland.gov.uk

The remarkably complete ruins of a Premonstratensian abbey. One of the four famous Border abbeys founded in the reign of David I by Hugh de Morville, Constable of Scotland. Mainly remains of transepts and cloisters. Sir Walter Scott and Field Marshall Earl Haig are buried here.

DRYHOPE TOWER   90 · 8 Q27

Off A708 near St Mary's Loch, 15 miles (24km) west of Selkirk. Access at all reasonable times. Free.

A stout tower, now ruinous but originally four storeys high, rebuilt circa 1613. Birthplace of Mary Scott, the Flower of Yarrow, who married the freebooter Auld Wat of Harden in 1576 – ancestors Sir Walter Scott was proud to claim.

DUMFRIES AND GALLOWAY AVIATION MUSEUM   91 · 8 N29

Heathhall Industrial Estate, Heathhall, Dumfries. Access from A75 Dumfries bypass, or from town centre via A701. Nearest railway station Dumfries, 2 miles (3km), bus to Heathhall stops within 0.5 mile (1km). Open first weekend in April (or Easter if sooner)–Oct, Sat–Sun 1000–1700; Jul and Aug also Wed–Fri 1100–1600; also some bank holidays. Charge ££. Group concessions by arrangement (including school groups). Group concessions. Guided tours. Explanatory displays. Gift shop. Light refreshments available. Garden. WC. Limited wheelchair access. Disabled WC. Car and coach parking. Telephone (01387) 251623. www.dumfriesaviation.com

Opened in 1977 and regarded as one of the foremost volunteer-run aviation museums in the UK. Various aircraft are on display and under restoration, including a spitfire, hawker, hunter and a trident airliner. There is an airborne forces display and in the former control tower is a varied collection of memorabilia ranging from aero engines to uniforms and documentation.

DUMFRIES ICE BOWL   92 · 8 N29

King Street, Dumfries. Nearest railway and bus stations Dumfries. Open all year, 0900–2200 except Christmas and New Year. Charge ££. Charge dependent on activity. Group concessions. Gift shop. Restaurant. WC. Wheelchair access. Disabled WC. Car and coach parking. Telephone (01387) 251300.

Curling, skating, ice disco, ice hockey matches and bowls hall.

DUMFRIES MUSEUM AND CAMERA OBSCURA 93 8 N29

The Observatory, Rotchell Road, Dumfries. 0.5 mile (1km) west of Dumfries centre. 15 minute walk from railway station, seven minute walk from bus station. Open Apr–Sep, Mon–Sat 1000–1700, Sun 1400–1700; Oct–Mar, Tue–Sat 1000–1300 and 1400–1700. Free. Charge £ for Camera Obscura. Explanatory displays. Leaflet in French, German, Spanish, Italian and Russian. Gift shop. Terraced gardens. WC. Wheelchair access (museum only). Disabled WC. Car parking. Telephone (01387) 253374. www.dumgal.gov.uk/museums

A treasure house of history in Dumfries and Galloway, Dumfries Museum tells the story of the land and people of the region. Look out for fossil footprints left by prehistoric animals, the wildlife of the Solway, tools and weapons of our earliest people, stone carvings by Scotland's first Christians and everyday things of the Victorian farm, workshop and home.

The Camera Obscura, installed in 1836, is on the top floor of the old windmill tower. From it you can see a fascinating panoramic view of Dumfries and the surrounding countryside.

DUNASKIN HERITAGE MUSEUM 94 8 L28

Dalmellington Road, Waterside, Patna, Ayrshire. Adjacent to A713 Ayr to Castle Douglas/ Dumfries road. Nearest railway station Ayr, buses from Ayr and Cumnock. Telephone (01292) 531144. www.dunaskin.co.uk

This open-air industrial museum closed to the public in June 2005. The site still, however, houses the Scottish Industrial Railway Centre, operated by the Ayrshire Railway Preservation Group (arpg.org.uk), which aims to preserve Scotland's industrial railway heritage. The group meets regularly and welcomes volunteers.

DUNDONALD CASTLE 95 9 L27

Dundonald, Kilmarnock, Ayrshire. On the A759, 5 miles (8km) west of Kilmarnock. Follow signs from A77 and A78. Bus from Kilmarnock, Irvine or Troon. Open Apr–Oct, daily 1000–1700. Charge £. Guided tours. Explanatory displays. Staff provide information. Visitor centre with interpretive display. Gift shop. Tearoom and picnic area. WC. Wheelchair access to visitor centre/interpretive display only. Disabled WC. Car and coach parking. Telephone (01563) 851489. www.dundonaldcastle.org.uk

A large prominent stone castle, built by Robert Stewart in the 1370s, probably to mark his succession to the Scottish throne as Robert II in 1371. Two great feasting halls, one above the other, with great vaults beneath. The third medieval castle to be built on the site, preceded by a hill fort between 500 and 200 BC. Remains of an earlier, but equally grand 13th-century castle of the Stewarts are visible.

DUNDRENNAN ABBEY 96 8 M31

HS. Dundrennan, Kirkcudbright. On the A711, 6.5 miles (10.5km) south east of Kirkcudbright. Bus to Dundrennan from Kirkcudbright or Dalbeattie. Open Apr–Sep, Mon–Sun 0930–1830; Oct–Mar, Sat–Sun 0930–1630. Charge £. Group concessions. WC. Blind visitors may touch carvings. Limited wheelchair access. Car and coach parking. Telephone (01557) 500262. www.historic-scotland.gov.uk

The beautiful ruins, amid a peaceful setting, of a Cistercian abbey founded in 1142 by King David I. Includes much later Norman and transitional work. The east end of the church and the chapter house are of high quality. It is believed that Mary, Queen of Scots spent her last night in Scotland here in May 1568.

DUNSKEY CASTLE   97   7 J30

Just south of Portpatrick. Access at all reasonable times. Free.

Impressive early 16th-century castle ruins in a dramatic cliff top setting. Reach the castle from the cliff top footpath which ascends from the old quarry at the south end of Portpatrick waterfront. Take care at the edge of the cliffs.

DUNSKEY GARDENS AND WOODLAND WALKS   98   7 J30

Dunskey House, Portpatrick. 1 mile (1.5km) from Portpatrick. Bus service to Portpatrick. Open Easter–Oct, daily 1000–1700. Charge ££. Group concessions. Guided tours by arrangement. Explanatory displays. Gift shop. Licenced tearoom. Plant sales. WC. Wheelchair access (except woodland gardens). Disabled WC. Car and coach parking. Telephone 01776810905. www.dunskey.com

A charming, recently renovated 18th-century walled garden with working greenhouses and interesting woodland gardens. See also 99 Dunskey Trout Lochs.

DUNSKEY TROUT LOCHS   99   7 J30

Dunskey House, Portpatrick, Stranraer. 1 mile (1.5km) from Portpatrick. Bus service to Portpatrick. Fishing from Mar–Oct. Charge £££. Car parking. Telephone (01776) 810364 or 810 848. www.dunskey.com

Two exclusive trout lochs for fly-fishing only. Boat and bank fishing. Licensed tearoom providing home made meals all day. See also 98 Dunskey Gardens and Woodland Garden.

DURISDEER CHURCH   100   8 N28

6 miles (9.5km) north east of Thornhill on A702. Access at all reasonable times. Free.

Dating from 1699, the church houses the Queensberry Marbles,which represent the recumbent figures of the second Duke and Duchess of Queensberry. In the vault lie lead coffins, containing ancient remains of the Clan Douglas.

EASTCOTE HOUSE ARCHERY CENTRE   101   8 R28

Eastcote, Hawick, Roxburghshire. On the A698, 2 miles (3km) east of Hawick. Bus from Hawick. Open Wed–Mon 1100–2100 (closed Tue). Open Wed–Mon 1100–2100. Charge dependent on activity. Archery shop. WC. Wheelchair access. Car parking. Telephone (01450) 870008. www.eastcote.net

A family-run archery centre offering introductory lessons, courses, coaching and use of archery facilities. Heated indoor range available.

THE EDINBURGH WOOLLEN MILL, JEDBURGH   102   8 R28

Bankend North, 1 Edinburgh Road, Jedburgh. In Jedburgh on the A68, 10 miles (16km) north of the English border. Bus from Edinburgh or Newcastle. Open all year (except Christmas Day), Apr–Oct, daily 0900–1730; Nov–Mar, daily 0900–1700. Free. Explanatory displays. Gift shop. Picnic area. WC. Wheelchair access with assistance. Disabled WC. Car and coach parking. Telephone (01835) 863585. www.ewm.co.uk

Visitors can trace their clan and tartan at the Clan Tartan Centre, fully authenticated by the Clan Chiefs of Scotland. A world of tartan from small mementos to full Highland Dress, the choice is immense. Also golf equipment, whisky shop (with over 100 different malts), selection of cashmere and ladies and gents clothing.

EDINS HALL BROCH   103   8 S26

HS. On the north eastern slope of Cockburn Law, off the A6112 about 4.5 miles (7km) from Grantshouse, Berwickshire. 1 mile (2km) walk from the Duns road, then footpath for 2 miles (3km). Access at all reasonable times. Free. Car parking. Telephone (0131) 5507603. www.historic-scotland.gov.uk

One of the few Iron Age brochs in the Scottish Lowlands. Unusually large, sitting in a fort defended by ramparts and ditches, partially overlain with a later settlement. Occupied in Roman times.

EDROM CHURCH   104   8 S26

HS. In Edrom churchyard, Berwickshire, off A6015, 3.5 miles (5.5km) north east of Duns. Access at all reasonable times. Free. Car parking. Telephone (0131) 5507603. www.historic-scotland.gov.uk

A fine Norman chancel arch from the church built by Thor Longus circa 1105.

EDROM NURSERIES   105   8 S26

Coldingham, Eyemouth, Berwickshire. On A1107, 12 miles (19km) north of Berwick upon Tweed. Follow brown tourist signs. Telephone to confirm opening times. Free. Explanatory displays. WC. Car and coach parking. Telephone (018907) 71386. www.edromnurseries.co.uk

Plant nursery offering a comprehensive selection of alpines, bulbous plants, ericaceous plants, ferns, woodland plants and trees and shrubs.

EGLINTON COUNTRY PARK   106   9 L27

Irvine. In Irvine, 2 miles (3km) south east of Kilwinning. Nearest railway stations at Irvine and Kilwinning, regular bus service passes entrance. Country park open all year, dawn to dusk. Visitor centre open Apr–mid Oct, daily, 1000–1630. Free. Explanatory displays. Ranger guided walks, events programme. Gift shop. Tearoom and picnic area. Children's play area, indoor soft play area (booking essential for parties). WC. Limited wheelchair access (electric scooters available). Disabled WC. Car and coach parking. Telephone (01294) 551776.

A 988 acre (400 ha) country park built around the ruin of Eglinton Castle. The visitor centre tells the story of the Eglinton Estate and the Eglinton/Montgomerie family. Country park comprises woodlands, wetlands and gardens. Ranger service provides guided walks and events. Opportunities for cycling, angling and horse riding.

ELECTRIC BRAE   107   8 K28

On A7, 20 miles (32km) south of Ayr (also known as Croy Brae). Access at all times. Free.

An optical illusion is created so that a car appears to be going down the hill when it is in fact going up.

ELLISLAND FARM   108   8 N29

Holywood, Dumfries. Off the A76, 6.5 miles (10.5km) north north-west of Dumfries. Bus from Dumfries. Open Easter–Sep, Mon–Sat 1000–1300 and 1400–1700, Sun

1400–1700; Oct–Easter same hours but closed Sun and Mon. Charge £. Guided tours. Explanatory displays. Picnic area. Riverside walk. WC. Limited wheelchair access. Car and coach parking. Telephone (01387) 740426. www.ellislandfarm.co.uk

The farm which Robert Burns took over in 1788, building the farmhouse and trying to introduce new farming methods. Unsuccessful, he became an exciseman in 1789, and when the stock was auctioned in 1791 he moved to Dumfries. Burns wrote some of his most famous works at the farm, including *Tam o' Shanter* and *Auld Lang Syne*. The granary houses an audio-visual display.

EYEMOUTH MUSEUM   109   8 T26

Auld Kirk, Manse Road, Eyemouth. Town centre. Nearest railway station Berwick-upon-Tweed, bus service from Berwick and Edinburgh. Open Apr–Jun and Sep, Mon–Sat 1000–1700, Sun 1000–1300; Jul–Aug, Mon–Sat 1000–1700, Sun 1000–1400; Oct, Mon–Sat 1000–1600. Charge £. Accompanied children free. Group concessions. Guided tours by arrangement. Explanatory displays. Shop and visitor information centre. Car and Coach parking nearby. Wheelchair access to main exhibition area. Telephone (01890) 750678.

The museum contains a magnificent tapestry which was sewn by local ladies to commemorate the Great East Coast Fishing Disaster of 1881, when 189 fishermen were drowned. Also exhibitions on farming, milling, blacksmith and wheelwright, and of course local fishing heritage.

FAST CASTLE   110   8 S25

Off A1107, 4 miles (6.5km) north west of Coldingham. Access at all times. Free. Car parking.

The scant, but impressive remains of a Home stronghold, perched on a cliff above the sea. Care should be taken on the cliffs.

FLAT CAT GALLERY   111   8 R26

2 Market Place, Lauder, Berwickshire. In Lauder town centre, off A68. Bus from Edinburgh to Jedburgh stops in town. Open all year, daily 0930–1700. Free. Explanatory displays. Gift shop. Coffee shop. Children's toy box. WC. Wheelchair access. Disabled WC. Car and coach parking. Telephone (01578) 722808. www.flatcatgallery.com

Changing exhibitions of paintings, sculpture, ceramics, jewellery and furniture by artists from the Borders and further afield. Also a resident restorer of middle-eastern rugs and textiles. A good stock of carpets on display.

FLODDEN MONUMENT   112   8 Q27

Town centre, Selkirk. Access at all times. Free.

The monument was erected in 1913 on the 400th anniversary of the battle and is inscribed O Flodden Field. The memorial is the work of sculptor Thomas Clapperton, and commemorates the lone survivor of the 80 Selkirk men who marched to Flodden.

FLOORS CASTLE   113   8 S27

Kelso, Roxburghshire. Open Apr–Oct, daily 1100–1700. Charge £££. Group concessions. Guided tours by prior arrangement. Explanatory displays. Gift shop. Restaurant and coffee shop (both with outdoor seating) and picnic area. Garden Centre. WC. No guide dogs. Wheelchair access. Disabled WC. Car and coach parking. Telephone (01573) 223333.

Floors Castle is the home of the Roxburghe family. The apartments display an outstanding collection of French 17th- and 18th-century furniture, many fine works of art and tapestries, Chinese and Dresden porcelain and a Victorian collection of birds. The extensive parkland and gardens overlooking the River Tweed provide delightful walks and picnic areas. The walled garden contains splendid herbaceous borders and is best seen in July, August and September.

FOULDEN TITHE BARN 114   8 T26

HS. On the A6105, 4 miles (6.5km) south east of Chirnside, Berwickshire. Bus from Berwick-upon-Tweed to Duns. View exterior only. Telephone (0131) 5507603. www.historic-scotland.gov.uk

A two-storey tithe barn with outside stair and crow-stepped gables.

GALLOWAY COUNTRY STYLE 115   8 M30

High Street, Gatehouse-of-Fleet. Bus from Dumfries or Stranraer. Open all year except Christmas and New Year, daily 1000–1700. Free. Guided tours by arrangement. Explanatory displays. Gift shop. Coffee shop. WC. Limited wheelchair access. Disabled WC. Car and coach parking. Telephone (01557) 814001.

A kilt-making workshop where visitors can see operations and learn about the history of kilts and how they are made.

GALLOWAY DEER RANGE 116   8 L30

Laggan O'Dee, New Galloway. 10 miles (16km) from Newton Stewart and 9 miles (14.5km) from New Galloway on A712. Open late Jun–mid Sep, walks Tue and Thu 1100 and 1400, Sun 1430. Charge £. Guided tours. Explanatory displays. No guide dogs. Car and coach parking. Telephone (07771) 748400 or 401. www.forestry.gov.uk/gallowayforestpark

Created in 1977 to enable visitors to see red deer in a semi-natural habitat of 500 acres (200ha). Good photo opportunities.

GALLOWAY HYDROS VISITOR CENTRE 117   8 M30

Kirkcudbright, Dumfries and Galloway. On A711, 2 miles (3km) north of Kirkcudbright. Bus service to Kirkcudbright. Open late May–early Sep, Mon–Fri 0930–1700. Charge £. Guided tours. Explanatory displays. Gift shop. Tearoom. WC. Written tour in large text on non-glare paper. Limited wheelchair access. Disabled WC. Car and coach parking. Telephone (01557) 330114. www.scottishpower.co.uk

Located at Tongland Power Station. The visitor centre tells the story of the construction of the Galloway Hydros Scheme in the 1930s and the operation of the power station. Tongland Dam and reservoir is nearby.

GALLOWAY SAILING CENTRE 118   8 M30

Parton, Castle Douglas, Dumfries and Galloway. On the A713, 10 miles (16km) north of Castle Douglas, on the shore of Loch Ken. Nearest railway station Dumfries, bus from Dumfries/Castle Douglas. Collection from station by arrangement. Open Apr–Oct, daily 0900–1800. Free. Charge for activities. Group concessions. Explanatory displays. Gift shop. Café and picnic area. Children's play area. WC. Wheelchair access with assistance. Disabled WC. Car and coach parking. Telephone (01644) 420626.

Tuition in sailing, windsurfing and canoeing. Also improvised raft-building, quad bikes and gorge scrambling. Residential courses and boat hire. Groups welcome.

GALLOWAY SMOKEHOUSE   119   8 L30

Carsluith, Newton Stewart, Wigtownshire. On A75, 2 miles south of Creetown. Bus service from Dumfries or Stranraer. Open all year, daily 0900–1730. Car parking. Telephone (01671) 820354. www.gallowaysmokehouse.co.uk

Visitors can take a tour around a traditional smokehouse. The shop sells award-winning smoked foods.

GALLOWAY WILDLIFE CONSERVATION PARK   120   8 M31

Lochfergus Plantation, Kirkcudbright, Dumfries & Galloway. 1 mile (2km) east of Kirkcudbright, on B727. Nearest bus stop Kirkcudbright. Open Feb–Nov, daily 1000–dusk; Dec–Jan, Fri–Sun 1000–1600. Charge ££. Group concessions. Explanatory displays. Gift shop. Cafe and picnic areas. Baby changing facilities, children's play area, gift shop. WC. British sign language guided tour. No guide dogs. Wheelchair access with assistance. Disabled WC. Car and coach parking. Telephone (01557) 331645. www.gallowaywildlife.co.uk

A varied collection of nearly 150 animals from all over the world can be seen within the peaceful and natural settings, where the woodland has been tailored to provide large and imaginative enclosures. Threatened species to be seen at the park inlcude red pandas, bush dogs, maned wolves, otters, lemurs and, of course, the famous Scottish wildcat.

LADY GIFFORD STATUE   121   8 P26

Village clock, in West Linton, 17 miles (27km) south south-west of Edinburgh. Access at all reasonable times.

Statue on the front of the village clock at West Linton, carved in 1666 by the Laird Gifford, a Covenanter and skilled stonemason. The clock is on the site of a well, disused since Victorial times. Laird Gifford also executed panels (1660 and 1678) on a house opposite, depicting Lady Gifford and the entire family genealogy.

GILNOCKIE TOWER   122   8 Q29

Hollows, Canonbie, Dumfries and Galloway. On the A7, 2 miles (3km) north of Canonbie. Bus from Carlisle or Galashiels. Tours Easter–Oct 1430 sharp; at other times by arrangement. Charge ££. Group concessions. Guided tours. Explanatory displays. Gift shop. WC. No guide dogs. Car and coach parking. Telephone (01387) 371876.

A tower house built in 1525 by the Border freebooter Johnie Armstrong and originally called Holehouse (from the quarry beside which it stands). Managed by the Clan Armstrong Centre.

THE GLAIDSTANE   123   9 K26

1 mile (1.6km) north of Millport, Isle of Cumbrae. Access at all reasonable times. Free. Picnic area. Car parking.

At 417 feet (127m), the highest point on Cumbrae. Excellent views to the Isles of Arran and Bute, the Ayrshire coast and Arrochar Alps to the north.

GLENLUCE ABBEY   124   8 K30

HS. Glenluce, Newton Stewart, Wigtownshire. Off the A75, 2 miles (3km) north west of Glenluce. Nearest railway station Stranraer (10 miles/16km), bus from Stranraer to Newton Stewart, then 1.5 mile (2.5km) walk. Open Apr–Sep, daily 0930–1830; Oct–Mar, Sat 0930–1630. Charge £. Group concessions. Explanatory displays. Gift shop. Tearoom. WC. Limited wheelchair access. Disabled WC. Car and coach parking. Telephone (01581) 300541. www.historic-scotland.gov.uk

The remains of a Cistercian abbey founded circa 1192, including a handsome early 16th-century chapter house. Includes an exhibition of *objets trouvés*. Lovely tranquil setting.

GLENTROOL VISITOR CENTRE   125   8 L29

FE. Glentrool, Newton Stewart. 8 miles (13km) north of Newton Stewart, 3 miles (5km) west of Loch Trool and Stroan Bridge in Galloway Forest Park. Open daily, Apr–Sep 1030–1730, Oct 1030–1630. Free. Explanatory displays. Gift shop. Tearoom and picnic area. Events schedule and details of waymarked trails and cycle routes at visitor centre. WC. Wheelchair access. Disabled WC. Car and coach parking. Telephone (01671) 840301. www.forestry.gov.uk

The gateway to Glen Trool, Scotland's largest forest park covering 18,780 acres (7600ha) of forest, moorland and loch. Exhibits on Loch Trool.

GLENWHAN GARDENS   126   8 K30

Dunragit, Stranraer, Wigtownshire. Off A75, 6 miles (10km) east of Stranraer. Bus from Stranraer. Open Apr–Sep, daily 1000–1700; other times by arrangement. Charge ££. Wheelchair users free admission. Group concessions. Guided tours (available in French). Explanatory displays. Small shop. Licensed restaurant. Dog walking area (dogs on lead allowed in garden). WC. Wheelchair access with assistance. Disabled WC. Car and coach parking. Telephone (01581) 400222. www.glenwhan.co.uk

A beautiful and spectacular 12 acre (5ha) garden overlooking Luce Bay and the Mull of Galloway, begun in 1979 and hewn from the hillside creating two small lakes. A rich habitat for many tender species, including alpines, scree plants and conifers. Woodland with bluebells, snowdrops, specie rhododendrons, azaleas and shrub roses. A plantsman's garden. Also rare ducks, guinea fowl, chickens peacocks and red squirrels. Primula Arena.

GOATFELL   127   7 J27

NTS. Isle of Arran. Access from Cladach on A841 Brodick to Lochranza road. Ferry from Ardrossan to Brodick. Open all year. Free. Explanatory displays. Car and coach parking. Telephone (01770) 302462. www.nts.org.uk

At 2866 feet (873m), Goatfell is the highest peak on Arran, dominating the skyline of the island and affording impressive views from the top. The climb includes fine rock climbing and ridge walking.

GRACEFIELD ARTS CENTRE   128   8 N29

28 Edinburgh Road, Dumfries. In centre of Dumfries. Open all year, Tue–Sat 1000–1700. Craft shop and café/bar. Wheelchair access wheelchair access to studios and assisted access to galleries. Car and coach parking. Telephone (01387) 262084. www.web-link.co.uk/gracefield.htm

Changing exhibitions and art courses. Also a regular Saturday Club for children.

GREENKNOWE TOWER   129   8 R27

HS. On the A6105, 0.5 mile (1km) west of Gordon on the Earlston road, Berwickshire. Bus from Kelso or Edinburgh to Gordon, then walk. Open at all reasonable times (see keyholder). Free. Telephone (0131) 5507603. www.historic-scotland.gov.uk

A handsome tower house on an L-plan, built in 1581 and still retaining its iron yett (gate).

GRETNA GREEN, WORLD FAMOUS OLD BLACKSMITH'S SHOP CENTRE   130   8 Q30

Gretna Green, Dumfries and Galloway. On the Scottish/English border off M74 or A75, 15 miles (24km) south of Lockerbie. Nearest railway station Gretna Green, bus from Dumfries or Carlisle. Open daily all year, 0900–1700 in winter; Jun and Sep 0900–1900; Jul–Aug 0900–2000; Oct–Nov and Apr–May 0900–1800. Charge £. Children under 16 free. Group concessions. Guided tours (leaflets and audio guide in seven languages). Explanatory displays. Gift shop. Restaurant, tearoom and picnic area. Sculpture park. Various art outlets. Children's play area. WC. Wheelchair access. Disabled WC. Car and coach parking. Telephone 01461 338441 or 338224. www.gretnagreen.com

The Blacksmith's Shop is famous around the world for runaway marriages. The unique *Gretna Green Story* involves the visitor in the legends of its romantic history and leads into the magnificent anvil and carriage museum. The Tartan Shop presents Scotland's finest independent collection of Scottish and UK merchandise – cashmere, tartans, crystal, luxury foods and gifts. Tartan information centre. Tax-free shopping and worldwide mailing services.

GRETNA HALL BLACKSMITH'S SHOP   131   8 Q30

Gretna Green. 1 mile (1.5km) north of the border with England. Nearest railway station Gretna Green (0.5 mile/1km). Open mid Apr–mid Oct, daily 0830–2100; mid Oct–mid Apr 0900–1700. Charge £. Children under 14 free. Guided tours (leaflets available in Dutch, French, German, Italian and Spanish). Explanatory displays. Gift shop. Restaurant, bar and picnic area. Gardens. WC. Wheelchair access. Disabled WC. Car and coach parking. Telephone (01461) 337635. www.gretna-green-weddings.com

Built in 1710, the Gretna Hall blacksmiths has an interesting history associated with weddings, which are still performed here.

GREY MARE'S TAIL   132   8 P28

NTS. Adjacent to A708, 10 miles (16km) north east of Moffat, Dumfries and Galloway. Site open all year. Visitor centre open Jun–Aug, Thur–Mon 1200–1600 . Free. Explanatory displays, remote camera link to waterfall and wildlife. Wheelchair access to reception area. Car and coach parking. Telephone (01683) 222714. www.nts.org.uk

Spectacular 200 feet (61m) waterfall in landscape of geological interest and rich in wild flowers. Herd of wild goats. Marked paths – please keep to these for your safety.

HALLIWELL'S HOUSE MUSEUM   133   8 Q27

Market Place, Selkirk. In Selkirk, 35 miles (56km) south of Edinburgh. Bus from Edinburgh, Carlisle or Berwick. Open Apr–Sep, daily 1000–1700, Sun 1000–1400; Jul and Aug 1000–1730, Sun 1000–1400; Oct, Mon–Sat 1000–1600. Free. Explanatory displays. Gift shop. WC. Wheelchair access. Disabled WC. Car and coach parking. Telephone (01750) 20096.

A local museum in a row of 19th-century cottages. One of the best collections of domestic ironmongery in the country. Based on local history, the museum traces the growth of Selkirk, from the Stone Age to its role as an important textile-producing centre.

HALLMUIR POW CHAPEL   134   8 P30

Halmuir Camp, Dalton Road, Lockerbie. Off A92, 2miles (3.6km) from Lockerbie.
Open Jan–Oct 0900–2100 and Nov–Dec 0900–1700. Free. Refreshments available.
WC. No guide dogs. Wheelchair access.

Hallmuir survives as a living memorial to several hundred Ukrainian prisoners
of war who in 1947 were sent from Italy to Scotland, rather than being handed
over to the Russians to face a potentially terrifying future.

HARBOUR ARTS CENTRE   135   9 K27

Harbour Arts Centre, Harbour Street, Irvine. Nearest railway station Irvine, then ten
minute walk. Open all year, Tue–Fri 1000–1600, Sat 1000–1300, Sun 1400–1700; also
open Fri 2000–0100. Free. Charge for performances and workshops. Group
concessions. WC. Wheelchair access. Disabled WC. Car parking. Telephone (01294)
274059. www.harbourarts.org.uk

The centre currently offers activities and events in a diverse range of art forms,
including theatre, music, visual art and literature. Located by scenic Irvine
Harbour.

HARBOUR COTTAGE GALLERY, KIRKCUDBRIGHT   136   8 M31

Castlebank, Kirkcudbright. Beside the harbour in Kirkcudbright. Bus from Dumfries.
Open Mar–Dec, daily 1030–1230 and 1400–1700; Apr–Oct, also Sun 1400–1700.
Charge £. Children free. Group concessions. Limited wheelchair access. Telephone
(01557) 330073. www.kirkcudbright.co.uk

An 18th-century cottage restored and opened in 1957 as a gallery exhibiting the
work of artists in Galloway.

KEIR HARDIE STATUE   137   8 M28

Cumnock town centre. Access at all times. Car parking.

Bust outside the Town Hall to commemorate James Keir Hardie (1856–1915), an
early socialist leader, and founder of the Independent Labour Party in 1893.

HARESTANES COUNTRYSIDE VISITOR CENTRE   138   8 R27

Ancrum, Jedburgh, Scottish Borders. 3 miles (5km) north of Jedburgh, well
signposted from A68, A698 and B6400. Buses from Jedburgh, Edinburgh, Galashiels,
and Hawick stop within one mile. Open Apr–Oct, daily 1000–1700. Free. Charges for
some activities/events. Explanatory displays. Gift shop. Tearoom and picnic area.
Children's play park. WC. Limited wheelchair access. Disabled WC. Car and coach
parking. Telephone (01835) 830306.

Housed in converted farm buildings and comprising both indoor and outdoor
attractions. Changing exhibitions, woodland paths and guided walks, activities
and events. Wildlife garden and wooden games room. Waymarked walks include
St Cuthbert's Way and the Waterloo monument, a prominent tower on the
summit of Peniel Heugh.

HARMONY GARDEN   139   8 R27

NTS. Melrose, Borders. Opposite Melrose Abbey. Bus from Edinburgh. Open
Apr–Sep, Mon–Sat 1000–1700, Sun 1300–1700. Charge £ (honesty box). Explanatory
displays. Limited wheelchair access. Car and coach parking. Telephone (01721)
722502. www.nts.org.uk

This attractive walled garden was built in the early 19th century, in a fine conservation area. The garden is lovely throughout the seasons, with a rich display of spring bulbs, colourful herbaceous and mixed borders, and fruiting apricots. The garden is set against the beautiful backdrop of Melrose Abbey ruins, with the Eildon Hills in the distance.

HAWICK CASHMERE COMPANY VISITOR CENTRE 140   8 R28

Trinity Mills, Duke Street, Hawick. Signposted in Hawick. Bus from Edinburgh or Carlisle. Open all year, Mon–Sat 0930–1700; May–Oct also Sun 1100–1600. Closed Christmas and New Year, and local holiday (first weekend in June). Free. Explanatory displays. Gift shop. WC. Wheelchair access. Car and coach parking. Telephone (01450) 371221. www.hawickcashmere.com

A specialist manufacturer of the finest quality knitwear, supplying some of the world's leading retailers, fashion houses and designers. Visitors can watch garments being knitted on the latest computer programmed machinery. The viewing gallery contains an informative display illustrating the cashmere fibre's long journey from goat to garment. Extensive retail area offering a wide range of classic and contemporary knitwear for men and women.

HAWICK MUSEUM AND THE SCOTT GALLERY 141   8 R28

Wilton Lodge Park, Hawick, Borders. In Hawick public park. Bus from Edinburgh or Carlisle. Open Apr–Sep, Mon–Fri 1000–1200 and 1300–1700; weekends 1300–1700; Oct–Mar, Mon–Fri 1300–1600, Sun 1400–1600. Free. Group concessions. Guided tours by arrangement. Explanatory displays. Gift shop. WC. Limited wheelchair access. Disabled WC. Car and coach parking. Telephone (01450) 373457. www.scotborders.gov.uk/museums

This 200-year-old mansion house, set in over 100 acres (40ha) of award-winning parkland, houses Hawick's long-established museum and art gallery. A programme of museum and art exhibitions complements permanent displays on local industrial history, natural history, ethnography, domestic bygones and militaria.

HAYES GARDEN LAND 142   8 L27

Tarbolton Road, Symington, Kilmarnock. On the A77, 4 miles (6.5km) west of Kilmarnock. Bus from Kilmarnock, Irvine, Troon, Ayr or Glasgow. Open all year (except Christmas–New Year), Mon–Sat 0900–1730, Sun 1000–1730. Free. Gift shop. Tearoom. Garden centre. WC. Wheelchair access. Disabled WC. Car and coach parking. Telephone (01563) 830204. www.hayesgardenland.com

Garden centre with coffee lounge offering home baking.

HEADS OF AYR PARK 143   8 K28

Dunure Road, Ayr. On the A719, 4 miles (6.5km) south of Ayr. Bus from town centre. Open daily Apr–Oct, 1000–1700. Charge for activities. Group concessions. Guided tours for schools. Explanatory displays. Gift shop. Snack bar barn. Garden, pets' corner. WC. Wheelchair access. Disabled WC. Car and coach parking. Telephone (01292) 441210. www.headsofayrpark.co.uk

Comprising 125 acres (50.5ha) with beautiful views over the Firth of Clyde. Animals include buffalo, wallabies, rhea and rabbits. Reptile house. Buggy rides. Trampolines, toy tractors. Quad biking. Indoor and outdoor play areas.

HERMITAGE CASTLE   144   8 R29

HS. Hawick, Roxburghshire. In Liddesdale, Roxburghshire, 5.5 miles (9km) north east of Newcastleton. Bus service from Hawick to Hermitage School House then 1 mile (2km) walk. Open Apr–Sep, daily 0930–1830. Charge £. Group concessions. Gift shop. Picnic area. Car and coach parking. Telephone (01387) 376222. www.historic-scotland.gov.uk

A vast eerie ruin of the 14th and 15th centuries, consisting of four towers and connecting walls, outwardly almost perfect. Much restored in the 19th century. Associated with the de Soulis family, but with the Douglases after 1341.

HIGHLAND MARY'S MONUMENT   145   8 L27

At Failford, on B743, 3 miles (4.5km) west of Mauchline. Access at all times. Free.

The monument commemorates the place where, it is said, Robert Burns parted from his Highland Mary, Mary Campbell. They exchanged vows, but she died the following autumn.

JAMES HOGG MONUMENT   146   8 Q28

By Ettrick, 1 mile (1.5km) west of B7009. Access at all times. Free. Car parking.

A monument on the site of the birthplace of James Hogg (1770–1835), a friend of Scott known as the Ettrick Shepherd. His grave is in the nearby church.

HUME CASTLE   147   8 R27

Hume, Kelso, Roxburghshire. On the B6364, 6 miles (9.5km) north of Kelso. Bus from Kelso, 6 miles (9.5km). Open daily 0900–2100. Free. Explanatory displays. Car parking.

A ruined castle, destroyed by Cromwell and partially rebuilt by the Earl of Marchmont. Good views of the Tweed valley and beyond.

ISLE OF ARRAN DISTILLERY VISITOR CENTRE   148   7 J27

Lochranza, Isle of Arran. 14 miles (22.5km) north of Brodick. By ferry to Brodick . Open mid Mar–end Oct daily, 1000–1800. Winter, telephone to confirm times. Charge ££. Children under 12 free. Group concessions. Guided tours. Explanatory displays. Gift shop. Restaurant and picnic area. Gardens. WC. Induction loop for audio-visual programme. Wheelchair access with assistance. Disabled WC. Car and coach parking. Telephone (01770) 830264. www.arranwhisky.com

This is the newest single malt whisky distillery in Scotland, and has been in production since August 1995. Tours explain how whisky is made. The visitor centre has interactive displays and a short film illustrating whisky production on Arran over the last 150 years. Audio-visual room set in mock 18th-century crofter's inn. Shop sells local goods and whisky products.

ISLE OF ARRAN HERITAGE MUSEUM   149   7 J27

Rosaburn, Brodick, Isle of Arran. 1.5 miles (2.5km) north of Brodick Pier. Bus from Brodick Pier. Open Easter–Oct daily, 1030–1630. Charge £. Children under 5 free. Group concessions. Guided tours. Explanatory displays. Gift shop. Tearoom and picnic area. Garden, children's play area. WC. Wheelchair access. Disabled WC. Car and coach parking. Telephone (01770) 302636. www.arranmuseum.co.uk

An original 18th-century croft farm with smiddy, cottage, coach house and stables. Extensive garden and special display area which is changed annually. Exhibits on shipping, geology, archaeology and local history.

JEDBURGH ABBEY   150   8 R28

HS. Abbey Bridge End, Jedburgh. Off the A68 in Jedburgh. Bus service from
Edinburgh, Kelso and Galashiels. Open Apr–Sep, daily 0930–1830; Oct–Mar, Mon–Sun
0930–1630. Charge ££. Group concessions. Explanatory displays and visitor centre.
Gift shop. Tearoom and picnic area. WC. Limited wheelchair access. Disabled WC. Car
and coach parking. Telephone (01835) 863925. www.historic-scotland.gov.uk

One of the Border abbeys founded by David I circa 1138 for Augustinian canons.
The remarkable complete church is mostly Romanesque and early Gothic. The
west front has a fine rose window and there is a richly carved Norman doorway.
The remains of the cloisters have recently been uncovered and finds from the
excavations are displayed. An exhibition portrays life in the monastery.

JEDBURGH CASTLE JAIL AND MUSEUM   151   8 R28

Castle Gate, Jedburgh. In Jedburgh. Nearest railway station Edinburgh or Carlisle,
bus from Edinburgh or Carlisle. Open Mon–Sat 1000–1630, Sun 1300–1600. Charge
£. Group concessions. Guided tours by arrangement. Explanatory displays. Gift shop.
Picnic area and vending machine. Baby changing facilities. WC. Limited wheelchair
access. Disabled WC. Car and coach parking. Telephone (01835) 864750.
www.scotborders.gov.uk/museums

A refurbished reform prison dating from 1824. Designed by Archibald Elliot to
principles advocated by John Howard, the prison reformer. New displays in the
Jailer's House provide an insight into the development of the Royal Burgh of
Jedburgh, while the history of the jail itself is told in the two adjoining cell
blocks. One of the few remaining examples of a Howard reform prison in
Britain.

JEDFOREST DEER AND FARM PARK   152   8 R28

Mervinslaw Estate, Camptown, Jedburgh. On the A68, 5 miles (8km) south of
Jedburgh. Open Easter–Aug, daily 1000–1730; Sep–Oct 1100–1630. Charge ££. Group
concessions. Guided tours. Explanatory displays. Gift shop. Tearoom, picnic and
barbecue area. Children's play area. WC. Limited wheelchair access. Disabled WC.
Car and coach parking. Telephone (01835) 840364. www.aboutscotland.com

A Borders working farm with sheep, suckler cows, and red deer. Large display of
rare breeds, including sheep, cattle, pigs, goats, poultry and waterfowl. Old and
new breeds are compared. Emphasis on physical contact with animals and
involvement with farm activities. Display with written and pictorial
information. Daily bulletin board, coded walks, adventure land, conservation
and wet areas. Birds of prey with daily displays, hawk walks and tuition.
Educational resources material and guide book. Ranger-led walks and activities.
Range of scenic, dedicated dog walks open all year at no charge.

JOHN PAUL JONES COTTAGE MUSEUM   153   8 N30

Arbigland, Kirkbean, Dumfries. Off the A710, 14 miles (22.5km) south of Dumfries.
Nearest railway station Dumfries, bus from Dumfries to Kirkbean then 1 mile walk.
Open Apr–Jun and Sep, Tue–Sun 1000–1700; Jul–Aug same hours but also open Mon.
Charge £. Group concessions. Guided tours. Audio-visual displays. Gift shop. WC.
Wheelchair access. Disabled WC. Car and coach parking. Telephone (01387) 880613.
www.jpj.demon.co.uk

Based around the cottage in which John Paul Jones, the Father of the American
Navy, spent his first 13 years before becoming an apprentice in the merchant

navy. The original building has been restored to the style of a gardener's cottage of the 1740s, with period furnishings, a replica of the cabin of the *Bonhomme Richard*, and a room containing a model of John Paul Jones and one of the cannons he is known to have used. The cottage gardens have been laid out in period style. Interpretive display and shop in former kennels. Caravan and camp site for Caravan Club members only

KAGYU SAMYE LING TIBETAN BUDDHIST MONASTERY   154   8 Q29

Eskdalemuir, Dumfries and Galloway. On the B709, 16 miles (25.5km) from Lockerbie. Nearest railway station Lockerbie, bus or taxi from Lockerbie. Open all year, daily, 0900–1800; café and shop 0900–1700. Admission by donation. Guided tours by arrangement. Explanatory displays. Gift shop. Restaurant, tearoom and picnic area. WC. Wheelchair access with assistance. Disabled WC. Car and coach parking. Telephone (01387) 373232. www.samyeling.org

A magnificent Tibetan temple in traditional Buddhist style, in beautiful surroundings. Also guest house for visitors who attend courses on meditation, therapy, arts and tai chi. Gardens and riverside walk.

KAILZIE GARDENS   155   8 Q27

by Peebles. 2.5 miles (4km) east of Peebles on B7062. Bus from Peebles. Open Mar–mid Oct daily, 1100–1730; in winter during daylight. Charge ££. Prices vary according to time of the year so telephone for further details. Group concessions. Guided tours. Explanatory displays. Gift shop. Licenced café, picnic area. Snacks available in fishing hut. WC. Wheelchair access with assistance. Disabled WC. Car and coach parking. Telephone (01721) 720007.

Seventeen acres (6.8ha) of gardens in the beautiful Tweed valley. The 1812 walled garden is semi-formal, with fine herbaceous borders and shrub roses. Formal rose garden and greenhouses. Woodland and burnside walks. Rhododendrons in season. Duck pond and stocked trout pond (rod hire available). Osprey viewing project. Children's play area and 18-hole putting green.

KELBURN CASTLE AND COUNTRY CENTRE   156   9 K26

South Offices, Fairlie, Ayrshire. On the A78, about 2 miles (3km) south of Largs. Bus from Largs and other towns (train to Largs). Centre open daily, Easter–Oct, 1000–1800; winter 1100–dusk. Castle open Jul–Aug; riding centre open all year. Charge £££. Group concessions. Guided tours. Explanatory displays. Gift shop. Licensed tearoom, café and picnic areas. Gardens, pets' corner, childrens play areas. WC. Limited wheelchair access. Disabled WC. Car and coach parking. Telephone (01475) 568685. www.kelburncountrycentre.com

Historic home of the Earls of Glasgow, and still lived in today. The original Norman keep is now enclosed in a castle built in 1581. A new mansion (Kelburn House) was added to this in 1700, followed later by a Victorian wing. The buildings are surrounded by spectacular natural scenery including waterfalls. Breathtaking views over the Firth of Clyde. Activities include glen walks, riding (with all-weather arena), assault and adventure courses, and Scotland's most unusual attraction – the Secret Forest, with fantasy follies and hidden secrets. Exhibitions and ranger centre. Special events most weekends.

KELSO ABBEY   157   8 S27

HS. In Bridge Street, Kelso, Roxburghshire. Bus service from Edinburgh and Galashiels. Open at all reasonable times. Free. Telephone (0131) 5507603. www.historic-scotland.gov.uk

The west end of the great abbey church of the Tironensians, who were brought to Kelso in 1128 by David I. One of the great Border abbeys – even in its fragmentary state, this is superb architecture.

KELSO RACECOURSE 158   8 S27

Kelso, Roxburghshire. Off A6089 and A699, north of Kelso. Nearest railway stations Berwick and Carlisle. Racing Oct–May, 14 fixtures a year (usually five before Christmas). Charges vary. Children under 16 free. Reductions for advance sales. Guided tours available by arrangement in advance. Two restaurants and fast food area. WC. Wheelchair access. Disabled WC. Car and coach parking. Telephone (01573) 224767 (race days only). www.kelso-races.co.uk

Britain's friendliest course, with a reputation for a fun day out for racing fanatics, families and new racegoers. Top quality National Hunt fixtures are held each season, culminating with the May Kelso Racing Carnival.

KID'Z PLAY 159   8 L27

The Esplanade, Prestwick, Ayrshire. In Prestwick, five minute walk from rail and bus stations. By rail or bus from Glasgow. Open daily (except Christmas, Boxing Day and New Year's Day): 0930–1900, Fri and Sat 0930–1930. Charge £ children, adults free. Group concessions. Café. Baby changing facilities. WC. Wheelchair access. Disabled WC. Car and coach parking. Telephone (01292) 475215. www.kidz-play.co.uk

An indoor adventure play area for children up to 12 years. Soft play adventure area for under 5s.

KILMORY CAIRNS 160   7 J27

At south end of Arran, 3.5 miles (5.5km) north east of Kilmory village, off A841. Access at all times. Free.

Cairn Baan is a notable Neolithic long cairn. Half a mile (0.5km) south west of A841 at the Lagg Hotel is Torrylin Cairn, a Neolithic chambered cairn.

KILPATRICK DUN 161   7 J27

HS. 1 mile (2km) south of Blackwaterfoot, Isle of Arran. By ferry from Ardrossan to Brodick, bus from Brodick to Blackwaterfoot. 0.5 mile (1km) walk to site. Free. Telephone (0131) 5507603. www.historic-scotland.gov.uk

The ruins of a circular drystone homestead of unknown date, with a more recent enclosure wall.

KILWINNING ABBEY 162   9 K27

HS. In Kilwinning, Ayrshire. Nearest railway station Kilwinning, bus service from Irvine. Access at all reasonable times but may be viewed from outside only. Free. Car parking. Telephone (0131) 5507603. www.historic-scotland.gov.uk

The ruins of a Tironensian-Benedictine abbey. Most of the surviving fragments, which consist of parts of the church and chapter house, appear to date from the 13th century.

KINSMAN BLAKE CERAMICS 163   8 R27

Barn House, Smailholm, Roxburghshire. On the A68, 6 miles (9.5km) east of St Boswells. Open all year, daily 1000–1700 (occasionally open in the evening). Free. Demonstrations given to groups on prior notice (charge). Gift shop. Wheelchair access. Car parking. Telephone (01573) 460666.

A small family pottery where visitors are welcome in the workshop. Demonstrations or explanations as required. Specialists in decorative techniques. Well-stocked showroom, includes paintings by Helen Tabor and Andrew Walker as well as furniture by Adrian McCurdy, and hand-carved wooden spoons by Rankin Kinsman-Blake.

KIRK YETHOLM   164   8 S27

Off B6352, 8 miles (12.5km) south east of Kelso.

Attractive village, once famous as the home of the Scottish gypsies, now the northern end of the Pennine Way.

KIRKCHRIST FISHINGS   165   8 K30

Kirkchrist Farm, Kirkcowan, Near Newton Stewart. 6 miles (9.5km) south west of Newton Stewart. Open all year, daily 0900–1 hour after sunset. Different charges for catch and release and two or three fish. Car parking. Telephone (01671) 830336.

Rainbow and brown trout fishing on nine stocked ponds, and salmon and brown trout fishing on the Ivy Tree and Boat Hill pools of the River Bladnoch. A high stocking level with an average weight of over 3.5lb is maintained in the stocked ponds. The record rainbow trout is 16.5lb and the brown trout is 10.5lb.

KIRKMADRINE EARLY CHRISTIAN STONES   166   7 J31

HS. In the Rhinns of Galloway, 2 miles (3km) south west of Sandhead, Wigtownshire. Nearest railway station Stranraer, bus from Stranraer. Access at all reasonable times. Free. Telephone (0131) 5507603. www.historic-scotland.gov.uk

Three of the earliest Christian memorial stones in Britain, dating from the 5th or early 6th century, displayed in a porch of a former chapel.

KIRROUGHTREE VISITOR CENTRE   167   8 L30

FE. Galloway Forest Park, Stronord, Newton Stewart. Open daily, Apr–Sep 1030–1700; Oct 1030–1630. Free. Guided tours. Gift shop. Café and picnic area. Adventure play area. WC. Wheelchair access. Disabled WC. Car and coach parking. Telephone (01671) 402165. www.forestry.gov.uk

The visitor centre runs various activities during the year. Also waymarked cycle trails, walks and a forest drive.

LADYKIRK   168   8 S26

4 miles (6.5km) east of Swinton and 0.5 miles (0.5km) from Norham off B6470. Access at all reasonable times. Car parking.

Ladykirk was built in 1500 by James IV, in memory of Our Lady who had saved him from drowning. As the Border was only 300 yards away and in constant dispute, he ordered it built to withstand fire and flood – hence the all-stone construction of the kirk with no wooden rafters and, until this century, stone pews. The Wardens of East March met regularly in the parish to resolve disputes between Scotland and England. In 1560, a copy of the last peace treaty between them was signed in Ladykirk, marking the end of sporadic warfare.

LAGGANGAIRN STANDING STONES   169   8 K30

HS. At Killgallioch, New Luce on the Southern Upland Way, Wigtownshire. Nearest railway station Stranraer, bus to New Luce on school days and Tue and Fri only.

Difficult access signposted through Forestry Commission land. Free. Telephone (0131) 5507603. www.historic-scotland.gov.uk

Two stones carved with early Christian crosses.

LARGS MUSEUM   170   9 K26

Kirkgate House, Manse Court, Largs, Ayrshire. Nearest railway station Largs, bus from Glasgow and Ayr. Open Jun–Sep, daily 1400–1700. Free. Guided tours. Explanatory displays. Wheelchair access. Telephone (01475) 687081.

The museum holds a small collection of local bygones and a library of local history books and photographs, put together by the local history society. Holds the key to the Skelmorlie Aisle, adjacent, which belongs to Historic Scotland.

LARGS OLD KIRK   171   9 K26

HS. In Bellman's Close, off High Street in Largs, Ayrshire. Nearest railway station Largs, bus from Glasgow and Ayr. Open late May–early Sep, Mon–Sun 1400–1700. Keys from Largs Museum. Free. Telephone (01475) 672450. www.historic-scotland.gov.uk

A splendid mausoleum with a painted ceiling illustrating the seasons. Added to the parish church in 1636 by Sir Robert Montgomerie of Skelmorlie. Contains an elaborate carved stone tomb in Renaissance style.

LEYDEN OBELISK AND TABLET   172   8 R28

Denholm, on A698 north east of Hawick. Access at all times. Free.

The village was the birthplace of John Leyden (1776-1811), poet, orientalist and friend of Sir Walter Scott. An obelisk was set up in 1861 and a tablet on a thatched cottage records his birth there. Another famous son of Denholm was Sir James Murray, editor of the *Oxford English Dictionary*, whose birth is commemorated on a tablet on a house in the Main Street.

LIDDESDALE HERITAGE CENTRE   173   8 R29

Townfoot Kirk, South Hermitage Street, Newcastleton, Roxburghshire. 21 miles (33.5km) from Hawick on B6399, 23 miles (37km) from Carlisle on A7; follow signposts to Newcastleton/Canonbie. Infrequent bus from Carlisle or Hawick to Newcastleton. Open Easter–Sep, Wed–Mon 1330–1630. Charge £. Residents of Liddesdale free. Group concessions by arrangement. Explanatory displays. Small gift shop. WC. Wheelchair access. Disabled WC. Car and coach parking. Telephone (01387) 375283. www.liddesdaleheritagecentre.scotshome.com

Liddesdale Heritage Association is a voluntary community group who run Liddesdale Heritage Centre and Museum in the former Congregational Church (built in 1804) within the planned village of Newcastleton (built 1793). Displays on the history of Liddesdale and its people, and a unique commemorative bicentenary tapestry. Many books and articles on the Borders region. Facilities available for genealogical research. Waverley Line railway memorabilia. Exhibitions are staged during July and August.

LINCLUDEN COLLEGIATE CHURCH   174   8 N29

HS. In Abbey Lane, on western outskirts of Dumfries, 1 mile (2km) from A76. Local bus service. Open at all reasonable times (contact keyholder). Charge £. Telephone (0131) 5507603. www.historic-scotland.gov.uk

The rich remains of a collegiate church founded in 1389 by Archibald the Grim, 3rd Earl of Douglas. The splendid chancel was probably added by his son,

Archibald, the 4th Earl, and houses the exquisite monumental tomb of his wife, Princess Margaret, daughter of King Robert III.

LINDEAN MILL GLASS 175   8 R27

Lindean Mill, Galashiels. On the A7, 1 mile (2km) north of Selkirk. Bus from Edinburgh or Carlisle. Open all year, Mon–Fri 0900–1700, weekends by appointment. Free. Gift shop. Limited wheelchair access. Car parking. Telephone (01750) 20173. www.lindeanmillglass.co.uk

Scotland's premier glass studio where visitors can watch glassware being made by hand. Seconds shop and gallery.

LOCH DOON CASTLE 176   8 L29

HS. Off the A713, 10 miles (16km) south of Dalmellington, Ayrshire. Nearest railway station Ayr, bus from Ayr. Access at all reasonable times. Free. Car parking. Telephone (0131) 5507603. www.historic-scotland.gov.uk

An early 14th-century castle with an eleven-sided curtain wall of fine masonry. Once known as Castle Balliol. Originally it stood on an island in Loch Doon but it was moved to its present site in the 1930s before its original site was flooded during the construction of a hydro-electric scheme.

LOCHCARRON CASHMERE WOOL CENTRE 177   8 R27

Waverley Mill, Huddersfield Street, Galashiels. In Galashiels centre. Bus from Edinburgh to within 1.25 miles (2km). Open all year, Mon–Sat 0900–1700; Jun–Sep, Sun 1200–1700. Tour £ (children under 14 free), museum free. Group concessions. Guided tours. Explanatory displays. Gift shop. WC. Personal guide for blind visitors. Wheelchair access. Disabled WC. Car parking. Telephone (01896) 751100. www.lochcarron.com

A woollen mill manufacturing cashmere from spun yarn to finished garment. Produces a huge range of pure wool tartans. Tour of mill and museum illustrating the history of Galashiels and its trade.

LOCHHILL EQUESTRIAN CENTRE 178   8 M30

Ringford, Castle Douglas, Dumfries and Galloway. 4 miles (6.5km) north of Kirkcudbright. From Ringford follow signs for New Galloway and Laurieston (A762). Take first left (concealed junction) as you leave Ringford. Straight on at crossroads. Lochhill is first farm on left. Open all year. Charge dependent on activity. WC. Wheelchair access with assistance. Car parking. Telephone (01557) 820225. www.kirkcudbright.co.uk/activity/lochhill.htm

Equestrian and trekking centre located in the Galloway hills. Lessons and hacks for beginners and more experienced riders. Children can spend a morning or afternoon learning how to groom and look after a pony. Riding parties organised.

LOCHMABEN CASTLE 179   8 P29

HS. On the south shore of Castle Loch, by Lochmaben, Dumfries and Galloway. Off the B7020, 9 miles (14.5km) east north-east of Dumfries. Nearest railway station Lockerbie, bus from Lockerbie or Dumfries. Access at all reasonable times but view exterior only. Car parking. Telephone (0131) 5507603. www.historic-scotland.gov.uk

The ruins of a royal castle, originally built by the English in the 14th century but extensively rebuilt during the reign of King James VI. Surrounded by extensive remains of earthworks, including a rectangular peel (timber pallisaded enclosure).

LOCHRANZA CASTLE   180   7 J26

HS. At Lochranza on the north coast of the Isle of Arran. Ferry from Ardrossan to Brodick, bus from Brodick. Open at all times (apply to custodian). Free. Car parking. Telephone (0131) 5507603. www.historic-scotland.gov.uk

A fine tower house, probably a 16th-century reconstruction of an earlier building. Reputed to be where King Robert the Bruce landed on his return in 1307.

LOGAN BOTANIC GARDEN   181   7 J31

Port Logan, Stranraer, Wigtownshire. 14 miles (22.5km) south of Stranraer, off the B7065. Open Mar and Oct, daily 1000–1700; Apr–Sep, daily 1000–1800. Charge ££. Group concessions. Guided tours for groups by arrangement (charge £). Explanatory displays. Gift shop. Licensed salad bar. WC. Limited wheelchair access. Disabled WC. Car and coach parking. Telephone (01776) 860231.

Experience the southern hemisphere in Scotland's most exotic garden. Logan's exceptionally mild climate allows a colourful array of tender plants to thrive. Tree ferns, cabbage palms, unusual shrubs, climbers and tender perennials are found within the Walled, Water, Terrace and Woodland Gardens. The Discovery Centre provides activities and information for all ages and the Soundalive self-guided tours enable visitors to make the most of the garden. Logan Botanic Garden is one of the National Botanic Gardens of Scotland.

LOGAN FISH POND MARINE LIFE CENTRE   182   7 J31

Port Logan, Stranraer, Wigtownshire. Off the B7056, 14 miles (22.5km) south of Stranraer, 1 mile (2km) from Logan Botanic Garden (see 181). Nearest railway and bus stations Stranraer. Open Mar–Oct, daily 1200–1700. Charge ££. Group concessions. Guided tours (available in Dutch, French, German and Spanish). Explanatory displays. Gift shop. Picnic area. Beach. WC. Limited wheelchair access. Car and coach parking. Telephone (01776) 860300. www.loganfishpond.co.uk

A fully restored Victorian fish larder in a unique setting – a tidal pool created by a blowhole which formed during the last Ice Age. The rock fissure through which the tide flows is now the setting for the unusual cave marine aquarium, containing a large variety of species from the Irish Sea.

LONGSHEDS EQUESTRIAN   183   8 M30

Kelton, Castle Douglas, Dumfries and Galloway. 2 miles (3km) south of Castle Douglas. Follow signs to Threave Gardens and take next road on right. Bus to Dumfries and Castle Douglas. Open all year, daily 1000–1700. Charge from £££, depending on activity. Visitors will be shown local places of interest when on a trek or hack. Hot and cold drinks and snacks available. Giftshop selling Longsheds clothing. WC. Limited wheelchair access. Car parking. Telephone (01556) 680498. www.longsheds.co.uk

Riding centre catering for all sizes and ages. Horses or ponies matched to each visitor. Lessons, treks and hacks available.

LOUDOUN HALL   184   8 L28

Boat Vennel, South Harbour Street, Ayr. In Ayr town centre, near cross. Open by arrangement only. Admission by donation. Guided tours. Explanatory displays. Refreshments available by arrangement. AV equipment for lectures and seminars. Limited wheelchair access (stairs suitable for ambient disabled only). Car and coach parking. Telephone (01292) 611290.

Loudon Hall is one of Ayr's oldest and finest buildings dating back to the late 15th century. Once in the garden ground there had been a brew house and bake house, the hall has been restored as a cultural centre. The forecourt is a public space with integrated art works and a performance space used for occasional music and drama events.

LOUDOUN HILL   185   9 M27

3 miles (4.8km) E of Darvel. Access at all reasonable times. Free.

An imposing rock, 1036 feet (316m) above sea level, offering far reaching views over the Ayrshire countryside. This unusual hill is the plug of an extinct volcano, and was the scene of victories over English forces by William Wallace in 1297, and Robert the Bruce in 1307. Bruce's victory is commemorated by a stone at the summit.

MABIE FARM PARK   186   8 N30

Burnside Farm, New Abbey Road, Mabie, Dumfries. 15 minutes from Dumfries and the A75. Farm lies on the edge of Mabie Forest – take A710 Solway Coast road towards New Abbey, through Islesteps and follow signposts after approximately 1 mile (1.5km). Open Apr–Oct, daily 1000–1700 (unless pre-booked for birthday party). Charge ££. Group concessions if pre-booked. Guided tours for educational visits. Gift shop. Tearoom, picnic areas and farm shop. WC. Wheelchair access. Disabled WC. Car and coach parking. Telephone (01387) 259666. www.mabiefarm.co.uk

Lots of animals to meet, including donkeys, horses and ponies, chicks and guinea pigs. Also adventure playground, giant flume slide, go-carts, quad bikes, grass sledge, astro slide and bouncy castles.

MABIE FOREST   187   8 N30

FE. 4 miles (6.5km) south of Dumfries. Free access at all times. Picnic areas and barbecues. Forest walks. Children's play area. Bike hire. Wheelchair access. Car parking. Telephone (01387) 247745. www.forestry.gov.uk

This popular forest attracts both locals and visitors, and offers a wide range of facilities and activities. Situated on the site of an old sawmill, it is the perfect place to relax, get some fresh air and take in the stunning views across the Solway Firth. Mountain biking for all abilities from quiet forest roads to technical single track. Programme of ranger-led activities throughout the year.

MACHRIE MOOR STONE CIRCLES   188   7 J27

HS. 3 miles (5km) north of Blackwaterfoot on the west coast of the Isle of Arran. Ferry from Ardrossan to Brodick, bus from Brodick then 1.5 mile (2.5km) walk to site. Access at all reasonable times. Free. Telephone (0131) 5507603. www.historic-scotland.gov.uk

The remains of five Bronze Age stone circles. One of the most important sites of its kind in Britain.

MACLELLAN'S CASTLE   189   8 M31

HS. Kirkcudbright. Off High Street (A711), Kirkcudbright. Bus from Dumfries and Stranraer. Open Apr–Sep, daily 0930–1830. Charge £. Group concessions. Explanatory displays. Gift shop. WC. Limited wheelchair access. Telephone (01557) 331856. www.historic-scotland.gov.uk

A handsome castellated mansion overlooking the harbour, dating from 1577, complete except for the roof. Elaborately planned with fine detail. A ruin since 1752.

MAGNUM LEISURE CENTRE   190   9 K27

Harbourside, Irvine, Ayrshire. At Irvine harbour, five minutes from Irvine railway
station. Open Tue–Thu 1000–2200; other days 0900–2200; closed Christmas and
New Year. Charge by activity or day ticket (££). Group concessions. Guided tours by
prior arrangement. Explanatory displays. Gift shop. Café, bar and vending machines.
WC. Wheelchair access with assistance. Disabled WC. Car and coach parking.
Telephone (01294) 278381.

Scotland's largest indoor leisure facility set in an attractive beachpark/
harbourside location. Leisure pool (also outdoor pool). Ice rink. Softplay area.
Ten court sports hall. Fitness/aerobic studio, steam room, sauna and spa baths.
Bowling rink.

MANDERSTON   191   8 S26

Duns, Berwickshire. Off the A6105, 2 miles (3km) east of Duns. Nearest railway
station Berwick-upon-Tweed, then bus to road end at Manderston. Open from
May–Sep, Thu and Sun; house 1400–1700, gardens open 1130 until dusk. Charge for
house and garden £££, gardens only ££. Group concessions. Guided tours by
arrangement (available in French). Gift shop. Tearoom and picnic area. Garden. WC.
Car and coach parking. Telephone (01361) 883450. www.manderston.co.uk

An Edwardian stately home set in 56 acres (22.6ha) and surrounded by formal
gardens, stables, dairy, lake and woodland garden. Features include the
sumptuous staterooms, the only silver staircase in the world, a racing room and
the first privately-owned biscuit tin museum. Domestic quarters in period style.

MARRBURY SMOKEHOUSE   192   8 L29

Marrbury Smokehouse, Whitecairn, Bargrennan, Newton Stewart. Directly on the
coastal road side of the A75 approx 6miles (10.6km) west Gatehouse of Fleet, 3 miles
(4.6km) east of Creetown. Nearest railway station Barrhill, local bus service. Open all
year, Tue–Fri 1100–1600, Sat 1000–1400. Opening hours occasionally extended
during summer months. Telephone or visit website for details. Free. Explanatory
displays and information on local facilities. Gift shop. Restaurant, coffee house and
bistro. WC. Wheelchair access. Telephone (01671) 820476. www.visitmarrbury.co.uk

Traditional Scottish smokehouse run by the Marr family, net and coble salmon
fishermen on the River Cree since 1920. A wide range of luxury smoked Scottish
foods are sold, with free recipes and cookery tips.

MARY, QUEEN OF SCOTS' HOUSE   193   8 R28

Queen Street, Jedburgh. In the centre of Jedburgh. Bus from Edinburgh or
Newcastle. Open Easter–Oct, Mon–Sat 1000–1630, Sun 1100–1630. Charge £. Group
concessions. Explanatory displays. Booklets in European languages. Gift shop.
Formal garden. Limited wheelchair access (ground floor). Car and coach parking.
Telephone (01835) 863331. www.scotborders.gov.uk/museums

A 16th-century castle which is now a visitor centre devoted to the memory of
Mary, Queen of Scots, who stayed here in 1566 while she was ill.

MAYBOLE COLLEGIATE CHURCH   194   8 K28

HS. South of the A77 in Maybole, Ayrshire. Nearest railway station Maybole, bus from
Ayr. Not open to the public – view exterior only. Telephone (0131) 5507603.
www.historic-scotland.gov.uk

The roofless ruin of a 15th-century church built for a small college established
in 1373 by John Kennedy of Dunure.

MELLERSTAIN HOUSE   195   8 R27

Gordon, Berwickshire. Off the A6089, 7 miles (11km) north west of Kelso. Bus from Galashiels or Kelso. Open Easter weekend, then May–Sep, Wed–Mon 1230–1700 (restaurant 1130–1730). Charge £££. Group concessions for pre-booked tours. Guided tours by arrangement. Explanatory displays. Gift shop. Restaurant. WC. Limited wheelchair access. Car and coach parking. Telephone (01573) 410225. www.mellerstain.com

A superb Georgian mansion designed by William and Robert Adam. Features exquisite plaster ceilings, beautiful interior decoration, fine period furniture, marvellous art collection. Award-winning terraced garden and grounds.

MELROSE ABBEY   196   8 R27

HS. Abbey Street, Melrose. Main Square, Melrose, Roxburghshire. In Melrose, off the A7 or A68. Bus services from Edinburgh, Kelso, Jedburgh and Galashiels. Open Apr–Sep, daily 0930–1830; Oct–Mar, Mon–Sun 0930–1630. Charge ££. Group concessions. Explanatory displays. Audio guide. Gift shop. Tearoom, picnic area. WC. Wheelchair access with assistance. Disabled WC. Car and coach parking. Telephone (01896) 822562. www.historic-scotland.gov.uk

The ruins of the Cistercian abbey founded by King David I circa 1136. It was largely destroyed by an English army in 1385 but rebuilt in the early 15th century. It is now probably the most famous ruin in Scotland because of the elegant and elaborate stonework which remains. The Commendator's House contains a large collection of *objets trouvés*.

MERKLAND CROSS   197   8 P30

HS. At Merkland Smithy, near Ecclefechan, Dumfries and Galloway. Nearest railway station Gretna, bus from Gretna, Lockerbie or Dumfries. Access at all reasonable times. Free. Telephone (0131) 5507603. www.historic-scotland.gov.uk

A fine carved wayside cross, dating from the 15th century.

MERSEHEAD RSPB NATURE RESERVE   198   8 N30

By Caulkerbush, Dumfriesshire. 18 miles (29km) south west of Dumfries on A710 just before Caulkerbush. First turn on left after Southwick Home Farm. Daily service from Dumfries stops 1 mile (1.5km) from reserve on A710. Reserve open at all times. Visitor centre open summer, daily 1000–1800; winter, daily 1000–1700. Free. Donation requested. Guided tours. Explanatory displays. Picnic area, two nature trails, two bird watching hides, viewing area. WC. Limited wheelchair access. Disabled WC. Car and coach parking. Telephone visitor centre (01387) 780679, reserve (01387) 780298. www.rspb.org.uk/scotland

Mersehead is an exciting reserve covering a large area of farmland, wet meadows, saltmarsh and mudflats on the north shore of the Solway. It is important for wintering wildfowl including barnacle geese, teals, wigeons and pintails. The RSPB are managing the reserve to encourage lapwings, snipe, redshanks and waterfowl to breed here, plus a range of farmland finches and buntings.

MILL ON THE FLEET   199   8 M30

High Street, Gatehouse-of-Fleet, Castle Douglas, Dunfries and Galloway. In Gatehouse-of-Fleet by the river. Buses from Dumfries or Stranraer. Open late Mar–Oct, daily 1030–1700. Last entry one hour before closing. Charge £. Group

concessions. Guided tours on request. Explanatory displays. Gift shop. Tearoom.
Baby changing facilities. WC. Wheelchair access (including car parking). Disabled
WC. Telephone (01557) 814099. www.gatehouse-of-fleet.co.uk

An exhibition housed in a restored 18th-century cotton mill, telling the history
of the town. Temporary and permanent exhibits. Craft shop.

MILNHOLM CROSS   200   8 R29

One mile (1.5km) south of Newcastleton beside B6357. Access at all times. Car
parking.

Erected circa 1320, and owned by the Clan Armstrong Trust, Milnholm Cross is a
memorial to Alexander Armstrong who was murdered in Hermitage Castle some
4 miles (6.5km) away. It faces the ruin of Mangerton Castle, seat of the Armstrong
chiefs for 300 years.

MOFFAT MUSEUM   201   8 P28

The Old Bakehouse, The Neuk, Church Gate, Moffat, Dumfries and Galloway. In
Moffat centre. Buses from Dumfries, Glasgow or Edinburgh. Open Easter and
May–Sep, Mon–Sat (except Wed pm) 1045–1615, Sun 1315–1615. Explanatory displays.
Gift shop. Telephone (01683) 220868.

Located in an old bakehouse with a Scotch oven. Tells the story of Moffat and its
people, border raids, Covenanters, education, sports and pastimes, famous
people. A short video presentation.

MOFFAT WOOLLEN MILL   202   8 P28

Ladyknowe, Moffat, Dumfries and Galloway. Located behind Esso filling station.
Nearest railway and bus stations Dumfries, bus to Moffat. Open Apr–Oct, daily
0900–1730; Nov–Mar, daily 0900–1700. Free. Explanatory displays. Gift shop.
Restaurant. WC. Wheelchair access. Disabled WC. Car and coach parking. Telephone
(01683) 220134. www.ewm.co.uk

Visit the working weaving exhibition. The mill offers a good selection of
cashmere, Aran, lambswool and traditional tartans and tweeds. Trace Scottish
clan history and heraldry at the Clan History Centre and receive a certificate
illustrating your clan history. Also whisky shop with over 200 malts, and golf
department.

MONREITH ANIMAL WORLD   203   8 L31

Low Knock Farm, Monreith, Wigtownshire. On the A747, 0.5 mile (1km) from
Monreith. Bus from Newton Stewart and Stranraer. Open Mar–Oct, daily 1000–1700.
Charge ££. Children under 3 free. Group concessions. Explanatory displays. Gift
shop. Picnic area. WC. No guide dogs. Limited wheelchair access. Disabled WC. Car
and coach parking. Telephone (01988) 700217.

Animal park set in 12 acres of scenic countryside. Tame owls, otters, alpacas,
minature donkeys, waterfowl, aviary birds, ponies, belted Galloway cattle, rabbits
and lots more. Peaceful pondside walk

MONTEVIOT HOUSE GARDENS   204   8 R28

Monteviot, Jedburgh, Roxburghshire. Off the B6400, 4 miles (6.5km) north of
Jedburgh (off A68). Nearest railway station Berwick-upon-Tweed 35 miles (56km).
Open Apr–Oct, daily 1200–1700. Charge £. Children under 16 free. Guided tours for
groups by prior arrangement. WC. Limited wheelchair access. Disabled WC. Car and
coach parking. Telephone (01835) 830380.

Gardens on the bank of the River Teviot with several feature areas – river garden, rose terraces and a water garden. Plants for sale.

MOONSTONE MINIATURES   205   8 M30

4 Victoria Street, Kirkpatrick Durham. 14 miles (22.5km) west of Dumfries, 4 miles (6.5km) east of Castle Douglas off the A75 at Springholm. Telephone to arrange a private viewing. Charge £. Children under 5 free. Explanatory displays. Gift shop. Wheelchair access with assistance (by appointment). Car parking. Telephone (01556) 650313. www.moonstone-miniatures.uk.com

One-twelfth size display of stately homes, shops and humble cottages. Cabinets of miniature marvels.

MORTON CASTLE   206   8 N28

HS. On the A702, 17 miles (27km) north north-west of Dumfries. Beside Morton Loch. Nearest railway station Dumfries, bus from Dumfries. Closed to the public – view exterior only. Telephone (0131) 5507603. www.historic-scotland.gov.uk

The well-preserved ruin of a fine late 13th-century hall house, a stronghold of the Douglases.

MOSS FARM ROAD STONE CIRCLE   207   7 J27

HS. 3 miles (5km) north of Blackwaterfoot, Isle of Arran. Ferry from Ardrossan to Brodick, bus from Brodick. Access at all reasonable times. Free. Telephone (0131) 5507603. www.historic-scotland.gov.uk

The remains of a Bronze Age cairn surrounded by a stone circle.

MOSSBURN ANIMAL CENTRE   208   8 P29

Hightae, Lockerbie. Off B7020 (Dalton) from Lochmaben. Open all year daily, 1000–1600. Admission by donation. Guided tours. Tearoom. Children's play areas. WC. Wheelchair access with assistance. Disabled WC. Car and coach parking. Telephone (01387) 811288.

Mossburn is an animal welfare centre where you can see and handle rescued animals, from pigs and horses to Thai water dragons, who now live in a healthy, happy and secure environment. Also shop selling antiques, crafts, bric a brac and gifts.

MOTTE OF URR   209   8 N30

Off B794, 5 miles (7.5km) north east of Castle Douglas. Access at all reasonable times. Free.

The most extensive motte and bailey castle in Scotland, dating from the 12th century AD, although the bailey may have been an earlier earthwork of hillfort type.

MULL OF GALLOWAY RSPB NATURE RESERVE   210   8 K31

RSPB. By Drummore, Mull of Galloway. 5 miles (8km) south of Drummore. Reserve open at all times. Free. Limited wheelchair access to reserve. Car and coach parking. Telephone 01671 402861, visitor centre (summer only) 01776 840539. www.rspb.org.uk/scotland

The most southerly point of Scotland offers excellent views over the Solway Firth. The cliffs are home to thousands of breeding birds, including razorbills, guillemots and puffins. Visit nesting birds between Apr and Jul. Over 2000 pairs of gannets breed on a small outcrop called Scare Rocks.

MULL OF GALLOWAY VISITOR CENTRE AND LIGHTHOUSE   211   8 K31

Mull of Galloway, near Drummore, Dumfries & Galloway. 5 miles (8km) south of
Drummore. Visitor centre open Apr–Oct, daily 1000–1600. Lighthouse tours
Apr–Sep, Sat–Sun 1000–1530 (118 steps,not suitable for babies, toddlers and visitors
with mobility difficulties). Admission to visitor centre free but donations
appreciated. Charge £ for lighthouse tour. Explanatory displays. WC. Disabled
parking available next to visitor centre. Wheelchair access. Disabled WC. Car and
coach parking. www.mull-of-galloway.co.uk

Run in conjunction with the RSPB, who have a warden on site five days a week.
The visitor centre is located in the building originally designed to house the
workmen who built the lighthouse in 1828. It was later used as a byre for the
lighthouse keepers. Impressive audio visual displays, including a DVD of local
scenery and wildlife. Visitors can listen to the calls of birds common to the area.
Also extensive information on the history and geology of the Mull of Galloway.

MUSEUM OF LEAD MINING   212   8 N28

Wanlockhead, Biggar, Lanarkshire. On the B797 between Abington (A74) and
Mennock (A76). Nearest railway station Sanquhar. Regular bus service to
Wanlockhead (9 miles). Open Apr–Oct, daily 1100–1630 (Jul and Aug 10.00–1700);
Nov–Mar by arrangement. Charge £££. Group concessions. Guided tours.
Explanatory displays and interactive computer presentations. Visitor centre. Gift
shop. Tearoom. WC. Wheelchair access. Disabled WC. Car and coach parking.
Telephone (01659) 74387. www.leadminingmuseum.co.uk

A museum tracing 300 years of lead mining in Scotland's highest village set in
the dramatic Lowther Hills. Features beam engine, tours of a lead mine, period
cottages, miners' library, displays of minerals. Seasonal gold panning centre
(you can take some gold home).

MUSEUM OF THE CUMBRAES   213   9 K26

Garrison Stables, Millport, Isle of Cumbrae. Just behind the garrison on Millport's
seafront. Ferry from Largs, bus from Cumbrae slip to Millport. Open Apr–Sep,
Thu–Mon 1000–1300 and 1400–1700. Free. Explanatory displays. Gift shop. Picnic
area. Wheelchair access (disabled WC on request). Car parking. Telephone (01475)
531191. www.northayrshiremuseums.org.uk

The museum tells the story of the islands of Great and Little (Wee) Cumbrae.
Displays show how the town of Millport developed and celebrate Millport's
heyday as a holiday resort.

NEIDPATH CASTLE   214   8 P27

Peebles, Tweeddale. 1 mile (2km) west of Peebles on A72. Bus service from Peebles
post office. Open Easter weekend and May–Sep, Wed–Sat 1030–1700 and Sun
1230–1700. Charge £. Historic House members/Great British Heritage passes
accepted. Group concessions. Guided tours by prior arrangement. Explanatory
displays. Gift shop. Picnic area. Grounds. WC. Limited wheelchair access. Car and
coach parking. Telephone (01721) 720333. www.neidpathcastle.co.uk

A rare example of a 14th-century castle converted into a tower house in the 17th
century. Displayed in the great hall is an exhibit of beautiful batiks depicting
the life of Mary, Queen of Scots. The Laigh Hall contains informative displays.
Good views from the parapet walks. Neidpath Castle is often used as a film
location. Resident ghost, the Maid of Neidpath.

NEVERLAND ADVENTURE PLAY CENTRE   215   8 N29

Park Lane, Dumfries. Near Dumfries Swimming Pool in the town centre. 0.75 mile (1km) from Dumfries railway station, local bus service. Open all year except Christmas and New Year's Day, daily 1000–1700. Charge £, accompanying adults free. Group concessions. Refreshments and seating area. Baby changing facilities. WC. Wheelchair access. Car parking. Telephone (01387) 249100.

Adventure play centre for children aged up to ten. Themed on J.M. Barrie's story of *Peter Pan*, the boy who would never grow up. There are rope bridges, slides, a ball pool, Indian encampment and Captain Hook's pirate ship. Special area for under fours. Located beside the River Nith, with a pleasant seating area for adults overlooking the river. Parent/guardian supervision is required.

NEW ABBEY CORN MILL   216   8 N30

HS. New Abbey, Dumfries. On the A710, in New Abbey, 7 miles (11km) south of Dumfries. Nearest railway station Dumfries, bus from Dumfries and Dalbeattie. Open Apr–Sep, daily 0930–1830; Oct–Mar, Mon–Sun 0930–1630, closed Thu and Fri. Charge £. Group concessions. Explanatory displays in visitor centre, with video about milling. Gift shop. Picnic area. Telephone (01387) 850620. www.historic-scotland.gov.uk

A carefully renovated water-driven oatmeal mill in working order and demonstrated regularly to visitors in the summer months.

NEWBARNS PROJECT   217   8 N30

Newbarns, Colvend, Dalbeattie. On A710 1 mile (1.5km) east of Colvend. Car parking in the field immediately adjacent to the A710. Open Jul–Sep, daily 1000–1300 and 1400–1600, weather permitting. Free. Donations welcome. Guided tours. Wheelchair access with assistance. www.sat.org.uk

Ongoing archaeological exhibition of two Neolithic kerb cairns some 80 metres apart with, initially, passage grave interments c 3300 BC followed by later use as Early Bronze Age funerary cairns c 2300 BC. Later occupation and change of use to a crannog in the Iron Age with a Roman connection c 1st/2nd centuries AD on one cairn and medieval occupation and change of use to a motte and bailey on the other cairn.

Evidence of later occupation by the Cistercian monks.

NEWTON STEWART MUSEUM   218   4 J20

York Road, Newton-Stewart, Wigtownshire. In Newton Stewart. Nearest railway station Stranraer, bus from Stranraer or Dumfries. Open Easter–Sep, Mon–Sat 1400–1700; Jul and Aug also Mon–Fri 1000–1230; Jul–Sep, Sun 1400–1700. Charge £. Explanatory displays. Gift shop. WC. Wheelchair access (except gallery). Disabled WC. Car and coach parking. Telephone (01671) 402472.

Contains a wealth of historical treasures and exciting and interesting displays of the natural and social history of Galloway.

NORTH AYRSHIRE MUSEUM   219   9 K27

North Ayrshire Museum, Manse Street, Saltcoats. Just beside Somerfield supermarket car park. Nearest railway and bus stations Saltcoats. Open all year, daily 1000–1300 and 1400–1700 (closed public holidays, Wed and Sun). Free. Guided tours. Explanatory displays. Gift shop. Children's activity area. WC. Wheelchair access. Disabled WC. Telephone (01294) 464174. www.north-ayrshire.gov.uk

Local history museum housed in a mid 18th-century parish church. Displays feature cottage life, Ayrshire whitework, fine art, maritime history, archaeology and natural history. Good reference and photographic collection. Children's activity and discovery area.

NORTH GLEN GALLERY AND WORKSHOP 220   8 N30

North Glen, Palnackie, Castle Douglas, Dumfries and Galloway. Off A711 between Dalbeattie and Auchencairn. Nearest railway station Dumfries, bus service to Palnackie (0.6 mile/1km). Open all year, daily 1000–1800 (telephone to confirm). Other times by appointment. Free. Glass-blowing demonstrations. Gift shop. Picnic area. Wheelchair access with assistance. Car parking. Telephone (01556) 600200. www.tipiglen.dircon.co.uk

Gallery, workshop and home base of international artist Ed Iglehart who works with many collaborators to produce individual works of glass. Glass-blowing demonstrations. Chandeliers, experimental structures, wine goblets and many other objects. Starting point for many walks.

OLD BRIDGE HOUSE MUSEUM 221   8 N29

Mill Road, Dumfries. In Dumfries town centre on the west bank of the River Nith at Devorgilla's Bridge. Nearest railway station 15 minute walk. Nearest bus station two minute walk. Open Apr–Sep, Mon–Sat 1000–1700, Sun 1400–1700. Free. Explanatory welcome in English, French and German. Leaflet (also available in Dutch, Italian, Russian and Spanish). Limited wheelchair access (steps to front door). Car and coach parking. Telephone (01387) 256904. www.dumgal.gov.uk/museums

Cross the fifteenth century Devorgilla Bridge to the Old Bridge House. Built in 1660 into the sandstone of the bridge itself, Dumfries's oldest house is now a museum of everyday life in the town. You can see the family kitchen, nursery and bedroom of a Victorian home, and pay a visit to an early dentist's surgery!

OLD GALA HOUSE 222   8 R27

Scott Crescent, Galashiels, Selkirk. In Galashiels, 0.25 mile (0.5km) from town centre. Bus from Edinburgh or Carlisle. Open Apr–Sep, Tue–Sat 1000–1600, Jun–Aug also Mon 1000–1600 and Sun 1400–1600; Oct Tue–Sat 1300–1600. Gardens open at all times. Free. Guided tours by arrangement. Explanatory displays. Gift shop. Refreshments and picnic area. Garden. WC. Limited wheelchair access. Disabled WC. Car and coach parking. Telephone (01896) 752611.

Dating from 1583 and set in its own grounds, the former home of the Lairds of Gala is now an interpretive centre. Displays tell the story of the house, its inhabitants and the early growth of Galashiels. Features painted ceilings (1635), a painted wall (1988) and the Thomas Clapperton Room. The Christopher Boyd Gallery hosts an exciting programme of exhibitions.

OLD PLACE OF MOCHRUM 223   8 K30

Off B7005, 11 miles (17.5km) west of Wigtown. No access to the public but can be seen from the road.

Known also as Drumwalt Castle, this is a mainly 15th- and 16th-century construction with two picturesque towers.

ORCHARDTON TOWER 224   8 N30

HS. Off A711, 6 miles (9.5km) south east of Castle Douglas, Dumfries and Galloway. Nearest railway station Dumfries, bus from Dumfries to Palnackie. Open at all reasonable times, apply to custodian at nearby cottage. Free. Car parking. Telephone (0131) 5507603. www.historic-scotland.gov.uk

A charming and unique circular 15th-century tower house. Built by John Cairns.

OWEN'S WAREHOUSE   225   9 N27

Mill 2, Level 3, New Lanark. 1 mile (2km) south of Lanark. Bus service from Lanark. Open all year, Mon–Sat 1000–1700, Sun 1100–1700. Free. Guided tours. Explanatory displays. Gift shop. Refreshments available on site. WC. Wheelchair access. Disabled WC. Car and coach parking. Telephone (01555) 662322. www.ewm.co.uk

A large selection of lambswool and Aran knitwear, wax jackets, waterproofs and high street fashions. Also the Golf Company for golf enthusiasts, containing clothing and equipment.

PAXTON HOUSE GALLERY AND COUNTRY PARK   226   8 T26

Paxton, Berwick-upon-Tweed. On the B6461, 5 miles (8km) west of Berwick-upon-Tweed. Nearest railway station Berwick-upon-Tweed, then connecting bus from railway and bus station to Paxton House. Open Apr–Oct, daily 1100–1700; grounds, shop and tearoom, 1000–1700. Charge £££. Charge for house and grounds £££, grounds only £. Group concessions. Guided tours (information in French and German). Explanatory displays. Gift shop. Restaurant, tearoom and picnic areas. Croquet, boathouse, museum, adventure playground, squirrel hide. WC. Tactile tour by arrangement. Limited wheelchair access. Disabled WC. Car and coach parking. Telephone (01289) 386291. www.paxtonhouse.com

Winner of several tourism awards and one of the finest 18th-century Palladian houses in Britain. Designed by John Adam and built in 1758 by Patrick Home for his intended bride, Sophie de Brandt, an aristocrat from the court of King Frederick the Great of Prussia. Interiors by Robert Adam. The largest collection of Chippendale furniture in Scotland, and fine Regency furniture by Trotter of Edinburgh. The largest art gallery in any Scottish house or castle, an outstation of the National Galleries of Scotland. Over 80 acres (32ha) of grounds and gardens, including a mile of the River Tweed.

PITLOCHRY KNITWEAR   227   8 P28

4 Bath Place, Moffat, Dumfries and Galloway. Bus from Lockerbie or Dumfries. Open daily (except Christmas Day and New Year's Day), Mon–Sat 0930–1700, Sun 1030–1700. Free. Explanatory displays. Gift shop. WC. Car and coach parking. Telephone (01683) 220354. www.ewm.co.uk

A shop specialising in ready-made tartan garments, a large selection of Aran and other quality knitwear lines. Souvenirs and gifts. Clan research and certificates.

POLMADDY SETTLEMENT   228   8 M29

FE. 6 miles (9.5km) north of New Galloway on the A713, just past Carsfard Loch on the right. Access at all times. Free. Explanatory displays. Car parking.

The last settlement in this area before the clearances of the 19th century. A short waymarked trail has interpretation boards explaining the layout of the settlement. There are some remaining features such as foundations.

A D POTTERY   229   8 P26

Kirkdean Farm, Blyth Bridge, West Linton. On A701, 0.5 mile (1km) south of Blythbridge. Open all year, daily 1000–1630 (please telephone in advance to confirm). Free. Gift shop. WC. Wheelchair access. Disabled WC. Car and coach parking. Telephone (01721) 752617.

The pottery offers a wide range of handmade thrown and decorated pottery goods, including mugs, jugs, blowls, clocks and lamps. Viewing workshop allows visitors to see how each item is made.

PRIORWOOD GARDEN AND DRIED FLOWER SHOP   230   8 R27

NTS. Melrose, Roxburghshire. Off A6091 in Melrose. By bus from Edinburgh. Open Easter–24 Dec, Mon Sat 1000–1700 and Sun 1300–1700. Charge £. Charge £ (honesty box). Group concessions. Explanatory displays. Gift shop. Picnic area in orchard. Garden. WC nearby. Wheelchair access with assistance. Disabled WC. Car and coach parking. Telephone (01896) 822493. www.nts.org.uk

A unique garden overlooked by ruins of Melrose Abbey, specialising in plants suitable for drying. Visitors can watch and learn about the drying process and buy or order dried flower arrangements in the shop. The adjacent orchard includes many varieties of historic apple trees.

RAMMERSCALES HOUSE   231   8 P29

Hightae, Lochmaben, Dumfries and Galloway. On the B7020, 2.5 miles (4km) from Lochmaben. Open late Jul–mid Aug, Sun–Fri 1400–1700. Charge ££. Group concessions. Guided tours for parties. WC. No guide dogs. Car and coach parking. Telephone (01387) 810229.

An 18th-century Georgian manor house with magnificent views over Annandale. In Adam style and mostly unaltered. Contains contemporary art and library with 6000 volumes. Extensive and attractive grounds.

RENNIE'S BRIDGE   232   8 S27

Kelso. Access at all times. Free.

A fine five-arched bridge built over the River Tweed in 1803 by Rennie to replace one destroyed by the floods of 1797. On the bridge are two lamp posts from the demolished Old Waterloo Bridge in London, which Rennie built in 1811. There is also a fine view to Floors Castle (see 113).

RHYMER'S STONE VIEWPOINT   233   8 R27

1 mile (1.5km) east of Melrose, off Melrose bypass. Bus service to Melrose. Access at all times. Free. Guided tours, information board. Picnic area. Wheelchair access. Car and coach parking. Telephone (01896) 822758.

Rhymer's Stone is situated in an area steeped in mythology and marks the site of the Eildon Tree, beneath which, legend says, Thomas the Rhymer met the Fairie Queen in the 13th century. There is an easy uphill stroll of approximately 200m to the stone and the attractive viewing area offers panoramic views over the Tweed valley and Eildon Hills.

RISPAIN CAMP   234   8 L31

HS. Behind Rispain Farm, 1 mile (2km) west of Whithorn, Wigtownshire on the A746. Nearest railway station Stranraer, bus from Stranraer or Newton Stewart, then walk 1 mile (2km). Access at all reasonable times. Free. Telephone (0131) 5507603. www.historic-scotland.gov.uk

A rectangular settlement defended by a bank and ditch. 1st or 2nd century AD.

ROCKCLIFFE 235   8 N30

NTS. Dumfries and Galloway. 7 miles (11km) south of Dalbeattie, off A710. Open all year. Free. Explanatory displays. Restaurant and tearoom in village. Ranger led walks in summer. WC. Car and coach parking. Telephone (01556) 502575. www.nts.org.uk

The NTS owns several sites in and around the picturesque village of Rockcliffe on the Solway Firth. These include the Mote of Mark which is an ancient hill fort, Rough Island which is a bird sanctuary with access on foot at low tide, and Muckle Lands and Jubilee Path which is a beautiful stretch of coastline between Rockcliffe and Kippford.

ROXBURGH CASTLE 236   8 R27

Off A699, 1 mile (1.5km) south west of Kelso. Access at all times. Free.

The earthworks are all that remain of the once mighty castle, destroyed by the Scots in the 15th century, and the walled Royal Burgh which gave its name to the county. The present village of Roxburgh dates from a later period.

ROZELLE HOUSE GALLERIES 237   8 L28

Rozelle Park, Monument Road, Ayr. In Rozelle Park, 2.5 miles (4km) from town centre. Nearest railway station Ayr. Open Apr–Oct, Mon–Sat 1000–1700, Sun 1400–1700; Nov–Mar, Mon–Sat only (closed Christmas and New Year's Day). Free. Gift shop. Coffee shop and picnic area. WC. Limited wheelchair access. Car and coach parking. Telephone (01292) 445447.

Built in 1760 by Robert Hamilton, in the style of Robert Adam. Rebuilt in 1830 by David Bryce. Now a gallery for art and museum exhibitions.

RUTHWELL CROSS 238   8 P30

HS. In Ruthwell Church on the B724, 8.5 miles (13.5km) south east of Dumfries. Nearest railway station Dumfries, buses from Dumfries, Gretna or Annan. Access at all reasonable times. Free. Car parking. Telephone 0131 668 8800. www.historic-scotland.gov.uk

An Anglian Cross, sculptured in high relief and dating from the end of the 7th century. Considered to be one of the major monuments of Dark Age Europe. Carved with Runic characters.

ST ABB'S HEAD 239   8 S25

NTS. Off A1107, 2 miles (3km) north of Coldingham, Berwickshire. By bus from Edinburgh, by rail to Berwick-upon-Tweed. Reserve open all year, daily. Centre open Apr–Oct, daily 1000–1700. Site free. Charge for centre and parking £. Group concessions. Explanatory displays. Tearoom. Guided walks by rangers. WC. Wheelchair access to centre. Disabled WC. Car and coach parking. Telephone (018907) 71443. www.nts.org.uk

A National Nature Reserve. The most important location for cliff-nesting sea birds in south east Scotland. Remote camera link to the centre provides glimpses of nesting birds. Spectacular walks around the headland, above 300 ft (91m) cliffs. Exhibition on wildlife.

ST MARY'S LOCH 240   8 Q27

Off A708, 14 miles (22.5km) east south-east of Selkirk. Access at all times. Free. Car parking.

Beautifully set among smooth green hills, this 3-mile (4.5km) long loch is used for sailing and fishing. On the neck of land separating it from Loch of the Lowes, at the south end, stands Tibbie Shiel's Inn. The inn was kept by Tibbie Shiel (Elizabeth Richardson, 1783–1878) from 1823, and was a meeting place for many 19th-century writers. Beside the road towards the north end of the loch is a seated statue of James Hogg, the Ettrick Shepherd, author of *Confessions of a Justified Sinner* and a friend of Scott, who farmed in this district. On the route of the Southern Upland Way.

ST NINIAN'S CAVE   241   8 L31

HS. At Physgill, on the shore 4 miles (6.5km) south west of Whithorn, Wigtownshire. Nearest railway station Stranraer, bus from Newton Stewart or Stranraer, alight at junction to Cave Walk, then 4 mile (6.5km) walk. Free. Car and coach parking. Telephone (0131) 5507603. www.historic-scotland.gov.uk

A cave traditionally associated with the saint. Early crosses found here are housed at Whithorn Museum. The crosses carved on the walls of the cave are now weathered.

ST NINIAN'S CHAPEL, ISLE OF WHITHORN   242   8 L31

HS. At Isle of Whithorn, 3 miles (5km) south east of Whithorn, Wigtownshire. Nearest railway station Stranraer, bus from Newton Stewart or Stranraer to Isle of Whithorn. Access at all reasonable times. Free. Car and coach parking. Telephone (0131) 5507603. www.historic-scotland.gov.uk

The restored ruins of a 13th-century chapel, probably used by pilgrims on their way to Whithorn.

ST RONANS WELLS INTERPRETIVE CENTRE   243   8 Q27

Wells Brae, Innerleithen, Peebleshire. On the A72, 6 miles (9.5km) from Peebles. Bus from Edinburgh. Open week before and week after Easter, and Jun–Oct, Mon–Fri 1000–1300 and 1400–1700, Sat–Sun 1400–1700. Free. Guided tours. Explanatory displays. Gift shop. Open air tearoom and picnic area. Garden. WC. Wheelchair access. Disabled WC. Car and coach parking. Telephone (01721) 724820.

A site associated with a novel by Sir Walter Scott. Memorabilia of Scott and James Hogg, information and photographs of local festival. The well water can be tasted.

ST RONANS WOOD   244   8 Q27

Innerleithen, . On the A72, 6 miles (9.5km) from Peebles. Bus from Edinburgh or Peebles to Innerleithen. Car and coach parking nearby. Access at all reasonable times. Free. Telephone (01764) 662554. www.woodland-trust.org.uk

St Ronans provides excellent public access and is criss-crossed by innumerable paths. To the north a path continues from the site to Lee Pen (a mountain 1647 feet/502m high). Visitors to St Ronans will enjoy fine views of Innerleithen, Walkerburn, the Tweed Valley and Traquair House.

SAMYE LING TIBETAN BUDDHIST MONASTERY   245

See 154 Kagyu Samye Ling Tibetan Buddhist Monastery.

SANQUHAR TOLBOOTH MUSEUM   246   8 M28

High Street, Sanquhar, Dumfries and Galloway. In the town centre near station. Nearest railway station Sanquhar, buses from Dumfries or Kilmarnock. Open

Apr–Sep, Tue–Sat 1000–1300 and 1400–1700, Sun 1400–1700. Free. Explanatory displays and audio-visual presentation. Gift shop. Limited wheelchair access. Car and coach parking. Telephone (01659) 50186.

Located in a fine 18th-century tolbooth. Tells the story of Upper Nithsdale. Features world famous Sanquhar knitting, mines and miners of Sanquhar and Kirkconnel, history and customs of the Royal Burgh of Sanquhar, three centuries of local literature, life in Sanquhar jail, the earliest inhabitants, and the people of Upper Nithsdale, at home and at work.

SAVINGS BANKS MUSEUM 247   8 P30

Ruthwell, Dumfries. Off the B724, 10 miles (16km) east of Dumfries. Bus from Dumfries or Annan. Open daily (except Sun–Mon in winter), 1000–1300 and 1400–1700. Free. Guided tours (leaflets in European languages, Russian, Chinese and Japanese). Explanatory displays. WC. Touch facilities for blind visitors. Wheelchair access. Car and coach parking. Telephone (01387) 870640. www.savingsbankmuseum.co.uk

Housed in the original 1800 village meeting place, the museum traces the savings bank movement from its founding here in 1810 by the Rev Henry Duncan, to its growth and spread worldwide. Features restoration of the 8th-century runic Ruthwell Cross (see 238).

SCOTS DYKE 248   8 Q29

Off A7, 7 miles (11km) south of Langholm. Access at all reasonable times, but not easily identified. Free.

The remains of a wall made of clods of earth and stones, which marked part of the border between England and Scotland.

SIR WALTER SCOTT'S COURTROOM 249   8 Q27

Market Place, Selkirk. In Selkirk, 25 miles (40km) south of Edinburgh. Bus from Edinburgh, Carlisle or Berwick. Open Apr–Sep, daily Mon–Fri 1000–1600, Sat 1000–1400; May–Aug also Sun 1000–1400; Oct, Mon–Sat 1300–1600. Free. Guided tours for groups by appointment. Explanatory displays. Gifts for sale. Tearoom. WC. Induction loop. Disabled WC. Car and coach parking. Telephone (01750) 20096.

The bench and chair from which Sir Walter Scott, as Sheriff of Selkirk, administered justice for 30 years are displayed, as are portraits of Scott, James Hogg, Mungo Park. Watercolours by Tom Scott RSA. Audio-visual display.

SCOTT'S VIEW 250   8 R27

B6356, 4 miles east of Melrose. Access at all reasonable times.

A view over the Tweed to the Eildon Hills, beloved by Scott. Here the horses taking his remains to Dryburgh for burial stopped, as they had so often before for Sir Walter to enjoy this panorama.

SCOTTISH MARITIME MUSEUM 251   9 K27

Laird Forge, Gottries Road, Irvine, Ayrshire. In Irvine, at Harbourside, five minute walk from station. Open Apr–Oct, daily 1000–1700. Charge £. Group concessions. Guided tours. Explanatory displays. Gift shop. Tearoom. WC. Limited wheelchair access. Disabled WC. Car and coach parking. Telephone (01294) 278283.

The museum reflects all aspects of Scottish maritime history. Vessels can be seen afloat in the harbour and under cover. Visitors can experience life in a 1910 shipyard worker's flat and visit the Linthouse Engine Shop, originally built in 1872, under reconstruction.

SELKIRK GLASS VISITOR CENTRE   252   8 Q27

Dunsdale Haugh, Selkirk. On the A7 to the north of Selkirk. Bus from Edinburgh or Carlisle. Open all year (except Christmas and New Year), Mon–Fri 0900–1700, Sat 0900–1700, Sun 1100–1700. Free. Explanatory displays. Gift shop. Award-winning coffee shop with patio. WC. Wheelchair access. Disabled WC. Car and coach parking. Telephone (01750) 20954.

Visitors can view the complete glassmaking process (Monday-Friday only to 1630) and can purchase quality seconds and other gifts in the shop.

SHAMBELLIE HOUSE MUSEUM OF COSTUME   253   8 N30

New Abbey, Dumfries. On the A710, 7 miles (11km) south of Dumfries. Car parking (coach parking by arrangment). Bus from Dumfries. Open Easter–Oct, daily 1000–1700 (grounds from 1030). Charge £. Children 12 and under and NMS Members free. Guided tours (leaflets in French, German and Dutch). Explanatory displays. Gift shop. Tearoom and picnic area. Gardens. WC. Limited wheelchair access (road from car park is steep, staff can open gate to allow parking by house). Telephone (01387) 850375.

Designed by renowned Scottish architect, David Bryce, for the Stewart family, this Victorian house presents a fascinating look at fashion and social etiquette from the 1850s to the 1950s. There are special exhibitions and events throughout the year. Part of the National Museums of Scotland.

ROBERT SMAIL'S PRINTING WORKS   254   8 Q27

NTS. 7-9 High Street, Innerleithen, Peebleshire. In Innerleithen, 30 miles (48km) south of Edinburgh. Buses from Edinburgh or Peebles. Open Easter and Jun–Sep, Thur–Mon 1200–1700 and Sun 1300–1700. Charge ££. Group concessions. Guided tours. Explanatory displays. Gift shop. Limited wheelchair access. Car and coach parking. Telephone (01896) 830206. www.nts.org.uk

Restored printing works using machinery and methods of the early 20th century. Visitors can watch the printer at work and try setting type by hand. Victorian office with many historic items. Reconstructed waterwheel.

SMAILHOLM TOWER   255   8 R27

HS. Off the B6404, 6 miles (9.5km) north west of Kelso, Roxburghshire. Occasional bus from Kelso and St Boswells then 1.5 mile (2.5km) walk. Open Apr–Sep, daily 0930–1830; Oct–Mar, Sat–Sun 0930–1630. Charge £. Group concessions. Explanatory displays. Gift shop. Car and coach parking. Telephone (01573) 460365. www.historic-scotland.gov.uk

A small rectangular 16th-century Border peel tower sited on a rocky outcrop within a stone barmkin wall. Well-preserved and containing an exhibition of costume figures and tapestries relating to Sir Walter Scott's *Minstrelsy of the Scottish Border*. Scott spent some of his childhood at nearby Sandyknowe Farm.

SOUTER JOHNNIE'S COTTAGE   256   8 K28

NTS. Main Road, Kirkoswald, Ayrshire. On A77 in Kirkoswald, 4 miles (6.5km) south west of Maybole. Buses from Ayr or Girvan. Open Apr–Sep, Fri–Tue 1130–1700. Charge ££. Group concessions. Explanatory displays. Cottage garden. Limited wheelchair access. Car and coach parking. Telephone (01655) 760603. www.nts.org.uk

Thatched cottage, home of the souter (cobbler) who inspired the character
Souter Johnnie in Robert Burns' poem *Tam O'Shanter*. Burns memorabilia and
reconstructed workshop. Restored alehouse with life-size stone figures of Burns'
characters.

THE STEWARTRY MUSEUM   257   8 M31

St Mary Street, Kirkcudbright. In Kirkcudbright centre. Nearest railway station
Dumfries, bus from Dumfries. Open May–Jun and Sep, Mon–Sat 1100–1700;
Jul–Aug, Mon–Sat 1000–1800 (Jun–Oct also Sun 1400–1700); Oct–Apr, Mon–Sat
1100–1600. Free. Group concessions. Guided tours for groups by arrangement.
Explanatory displays. Gift shop. Picnic area. WC. Wheelchair access with assistance.
Telephone (01557) 331643. www.dumgal.gov.uk/museums

A wide range of exhibits reflecting the social and natural history of the
Stewartry of Kirkcudbright. Features illustrations, pottery and jewellery by
Jessie M. King and the work of her husband, E. A. Taylor, Phyllis Bone and other
Kirkcudbright artists. Special temporary exhibitions, family and local history
information services.

STRANRAER MUSEUM   258   7 J30

Old Town Hall, George Street, Stranraer. In town centre, five minutes walk from ferry
terminals. Nearest railway station Stranraer, trains from Glasgow and Ayr. Open all
year, Mon–Fri 1000–1700, Sat 1000–1300 and 1400–1700 (closed Christmas, New
Year, and on bank holidays). Free. Explanatory displays. Gift shop. WC. Wheelchair
access. Disabled WC. Telephone (01776) 705088. www.dumgal.gov.uk/museums

Permanent display on local history, archaeology, farming and polar exploration.
Temporary exhibition programme throughout the year with supporting
educational and family activities. Enquiry and identification service available.

SWEETHEART ABBEY   259   8 N30

HS. New Abbey, Dumfries. 7 miles (11km) south of Dumfries. Nearest railway station
Dumfries; bus from Dumfries and Dalbeattie. Open Apr–Sep, daily 0930–1830;
Oct–Mar, Mon–Sun 0930–1630, (closed Thu and Fri). Charge £. Group concessions.
WC. Limited wheelchair access. Disabled WC. Car and coach parking. Telephone
(01387) 850397. www.historic-scotland.gov.uk

Splendid ruin of a late 13th-century and early 14th-century Cistercian abbey
founded by Dervorgilla, Lady of Galloway, in memory of her husband John
Balliol. Apart from the abbey, the principal feature is the well-preserved precinct
wall, enclosing 30 acres (12ha).

SYMINGTON PARISH CHURCH   260   8 L27

Brewlands Road, Symington, near Kilmarnock, Ayrshire. Just off A77, 4 miles (6.5km)
north of Prestwick airport. Regular bus service from Glasgow and Ayr. On-street
parking only. Workship takes place all year, Sun 1030. The church can always be opened
on request – see church notice board and local press. Free. Guided tours can be
arranged. Refreshments available locally. WC. Wheelchair access with assistance.
Telephone Session Clerk on (01563) 830289. www.symingtonchurch.com

This Norman church was founded in 1160 AD by a local landowner Simon
Loccard. It is understood that the village derived its original name of
'Symonstown' from him. The church is without doubt one of the oldest and most
beautiful in Scotland. The oak beam roof with some of the original timbers,
along with the fine stained glass windows by some of the finest artists of their
generation make it a remarkably well-preserved part of our heritage.

TAM O' SHANTER EXPERIENCE   261   8 L28

Murdochs Lone, Alloway, Ayr. 2 miles (3km) south of Ayr. Nearest railway station Ayr, bus service from centre of Ayr. Open Apr–Sep, daily 0930–1730; Oct–Mar, daily 1000–1700. Closed Christmas and New Year. Charge £. Admission to restaurant, shop and gardens free. Charge £ for audio visual theatre. Group concessions. Explanatory displays. Gift shop. Restaurant. Children's play area, baby changing facilities. WC. Wheelchair access. Disabled WC. Car and coach parking. Telephone (01292) 443700. www.burnsheritagepark.com

Walk your way through history, and experience the Burns mystery and magic with our audio-visual presentations. The presentation is the poem *Tam O'Shanter* in the words of Burns, using the latest technology. See also 39 Burns National Heritage Park.

TEVIOT WATER GARDENS   262   8 S27

Kirkbank House, Kelso, Roxburghshire. Midway between Kelso and Jedburgh on A698. Nearest railway stations Berwick and Carlisle, bus from Kelso. Gardens open Apr–Oct, daily 1000–1700. Smokery open Apr–Sep, Mon–Sat 1000–1630; Oct–Mar, Mon–Sat closes 1630. Free. Guided tours by arrangement. Explanatory displays. Gift shop. Tearoom. WC. Limited wheelchair access. Disabled WC. Car parking. Telephone (01835) 850734.

The water gardens are on four levels, set amidst scenic Borders countryside. The lowest garden flows down to the River Teviot. Teviot Game Fare Smokery is produced and sold here.

THIRLESTANE CASTLE   263   8 R26

Lauder, Berwickshire. Off A68 at Lauder. Bus from Edinburgh. Check website or telephone for opening times. Charge for castle and grounds £££, grounds only £. Group concessions. Guided tours until 1400. Explanatory displays. Gift shop. Café and picnic tables in grounds. Adventure playground, woodland walk. WC. Limited wheelchair access. Disabled WC. Car and coach parking. Telephone (01578) 722430. www.thirlestanecastle.co.uk

Nestling in the gentle Border Hills, with its rose pink sandstone and fairytale turrets, Thirlestane Castle holds a uniquely important place in Scottish history. It is one of the oldest and finest castles in the land, and home to one of the country's most distinguished families.

The ancient seat of the Earls & Duke of Lauderdale, Thirlestane Castle has exquisite 17th centuary ceilings; victorian kitchens; historic toys and country life exhibition; gift shop; adventure playground; woodland walk and picnic tables. Lunches and teas are served in the Old Servants Hall.

THREAVE CASTLE   264   8 M30

HS. Castle Douglas, Dumfries and Galloway. North of the A75, 3 miles (5km) west of Castle Douglas. Nearest railway station Dumfries, bus from Dumfries, then 30 min walk to the boat over to island. Open Apr–Sep, daily 0930–1830. Charge £. Charge includes ferry. Group concessions. Picnic area. WC. Car and coach parking. Telephone (07711) 223101. www.historic-scotland.gov.uk

A massive tower built in the late 14th century by Archibald the Grim, Lord of Galloway. Round its base is an artillery fortification built before 1455, when the castle was besieged by James II. The castle is on an island, approached by boat.

THREAVE GARDEN AND ESTATE   265   8 M30

NTS. Castle Douglas, Dumfries and Galloway. Off A75, 1 mile (2km) west of Castle Douglas. Bus to Castle Douglas. Walled garden open all year, daily 0930–1700; visitor centre open Feb-Mar and Nov–Dec, daily 1000–1600; Apr–Oct, daily 0930–1730. Charge £££. Group concessions. Guided tours. Explanatory displays, information in four languages. Gift shop. Restaurant. Plant sales. WC. Induction loop in visitor centre. Wheelchair access (wheelchairs and batricars available). Disabled WC. Car and coach parking. Telephone (01556) 502575. www.nts.org.uk

Threave Garden has a spectacular springtime display of daffodils, colourful herbaceous beds in summer, and striking trees and heathers in autumn. The visitor centre has an exhibition and delightful terraced restaurant. Threave Estate is a wildfowl refuge, with bird hides and waymarked trails.

THE THREE HILLS ROMAN HERITAGE CENTRE   266   8 R27

The Ormiston, The Square, Melrose, Roxburghshire. Train to Berwick or Edinburgh, then bus to Galashiels or Earlston, then Melrose. Open Apr–Oct, daily 1030–1630. Charge £. Guided tours of the site Thu 1320-1700, (£) includes tea/juice and biscuits. Additional tours Jul–Aug, Tue, telephone to confirm. Explanatory displays and audio guide. Gift shop. Refreshments nearby. Baby changing facilities. WC. Wheelchair access. Disabled WC. Car and coach parking. Telephone (01896) 822651. www.trimontium.net

An exhibition illustrating daily life on the Roman frontier at Trimontium fortress, the remains of which can be seen on the tour. Museum contains *objets trouvés*.

TOLBOOTH ART CENTRE   267   8 M31

High Street, Kirkcudbright. In Kirkcudbright centre. Nearest railway station Dumfries, bus from Dumfries. Open May–Jun and Sep, Mon–Sat 1100–1700, Jul–Aug, Mon–Sat 1000–1700 (Jun–Oct also Sun 1400–1700); Oct–Apr, Mon–Sat 1100–1600. Free. Group concessions. Guided tours by arrangement. Explanatory displays. Gift shop. Tearoom. WC. Wheelchair access. Disabled WC. Telephone (01557) 331556.

An interpretive centre located in the 17th-century tolbooth. Exhibition about the town's history as an artists' colony, including paintings by important Kirkcudbright artists. Audio-visual presentations about the town's art heritage and the artist Jessie M King. Temporary exhibitions programme.

TORHOUSKIE STONE CIRCLE   268   8 L30

HS. Off the B733, 4 miles (6.5km) west of Wigtown. Nearest railway station Stranraer, buses from Stranraer, Newton Stewart or Dumfries, alight at Kirkcowan (5 miles/8km) or Wigton (4 miles/6.5km). Access at all reasonable times. Free. Telephone (0131) 5507603. www.historic-scotland.gov.uk

A Bronze Age recumbent circle of 19 boulders on the edge of a low mound.

TORR A'CHAISTEAL FORT   269   7 J27

HS. 4 miles (6.5km) south of Blackwaterfoot, Isle of Arran. Ferry from Ardrossan to Brodick, bus from Brodick. Access at all reasonable times. Free. Telephone (0131) 5507603. www.historic-scotland.gov.uk

A circular Iron Age fort on a ridge.

TORRYLIN CAIRN   270   7 J28

HS. 0.25 miles (0.5km) south east of Lagg on the south coast of the Isle of Arran. By ferry from Ardrossan to Brodick, bus from Brodick to Lagg. Access at all reasonable times. Free. Telephone (0131) 5507603. www.historic-scotland.gov.uk

A Neolithic chambered cairn with its compartments visible.

TRAQUAIR HOUSE   271   8 Q27

Innerleithen, Peeblesshire. 6 miles (10km) south east of Peebles, 29 miles (46.5km) south of Edinburgh. Off A72 on B709, signposted. Nearest railway station Edinburgh, bus to Innerleithen then 1.5 mile (2.5km) walk. Open mid Apr–Sep, daily 1200–1700; Oct, daily 1100–1600; Nov, Sat–Sun 1200–1600. Charge £££. Group concessions. Guided tours. Explanatory displays. Gift shop. Restaurant. WC. Limited wheelchair access. Disabled WC. Car and coach parking. Telephone (01896) 830323. www.traquair.co.uk

Dating back to the 12th century, this is said to be the oldest continuously inhabited house in Scotland. Twenty-seven Scottish and English monarchs have visited the house, including Mary, Queen of Scots, of whom there are relics. William the Lion held court here in 1175. The well-known Bear Gates were closed in 1745, not to be reopened until the Stuarts should ascend the throne. Ale is regularly produced at the 18th-century brewhouse. Exhibitions and special events are held during the summer months. Craft workshops, brewery with ale tasting (£), woodland and River Tweed walks and maze.

TURNBERRY CASTLE   272   8 K28

Off A719, 6 miles (9.5km) north of Girvan. Access at all reasonable times. Free.

The scant remains of the castle where Robert the Bruce was probably born in 1274.

TWEED BRIDGE   273   8 S27

A698 at Coldstream, 9 miles (14.5km) east north east of Kelso.

The 300-feet (91-m) long bridge was built in 1766 by Smeaton. In the past the bridge was a crossing into Scotland for eloping couples taking advantage of Scotland's easier marriage laws.

TWEEDDALE MUSEUM AND GALLERY   274   8 Q27

Chambers Institute, High Street, Peebles. In the town centre. Bus from Edinburgh. Open all year, Mon–Fri 1000–1200 and 1400–1700; Easter–Oct also Sat 1000–1300 and 1400–1600. Free. Guided tours. Explanatory displays. WC. Car and coach parking. Telephone (01721) 724820.

A 19th-century building housing a museum and gallery. Temporary exhibitions of art and craftwork. Gallery of local history and ornamental plasterwork.

TWELVE APOSTLES   275   8 N29

400m off B729 towards Dunscore, north of Dumfries. Park beside first road on left and walk 100m to waymark and stile. Access at all reasonable times. Free.

The largest stone circle on the Scottish mainland.

UNION SUSPENSION BRIDGE   276   8 S26

Across River Tweed, 2 miles (3km) south of Paxton on unclassified road.

This suspension bridge, the first of its type in Britain, was built by Samuel Brown in 1820, and links England and Scotland.

VENNEL GALLERY 277   9 K27

10 Glasgow Vennel, Irvine, Ayrshire. In Irvine town centre off High Street. Nearest railway and bus stations Irvine. Open all year (except public holidays), Fri– Sun 1000–1300 and 1400–1700. Free. Guided tours. Explanatory displays. Gift shop. WC. Wheelchair access. Telephone (01294) 275059. www.northayrshiremuseums.org.uk

Gallery with a programme of changing exhibitions of contemporary art and crafts. The gallery includes the Heckling Shop, where Robert Burns worked, and the Lodging House where he lived in 1781.

VIKINGAR 278   9 K26

Greenock Road, Largs, Ayrshire. 25 miles (40km) from Glasgow on A78. Nearest railway station Largs, bus from Glasgow. Open all year, Apr–Sep, daily 1030–1730; Oct and Mar, daily 1030–1530; Nov–Feb, Sat–Sun 1030–1530. Charge dependent on activity. Group concessions. Guided tours (language sheets available). Explanatory displays. Gift shop. Café and vending machine. Swimming pool. Soft play area. WC. Braille sheet. Written tour for hearing impaired. Wheelchair access. Disabled WC. Car and coach parking. Telephone (01475) 689777. www.vikingar.co.uk

The history of the Vikings in Scotland, including the Battle of Largs in 1263, is told here using multimedia. Other facilities include a swimming pool, sauna and health suite, as well as a 500-seat cinema. There is a Winter Garden café, children's play area and an activity room.

WANLOCKHEAD BEAM ENGINE 279   8 N28

HS. In Wanlockhead, Dumfries and Galloway, on the A797. Nearest railway station Sanquhar, buses from Sanquhar, Ayr or Dumfries. Access at all reasonable times. Free. Telephone (0131) 5507603. www.historic-scotland.gov.uk

An early 19th-century wooden water-balance pump for draining a lead mine, with the track of a horse engine beside it. Nearby is the privately-operated Museum of Lead Mining (see 212).

WESTLANDS ACTIVITIES 280   8 Q30

Westlands, Annan, Dumfries and Galloway. On the B6357 between Annan and Kirkpatrick Fleming, 2 miles (3.5km) from junction 21 on the M74. Open Easter–Oct, Mon–Tue and Thu–Sun 1000–1700; after 1700 and during winter by appointment. Charge per activity. Group concessions. Explanatory displays. Tearoom and picnic area. WC. Limited wheelchair access. Disabled WC. Car and coach parking. Telephone (01461) 800274. www.westlands-activities.co.uk

The 70 acre (29ha) site has activities for all the family: quad bike tracks, paintball, fishing pond, fly fishing lochans, clay pigeon shooting, go-karts for children and adults. The ages for activities start at 9 years. All equipment available for hire.

WHITHORN PRIORY AND MUSEUM 281   8 L31

HS. 6 Bruce Street, Whithorn, Newton Stewart. In Whithorn. Nearest railway station Dumfries, bus from Newton Stewart and Stranraer. Open Easter–Oct, 1030–1700. Free. For details of charges see 282 Whithorn Trust Discovery Centre. Priory museum free to Historic Scotland Members. Explanatory displays. Gift shop. WC. Wheelchair access with assistance. Telephone (01988) 500508. www.historic-scotland.gov.uk

The cradle of Christianity in Scotland, founded in the 5th century. The priory for Premonstratensian canons was built in the 12th century and became the

cathedral church of Galloway. In the museum is a fine collection of early
Christian stone, including the Latinus stone, the earliest Christian memorial in
Scotland, and the Monreith Cross, the finest of the Whithorn school of crosses.

WHITHORN TRUST DISCOVERY CENTRE   282   8 L31

45-47 George Street, Whithorn. Off A75 between Glenluce and Newton Stewart. Bus
service from Newton Stewart, Stranraer and Dumfries. Open Apr–Oct, daily
1030–1700. Charge £. Joint ticket with Whithorn Priory and Museum (see 281). Group
concessions. Guided tours. Explanatory displays and audio-visual show. Gift shop.
Tearoom and picnic area. WC. Limited wheelchair access. Disabled WC. Car and
coach parking. Telephone (01988) 500508.

Since 1986 archaeologists have been investigating the site of an abandoned
town. One thousand years ago the Anglo-Saxons called it *Hwiterne*; earlier it was
called *Candida Casa*, the Shining House. Fifteen hundred years ago St Ninian,
Scotland's first saint, built a church here. Guided tour of original dig site,
priory, museum and crypts, discovery centre with archaeology puzzle. Audio-
visual show, exhibitions.

WIGTOWN MARTYRS' MONUMENT   283   8 L30

In Wigtown. Access at all reasonable times. Free. Car parking.

Hilltop monument to the 17th-century Covenanters who died for their beliefs.
Their gravestones are in the churchyard and a stone shaft on the shore marks
the spot where two women were drowned at the stake in 1685.

WILTON LODGE PARK AND WALLED GARDEN   284   8 R28

Wilton Park Road, Hawick. 0.5 mile (1km) from the town centre. Open all year, 24
hours daily. Free. Tearoom open Apr–Oct (variable). Bowling, putting, crazy golf, and
tennis. WC. Wheelchair access. Car and coach parking. Telephone (01450) 378023.

Comprises 107 acres (43ha) of parkland and gardens with extensive shrubberies
and a large selection of mature trees.

WILTONBURN COUNTRY CASHMERES   285   8 R28

Wiltonburn Farm, Hawick. Pleasant walk or taxi ride from town, 2 miles (3km) from
A7. Take B711 signposted Robertson Road. Cross bridge and turn right. Follow road
along riverside and straight on through signs for No Through Road. Open all year
(except Christmas Day and New Year's Day) from 1000. Please telephone to confirm.
Free. Guided tours. Explanatory displays. Gift shop. WC. Wheelchair access with
assistance. Car parking. Telephone (01450) 372414. www.wiltonburnfarm.co.uk

Situated on a working hill farm, the showroom contains designer cashmere
knitwear, costume jewellery, paintings, furniture and country gifts. Also art
courses.

WOODSIDE WALLED GARDEN   286   8 R27

Near Harestanes, Ancrum, Jedburgh. 4 miles (6.5km) north of Jedburgh. Turn right
off A68 onto B6400 and continue for 0.5 mile (1km). Buses from Jedburgh,
Edinburgh, Kelso, Galashiels, Hawick. Open daily 1000–1700. Closed Christmas and
Jan–Feb. Free. Explanatory displays. Plant sales. Picnic area. Occasional sculpture
displays. Organic demonstrations and trials. WC. Wheelchair access. Disabled WC.
Car parking. Telephone (01835) 830315.

Situated in a secluded and sheltered Victorian walled garden, the retail sales
area is open to the public. The developing gardens on the rest of the 2 acre (1ha)

site include stunning herbaceous borders, organic demonstration garden (including composting), and wildlife pond.

WWT CAERLAVEROCK WETLANDS CENTRE   287   8 P30

East Park Farm, Caerlaverock, Dumfries. 9 miles (14.5km) south east of Dumfries. Nearest railway station Dumfries, bus from Dumfries. Open daily (except Christmas Day), 1000–1700. Charge ££. Carers of disabled visitors free. Group concessions. Guided tours. Explanatory displays. Gift shop. Tearoom and picnic area. Waymarked trails. WC. No dogs apart from guide dogs. Limited wheelchair access. Car and coach parking. Telephone (01387) 770200. www.wwt.org.uk and www.snh.org.uk

A 1350 acre (546ha) nature reserve of mudflats and merse. Duck, geese and waders; the rare natterjack toad; many beautiful flowers. Hides and observation towers.

YARROW   288   8 Q27

A708, west from Selkirk. Car parking.

A lovely valley praised by many writers including Scott, Wordsworth and Hogg. Little Yarrow Kirk dates from 1640, Scott's great-great-grandfather was minister there. Deuchar Bridge dates from the 17th century. On the surrounding hills are the remains of ancient Border keeps.

EDINBURGH AND LOTHIANS

ABERCORN CHURCH AND MUSEUM   289   10 P25

Hopetoun Estate, South Queensferry. 4 miles (6.4km) west of South Queensferry off the A904. Open all year daily. Free. Explanatory displays and brochure. Wheelchair access. Car parking. Telephone (01506) 834331.

There has been a church on this site for 1500 years. Abercorn was the first bishopric in Scotland, dating from 681 AD. The present church (dedicated to St Serf) developed from the Reformation to the present day – the present building, on the site of a 7th-century monastery, dates from the 12th century. The museum contains Viking burial stones.

ALMOND VALLEY HERITAGE CENTRE   290   10 P26

Millfield, Livingston Village, West Lothian. Off A705, 2 miles (3km) from junction 3 on M8, 15 miles (24km) west of Edinburgh. Bus and train service from Edinburgh to Glasgow to local stations. Open all year, daily 1000–1700. Charge £. Group concessions. Explanatory displays. Gift shop. Tearoom. WC. Wheelchair access. Disabled WC. Car and coach parking. Telephone (01506) 414957. www.almondvalley.co.uk

The history and environment of West Lothian brought to life in an exciting and innovative museum combining a working farm, restored watermill and museum of social and industrial history. Award-winning interactive displays for children, indoor play areas, nature trail, trailer rides and a narrow-gauge railway.

ALMONDELL AND CALDERWOOD COUNTRY PARK   291   10 P25

Broxburn, West Lothian. On B7015 (A71) at East Calder or off A89 at Broxburn. 12 miles (19km) south west of Edinburgh. Park open all year. Visitor centre open Apr–Sep, Mon, Tue and Thu 0930–1700, Wed 0930–1630, Sat 1000–1700 (Sun closes 1730); Oct–Mar, Mon–Thu 0915–1700, Sat and Sun 1000–1630. Closed for lunch 1200–1300. Free. Guided tours cost £, varied for guided walks. Explanatory displays.

Gift shop. Refreshments in visitor centre. Garden. WC. Wheelchair access to visitor centre, partial access to country park. Disabled WC. Car and coach parking. Telephone (01506) 414957. www.beecraigs.com

Extensive riverside and woodland walks in former estate, with large picnic and grassy areas. The visitor centre, housed in an old stable block, has a large freshwater aquarium, displays on local and natural history, and a short slide show. Ranger service, guided walks programme.

AMAZONIA RAINFOREST EXPERIENCE   292   10 P26

Freeport Leisure Village, West Calder, West Lothian. 4 miles (6.5km) from junction 4 off M8. Rail and bus service to West Calder. Open all year, daily 1000–1730. Charge £££. Group concessions. Guided tours available for parties of ten or more (book in advance). Explanatory displays. Gift shop. Picnic area. WC. Limited wheelchair access. Disabled WC. Car and coach parking. Telephone (01501) 763746. www.ama-zone-ia.com

An indoor tropical environment giving visitors the opportunity to explore a recreated rainforest, waterfalls and lush vegetation. Hundreds of free-flying butterflies. Many animals and birds, including parrots, toucans, poison dart frogs, snakes, spiders and the world's smallest monkeys. Daily animal handling sessions. Admission includes entry into West Lothian's largest outdoor adventure playground.

ARNISTON HOUSE   293   10 Q26

Gorebridge, Midlothian. On the B6372, 1 mile (2km) from the A7 and 10 miles (16km) from Edinburgh. Bus on A7. View house by guided tour only: Apr, May and Jun Tue and Wed 01400 and 1530; Jul–mid-Sep Sun–Fri 1400 and 1530. Grounds open 1400–1700 on these days. Charge ££. Children under 5 years free. Grounds free. Guided tours. WC. Limited wheelchair access. Disabled WC. Car and coach parking. Telephone (01875) 830515. www.arniston-house.co.uk

An outstanding example of the work of William Adam, built in the 1720s. Contains an important collection of furniture, Scottish portraiture and other fascinating items.

ATHELSTANEFORD, FLAG HERITAGE CENTRE   294   10 R25

Athelstaneford, East Lothian. Behind Athelstaneford Church. Off B1347, 3 miles (4.5km) off the A1, 2.5 miles (4km) east of Haddington off B1343. Nearest railway station Drem, 2.5 miles (4km). Bus from North Berwick to Haddington stops in village. Open Apr–Oct, daily 0900–1800 and St Andrews day November 30. Free. Explanatory displays. WC. Wheelchair access. Disabled WC. Car and coach parking. Telephone (01620) 880378.

A 16th-century dovecot restored to house an audio-visual dramatisation of the battle in 832 AD at which an army of Picts/Scots encountered a larger force of Saxons under Athelstan. The appearance of a cloud formation of a white saltire (the diagonal cross on which St Andrew had been martyred) against a blue sky inspired the Scots to victory. Since that time, the St Andrew's Cross has been the national flag of Scotland. There is a viewpoint overlooking the battle site, and visitors can also inspect the Saltire Memorial, the *Book of the Saltire*, and walk through the historic churchyard.

AUBIGNY SPORTS CENTRE   295   10 R25

Mill Wynd, Haddington. In Haddington, five minute walk from High Street. Bus from Edinburgh. Open daily all year (except Christmas and New Year) Mon–Fri

0900–2200, weekends 0900–1700. Charges dependent on activity. Group concessions. Café. Crèche. WC. Wheelchair access. Disabled WC. Car and coach parking. Telephone (01620) 826800.

Sports centre with a swimming pool, a toddlers pool, sauna, steam room, activity hall, bodyworks gym, aerobics studio, soft play area and a variety of coached activities.

BASS ROCK   296   10 R25

Off North Berwick. Boat trips from North Berwick go round the Bass Rock. Telephone (01620) 892838 (boat trips) or (01620) 892197 (Tourist Information Centre). Car parking.

A massive 350-feet (106.5m) high rock whose many thousands of raucous sea birds include the third largest gannetry in the world.

BEECRAIGS COUNTRY PARK   297   10 N25

The Park Centre, Linlithgow, West Lothian. 2 miles (3km) south of Linlithgow. Nearest railway station Linlithgow. Open all year, daily until dusk. Park centre closed 25–26 Dec and 1–2 Jan. Free. Charge for activities. Guided tours, ranger service events programme and outdoor activities. Explanatory displays. Gift shop. Restaurant and refreshments. Barbecues to hire. WC. Braille map of park. Limited wheelchair access to park centre. Disabled WC. Car and coach parking. Telephone (01506) 844516. www.beecraigs.com

Nestled high in the Bathgate hills, Beecraigs offers a wide range of leisure and recreational pursuits within its 915 acres (370ha). Archery, orienteering, fly-fishing, walks and trails. Trim course, play area, picnic areas, barbecue sites, fish farm, deer farm, caravan and camping site. Ranger service.

BENNIE MUSEUM   298   10 N25

9-11 Mansefield Street, Bathgate, West Lothian. 3 miles (5km) east of Livingston off M8. Nearest railway station Bathgate. Bus service from Edinburgh. Open Apr–Sep, Mon–Sat 1000–1600; Oct–Mar, Mon–Sat 1100–1530. Closed Christmas and New Year. Free. Guided tours on request. Explanatory displays. Gift shop. WC. Limited wheelchair access. Disabled WC. Car and coach parking. Telephone (01506) 634944. www.benniemuseum.homestead.com

Local heritage museum with almost 5000 artefacts illustrating the social, industrial, religious and military history of Bathgate, a former burgh town. Displays of postcards and photographs from the 1890s onwards. Fossils, Roman glass and coins, relics from Prince Charles Edward Stuart and the Napoleonic Wars.

BLACKNESS CASTLE   299   10 P25

HS. Blackness, West Lothian. On the B903, 4 miles (6.5km) north east of Linlithgow, West Lothian. Nearest railway station Linlithgow, buses from Bo'ness and Linlithgow to Blackness. Open Apr–Sep, daily 0930–1830; Oct–Mar, Mon–Sun 0930–1630 (closed Thu and Fri). Charge £. Group concessions. Explanatory displays. Gift shop. Picnic area. WC. Car parking. Telephone (01506) 834807. www.historic-scotland.gov.uk

A 15th-century stronghold, once one of the most important fortresses in Scotland and one of the four castles which the Articles of Union left fortified. A state prison in Covenanting times; a powder magazine in the 1870s. More recently, for a period, a youth hostel.

CAIRNPAPPLE HILL   300   10 N25

HS. Near Torphichen, off the B792, 3 miles (5km) north of Bathgate, West Lothian.
Bus from Linlithgow to Bathgate via Torphichen, then a 3 mile (5km) walk. Open
Apr–Sep, daily 0900–1830; Closed Oct–Mar. Charge £. Group concessions.
Explanatory displays. Car parking. Telephone (01506) 634622. www.historic-
scotland.gov.uk

One of the most important prehistoric monuments in Scotland. It was used as a
burial and ceremonial site from around 3000 to 1400 BC. Excellent views.

CASTLELAW HILL FORT   301   10 P26

HS. 1 mile north west of Glencorse, Midlothian, off the A702, 7 miles (11km) south of
Edinburgh. Nearest railway station Edinburgh, bus from Edinburgh then 1 mile
(2km) walk. Access at all reasonable times. Free. Car and coach parking. Telephone
(0131) 5507603. www.historic-scotland.gov.uk

A small Iron Age hill fort consisting of two concentric banks and ditches. An
earth house is preserved in the older rock-cut ditch. Occupied in Roman times.

CHESTERS HILL FORT   302   10 R25

HS. 1 mile (2km) south of Drem off the B1377, near Haddington, East Lothian.
Nearest railway station Drem, bus from Edinburgh to North Berwick, then bus to
Drem, then walk 1 mile (2km). Open all year. Free. Car parking. Telephone (0131)
5507603. www.historic-scotland.gov.uk

One of the best examples of an Iron Age hill fort with multiple ramparts. A
souterrain is built into one of the ditches.

CRICHTON CASTLE   303   10 Q26

HS. Crichton, Pathhead, Midlothian. Off the A68, 2.5 miles (4km) south south-west of
Pathhead. Bus from Edinburgh to Pathhead then 2.5 mile (4km) walk. Open Apr–Sep,
daily 0930–1830. Charge £. Group concessions. Blind visitors may touch carvings.
Limited wheelchair access. Car and coach parking. Telephone (01875) 320017.
www.historic-scotland.gov.uk

A large and sophisticated castle built around a 14th-century keep. The most
spectacular part is the arcaded range erected by the Earl of Bothwell between
1581 and 1591. This has a façade of faceted stonework in an Italian style. The
small Collegiate Church nearby dates from 1499 and is notable for its tower and
barrel vaulting.

CURRIE WOOD   304   10 Q26

Borthwick, Midlothian. On A772/A7, 12 miles (19km) south east of Edinburgh and 1.5
miles (2.5km) south est of Gorebridge. Access at all times. Free. Car parking.
Telephone (01764) 662554. www.woodland-trust.org.uk

A 52-acre (21-ha) site of diverse woodland in a steep sided, sheltered valley with a
burn running through it. The wood is of local and regional significance for
wildlife. A footbridge over the Middleton South burn and a series of boardwalks
through the wetter areas enable visitors to complete a satisfying circular route
around the wood. Good spring and autumn colour.

DALKEITH COUNTRY PARK   305   10 Q25

Dalkeith, Midlothian. In Dalkeith High Street, off A68, 7 miles (11km) south of
Edinburgh. Bus from Edinburgh. Open Apr–Sep, daily 1000–1800. Charge £.
Children under 5 free. Group concessions. Guided tours. Explanatory displays. Gift

shop. Restaurant, tearoom and picnic area. WC. Wheelchair access. Disabled WC. Car and coach parking. Telephone 0131 654 1666 or 663 5684.

The extensive grounds of Dalkeith Palace (not open to the public), an 18th-century planned landscape. Farm animals, including working Clydesdale horses, adventure woodland play area, nature trails, woodland walks, 18th-century bridge, orangery and ice house. Ranger service.

DALMENY HOUSE   306   10 P25

South Queenferry, West Lothian. Off the B924, 7 miles (11km) west of Edinburgh. Bus or rail (Dalmeny station) from Edinburgh. Open Jul–Aug, Sun–Tue 1400–1730; groups by special arrangement at other times. Charge ££. Group concessions. Guided tours. Tearoom. WC. Limited wheelchair access. Disabled WC. Car and coach parking. Telephone 0131 331 1888. www.dalmeny.co.uk

The home of the Earls of Rosebery for over 300 years, but the present Tudor Gothic building, by William Wilkins, dates from 1815. Interior Gothic splendour of hammer-beamed hall, vaulted corridors and classical main rooms. Works of art include a magnificent collection of 18th-century British portraits, 18th-century French furniture, tapestries, porcelain from the Rothschild Mentmore collection and the Napoleon collection. Lovely grounds and a 4.5 mile (7km) shore walk.

DALMENY PARISH CHURCH   307   10 P25

Main Street, Dalmeny, West Lothian. 10 miles (16km) west of Edinburgh. A90 to South Queensferry then follow signs to Dalmeny. Nearest railway station Dalmeny then 1 mile (1.6km) walk, bus service from Edinburgh. Open Apr–Sep, Sun 1400–1630; other times by request. Admission by donation. Guided tours by arrangement. Leaflets (available in French, German and Japanese). Gifts available. WC. Wheelchair access. Disabled WC. Car and coach parking. Telephone 0131 331 1479.

The best preserved Romanesque (Norman) church in Scotland, dating from the 12th century. Coach tours should book in advance.

DEER PARK GOLF AND COUNTRY CLUB   308   10 P25

Golf Course Road, Livingston, West Lothian. Signposted from M8, junction 3. Open all year, daily. Charges vary. Several bars and dining areas. WC. Wheelchair access with assistance. Disabled WC. Car and coach parking. Telephone (01506) 446699.

A regional qualifying course for the British Open and host to Scottish PGA championships – a 6688 yard, 18 hole, par 72 parkland course. Also squash courts, gym, tenpin bowling, snooker, pool, spa and sauna.

DERE STREET ROMAN ROAD   309   10 Q26

HS. On the B6368 (off the A68) beside Soutra Aisle, Midlothian. Bus from Edinburgh to Jedburgh, alight at top of Soutra Hill then 0.6 mile (1km) walk. Access at all reasonable times. Free. Telephone (0131) 5507603. www.historic-scotland.gov.uk

A good stretch of the Roman road which ran from Corbridge beside Hadrian's Wall to Cramond on the Firth of Forth. Beside the road are scoops, pits from which the gravel for building the road was taken.

DIRLETON CASTLE AND GARDENS   310   10 R25

HS. Dirleton, North Berwick. On A198 in Dirleton village, 3 miles (4.8km) west of North Berwick, East Lothian. Nearest railway station North Berwick, bus to Dirleton from Edinburgh and North Berwick. Open Apr–Sep, daily 0930–1830; Oct–Mar, daily 0930–1630. Charge £. Group concessions. Explanatory displays. Gift shop. Main garden has a selection of scented flowers and plants. Limited wheelchair access. Car and coach parking. Telephone (01620) 850330. www.historic-scotland.gov.uk

A romantic castle dating from the 13th century with 15th- to 17th-century additions. First besieged in 1298 by Edward I. Destroyed in 1650. The adjoining gardens include an early 20th-century Arts and Crafts garden and a restored Victorian garden. Also a 17th-century bowling green.

DOONHILL HOMESTEAD   311   8 R25

HS. Off the A1, 2 miles (3km) south of Dunbar, East Lothian. Nearest railway station Dunbar. Bus from Edinburgh to Dunbar, then 2 mile (3km) walk. Access at all reasonable times. Free. Car parking. Telephone (0131) 5507603. www.historic-scotland.gov.uk

The site of a wooden hall of a 6th-century British chief, and of an Anglian chief's hall which superseded it in the 7th century. A rare record of the Anglian occupation of south east Scotland.

DUNBAR LEISURE POOL   312   8 R25

Castle Park, Dunbar. Above the harbour in Dunbar. Nearest railway station Dunbar, bus from Edinburgh. Open all year except Christmas and New Year, daily from 0900. Charge dependent on activity. Group concessions. Café. Crèche. WC. Wheelchair access. Disabled WC. Car and coach parking. Telephone (01368) 865456.

Leisure pool with large flume, bubble bed, sprays, tropical temperatures and gently sloping beach. Also sauna, steam room, activity hall and gym. The café has spectacular views of the harbour and coast.

DUNBAR TOWN HOUSE MUSEUM   313   8 R25

High Street, Dunbar, East Lothian. In Dunbar High Street, at corner of Silver Street. Bus or rail from Edinburgh. Open Apr–Oct, daily 1230–1630. Free. Explanatory displays. Gift shop. Limited wheelchair access. Car and coach parking. Telephone (01368) 863734.

A 16th-century town house now containing a museum of local history and archaeology.

DUNGLASS COLLEGIATE CHURCH   314   8 S25

HS. On an estate road west of A1 (signposted Bilsdean), 1 mile (2km) north west of Cockburnspath, East Lothian. Nearest railway station Dunbar, bus to Cockburnspath, then 1 mile (2km) walk. Access at all reasonable times. Free. Car parking. Telephone (0131) 5507603. www.historic-scotland.gov.uk

A handsome cross-shaped church with vaulted nave, choir and transepts, all with stone slab roofs. Founded in 1450 for a college of canons by Sir Alexander Hume.

EAST LINKS FAMILY PARK   315   10 R25

Dunbar, East Lothian. Just off A1 Beltonford roundabout near Dunbar. Nearest railway station at Dunbar. Regular bus service (request Tilton Stables stop). First bus service X6. Open daily, 1000–1700 (closes1800 during school summer holidays; closed 5 Jan–14 Feb). Charge ££ (all inclusive ticket). Group concessions. Guided tours. Explanatory displays. Tea room and picnic area. WC. Wheelchair access. Disabled WC. Car and coach parking. Telephone 07775 713646 or 01368 863607. www.eastlinks.co.uk

A 20-acre (8-ha) farm, featuring a narrow gauge railway that carries visitors on a train safari around the farm, past all the animals. Also level walkway throughout the farm. Go-karting, all-weather sledging, milkcan skittles, horse shoe pitching, child-sized rabbit warren, sand diggers, soft play, trampolines, toy tractors, roller racers, play barn and picnic barn, bouncy castle and 2-acre (1ha) woodland maze.

EDINBURGH, THE ADAM POTTERY   316   10 Q25

76 Henderson Row, Edinburgh. 1 mile (2km) north of Princes Street. Bus from city centre. Metered on-street parking (free on Sat). Open Mon–Sat 1000–1730, except Christmas and New Year. Free. Gift shop. Telephone 0131 557 3978.

Wheel-thrown stoneware and porcelain with colourful high-fired glazes. Functional and decorative items. Work by other ceramicists also made on the premises. Visitors are welcome to watch any work in progress.

EDINBURGH, AULD REEKIE TOURS   317   10 Q25

45-47 Niddry Street, (just off Royal Mile). Tours leave from Tron Church on the Royal Mile. Exhibition open all year, daily 1000–1900. Tours at various times. Telephone for information. Exhibition £, tours ££.

Costumed guides take visitors back into Edinburgh's grisly past on Underground and Witchcraft tours. Also Medieval Torture Exhibition.

EDINBURGH, BRASS RUBBING CENTRE   318   10 Q25

Chalmers Close, 81 High Street, Edinburgh. Just off the Royal Mile opposite the Museum of Childhood (see 358), also access from Jeffrey Street. Nearest railway station Waverley; tour bus from station or ten minute walk. Open Apr–Sep, Mon–Sat 1000–1645 (last rubbings at 1545); during Edinburgh Festival also Sun 1200–1700. Free. Charge for making rubbings. Group concessions. Explanatory displays. Gift shop. Car parking. Telephone 0131 556 4364. www.cac.org.uk

Housed in the historic Trinity Apse, thought to have been founded in 1460 by Queen Mary of Gueldres, consort of King James II of Scotland, as a memorial to her husband. Offers a fine collection of replicas moulded from ancient Pictish stones, medieval church brasses and rare Scottish brasses. No experience needed to make a rubbing; instruction and materials provided.

EDINBURGH, BRITANNIA   319

See 382 Edinburgh, The Royal Yacht Britannia.

EDINBURGH BUS TOURS   320   10 Q25

Waverley Bridge, Edinburgh. All tours depart from Waverley Bridge in the centre of Edinburgh. Waverley Bridge is next to Waverley Railway Station and passed by all main bus routes. Tours all year, departing regularly each day. Telephone or visit website for details. Charge £££. Group concessions. Limited wheelchair access. Telephone 0131 220 0770. www.edinburghtour.com

Edinburgh Bus Tours incorporates City Sightseeing, The Edinburgh Tour, MacTours and the Majestic, taking in places of historic and cultural interest in the city centre and outlying areas. All tours operate on a hop on, hop off basis and tickets are valid for 24 hours.

EDINBURGH BUTTERFLY AND INSECT WORLD   321   10 Q26

Dobbies Garden World, Lasswade, Midlothian. Just off A720 Edinburgh city bypass at the Gilmerton junction. Bus from Edinburgh No 3. Open all year (except Christmas and New Year's Day), 0930–1730; winter 1000–1700. Charge ££. Group concessions. Guided tours for groups by arrangement. Explanatory displays. Gift shop. Restaurant, tearoom and picnic areas. WC. Wheelchair access. Disabled WC. Car and coach parking. Telephone 0131 663 4932. www.edinburgh-butterfly-world-co.uk

Visitors can walk through an indoor tropical rainforest inhabited by thousands of the world's most beautiful butterflies. Also Bugs and Beasties exhibition, featuring hundreds of live creepy crawlies, snakes, lizards and frogs. Daily 'meet the beasties' handling sessions. Garden centre, birds of prey centre and children's play parks.

EDINBURGH, CALEDONIAN BREWERY VISITOR CENTRE 322   10 P25

42 Slateford Road, Edinburgh. On A7 Lanark road, 2 miles (3km) from Princes Street. Local bus service. Open all year. Tour times vary, please telephone to confirm. Charge £££. Group concessions. Guided tours. Explanatory displays. Gift shop. WC. No guide dogs. Disabled WC. Car and coach parking. Telephone 0131 337 1286. www.caledonian-brewery.co.uk

A unique reminder of a bygone era when the city boasted over 40 breweries and was one of the great brewing capitals of Europe. Beer is still brewed today using hand selected natural ingredients and the original brewers' equipment – still fired by direct flame and the last of their kind still working in any British brewery.

EDINBURGH, CAMERA OBSCURA 323   10 Q25

Camera Obscura and World of Illusions, Castlehill, The Royal Mile, Edinburgh. Adjacent to Edinburgh Castle (see 326) at the top of the Royal Mile. Nearest railway station Waverley, then ten minute walk from Princes Street. Open daily (except Christmas Day), summer 0930–1800 (later in high summer); winter 1000–1700. Charge £££. Group concessions. Guided tours (available in foreign languages by arrangement). Explanatory displays in six languages. Gift shop. WC. Telephone 0131 226 3709.

Edinburgh's oldest attraction. An 1850s camera obscura captures a live panorama of the city below while guides tell Edinburgh's story. Visitors can spy on passers-by or pick vehicles up in the palm of their hand. Superb views of Edinburgh from the terrace (telescopes free). Seeing is not believing in three floors of exhibitions of hands-on exhibits on light, photography and optical illusions.

EDINBURGH CANAL CENTRE 324   10 P25

The Bridge Inn, 27 Baird Road, Ratho, Midlothian. In Ratho, 7 miles (11km) west of Edinburgh off the A8 or A71. Bus from Waterloo Place, Edinburgh. Sightseeing cruises, Easter–Jun, Sat–Sun 1430; Jul–Sep daily 1430. Santa cruises, Dec, Sat–Sun hourly from 1000 (daily during Christmas week). Restaurant cruises also available, booking required. Charge by facility. Explanatory displays. Sightseeing canal cruises Apr-Oct. Gift shop. Restaurant/bar and restaurants on boats. Garden. Play area. Wildfowl reserve. Towpath for walks and cycling. WC. Wheelchair access with assistance to building and restaurant boat. Disabled WC. Car and coach parking. Telephone 0131 333 1320 or 1251. www.bridgeinn.com

Built circa 1750, the inn became a canalside inn with the opening of the Union Canal in 1822. Canal boat restaurants cater for meals, dances, weddings, etc. Sightseeing cruises and Santa cruises in December.

EDINBURGH, CANONGATE KIRK 325   10 Q25

The Kirk of Holyroodhouse, Canongate, Edinburgh. Opposite Huntly House Museum in the Royal Mile. Nearest railway station Waverly 15 minute walk, local bus service and tour buses. Open all year, Sun 1000–1230; also Jun–Sep, Mon–Sat 1030–1630. Free. Guided tours for groups by arrangement. Information sheets in thirty languages. Gift shop. WC. Wheelchair access. Disabled WC. Telephone 0131 556 3515. www.canongatekirk.com

Historic 300-year-old Church of Scotland, recently renovated and restored. Parish church of the Palace of Holyroodhouse and Edinburgh Castle, with Frobenius organ and Normandy tapestry.

EDINBURGH CASTLE   326   10 Q25

HS. Castlehill, Edinburgh. In the centre of Edinburgh at the top of the Royal Mile. Nearest railway station Waverley. Local bus service and tour buses. Open all year (except Christmas Day and Boxing Day), Apr–Sep, daily 0930–1800; Oct–Mar 0930–1700. Last entry 45 minutes before closing. Charge £££. Guided tours, audio guides available for hire. Explanatory displays. Gift shop. Restaurant. WC. Braille texts and models of Crown Jewels for handling. Wheelchair access. A courtesy vehicle (provided by the Bank of Scotland) takes disabled visitors to the top of the castle; there are ramps and lift access to the Crown Jewels, Stone of Destiny and associated exhibition; a wheelchair stair climber gives access to the War Memorial. Disabled WC. Car and coach parking. Telephone 0131 225 9846. www.historic-scotland.gov.uk

One of the most famous castles in the world with battlements overlooking the Esplanade where the floodlit Military Tattoo is staged each year. The oldest part, St Margaret's Chapel, dates from the Norman period. The Great Hall was built by James IV; the Half Moon Battery by the Regent Morton in the late 16th century. The Scottish National War Memorial was erected after World War I. The castle houses the Crown Jewels (Honours) of Scotland, the Stone of Destiny, the famous 15th-century gun Mons Meg and the One o'clock gun. See also 365 Edinburgh, National War Museum of Scotland and 377 Edinburgh, Regimental Museum of The Royal Scots.

EDINBURGH, CERAMIC EXPERIENCE   327   10 Q25

8 Hopetoun Street, Edinburgh. Off Leith Walk, close to John Lewis. Waverley Railway Station and Lothian Bus Station nearby. Open all year (except Christmas and New Year), daily 1000–1730; Sep–Mar, Tue and Thu closes 2230. Free admission. Charge from £ for materials. Café. WC. Wheelchair access. Disabled WC. Car and coach parking. Telephone 0131 556 0070. www.ceramicx.biz

A painting studio with a difference. Hundreds of items to decorate, from tiles to teapots, dogs to dinner plates and a large, friendly environment in which to paint. Two ball pools for small children and quiet seating areas with sofas for nursing mothers. Friendly and helpful staff. All pieces are glazed to a professional and dishwasher safe finish.

EDINBURGH, CITY ART CENTRE   328   10 Q25

2 Market Street, Edinburgh. In city centre opposite Waverley station. Open all year (except Christmas), Mon–Sat 1000–1700, Sun 1200–1700. Free. Charge for special exhibitions. Guided tours on request (book in advance). Explanatory displays. Gift shop. Licensed restaurant/café. WC. Induction loop. Wheelchair access. Disabled WC. Telephone 0131 529 3993. www.cac.org.uk

Houses the City of Edinburgh's permanent fine art collection and stages a programme of temporary exhibitions from all over the world. Six floors of display galleries (with escalators and lifts). Education programme of workshops, lectures, events and educational publications.

EDINBURGH, CITY OF THE DEAD HAUNTED GRAVEYARD TOUR   329   10 Q25

40 Candlemaker Row, Edinburgh. Tours depart from large black signs, next to St
Giles Cathedral, Royal Mile. Close to railway and bus station. Tours operate daily all
year. Apr–Oct at 2030, 2115 and 2200; Nov–Mar at 1930 and 2030. Office open for
bookings 1000–2200. Charge £££. Group concessions. Guided tours. Gift shop. WC.
Wheelchair access with assistance. Car parking. Telephone 0131 225 9044.
www.blackhart.uk.com

In a locked mausoleum, in a locked prison, in ancient Greyfriars graveyard lurks
the Mackenzie Poltergeist – the best documented supernatural case in history.
Only this tour has the key. Hundreds of tour members have experienced cold
spots, rapping noises, cuts, bruising and physical attacks. In the past three years,
over 180 visitors have been knocked unconcious. Through Edinburgh's hidden
Old Town wynds, the expert guides will weave tales of humour, horror and
fascinating history.

EDINBURGH, CRAIGMILLAR CASTLE   330   10 Q25

HS. Craigmillar Castle Road, Edinburgh. Off A68 (Dalkeith road), 2.5 miles (4km)
south east of Edinburgh city centre. Take any bus for the new Royal Infirmary/Little
France on Old Dalkeith Road then follow footpath. Open Apr–Sep, Mon–Sun
0930–1830; Oct–Mar, Mon–Sun 0930–1630 (closed Thu and Fri) . Charge £. Group
concessions. Explanatory displays and visitor centre. Gift shop. Tearoom. WC.
Limited wheelchair access. Disabled WC. Car and coach parking. Telephone 0131 661
4445. www.historic-scotland.gov.uk

Imposing ruins of massive 14th-century keep enclosed in the early 15th century
by an embattled curtain wall. Within are the remains of the stately ranges of
apartments dating from the 16th and 17th centuries. The castle was burned by
Hertford in 1544. Strong connections with Mary, Queen of Scots.

THE EDINBURGH CRYSTAL VISITOR CENTRE   331   10 P26

Eastfield, Penicuik, Midlothian. In Penicuik, south of Edinburgh. LRT number 37.
Open all year, Mon–Sat 1000–1700, Sun 1100–1700. Free. Group concessions.
Explanatory displays. Self guided tour (available in foreign languages). Gift shop.
Coffee shop and picnic area. WC. Tour synopsis in braille and large print. Wheelchair
access. Disabled WC. Car and coach parking. Telephone (01968) 672244.
www.edinburgh-crystal.com

Get the chance to see plain crystal being transformed into exquisite pieces of
art! Marvel at the wealth of designs and history in this heritage centre. There is a
shop full of crystal, and a restaurant.

EDINBURGH, THE DEAN GALLERY   332   10 P25

Belford Road, Edinburgh. In the centre of Edinburgh, 15 minute walk from Princes
Street and ten minutes from Haymarket railway station. Local bus service to Belford
Road or Queensferry Road, then walk. Open all year, Mon–Sun 1000–1700. Closed
Christmas Day and Boxing Day. Free. Charge for temporary exhibitions. Group
concessions. Guided tours by arrangement (0131 624 6410). Explanatory displays. Gift
shop. Restaurant. WC. Wheelchair access. Disabled WC. Car parking. Telephone 0131
624 6200. www.natgalscot.ac.uk

Situated across the road from the Scottish National Gallery of Modern Art (see
389), the Dean Gallery houses the Gallery of Modern Art's extensive collections
of Dada and Surrealism. In 1994, Edinburgh-born sculptor Sir Eduardo Paolozzi

offered a large body of his work to the National Galleries of Scotland. This collection of prints, drawings, plaster maquettes, moulds and the contents of his studio is how housed in the Dean Gallery. The gallery also accommodates a remarkable library and archive of artists' books, catalogues and manuscripts relating in particular to the Dada and Surrealist movement, but also to 20th century art as a whole. Landscaped gardens and commanding views south over Edinburgh.

EDINBURGH, DOM GALLERY IN EDINBURGH'S OLDEST HOUSE   333   10 Q25

8 Advocates Close, 357 High Street, Edinburgh. In the centre of Edinburgh. Nearest railway station Waverley, within one minute walk, close to all bus routes. Open all year, Thu–Tue 1100–1730 (closed Wed). Admission by donation. Explanatory displays. Gift shop. WC. Telephone 0131 225 9271.

DOM is an international collective of artists, musicians and writers, whose work at Advocate's Close includes an ever-evolving exhibition of works. Number 8 Advocate's Close is Edinburgh's oldest surviving house. Known as Henry Cant's tenement, it was built in the 1480s. This would have been a very prestigious home and the fireplaces bear favourable comparison to those found in Scottish castles of the same period.

THE EDINBURGH DUNGEON   334   10 Q25

31 Market Street, Edinburgh. Adjacent to Edinburgh Tattoo office. Car and coach parking nearby. Open all year, daily from 1000; Jul–Aug closes late (telephone for details). Closed Christmas Day. Charge £££. Children under 15 must be accompanied by an adult. Group concessions. Gift shop. Refreshments available in shop. WC. Wheelchair access. Disabled WC. Telephone 0131 240 1000. www.thedungeons.com

The Edinburgh Dungeon transports visitors back to the darkest chapters of Scotland's history. Visitors come face to face with the notorious murderers, Burke and Hare, join in the clan wars, wander through the plague ravaged streets of old Edinburgh and join James VI on a one-way boatride to confront the infamous cannibal Sawney Bean in Witchfynder.

EDINBURGH, EAGLE ROCK   335   10 P25

HS. On the shore of the River Forth about 2.5 mile (0.5km) west of Cramond, Edinburgh. Nearest railway station Edinburgh, bus from city centre to Cramond, then short walk. Access at all reasonable times. Free. Telephone (0131) 5507603. www.historic-scotland.gov.uk

A much-defaced carving on natural rock, said to represent an eagle.

EDINBURGH, FORTH RAIL BRIDGE   336   10 P25

South Queensferry, 10 miles (16km) north west of Edinburgh. Access at all times. Telephone 0131 319 1699.

Opened on 4 March 1890 by the Prince of Wales. The bridge was designed on the cantilever principle with three towers 340 feet (104m) high. The engineers were Sir John Fowler and Benjamin Baker. See also 939 Forth Bridges Exhibition.

EDINBURGH, THE FRUITMARKET GALLERY   337   10 Q25

45 Market Street, Edinburgh. In city centre adjacent to Waverley station. Two car parks nearby. Bus stop outside gallery. Open Mon–Sat 1100–1800, Sun 1200–1700 (later during Festival). Free. Guided tours by arrangement. Explanatory displays. Gift

and bookshop. Restaurant. WC. Induction loop. Disabled lift. Wheelchair access.
Disabled WC. Telephone 0131 225 2383. www.fruitmarket.co.uk

Originally built in 1938 as a fruit and vegetable market, the building now
contains an acclaimed art gallery with a national and international reputation
for diverse and challenging contemporary exhibitions and an extensive
education and events programme, along with an acclaimed contemporary
bookshop and café.

EDINBURGH, FUN PARK   338   10 Q25

Portobello Promenade, Edinburgh. Bus from city centre. Open daily 1000–2300
(except Christmas Day). Charge for entertainments. Group concessions. Explanatory
displays. Gift shop. Restaurant and tearoom. WC. Limited wheelchair access.
Disabled WC. Car and coach parking. Telephone 0131 669 1859.

A family entertainment centre with various amusements – soft play area,
dodgems, carousel, juvenile rides (merry-go-round), full-size ten-pin bowling
lanes, American pool hall and full-size snooker tables.

EDINBURGH, GEOFFREY (TAILOR'S) TARTAN WEAVING MILL
AND EXHIBITION   339   10 Q25

555 Castlehill, Edinburgh. Beside Edinburgh Castle at the top of the Royal Mile. Car
parking nearby. Nearest railway station Waverley, then five minute walk. Open all
year (except Christmas Day and New Year's Day), Mon–Sat 0900–1730, Sun
1000–1730; Mar–Oct closes 1830. Free. Charge for photo in Scottish costume and to
try weaving on pedal loom. Guided tours for groups of ten or more (charge, pre-
booking required). Explanatory displays. Gift shop. Restaurant and café. Baby
changing facilties. WC. Limited wheelchair access. Disabled WC. Telephone 0131 226
1555. www.tartanweavingmill.co.uk

A working tartan weaving mill where visitors can see the production of tartan
cloth and try weaving on a 60-year-old pedal loom. Visitors can also have their
photo taken in ancient Scottish costume and search for a tartan in the Clans and
Tartans Information Bureau. Specialist Highland dress, cashmere, crystal,
ceramics and Scottish gifts for sale.

EDINBURGH, GEORGIAN HOUSE   340   10 Q25

NTS. 7 Charlotte Square, Edinburgh. Near city centre, ten minute walk from
Waverley railway station. Open Mar and Nov, daily 1100–1500; Apr–Jun and Sep–Oct,
daily 1000–1700; Jul–Aug, daily 1000–1900. Charge ££. Group concessions. Guided
tours by arrangement. Explanatory displays. Information sheets in 12 languages. Gift
shop. WC. Audio-visual programme with induction loop, Braille guidebook. Limited
wheelchair access. Telephone 0131 226 3318. www.nts.org.uk

On the north side of Charlotte Square, designed by Robert Adam. A typical house
in Edinburgh's New Town, furnished as it would have been by its first owners in
1796. Video programmes on the building of the New Town and A Day in the Life
of the Georgian House.

EDINBURGH, GEOWALKS VOLCANO TOURS   341   10 Q25

Walks available for groups in the Edinburgh area. Walks usually start within reach of
public transport. Changing and varied programme Mar–Oct; please contact for
details. Charge ££–£££ dependent on walk. Guided tours. WC usually available in
locality. Car and coach parking. Telephone 0131 555 5488. www.geowalks.co.uk

Discover extinct volcanos, hidden views, stunning scenery, the secrets of the local landscape and over 400 million years of history. Explore the beautiful surroundings of Fife and the Lothians, and the dramatic cityscape of Edinburgh. Join Dr Angus Miller for a walk back in time. Walks vary from 2–5 hours, covering a variety of terrain.

EDINBURGH, GLADSTONE'S LAND   342   10 Q25

NTS. 477b Lawnmarket, Royal Mile, Edinburgh. Near city centre, ten minutes walk from Waverley railway station. Open Apr–Jun and Sep–Oct, daily 1000–1700; Jul–Aug, daily 1000–1900. Charge ££. Group concessions. Guided tours by arrangement. Explanatory displays. Information sheets in European languages and Japanese. Gift shop. Refreshments nearby. Tours for blind visitors by arrangement, Braille guidebook. Limited wheelchair access. Telephone 0131 226 5856. www.nts.org.uk

Typical example of the 17th-century tenements of Edinburgh's Old Town, clustered along the ridge between the Castle and the Palace of Holyroodhouse – the Royal Mile. Completed in 1620 and originally home to a prosperous Edinburgh merchant, Thomas Gledstanes, the house contains original painted ceilings and some contemporary furniture.

EDINBURGH, GORGIE CITY FARM   343   10 P25

51 Gorgie Road, Edinburgh. On the A71 Kilmarnock road, 1 mile (2km) south west of Haymarket station. Bus from city centre. Open daily (except Christmas and New Year's Day), summer 0930–1630; winter 0930–1600. Free. Guided tours (charge £). Explanatory displays. Gift shop. Café and picnic area. Baby changing facilities. Play park. WC. Induction loop for talks/tours. Wheelchair access. Disabled WC. Car parking. Telephone 0131 337 4202.

A 2 acre (1ha) farm with various farm animals, commonly kept pets, herbs, vegetables and a wildlife garden. Special events throughout the year, craft classes, educational workshops and tours. Education centre.

EDINBURGH, GRAYLINE SIGHTSEEING TOURS   344   10 Q25

Lower Floor, 81 Salamander Street, Leith, Edinburgh. Courtesy collections from hotels and guest houses in Edinburgh. Tours take place all year. Booking lines open all year, daily 0700–2200. Charge £££. Group concessions. Regular stops ensure opportunities to visit gifts shops and get a meal. Larger coaches have WC on board. Deaf and blind passengers encouraged to join tours. Assistance always given to ensure passengers get most from the tours. Wheelchair access with assistance (coaches can carry wheelchair in luggage hold). Telephone 0131 555 5558. www.graylinetours.com

Comprehensive daily guided sightseeing tours to various locations in Scotland. The tours incorporate wonderful countryside, history and music. Also airport transfers, conference transfers, spouse programmes and short breaks. Assistance with itineraries.

EDINBURGH, GREYFRIARS BOBBY   345   10 Q25

By Greyfriars churchyard, corner of George IV Bridge and Candlemaker Row. Access at all times. Free.

Statue of Greyfriars Bobby, the Skye terrier who, after his master's death in 1858, watched over his grave in the nearby Greyfriars Churchyard for 14 years.

EDINBURGH, GREYFRIARS KIRK   346   10 Q25

2 Greyfriars Place, Edinburgh. In Edinburgh Old Town, 15 minute walk from Waverley railway station. Bus from city centre to George IV Bridge. Open Easter–Oct, Mon–Fri 1030–1630, Sat 1030–1430; churchyard open every day 0900–1800 (except New Year's Day). Free. Group visits by prior arrangement (£); donation requested from children's groups. Guided tours (available in French and Gaelic by arrangement). Explanatory displays and videos. Gift shop. Refreshments for groups available with advance notice. Baby changing facilities. WC. Tours to suit blind visitors (by arrangement). Loop induction (services and talks). Wheelchair access and disabled parking. Disabled WC. Telephone 0131 225 1900/226 5429. www.greyfriarskirk.com

Edinburgh's first Reformed Church (1620). On display is the National Covenant (signed at the church in 1638), Scotland's finest collection of 17th- and 18th-century funeral monuments, fine 19th-century windows by Ballantyne, Peter Collins' organ (1990) with carvings of Scottish flora and fauna, memorabilia about Greyfriars Bobby (see 345). Millennium window by Douglas Hogg and Millennium kneelers portraying kirk history.

EDINBURGH, HEART OF SCOTLAND TOURS   347   10 Q25

Stand E, Waterloo Place, Edinburgh. Tours leave from stand E Waterloo Place in Edinburgh city centre (eastern extension of Princes Street). Five minute walk from Waverley Railway Station, on main bus routes. Tours take place throughout the year. Booking hotline open daily, Apr–Oct 0700–2200; Nov–Mar 0700–2000. Charge £££. Group concessions. Car and coach parking. Telephone 0131 558 8855. www.heartofscotlandtours.co.uk

One-day minibus tours to Loch Ness, Loch Lomond, Stirling Castle, St Andrews and other beautiful parts of Scotland. The tours have been specially designed to include famous sights and some hidden gems, with lots of interesting stops, including the well-liked Heart of Scotland 'walk and talk' in the Scottish countryside. Fully guided by knowledgeable driver/guides who share their passion for Scotland's story. Small tour groups make for a welcoming atmosphere.

EDINBURGH, HOLYROOD ABBEY   348   10 Q25

HS. At the foot of the Canongate (Royal Mile), Edinburgh, in the grounds of the Palace of Holyroodhouse. Local bus service and tour bus. Access and charges same as Palace of Holyroodhouse. No free entry for Friends of Historic Scotland at this site. Telephone (0131) 5507603. www.historic-scotland.gov.uk

The ruined nave of the 12th- and 13th-century Abbey church, built for Augustinian canons. The abbey and palace are administered by the Lord Chamberlain. See also 370 Edinburgh, Palace of Holyroodhouse.

EDINBURGH, HOLYROOD PARK   349   10 Q25

HS. In Edinburgh, immediately to the east of Holyrood Palace and Abbey. Local bus service and tour buses. Open at all times. Free. Car parking. Telephone 0131 556 1761. www.historic-scotland.gov.uk

There has probably been a royal park here since the Augustinian Abbey was founded in the early 12th century; but it was formally enclosed in 1541 during James V's reign. Within the park is a wealth of archaeology, including the remains of four hill forts, other settlements and round them a fascinating landscape of prehistoric and early-medieval farming activity.

EDINBURGH, THE HUB (EDINBURGH FESTIVAL CENTRE)   350   10 Q25

348 Castlehill, Edinburgh. On the Royal Mile, close to Edinburgh Castle. Nearest railway station Waverley. Open all year except Christmas Day, daily 0930–2200. Charge for performances. Café bar. WC. Festival Brochure available in braille and audio tape. Induction loop. Wheelchair access. Disabled WC. Telephone 0131 473 2015. www.eif.co.uk/thehub

The Hub is the home of the Edinburgh International Festival (EIF). This magnificent Gothic building also houses its own restaurant Cafe Hub, and Hub Tickets, the central box office for the EIF and a range of other events. It is a popular venue for concerts, ceilidhs, banquets and parties and the best place in town to soak up the Festival atmosphere and find information on all the festivals.

EDINBURGH, INGLEBY GALLERY   351   10 Q25

Ingleby Gallery, 6 Carlton Terrace, Edinburgh. Nearest railway station Waverley, then 15 minute walk. Open Mon–Sat 1000–1700. Free. Explanatory displays, information provided. WC. Wheelchair access. Car parking. Telephone 0131 556 4441. www.inglebygallery.com

The Ingleby Gallery is one of Scotland's leading private galleries and presents a curated program of exhibitions with an emphasis on contemporary painting, sculpture and photography. The gallery exhibits and represents internationally renowned artists such as Craigie Aitchison, Ian Davenport, Ian Hamilton Finlay, Howard Hodgkin, Callum Innes, Sean Scully and Alison Watt.

EDINBURGH, JOHN KNOX HOUSE   352   10 Q25

43-45 High Street, Edinburgh. In the Royal Mile within easy walking distance of Waverley railway station. Open all year, Mon–Sat 1000–1800; Jul–Sep, Sun 1200–1800. Also open in evenings if show on at Netherbow Theatre. Charge £. Group concessions. Explanatory displays. Gift shop. Café. Courtyard. WC. Staff have been trained to assist deaf and blind visitors. Limited wheelchair access. Computer virtual tour for those unable to manage the stairs. Disabled WC. Telephone 0131 556 9579. www.scottishstorytellingcentre.co.uk

A picturesque 15th-century house associated with John Knox, the religious reformer, and James Mossman, keeper of the Royal Mint to Mary, Queen of Scots. The house contains many original features including the painted ceiling in the Oak Room, and an exhibition on the life and times of John Knox and James Mossman.

EDINBURGH, LAURISTON CASTLE   353   10 P25

Cramond Road South, Edinburgh. At Davidson's Mains, 3 miles (5km) west of Edinburgh centre. Bus from city centre. Admission to castle by guided tour only. Apr–Oct, Sat–Thu tours at 1120, 1220, 1420, 1520 and 1620; Nov–Mar, Sat–Sun tours at 1420 and 1520. Tours last approximately 50 minutes. Castle grounds open all year, daily 0900–dusk. Charge ££. Foreign language guide sheets available. Picnic area. WC. Disabled WC. Car and coach parking. Telephone 0131 336 2060. www.cac.org.uk

A 16th-century tower house with extensive 19th-century additions. Built about 1590 by Archibald Napier whose son John invented logarithms. In the early 18th century Lauriston was owned by financier John Law who held high office in the court of pre-revolution France. The last private owners were the Reid family, and the castle contains William Reid's extensive collections of furniture and antiques – a snapshot of the interior of a Scottish country house in the

Edwardian era. Thirty acres (12ha) of beautiful gardens and parkland with panoramic views of the Firth of Forth.

EDINBURGH, LITERARY PUB TOUR   354   10 Q25

The Beehive Inn, Grassmarket, Edinburgh. In Edinburgh old town, ten minutes walk from Princes Street and the Royal Mile. Nearest railway station Waverley, then 15 minute walk. Tours Jun–Sep, daily 1930; Mar–May and Oct–Nov, Thu–Sun 1930; Dec–Feb, Fri 1930. Additional tours Jul–Aug, telephone to confirm. Charge £££. Customised tours for groups arranged. Guided tours. Four pubs visited. WC. Limited wheelchair access. Car and coach parking. Telephone 0131 226 6665. www.scot-lit-tour.co.uk

This two hour promenade performance, led by professional actors, begins at the historic Beehive Inn, in the Grassmarket, and follows a route through the streets, wynds, courtyards and old taverns of the Old and New Towns of Edinburgh. The lives and work of Scotland's great poets, writers and colourful characters from the past 300 years are described, from Robert Burns and Walter Scott to Muriel Spark and Trainspotting.

EDINBURGH, MALLENY GARDEN   355   10 P26

NTS. Balerno. Off the A70 Lanark road in Balerno near Edinburgh. By bus from Edinburgh centre. Open all year, daily 1000–1800. Charge £. Charge £ (honesty box). Group concessions. WC. Limited wheelchair access. Car and coach parking. Telephone 0131 449 2283. www.nts.org.uk

Dominated by four 400-year-old clipped yew trees, this peaceful garden features fine herbaceous borders and a large collection of old-fashioned roses. The National Bonsai Collection for Scotland is also housed here.

EDINBURGH, MERCAT TOURS   356   10 Q25

Mercat House, 12 Niddry Street South, Edinburgh. All tours leave from the Mercat Cross (Royal Mile) beside St Giles Cathedral. Nearest railway station Waverley, then five minute walk. All year, daily 1030–2130. Charge £££. Group concessions. Guided tours (available in Dutch, French, German, Italian). Explanatory displays. Gift shop. WC. Car and coach parking. Telephone 0131 557 6464. www.mercattours.com

Award-winning dramatised history and ghost tours of the Royal Mile. Tours visit the wynds and closes of Old Edinburgh and include a visit to the most extensive underground vaults open to the public beneath the South Bridge.

EDINBURGH, MIDLOTHIAN SKI CENTRE   357   10 Q26

Hillend, Near Edinburgh. Just south of the city bypass off the A702 at Lothianburn junction. Nearest railway station Edinburgh, bus from city centre. Open winter, Mon–Sat 0930–2100, Sun 0930–1900; summer Mon–Fri 0930–2100 weekends 0930–1700. Chairlift ride £. Group concessions. Explanatory displays. Refreshments available at Cafe 360. WC. Limited wheelchair access. Disabled WC. Car and coach parking. Telephone 0131 445 4433. www.ski.midlothian.gov.uk

Europe's longest and most challenging artificial ski slope. Two main slopes, a fun slope and two nursery slopes. Equipment hire, skiing/snowboarding, coaching and instruction for all levels, chair lift and two ski tows. Chairlift open to all visitors, with terrific views.

EDINBURGH, MUSEUM OF CHILDHOOD   358   10 Q25

42 High Street, Edinburgh. In the Royal Mile. Open all year, Mon–Sat 1000–1700; Jul–Aug also Sun 1400–1700. Free. Explanatory displays. Gift shop. WC. Mini-com for

the deaf, blind visitors may handle artefacts. Limited wheelchair access. Disabled
WC. Telephone 0131 529 4142. www.cac.org.uk

This unique museum has a fine collection of childhood-related items including
toys, dolls, dolls' houses, costumes and nursery equipment. It has a programme
of changing exhibitions and activities.

EDINBURGH, MUSEUM OF EDINBURGH 359   10 Q25

142 Canongate, Royal Mile, Edinburgh. In the Royal Mile. Nearest railway station
Waverley 15 minute walk, local bus service and tour buses. Open all year (except
Christmas and New Year), Mon–Sat 1000–1700. During Festival open Sun
1400–1700. Free. Explanatory displays. Gift shop. WC. Telephone 0131 529 4143.
www.cac.org.uk

A restored 16th-century mansion, the Museum of Edinburgh is the city's main
museum of local history, with period rooms and reconstructions relating to the
city's traditional industries. There are also collections of Edinburgh silver and
glass, Scottish pottery, shop signs and relics relating to Field Marshall Earl
Haig, the First World War general.

EDINBURGH, MUSEUM OF FIRE   360   10 Q25

Lothian and Borders Fire Brigade Headquaters, Lauriston Place, Edinburgh. In city
centre. Nearest railway station Waverley, then 20 minute walk or local bus. Open all
year (except for first two weeks in Aug, and Christmas and New Year), Mon–Fri
0900–1630 by appointment. Free. Guided tours. Explanatory displays. WC.
Wheelchair access. Disabled WC. Telephone 0131 228 2401. www.lothian.fire-uk.org

An integral part of the brigade's fire education programme, the museum tells
the history of the oldest municipal fire brigade in the United Kingdom. Housed
in the historic headquarters building, it shows the development of fire fighting
in an exciting and educational way. Displays a range of fire engines from 1806,
and many other fire related items.

EDINBURGH, MUSEUM OF SCOTLAND   361   10 Q25

Chambers Street, Edinburgh. In the centre of Edinburgh's Old Town. Within ten
minutes walk of Princes Street and Waverley railway station; close to most major bus
routes. Open all year, Mon–Sat 1000–1700 (Tue closes 2000), Sun 1200–1700. Free.
Group concessions. Guided tours (also audio tours). Explanatory displays. Gift shop.
Restaurant (tearoom and bistro in adjoining Royal Museum). Rooftop garden. WC.
Free radio aids and personal access guides, telephone 0131 247 4206. Wheelchair
access (level access at Tower entrance). Disabled WC. Telephone 0131 225 7534 or 0131
247 4027 minicom. www.nms.ac.uk

The Museum of Scotland tells the history of Scotland from its geological
beginnings to the present day. A striking piece of architecture to hold the
treasured objects of Scotland's past and present.

EDINBURGH, MUSEUM ON THE MOUND   362   10 Q25

HBOS Plc head office, The Mound, Edinburgh. Between the Old and New Towns, just
off the Royal Mile and five minutes walk from Waverley station . Closed for
refurbishment until Sep 2006. Will be open 6 days a week 1000–1700. Please
telephone for details. Free. Guided tours on request. Explanatory displays. Gift shop.
WC. Wheelchair access. Disabled WC. Telephone 0131 529 1288.
www.museumonthemound.co.uk

The museum looks at the origins and development of banks and banking services in Scotland and the rest of the UK. Displays cover the history of the building, the manufacture of money and changes in working life over the last 300 years. They feature maps, bullion chests, exotic currencies, coins, banknotes, old banking equipment and a million pounds.

EDINBURGH, NATIONAL GALLERY OF SCOTLAND   363   10 Q25

The Mound, Edinburgh. In city centre, just off Princes Street. Nearest railway and bus stations ten minute walk. Open all year, Mon–Sun 1000–1700 (open until 1900 on Thur). Closed Christmas Day and Boxing Day. Free. Small charge for temporary exhibitions. Guided tours by prior arrangement (telephone 0131 624 6506). Room plan. Gift shop. WC. Acoustic guide for visually impaired. Limited wheelchair access. Disabled WC. Telephone 0131 624 6332. www.natgalscot.ac.uk

The building was designed by William Henry Playfair and the foundation stone laid by Prince Albert in 1850. The gallery opened to the public in 1859. The collection contains outstanding paintings, drawings and prints by the greatest artists from the Renaissance to Post-Impressionism, including Velásquez, El Greco, Titian, Vermeer, Constable, Monet and Van Gogh. It also houses the national collection of Scottish art featuring works by Taggart, Wilkie, Ramsay and Raeburn.

EDINBURGH, NATIONAL LIBRARY OF SCOTLAND   364   10 Q25

George IV Bridge, Edinburgh. In the Old Town just off the High Street. Nearest railway station Waverley, then ten minute walk, or bus from Princes Street. Open all year (except Easter, Christmas, New Year and Edinburgh autumn holiday in Sep). Exhibitions open year round (summer only) Mon–Sat 1000–1700, Sun 1400–1700. Free. Guided tours, free events, talks, and workshops. Explanatory displays. Gift shop. Self-service refreshment area. WC. Wheelchair access with assistance. Disabled WC. Telephone 0131 623 3700. www.nls.uk

Founded in 1682, the library is a treasure house of books and manuscripts, maps and music with reading rooms open for research and a diverse programme of events and exhibitions, reflecting the ideas and cultures of Scotland and the wider world.

EDINBURGH, NATIONAL WAR MUSEUM OF SCOTLAND   365   10 Q25

Edinburgh Castle, Edinburgh. Within Edinburgh Castle at the heart of the city. Nearest railway station Waverley, then 15 minute walk, close to most major bus routes. Open Apr–Oct, daily 0945–1745; Nov–Mar, daily 0945–1645. Museum entry included in admission charge for Edinburgh Castle. Explanatory displays and audio guide (English). Gift shop. Café within castle. Reference library available by appointment. WC. Induction loop. Wheelchair access. Disabled WC. Car and coach parking. Telephone 0131 225 7534. www.nms.ac.uk

The National War Museum of Scotland explores the Scottish experience of war and military service over the last 400 years – presented in galleries housed in mid-18th century buildings within Edinburgh Castle. See also 326 Edinburgh Castle and 377 Edinburgh, Regimental Museum of The Royal Scots.

EDINBURGH, NELSON MONUMENT   366   10 Q25

32 Calton Hill, Edinburgh. On Calton Hill, above Waterloo Place at the east end of Princes Street. Nearest railway station Waverley, then 15 minute walk. Open Apr–Sep, Mon 1300–1800, Tue–Sat 1000–1800; Oct–Mar, Mon–Sat 1000–1500. Charge £.

Explanatory displays. Gift shop. Picnic area. WC. Car and coach parking. Telephone 0131 556 2716. www.cac.org.uk

One of the first monuments to Admiral Nelson, built between 1807 and 1815. A telescope-shaped tower with a time-ball on the top. The latter is wound up every day (except Sunday) and dropped at 1300. The timeball was linked to the 1 o'clock gun at Edinburgh Castle and acted as a visual signal to ships in Leith docks to set their chronometers, enabling them to calculate longitude. Nelson's Trafalgar signal is flown every year on 21 October. Good views from top.

EDINBURGH, NEWHAVEN HERITAGE MUSEUM   367   10 Q25

24 Pier Place, Edinburgh. Bus service from Princes Street. Open all year, daily 1200–1700. Free. Explanatory displays. Gift shop. Induction loop for video. Wheelchair access. Car and coach parking. Telephone 0131 551 4165. www.cac.org.uk

This museum is situated in the historic fishmarket overlooking the harbour. It tells the story of Newhaven and its people. Find out about fishing and other sea trades, customs and superstitions. Displays tell the stories of the Society of Free Fishermen and the development of this tightly-knit community. Reconstructed sets of fishwives and fishermen, displays of objects and photographs, and first-hand written and spoken accounts of people's lives. Hands-on exhibits, music and video.

EDINBURGH, NO. 28 CHARLOTTE SQUARE   368   10 Q25

NTS. 28 Charlotte Square, Edinburgh. In the city centre. Nearest railway station Waverley, then ten minute walk. Open Jan–24 Dec, Mon–Sat 09.30–1700. Gallery open Jan–24 Dec, Mon–Fri 1100–1500. Free. Explanatory displays. Gift shop. WC. Wheelchair access. Telephone 0131 243 9300. www.nts.org.uk

An attractive gallery overlooking Charlotte Square and displaying a collection of 20th-century Scottish paintings.

EDINBURGH, OUR DYNAMIC EARTH   369   10 Q25

107 Holyrood Road, Edinburgh. Nearest railway station Waverley. Local bus or tour bus. Open Apr–Oct, daily 1000–1800 (last entry 1650); Nov–Mar, Wed–Sun 1000–1700 (last entry 1550). Charge £££. Carers of disabled visitors free. Group concessions. Explanatory displays. Gift shop. Restaurant and bar. Children's play area, terrace. WC. Large print text. Wheelchair access. Disabled WC. Car and coach parking. Telephone 0131 550 7800. www.dynamicearth.co.uk

Through dramatic special effects, stunning wrap-around images and state-of-the-art interactives, visitors discover the story of the planet, from the start of time to an unknown future. See the Restless Earth volcano erupt, walk through the tropical rainforest thunderstorm and meet an ever-changing menagerie of animals. Take a dramatic helicopter flight over the magnificent Scottish mountains and feel the chill of ice in the polar region.

EDINBURGH, PALACE OF HOLYROODHOUSE   370   10 Q25

Canongate, Edinburgh. At the foot of the Royal Mile, 15 minute walk from Waverley railway station. By tourist bus. Open all year, daily Apr–Oct 0930–1800 (last entry 1715); Nov–Mar, 0930–1630 (last entry 1545). Closed Christmas and Good Friday; before, during and after Royal and State visits; and also at other times. Charge £££. Children under 5 free. Group concessions. Guided tours Nov–Mar (available in foreign languages). Gift shop. Picnic area. Garden in summer. WC. Guide for blind visitors. Limited wheelchair access. Disabled WC. Car and coach parking. Telephone 0131 556 7371; recorded information on 0131 556 1096. www.royal.gov.uk

The official residence of The Queen in Scotland. The oldest part is built against the monastic nave of Holyrood Abbey (see 348), little of which remains. The rest of the palace was reconstructed by the architect Sir William Bruce for Charles II. Home of Mary, Queen of Scots for six years and where she met John Knox. Rizzio was murdered here and Prince Charles Edward Stuart held court here in 1745. The State Apartments house tapestries and paintings. The Picture Gallery has portraits of over 80 Scottish kings painted by De Wet 1684–6.

EDINBURGH, PARISH CHURCH OF ST CUTHBERT   371   10 Q25

5 Lothian Road, Edinburgh. St Cuthbert's Church lies in a graveyard below the castle just beyond the west end of Princes Street Gardens. Local bus to Princes Street and Lothian Road. Open end Apr–early Sep, Mon–Sat 1000–1600. Sun open for worship. Free. Guided tours (leaflets in English, Czech, Dutch, French, German, Italian, Russian, Portuguese, Spanish, Swedish, Danish, Polish, Chinese, Japanese, and Korean). Explanatory displays. Gift shop. Refreshments available. WC. Induction loop during services. Wheelchair access. Disabled WC. Car parking. Telephone 0131 229 1142. www.st-cuthberts.net

This is the seventh church on this site. Tradition has it that St Cuthbert had a small cell church here at the head of the Nor'Loch. Recorded history tells that King David I gifted lands to 'the Church of St Cuthbert, hard by the Castle of Edinburgh'. The present building was built in 1894 to a design by Hippolyte Blanc, but retained the 1790 tower. Interior was reorganised in 1990 by Stewart Tod. Features Renaissance style stalls, marble communion table, alabaster mural, stained glass by Tiffany. Famous names in graveyard.

EDINBURGH, PARLIAMENT HOUSE   372   10 Q25

11 Parliament Square, Edinburgh. Behind the High Kirk of St Giles, Royal Mile. Open all year, Mon–Fri 1000–1600. Free. Explanatory displays. Postcards and booklets for sale. WC. Disabled WC. Telephone 0131 240 6751.

Built 1632–9, this was the seat of Scottish government until 1707, when the governments of Scotland and England were united. Now the Supreme Law Courts of Scotland, Parliament Hall has a fine hammer beam roof and portraits by Raeburn and other major Scottish artists. Access (free) to the splendid Signet Library on an upper floor is by prior written request only, to: The Librarian, Signet Library, Parliament House, Edinburgh. Outside is the medieval Mercat Cross, which was restored in 1885 by W. E. Gladstone. Royal proclamations are still read from its platform.

EDINBURGH, THE PEOPLES STORY   373   10 Q25

Canongate Tolbooth, 163 Canongate, Edinburgh. Near the foot of the Royal Mile, ten minute walk from Waverley station and bus station. Open all year (except Christmas and New Year), Mon–Sat 1000–1700; Jun–Sep 1000–1800; during the Edinburgh Festival, also Sun 1400–1700. Free. Explanatory displays. Gift shop. WC. Induction loop. Limited wheelchair access, to ground and first floor only. Disabled WC. Telephone 0131 529 4057. www.cac.org.uk

In the picturesque Canongate Tolbooth, built in 1591. Tells the story of the life, work and pastimes of the ordinary working people of Edinburgh from the late 18th century. Sights, sounds and smells. Room reconstructions, rare artefacts and everyday objects.

EDINBURGH, JAMES PRINGLE WEAVERS LEITH MILLS   374   10 Q25

70-74 Bangor Road, Leith, Edinburgh. In Leith, 1 mile (2km) from Edinburgh city centre. Bus from Edinburgh centre. Open Apr–Oct, Mon–Sat 0900–1730, Sun 1000–1700; Nov–Mar, Mon–Sat 0900–1700, Sun 1000–1700. Free. Explanatory displays. Gift shop. Restaurant. WC. Wheelchair access. Disabled WC. Car and coach parking. Telephone 0131 553 5161. www.ewm.co.uk

Large shop selling woollens, tartans, clothing and gifts. Tailor-made outfits. Clan Tartan Centre with a computer which will provide visitors with a printed certificate detailing any clan connection, information on the clan chief, origins, heraldic emblems, plant badge and other historic information. Also whisky shop, golf shop and designer brand shop.

EDINBURGH PRINTMAKERS   375   10 Q25

23 Union Street, Edinburgh. At the east end of Edinburgh near the Playhouse Theatre. Nearest railway station Waverley, then 15 minute walk, or bus from city centre. Open all year (except Christmas and New Year), Tue–Sat 1000–1800. Free. Guided tours of studios by appointment. Explanatory displays. WC. Limited wheelchair access. Telephone 0131 557 2479. www.edinburgh-printmakers.co.uk

Edinburgh's main studio for practising artists who make limited edition prints. Visitors can watch artists at work and see the huge range of prints for sale in the gallery. Courses in print-making.

EDINBURGH, RABBIE'S TRAIL BURNERS   376   10 Q25

207 High Street, Edinburgh. In the Royal Mile, five minute walk from Waverley station. Open all year, May–Sep 0815–2000; Oct–Apr 0815–1800. Charge £££. Group concessions on application. Guided tours. Gift shop. Wheelchair access with assistance. Telephone 0131 226 3133. www.rabbies.com

Scottish Highland minicoach tours depart all year to all areas of the Highlands. Bespoke tours, individually arranged, also available.

EDINBURGH, REGIMENTAL MUSEUM OF THE ROYAL SCOTS   377   10 Q25

Edinburgh Castle, Edinburgh. In the castle at the top of the Royal Mile. Car and coach parking in winter only. Nearest railway station Waverley, then ten minute walk. Open daily Apr–Sep, 0930–1730; Oct–Mar, Mon–Fri 0930–1600. Free but charge for entry to castle. Explanatory displays. Gift shop. Restaurant and tearoom. WC. Wheelchair access with assistance (courtesy coach within castle, wheelchair access to museum). Disabled WC. Telephone 0131 310 5017.

The museum of the oldest regiment in the British Army, housed in Edinburgh Castle. Contains paintings, artefacts, silver and medals which tell the story of the regiment from its formation in 1633 to the present day. See also 326 Edinburgh Castle and 365 Edinburgh, National War Museum of Scotland.

MERCAT TOURS – GUIDED WALKING HISTORY + GHOST TOURS OF EDINBURGH   378   10 Q25

Mercat House, 12 Niddry Street South, Edinburgh. All tours begin from the Mercat Cross, High Street, next to St Giles Cathedral.. Tours run daily all year, daily (except Christmas). Times vary. Telephone or visit website for confirmation. Charge £££. Group concessions. Guided tours. Telephone 0131 557 6464. www.mercattours.com

Discover the hidden history of Edinburgh with Scotland's original, biggest and best ghost and history walking tours. By day the guides escort visitors through the heart of Edinburgh's proud and notable Old Town. At night ghost tours recall tales of ghastly, grisly crimes, witchcraft and unexplained incidents from Edinburgh's past. Includes visits to the underground vaults – "probably the most haunted place in Britain" (BBC News).

EDINBURGH, ROYAL BOTANIC GARDEN 379   10 Q25

20a Inverleith Row, Edinburgh. 1 mile (2km) north of the city centre.Entrances on Inverleith Row (East Gate) and Arboretum Place (West Gate). On-street parking. Bus from city centre to the east gate. Open daily (except Christmas Day and New Year's Day) from 1000; closes Nov–Feb at 1600; Mar and Oct 1800; Apr–Sep 1900. Free. Guided tours (Apr–Sep). Explanatory displays. Gift shop. Licensed café. Baby changing facilities, exhibitions and events, wedding and conference facilities. WC. Wheelchair access (wheelchairs available). Disabled WC. Telephone 0131 552 7171. www.rbge.org.uk

Just one mile from the city centre, the Royal Botanic Garden Edinburgh offers visitors peace and tranquility amongst its stunning 72 acres of beautifully landscaped grounds. Founded in 1670 , the garden is acknowledged to be one of the finest gardens in the world with its magnificent glasshouses, exhibitions, events, cafe and shop.

EDINBURGH, ROYAL MUSEUM 380   10 Q25

Chambers Street, Edinburgh. In the centre of Edinburgh's Old Town. Within ten minute walk of Princes Street and Waverley railway station; close to most major bus routes. Open all year (except Christmas Day), Mon–Sat 1000–1700 (Tue closes 2000), Sun 1200–1700. Free. Guided tours and audio tours. Explanatory displays.
Gift shop. Tearoom and bistro (restaurant in ajoining Museum of Scotland). Lecture theatre. Baby changing facilities. WC. Induction loop; free radio aids and personal access guides, telephone 0131 247 4206. Wheelchair access (level access at Tower entrance). Disabled WC. Telephone 0131 225 7534 or 0131 247 4027 minicom. www.nms.ac.uk

The museum houses international collections in a wonderful Victorian glass-topped building. Collections include applied arts, geology and zoology, natural history, social and technical history, jewellery and costume, Egyptian and African treasures, many new permanent galleries as well as exciting temporary exhibition programme. Lectures, concerts and activities for children.

EDINBURGH, ROYAL SCOTTISH ACADEMY 381   10 Q25

The Mound, Edinburgh. Located on Princes Street at the foot of the Mound. Nearest railway and bus stations five minute walk. Mon–Sat 1000–1700, Sun 1200–1700. Most exhibitions are free. WC. Wheelchair access. Disabled WC. Telephone 0131 225 6671. www.royalscottishacademy.org

The Royal Scottish Academy maintains a unique position in Scotland as an independently funded institution led by eminent artists and architects whose purpose is to promote and support the creation, understanding and enjoyment of the visual arts through exhibitions and related educational events.

The RSA also administers scholarships, awards and residencies for artists living and working in Scotland and has a historic collection of important artworks and an extensive archive of related material chronicling art and literature in Scotland over the last 180 years.

EDINBURGH, THE ROYAL YACHT BRITANNIA   382   10 Q25

Ocean Drive, Leith, Edinburgh. 2 miles (3km) from the centre of Edinburgh, at Ocean Terminal shopping and leisure centre in the port of Leith. Service no 22 runs direct from Princess Street. Open all year, Apr–Sep daily, 0930–1630; Oct–Mar daily, 1000–1530. Charge £££. Group concessions. Guided tours by audio handset (also available in French, German, Italian, Spanish, Dutch, Danish, Norwegian, Japanese, Urdu, Mandarin, Russian and Arabic). Explanatory displays. Gift shop. Refreshments in Ocean Terminal. WC. Audio script for deaf visitors and a special audio facility for the visually impared. Wheelchair access. Disabled WC. Car and coach parking. Telephone 0131 555 5566. www.royalyachtbritannia.co.uk

Visitors can experience life on board by exploring the five decks of *Britannia*, from the top of the bridge to the depths of the gleaming engine room. Described by the BBC as "Scotland's leading visitor attraction".

EDINBURGH, ST GILES' CATHEDRAL   383   10 Q25

High Street, Edinburgh. In the Royal Mile, halfway between Edinburgh Castle and Palace of Holyroodhouse. Bus from city centre. Five minute walk from Waverley railway station. Open all year. Sat 0900–1700, Sun 1300–1700; May–Sep, Mon–Fri 0900–1900; Oct–Apr, Mon–Fri 0900–1700. Recommended donation £1.00 per person. Guided tours for groups by arrangement. Explanatory displays. Gift shop. Restaurant. WC. Wheelchair access with assistance. Telephone 0131 225 9442. www.stgilescathedral.org.uk

Discover 1000 years of history in the heart of Edinburgh. St Giles' Cathedral was founded in the 1120s and was the church of John Knox during the Reformation. Highlights of a visit include the beautiful stained glass windows, impressive Rieger organ (1992) and famous Thistle Chapel, home of the Knights of the Order of the Thistle. The cathedral also houses memorials to many prominent Scots. Regular concerts held throughout the year, contact us for details.

EDINBURGH, ST JOHN'S   384   10 Q25

Princes Street, Edinburgh. Located at the west end of Princes Street. Car park nearby. Nearest railway and bus stations 15 minute walk. Open all year, Mon–Fri 0730–1600, Sat 0800–1230, Sun for worship. Free. Guided tours by arrangement. Gift shop. Café. Wheelchair access with assistance. Disabled WC. Car parking. Telephone 0131 229 7565.

St John's, The Church of St John the Evangelist, is one of architect William Burn's finest early 19th-century buildings. It also has one of the finest collections of stained glass in the country. There is a fine collection of modern paintings and sculptures. Outside are the graves of many famous Scots such as Sir Henry Raeburn, Scotland's finest portrait painter, and James Donaldson, the founder of the School for the Deaf.

EDINBURGH, ST MARY'S CATHEDRAL   385   10 P25

Palmerston Place, Edinburgh. At the West End, near Haymarket. Nearest railway station Haymarket, then five minute walk. Bus from city centre. Open all year, Mon–Fri 0730–1800; Sat–Sun 0730–1700. Free. Guided tours by arrangement. Explanatory displays. Gift stall. Crèche on Sun at 1030. WC. Induction loop. Wheelchair access. Disabled WC. Telephone 0131 225 6293. www.cathedral.net

An Episcopal cathedral built in 1879, with the western towers added in 1917. The central spire is 276 feet (84m) high. Impressive interior. Nearby is the charming

Old Coates House, built in the late 17th century and now the Episcopal Church's Theological Institute.

EDINBURGH, ST TRIDUANA'S CHAPEL 386   10 Q25

HS. At Restalrig Church, off Restalrig Road South, 1.5 miles (2.5km) east of Edinburgh city centre. Nearest railway station Waverley, bus from city centre. Telephone for opening times. Free. Telephone 0131 554 7400. www.historic-scotland.gov.uk

The lower part of the chapel built by James III, housing the shrine of St Triduana, a Pictish saint. The hexagonal vaulted chamber is unique.

EDINBURGH, SCOTCH WHISKY HERITAGE CENTRE 387   10 Q25

354 Castlehill, Edinburgh. At the top of the Royal Mile in Edinburgh. Waverley station within walking distance. Open daily (except 25 Dec) 1000–1700, hours extended in summer. Charge £££. Reduced admission for disabled. Group concessions. Guided tours (translations in ten languages). Explanatory displays. Gift shop. Whisky bar, coffee shop and restaurant. WC. Script available for deaf, braille also available. Wheelchair access. Disabled WC. Telephone 0131 220 0441. www.whisky-heritage.co.uk

The mystery of Scotch whisky revealed – learn about malt, grain and blended whisky, take a barrel ride through whisky history and meet the resident ghost. Also free taste of whisky for adults. Whisky Bar selling over 300 different whiskies.

EDINBURGH, SCOTT MONUMENT 388   10 Q25

East Princes Street Gardens, Edinburgh. Close to Waverly train station and St Andrew's bus station. Open Apr–Sep, Mon–Sat 0900–1800, Sun 1000–1800; Oct–Mar, daily 0900–1500. Charge £. Group concessions. Explanatory displays. Refreshments nearby. Telephone re disabled access. Telephone 0131 529 4068.

One of Edinburgh's most famous landmarks, completed in 1844. The monument commemorates the great Scottish writer, Sir Walter Scott. At 200 feet high (61m) there are 287 steps to the top rewarding the visitor with superb views of Edinburgh and its surroundings. The statue of Sir Walter Scott was sculpted by Sir John Steell in Carrara marble.

EDINBURGH, SCOTTISH NATIONAL GALLERY OF MODERN ART 389   10 P25

Belford Road, Edinburgh. 20 minute walk from west end of the city centre. Nearest railway station Edinburgh Haymarket, limited bus service. Open all year, Mon–Sun 1000–1700. Closed Christmas Day and Boxing Day. Free. Small charge for temporary exhibitions. Guided tours by prior arrangement (telephone 0131 624 6410). Room plan. Gift shop. Restaurant and picnic area. WC. Wheelchair access. Disabled WC. Car and coach parking. Telephone 0131 624 6200. www.natgalscot.ac.uk

The building was designed in the 1820s by Sir William Burn and was formerly a school. It has bright spacious rooms and extensive grounds providing the perfect setting for sculptures by Barbara Hepworth, Eduardo Paolozzi, Henry Moore and others. The bulk of the collection, which amounts to almost 4000 works of art, has been amassed since 1960. There are examples of work by Matisse, Kirchner, Picasso, Magritte, Miró, Dali and Ernst. The gallery houses an unrivalled collection of 20th-century Scottish art including work by Charles Rennie Mackintosh, Peploe, Fergusson and Cadell. The greatest strengths of the gallery's modern international collection are works by surrealist, German expressionist and French artists.

EDINBURGH, SCOTTISH NATIONAL PORTRAIT GALLERY   390   10 Q25

1 Queen Street, Edinburgh. In city centre, five minute walk from Princes Street. Nearest railway and bus stations ten minute walk. Open all year, Mon–Sun 1000–1700 (open until 1900 on Thur). Closed Christmas Day and Boxing Day. Free. Small charge for temporary exhibitions. Guided tours by prior arrangement (telephone 0131 624 6410). Explanatory displays. Gift shop. Restaurant. WC. Wheelchair access with assistance. Disabled WC. Telephone 0131 624 6200. www.natgalscot.ac.uk

The gallery, built in the 1880s and designed by Sir Robert Rowland Anderson, provides a unique visual history of Scotland, told through the portraits of the figures who shaped it – royalty, poets, philosophers, heroes and rebels. All the portraits are of Scots but not all are by Scots. The collection holds works by great English, European and American masters such as Van Dyck, Gainsborough, Copley, Rodin, Kokoschka and Thorvaldsen. The gallery also houses the National Photography Collection.

EDINBURGH, SCOTTISH PARLIAMENT VISITOR CENTRE   391   10 Q25

Holyrood, Edinburgh. In the centre of Edinburgh at the junction of George IV Bridge and the Royal Mile. Nearest railway station Waverley, then ten minute walk. Local bus service. Open all year Tue–Thur 0900–1900. Free. Guided tours avaliable on non-business days. Explanatory displays. Gift shop. WC. Tactile map in visitor centre. Wheelchair access. Disabled WC. Car parking. Telephone 0131 348 5200. www.scottish.parliament.uk

The displays explain the past, present and future of Scotland's Parliaments through colourful displays, exhibitions and state-of-the-art interactive computer systems.

EDINBURGH, STILLS GALLERY   392   10 Q25

23 Cockburn Street, Edinburgh. In the Old Town just off the High Street. Nearest railway station Waverley, then two minute walk. Contact for opening hours. Free. Guided tours on request. Explanatory displays. Gift shop. WC. Wheelchair access. Disabled WC. Telephone 0131 622 6200.

A contemporary art gallery. Open access photography and digital imaging labs open to visitors.

EDINBURGH, SUNTRAP GARDEN   393   10 P25

43 Gogarbank, Edinburgh. Between the A8 and A71, 1 mile (2km) west of city centre. Bus service from Waterloo Place. Open daily all year except Christmas and New Year, daily 1000–1600. Charge £. Free to NTS members and children. WC. Wheelchair access. Disabled WC. Car parking. Telephone 01506 854387 and 0131 339 2891. www.suntap-garden.org.uk

A 3 acre (1.2ha) site with several gardens in one – Italian, rock, oriental, formal, pond, peat and woodland. Started in 1957 by philanthropist and keen amateur gardener George Boyd Anderson, bequeathed to the National Trust for Scotland and Lothian region as a centre for gardening advice and horticultural excellence. Now run by Oatridge College, with excellent demonstration facilities.

EDINBURGH, TALBOT RICE GALLERY   394   10 Q25

University of Edinburgh, Old College, South Bridge, Edinburgh. In the Old Town, 0.25 mile (0.5km) from east end of Princes Street and Waverley station. Open during exhibitions, Tue–Sat 1000–1700. Opening times extended during Edinburgh Festival, telephone for information. Free. Guided tours available by arrangment. Explanatory displays. Book shop. WC. Wheelchair access to White Gallery. Telephone 0131 650 2210. www.trg.ed.ac.uk

The White Gallery shows around seven contemporary exhibitions each year, focusing on Scottish artists, but also artists from further afield and occasional historical exhibitions. The Red Gallery shows the University of Edinburgh's Torrie Collection.

EDINBURGH, TIMBERBUSH TOURS   395   10 Q25

555 Castlehill, The Royal Mile, Edinburgh. Close to Edinburgh Castle. A short walk from Waverley railway station and on many bus routes. Tours available all year. Shop open Mon–Sat 0900–1800, Sun 1000–1800. Charges dependent on tour. Group concessions. Gift shop. WC. Limited wheelchair access. Telephone 0131 226 6066. www.timberbushtours.com

Tours (1, 2, 3 and 5 day) for both independent travellers and organised groups, taking in many different locations including the Highlands and the Isle of Skye. All tours are led by knowledgeable and enthusiastic guides and there is plenty of time off the vehicle to enjoy the countryside and take photographs.

EDINBURGH, TRON KIRK VISITOR CENTRE   396   10 Q25

122 High Street, Edinburgh. On the Royal Mile. Close to bus and railway stations. Open all year, daily Apr–Oct 1000–1730; Nov–Mar 1200–1630. Free. Guided tours. Explanatory displays. Gift shop. WC. Wheelchair access with assistance. Telephone 0131 225 8408.

Inside this magnificently converted 17th-century church lies Marlyn's Wynd – Edinburgh's first cobbled street and part of the legendary Underground City. Exhibition, craft shop, superb stained glass and an exhibition of haunted Edinburgh.

EDINBURGH UNIVERSITY COLLECTION OF HISTORIC MUSICAL INSTRUMENTS   397   10 Q25

Reid Concert Hall, Bristo Square, Edinburgh. Near the McEwan Hall and Students' Union in the south west corner of Bristo Square. Bus from Waverley railway station. Open Wed 1500–1700, Sat 1000–1300 (and Mon–Fri 1400–1700 during the Edinburgh International Festival); closed Christmas and New Year. Free. Guided tours by arrangement. WC. Wheelchair access. Disabled WC. Car parking. Telephone 0131 650 2423. www.music.ed.ac.uk/euchmi

Founded circa 1850 and opened to the public in 1982. The galleries, built in 1859 and still with their original showcases, are believed to be the earliest surviving purpose-built musical museum in the world. On display are 1000 items including stringed, woodwind, brass and percussion instruments from Britain, Europe and from distant lands. The history of the instruments of the orchestra, the wind band, theatre, dance, popular music, domestic music-making and brass bands is shown. Displays include many beautiful examples of the instrument-maker's art over the past 400 years.

EDINBURGH, WATER OF LEITH CONSERVATION TRUST   398   10 P25

Water of Leith Centre, 24 Lanark Road, Edinburgh. On Lanark Road, Slatefor, 5 miles (8km) west of city centre. Bus from city centre. Open daily 1000–1600, closed Christmas and New Year. Charge £. Members free. Guided tours. Explanatory displays. Gift shop. Picnic area. Tea and coffee available. Drinks vending machine. Education programme. WC. Wheelchair access. Disabled WC. Car parking. Telephone 0131 455 7367. www.waterofleith.org.uk

The trust operates a visitor centre with fantastic interactive exhibition about the Water of Leith, its heritage and wildlife. A central point for information about the river, Water of Leith Walkway. Regular events, telephone for details

EDINBURGH, WHITE HORSE CLOSE   399   10 Q25

Off Canongate, Royal Mile.

A restored group of 17th-century buildings off the High Street. The coaches to London left from White Horse Inn (named after Queen Mary's Palfrey), and there are Jacobite links.

EDINBURGH, THE WRITERS' MUSEUM   400   10 Q25

Lady Stair's Close, Lawnmarket, Edinburgh. City centre. Open all year, Mon–Sat 1000–1700; during Edinburgh Festival only, Sun 1400–1700. Free. Explanatory displays. Gift shop. Baby changing facilities. WC. Telephone 0131 529 4901. www.cac.org.uk

Treasure house of portraits, relics and manuscripts relating to Scotland's three great writers – Robert Burns, Sir Walter Scott and Robert Louis Stevenson. Temporary exhibitions on other writers and literary organisations.

EDINBURGH ZOO   401   10 P25

134 Corstorphine Road, Edinburgh. On the A8, 3 miles (5km) west of the city centre. Buses from city centre. Open daily, Apr–Sep 0900–1800; Oct and Mar 0900–1700; Nov–Feb 0900–1630. Charge £££. Group concessions. Guided tours by prior arrangement. Explanatory displays. Gift shop. Cafeterias and snack kiosks. Children's play area. WC. Reduced admission for blind visitors, companion admitted free of charge. Guide dogs allowed into selected areas. Wheelchair access with assistance. Disabled WC. Car and coach parking. Telephone 0131 334 9171. www.edinburghzoo.org.uk

Established in 1913 by the Royal Zoological Society of Scotland, this is one of Britain's largest and most exciting wildlife attractions. Explore the hillside parkland to discover over 1000 beautiful animals, many threatened in the wild. Daily penguin parade, sealion feeding, hilltop safari and lots of interesting keeper talks and events.

FENTON BARNS ARTS AND CRAFTS GALLERY   402   10 R25

Fenton Barns Retail Village, North Berwick, East Lothian. 3 miles (5km) from North Berwick, between Drem and Direlton. Nearest railway station at Drem. Open all year, daily 1000–1700. Free. Tours on request. Explanatory displays. Gift shop. Tearoom and picnic area. Garden and pets corner. WC. Wheelchair access. Disabled WC. Car and coach parking. Telephone (01620) 850355. www.fentonbarnsworld.com

Four unique galleries, three working studios housed in the former RAF Drem buildings, and the largest arts and crafts supply store in the area. Scottish sculpture gardens, classes and workshops, make and take projects for all.

FENTON BARNS GOLF CENTRE   403   10 R25

Fenton Barns, North Berwick, East Lothian. On the B1345, between Drem and North Berwick. Nearest railway station Drem. Open daily all year (except Christmas Day)

0900–2100. Free. Charge for balls. Restaurant. Playground. WC. Wheelchair access with assistance. Disabled WC. Car and coach parking. Telephone (01620) 850475.

A floodlit driving range and nine-hole 3-par golf course. Part of a retail and leisure village, including a farm shop, coffee shop and archery centre.

FLAG HERITAGE CENTRE   404

See 294 Athelstaneford, Flag Heritage Centre.

GLENEAGLES CRYSTAL   405   10 P25

9 Simpson Road, East Mains Industrial Estate, Broxburn, West Lothian. In Broxburn, 4 miles (6.5km) from Newbridge on the M8/M9 junction. Bus from Edinburgh. Open daily except Christmas and New Year, Mon–Sat 0930–1700, Sun 1100–1600. Free. Viewing window. Gift shop. Coffee and juice available. Wheelchair access. Car and coach parking. Telephone (01506) 505120. www.gleneaglescrystal.com

A factory shop with excellent lead crystal, fine bone china and collectables

GLENKINCHIE DISTILLERY   406   10 Q25

Pencaitland, Tranent, East Lothian. 2 miles (3km) from Pencaitland on the A6093 (signposted). Nearest railway station Longniddry, bus from Edinburgh to Pencaitland. Open all year, Mon–Fri 1200–1600; Easter–Oct also Sat–Sun. Charge ££. Under 18s free. Group concessions. Guided tours (available in French, German, Italian or Spanish). Explanatory displays. Gift shop. WC. Wheelchair access. Disabled WC. Car and coach parking. Telephone (01875) 342004.

Set in a small valley, the only remaining malt whisky distillery close to Edinburgh. Visitors can see all aspects of the traditional distilling craft, with sample tasting. Exhibition includes a scale model of a malt distillery made for the British Empire Exhibition of 1924.

HAILES CASTLE   407   10 R25

HS. Off the A1, 1.5 miles (2.5km) south west of East Linton, East Lothian. Nearest railway station Dunbar, bus to Pencraig (request stop), then 15 minute walk. Access at all reasonable times (see keyholder). Free. Picnic area. Car parking. Telephone (0131) 5507603. www.historic-scotland.gov.uk

A beautifully-sited ruin incorporating a 13th-century fortified manor which was extended in the 14th and 15th centuries. Includes a fine 16th-century chapel and two vaulted pit-prisons.

HOPETOUN HOUSE   408   10 P25

South Queensferry, West Lothian. 12 miles (19km) north west of Edinburgh. Nearest railway station Dalmeny, bus from Edinburgh to South Queensferry then 2 mile (3km) walk. Open end Mar–Sep, daily 1000–1730 (last entry 1630). House can be opened out of season by prior arrangement. Charge £££. No charge for admission to restaurant only. Group concessions. Guided tours. Explanatory displays. Gift shop. Restaurant, tearoom and picnic area. WC. Limited wheelchair access (many of trails in grounds are accessible by wheelchair but house accessed via steps). Disabled WC. Car and coach parking. Telephone 0131 331 2451. www.hopetounhouse.com

A gem of Europe's architectural heritage and the residence of the Marquis of Linlithgow. Set in 100 acres (40ha) of magnificent parkland on the shore of the Firth of Forth with fine views of the famous bridges. Built 1699–1707 by William Bruce and extended by William Adam from 1721. Features original furniture, carriage collection, paintings by famous artists, 17th-century tapestries, rococo ceilings and Meissen ceramics.

HOUSE OF THE BINNS   409   10 P25

NTS. Linlithgow, West Lothian. Off A904, 15 miles (24km) west of Edinburgh, 3 miles (5km) east of Linlithgow. By bus from Linlithgow. Open Jun–Sep, daily (except Fri) 1400–1700. Charge £££. Group concessions. Guided tours. Explanatory displays. Information sheets in seven languages. Picnic area. Parkland. WC. Braille information sheets. Photo album of upper rooms available at reception. Limited wheelchair access. Disabled WC. Car and coach parking. Telephone (01506) 834255. www.nts.org.uk

Home of the Dalyell family since 1612. General Tam Dalyell raised the Royal Scots Greys here in 1681. The architecture reflects the early 17th-century transition from fortified stronghold to spacious mansion. Elaborate plaster ceilings dating from 1630. Woodland walk to panoramic viewpoint over Firth of Forth. Famous for snowdrops and daffodils in spring.

INVERESK LODGE GARDEN   410   10 Q25

NTS. Inveresk Village, Musselburgh, East Lothian. On A6124, just south of Musselburgh. By bus from Edinburgh or Musselburgh. Open all year, daily 1000–1800. Charge £. Group concessions. Explanatory displays. WC. Wheelchair access with assistance. Disabled WC. Car and coach parking. Telephone (01721) 722502. www.nts.org.uk

Attractive terraced garden in historic village of Inveresk. Excellent range of roses and shrubs and a beautiful display of colour in autumn. The peaceful atmosphere of a secret garden, yet very accessible from the centre of Edinburgh.

KIRK OF CALDER   411   10 P25

Main Street, Mid Calder, West Lothian. 12 miles (19km) west of Edinburgh, off A71 on B7015 in the village of Mid Calder. Nearest railway station Livingston, bus service from Edinburgh. Open May–Sep, Sun 1400–1600. Free. Guided tours. Explanatory displays. Gift shop. Tearoom. WC. Induction loop. Limited wheelchair access. Car and coach parking. www.kirkofcalder.co.uk

This 16th-century parish church won the West Lothian award for conservation in 1992. Famous visitors include John Knox, David Livingstone, Frederick Chopin and James 'Paraffin' Young. Fine stained glass windows. Visitors can learn about four centuries of Scottish history.

LAUDERDALE AISLE, ST MARY'S CHURCH, HADDINGTON   412   10 R25

HS. In Haddington, East Lothian. Nearest railway station Drem, bus from Edinburgh. Access at all reasonable times. Free. Telephone (0131) 5507603. www.historic-scotland.gov.uk

The former sacristy of the great 15th-century parish church. Contains a splendid early 17th-century monument in marble with alabaster effigies.

LENNOXLOVE HOUSE   413   10 R25

Lennoxlove Estate, Haddington, East Lothian. On the B6369, 1 mile (2km) from Haddington. Bus from Haddington. Open Wed, Thu and Sun 1330–1630. Charge ££. Group concessions. Guided tours (available in French, German and Spanish). Garden café. Garden. WC. Limited wheelchair access. Disabled WC. Car and coach parking. Telephone (01620) 823720. www.lennoxlove.com

The home of the Duke of Hamilton. It features a 14th-century keep originally built for Maitland of Lethington, Secretary of State to Mary, Queen of Scots, and houses mementoes belonging to Mary, together with furniture, paintings and porcelain once part of the Hamilton Palace collection. House will not be available to public during 2006 and re-opens in Jul 2007.

LINLITHGOW CANAL CENTRE   414   10 N25

Canal Basin, Manse Road, Linlithgow, West Lothian. In Linlithgow, five minute walk from station. Bus or rail from Edinburgh or Glasgow. Open Easter–Sep, weekends 1400–1700; Jul–Aug, daily 1400–1700. Museum free, charge for boat trips. Explanatory displays. Gift shop. Tearoom and picnic area. WC. Wheelchair access to museum and tearoom. Disabled WC. Telephone (01506) 671215. www.lucs.org.uk

Historic canal basin on the Edinburgh and Glasgow Union Canal with small museum in former stable. Trip boats *Victoria* (replica 12-seater Victorian steam packet boat, 1/2 hour town stretch trips) and *St Magdalene* (40 seater, 2½ hour trip to Avon Aqueduct). Trips to Falkirk Wheel (4 hours), last Sunday of certain months. Booking essential on 01506 843194.

LINLITHGOW PALACE   415   10 N25

HS. Kirkgate, Linlithgow, West Lothian. Nearest railway station Linlithgow, then ten minute walk. Bus from Falkirk and Edinburgh. Open Apr–Sep, daily 0930–1830; Oct–Mar, Mon–Sun 0930–1630. Charge £. Group concessions. Gift shop. Picnic area. WC. Limited wheelchair access. Car and coach parking. Telephone (01506) 842896. www.historic-scotland.gov.uk

The magnificent ruin of a great royal palace set in its own park beside Linlithgow Loch. The Great Hall and Chapel (late 15th century) are particularly fine. The quadrangle has a richly-carved 16th-century fountain. A favoured residence of the Stewart monarchs from James I. Works commissioned by James I, III, IV, V and VI can be seen. Both King James V and Mary, Queen of Scots were born here.

THE LINLITHGOW STORY   416   10 N25

Annet House, 143 High Street, Linlithgow, West Lothian. In Linlithgow 800 yards (731m) from the station. Bus or rail from Edinburgh or Glasgow. Open Apr–Oct, Mon–Sat 1000–1700, Sun 1300–1600. Charge £. Group concessions. Guided tours by prior arrangement. Explanatory displays. Gift shop. Picnic area in terraced garden. WC. Limited wheelchair access. Car and coach parking. Telephone (01506) 670677. www.linlithgowstory.org.uk

A small museum of local history which tells the story, not only of the Stewart kings of Scotland who built and lived in Linlithgow Palace (see 415), but also of the ordinary people who lived and worked in the burgh. Housed in a late 18th-century merchant house.

LOCH CENTRE   417   10 Q25

Well Wynd, Tranent, East Lothian. In Tranent centre. Bus from Edinburgh. Open all year (except Christmas and New Year), Mon–Fri 0900–2200, weekends 0900–1700. Charge by activity. Group concessions. Café. Crèche. WC. Wheelchair access. Disabled WC. Car and coach parking. Telephone (01875) 611081.

Swimming pool with sauna, steam room, bodyworks gym, activity hall, dance studios, soft play area and meeting rooms.

MARKLE FISHERIES   418   10 R25

Markle, East Linton, East Lothian. Just off the A199, 4 miles (6.5km) south of Haddington. Bus to East Linton, then ten minute walk. Open all year (weather permitting) except Christmas Day and New Year's Day, 0800–dusk. Various charges (prices from £6.00). Group concessions. Explanatory displays. Shop. Vending machine for drinks and snacks. WC. Limited wheelchair access. Disabled WC. Car and coach parking. Telephone (01620) 861213. www.marklefisheries.com

Three spring-fed lakes, totalling 9.5 acres (3.8ha), which are regularly stocked with trout and coarse fish. Bank fishing. Children's bait pond. Tackle hire and shop and tuition. Also ornamental fish such as coy carp for sale.

MEADOWMILL SPORTS CENTRE   419   10 Q25

Meadowmill, Tranent, East Lothian. Off the A198, north of the A1 and 2 miles (3km) outside Tranent. Prestonpans station, bus from Edinburgh. Open daily (except Christmas and New Year); Mon–Fri 0900–2200, weekends 1000–1700. Charge by activity. Group concessions. Café and vending machines. Crèche. WC. Wheelchair access. Disabled WC. Car and coach parking. Telephone (01875) 614900.

A general sports centre offering all kinds of activities including a gym, free weights room, soft play room, activity hall and sports pitches.

MELVILLE GOLF CENTRE   420   10 Q26

South Melville, Lasswade, Near Edinburgh. 7 miles (11km) south of Edinburgh centre, just off the city bypass. Bus from Edinburgh. Golf course open all year, daily dawn to dusk. Golf range and shop open Mon–Fri 0900–2200, weekends 0900–2000. Happy Hour daily, 1700–1800. Charge for range £, course £££. Group concessions. Golf shop, equipment and clothing. Picnic area and hot and cold vending machines. WC. Wheelchair access. Disabled WC. Car and coach parking. Telephone 0131 663 8038 (range and shop) 0131 654 0224 (bookings). www.melvillegolf.co.uk

Golf centre. Nine-hole pay-and-play course, floodlit range, four-hole short game area and putting. Full shoe and equipment hire. PGA tuition.

JOHN MUIR BIRTHPLACE   421   8 R25

126-128 High Street, Dunbar. In centre of town. Nearest railway station Dunbar, buses from Edinburgh and Berwick-upon-Tweed. Open Apr–Jul, Mon–Sat 1100–1300 and 1400–1700, Sun 1400–1700. Free. Explanatory displays. Gift shop. Limited wheelchair access. Car and coach parking. Telephone (01368) 860187.

The birthplace of John Muir, founding figure of the worldwide conservation movement. He was born in 1838 in this house. On the ground floor his father ran a business. His boyhood was spent in Dunbar until his family emigrated in 1849. Recently extensively refurbished.

MUSEUM OF FLIGHT   422   10 R25

East Fortune Airfield, North Berwick, East Lothian. 20 miles (32km) east of Edinburgh. Bus from Haddington or North Berwick. Open all year (except Christmas and New Year), daily, Easter–Oct 1000–1700; Nov–Easter, Sat–Sun 1000–1700. Charge £. Children under 12 and NMS members free. Group concessions. Guided tours. Explanatory displays. Gift shop. Tearoom and picnic area. Baby changing facilities. Garden. WC. Wheelchair access and disabled parking. Disabled WC. Car and coach parking. Telephone (01620) 880308. www.nms.ac.uk/flight

Scotland's national museum of aviation with a large collection of over 40 aircraft (including Britain's oldest aeroplane, a Spitfire and a Vulcan bomber) in the hangars of a wartime airfield. Now home to Scotland's Concorde, visit The Concorde Experience and take an onboard tour (advance booking highly recommended). Special exhibitions on space flight, early aviation, air traffic control and the R34 airship. Regular events. Part of the National Museums of Scotland.

MUSSELBURGH LINKS, THE OLD GOLF COURSE   423   10 Q25

Balcarres Road, Musselburgh. At the east end of Musselburgh High Street. Nearest railway station Musselburgh, bus from Edinburgh. Open all year during daylight hours. Charges on application. Group concessions. Explanatory displays. Gift shop. Refreshments available. WC. No guide dogs. Limited wheelchair access. Car and coach parking. Telephone 0131 665 5438. www.musselburgholdlinks.co.uk

Mary, Queen of Scots is said to have played this course in 1567, although the oldest documentary evidence dates from 1672. Between 1874 and 1889 the course hosted six Open Championships and was the scene of many great matches between the leading players of the day. Today golfers can hire hickory clubs and replica balls to emulate the masters of the past.

MUSSELBURGH RACECOURSE   424   10 Q25

Linkfield Road, Musselburgh, East Lothian. Off A1, 6 miles (9.5km) east of Edinburgh. Nearest railway station in Edinburgh and Wallyford. On race days a courtesy bus runs from Wallyford station. Twenty-four racedays throughout the year. Charges vary. Children under 16 free. Telephone or visit website for information. Restaurants, bars and snack outlets. WC. Wheelchair access with assistance. Disabled WC. Car and coach parking. Telephone 0131 665 2859. www.musselburgh-racecourse.co.uk

A venue for horseracing since 1816, originally known as Edinburgh Races with meetings held on Leith Sands. Today the course hosts Flat racing and National Hunt meetings and is one of the UK's most stylish racecourses. There is a nine-hole golf course within the racecourse. Refurbished Edwardian grandstand and landscaped lawns.

MUSSELBURGH SPORTS CENTRE   425   10 Q25

Newbigging, Musselburgh. On the A6124 to Inveresk, on the outskirts of Musselburgh. Nearest railway station Musselburgh, bus from Edinburgh. Open all year (except Christmas and New Year), Mon, Wed and Fri 0700–2130, Tue and Thu 0900–2130, weekends 0900–1700. Charge by activity. Group concessions. Café. Crèche. WC. Wheelchair access. Disabled WC. Car and coach parking. Telephone 0131 653 6367.

A sports centre with swimming pool, sauna, steam room, squash courts, gym and coached activities.

MYRETON MOTOR MUSEUM   426   10 Q25

Myreton, Aberlady, East Lothian. Off the A198 just east of Aberlady. Nearest railway station Drem or bus from Edinburgh. Open Apr–Oct, daily 1000–1600; Nov–Mar, Sat–Sun 1100–1500. Charge ££. Group concessions. Explanatory displays. Small gift shop. Picnic area. WC. Wheelchair access. Car and coach parking. Telephone (01875) 870288/(079470) 66666.

A varied collection of road transport from 1897, including motor cars, cycles, motorcycles, commercials. Period advertising, posters and signs. Pedal cars.

NEWHAILES 427   10 Q25

NTS. Newhailes Road, Musselburgh. In Musselburgh on A6095. Lothian Buses from
Edinburgh; 15 minute walk from Newcraighall or Musselburgh stations. Open Easter
weekend and May–Sep, Thur–Mon 1200–1700. Charge £££. Group concessions.
Guided tours. Explanatory displays. Gift shop. Tearoom. Picnic area. WC. Wheelchair
access. Disabled WC. Car and coach parking. Telephone (0131) 6535599.
www.nts.org.uk

17th century house developed further in 18th century, with much of the original
decorative scheme intact. Family home of the Dalrymples who played a key role
in Scottish political, legal, and cultural life.

NORTH BERWICK SPORTS CENTRE 428   10 R25

Grange Road, North Berwick, East Lothian. On the outskirts of North Berwick near
The Law. Nearest railway station North Berwick, bus from Edinburgh. Open all year
(except Christmas and New year), Mon–Fri 0900–2200, weekends 0900–1700.
Charge by activity. Group concessions. Café. Crèche. WC. Wheelchair access.
Disabled WC. Car and coach parking. Telephone (01620) 893454.

Swimming pool, sauna, steam room, activity hall, squash courts, trampolines,
body conditioning and many coached activities.

ORMISTON MARKET CROSS 429   10 Q25

HS. On the B6371 in Ormiston. 2 miles (3km) south of Tranent, East Lothian. Nearest
railway station at Wallyford, bus from Edinburgh to Ormiston. Telephone (0131)
5507603. www.historic-scotland.gov.uk

A 15th-century cross on a modern base in the main street. A symbol of the right
of the inhabitants to hold a market.

POLKEMMET COUNTRY PARK 430   9 N26

Park Centre, Polkemmet Country Park, Whitburn, West Lothian. On the B7066 west
of Whitburn. Nearest railway station Fauldhouse or Bathgate. Open all year. Please
telephone for opening times of golf course and driving range. Free. Charge for
activities. Restaurant, bar, picnic and barbecue sites. WC. Limited wheelchair access.
Disabled WC. Car and coach parking. Telephone (01501) 743905.

A public park with mature woodland, a 9-hole golf course, golf driving range
and bowling green. Also barbecue site (bookable) and large children's play area
(the Fantasy Forest). Rhododendrons in summer. Reception and restaurant/bar
at the Park Centre.

PRESTON MARKET CROSS 431   10 Q25

HS. 0.5 mile (1km) south of Prestonpans, East Lothian. Nearest railway station
Prestonpans, bus from Edinburgh to Prestonpans, then 0.5 mile (1km) walk. Access at
all reasonable times. Free. Telephone (0131) 5507603. www.historic-scotland.gov.uk

The only surviving example of a market cross of its type on its original site. A
fine early 17th-century design with a cylindrical base surmounted by a cross-
shaft headed by a unicorn.

PRESTON MILL AND PHANTASSIE DOOCOT 432   10 R25

NTS. East Linton, East Lothian. Off A1, in East Linton, 23 miles (37km) east of
Edinburgh. By bus from Edinburgh. Open Easter–Sep, Thur–Mon 1200–1700. Charge
££. Group concessions. Guided tours by arrangement. Explanatory displays.
Information sheets in six languages. Gift shop. Picnic area. WC. Limited wheelchair

access. Disabled WC. Car and coach parking. Telephone (01620) 860426. www.nts.org.uk

Picturesque mill with stone buildings dating from the 18th century. The water wheel and grain milling machinery are still intact and visitors can see them in operation. Attractive surroundings with ducks and geese on millponds and short walk through fields to 16th-century Phantassie Doocot, once home to 500 pigeons.

PRESTONGRANGE INDUSTRIAL HERITAGE MUSEUM   433   10 Q25

Morison's Haven, Prestonpans, East Lothian. In Prestonpans, 9 miles (14.5km) east of Edinburgh, 15 minute walk from Prestonpans station. Bus from Edinburgh. Open Apr–Oct, daily 1100–1600. Free. Guided tours. Explanatory displays. Gift shop. Café and picnic area. WC. Wheelchair access with assistance. Disabled WC. Car and coach parking. Telephone 0131 653 2904.

A museum telling the story of many local industries. Displays include a historic Cornish beam engine. Special activities and steam days.

PRESTONPANS BATTLE CAIRN   434   10 Q25

East of Prestonpans on A198. Access at all times. Free. Car parking.

The cairn commemorates the victory of Prince Charles Edward over General Cope at the Battle of Prestonpans in 1745.

QUEENSFERRY MUSEUM   435   10 P25

53 High Street, South Queensferry, West Lothian. Off the A90, 12 miles (19km) west of Edinburgh. Bus from Edinburgh. Open all year, Mon and Thu–Sat 1000–1300 and 1415–1700, Sun 1200–1700. Free. Explanatory displays. Gift shop. Car and coach parking nearby. Mini induction loop. Telephone 0131 331 5545. www.cac.org.uk

A museum telling the story of the town, known as the Queen's Ferry in honour of the saintly Queen Margaret (died 1093), who encouraged pilgrims to use the ferry crossing to travel to the shrine of St Andrew in Fife. Describes the development of the Queensferry Passage, the growth of the former Royal Burgh and the building of the Forth Bridges. Displays on life, work and pastimes, including the annual Ferry Fair and a life-size model of the Burry Man.

ROSSLYN CHAPEL   436   10 Q26

Roslin, Midlothian. In Roslin, 7 miles (11km) south west of Edinburgh. Nearest railway station Edinburgh, bus from Edinburgh. Open all year, Mon–Sat 0930–1800 (Oct–Apr closes at 1700), Sun 1200–1645.. Charge £££. Group concessions. Guided tours (information in French, German, Italian and Spanish). Explanatory displays. Gift shop. Tearoom. Garden. WC. Wheelchair access (except for crypt). Disabled WC. Car and coach parking. Telephone 0131 440 2159. www.rosslynchapel.com

A 15th-century chapel with unique carving throughout, including the legendary Apprentice Pillar, many references to Freemasonry and the Knights Templar. The only medieval church in Scotland used by the Scottish Episcopal Church.

ST MARTIN'S KIRK, HADDINGTON   437   10 R25

HS. On the eastern outskirts of Haddington, East Lothian. Nearest railway station Drem, bus from Edinburgh. Access at all reasonable times. Free. Telephone (0131) 5507603. www.historic-scotland.gov.uk

The ruined nave of a Romanesque church, altered in the 13th century.

ST MARY'S COLLEGIATE CHURCH, HADDINGTON   438   10 R25

Sidegate, Haddington. In Haddington. Bus from Edinburgh. Open May–Sep, Mon–Sat 1100–1600, Sun 1430–1630. Free. Guided tours (leaflets in foreign languages), tours by arrangement. Explanatory displays. Tearoom and picnic area. Gift shop and book shop. Brass rubbing centre open by arrangement. WC. Wheelchair access. Disabled WC. Car and coach parking. Telephone (01620) 826275. www.kylemore.btinternet.co.uk/stmarys.htm

A magnificent 14th-century medieval cruciform church, East Lothian's Cathedral. Destroyed during the Siege of Haddington in 1548, but completely restored 1971–3. Features Burne Jones and Sax Shaw windows; Lammermuir pipe organ. The Lauderdale Chapel is a focus for ecumenical unity. A popular venue for televised services and commercial recordings, concerts and art exhibitions. In picturesque surroundings beside the River Tyne.

ST MICHAEL'S PARISH CHURCH, LINLITHGOW   439   10 N25

Kirkgate, Linlithgow. In the centre of the town. By rail or bus from Edinburgh then five minute walk. Open Jun–Sep, daily 1000–1600; Oct–May, Mon–Fri 1000–1530. Free. Guided tours by prior arrangement (available in French or German). Explanatory displays. Gift shop. Picnic area. Wheelchair access. Car parking. Telephone (01506) 842188. www.stmichaels-parish.org.uk

A medieval parish church consecrated in 1242 on the site of an earlier church. Close association with the royal house of Stewart and Mary, Queen of Scots, born in nearby Linlithgow Palace (see 415) and baptized in the church. The church is recognisable from afar by the contemporary aluminium crown on the tower, replacing the medieval stone crown removed in 1820. A restored Willis organ was installed in 2002.

SCOTTISH MINING MUSEUM   440   10 Q26

Lady Victoria Colliery, Newtongrange, Midlothian. On the A7, 10 miles (16km) south of Edinburgh. Bus from Edinburgh. Open Mar–Oct, daily 1000–1700; Nov–Feb, daily 1100–1600. Charge ££. Group concessions. Guided tours by prior arrangement (ex-miners as guides). Audio guides in French, German and Italian. Explanatory displays. Gift shop. Restaurant and picnic area. Children's play area, tourist information. WC. Wheelchair access. Disabled WC. Car and coach parking. Telephone 0131 663 7519. www.scottishminingmuseum.com

Visitors will marvel at the sheer size of the Scottish Mining Museum, and be astounded by the engineering brilliance behind all the machinery. Retrace the footsteps of thousands of miners and their families. Exhibitions, interactive film theatres, coalface, roadway, magic helmets.

SCOTTISH SEABIRD CENTRE   441   10 R25

The Harbour, North Berwick. Car parking (coach parking by arrangement). By train or bus from Edinburgh, bus from Dunbar and Haddington. Open all year, summer, daily 1000–1800; winter telephone to confirm times (closed Christmas). Charge £££. Children under 5 free. Explanatory displays. Gift shop. Restaurant/café. WC. Wheelchair access. Disabled WC. Telephone (01620) 890202. www.seabird.org

Visitors can discover the secret and fascinating world of Scotland's sea birds by studying the birds close up, in their natural environment – without disturbing them. Remote cameras and the latest technology provide amazing live pictures of puffins, gannets and many other sea birds. Breathtaking views across the Firth of Forth to the Bass Rock and Fife.

SETON COLLEGIATE CHURCH   442   10 Q25

HS. Longniddry, East Lothian. Off the A198, 1 mile (2km) south east of Cockenzie. Nearest railway station Longniddry, bus to Seton Church road end from Edinburgh or North Berwick. Open Apr–Sep, daily 0930–1830. Charge £. Group concessions. Explanatory displays. Car and coach parking. Telephone (01875) 813334. www.historic-scotland.gov.uk

The chancel and apse of a fine 15th-century church. Transept and steeple added in 1513.

STENTON GALLERY   443   10 R25

Stenton, East Lothian. On the B6370 (Hillfoots Trail), signposted from A1 and A199. Transport can be arranged for groups. Open Fri–Wed, 1100–1700 during exhibitions (telephone or email for details). Free. Guided tours by arrangement (multi-lingual). Talks, lectures and demonstrations. Coffee available. WC. Limited wheelchair access. Car parking. Telephone (01368) 850256. www.stentongallery.com

Contemporary art from throughout Scotland in a regularly changing programme of exhibitions.

TANTALLON CASTLE   444   10 R25

HS. North Berwick, East Lothian. Off the A198, 3 miles (5km) east of North Berwick. Nearest railway station North Berwick, buses from North Berwick and Dunbar pass Tantallon Castle road end. Open Apr–Sep, daily 0930–1830; Oct–Mar, Mon–Sun 0930–1630, (closed Thu and Fri). Charge £. Group concessions. Explanatory displays. Gift shop. Picnic area, refreshments available in shop. WC. Limited wheelchair access. Car and coach parking. Telephone (01620) 892727. www.historic-scotland.gov.uk

Set on the edge of the cliffs looking out to the Bass Rock, this formidable castle was a stronghold of the Douglas family. It features earthwork defences and a massive 50 foot (15m) high curtain wall. Display includes replica gun.

TORPHICHEN PRECEPTORY   445   10 N25

HS. In Torphichen village on the B792, 5 miles (8km) south south-west of Linlithgow, West Lothian. Bus from Linlithgow to Bathgate via Torphichen. Open Apr–Sep, Sat 1000–1700, Sun and bank holidays 1400–1700. Charge £. Explanatory displays. WC. Car and coach parking. Telephone (01506) 653733. www.historic-scotland.gov.uk

The tower and transepts of a church built by the Knights Hospitaller of the Order of St John of Jerusalem in the 13th century, but much altered.

TRAPRAIN LAW   446   10 R25

Off A1, 5 miles (7.5km) west of Dunbar. Access at all times. Free.

A whale-backed hill, 734 feet (224m) high, with Iron Age fortified site, probably continuing in use as a defended Celtic township until the 11th century. A treasure of 4th-century Christian and pagan silver excavated here in 1919 is now in the Museum of Antiquities, Queen Street, Edinburgh.

VOGRIE COUNTRY PARK   447   10 Q26

Gorebridge, Midlothian. 2 miles (3km) east of Gorebridge on B6372. Open all year daily, from dawn to dusk. Free. Small charge for parking. Guided tours by arrangement. Explanatory displays. Tearoom during summer. Picnic areas and two

barbecue sites (book in advance). WC. Sensory garden. Limited wheelchair access.
Disabled WC. Car and coach parking. Telephone (01875) 821990.
www.midlothiancouncil.gov.uk

Over 5 miles (8km) of woodland and riverside walks with year-round interest.
Nature trails, interpretation and guided walks. Historic house open to visitors.
Model railway, golf course and an adventure play area. Events field for hire.

WINTON HOUSE   448   10 Q25

Pencaitland, East Lothian. 14 miles (22.5km) east of Edinburgh off A1 at Tranent.
Lodge gates south of New Winton (B6355) or Pencaitland (A6093). Bus from
Edinburgh to Pencaitland, then 1 mile (2km) walk. Open Apr, Jul and Aug, first
weekend 1230–1630; other times by prior arrangement. Charge ££. Group
concessions. Guided tours. Explanatory displays. Tearoom and picnic area. Garden,
walks. WC. Limited wheelchair access. Disabled WC. Car and coach parking.
Telephone (01875) 340222. www.wintonhouse.co.uk

A 15th-century tower house restored palatially with famous stone twisted
chimneys and magnificent plaster ceilings. Still a family home, it houses many
treasures including paintings by many of Scotland's notable artists, fine
furniture and an exhibition of family costumes and photographs. The grounds
contain specimen trees, woodland walks, terraced gardens and loch.

WINTON POTTERY   449   10 Q25

Winton Estate, Pencaitland, East Lothian. 14 miles (22.5km) south east of Edinburgh
on B6355. Bus from Edinburgh to Pencaitland, then 1 mile (2km) walk. Open by
arrangement all year, and during Apr, Jun and Dec. Free. Guided tours. Gift shop.
Limited wheelchair access. Car and coach parking. Telephone (01875) 340188.

The pottery is situated in the grounds of a stately home (see 448 Winton House)
in a former stable block. Specialising in thrown and hand-built stoneware for
domestic use, as well as plant holders and sundials. Demonstrations are
available by arrangement.

WOOL STONE   450   10 R25

In Stenton, B6370, 5 miles (7.5km) south west of Dunbar. Access at all reasonable
times. Free. Car parking.

The medieval Wool Stone, used formerly for the weighing of wool at Stenton
Fair, stands on the green. See also the 14th-century Rood Well, topped by a
cardinal's hat, and the old doocot.

GREATER GLASGOW AND CLYDE VALLEY

ANTARTEX VILLAGE   451   9 L25

Lomond Industrial Estate, Heather Avenue, Alexandria. 1 mile (2km) from A82, 15
miles (24km) north of Glasgow. Bus and rail service from Glasgow. Open daily all
year, 1000–1800 (except Christmas and New Year). Free. Explanatory displays and
sheepskin cutting demonstrations. Gift shop. Restaurant. WC. Wheelchair access.
Disabled WC. Car and coach parking. Telephone (01389) 752393. www.ewm.co.uk

Watch the famous Antartex sheepskins being made and choose from a vast
selection of sheepskin and leather goods. Also golfing equipment and whisky
tasting. Restaurant offers traditional Scottish dishes. Large Edinburgh Woollen
Mill section with gifts, shoes and clothing.

AQUATEC   452   9 M26

1 Menteith Road, Motherwell. Five minute walk from Motherwell railway station.
Open daily all year, 1000–2200 (except Christmas Day and New Year's Day). Charges
vary. Children under 3 years free. Group concessions. Gift shop. Café and vending
machines. WC. Wheelchair access. Disabled WC. Car and coach parking. Telephone
(01698) 276464. www.northlan.gov.uk

The Aquatec is a leisure facility with a free form leisure pool with tyre ride, wild
water channel and outdoor pool, children's beach area and lagoon. A leisure ice
rink and ice cavern, snow machines and video wall. Health suite and
conditioning gym.

AUCHENTOSHAN DISTILLERY   453   9 L25

By Dalmuir, Clydebank, Glasgow. 20 mins from Glasgow city centre, on westbound
A82 just before the Erskine bridge. No 66 bus from George Square in Glasgow stops
a 5 min walk away from distillery. Nearest train station is Kilpatrick. Open all year,
Mon–Sat 0900–1700. Charge ££. Guided tours on the hour from 1000–1600.
Explanatory displays. Gift shop. All visitors recieve a dram of Auchentoshan single
malt Scotch whisky. VIP tours and whisky masterclasses can be arranged. Conference
and meeting room facilities are available. WC. Wheelchair access. Disabled WC.
Telephone (01389) 878561. www.auchentoshan.com

Auchentoshan Distillery was established in 1823 and has been producing its
characteristically delicate, smooth single malt since then. The subtle aromas and
flavours of Auchentoshan are created by its unique triple distillation
method—something you will see in no other distillery in Scotland.You really get a
sense of the magic behind the distillation of the worlds No 1 Lowland single malt.

AULD KIRK MUSEUM   454   9 M25

Cowgate, Kirkintilloch, Glasgow. Take A803 from Glasgow to Kirkintilloch. Bus
service to Kirkintilloch from Buchanan Bus Station, Glasgow. Open all year, Tue–Sat
1000–1300 and 1400–1700. Closed Sun and Mon. Free. Explanatory displays. Gift
shop. WC. Wheelchair access. Disabled WC. Car parking. Telephone 0141 578 0144.
www.eastdunbarton.gov.uk

The award-winning Auld Kirk Museum is an opportunity to experience a time
journey that traces the town from Roman times to the present day. The building
dates back to 1644 when it was the parish church of Kirkintilloch. The museum
describes the domestic and working life of people in the area. Temporary
exhibition programme of crafts, photography and local history throughout the
year.

BAR HILL FORT   455   9 M25

HS. 0.5 mile (1km) east of Twechar, Stirlingshire (signposted from the village).
Nearest railway station Glasgow, bus from Glasgow (Buchanan Street). Access at all
reasonable times. Free. www.historic-scotland.gov.uk

The highest on the line of the Antonine Wall, containing the foundations of the
headquarters building and bathhouse. A small Iron Age fort lies to the east. See
573 Antonine Wall.

BAROCHAN CROSS   456   9 L26

HS. In Paisley Abbey (see 554), in the centre of Paisley. Nearest railway station Paisley
Gilmour Street. For access see guide entry for Paisley Abbey. Free. Telephone (0131)
5507603. www.historic-scotland.gov.uk

A fine free-standing Celtic cross that formerly stood in Houston parish, west of Paisley.

BARON'S HAUGH RSPB NATURE RESERVE   457   9 M26

RSPB. Motherwell, Lanarkshire, off North Lodge Avenue. Nearest railway station Airbles (Motherwell), local bus services stop near reserve (Adele Street). Reserve open at all times. Free. Explanatory displays and scheduled events. Limited wheelchair access. Car and coach parking. Telephone (0141) 3310993. www.rspb.org.uk/scotland

Baron's Haugh is an urban nature reserve with a variety of habitats: flooded meadow (or haugh), marshland, river, woodland and scrub. This rich mix is important for a wide variety of wildlife.

BIGGAR GASWORKS MUSEUM   458   8 P27

HS. On the A702 in Biggar, Lanarkshire. Nearest railway station Lanark, bus from Lanark and Edinburgh. Open daily, Jun–Sep 1400–1700. Charge £. Group concessions. Guided tours. Explanatory displays. Picnic area. WC. Wheelchair access with assistance. Car parking. Telephone (01899) 221050. www.historic-scotland.gov.uk

Typical of a small town coal-gas works, the only surviving example in Scotland (dates from 1839). Managed by the Biggar Museum Trust.

BIGGAR KIRK   459   8 P27

High Street, Biggar, Lanarkshire. In the centre of Biggar, 28 miles (45km) south west of Edinburgh, 12 miles (19km) east of M74 junction 13. Nearest railway station Lanark, bus service from Lanark and Edinburgh. Open daily during summer months. Free. Explanatory displays. Induction loop for church services. Car parking. Telephone (01899) 220227.

Cruciform 16th-century church with fine examples of modern stained glass.

BLACK HILL   460   9 N27

NTS. South Lanarkshire. Off B7018 between Kirkfieldbank and Lesmahagow, 3 miles (5km) west of Lanark. Open all year. Free. Explanatory displays. www.nts.org.uk

This is the site of a Bronze Age burial cairn, Iron Age hill fort, and outlook point over the Clyde Valley.

BOTHWELL CASTLE   461   9 M26

HS. Uddingston, near Glasgow. At Uddingston off the B7071, 7 miles (11km) south east of Glasgow. Nearest railway station Uddingston, bus from Glasgow or Hamilton. Open Apr–Sep, daily 0930–1830; Oct–Mar, Mon–Sun (closed Thu and Fri) 0930–1630. Charge £. Group concessions. Explanatory displays. Gift shop. WC. Limited wheelchair access. Car and coach parking. Telephone (01698) 816894. www.historic-scotland.gov.uk

In a picturesque setting above the Clyde valley, the largest and finest 13th-century stone castle in Scotland. Much fought over during the Wars of Independence. Most of the castle dates from the 14th and 15th centuries.

BOTHWELL PARISH CHURCH   462   9 M26

Main Street, Bothwell. On B7071 in centre of Bothwell, 2 miles (3km) from Hamilton. Nearest railway station at Uddingston (1.5 miles/2.5km). Local bus service. Open May–Sep, Mon–Fri 1030–1230 and 1400–1600. Free. Explanatory displays. Gift shop. Wheelchair access with assistance. Car parking. Telephone (01698) 853189.

The oldest collegiate church in Scotland. Choir built in 1398 with stone vaulted roof and knave built in 1833. Beautiful stained-glass windows and embroideries.

CADZOW CASTLE   463   9 M26

HS. Chatelherault Country Park, Hamilton. In the grounds of Chatelherault Country Park, Hamilton, Lanarkshire. Nearest railway and bus stations Hamilton, bus from Hamilton. Access at all reasonable times. View exterior only. Telephone (0131) 5507603. www.historic-scotland.gov.uk

Constructed between 1500 and 1550, the castle was known as 'the castle in the woods of Hamilton'.

CALDERGLEN COUNTRY PARK   464   9 M26

Strathaven Road, East Kilbride, South Lanarkshire. 1 mile (1.5km) from East Kilbride town centre on A726/Strathaven Road. Nearest railway and bus station East Kilbride. Country park open all year at all times. Visitor centre open summer Mon–Fri 1030–1700, weekends and public holidays 1100–1830; winter, daily 1100–1600. Free. Guided tours by arrangement. Explanatory displays. Gift shop. Courtyard café, snack bar and picnic area. Conservatory and children's zoo. WC. Large print text leaflet. Wheelchair access to buildings. Partial access to nature trails. Disabled WC. Car and coach parking. Telephone (01355) 236644.

The park consists of over 440 acres (180ha) of attractive wooded gorge and parkland, including several fine waterfalls. All are accessible by an extensive network of paths and nature trails. Visitor centre, conservatory, ornamental garden, children's zoo, pets' corner, toddlers' play area, adventure and special needs play area centred around the historic Torrance House. Horticultural staff, animal keepers and a countryside ranger service run a year-round programme of activities and events.

CARMICHAEL HERITAGE CENTRE   465   9 N27

Warrenhill Farm, by Biggar. 4 miles (6.5km) south of Lanark on A73. Nearest railway and bus stations Lanark, bus to Biggar. Open all year except Jan and Feb, daily 1000–1700. Farm and gift shop open all year, daily (except Christmas and New Year) 1000–1700. Oct–Mar hours may vary, please telephone to confirm. Charge ££. Group concessions. Guided tours by prior arrangement (available in French and German). Explanatory displays. Gift shop. Restaurant and picnic area. WC. Wheelchair access. Disabled WC. Car and coach parking. Telephone 01899 308336 or 01899 030169. www.carmichael.co.uk

Scotland's only wax model collection tells Scotland's and Carmichael's story using Madame Tussaud quality models. The Clan Centre for southern Scotland concentrates on the Carmichaels who have lived here throughout the Millennium. It also includes information on many other southern Scottish families and clans as well as the history of the estate's agriculture and environment. Wind energy exhibit. Deer park. Venison farm shop. Adventure playground. Animal farm. Heritage walks. Orienteering and way-finding. Ladies Nightingales fashion shop.

CARTLAND BRIDGE   466   9 N26

On A73 west of Lanark. Access at all times. Free.

An impressive bridge built by Telford in 1822 over a gorge, carrying the Mouse Water. It is one of the highest road bridges in Scotland.

CASTLE SEMPLE COLLEGIATE CHURCH   467   9 L26

HS. Castle Semple, Ayrshire, 2 miles (3km) west of Howwood on the B787 then on to the B776. Access at all reasonable times, view exterior only. Telephone (0131) 5507603. www.historic-scotland.gov.uk

A late gothic church with a three-sided east end with windows of an unusual style. See also 473 Clyde Muirshiel, Castle Semple Visitor Centre.

CASTLECARY   468   9 M25

HS. On the B816, east of Castlecary village, Stirlingshire. Nearest railway and bus stations Falkirk. Access at all reasonable times. Free. Telephone (01786) 431326. www.historic-scotland.gov.uk

The reduced earthworks of a fort on the Antonine Wall (see 573).

CHATELHERAULT COUNTRY PARK   469   9 M26

Carlisle Road, Ferniegair, Hamilton. Nearest railway station Ferniegar, bus from Hamilton. Open all year. Visitor centre, Mon–Sat 1000–1700, Sun 1200–1700; Lodge, Mon–Thu and Sat 1030–1630, Sun 1230–1630. Free. Guided tours. Explanatory displays. Gift shop. Tearoom and picnic area. Children's play area. WC. Large print text. Limited wheelchair access. Disabled WC. Car and coach parking. Telephone (01698) 426213.

A magnificent hunting lodge and kennels built in 1732 by William Adam for the Duke of Hamilton, since restored. Extensive country walks. Exhibition on the Clyde Valley, geology and natural history of the park, 18th-century gardens, terraces and parterre.

CLOCH LIGHTHOUSE   470   9 K25

A770, 3 miles (4.5km) south west of Gourock. View exterior only.

This notable landmark stands at Cloch Point with fine views across the upper Firth of Clyde estuary. The white-painted lighthouse was constructed in 1797.

CLYDE MARINE CRUISES   471   9 K25

Victoria Harbour, Greenock. 25 miles (40km) west of Glasgow. Nearest railway station Greenock Central then five minute walk. Sailings all year (Kenilworth); May–Sep (Second Snark). Charges variable. Group concessions. Licensed bar with refreshments. Commentary in English. WC. Car and coach parking. Telephone (01475) 721281. www.clyde-marine.co.uk

Set sail for spectacular west coast scenery on board the *Second Snark*. Day trips to the islands of Arran, Bute, Cumbrae and the highland village of Tighnabruaich via the magnificent scenery of the Kyles of Bute. Frequent sightings of seals, dolphins and porpoises. Departures from Greenock, Helensburgh, Dunoon, Largs, Millport, Rothesay and Tighnabruaich.

CLYDE MUIRSHIEL REGIONAL PARK, BARNBROCK CAMPSITE   472   9 L26

Park headquarters and campsite, Barnbrock, near Lochwinnoch, Renfrewshire. 4 miles (6.5km) north of Lochwinnoch just off B786. Nearest railway and bus service Lochwinnoch. Strathclyde Passenger Transport Ring & Ride service 965 operates to Bambrock. Open all year, Mon–Fri 0900–1630; campsite open Apr–Oct at all times. Free. Charge for camping and wigwams. Guided tours by arrangement. Picnic area. WC. Car and coach parking. Telephone (01505) 614791. www.clydemuirshiel.co.uk

Barnbrock Farm incorporates the headquarters of the Clyde Muirshiel Regional Park. Campsite, wigwams, picnic area and easy access to nearby Locherwood Community Woodland.

CLYDE MUIRSHIEL REGIONAL PARK, CASTLE SEMPLE CENTRE   473   9 L26

Castle Semple Centre, Lochlip Road, Lochwinnoch, Renfrewshire. Just off A760 in Lochwinoch. Nearest railway station Lochwinnoch 1 mile (1.5km) from visitor centre, bus from Glasgow, Paisley or Largs. Open daily, summer months 1000–1900 or dusk, whichever is earlier; winter months 1000–1600. Free. Guided tours. Explanatory displays. Gift shop. Tearoom, picnic areas. WC. Wheelchair access. Disabled WC. Car and coach parking. Telephone (01505) 842882. www.clydemuirshiel.co.uk

The centre is located on the edge of Castle Semple loch. Ranger service, woodland walks and nature trails in Parkhill Wood (formerly part of the Castle Semple Estate). Historical landmarks in the vicinity include Peel Castle, Collegiate Church, grotto, maze and fishponds. Outdoor activities available from the centre (for taught courses, group taster sessions and equipment hire) include kayaking, sailing, rowing boats, trail biking, hill walking, orienteering and archery. Fishing permits are also available. See also 467 Castle Semple Collegiate Church.

CLYDE MUIRSHIEL REGIONAL PARK, CORNALEES CENTRE   474   9 K25

Loch Thom, near Inverkip, Inverclyde. Nearest railway and bus service Greenock (Branchton or Inverkip stations) 3 miles (5km). Open Apr–Oct, daily 1100–1600; Nov–Mar weekends 1100–1500. Free. Guided tours. Explanatory displays. Gift shop. Drinks and snacks available. Picnic and barbecue areas. WC. Wheelchair access. Disabled WC. Car and coach parking. Telephone (01475) 521458 . www.clydemuirshiel.co.uk

By scenic Loch Thom. Stepped boardwalk trails and woodland walks through Sheilhill Glen, access to the Greenock Cut and Kelly Cut for scenic walks and views of the Clyde estuary. Natural and local history exhibitions. Children's nature club, special events, guided walks. Ranger service.

CLYDE MUIRSHIEL REGIONAL PARK, LUNDERSTON BAY   475   9 K25

Lunderston Bay, near Inverkip, Inverclyde. On A78 Gourock to Inverkip road. Nearest railway station Inverkip 2 miles (3km). Open all year, daily. Free. Guided tours. Snack bar, picnic area. Children's play area. WC. Sensory garden. Wheelchair access. Car and coach parking. Telephone (01475) 521129 or 521458. www.clydemuirshiel.co.uk

On the Clyde Coast. The bay offers panoramic views to the Cowal peninsula. Ranger service, coastal walks, rock pools, marine birds and plants, children's play area, beach and picnic spots.

CLYDE MUIRSHIEL REGIONAL PARK, MUIRSHIEL VISITOR CENTRE   476   9 L26

Calder Glen Road, near Lochwinnoch. 4 miles (6.5km) north west of Lochwinnoch, off B786. Nearest railway and bus service Lochwinnoch. Open Apr–Oct, daily 1100–1600; Nov–Mar weekends 1100–1500. Free. Guided tours. Explanatory displays. Gift shop. Drinks and snacks available, picnic and barbecue sites. WC. Wheelchair access. Disabled WC. Car and coach parking. Telephone (01505) 842803 or 842882. www.clydemuirshiel.co.uk

On top of Calder Glen, originally a Victorian sporting estate. Woodland, riverside and waterfall walks along signposted rails, picnic and barbecue sites and boardwalk access to scenic viewpoint, Windy Hill. The area is rich in archaeological sites including a Barytes Mine with much to offer the botanist and ornithologist. Orienteering and navigation courses run throughout the year. Ranger service. Special events.

CLYDEBANK MUSEUM   477   9 L25

Town Hall, Dumbarton Road, Clydebank. 6 miles (10km) north west of Glasgow on A814. Nearest railway stations Clydebank Central and Singer, frequent bus service. Open Tue–Sat 1000–1300 and 1400–1630 all year except public holidays and Christmas period. Free. Guided tours book in advance for groups. Explanatory displays and audio-visual presentation. Gift shop. Refreshments nearby. WC. Wheelchair access. Disabled WC. Car and coach parking. Telephone (01389) 738702.

Community museum describing local social and industrial history. Displays on ship building, the Clydebank blitz, and Singer sewing machines. Please note that exhibitions and opening times may change so please telephone to avoid disappointment.

COATS OBSERVATORY   478   9 L26

49 Oakshaw Street West, Paisley. 7 miles (11km) west of Glasgow. Nearest railway station Paisley Gilmour Street. Open all year, Tue–Sat and bank holidays, 1000–1300 and 1400–1700, Sun 1400–1700. Last entry 15 minutes before closing. Telescope viewing end Oct–Mar, Thu 1900–2100. Free. Groups by prior arrangement. Explanatory displays. Telephone 0141 889 2013.

Designed by John Honeyman, Coats Observatory continues a tradition of astronomical, meteorological and seismic observing which started in 1883. Displays relate to the history and architecture of the building, astronomy and astronautics, meteorology and seismicity.

COLZIUM ESTATE   479   9 M25

Colzium Lennox Estate, Stirling Road, Kilsyth. From Glasgow follow A803 to Kilsyth from where Colzium House is well signposted. Bus from Kilsyth. Open daily, dawn to dusk. Free. WC. Limited wheelchair access. Car and coach parking. Telephone 0141 304 1800. www.northlan.gov.uk

Outstanding collection of conifers and rare trees in a beautifully designed small walled garden. All trees well labelled – excellent for learning the difference between varieties of conifers. Fabulous display of snowdrops and crocuses in spring. Other attractions include a 17th-century ice house, glen walk, 15th-century tower house, arboretum, curling pond, clock theatre and pitch and putt course.

COULTER MOTTE   480   8 N27

HS. Off A72, 2 miles (3km) north of Coulter, 1.5 miles (2.5km) south west of Biggar, Lanarkshire. Nearest railway station Lanark, bus from Edinburgh or Lanark to Biggar. Telephone (0131) 5507603. www.historic-scotland.gov.uk

Early medieval castle mound, originally moated and probably surrounded by a palisade enclosing a timber tower.

CRAIGNETHAN CASTLE   481   9 N26

HS. Blackwood, Lesmahagow, Lanarkshire. 2.5 miles (4km) west of A72 at Crossford, 5 miles (8km) north west of Lanark. Nearest railway station Carluke then bus to Lanark. Bus from Lanark or Hamilton to Crossford then 15 minute walk. Open Apr–Sep, daily 0930–1830; Oct–Mar, Sat–Sun 0930–1630. Charge £. Group concessions. Explanatory displays. Gift shop. Tearoom, open at weekends only. WC. Limited wheelchair access. Car parking. Telephone (01555) 860364. www.historic-scotland.gov.uk

An extensive and well-preserved ruin of an unusual and ornate tower house built by Sir James Hamilton of Finnart in the 16th century. It is defended by an outer wall pierced by gun ports, also by a wide and deep ditch with a most unusual caponier (a stone vaulted chamber for artillery). Attacked and dismantled by the Protestant party in 1579. In a very picturesque setting overlooking the River Nethan.

CROOKSTON CASTLE   482   9 L26

HS. Off Brockburn Road, Pollock, 4 miles (6.5km) south west of Glasgow city centre. Nearest railway station Glasgow Central, bus from Union Street. Open at all reasonable times (see keyholder). Free. Telephone (0131) 5507603. www.historic-scotland.gov.uk

The altered ruin of an unusual 15th-century castle. It consists of a central tower with four square corner towers, set within 12th-century earthworks. Affords excellent views of south west Glasgow.

CROSS OF LORRAINE   483   9 K25

Lyle Hill, Greenock (access via Newton Street). Access at all reasonable times. Free. Car parking.

Monument to the contribution made by the Free French Navy during World War II. The Cross of Lorraine is situated at a popular viewpoint overlooking the Clyde.

CROY HILL   484   9 M25

HS. Between Croy and Dullatur. Access from B802. Nearest railway station Croy. Access at all reasonable times. Free. Telephone (0131) 5507603. www.historic-scotland.gov.uk

The site of a Roman fort (not visible) on the Antonine Wall. Part of the wall ditch can be seen, beside two beacon platforms on the west side of the hill. See also 573 Antonine Wall.

CUMBERNAULD MUSEUM   485   9 M25

Cumbernauld Library, 8 Allander Walk, Cumbernauld. In Cumbernauld town centre. Nearest railway station Cumbernauld, local bus service. Open all year, Mon–Fri 0900–1900 (Wed closes 1200), Sat 0900–1700. Free. Guided tours. Explanatory displays. WC. Wheelchair access. Car and coach parking. Telephone (01236) 725664. www.northlan.gov.uk

Telling the history of Cumbernauld from the setting of a Roman camp, past the fireside chat of a medieval lord, to the parlour of a 1930s miner. Audio-visual techniques bring the past to life.

DALZELL PARK   486   9 M26

Adele Street, Motherwell. Nearest railway station Motherwell, bus from Glasgow. Open from dawn to dusk. Free. Limited wheelchair access. Car and coach parking. Telephone (01698) 266155. www.northlan.gov.uk

Peaceful woodland with spectacular scenery and heritage monuments such as Dalzell House and Lord Gavin's Temple. Wildlife includes woodpeckers, roe deer and squirrels. Ranger service.

DRUMPELLIER COUNTRY PARK   487   9 M26

Townhead Road, Coatbridge. 2 miles (3km) from Coatbridge. By rail to Coatbridge
Sunnyside or Central stations, then bus to park. Park open all year during daylight.
Visitor centre open daily, May and Sep 1100–1730; Jun–Aug 1030–1930; Oct–Apr
1200–1600. Free. Explanatory displays. Ranger guided walks. Gift shop. Tearoom.
WC. Limited wheelchair access. Disabled WC. Car and coach parking. Telephone
(01236) 422257. www.northlan.gov.uk

Five hundred acres (202ha) of woodland, heathland and a loch. There is a visitor
centre, café, ranger service, road train as well as angling, boating, nature trails,
18-hole golf course and driving range, butterfly house, pets' corner,
birdwatching and play areas.

DULLATUR   488   9 M25

HS. Dullatur. 0.6 mile (1km) east of Dullatur off the A803. Nearest railway station
Croy, bus from Glasgow (Buchanan Street). www.historic-scotland.gov.uk

A well-preserved section of ditch. Part of the Antonine wall (see 573).

FALLS OF CLYDE WILDLIFE RESERVE AND VISITOR CENTRE   489   9 N27

The Scottish Wildlife Trust Visitor Centre, New Lanark, Lanarkshire. 30 miles (48km)
south east of Glasgow. Nearest railway station Lanark, bus from Lanark. Open all
year, Mon–Sun 1100–1700. Reserve open daylight hours. Free. Guided tours.
Explanatory displays. Gift shop. Picnic area. WC. Wheelchair access to visitor centre,
partial access to reserve. Disabled WC. Car and coach parking. Telephone (01555)
665262. www.swt.org

The reserve comprises one of Britain's most spectacular waterfalls set in a
mosaic of ancient woodland, meadow and ancient monuments. Over 100 species
of birds have been recorded on the reserve, with unsurpassed views of breeding
peregrine falcons. The visitor centre has a small exhibition with interactive
computers and wildlife-inspired gifts for sale. The ranger service based at the
visitor centre provides a comprehensive events programme, including badger
watches, bat walks, insect expeditions and waterfall day walks.

FINLAYSTONE COUNTRY ESTATE   490   9 L25

Finlaystone Country Estate, Langbank, Renfrewshire. 3 miles (4km) east of Port
Glasgow. Bus service to Langbank. Open all year, daily 1100–1700. Charge ££.
Guided tours for groups and schools must be booked in advance. Explanatory
displays. Gift shop. Tearoom and picnic areas. WC. Scented garden. Limited
wheelchair access. Disabled WC. Car and coach parking. Telephone (01475) 540505.
www.finlaystone.co.uk

Finlaystone Country Estate is a combination of spectacular gardens, with views
overlooking the River Clyde, and mixed woodlands with burn and waterfalls.
Extensive woodland play areas, including a pirate ship, fort and wigwams.

FORTH AND CLYDE CANAL   491   9 M26

The Forth and Clyde Canal flows from Bowling on the River Clyde on Scotland's west
coast, to the town of Grangemouth on the River Carron in the east, joining with the
Union Canal to Edinburgh at the Falkirk Wheel. Excellent links all along the canal's
route. Access at all times to the towpath unless stoppage work prevents access. Free.
Fishing (permits available through Lowland Canals Angling Partnership Scotland),
canoeing, cycling, boat hire, boat trips, guided walks, picnic spots and charity,

British Waterways Scotland and canal society events and activities. Telephone (01324) 671217. www.britishwaterways.co.uk/scotland

The Forth and Clyde Canal (F&C) passes through a whole range of landscapes – tranquil rural and bustling urban – as it nears the heart of the city of Glasgow. There is lots to see and do all along its length and each of the towns it passes through is worth a stop in itself. Sailing the F&C takes visitors right to the doorstep of the magnificent Falkirk Wheel (see 658) which links the F&C with the Union Canal (see 804).

GLADSTONE COURT MUSEUM   492   8 P27

North Back Road, Biggar, Lanarkshire. On the A702, 26 miles (41.5km) south of Edinburgh. Bus from Biggar or Edinburgh. Open Easter–mid Oct, Mon–Sat 1100–1630, Sun 1400–1630. Charge £. Group concessions. Guided tours. Explanatory displays. Gift shop. Activity sheets and hands-on sessions for children. WC. Limited wheelchair access. Car and coach parking. Telephone (01899) 221573.

An indoor street museum of shops and windows. Grocer, photographer, dress maker, bank, school, library, ironmonger, chemist, china merchant, telephone exchange.

GLASGOW ART GALLERY AND MUSEUM, KELVINGROVE   493   9 M26

Kelvingrove, Glasgow. Located in the west end of Glasgow. Nearest railway station Partick, nearest underground station Kelvinhall. Bus service from city centre. Open all year, Mon–Thu and Sat 1000–1700, Fri and Sun 1100–1700. Free. Guided tours. Explanatory displays. Gift shop. Café and picnic area. WC. Wheelchair access. Disabled WC. Car and coach parking. Telephone 0141 287 2699. www.glasgow.gov.uk

This fine national art collection contains superb paintings and sculptures, silver and ceramics, European armour, weapons and firearms, clothing, and furniture. The natural history of Scotland is treated in depth and there are displays of relics from Scotland's history and prehistory. Activities for children and temporary exhibitions. NB: Glasgow Art Gallery and Museum will close for refurbishment, reopening in the summer of 2006. See 510 Glasgow, McLellan Galleries.

GLASGOW, THE BARRAS   494   9 M26

Gallowgate, 0.25 miles (0.5km) east of Glasgow Cross. Open all year, Sat and Sun 0900–1700, Wed–Fri 1000–1600. Free.

Glasgow's world-famous market, with an amazing variety of stalls and shops. Founded one hundred years ago, the Barras is now home to over 800 traders. Look out for the Barras archways, children's crèche and buskers. Numerous licensed premises and cafés. All markets are covered.

GLASGOW, BEARSDEN BATHHOUSE   495   9 L25

HS. On Roman Road, Bearsden, near Glasgow. Nearest railway station Glasgow, bus from city centre. Access at all reasonable times. Free. Wheelchair access with assistance. Telephone (0131) 5507603. www.historic-scotland.gov.uk

The well-preserved remains of a bathhouse and latrine built in the 2nd century AD to serve a fort. See also 573 Antonine Wall.

GLASGOW BOTANIC GARDEN   496   9 L25

730 Great Western Road, Glasgow. At the west end of Glasgow off the A82, 1.5 miles (2.5km) from the city centre. Bus from city centre or underground to Hillhead

station. Open all year, 0700–dusk; glasshouses open 1000–1645 (1615 in winter). Free. Guided tours by arrangement. Explanatory displays. Café. WC. Wheelchair access. Disabled WC. Telephone 0141 334 2422.

The gardens were formed in 1817 to provide a source of plant material for use in teaching medicine and botany. Today they are valued by tourists and as a centre for education, conservation and research. Specialist plant collections include exotic Australian tree and filmy ferns, orchids and tropical begonias.

GLASGOW, THE BURRELL COLLECTION   497   9 L26

Pollok Country Park, 2060 Pollokshaws Road, Glasgow. Nearest railway stations, Pollokshaws West or Shawlands, bus service from city centre. Park bus runs every hour, on the half hour, from front entrance of Pollok Country park to the Burrell. Open all year, Mon–Thu and Sat 1000–1700, Fri and Sun 1100–1700. Free. Guided tours (available in French and German). Explanatory displays. Gift shop. Restaurant and café. WC. Audio guides for visually impaired visitors. Wheelchair access. Disabled WC. Car and coach parking. Telephone 0141 287 2550. www.glasgow.gov.uk

This award-winning building houses a world-famous collection gifted to Glasgow by Sir William Burrell. Visitors can see art objects from Iraq, Egypt, Greece and Italy. Tapestries, furniture, textiles, ceramics, stained glass and sculptures from medieval Europe, and drawings from the 15th to 19th centuries. Regular temporary exhibitions.

GLASGOW CATHEDRAL   498   9 M26

HS. Cathedral Square, Glasgow. At the east end of Cathedral Street. Nearest railway station Glasgow Queen Street, bus from city centre. Open Apr–Sep, Mon–Sat 0900–1800, Sun 1300–1700; Oct–Mar, Mon–Sat 0900–1600, Sun 1400–1600. Free. Gift shop. Limited wheelchair access. Telephone 0141 552 6891. www.historic-scotland.gov.uk

The only Scottish mainland medieval cathedral to have survived the Reformation complete (apart from its western towers). Built during the 12th and 13th centuries over the supposed tomb of St Kentigern. Notable features are the elaborately vaulted crypt, the stone screen and the unfinished Blackadder Aisle. The parish church of Glasgow.

GLASGOW, CLYDEBUILT   499   9 L26

Scottish Maritime Museum at Braehead, King's Inch Road, Glasgow. Located at Braehead shopping centre. Nearest railway station Paisley, regular bus service. Open all year Mon–Sat 1000–1730 and Sun 1100–1730. Charge ££. Group concessions. Guided tours on request. Explanatory displays. Gift shop. Children's play area. WC. Wheelchair access. Disabled WC. Car and coach parking. Telephone 0141 886 1013. www.scottishmaritimemuseum.rg

Clydebuilt tells the history of Glasgow's river, its ships and its people, over the past 300 years. Hands-on and interactive computer activities. Also *Kyles*, the oldest Clyde built ship afloat in the UK.

GLASGOW, COLLINS GALLERY   500   9 M26

University of Strathclyde, 22 Richmond Street, Glasgow. Glasgow city centre. Nearest railway station Glasgow Queen Street, then five minute walk. Open all year Mon–Fri 1000–1700, Sat 1200–1600, closed Sun, public holidays and exhibition changeover weeks. Free. Guided tours by arrangement. Explanatory displays. Gift shop. Refreshments. WC. Wheelchair access. Disabled WC. Telephone 0141 548 2558 or 0141 553 4145. www.strath.ac.uk/culture/collins

Temporary exhibition gallery showing annual programme of ten shows ranging from contemporary, fine and applied art, photography, technology and design, and multi-media installations. Active education programme. Most works are for sale.

GLASGOW, FOSSIL GROVE 501   9 L25

Victoria Park, Glasgow. Nearest railway station Jordanhill, bus from Argyle Street or from Hope Street. Open daily Apr–Sep, 1200–1700. Free. Explanatory displays. Gift shop. WC. Wheelchair access. Disabled WC. Car and coach parking. Telephone 0141 950 1448. www.glasgow.gov.uk

Glasgow's oldest tourist attraction, discovered by accident and now designated a Site of Special Scientific Interest by Scottish National Heritage. Fossil stumps and roots of trees which grew here 350 million years ago.

GLASGOW, GALLERY OF MODERN ART 502   9 M26

Royal Exchange Square, Glasgow. In Glasgow city centre. Nearest railway stations Glasgow Queen Street and Central station; or by underground to Buchanan Street. Open all year (except Christmas and New Year), Mon–Thu and Sat 1000–1700, Fri and Sun 1100–1700. Free. Guided tours. Explanatory displays. Gift shop. Restaurant/tearoom. WC. Wheelchair access. Disabled WC. Telephone 0141 229 1996. www.glasgow.gov.uk

The elegant Royal Exchange building displays works by living artists from across the world. A wide range of contemporary temporary exhibitions plus a programme of events including music, drama, dance and workshops.

GLASGOW, GEORGE SQUARE 503   9 M26

Glasgow city centre. Access at all times. Free.

The heart of Glasgow with the City Chambers and statues of Sir Walter Scott, Queen Victoria, Prince Albert, Robert Burns, Sir John Moore, Lord Clyde, Thomas Campbell, Dr Thomas Graham, James Oswald, James Watt, William Gladstone and Sir Robert Peel.

GLASGOW, GREENBANK GARDEN 504   9 M26

NTS. Flenders Road, Clarkston, Glasgow. Off M77 and A726, 6 miles (10km) south of city centre. By bus from city centre. Open all year except Christmas and New Year, daily 0930–sunset (walled garden closes 1700). Charge ££. Group concessions. Guided tours of garden. Explanatory displays. Gift shop. Tearoom in summer, picnic area. WC. Gardening advice for disabled. Wheelchair access (wheelchairs available). Disabled WC. Car and coach parking. Telephone 0141 639 3281. www.nts.org.uk

Attractive garden surrounding an elegant Georgian house (only open summer, Sunday 1400–1700). Wide range of ornamental plants, annuals, perennials, shrubs and trees – especially interesting for owners of small gardens. Fountain garden and woodland walks.

GLASGOW, HORROR WALKING TOUR 505   9 M26

Tours leave from Glasgow Cathedral, Glasgow. Close to railway and bus stations. Booking line open all year, daily. Charge £££. Group concessions. Wheelchair access. Telephone 0141 586 5378. www.mercat-glasgow.co.uk

A guided horror walk of Glasgow by fully costumed, knowledgable guide. Informative fun.

GLASGOW, HOUSE FOR AN ART LOVER   506   9 L26

Bellahouston Park, 10 Dumbreck Road, Glasgow. 3 miles (5km) south of city centre. Bus from city centre, by underground to Ibrox or train to Dumbreck. Open Apr–Sep, Thur–Sun 1000–1300, Mon–Wed 1000–1600; Oct–Mar, weekends 1000–1300, Mon–Fri by arrangement. Charge ££. Children under 10 free. Group concessions. Guided tours. Explanatory displays. Gift shop. Café/restaurant. WC. Audio loop with video. Wheelchair access. Disabled WC. Car and coach parking. Telephone 0141 353 4770. www.houseforanartlover.co.uk

A house designed in 1901 by Charles Rennie Mackintosh but not built until 1989–96. Exhibition and film showing the construction. Permanant exhibition of Mackintosh rooms. Sculpture park. Situated in parkland adjacent to magnificent Victorian walled gardens.

GLASGOW, HUNTERIAN ART GALLERY   507   9 M26

82 Hillhead Street, Glasgow. In the west end of Glasgow, near Hillhead underground station. Bus or underground from city centre. Open all year, Mon–Sat 0930–1700. Admission to the art gallery is free. Admission to the Mackintosh house is £2.50 with free admission on Wed after 1400. Explanatory displays. Gift shop. Sculpture courtyard. Childrens activities arranged by Hunterian Museum and Art Gallery during Jul and Aug (0141 330 2838). WC. Limited wheelchair access. Disabled WC. Telephone 0141 330 5431.

A prestigious art gallery housing many important works by old masters, impressionists and Scottish paintings from the 18th century to the present day. The William Hunter collection includes works by Chardin, Rembrandt and Koninck. Many important works by Whistler. The print gallery has a changing display from a collection of 15,000 prints. Also houses the Mackintosh House, a reconstructed interior of the architect's own house in Glasgow, using original furniture, prints and designs.

GLASGOW, HUNTERIAN MUSEUM   508   9 M26

University of Glasgow, University Avenue, Glasgow. In the west end of Glasgow. Nearest underground station Hillhead or Kelvinbridge. Open all year (except public holidays), Mon–Sat 0930–1700. Free. Charge for some temporary exhibitions. Explanatory displays. Gift shop. Refreshments in visitor centre. Childrens activities arranged by Hunterian Museum and Art Gallery during Jul and Aug (0141 330 2193). WC. Wheelchair access. Disabled WC. Car parking. Telephone 0141 330 4221. www.hunterian.gla.ac.uk

Scotland's first public museum was established in 1807 based on the vast collections of Dr William Hunter (1718–83). Many items from his valuable collections are on display together with new and exciting additions. See displays of dinosaurs from Scotland, Romans in Scotland, geology, archaeology, the history of science and coins.

GLASGOW, THE LIGHTHOUSE   509   9 M26

The Lighthouse, Scotland's Centre for Architecture, Design, and the City, 11 Mitchell Lane, Glasgow. In city centre, between Buchanan Street and Mitchell Street. Within walking distance of Glasgow Central and Queen Street railway stations, St Enoch and Buchanan Street underground stations, and all city centre buses. Open all year, Mon and Wed–Sat 1030–1700, Tue 1100–1700, Sun 1200–1700. Charge £. Group rates, family tickets and membership available on request. Group concessions. Guided tours. Explanatory displays. Gift shop. Restaurant and café. WC. Wheelchair access. Disabled WC. Car parking. Telephone 0141 221 6362. www.thelighthouse.co.uk

An unrivalled opportunity to experience architecture and design through a changing programme of world-class exhibitions, displays and events. Spanning six floors, The Lighthouse also contains the award-winning Mackintosh Centre, Mackintosh Tower with stunning city views, Wee People's City, design shop and stylish rooftop café/bar.

GLASGOW, MCLELLAN GALLERIES   510   9 M26

270 Sauchiehall Street, Glasgow. Nearest railway station Queen Street, nearest underground station Cowcaddens. Open for temporary exhibitions only, telephone for details. Charges vary. Explanatory displays. Gift shop. WC. Wheelchair access. Disabled WC. Telephone 0141 565 4100. www.glasgow.gov.uk

This purpose-built exhibition gallery which opened in 1854 provides Glasgow with a superb temporary exhibition venue, the largest outside London.

GLASGOW, MARTYRS' SCHOOL   511   9 M26

Parsons Street, Glasgow. In centre of Glasgow, close to bus and train stations. Car parking nearby. Open all year, Mon–Sat 1000–1700, Sun 1100–1600. Free. WC. Limited wheelchair access. Disabled WC. Telephone 0141 271 8301. www.glasgowmuseums.com

One of the earliest buildings by Charles Rennie Mackintosh, commissioned in 1895. Although some of the building is used as offices for Glasgow's museum staff, much of the building is open to the public.

GLASGOW, MUSEUM OF TRANSPORT   512   9 M26

Kelvin Hall, 1 Bunhouse Road, Glasgow. Located in the west end of Glasgow. Nearest railway station Partick, nearest underground station Kelvinhall. Bus service from city centre. Open all year, Mon–Thu and Sat 1000–1700; Fri and Sun 1100–1700. Free. Guided tours. Explanatory displays. Gift shop. Café. WC. Wheelchair access. Disabled WC. Car and coach parking. Telephone 0141 287 2720. www.glasgow.gov.uk

The history of transport on land and sea with vehicles from horse-drawn carriages to motor cycles, fire engines, railway engines, steam and motor cars. The Clyde Room contains ship models. Also a recreated Glasgow street circa 1938, and a reconstructed underground station.

GLASGOW, NECROPOLIS   513   9 M26

Castle Street, behind Glasgow Cathedral. Access restricted: contact Cemeteries and Cremations, Port Dundas Place, Glasgow. Telephone 0141 287 3961.

Remarkable and extensive burial ground laid out in 1833, with numerous elaborate tombs of 19th-century illustrious Glaswegians and others; of particular interest is the Menteith Mausoleum of 1842.

GLASGOW, PEOPLE'S PALACE   514   9 M26

Glasgow Green, Glasgow. Nearest railway station Central and Queen Street, bus from city centre. Open all year, Mon–Thu and Sat 1000–1700, Fri and Sun 1100–1700. Free. Guided tours. Explanatory displays. Gift shop. Café. Winter Garden. WC. Wheelchair access. Disabled WC. Car and coach parking. Telephone 0141 554 0223. www.glasgow.gov.uk

Opened in 1898, this collection displays the story of Glasgow and its people, and its impact on the world from 1175 to the present day. Important collections relating to the tobacco and other industries, stained glass, ceramics, political and social movements including temperance, co-operation, woman's suffrage and socialism. Photographs, film sequences and reminiscences bring to life the city's past.

GLASGOW, POLLOK HOUSE   515   9 L26

NTS. Pollok Country Park, 2060 Pollokshaws Road, Glasgow. Off M77, 3 miles (5km) south of Glasgow city centre. Nearest railway stations Pollokshaws West or Shawlands, frequent buses from city centre. Open all year, daily 1000–1700 (closed Christmas). Charge £££. Group concessions. Guided tours by arrangement. Explanatory displays. Gift shop. Restaurant. WC. Limited wheelchair access. Car and coach parking. Telephone 0141 616 6410. www.nts.org.uk

The house was built in 1740 and extended in 1890 by Sir John Stirling Maxwell. Set within Pollok Country Park (not NTS), the house contains a renowned collection of paintings and furnishings appropriate for an Edwardian country house. Fascinating servants quarters.

GLASGOW, PROVAND'S LORDSHIP   516   9 M26

3 Castle Street, Glasgow. Opposite St Mungo's Museum. Nearest railway and bus stations in city centre. Open all year (except Christmas and New Year) Mon–Thu and Sat 1000–1700, Fri and Sun 1100–1700. Free. Guided tours by arrangement. Explanatory displays. Limited wheelchair access. Car and coach parking. Telephone 0141 552 8819. www.glasgow.gov.uk

The oldest dwelling in Glasgow, built in 1471 as a manse for the St Nicholas Hospital, just opposite Glasgow Cathedral. Period displays and furniture. Tranquil recreated medieval/renaissance herb garden. See 520 Glasgow, St Mungo's Museum for facilities.

GLASGOW, QUEEN'S CROSS CHURCH   517   9 M25

870 Garscube Road, Glasgow. 0.5 mile (1km) west of city centre. Bus from city centre. Open all year, Mon–Fri 1000–1700, Sun 1400–1700; Nov–Feb closed Sun. Charge £. Children free. Guided tours by arrangement. Gift shop. Refreshments. WC. Wheelchair access with assistance. Car parking. Telephone 0141 946 6600. www.crmsociety.com

The only church designed by Charles Rennie Mackintosh and now the headquarters of the Charles Rennie Mackintosh Society, which has extensively restored the building. Built 1897–9 in a perpendicular Gothic style. Reference library and specialist shop.

GLASGOW, ROUKEN GLEN   518   9 L26

Thornliebank, south Glasgow. Access at all reasonable times. Free. Information centre. Restaurant and tearoom. WC. Limited wheelchair access. Telephone 0141 577 3913.

One of Glasgow's most attractive parks with lovely shaded walks and a waterfall. Children's playground, boating pond and garden centre.

GLASGOW, ROYAL HIGHLAND FUSILIERS REGIMENTAL MUSEUM   519   9 M26

518 Sauchiehall Street, Glasgow. In Charing Cross area of Glasgow. Bus from city centre. Open all year, Mon–Thu 0830–1630, Fri 0830–1600. Free. Guided tours. Explanatory displays. Gift shop. WC. Induction loop. Wheelchair access with assistance. Disabled WC. Car parking. Telephone 0141 332 0961. www.rhf.org.uk

A museum exhibiting medals, badges, uniforms and records which illustrate the histories of The Royal Scots Fusiliers, The Highland Light Infantry, the Royal Highland Fusiliers and Princess Margaret's Own Glasgow and Ayrshire Regiment.

GLASGOW, ST MUNGO MUSEUM OF RELIGIOUS LIFE AND ART   520   9 M26

2 Castle Street, Glasgow. Next to Glasgow Cathedral. Nearest railway station Glasgow Queen Street, bus from city centre. Open daily (except Christmas and New Year), Mon–Thu and Sat 1000–1700, Fri and Sun 1100–1700. Free. Guided tours. Explanatory displays. Gift shop. Restaurant. Zen garden. WC. Wheelchair access. Disabled WC. Telephone 0141 553 2557. www.glasgow.gov.uk

A unique museum exploring the universal themes of life, death and the hereafter through beautiful and evocative art objects associated with different religious faiths. Three galleries focus on art, world religions and religion in Scottish history. Includes Britain's only authentic Japanese Zen garden.

GLASGOW SCHOOL OF ART   521   9 M26

167 Renfrew Street, Glasgow. In Glasgow city centre, 10-15 minute walk from both railway stations. Entry by guided tour only. Tours run all year, Mon–Fri 1100 and 1400, Sat 1030 and 1130. Additional tours Jul–Sep, Sat–Sun 1030, 1130 and 1300. Depending on demand, extra tours are often run during this period. Telephone for further information. Charge ££. Children under 10 free. Group concessions. Guided tours. Gift shop. Café. WC. Limited wheelchair access. Disabled WC. Telephone 0141 353 4526. www.gsa.ac.uk

The Glasgow School of Art is Charles Rennie Mackintosh's architectural masterpiece. Still a working art school, the Mackintosh building continues to be admired and respected and has taken its place as one of the most influential and significant structures of the 20th century. Regular guided tours let you experience this famous and fascinating art school.

GLASGOW, SCIENCE CENTRE   522   9 M26

50 Pacific Quay, Glasgow. On the south bank of the River Clyde, across from SECC. Take junction 24 off M8 and follow brown tourist signs. From M77, stay in left hand lane as motorway merges with M8, exit at junction 21 and follow brown tourist signs. Nearest underground Ibrox or Cessnock, by bus from city centre, or rail to SECC and walk over Bells Bridge or Millennium Bridge. Open Apr–Oct, daily 1000–1800; Nov–Mar, Tue–Sun 1000–1800. Charge £££ (joint ticket for Science Centre and IMAX(r) theatre available). Group concessions. Explanatory displays. Gift shop. Tearoom. WC. Interpretation facilities for deaf and blind visitors. Theatres fitted with induction loops. Wheelchair access. Disabled WC. Car and coach parking. Telephone 0141 420 5000. www.glasgowsciencecentre.org

The award-winning Glasgow Science Centre (GSC) is one of Scotland's must-see visitor attractions. GSC encapsulates the world of science and technology in new, fun and exciting ways. With hundreds of interactive exhibits based over three floors, the Science Mall also offers live science shows, workshops and demonstrations, as well as the Climate Change Theatre and the ScottishPower Planetarium, one of the finest planetariums in the world. Scotland's only IMAX(r) Theatre shows film in both 2D and 3D large-format that will amaze and astound visitors. With a screen the height of five double-decker buses and a 12,000 watt sound system, the IMAX(r) gives visitors a unique view of the world.

GLASGOW, SCOTLAND STREET SCHOOL MUSEUM   523   9 M26

225 Scotland Street, Glasgow. 1 mile (2km) south of the city centre, opposite Shields Road underground station. Open daily excluding public holidays, Mon–Thu and Sat 1000–1700, Fri and Sun 1100–1700. Free. Guided tours. Explanatory displays. Gift shop. Vending machines. WC. Wheelchair access. Disabled WC. Car and coach parking. Telephone 0141 287 0500.

A magnificent building with twin leaded towers and Glasgow style stone carving designed by Charles Rennie Mackintosh in 1904. Now housing a permanent exhibition on the history of education. There are Victorian, World War II, 1950s and 1960s classrooms, a drill hall and an Edwardian cookery room. Regularly changing exhibitions include subjects such as other cultures, Mackintosh, art, craft, and exhibitions designed for children. Activity sessions. The museum is run by Glasgow City Council.

GLASGOW, SCOTTISH FOOTBALL MUSEUM   524   9 M26

Hampden Park, Letherby Drive, Glasgow. Mount Florida area in the south of Glasgow off B768. Nearest railway station Mount Florida, Glasgow, bus service from city centre. Open all year, Mon–Sat 1000–1700, Sun 1100–1700 (closed subject to events). Charge ££. Additional charge for stadium tour (booking advised). Guided tours. Explanatory displays. Gift shop. Tearoom. WC. Wheelchair access. Disabled WC. Car and coach parking. Telephone 0141 616 6104. www.scottishfootballmuseum.org.uk

Over 2500 items and interactive areas in 14 galleries, admission includes entry into the Scottish Football Hall of Fame. Stadium tours also available. Experience the stadium as players do on matchdays–underground roadway, changing rooms, players tunnel and out to pitchside–and test the speed of your shot in the warm up area

GLASGOW, THE TALL SHIP AT GLASGOW HARBOUR   525   9 M26

100 Stobcross Road, Glasgow. From Glasgow city centre, follow signs for SECC West off Clydeside Expressway. Nearest railway station Finnieston/Exhibition Centre. Open all year daily, Mar–Oct 1000–1700; Nov–Feb 1000–1600. Charge ££. Child free with paying adult. Group concessions. Guided tours on request. Explanatory displays. Gift shop. Restaurant and picnic area. Children's activities. WC. Wheelchair access with assistance. Disabled WC. Car and coach parking. Telephone 0141 222 2513. www.thetallship.com

Glasgow's maritime heritage is brought to life at the Tall Ship at Glasgow Harbour, home to the *Glenlee* (1896). Exhibitions and children's activities.

GLASGOW, TENEMENT HOUSE   526   9 M26

NTS. 145 Buccleuch Street, Glasgow. A short walk from both city centre railway stations. Open Mar–Oct, daily 1300–1700. Charge ££. Group concessions. Guided tours by arrangement. Explanatory displays. Guidebook available in French and German. WC. Braille guide, audio tour. Disabled WC. Telephone 0141 333 0183. www.nts.org.uk

A typical late Victorian Glasgow tenement flat, retaining many original features. The furniture and possessions of the woman who lived here for 50 years give a fascinating glimpse of life in the early 20th century. Exhibition on ground floor about tenement life.

GLASGOW, THE NATIONAL PIPING CENTRE   527   9 M26

30-34 McPhater Street, Cowcaddens, Glasgow. In city centre, five–ten minute walk
from railway stations and close to the Royal Scottish Academy of Music and Drama.
Five minute walk from Buchanan bus station, two minute walk from Cowcaddens
underground. Museum open all year, daily 1000–1600. Café bar open all year,
Mon–Sat 0800–2200; Jun–Sep, Sun 0800–1800. Charge £. Group concessions.
Guided tours (recordings in French, German or Italian). Explanatory displays. Gift
shop. Café. WC. Wheelchair access with assistance. Disabled WC. Telephone 0141 353
0220. www.thepipingcentre.co.uk

A national and international centre of excellence for the bagpipes and their
music, incorporating a school with rehearsal rooms and a performance hall, a
museum and interpretation centre, a reference library and conference facilities.
Housed in a fine listed building.

GLASGOW, VICTORIA PARK   528

See 501 Glasgow, Fossil Grove.

GLASGOW, WAVERLEY PADDLE STEAMER   529   9 M26

Glasgow Science Centre, Glasgow. Nearest railway station Glasgow city centre or
Cessnock. Buses from city centre. Sailings from Easter–Oct, various times.
Telephone for full details of departure points and times. Charge £££. Group
concessions. Explanatory displays. Some tours have inclusive commentary. Gift
shop. Bar meals and light refreshments. Baby changing facilities. WC. Limited
wheelchair access. Disabled WC. Car and coach parking. Telephone (0845) 1304647.
www.waverleyexcursions.co.uk

Historically one of the most interesting vessels still in operation in the country,
the *Waverley* is the last paddle steamer to be built for service on the Clyde, and is
now the last sea-going paddle steamer in the world. A variety of cruises from
Glasgow and Ayr along the Clyde coast.

GLASGOW, WILLOW TEA ROOMS   530   9 M26

217 Sauchiehall Street, Glasgow. In precinct area above Henderson the Jeweller.
Open all year, except Christmas Day and 1–2 Jan, Mon–Sat 0930–1630, Sun and bank
holidays 1200–1600. Free. Gift shop. Restaurant. High chairs available. WC.
Telephone 0141 332 0521. www.willowtearooms.co.uk

The Willow Tea Rooms are housed in an original Charles Rennie Mackintosh
building, designed for Miss Cranston 1904–28. Re-opened in 1983, the tearoom
still has the original glass and mirror work and doors, and functions as a
restaurant serving light meals, teas and coffees.

GREENHILL COVENANTER HOUSE   531   8 P27

Burnbraes, Biggar, Lanarkshire. In Biggar, on the A702, 26 miles (41.5km) from
Edinburgh. Bus from Edinburgh or Lanark. Open May–Sep, Sat–Sun 1400–1630, at
other times by appointment. Charge £. Group concessions. Guided tours.
Explanatory displays. Picnic area. Garden. Children's activity sheets. Limited
wheelchair access. Car and coach parking. Telephone (01899) 221572.

Farmhouse, rescued in a ruinous condition and rebuilt at Biggar, 10 miles
(16km) from its original site. Exhibits include relics of local Covenanters,
Donald Cargill's bed (1681), 17th-century furnishings and costume dolls.

HAMILTON PARK RACECOURSE   532   9 M26

Bothwell Road, Hamilton, . On A723, 10 miles (16km) south of Glasgow, accessed from M74, junction 5 and M8, junction 6. Nearest railway station at Hamilton. Charge £££. Children under 16 free. Group concessions. Restaurants. WC. Wheelchair access (special viewing area, lifts to all levels). Disabled WC. Car and coach parking. Telephone (01698) 283806. www.hamilton-park.co.uk

A world of manicured lawns and leafy paddocks. The course hosts flat racing from April through to September, and the summer evening meetings are popular social occasions. Grandstand and grounds available for hire.

JOHN HASTIE MUSEUM   533   9 M26

8 Threestanes Road, Strathaven, Lanarkshire. On the A726, 6 miles (10km) south of East Kilbride, beside Strathaven Park. Bus from East Kilbride and Hamilton. Coach parking nearby. Open Apr–Sep, daily 1230–1630. Free. Guided tours by arrangement. Explanatory displays. Gift shop. Adjacent to Strathaven Park. Wheelchair access with assistance. Telephone (01357) 521257.

A local history museum with displays on the town, weaving, commerce, Covenanters, ceramics. Temporary display gallery.

HM CUSTOMS AND EXCISE MUSEUM AND EXHIBITION   534   9 K25

Custom House, Custom House Quay, Greenock. 25 miles (40km) west of Glasgow, two minute walk from Greenock station. Open all year (closed some bank holidays), Mon–Fri 1000–1600. Free. Guided tours. Explanatory displays. WC. Disabled WC. Car parking. Telephone (01475) 881450.

A magnificent building which has been used a customs office since its completion in 1819. The museum shows the diverse and colourful history of the organisation and highlights the great variety of work undertaken by the department.

HOLMWOOD HOUSE   535   9 M26

NTS. 61-63 Netherlee Road, Glasgow. Off B767 in Cathcart, Glasgow. Nearest railway station Cathcart, frequent buses from Glasgow city centre. Open Apr–Oct, daily 1200–1700. Charge ££. Groups must pre-book. Group concessions. Guided tours by arrangement (audio tour in French and German). Explanatory displays. Grounds, riverside walk. WC. Induction loop. Adapted audio tour for visitors with learning difficulties. Wheelchair access. Disabled WC. Car and coach parking. Telephone 0141 637 2129. www.nts.org.uk

Alexander Greek Thomson, Glasgow's greatest Victorian architect, designed this villa for a local mill owner in 1857. Many rooms are richly ornamented in wood, plaster and marble and visitors can see in progress the restoration of Thomson's original stencilled decoration and elaborate friezes.

HUNTER HOUSE   536   9 M26

Maxwelton Road, Calderwood, East Kilbride. 3 miles (4.5km) east of East Kilbride town centre. Nearest railway station East Kilbride, bus from town centre. Open Apr–Sep, daily 1230–1630. Free. Guided tours by arrangement. Explanatory displays with interactive computers and touch table. Gift shop. Tearoom. Soft play area. WC. Large print text. Wheelchair access. Disabled WC. Car and coach parking. Telephone (01355) 261261.

An exhibition about the lives of John and William Hunter, pioneering 18th-century medical surgeons. Audio-visual presentation on East Kilbride new town.

INTERNATIONAL PURVES PUPPETS   537   8 P27

Biggar Puppet Theatre, Broughton Road, Biggar, South Lanarkshire. Bus from Edinburgh or Hamilton, nearest railway station Lanark. Open all year round for group bookings and public shows but please telephone or check website for scheduled performances. . Charge £££. Guided tours £ (please book). Group concessions. Guided tours (also available in French). Explanatory displays. Gift shop. Tearoom and picnic area. Play area, gardens and pets' corner. WC. Wheelchair access (telephone to confirm for theatre performances). Disabled WC. Car and coach parking. Telephone (01899) 220631. www.purvespuppets.com

A unique Victorian puppet theatre seating 100 and set in beautiful grounds. Ultraviolet spectacular puppet performances, large-scale puppets, secret passages and magical starry ceiling. Regular performances in many languages for all ages. Backstage and museum tours.

KEMPOCK STONE   538   9 K25

Castle Mansions of Gourock. Access at all reasonable times. Free.

Granny Kempock's stone, of grey schist 6 feet (2m) high, was probably significant in prehistoric times. In past centuries it was used by fishermen in rites to ensure fair weather. Couples intending to wed used to encircle the stone to get Granny's blessing.

LEADHILLS AND WANLOCKHEAD RAILWAY   539   8 N28

The Station, Leadhills, South Lanarkshire. 6 miles (9.5km) from M74, junction 13 or 14. Car parking, limited coach parking by arrangement. Nearest railway station Sanquhar or Lanark, then bus. Open May–Oct, Sat–Sun 1100–1700. Charge £. Members free. Group concessions. Guided tours. Gift shop. Picnic area. WC in village. Wheelchair access with assistance. Telephone (01555) 820778. www.leadhillsrailway.co.uk

Britain's highest adhesion railway, reaching 1498 feet (456.5m) above sea level. Originally built in 1900 for the transport of refined lead to central Scotland. Today the railway runs through picturesque countryside. The diesel-hauled journey takes approximately 25 minutes. Steam weekend in July/August. See also 540 Leadhills Miner's Library and Reading Room.

LEADHILLS MINER'S LIBRARY AND READING ROOM   540   8 N28

15 Main Street, Leadhills, Lanarkshire. On the B797, south of Abington; take junction 13 (Abington) from M74. Nearest railway station Lanark, bus service from Lanark. Open May–Sep, Wed, Sat and Sun 1400–1600. Charge £. Explanatory displays. Car and coach parking. Telephone (01659) 74456. www.lowtherhills.fsnet.co.uk

The lead miner's subscription library established in 1741 with rare books, detailed 18th-century mining documents, and local records and history. Public park. See also 539 Leadhills and Wanlockhead Railway.

DAVID LIVINGSTONE CENTRE   541   9 M26

NTS. 165 Station Road, Blantyre, Glasgow. Off the A724 in Blantyre, within walking distance of Blantyre station. Open Easter–24 Dec, Mon–Sat 1000–1700 and Sun 1230–1700. Charge ££. Explanatory displays. Gift shop. Tearoom. Playground, riverside walks. WC. Limited wheelchair access. Disabled WC. Car and coach parking. Telephone (01698) 823140. www.nts.org.uk

In the tenement where Livingstone was born. Displays chart his life, from his childhood in the Blantyre mills to his exploration of Africa.

LOCHWINNOCH RSPB NATURE RESERVE 542   9 L26

RSPB. Largs Road, Lochwinnoch, Renfrewshire. South west of Glasgow on A737 Irvine road, near Lochwinnoch village. Lochwinnoch railway station adjacent to reserve, for bus services telephone reserve. Visitor centre open all year daily, 1000–1700 (except Christmas and New Year). Reserve open at all times. Charge £. RSPB members free. Charge for some events. Guided tours as per events schedule or by prior arrangement. Explanatory displays. Gift shop. Light snacks available, picnic area. Wildlife garden, birdwatching hides. WC. Wheelchair access. Disabled WC. Car and coach parking. Telephone (01505) 842663. www.rspb.org.uk/scotland

A varied nature reserve encompassing marshland, open water and woodland. A range of wildlife can be seen all year round, including great-crested grebes and the elusive otter. The visitor centre, with telescopes and reading material, will help visitors get the most from their visit.

LOW PARKS MUSEUM 543   9 M26

129 Muir Street, Motehill, Hamilton, Lanarkshire. Off junction 6 on the M74. Nearest railway station Hamilton, bus from Glasgow. Open all year, Mon–Sat 1000–1700, Sun 1200–1700. Free. Guided tours. Explanatory displays. Gift shop. Garden. WC. Large print text. Wheelchair access. Disabled WC. Car and coach parking. Telephone (01698) 328232.

Combines the former Hamilton District Museum with the Cameronians (Scottish Rifles) Regimental Museum. Displays on the Hamilton Estate and settlement in the area, coal mining, textiles, agriculture, covenantors and Cameronians (Scottish Rifles) Regiment. Changing exhibition programme and activities. Tours of Hamilton Mausoleum.

MACKINNON MILLS 544   9 M26

Kirkshaws Road, Coatbridge, North Lanarkshire. Just off the A8, 10 miles (16km) east of Glasgow. Nearest railway station Whifflet, bus from Glasgow. Open all year, daily; Jan–Nov, Mon–Fri 1000–1730, Sat–Sun 1000–1800; Dec 0900–1800. Free. Explanatory displays. Gift shop. Refeshments from snacks to three-course meals available. WC. Wheelchair access. Disabled WC. Car and coach parking. Telephone (01236) 440702. www.ewm.co.uk

Mackinnon Mills offers factory shopping – classic and fashion knitwear, designer label garments, co-ordinated casuals and everything for the golfer. Also gift department.

MCLEAN MUSEUM AND ART GALLERY 545   9 K25

15 Kelly Street, Greenock, Renfrewshire. At the west end of Greenock close to rail and bus stations. By rail or bus from Glasgow, railway station Greenock. Open all year (except national and local public holidays) Mon–Sat 1000–1700. Free. Guided tours by arrangement. Explanatory displays. Gift shop. Small garden with seats. WC. Wheelchair access except top floor. Disabled WC. Telephone (01475) 715624.

A museum showing local history, maritime exhibits, ethnography, Egyptology, big game mounts and fine art. Also items relating to James Watt. Programme of temporary exhibitions in the art galleries.

MOAT PARK HERITAGE CENTRE 546   8 P27

Kirkstyle, Biggar, Lanarkshire. In Biggar. Bus from Edinburgh. Open Easter–mid Oct, Mon–Sat 1100–1630, Sun 1400–1630. Charge £. Group concessions. Guided tours. Explanatory displays. Gift shop. Picnic area. Children's activity sheets. WC.

Blind visitors may handle artefacts by arrangement. Limited wheelchair access. Disabled WC. Car parking. Telephone (01899) 221050.

A former church adapted to display the history of the Upper Clyde and Tweed Valleys, from the days of the volcano and the glacier to the present. A fine collection of embroidery, including the largest known patchwork cover containing over 80 figures from the 1850s. Archaeology collection.

MOTHERWELL CONCERT HALL AND THEATRE   547   9 M26

Civic Centre, Motherwell. Off junction 6 on M74, then to Airles Road to town centre. Nearest railway station Motherwell. Telephone to confirm times and charges which are dependent on performances. Bar and refreshments. WC. Wheelchair access. Disabled WC. Car and coach parking. Telephone (01698) 302993. www.northlan.gov.uk

The refurbished Theatre and Concert Hall at the Civic Centre is the venue for performances by some of the finest and foremost stars of theatre, television and stage. Doubles as Motherwell Moviehouse showing a programme of popular films.

MOTHERWELL HERITAGE CENTRE   548   9 M26

1 High Road, Motherwell. Opposite library in Motherwell. Off junction 6 on M74, then to Hamilton Road to town centre. Nearest railway station Motherwell, then five minute walk. Regular bus service. Open all year, Mon–Sat 1000–1700 (Thu closes 1900) Sun 1200–1700; closed 25–26 Dec and 1 Jan. Free. Guided tours on request. Explanatory displays. Gift shop. Tearoom. Garden. WC. Wheelchair access. Disabled WC. Car and coach parking. Telephone (01698) 251000. www.northlan.gov.uk

A superb new heritage attraction, telling the story of the Motherwell area from Roman times to the present day. Visit the Technopolis interactive media display and walk through time to see the industrial heyday of the area, social and political upheavals and the development of the modern town. Family history research room, exhibition gallery and special events programme.

MUGDOCK COUNTRY PARK   549   9 L25

Craigallian Road, Milngavie, Glasgow. 10 miles (16km) north of Glasgow. Nearest railway station Milngavie, bus from Glasgow. Summer shuttle to visitor centre from railway station. Open daily all year (except Christmas Day). Free. Charge for events and barbecue hire. Castle tours on request. Explanatory displays. Countryside events programme. Gift shop. Tearoom, picnic and barbecue areas. WC. Tactile map. Wheelchair access. Disabled WC. Car and coach parking. Telephone 0141 956 6100. www.mugdock-country-park.org.uk

Seven hundred acres (260ha) of beautiful countryside – lakes, woodland and moorland. Mugdock and Craigend Castles. Countryside events – orienteering, archery, cycling and bridle ways. Visitor centre, garden centre, craft shops, play areas, walks and Victorian walled garden

MUSEUM OF SCOTTISH COUNTRY LIFE   550   9 M26

Philipshill Road, Wester Kittochside, East Kilbride, South Lanarkshire. Nearest railway stations East Kilbride (3 miles/5km), or Hairmyres (1 mile/1.6km), regular bus service from Glasgow. Open all year, daily 1000–1700. Charge £. Children 12 and under free. NMS and NTS Members free (excluding some special events). Guided tours. Explanatory displays. Gift shop. Café and picnic area. WC. Induction loop in lecture theatre. Limited wheelchair access. Disabled WC. Car and coach parking. Telephone (01355) 224181. www.nms.ac.uk

This unique museum offers visitors an insight into the working lives of people in rural Scotland and shows how the countryside was once worked by generations of farmers. Built on a 170 acres (69ha) farm, the museum houses the National Country Life Collection. There is also an events area and the original Georgian farmhouse and steading. The farm follows a pattern of seasonal work to show ploughing, seed time, haymaking and harvest. Special events are held throughout the year.

NEW LANARK WORLD HERITAGE SITE   551   9 N27

New Lanark Mills, Lanark. Less than 1 hour from Glasgow (M74) and Edinburgh (A70). 1 mile (2km) south of Lanark. Nearest railway station Lanark, then local bus service. Open all year, daily 1100–1700. Closed Christmas Day and New Year. Charge £££. Group concessions. Guided tours. Explanatory displays. Gift shop. Tearoom and picnic areas. Children's play area, hotel and self-catering accommodation. WC. Induction loop for dark ride and audio-visual show. Wheelchair access with assistance. Disabled WC. Car and coach parking. Telephone (01555) 661345. www.newlanark.org

Long famous as a beauty spot and the site of Robert Owen's (1771–1858) social and educational reforms, this 18th-century cotton mill village is Scotland's latest UNESCO World Heritage Site, carefully restored as a living community, with award-winning visitor centre and hotel. Highlights include a futuristic dark ride and a theatre show. Other attractions include working textile machinery, historic classroom, Saving New Lanark exhibition, interactive gallery, millworker's house, village store and Robert Owen's house. The village is surrounded by native woodlands, now protected as a wildlife reserve. See 489 Falls of Clyde Wildlife Reserve and Visitor Centre.

NEWARK CASTLE   552   9 L25

HS. Port Glasgow, Renfrewshire. On the A8 in Port Glasgow, Renfrewshire. Nearest railway and bus station Port Glasgow, then 15 minute walk. Open Apr–Sep, daily 0930–1830. Charge £. Group concessions. Gift shop. WC. Limited wheelchair access. Car and coach parking. Telephone (01475) 741858. www.historic-scotland.gov.uk

A large turreted mansion house in a remarkably good state of preservation, with a 15th-century tower, a courtyard and hall.

OLD PARISH CHURCH, HAMILTON   553   9 M26

Strathmore Road, Hamilton. In the centre of town, five minute walk from railway and bus stations. Nearest railway and bus stations Hamilton. Open all year, Mon–Fri 1030–1530, Sat 1030–1200, Sun after the 1045 service. Evenings by appointment. Free. Guided tours. Refreshments by arrangement. WC. Induction loop. Limited wheelchair access. Disabled WC. Car and coach parking. Telephone (01698) 281905. www.hope.fsnet.co.uk

The oldest building in Hamilton, a Georgian masterpiece designed by William Adam 1732–34, and the only church designed by him. The roof timbers are full of lead shot as Adam used timbers from an old man of war. Embroidery work by Hannah Frew Paterson and exceptionally detailed engraved glass windows depicting the history of church, by Anita Pate. Well-preserved and maintained 11th-century Netherton Cross and Covenanting memorials.

PAISLEY ABBEY   554   9 L26

Abbey Close, Paisley, Renfrewshire. In central Paisley. Nearest railway station Paisley Gilmour Street. Open all year, Mon–Sat 1000–1530, Sun for services only (1100, 1215 and 1830). Free. Guided tours by arrangement. Explanatory displays. Gift shop. Tearoom. WC. Induction loop system. Wheelchair access with assistance. Disabled WC. Telephone 0141 889 7654. www.paisleyabbey.org.uk

A fine Cluniac abbey church founded in 1163. Some 12th-century walls remain, but most of the nave dates from the 14th and 15th centuries. The transept and choir lay in ruins from 16th to 19th centuries, but are now fully restored. Fine medieval carvings in St Mirin Chapel. Also tombs of Princess Marjory Bruce and King Robert III in the choir. Fine stained glass and Cavaille-Coll Organ. The Abbey contains the Barochan Cross, a weathered Celtic cross attributed to the 10th century. See also 849 Brechin Cathedral Round Tower.

PAISLEY MUSEUM AND ART GALLERIES   555   9 L26

High Street, Paisley. In Paisley centre. Nearest railway station Paisley Gilmour Street. Open all year Tue–Sat 1000–1700, Sun 1400–1700, public holidays 1000–1700. Free. Explanatory displays. Gift shop. WC. Limited wheelchair access. Disabled WC.

Displays a world-famous collection of Paisley shawls. Also the local, industrial and natural history of Paisley and Renfrewshire. Important ceramic collection and many 19th-century Scottish paintings.

PALACERIGG COUNTRY PARK   556   9 M25

Palacerigg Road, Cumbernauld, Glasgow. 3 miles (5km) east of Cumbernauld. Nearest railway station Cumbernauld, then 1.5 mile (2.5km) walk to park, bus from Glasgow to Cumbernauld, but no link to park. Visitor centre open all year, Apr–Sep 1000–1800; Oct–Mar 1000–1630. Free. Explanatory displays. Gift shop. Tearoom and picnic areas. WC. Limited wheelchair access. Disabled WC. Car and coach parking. Telephone (01236) 720047. www.northlan.gov.uk

A 700 acre (283ha) country park with a Scottish and north European animal collection. Home to populations of roe deer, owls, bison, wildcat, lynx and moufflon. Approximately 7 miles (11km) of nature trails and bridle paths. Eighteen-hole golf course. Ranger service.

ST BRIDE'S CHURCH, DOUGLAS   557   8 N27

HS. In Douglas, 12 miles (19km) south south-west of Lanark. Nearest railway station Lanark, bus from Lanark. Open at all reasonable times (apply to keyholder). Free. Telephone (01555) 851657. www.historic-scotland.gov.uk

The restored choir and south side of the nave of a late 14th-century parish church. The choir contains three canopied monuments to the Douglas family.

SCOTKART INDOOR KART RACING CENTRE, CAMBUSLANG   558   9 M26

Westburn Road, Cambuslang, Glasgow. 4 miles (6.5km) from city centre (off M74 at Cambuslang exit). Bus from Glasgow centre or train to Cambuslang. Track open daily (except Christmas Day and New Year's Day), 1200–2130. Booking office open 0930–1800. Charge £££. Also race meetings. Group concessions. Snack bar. Viewing gallery and changing rooms. WC. Limited wheelchair access. Disabled WC. Car and coach parking. Telephone 0141 641 0222. www.scotkart.co.uk

A large indoor motorsport centre featuring 200cc pro-karts capable of over 40mph with a unique flyover tunnel. The track is available for practice lapping or groups can compete in a professionally organised race meeting. All equipment and instruction provided. See also 559 Scotkart Indoor Kart Racing Centre, Clydebank.

SCOTKART INDOOR KART RACING CENTRE, CLYDEBANK   559   9 L25

Scotkart Indoor Kart Racing Centre, John Knox Street, Clydebank. 5 miles (8km) from Glasgow city centre, off Dumbarton Road. Nearest railway station Yoker. Track open daily (except Christmas Day and New Year's Day), Mon–Fri 1200–2130, Sat–Sun and school holidays 1200–2130. Booking office open daily 1000–1800. Charge £££. Race meetings £££. Snack bar. Corporate meeting room, viewing gallery and changing rooms. WC. Limited wheelchair access. Disabled WC. Car and coach parking. Telephone 0141 641 0222. www.scotkart.co.uk

A large indoor motorsport centre featuring 200cc pro-karts capable of over 40mph. The track can be booked for practice lapping or visitors can compete in a professionally organised race meeting. All equipment and instruction provided. See also 558 Scotkart Indoor Kart Racing Centre, Cambuslang.

SHOTTS HERITAGE CENTRE   560   9 N26

Shotts Library, Benhar Road, Shotts, Lanarkshire. In Shotts town centre. Nearest railway station Shotts, buses from Motherwell or Wishaw. Open all year (except public holidays), Mon–Tue 0930–1900, Wed 0930–1200, Thu–Sat 0930–1700. Free. Guided tours by arrangement (telephone 0141 304 1841). Explanatory displays. Headphone sets. Wheelchair access. Car and coach parking. Telephone (01501) 821556. www.northlan.gov.uk

Displays three life-size exhibits – Covenanters, a coal mine and 1940s shop front scene. Photographs and illustrations of local history and heritage.

SMA' SHOT COTTAGES   561   9 L26

11-17 George Place, Paisley. By rail or bus from Glasgow. Open Apr–Sep, Wed and Sat 1200–1600. Free. Guided tours. Gift shop. Tearoom. Garden. WC. Limited wheelchair access. Telephone 0141 889 1708.

A former 18th-century weaver's cottage, with domestic accommodation and loom shop, linked by a garden to a 19th-century artisan's house, both fully furnished. Exhibition of historic photographs and a fine collection of china and linen. Run by the Old Paisley Society.

STRATHCLYDE COUNTRY PARK   562   9 M26

366 Hamilton Road, Motherwell, Lanarkshire. 10 miles (16km) south of Glasgow on the M74, exit at junction 5 or 6. Nearest railway station Motherwell, buses from Motherwell and Hamilton. M&D's Theme Park (located in park) provide special bus service at weekends/public holidays. Park grounds open all year daily, dawn to dusk; watersports centre open daily 0800–2000. Free. Charge for watersports (group concessions by prior arrangement). Guided tours. Explanatory displays in visitor centre. Restaurant, tearoom, barbecue and picnic areas. Ranger service. WC. Wheelchair access. Disabled WC. Car and coach parking. Telephone (01698) 266155. www.northlan.gov.uk

A 1000 acre (404ha) park set in the Clyde valley. Artificial lake, mixed parkland and woodlands, and a variety of recreational facilities, including watersports. Woodland trails, countryside walks, sports pitches, sandy beaches, caravan site, hotel, inn and M & Ds, Scotland's first theme park. The visitor centre depicts the history and wildlife of the park. Also remains of a Roman bathhouse.

SUMMERLEE HERITAGE PARK   563   9 M26

Heritage Way, Coatbridge, Lanarkshire. In the centre of Coatbridge near the stations. Nearest railway station Coatbridge, bus from Glasgow. Open daily, Apr–Oct

1000–1700; Nov–Mar 1000–1600 (closed Christmas and New Year). Free. Charge for tram ride. Guided tours. Explanatory displays. Gift shop. Tearoom and picnic areas. Play area and extensive grounds. WC. Limited wheelchair access. Disabled WC. Car and coach parking. Telephone (01236) 431261. www.northlan.gov.uk

Summerlee Heritage Park is described as Scotland's noisiest museum, interpreting the history of the local steel and engineering industries and of the communities that depended upon them. It contains reconstructed miners rows, a mine and a tramway. Guided tours include the coal mine where visitors see the underground workings of a mine. The Ironworks Gallery houses a programme of temporary exhibitions. Regular workshops and craft demonstrations.

TIME CAPSULE   564   9 M26

100 Buchanan Street, Coatbridge, North Lanarkshire. Off M8 in Coatbridge. Nearest railway stations Whifflet or Sunnyside stations, Coatbridge, bus from Glasgow. Open all year (except Christmas and New Year), daily 1000–2100. Charge dependent on activity. Group concessions. Small gift shop. Café/bar. WC. Wheelchair access. Disabled WC. Car and coach parking. Telephone (01236) 449572. www.northland.gov.uk

Swim through primeval swamps, ride the rapids, skate with a 14 foot (4m) woolly mammoth and slide down the time tunnel. Also Nardini's Water Babies park, ideal for toddlers.

VIEWPARK GARDENS   565   9 M26

New Edinburgh Road, Viewpark, Uddingston. Off M74 at Bellshill exit. Open Apr–Sep, Mon–Thu 1000–1600, Fri 1000–1500, Sat–Sun 1000–1700; Oct–Easter, Mon–Thu 1000–1600, Fri 1000–1200. Free. Guided tours by prior arrangement. WC. Wheelchair access. Car and coach parking. Telephone (01698) 818269.

With its ornamental gardens and colourful displays, the gardens comprise glasshouse displays, plant collections, horticultural demonstrations, and various themed gardens including Highland, Japanese and Demonstration.

WEAVERS COTTAGE   566   9 L26

NTS. Shuttle Street, Kilbarchan, Paisley. Off A737, 5 miles (8km) west of Paisley. Nearest railway station Johnstone (2 miles/3.5km), bus from Paisley, Glasgow or Johnstone. Open Apr–Sep, Fri–Tue 1330–1730; weekends in Oct, 1330–1730. Charge ££. Group concessions. Explanatory displays and subtitled video. Explanatory text (available in Spanish). Cottage garden. WC. Subtitled video. Car parking. Telephone (01505) 705588. www.nts.org.uk

This typical cottage of an 18th-century handloom weaver contains looms, weaving equipment and domestic utensils. Displays of local, historical and weaving items. Attractive cottage garden. Weaving demonstrations (check for times). Video programme.

WEST HIGHLANDS & ISLANDS, LOCH LOMOND, STIRLING AND TROSSACHS

ACHNABRECK CUP AND RING MARKS   567   5 H24

HS. Kilmartin Glen. 1.5 miles (2.5 km) north west of Lochgilphead, Argyll. Nearest railway station Oban, then Lochgilphead bus to Kilmartin. Access at all reaonable times. Free. Telephone 01786 431 326. www.historic-scotland.gov.uk

The exposed crest of a rocky ridge with well-preserved cup and ring marks. Bronze Age.

ACHNALARIG RIDING CENTRE   568   5 J23

Achnalarig Farm, Glencruittein, Oban, Argyll. 1.5 miles (2.5km) from Oban town centre. Open all year (except Christmas Day and New Year's Day). Reduced hours during winter. Charge £££. Group concessions. WC. Wheelchair access with assistance. Car and coach parking. Telephone (01631) 562745.

Hacking, riding and trekking through beautiful countryside. Lessons available for all ages. Advanced booking necessary.

ADAM'S GRAVE   569   9 K25

Dunoon. Near Ardnadam Farm, 3 miles (5km) north of Dunoon on A815. Access at all times. Free.

Local name for a neolithic cairn. Two portals and one cap stone still remain and are believed to date from 3500 BC.

ALLOA TOWER   570   10 N24

NTS. Alloa Park, Alloa. On A907 in Alloa. Bus from Alloa centre. Open Apr–Oct, daily 1200–1700. Charge ££. Group concessions. Explanatory displays. WC. Limited wheelchair access. Disabled WC. Car parking. Telephone (01259) 211701. www.nts.org.uk

Alloa Tower was the ancestral home of the Earls of Mar and Kellie for four centuries. The present building dates from 1497 and was built by the 3rd Lord Erskine. In the early 18th century, the 6th Earl remodelled the tower to tie in with the adjoining mansion house, which was destroyed by fire in 1800. Impressive parapet walk around the tower's battlements offering spectacular views of the Forth. Fine collection of family portraits, including works by Jamesone and Raeburn.

ALVA GLEN   571   10 N24

Alva. 0.3 miles (0.5km) north of Alva village, at foot of Ochil Hills. Bus from Alloa and Stirling. Access at all times. Free. Explanatory displays. Refreshments and facilities in Alva. Limited wheelchair access. Car parking. Telephone (01259) 450000. www.clacksweb.org.uk

Situated above the village of Alva, at the foot of the Ochil Hills. Formal gardens and a more rugged area (where care is required), offering views down into a steep gorge. Also the remnants of an old dam that supplied the mills with fast flowing water to drive their machines. A kestrel is often spotted in the upper part of the glen around the rocky cliffs. The long tailed grey wagtail can also be seen in the lower part of the glen all year round.

AN TOBAR ARTS CENTRE, GALLERY AND CAFÉ   572   5 G22

Argyll Terrace, Tobermory, Isle of Mull. Ferry from Oban to Craignure, then bus to Tobermory. Open Mar–Jun and Sep–Dec, Tue–Sat 1000–1600; Jul–Aug, Mon–Sat 1000–1700, Sun 1300–1600. Free. Explanatory displays. Gift shop. Café and picnic area. WC. Wheelchair access. Disabled WC. Car parking. Telephone (01688) 302211. www.antobar.co.uk

Based in a renovated Victorian primary school, the building has retained its historic detail and atmosphere and commands breathtaking views over Tobermory Bay. Monthly touring local art and craft exhibitions. The best of traditional and contemporary music. Concerts and informal ceilidhs, usually on Tuesday and Friday evenings. Art, craft and music workshops with local and visiting artists.

ANTONINE WALL   573   9 N25

HS. From Bo'ness to Old Kilpatrick, best seen off A803 east of Bonnybridge, 12 miles (19km) south of Stirling. Access at all reasonable times. Free. Explanatory board. Telephone 01786 431 326. www.historic-scotland.gov.uk

This Roman fortification stretched from Bo'ness on the Forth to Old Kilpatrick on the Clyde. Built circa 142-3 AD, it consisted of a turf rampart behind a ditch, with forts approximately every two miles. It was probably abandoned around 163 AD. Remains are best preserved in the Falkirk/Bonnybridge area. See 455 Bar Hill Fort, 468 Castlecary, 484 Croy Hill, 488 Dullatur, 495 Glasgow Bearsden Bathhouse, 766 Rough Castle, 777 Seabegs Wood, and 574 Watling Lodge.

ANTONINE WALL – WATLING LODGE   574   9 N25

HS. In Falkirk, signposted from the A9. Nearest railway and bus stations Falkirk. There is no access to the house or grounds. Free. Telephone (01786) 431326. www.historic-scotland.gov.uk

The best section of the ditch of the Antonine Wall (see 573).

ARDANAISEIG GARDENS   575   5 J23

Ardanaiseig Hotel, Kilchrenan, Taynuilt, Argyll. On the B845, 10 miles (11.5km) east of Taynuilt. Nearest railway station Taynuilt. Open all year (except Jan and first two weeks of Feb) 0900–dusk. Charge £. Explanatory displays. Refreshments and WC in hotel. WC. Car parking. Telephone (01866) 833333. www.ardanaiseig.com

Ardanaiseig Gardens comprise over 100 acres (40.5ha) of Victorian woodlands on the shores of Loch Awe, under the shadow of Ben Cruachan. Many exotic shrubs and trees.

ARDBEG DISTILLERY VISITOR CENTRE   576   7 F26

Port Ellen, Isle of Islay. 3 miles (5km) east of Port Ellen on the southern tip of Islay. Ferry from Kennacraig; by air from Glasgow to Islay. Open Jun–Aug, daily 1000–1700; Sep–May, Mon–Fri 1000–1600. Charge £. Guided tours. Explanatory displays. Gift shop. Restaurant. WC. Limited wheelchair access to restaurant and shop. Disabled WC. Car and coach parking. Telephone (01496) 302244. www.ardbeg.com

Take a step back in time and experience the history and mystique of the Ardbeg Distillery. Visitors enjoy a personal guided tour and a dram of Ardbeg's extraordinary malt whisky.

ARDCHATTAN GARDENS   577   5 J22

Ardchattan Priory, Connel, Oban. On the north shore of Loch Etive, 5 miles (8km) east of Connel. Bus from Oban. Open Apr–Oct, daily 0900–1800. Charge £. Children under 16 free. WC. Wheelchair access. Disabled WC. Car and coach parking. Telephone (01796) 481355. www.gardens-of-argyll.co.uk

Four acres (1.6ha) of garden surrounding Ardchattan Priory, a private home, with a ruined chapel and interesting stones. Herbaceous borders and extensive lawn facing the loch. Rose, Sorbus and many varieties of Hebe.

ARDCHATTAN PRIORY   578   5 J22

HS. On the north side of Loch Etive, 6.5 miles (10.5km) north east of Oban, Argyll. Nearest railway station Oban. Access at all reasonable times. Free. There is a charge to go through the gardens (not in HS care). Telephone (01786) 431326. www.historic-scotland.gov.uk

The ruins of a Valliscaulian priory founded in 1230 and later converted to secular use. The meeting place in 1308 of one of Robert the Bruce's parliaments. Burned by Cromwell's soldiers in 1654. The remains include some carved stones.

ARDENCRAIG GARDENS   579   9 J26

Ardencraig Lane, Rothesay, Isle of Bute. 2 miles from Rothesay. Bus service from Rothesay. Open May–Sep, Mon–Fri 0900–1630, Sat and Sun 1300–1630. Free. WC. Wheelchair access. Car parking. Telephone (01700) 504644.

A working greenhouse and garden which produces plants for floral displays on Bute, built between 1919 and 1923. A collection of rare plants, an aviary with many foreign bird species and ornamental fish ponds.

ARDFERN RIDING CENTRE   580   7 H25

Craobh Haven, Lochgilphead, Argyll. 25 miles (40km) south of Oban on A816. Open all year, daily. Charges vary. Group concessions. WC. Riding for the disabled. Wheelchair access with assistance. Car parking. Telephone (01852) 500632. www.aboutscotland.com/argyll/appaloosa

Day rides along the seashore or into the hills and glens on Quarterhorses and Appaloosas, bred, born and trained at this riding centre. Western riding, Natural Horsemanship and various courses.

ARDGARTAN VISITOR CENTRE   581   5 K24

FE. Glen Croe, Arrochar, Argyll. On A83 west of Arrochar on Cowal Peninsula. Nearest railway station Tarbet then local bus service. Open Apr–Oct, daily 1000–1700. Free. Explanatory displays. Gift shop. Picnic area. Forest walks and cycleways. Wheelchair access. Car and coach parking. Telephone (01301) 702432. www.forestry.gov.uk

Situated in Argyll Forest Park and close to the Arrochar Alps, the visitor centre is a good access point for the forest and its surroundings. Many special events are held throughout the year (nominal charge) and include Deer Watch, guided walks on the hills to see local wildlife and archaeology, and barbecues.

ARDKINGLAS WOODLAND GARDEN   582   5 K24

Ardkinglas Estate, Cairndow, Argyll. In Cairndow, on the A83, 8 miles (13km) north of Inveraray. Buses from Glasgow, Oban or Campbeltown. Open daily, dawn to dusk. Charge £. Children under 16 free. Group concessions. Guided tours for groups. Explanatory displays. Gift shop nearby. Picnic area. WC. Limited wheelchair access. Car and coach parking. Telephone (01499) 600261. www.ardkinglas.com

One of the finest collections of conifers in Britain, including Europe's mightiest conifer, a silver fir with a girth over 9.6m. Watch out for the red squirrels. Also a spectacular display of rhododendrons and a gazebo.

ARDNADAM HERITAGE TRAIL   583   9 K25

Dunoon. Near to the village of Sandbank, 3 miles (5km) north of Dunoon on A815. Access at all times. Free.

Excellent walk including a climb to the Dunan viewpoint, approximately 2 miles (3km) long.

ARDUAINE GARDEN   584   5 H24

NTS. Arduaine, Argyll. On A816, 20 miles (32km) south of Oban. Infrequent bus service from Oban. Open all year, daily 0930–sunset. Charge £££. Group concessions. Explanatory displays (information sheets in French and German). Plant sales. WC. Wheelchair access (wheelchair available). Disabled WC. Car and coach parking. Telephone (01852) 200366. www.nts.org.uk

Twenty acre (8ha) garden on promontory with fine views overlooking Loch Melfort. Noted for rhododendrons, azaleas, magnolias and other interesting trees and shrubs. The garden also has a series of ponds and watercourses and many beautiful herbaceous perennials flowering throughout the season.

ARGYLL AND SUTHERLAND HIGHLANDERS REGIMENTAL MUSEUM 585   10 N24

Stirling Castle, Stirling. In Stirling Castle. Nearest railway station Stirling, buses from Glasgow and Edinburgh. Open daily, Easter–Sep 0930–1700; Oct–Easter 1000–1615. Free. Fee for entry to castle. Explanatory displays. Gift shop. Refreshments and WC in castle. Car and coach parking. Telephone (01786) 475165. www.argylls.co.uk

A fine museum which brings alive the history of the Regiment from 1794 to the present day. Features weapons, silver, colours, uniforms, medals, pictures, music, World War I trench. See 783 Stirling Castle.

ARGYLL POTTERY 586   5 J22

Barcaldine, Oban, Argyll. On the A828, on the south shore of Loch Creran. Infrequent bus from Oban. Open all year, Mon–Fri 1000–1800, Sat 1300–1800. Free. Explanatory displays. Gift shop. Wheelchair access. Car parking. Telephone (01631) 720503. www.argyllpottery.co.uk

A pottery producing mostly domestic ware on the wheel, with some individual pieces.

ARGYLL RIDING 587   5 J24

Dalchenna Farm, Inveraray, Argyll. 2 miles (3km) south of Inveraray on A83. Bus service to Inveraray from Oban and Glasgow. Open all year, daily. Charges vary. WC. Limited wheelchair access. Car parking. Telephone (01499) 302611. www.horserides.co.uk

Scenic pony trekking, lessons and children's pony rides.

ARGYLL TRAIL RIDING 588   7 H25

Brenfield Farm, Ardrishaig, Argyll. 2 miles (3km) south of Ardrishaig on the A83. Bus service from Glasgow. Open all year for day rides; Apr–Oct for week trails. Charge varies. Group concessions. Car parking. Telephone (01546) 603274. www.brenfield.co.uk

Riding for everyone, from beginner to expert – one and a half, and two hour treks, a full day's pub ride with beach gallop, swimming with horses, picnic rides, family and children's holidays, tuition and training. Also clay pigeon shooting and mountain bike hire.

ARGYLL'S LODGING 589   10 N24

HS. Castle Wynd, Stirling. At the top of Castle Wynd in centre of the town. Nearest railway station Stirling, buses from Glasgow and Edinburgh. Open Apr–Sep, daily 0930–1800; Oct–Mar, daily 0930–1800. Charge ££. Joint ticket with Stirling Castle (see 783) available. Group concessions. Explanatory displays. Gift shop. WC. Limited wheelchair access. Disabled WC. Car and coach parking. Telephone (01786) 431319. www.historic-scotland.gov.uk

A superb mansion built around an earlier core in about 1630 and further extended by the Earl of Argyll in the 1670s. It is the most impressive town house of its period in Scotland. The principal rooms are now restored to their former glory.

ASCOG HALL FERNERY AND GARDENS   590   9 J26

Ascog Hall, Ascog, Isle of Bute. 3 miles (5km) south of Rothesay on A886. Nearest railway station Wemyss Bay, then ferry (30 minutes) to Rothesay. Bus service from Rothesay to Ascog Hall (request stop). Open Easter–end Oct, Wed–Sun 1000–1700, closed Mon and Tue. Charge £. Children free. Group concessions. Guided tours. Explanatory displays. Picnic area. Wheelchair access with assistance. Car and coach parking. Telephone (01700) 504555. www.ascoghallfernery.co.uk

Built circa 1870, this magnificent Victorian fernery, with beautiful rock work and water pools, has been restored and refurnished with an impressive collection of sub-tropical ferns. The only surviving fern from the original collection is said to be 1000 years old. After decades of neglect, the garden has been lovingly restored and an hour or so spent meandering through its colourful beds and borders is a truly delightful experience.

AUCHINDRAIN TOWNSHIP OPEN AIR MUSEUM   591   5 J24

By Inveraray, Argyll. 6 miles (10km) south west of Inveraray on A83. Nearest railway station Arrochar, bus from Glasgow or Oban to Inveraray. Open Apr–Sep, daily 1000–1700. Charge ££. Group concessions. Explanatory displays. Gift shop. WC. Car and coach parking. Telephone (01499) 500235. www.auchindrain-museum.org.uk

Auchindrain is an original West Highland township of great antiquity and the only communal tenancy township in Scotland to have survived on its centuries-old site, much of it in its original form. The various township buildings and surrounding lands look as they would have done at the end of the 19th century and give visitors a fascinating glimpse of Highland life.

BALLIVICAR PONY TREKKING CENTRE   592   7 F26

Ballivicar Farm, Port Ellen, Isle of Islay. 2 miles (3km) from Port Ellen on Kintra road. Open all year. Jun–Aug treks at 1100 and 1400; winter afternoons only. Charge £££. WC. Rides tailored to suit abilities/disabilities. Wheelchair access. Car and coach parking. Telephone (01496) 302251. www.ballivicar.co.uk

Family-run trekking centre catering for all abilities. Beach rides.

BALLYGOWAN CUP AND RING MARKS   593   5 H24

HS. Kilmartin Glen. 1 mile (2km) south west of Kilmartin, near Poltalloch, Argyll. Nearest railway station Oban, then bus to Kilmartin. Access at all reasonable times. Free. Telephone (01786) 431326. www.historic-scotland.gov.uk

Bronze Age cup and ring marks on natural rock faces.

BALUACHRAIG CUP AND RING   594   5 H24

HS. Kilmartin Glen. 1 mile (2km) south south-east of Kilmartin, Argyll. Nearest railway station Oban, then bus to Kilmartin. Access at all reasonable times. Free. Telephone (01786) 431326. www.historic-scotland.gov.uk

Several groups of Bronze Age cup and ring marks on natural rock faces.

BANNOCKBURN HERITAGE CENTRE   595   10 N24

NTS. Glasgow Road, Stirling. 2 miles (3.2km) south of Stirling, off M80/M9 at junction 9. By bus from Stirling. Open daily, Mar and Nov–Christmas 1030–1600;

Apr–Oct 1000–1730. Charge ££. Group concessions. Explanatory displays, audio-visual programme and guidebook in French and German. Gift shop. Café. WC. Induction loop system, braille guidebook. Wheelchair access (wheelchair available). Disabled WC. Car and coach parking. Telephone (01786) 812664. www.nts.org.uk

Site of the famous battle in 1314 when Robert the Bruce, King of Scots, defeated the English army of Edward II. Colourful exhibition with life-size figures of Bruce and William Wallace, heraldic flags. Equestrian statue of Bruce outside.

BARGUILLEAN'S ANGUS GARDEN   596   5 J23

Barguillean Farm, Taynuilt, Argyll. 2 miles (3km) from Taynuilt along Glen Lonan road. Nearest railway and bus station in Taynuilt. Open all year, daily 0900–1800. Charge £. Children free. Group concessions. Guided tours on request. Explanatory displays. Limited wheelchair access. Car and coach parking. Telephone (01866) 822335.

The garden was established in 1957 and is set within semi-natural woodland, bordered by Loch Angus with magnificent views of Ben Cruachan and Glen Etive. Famous for its collections of hybrid rhododendron and azaleas, the garden is noted for its charm and tranquility. Created in memory of Angus MacDonald, journalist and writer, who was killed in Cyrpus in 1956. Woodland walks for all abilities.

BARNALINE WALKS   597   5 J23

Dalavich, on an unclassified road along west shore of Loch Awe. Access at all times. Free. Car parking.

Three walks starting from Barnaline car park and picnic site, taking in Dalavich Oakwood Forest Nature Reserve (an interpretive trail with information point), Avich Falls and Loch Avich. Panoramic views of Loch Awe.

BARNLUASGAN VISITOR CENTRE   598   5 H24

FE. Near Lochgilphead. Follow B841 towards Crinan then B8025 from Bellanoch towards Tayvallich. Barnluasgan visitor centre is at the junction of the road to Achnamara village. Access at all times. Free. Explanatory displays. Wheelchair access. Car parking. www.forestry.gov.uk

This unstaffed visitor centre provides information on Knapdale Forest with exhibits on local and natural history. See also 714 Knapdale Forest.

BEN LOMOND   599   5 L24

NTS. Ardess Lodge, Rowardennan, by Drymen, Stirlingshire. By B837, 11 miles (17.5km) beyond Drymen off A811. By bus from Glasgow to Drymen, then to Balmaha. Open all year. Free. Explanatory displays. Guided walks by rangers. WC. Car and coach parking. Telephone (01360) 870224. www.nts.org.uk

Rising from the east shore of Loch Lomond to 3194 feet (973.5m), the mountain offers exhilarating walking and spectacular views. It is part of the Ben Lomond National Memorial Park commemorating war dead. See also 726 Loch Lomond National Park, 725 Loch Lomond, 729 Lomond Shores and 731 Maid of the Loch.

BENMORE BOTANIC GARDEN   600   5 K25

Benmore Botanic Garden, Dunoon, Argyll. 7 miles (11km) north of Dunoon, on A815. Bus from Dunoon. Open Mar–Oct, daily from 1000; Mar and Oct closes 1700;

Apr–Sep closes 1800. Charge ££. Group concessions. Guided tours Tue–Thu and Sun 1400. Explanatory displays. Gift shop. Licensed café with indoor and outdoor seating. Exhibitions and events. WC. Limited wheelchair access. Disabled WC. Car and coach parking. Telephone (01369) 706261. www.rbge.org.uk

Some of Britain's tallest trees can be found here, as can over 250 species of rhododendrons and an extensive magnolia collection. Other features include an avenue of giant redwoods planted in 1863, a formal garden, and a variety of waymarked trails. Benmore Botanic Garden is a regional garden of the Royal Botanic Garden Edinburgh (see 379). See also 757 Puck's Glen.

BIRKHILL FIRECLAY MINE   601   10 N25

3 miles (5km) west of Bo'ness. Accessed by the Bo'ness and Kinneil Railway, no bus service. Open Apr–Jun and Sep–Oct, weekends; Jul–Aug, daily except Mon; telephone for other opening. Charge £. Joint ticket with Bo'ness and Kinneil Railway available. Group concessions. Guided tours. Explanatory displays. Picnic area. WC. No guide dogs. Car parking. Telephone (01506) 825855. www.srps.org.uk

The caverns of Birkhill Fireclay Mine are set in the picturesque Avon Gorge. A mine guide takes visitors on a tour of the mine workings where you can discover how fireclay was mined. There are also fossils which are over 300 million years old. The mine can only be reached by descending 130 steps into the Avon Gorge so access for the disabled and elderly is difficult. See also 605 Bo'ness and Kinneil Railway.

BISHOP'S GLEN   602   9 K25

Dunoon, main entrance Nelson Street.

Once the source of Dunoon's water supply, now a favoured beauty spot and delightful walk leading to the Bishop's Seat, 1655ft (504m).

BLAIR DRUMMOND SAFARI AND ADVENTURE PARK   603   5 M24

Blair Drummond, Stirling. 4 miles (6.5km) towards Doune on A84, take junction 10 off M9. Nearest railway and bus stations Stirling. There is transport around the park for visitors without vehicles. Open Apr–Oct, daily 1000–1730, last admission 1630. Telephone to confirm details. Charge £££. Children under 3 free. Group concessions. Explanatory displays, guide books with maps. Gift shop. Restaurant, bar, picnic and barbecue areas. WC. Wheelchair access. Disabled WC. Car and coach parking. Telephone (01786) 841456. www.blairdrummond.com

Drive through wild animal reserves, boat safari around chimpanzee island, pets' farm, adventure playground. Giant astra-glide and flying-fox cable slide across lake. Five-seater pedal boats. Amusement arcade, bouncy castle, dodgem cars.

BONAWE IRON FURNACE   604   5 J23

HS. Taynuilt, Argyll. At Bonawe, close to Taynuilt on the A85, 12 miles (19km) east of Oban. Nearest railway station Taynuilt, bus to Oban via Taynuilt then 15 minute walk. Open Apr–Sep, Mon–Sun 0930–1830. Charge £. Group concessions. Explanatory displays. Gift shop. Picnic area. WC. Limited wheelchair access. Disabled WC. Car parking. Telephone (01866) 822432. www.historic-scotland.gov.uk

The restored remains of a charcoal furnace for iron smelting. Established in 1753, it functioned until 1876. The most complete example of its type. Displays illustrate how iron was made here.

BO'NESS AND KINNEIL RAILWAY   605   10 N25

Bo'ness Station, Bo'ness. On A904 and A706. Buses from Edinburgh, Glasgow and Falkirk, nearest railway station Linlithgow. Open Apr–Oct (weekends) and Jul–Aug daily except Monday; exhibition 1130–1700, steam train journeys between 1100 and 1615. Charge ££. Children under 5 free (except for special events). Group concessions. Explanatory displays. Gift shop. Tearoom and picnic area. WC. Wheelchair access and adapted coach for wheelchair users and companions. Disabled WC. Car and coach parking. Telephone (01506) 822298. www.srps.org.uk

Savour the nostalgia of the railway age and travel by steam train from Bo'ness to visit the man-made caverns of Birkhill Fireclay Mine (see 601). Also at Bo'ness the Scottish Railway exhibition tells the story of the movement of goods and people in the days before motorway travel, with a display of carriages, wagons and locomotives, some over 100 years old.

BOWMORE DISTILLERY VISITOR CENTRE   606   7 F26

School Street, Bowmore, Isle of Islay. Located in the centre of town of Bowmore on Islay. Bus service to Bowmore from ferry terminals and airport. Open all year round, Mon–Sat, guided tours at 1000, 1100, 1400 and 1500. Charge £. Under 18s free. Cost of entry refunded on a purchase in the distillery shop. Group concessions. Guided tours (foreign language video). Gift shop. Visitors receive a dram of whisky. VIP tours or whisky masterclasses can be arranged. Bowmore Distillery cottages are available for holiday lets. WC. Wheelchair access. Disabled WC. Car and coach parking. Telephone (01496) 810671. www.bowmore.com

Established in 1779, Bowmore, the oldest distillery on Islay is ideally located right in the heart of Bowmore. Come and join us for a tour of the distillery where you will see the rare sight of barley being malted in the maltbarns, the firing of the enormous peat kilns, the stillroom by the shores of Loch Indaal and the famous No 1 Vaults where the Bowmore spirit slowly matures. There is also the opportunity to stay in one of the charming distillery cottages.

BRACKLINN FALLS   607   5 M24

1 mile (2km) east of Callander. Follow minor road from Callander, signposted Bracklinn Falls/Golf Course. Bus to Callander. Access at all times. Free. Car parking.

A series of dramatic waterfalls on the Keltie Water to the north east of Callander. The falls are approached along a woodland walk from a car park by the Callander Crags at Callander. Take care as ground can be muddy and slippery.

BREADALBANE FOLKLORE CENTRE   608   5 M23

Falls of Dochart, Killin, Perthshire. 2 miles (3km) along A827 from A85 at Lix Toll junction. 12 miles (19km) east of Crianlarich, 20 miles (32km) north west of Callander. Car and coach parking nearby. Nearest railway station Crianlarich, post and school bus from Callander, Mon–Fri, term-time only. Open Mar-Oct, daily; Mar–May 1000–1700; Jun 1000–1800; Jul–Aug 0930–1830; Sep 1000–1800; Oct 1000–1700. Closed Nov–Jan, Feb open weekends only 1000–1600. Charge £. Group concessions. Explanatory displays. Gift shop. WC. Induction loop. Limited wheelchair access (to ground floor only). Disabled WC. Telephone (01567) 820254.

Scotland's Celtic and Christian peoples lived in a world where devils and demons, sprites and spirits, mystic visions and miraculous events were very real and part of their everday lives. Housed in a restored working watermill overlooking the Falls of Dochart, the centre brings to life the folklore and fables of ancient Breadalbane. The centre includes a Tourist Information Centre.

BUNNAHABHAIN DISTILLERY   609   7 G25

Port Askaig, Isle of Islay. Limited post bus service from Bowmore. Telephone
Mundells (01496) 840273 from ferry terminals and airport. Tours available Apr–Oct,
Mon–Fri 1030, 1245, 1400, and 1515; Oct–Apr by appointment only. Free. Guided
tours and tasting. Gift shop. Free tea and coffee. WC. Car and coach parking.
Telephone (01496) 840646.

Visitors can see the malt whisky distillation process and sample the results.
Individuals and groups welcome.

BURG   610   5 F23

NTS. Isle of Mull, 7 miles (11km) west of Tiroran off B8035, then rough path. Car
parking at Tiroran. Access at all times. Free. Telephone (01631) 570000. www.nts.org.uk

Covering a distance of 1405 acres (568.5ha), this is a spectacular and remote part
of Mull. The high cliffs here are known as the Wilderness. MacCulloch's Fossil
Tree is 50 million years old, and can be reached by a steep iron ladder down to
the beach at low tide.

BUTE MUSEUM   611   9 J26

Stuart Street, Rothesay, Isle of Bute. Located in the centre of Rothesay. Car ferry
from Wemyss Bay to Rothesay Pier or from Colintraive to Rhubodach at north end of
Bute. Open Apr–Sep, Mon–Sat 1030–1630, Sun 1430–1630; Oct–Mar, Tue–Sat
1430–1630. Charge £. Groups normally admitted by donation. Accompanied school
parties free by prior arrangement. Guided tours by arrangement. Explanatory
displays. Gift shop. WC. Touch table for blind visitors. Wheelchair access. Car and
coach parking. Telephone (01700) 505067.

Custom-made museum, gifted by the fourth Marquess of Bute in 1926. A
recognised source of information on the Island of Bute. Archaeology, natural
history, geology, photography, archives and social history.

CAIRNBAAN CUP AND RING MARKS   612   5 H24

HS. Kilmartin Glen. Near to the Cairnbaan Hotel on the A841, 2.5 miles (4km) north
west of Lochgilphead, Argyll. Nearest railway station Oban, then bus to
Lochgilphead. Access at all reasonable times. Free. Telephone (01786) 431326.
www.historic-scotland.gov.uk

Cup and ring marks on a natural rock surface.

CALLENDAR HOUSE   613   9 N25

Callendar Park, Falkirk. 1 mile (2km) east of town centre. Ten minute walk from
railway and bus station. Open all year, Mon–Sat 1000–1700 (also Suns from Apr–Sep
1400–1700 and most public holidays). Charge £. Children under 6 free. Group
concessions. Guided tours by arrangement (£££). Explanatory displays. Gift shop.
Tearoom. Garden and children's play area, leisure facilities in park. WC. Braille map
of exhibition. Wheelchair access. Disabled WC. Car and coach parking. Telephone
(01324) 503770. www.falkirkmuseums.demon.co.uk

Callendar House encapsulates 600 years of Scotland's history from medieval
times to the 20th century and was visited by great historical figures like Mary,
Queen of Scots, Cromwell and Bonnie Prince Charlie. Permanent attractions
include displays on the Story of Callendar House, and on the Falkirk area during
the great social revolution of 1750–1850. Costumed interpretations bring this
history to life, while a programme of temporary exhibitions provides for a wide

range of interests. The house's research centre contains an extensive archive and other material on the area's history.

CAMBUSKENNETH ABBEY   614   10 N24

HS. 1 mile (2km) east of Stirling. Nearest railway station Stirling, bus from Glasgow and Edinburgh. Access at all reasonable times. View exterior only. Telephone (01786) 431326. www.historic-scotland.gov.uk

Ruins of an abbey founded in 1147 as a house of Augustinian canons. Scene of Robert the Bruce's parliament in 1326 and the burial place of James III and his queen. The fine detached tower is the only substantial survivor, but extensive foundations remain of the rest.

CAMPBELTOWN HERITAGE CENTRE   615   7 H28

Big Kiln, Campbeltown, Argyll. 38 miles (61km) south of Tarbet, Loch Fyne on A82. Daily bus service from Glasgow. Open Easter–Sep, Mon–Sat 1200–1700, Sun 1400–1700. Charge £. Group concessions. Explanatory displays. Gift shop. Refreshments available. WC. Wheelchair access. Disabled WC. Car and coach parking. Telephone (07783) 485387.

A treasure-trove of information and exhibits covering many aspects of the history and development of south Kintyre, including a working model of the Campbeltown/Machrihanish Light Railway. Many of the countless commercial and industrial enterprises over the centuries are depicted in the centre.

CAMPBELTOWN MUSEUM   616   7 H28

Hall Street, Campbeltown, Argyll. 38 miles (61km) south of Tarbet, Loch Fyne on A82. Daily bus service from Glasgow. Open all year, Tue and Thu 1000–1300, 1400–1700 and 1730–1930, Wed, Fri and Sat 1000–1300 and 1400–1700. Closed Sun and Mon. Free. Explanatory displays. WC. Wheelchair access with assistance. Car parking. Telephone (01586) 552366.

A listed building, designed by the renowned Scottish architect J. J. Burnet. The collections are mainly archaeology and natural history with some local history and maritime material. Natural history displays and a diorama depicting the landscape and birdlife of Kintyre.

CAOL ILA DISTILLERY   617   7 G25

Port Askaig, Isle of Islay. On the A846, on the east side of Islay, just by Port Askaig. Bus on island, 1.5 mile (2km) walk to distillery. Open Apr–Oct, Mon–Fri by appointment only. Charge ££. No children under 8. Guided tours by arrangement. Visitor centre. Gift shop. WC. Car parking. Telephone (01496) 302760.

A distillery built in 1846 by Hector Henderson. It stands in a picturesque setting at the foot of a steep hill with its own small pier overlooking the Sound of Islay and Paps of Jura.

CARNASSERIE CASTLE   618   5 H24

HS. Off A816, 9 miles (14.5km) north of Lochgilphead, 2 miles (3km) north of Kilmartin, Argyll. Nearest railway station Oban, then bus to Kilmartin. Open at all times. Free. Picnic area. Car and coach parking. Telephone (01786) 431326. www.historic-scotland.gov.uk

A handsome combined tower house and hall, home of John Carswell, first Protestant Bishop of the Isles and translator of the first book printed in Gaelic.

Fine architectural details of the late 16th century. The castle was captured and partly blown up during Argyll's rebellion in 1685.

CASTLE CAMPBELL   619   10 N24

HS. Dollar, Clackmannanshire. In Dollar Glen, 1 mile (2km) north of Dollar. Bus via Dollar from Stirling or St Andrews then 20 minute walk. Open Apr–Sep, daily 0930–1830; Oct–Mar, Mon–Sun (closed Thu and Fri) 0930–1630. Charge £. Group concessions. Explanatory displays. Gift shop. Tearoom. Garden. WC. Limited wheelchair access. Car parking. Telephone (01259) 742408. www.historic-scotland.gov.uk

Once known as Castle Gloom, the castle was built towards the end of the 15th century by the 1st Earl of Argyll. Located on a steep mound with extensive views to the plains of the Forth. Burned by Cromwell in the 1650s. The original tower is well preserved. The 60 acres (24ha) of woodland in the glen make an attractive walk to the castle. See also 640 Dollar Glen.

CASTLE HOUSE MUSEUM   620   9 K25

Castle Gardens, Dunoon, Argyll. Opposite the pier in Dunoon. Open Easter–late Oct, Mon–Sat 1030–1630, Sun 1400–1630. Charge £. Accompanied children free. Group concessions. Guided tours. Explanatory displays and audio-visual presentation. Gift shop. Picnic area in grounds. Ornamental gardens. WC. Wheelchair access. Car parking. Telephone (01369) 701422. www.castlehousemuseum.org.uk

The museum illustrates the history of Dunoon and district from pre-history to the recent past. Four rooms have been set aside to give the visitor a reflection of life in Victorian times. Set in pleasant gardens, opposite Dunoon's beautiful Victorian Pier with excellent views of the surrounding area.

CASTLE LACHLAN   621   5 J24

4 miles (6.5km) south west of Strachur on A886/B8000. Access at all times. Free.

Ruins dating from the 12th century. The MacLachlans are believed to have had lands in Strathlachlan for over 900 years.

CASTLE SWEEN   622   7 H25

HS. On the east shore of Loch Sween, 15 miles (24km) south west of Lochgilphead, Argyll. Bus from Lochgilphead to Achanamara, then 14 mile (22.5km) walk. Access at all reasonable times. Free. Telephone (01786) 431326. www.historic-scotland.gov.uk

Probably the oldest stone castle on the Scottish mainland. Built in the mid 12th century with later towers in addition to now vanished wooden structures. Destroyed by Sir Alexander Macdonald in 1647.

CHURCH OF THE HOLY RUDE   623   10 N24

St John Street, Stirling. Nearest railway and bus station Stirling. Sunday services Jan–Jun 1000, Jul–Dec 1130; Open May–Sep, every day 1100–1600. Other opening by prior arrangement . Free. Guided tours by prior arrangement. Explanatory displays, postcards and leaflets available. WC. Induction loop system. Wheelchair access. Telephone (01786) 475275. www.holyrude.org

Believed to be the only church in the United Kingdom apart from Westminster Abbey which has held a coronation, that of James VI, son of Mary, Queen of Scots. John Knox preached the coronation sermon. Scottish monarchs of the 15th and 16th centuries worshipped here. Significant traditional and modern stained glass windows. Magnificent Rushworth & Dreaper Ltd romantic organ.

CLACHAN BRIDGE   624   5 H23

B844 off A816, 12 miles (19k) south west of Oban. Access at all times. Free.

This picturesque single-arched bridge, built in 1792 and linking the mainland with the island of Seil, is often claimed to be the only bridge to span the Atlantic (although there are others similar). The waters are actually those of the narrow Seil Sound, which joins the Firth of Lorne to Outer Loch Melfort, but they can, with some justification, claim to be an arm of the Atlantic.

THE COBBLER   625   5 K24

Part of the Arrochar Alps, overlooking Arrochar and Loch Long. Access at all times. Free.

So-called because of its curious rock formation summit, The Cobbler – or Ben Artuur – is one of Scotland's most distinctive peaks.

COLL RSPB NATURE RESERVE   626   5 F22

Isle of Coll, Argyll and Bute. 6 miles (9.5km) west of Arinagour. Ferry from mainland. Reserve open at all times. Please avoid walking through fields of hay and crops. Free. Guided walks available in summer. Information bothy and corncrake viewing platform (summer only). Limited wheelchair access. Car and coach parking. Telephone (01879) 230301. www.rspb.org.uk/scotland

The reserve on the island of Coll has long, white shell sand beaches, sand dunes and machair grassland, all typical Hebridean habitats. The reserve is a stronghold for the rare corncrake. The RSPB are managing the reserve with local farmers to help corncrake numbers recover. There are also many other breeding birds on the reserve, including redshanks, lapwings and snipe. In the winter, large numbers of barnacle and Greenland white-fronted geese use the site.

COLONSAY HOUSE GARDENS   627   5 F24

Kiloran, Isle of Colonsay, Argyll. 2 miles (3km) from pier. Car ferry from Oban. Open Easter–Sep, Wed 1200–1700 and Fri 1500–1730. Charge £. Group concessions. Explanatory displays. Gift shop. Tearoom and picnic area. Children's play area. WC. Limited wheelchair access. Car and coach parking. Telephone (01951) 200211. www.colonsay.org.uk

Famous rhododendron garden of 20 acres (8ha), adjacent to Colonsay House, home of Lord Strathcona. In the woods surrounding the house, rocks, streams and contours of land have been used to create a natural woodland garden where native trees and rare rhododendrons, bluebells and mecanopsis flourish together. Due to the mildness of the climate and the shelter of the woods, many tender and rare shrubs from all parts of the world grow happily including mimosa, eucalyptus and palm trees.

COLUMBA'S FOOTSTEPS   628   7 H28

West of Southend at Keil, Mull of Kintyre.

Traditionally it is believed that St Columba first set foot on Scottish soil near Southend. The footsteps are imprinted in a flat topped rock near the ruin of an old chapel.

CORRYVRECKAN WHIRLPOOL   629   5 H24

Between the islands of Jura and Scarba.

This treacherous tide race, dangerous for small craft, covers an extensive area and may be seen from the north end of Jura or from Craignish Point. The noise can sometimes be heard from a considerable distance.

CRAFT DAFT ON A RAFT 630 9 M25

Forth & Clyde Canal, Glasgow Bridge, Kirkintilloch Road, Kirkintilloch. On A803 between Bishopbriggs and Kirkintilloch. Nearest railway station in Bishopbriggs. Local bus service. Open during school term Thu and Fri 1300–2100, Sat 1030–1730, and Sun 1230–1730, . During school holidays, Mon–Sat 1030–1730, Sun 1230–1730. ££ plus cost of piece. Group concessions. Car and coach parking. Telephone (01292) 280844.

Drop in craft studio located on a canal boat on the Forth and Clyde Canal. Suitable for all ages and abilities. Ceramic painting, silk painting, glass painting and pyrography. Parties welcome.

CRARAE GARDENS 631

NTS. Crarae, Inveraray, Argyll. On A83, 10m south of Inveraray. Garden open all year, daily 0930–sunset; visitor centre Good Friday–Sep, daily 1000–1700. Charge ££. Group concessions. Explanatory displays. Gift shop. Plant sales. WC. Wheelchair access with assistance. Disabled WC. Car and coach parking. Telephone (01546) 886614. www.nts.org.uk

The nearest Scotland has to a Himalayan garden. This is a spectacular site at any time of the year, but spring and Autumn are particularly good.

CRINAN CANAL 632 5 H24

Crinan Canal Office, Pier Square, Ardrishaig. Crinan to Ardrishaig, by Lochgilphead. Nearest bus station Ardrishaig. Open all year (except during winter maintenance), daily 0830–1700. Telephone to confirm times. Free. Explanatory displays. Picnic area. Limited wheelchair access. Car parking. Telephone (01546) 603210. www.scottishcanals.co.uk

Constructed between 1793 and 1801 to carry ships from Loch Fyne to the Atlantic without rounding Kintyre. The 9-mile (14.5km) stretch of water with 15 locks is now almost entirely used by pleasure craft. The towing path provides a pleasant, easy walk with the interest of canal activity. There are magnificent views to the Western Isles from Crinan. The Crinan basin, coffee shop, boatyard and hotel make a visit well worthwhile.

CRINAN WOOD 633 5 H24

Crinan, Argyll & Bute. Crinan, 6 miles (9.5km) north west of Lochgilphead on B841. Nearest railway station Oban; bus from Oban to Lochgilphead , then from Lochgilphead to Crinan (infrequent service). Access at all times. Free. Explanatory displays. Wheelchair access along woodland edge, on Crinan canal towpath. Car parking. Telephone (01764) 662554. www.woodland-trust.org.uk

Crinan Wood is categorised as a temperate rainforest, benefitting from sea mists and plentiful rain. Over 13 types of fern grow here, together with many varieties of mosses and lichens. Waymarked trails and good views of Jura and Corryvreckan to the west, Ben More to the north.

CRUACHAN POWER STATION 634 5 J23

Dalmally, Argyll. 18 miles (29km) east of Oban on A85. Nearest railway station Cruachan, bus service from Oban and Glasgow. Open Easter–Nov, daily 0930–1700.

Jul–Aug closes at 1800. Charge £. Group concessions. Guided tours. Explanatory displays. Gift shop. Café and picnic area. WC. Wheelchair access with assistance. Disabled WC. Car and coach parking. Telephone (01866) 822618.

A guided tour takes visitors 0.5 mile (1km) inside Ben Cruachan to see a reversible pumped storage scheme. An exhibition houses touch screen and computer video technology.

CRUISE LOCH LOMOND   635   5 K24

The Boatyard, Tarbet, Loch Lomond, Argyll & Bute. On A82, on west shore of Loch Lomond. Daily cruises for coach tours, groups and individuals – telephone to confirm departure times. Lunch cruise to Inversnaid Hotel departs most days at 1130. Charge dependent on cruise. Group concessions. WC. Wheelchair access with assistance. Car parking. Telephone (01301) 702356. www.cruiselochlomond.co.uk

Daily cruises around the scenic, northern fjord-like end of the loch.

CULCREUCH CASTLE AND COUNTRY PARK   636   5 M25

Fintry, Stirling. Nearest railway station Stirling, nearest bus station Balfron. Open all year, daily 1100–2300. Free. Guided tours for groups only by prior arrangement. Gift shop. Refreshments available. WC. Limited wheelchair access. Disabled WC. Car and coach parking. Telephone (01360) 860555. www.culcreuch.com

A 14th-century castle, ancestral home of the Clan Galbraith, set in a 1600 acre (647.5ha) estate. Woodland, river and moorland walks. Pinetum. Walled garden and children's play area. The castle houses a hotel and conference centre.

CUNNINGHAME GRAHAM MEMORIAL   637   5 L24

NTS. Gartmore, Stirling. 2 miles (3km) south west of Aberfoyle, off A81. Access at all times. Free. Explanatory displays. Wheelchair access with assistance. Car and coach parking. www.nts.org.uk

A cairn commemorates the extraordinary life of R. B. Cunninghame Graham (1852–1936). He was a radical politician, writer, traveller and renowned horseman. An interpretive panel gives details of his life and the estate of Gartmore, his family home.

BARBARA DAVIDSON POTTERY   638   9 N25

Muirhall Farm, Larbert, Stirlingshire. On the A88 north side of Larbert, 9 miles (14.5km) south of Stirling, signposted from the A9 at the Inches roundabout.. Nearest railway station Larbert, then 12 minute walk, or bus from Stirling or Falkirk. Open all year, Mon–Sat 1000–1700; closed Christmas, New Year and local holidays – telephone to confirm. Free. Guided tours by arrangment; demonstration (£). Gift shop. Wheelchair access. Car parking. Telephone (01324) 554430. www.barbara-davidson.com

A working pottery in a picturesque converted 17th-century farm steading. Products are hand-thrown stoneware, mostly functional. In July and August, visitors can try their hand at making a pot or painting a pot (small charge).

DENNY SHIP MODEL EXPERIMENT TANK   639   9 L25

Castle Street, Dumbarton, Dunbartonshire. 200 yards (182m) east of Dumbarton town centre. Bus or rail from Glasgow. Open all year (except Christmas and New Year), Mon–Sat 1000–1600. Charge £. Group concessions. Guided tours on request. Explanatory displays. Gift shop. Picnic area. WC. Limited wheelchair access. Car and coach parking. Telephone (01389) 763444.

A ship model experiment tank constructed in 1882 and retaining many of its original features. Fully restored to working order by the Scottish Maritime Museum so that the original process can be demonstrated.

DOLLAR GLEN   640   10 N24

0.3 miles (0.5km) north of Dollar, Clackmannanshire. Bus from Alloa and Stirling. Access at all times. Free. Explanatory displays. Refreshments and facilities in Dollar. Limited wheelchair access. Car parking.

At the foot of the Ochil Hills, Dollar Glen is unmistakable with its imposing castle, Castle Campbell, at its head. A path crosses Dollar Burn and follows the west side of the glen to emerge at the rear of the castle. See also 619 Castle Campbell.

DOLLAR MUSEUM   641   10 N24

Castle Campbell Hall, 1 High Street, Dollar. At the top of East Burnside. Open from Easter–Christmas, Sat 1100–1300 and 1400–1630, Sun 1400–1630, and by appointment (contact curator on 01259 742895). Free. Guided tours on request. Explanatory displays. Gift shop. Children's corner. WC. Wheelchair access (except reading room). Disabled WC. Car parking. Telephone (01259) 742895. www.scottishmuseums.org.uk

A small award-winning museum with frequently changing, temporary exhibitions. Also permanent exhibitions on the history of Dollar, Castle Campbell, Dollar Academy, the Devon Valley Railway and the prehistory of Dollar. Reading room with local history material, including many photographs.

DOUNE CASTLE   642   5 M24

HS. Castle Road, Doune. Off A84 at Doune, 10 miles (16km) north west of Stirling. Nearest railway station Dunblane, bus via Doune from Stirling or Callander. Open Apr–Sep, daily 0930–1830; Oct–Mar, Mon–Sun 0930–1630, closed Thu and Fri. Charge £. Group concessions. Explanatory displays. Gift shop. Picnic area. Blind visitors may touch carvings. Limited wheelchair access. Car parking. Telephone (01786) 841742. www.historic-scotland.gov.uk

A magnificent late 14th-century courtyard castle built for the Regent Albany. Its most striking feature is the combination of tower, gatehouse and hall with its kitchen in a massive frontal block. Later possessed by the Stuarts of Doune, Earls of Moray.

DRYMEN POTTERY   643   5 L25

The Square, Drymen, Stirlingshire. 20 miles (32km) north of Glasgow. Car and coach parking nearby. Bus from Glasgow or Balloch (by train to Balloch). Open all year (except Christmas Day and New Year), daily 1000–1600. Free. Gift shop. Coffee shop. WC. Wheelchair access to shop and tearoom only. Disabled WC. Telephone (01360) 660458.

Pottery studio with a large coffee and gift shop. Licenced pub upstairs.

DUART CASTLE   644   5 H23

Craignure, Isle of Mull, Argyll. Take A849 to Iona and after 1.5 miles (2km) turn right at the turning to Kilpatrick. Duart is at the end of this road.. By ferry from Oban to Craignure, coach (Mull Experience) from Craignure. By launch from Oban to Castle jetty, weather permitting. Open Apr Sun–Thur 1100–1600 (castle only), and May–Oct, daily 1030–1730. Charge ££. Grounds free. Group concessions. Guided tours, there is a guide in the castle at all times. Explanatory displays. Leaflet in French, German, Italian and Spanish. Gift shop. Tearoom and picnic area. WC. Limited wheelchair access to shop and tearoom only. Car and coach parking. Telephone (01680) 812309. www.duartcastle.com

A fortress and a family home, Duart is a focal point for Macleans from all over the world. Clearly visible from the ferry as you approach the Isle of Mull, the castle stands on a cliff overlooking the sea. There are kitchens, dungeons, a banqueting hall, an exhibition area and state bedroom.

There is a video for those who do not wish to climb the turnpike stairs. Children can follow their own tour. Fresh soup, scones and soda bread prepared on site, as well as a wide variety of cakes.

There is a gift shop, you can pick up emails, hire a kilt, or even have a game of draughts. Walk in the grounds and through the Millennium Wood. Weather permitting you can sail from Oban on the launch, The Duchess, direct to the castle's own jetty.

DUMBARTON CASTLE   645   9 L25

HS. Castle Road, Dumbarton. Off the A814 in Dumbarton on Dumbarton Rock. Nearest railway station Dumbarton East, bus from Glasgow then 20 minute walk. Open Apr–Sep, Mon–Sun 0930–1830; Oct–Mar, Mon–Sun 0930–1830 (closed Thu pm and Fri). Charge £. Group concessions. Explanatory displays. Gift shop. Picnic area. WC. Car parking. Telephone (01389) 732167. www.historic-scotland.gov.uk

Spectacularly sited on a volcanic rock, the site of the ancient capital of Strathclyde. The most interesting features are the 18th-century artillery fortifications, with the 19th-century guns. Also a mostly modern barrack, a dungeon, a 12th-century gateway and a sundial gifted by Mary, Queen of Scots.

DUNADD FORT   646   5 H24

HS. Kilmartin Glen. 1 mile (2km) west of Kilmichael Glassary, Argyll. Nearest railway station Oban, then bus to Lochgilphead. Access at all reasonable times. Free. Telephone (01786) 431326. www.historic-scotland.gov.uk

A spectacular site occupied since the Iron Age. The well-preserved hill fort is part-Roman, when it was a stronghold of Dalriada, the kingdom of the Scots.

DUNAGOIL VITRIFIED FORT   647   9 J26

Isle of Bute. From A844, turn left after Kingarth Hotel onto unclassified road to Dunagoil for 0.25 mile (0.5km).

On a commanding site at the south of the island, this ancient fort is clear evidence of Iron Age habitation.

DUNAVERTY ROCK   648   7 H28

At Southend, Mull of Kintyre, dominating beach and golf course. Access at all times. Free.

Formerly the site of Dunaverty Castle, a Macdonald stronghold. In 1647, about 300 people were put to death here by Covenanters under General Leslie. The rock is known locally as Blood Rock.

DUNBLANE MUSEUM   649   10 M24

The Cross, Dunblane, Perthshire. 6 miles (9.5km) north of Stirling. Bus from Perth, Stirling or Glasgow. Railway station within 500 yards (457m). Open May–Sep,

Mon–Sat 1030–1630. Free. Guided tours on request. Explanatory displays and video. Gift shop. WC. Limited wheelchair access. Car and coach parking. Telephone (01765) 823440. www.dunblanemuseum.org.uk

A museum located in barrel-vaulted rooms built in 1624. Contents include paintings, books, and artefacts which illustrate the life of the cathedral and its congregation from St Blane to the restoration in 1893. Large collection of communion tokens.

DUNCHRAIGAIG CAIRN   650   5 H24

HS. Kilmartin Glen. 1.25 miles (2km) south of Kilmartin, Argyll. Nearest railway station Oban, then bus to Lochgilphead. Access at all reasonable times. Free. Picnic area. Car parking. Telephone (01786) 431326. www.historic-scotland.gov.uk

A Bronze Age cairn excavated in the last century.

DUNCRYNE HILL   651   5 L25

Between Balloch and Drymen, just off A811 at the east end of Gartocharn. Access at all times. Free.

Known locally as The Dumpling, due to its shape, this small hill can be climbed using a short steep path. The reward at the top is one of the best views of Loch Lomond.

DUNGLASS CASTLE AND HENRY BELL OBELISK   652   9 L25

On the shore of the River Clyde near the village of Bowling. A right of way exists from A814 to the Castle but visitors should ask for access at main gate of Esso terminal. Access at all times. Free.

Ruined castle on the shore of the River Clyde. Former seat of the Colquhoun family which dates back to the 14th century. Obelisk erected within the grounds to the memory of Henry Bell, first provost of Helensburgh and pioneer of the steam boat.

DUNSTAFFNAGE CASTLE AND CHAPEL   653   5 H23

HS. Off the A85 by Loch Etive, 3.5 miles (5km) north of Oban, Argyll. Nearest railway station Oban, bus from Oban to Dunbeg then 1 mile (2km) walk. Open Apr–Sep, Mon–Sun 0930–1830; Oct–Mar 0930–1630 (closed Thu and Fri). Charge £. Group concessions. Explanatory displays. Gift shop. WC. Limited wheelchair access. Car and coach parking. Telephone (01631) 562465. www.historic-scotland.gov.uk

A fine, well-preserved 13th-century castle built on rock. Nearby, ruins of what was an exceptionally beautiful chapel.

EASDALE ISLAND FOLK MUSEUM   654   5 H23

Easdale Island, by Oban, Argyll. On B844, 16 miles (25.5km) south of Oban. Car and coach parking on the mainland. Nearest railway station at Oban. Bus to Seil Island. Passenger ferry to Easdale Island. Open Apr–mid Oct, daily 1030–1730. Charge £. Group concessions. Guided tours. Explanatory displays. Tearoom on the island. WC. Braille information available. Wheelchair access (access to the museum is by one step; however, ferry access can be difficult). Telephone (01852) 300370. www.slate.org.uk

The museum contains a fascinating pictorial collection showing the industrial and domestic life of the Slate Islands in the 19th century. Records of the slate quarriers, the volunteers, Friendly Societies, education and public health. Also a comprehensive study of the area's geology.

EILEACH AN NAOIMH   655   5 G24

HS. On an island of that name in the Garvellach group, north of Jura, Argyll.
Transport by boat on request, dependent on weather. Telephone Craobh Haven Boat
Trips (01852) 500664 or Ruby Cruises (01852) 500616 for details. Access at all
reasonable times. Free. Telephone (01786) 431326. www.historic-scotland.gov.uk

The ruins of beehive cells, a chapel and a graveyard. Associated by local tradition
with St Columba.

EILEAN MOR – ST CORMAC'S CHAPEL   656   7 H25

HS. On Eilean Mor, a small island off the coast of Knapdale in the Sound of Jura. Bus
from Lochgilphead to Tayvallich, from there no public transport. Half-day charter
boat trips for groups from Crinan, telephone Gemini Cruises (01546) 830238. Access
at all reasonable times. Free. Telephone (01786) 431326. www.historic-scotland.gov.uk

A chapel with a vaulted chancel containing the effigy of an ecclesiastical figure.
Probably 12th century.

ETTRICK BAY   657   9 J26

On the Isle of Bute. From A844 take Ettrick Bay turning, 2.5 miles (4km) north of
Rothesay, then continue for 3 miles (5km). Access at all times. Free. Tearoom. WC.

A popular and safe beach with tearoom and toilet facilities.

THE FALKIRK WHEEL   658   9 N25

Lime Road, Tamfourhill, Falkirk. At the interchange between the Union and the Forth
and Clyde canals, close to Tamfourhill, south Falkirk. Bus service or taxi from Falkirk
High railway station. Open Apr–Oct, daily 0900–1800; Nov–Mar, daily 1000–1500
(closed Christmas Day and during Jan for scheduled maintenance). Charge £££.
Group concessions. Guided tours. Explanatory displays. Gift shop. Café. Children's
play area. WC. Written script available for barge ride interpretation. Dedicated
disabled car parking spaces. Fresh drinking water for guide and hearing dogs in
visitor centre. Wheelchairs available for use in visitor centre and around the site.
Wheelchair access (but no wheelchair access onto trip boats at present). Disabled
WC. Car and coach parking. Telephone (01324) 619888. www.thefalkirkwheel.co.uk

The world's first and only rotating boat lift. Linking two canals with water levels
115 feet (35m) apart, it is has replaced 11 locks and is the centrepiece of the
Millennium Link, the project that re-established the waterway link between the
west and east coasts of Scotland. Visitor centre and boat trips through the wheel
(pre-booking required on 08700 500208). Events take place throughout the year.

FALLS OF DOCHART   659   5 M23

Killin. Access to this island and to the graveyard available from Tourist Information
Centre in Killin. Free.

Dramatic waterfalls rushing through the centre of this picturesque Highland
village. On the island of Inchbuie in the river is the burial ground of Clan McNab.

FINLAGGAN TRUST   660   7 F26

The Cottage, Ballygrant, Isle of Islay. 2 miles (3km) off A846 from Port Askaig. Open
Apr, Sun, Tue and Thu 1300–1630; May–Sep, daily 1300–1630; Oct, Sun, Tue and Thu
1300–1600. Charge £. Group concessions. Guided tours by prior arrangement.
Explanatory displays. Gift shop. WC. Wheelchair access to visitor centre. Car and
coach parking. Telephone (01496) 840644. www.islay.com

Islay, known as the Cradle of Clan Donald and Finlaggan, is the main headquarters of the Lords of the Isles and a place of pilgrimage for clan members today. The interpretive centre describes the history of the area and details the archaeological finds to-date.

FISHING MULL'S RIVERS AND LOCHS   661   5 F22

Tostarie, Torloisk, Ulva Ferry, Isle of Mull. On island of Mull. Transport can be provided locally. Open Mar–Oct, daily. Charge £££ by half or full day. Telephone (01688) 500249.

Mull offers fantastic fishing for salmon, sea trout and brown trout. The proprietor will guide visitors around the rivers and lochs, showing the best spots for fish, taking into account weather and water conditions. As well as outstanding fishing, Mull has spectacular scenery and abundant wildlife, and it is all taken in during a half or whole day's fishing. Novices and professionals catered for. Everything, from tackle to transport, can be arranged.

GAIRLOCH HARBOUR   662   4 H16

Gairloch, Ross-shire. 75 miles (120km) west of Inverness. Local bus service. Harbour open all year, daily. For navigation information, contact the Harbour Master. Free. Refreshments available nearby. Usual harbour facilities, including chandlery. WC. Wheelchair access with assistance. Disabled WC. Car and coach parking. Telephone (01445) 712140. www.gairloch.co.uk

The area offers clean, sandy beaches and lots of wildlife. Various boat and fishing trips can be made from the harbour.

GARTMORN DAM COUNTRY PARK   663   10 N24

Sauchie, Near Alloa. 1.25 miles (2km) east of A908, Sauchie. Bus to Sauchie from Alloa. Open all year. Free. Explanatory displays. Gift shop, refreshments, WC and disabled WC available during summer and winter weekends. Sunken garden, orienteering course. WC. Wheelchair access. Disabled WC. Car parking. Telephone (01259) 214319. www.clacksweb.org.uk

The country park is a peaceful retreat for visitors to walk, cycle, horse ride or fish. Extensive network of paths. Gartmorn Dam itself is a 170 acre (69ha) resevoir engineered by Sir John Erskine to power pumps which drained mines.

GEILSTON GARDEN   664   9 L25

NTS. Cardross, Dumbarton. On A814 at west end of Cardross, 18 miles (29km) north of Glasgow. Nearest railway station Cardross, then 1 mile (1.5km) walk. Bus from Helensburgh or Dumbarton. Open Apr–Oct, daily 0930–1700. Charge £ (honesty box). Explanatory displays. WC. Limited wheelchair access. Disabled WC. Car and coach parking. Telephone (01389) 841867. www.nts.org.uk

Small estate typical of those owned on the banks of the Clyde by tobacco barons and factory owners who made their money in 19th-century Glasgow. Charming garden with walled area and wooded glen.

GLEBE CAIRN   665   5 H24

HS. In Kilmartin Glen, Argyll. Nearest railway station Oban, then bus to Kilmartin. Access at all reasonable times. Free. Telephone (01786) 431326. www.historic-scotland.gov.uk

An early Bronze Age burial cairn with two burial chambers (cists).

GLEN FINGLAS 666 5 L24

Off A821, approx 5 miles (8km) west of Callander. Access at all times. Free. Explanatory displays. Refreshments at Brig O'Turk. Car parking. Telephone (01764) 662554. www.woodland-trust.org.uk

Enjoy walks from 15 minutes to 15 miles at the Woodland Trust's largest and most spectacular site. There are mountains, glens, lochs and wildlife.

GLENARN GARDENS 667 5 K25

Glenarn Gardens, Glenarn Road, Rhu, by Helensburgh, Argyll & Bute. In the village on Glenarn Road. Coach parking by arrangment only. Open Mar–Sep, from dawn to dusk. Charge £. Guided tours, by arrangement. Explanatory displays, leaflet provided. Refreshments by arrangement for groups. Plant sales. Limited wheelchair access. Telephone (01436) 820493.

A west coast garden in a sheltered glen overlooking the Gareloch, famous for the collection of rare and tender rhododendrons. Also fine magnolias and many other interesting ericaceous plants. Colour all year round. A network of paths with small bridges connect the different parts of the garden – the pond, rock garden, woodland, greenhouse and the productive vegetable patch.

GLENBARR ABBEY VISITOR CENTRE 668 7 H27

Glenbarr, Tarbert, Argyll. On the A83, 12 miles (19km) north of Campbeltown. Bus from Glasgow. Open Easter–Oct daily (except Tue), 1000–1700. Charge £. Group concessions. Guided tours (available in German). Explanatory displays. Gift shop. Tearoom. Short woodland walk. WC. Limited wheelchair access. Car and coach parking. Telephone (01583) 421247.

A house in the 18th-century Gothic Revival style, the seat of the lairds of Glenbarr since 1796, designed by James Gillespie Graham. Tours are conducted by the 5th laird, Angus Macalister, whose home this is. Among items displayed are 19th-century fashions, Spode, Sèvres and Derby china, gloves worn by Mary, Queen of Scots, thimble collection.

GLENGOYNE DISTILLERY 669 5 L25

Dumgoyne, Killearn, Glasgow. On the A81, 3 miles (5km) north of Strathblane. Bus from Glasgow or Stirling. Open all year, Mon–Sat 1000–1600, Sun 1200–1600. Charge ££. Accompanied children under 18 free. Group concessions. Guided tours (video presentation and literature available in various different languages). Explanatory displays. Gift shop. Scenic waterfall walk. WC. Wheelchair access. Disabled WC. Car and coach parking. Telephone (01360) 550254. www.glengoyne.com

First licensed in 1833, Glengoyne Distillery is often described as Scotland's most beautiful distillery. Close to Glasgow, Stirling and Loch Lomond. Visitors can enjoy dram of whisky in reception room, overlooking the beautiful waterfall and glen, before being taken on a guided tour of the distillery. No visit to Glengoyne is complete without a look in the heritage room and shop which is full of different whiskies, gifts and collectables.

HAMILTON TOY COLLECTION 670 5 M24

111 Main Street, Callander. On the High Street in Callandar, 16 miles (25.5km) north west of Stirling on A84. Nearest railway station Stirling, bus service to Callander passes door. Open Easter–Oct, Tue–Sun 1200–1630. Charge £. Group concessions. Guided tours for groups by special arrangement only. Gift shop. WC. Limited wheelchair access. Disabled WC. Car parking. Telephone (01877) 330004.

A family-run toy museum comprising five rooms of toys dating from between 1880 and 1980. Teddy bears, trains (running layout), dolls, toy soldiers, dolls houses and accessories, cars, bygones, planes, ships, children's books, science fiction toys and associated memorabilia.

HEBRIDEAN WHALE AND DOLPHIN TRUST   671   5 G22

28 Main Street, Tobermory, Isle of Mull. In the centre of Tobermory. Bus service from Craignure ferry terminal. Open all year, Mon—Sat 1000–1700, Sun 1100–1600. Free. Guided tours on request. Explanatory displays. Gift shop. Children's corner with computer games. Wheelchair access. Car parking. Telephone (01688) 302620. www.hwdt.org

Visitor centre offering information on marine issues and local species, The trust carries out research projects (such as eco-tourism, minke whale photo ID) and education (school visits).

HERMITAGE PARK   672   9 K25

In Helensburgh town centre. Nearest railway station Helensburgh. Access at all times. Free.

Formal gardens, play area, putting green, bowling green. Features a memorial bust to John Logie Baird, the inventor of television, who was born in Helensburgh.

HIGHLAND MARY'S STATUE   673   9 K25

Castle gardens, near Dunoon pier. Access at all times. Car parking.

The statue of Burns' Highland Mary at the foot of the Castle Hill. Mary Campbell was born on a farm in Dunoon and exchanged vows with Burns. However, she died the following autumn and Burns went on to marry Jean Armour.

HILL HOUSE   674   9 K25

NTS. Upper Colquhoun Street, Helensburgh. Off B832, 23 miles (37km) north west of Glasgow. Nearest railway station Helensburgh, then 1.5 mile (2.5km) walk. Open Apr–Oct, daily 1330–1730. Charge £££. Groups must pre-book and arrive prior to 1300. Explanatory displays in gift and design shops. Gift shop. Tearoom. Garden. WC. Braille information sheet. Limited wheelchair access. Disabled WC. Car parking. Telephone (01436) 673900. www.nts.org.uk

Charles Rennie Mackintosh designed this house for the publisher Walter Blackie in 1904. A masterpiece of domestic architecture synthesizing traditional Scottish style with avant-garde innovation, this extraordinary building still looks modern today. Mackintosh, with his wife Margaret, also designed the interiors and most of the furniture.

BRIDGE OF ALLAN PARISH CHURCH   675   10 N24

12 Keir Street, Bridge of Allan, Stirling. 2 miles (3km) south of exit 11 on M9. Nearest railway station Bridge of Allan, then ten minute walk. Bus from Stirling. Open Jun–Sep (except during weddings), Sat 1000–1600. Free. Guided tours. Explanatory displays. Gift shop. WC. Wheelchair access. Car and coach parking. Telephone (01786) 834155. www.bridgeofallanparishchurch.org.uk

An attractive 19th-century building with fine timbered roof and excellent stained glass windows. The chancel furnishings, consisting of pulpit, communion table, chair, organ screen and choir rail, were designed in 1904 by Charles Rennie Mackintosh in light oak and represent a unique aspect of Mackintosh's style. Four complementing chairs, gifted in 1999, and a font in light oak add modern interest.

INCHCAILLOCH NATURE RESERVE   676   5 L24

On Inchcailloch island, Loch Lomond opposite Balmaha. Ferry from McFarlanes boatyard, Balmaha (01360) 870214. Access all year, warden service from Easter–mid Sep. Free. Charge for camping (telephone to arrange) and ferry crossing. Picnic and barbecue area at Port Bawn. Telephone for disabled access. Car and coach parking. Telephone (01786) 450362.

Protected oak woodland of European importance. The island lies on the highland boundry fault providing a great opportunity to see the distinction between lowland and highland areas of Loch Lomond. Woodland birds, deer, bluebell wood. Two miles (3km) of waymarked paths, taking visitors to a beach with picnic and barbecue facility.

INCHKENNETH CHAPEL   677   5 G22

HS. On the island of Inch Kenneth off the west coast of the Isle of Mull, Argyll. Access at all reasonable times. Free. Telephone (01786) 431326. www.historic-scotland.gov.uk

A simple building of a distinctive west Highland type, with good medieval monuments in the graveyard.

INCHMAHOME PRIORY   678   5 M24

HS. On an island in the Lake of Mentieth, Perthshire. Access by boat from Port of Menteith, on A81, 4 miles (6.5km) east of Aberfoyle. Bus from Glasgow or Stirling to Port of Menteith, then short walk to ferry. Open Apr–Sep, daily 0930–1830 (last outward sailing at 1715). Charge ££. Group concessions. Gift shop. Picnic area. WC. Limited wheelchair access. Disabled WC. Car parking. Telephone (01877) 385294. www.historic-scotland.gov.uk

The beautifully situated ruins of an Augustinian monastery founded in 1238, with much 13th-century building surviving. Briefly housed Mary, Queen of Scots as an infant in 1547.

INVERARAY BELL TOWER   679   5 J24

The Avenue, Inveraray, Argyll. In centre of town. Approach through the arches by the Argyll Hotel, then up the avenue. Nearest railway station Arrochar, bus from Glasgow or Oban. Open May–Sep, daily 1000–1300 and 1400–1700. Charge £. Children under 5 free. Group concessions. Explanatory displays. Gift shop. Picnic area and garden. Limited wheelchair access. Car and coach parking.

This 126 feet (38.5m) high granite tower houses Scotland's finest ring of bells and the world's second-heaviest ring of ten bells. Excellent views, pleasant grounds. Opportunities to see bells and ringers in action. Recordings always available when tower open. Easy staircase to top viewing gallery in bell chamber.

INVERARAY CASTLE   680   5 J24

Inveraray, Argyll. On the A83, 0.5 mile (1km) north of Inveraray. Nearest railway station Arrochar, bus from Glasgow or Oban. Open Apr, May and Oct, Mon, Thu and Sat 1000–1300 and 1400–1745, Sun 1300–1745; Jun–Sep, Mon–Sat 1000–1745, Sun 1300–1745. Charge £££. Group concessions. Guided tours (available in French and

German by arrangement). Explanatory displays. Gift shop. Tearoom and picnic area. WC. Limited wheelchair access. Disabled WC. Car and coach parking. Telephone (01499) 302203. www.inveraray-castle.com

The Duke of Argyll's family, the senior branch of the Campbell Clan, moved from Loch Awe to Inveraray in the first half of the 15th century. The present building, in the style of a castle, was erected between 1745 and 1790 to replace an earlier traditional fortified keep, and marks the start of more settled times. It was designed by Roger Morris and Robert Mylne. On display are the famous collections of armour, French tapestries, fine examples of Scottish and European furniture, and a wealth of other works of art together with a genealogical display in the Clan Room. Gardens open by appointment only.

INVERARAY JAIL   681   5 J24

Church Square, Inveraray, Argyll. In Inveraray centre. Nearest railway station Arrochar, bus from Glasgow or Oban. Open Apr–Oct, daily 0930–1700; Nov–Mar, daily 1000–1600 (closed Christmas Day and New Year's Day). Last entry one hour before closing. Charge £££. Group concessions. Explanatory displays (translated to French, German, Dutch and Italian). Costumed guides. Gift shop. WC. Induction loop in courtroom. Limited wheelchair access to ground floor (free of charge). Disabled WC. Telephone (01499) 302381. www.inverarayjail.co.uk

Award-winning attraction. Visitors can see a medieval punishment exhibition, listen to trials in the superb 1820 courtroom, visit the airing yards, talk with guides dressed as warders, prisoners and matron, experience life inside prison and try the crank machine, whipping table and hammocks, before comparing all this with a new exhibition *In Prison Today*.

INVERARAY MARITIME MUSEUM   682   5 J24

Arctic Penguin, The Pier, Inveraray, Argyll. In Inveraray centre. Nearest railway station Arrochar, bus from Glasgow or Oban. Open all year, daily 1000–1800, closed Christmas and New Year's Day. Charge ££. Group concessions. Guided tours by prior arrangement. Explanatory displays. Gift shop. Play area. WC. Limited wheelchair access. Disabled WC. Car and coach parking. Telephone (01499) 302213.

A fascinating collection of maritime displays, memorabilia, archive film and entertaining hands-on activities on board one of the last iron ships built (1911). Graphic tableaux in the hold depict the hardships suffered on emigrant ships during the Highland clearances. Inveraray was the birthplace of Neil Munro, author of the *Para Handy* stories. Scotland's last working Clyde Puffer (a small cargo vessel) takes visitors on a short cruise of Loch Fyne.

INVERARAY WOOLLEN MILL   683   5 J24

The Anvil, Inveraray, Argyll, . Off the A83. Nearest railway station Arrochar, bus from Glasgow or Oban. Open all year, daily summer 0900–1700; spring and autumn 1000–1730; winter 1000–1700. Free. Explanatory displays. Gift shop. Coffee shop. WC. Limited wheelchair access. Car and coach parking. Telephone (01499) 302166. www.ewm.co.uk

Situated in an old blacksmith's shop dating back to 1787, the mill shop has a wide selection of quality knitwear, clothing accessories and gifts.

INVERBEG GALLERIES   684   5 L24

Inverbeg, Loch Lomond. At Inverbeg on the A82, 3 miles (5km) north of Luss. Bus from Glasgow. Open daily all year (except Christmas Day), 1000–1800, closed Thu pm. Free. Guided tours. Explanatory displays. Wheelchair access with assistance. Car and coach parking. Telephone (01436) 860277. www.inverbeggalleries.co.uk

An internationally renowned art gallery with one of the largest selections of oil and watercolour paintings and prints in Europe, all for sale. Also gifts for sale.

INVERSNAID RSPB NATURE RESERVE   685   5 L24

RSPB. By Aberfoyle, Stirlingshire. 15 miles (24km) west of Aberfoyle at end of B829 and an unclassified road. Nearest railway station at Stirling (35 miles/56km). Post bus from Aberfoyle and minibuses from Callander and Aberfoyle. Bus stop at Inversnaid Hotel is 0.5 mile (1km) from reserve. Reserve open at all times. Free. WC Mar–Oct only. Nature trail. Car and coach parking. Telephone 0141 331 0993. www.rspb.org.uk/scotland

Inversnaid is set on the east shore of Loch Lomond. The woodland rises steeply from the shores of the loch and then gives way to open moorland. In the summer, pied flycatchers and redstarts breed here, along with resident birds. Buzzards nest on the crags in the wood and black grouse can sometimes be seen on the moorland.

IONA   686   5 F23

NTS. Argyll. An island off the south west tip of the Isle of Mull. Car and coach parking at Fionnphort. By ferry from Oban to Craignure, bus from Craignure to Fionnphort, by ferry to Iona. Day tours from Oban in summer. Open all year. Free. Explanatory displays. Gift shop. Coffee shop at Abbey (not NTS). WC. Limited wheelchair access. Telephone Telephone NTS Regional Office (01631) 570000. www.nts.org.uk

The island where Columba began to spread the gospel in 563 AD. Superb long sandy beaches and turquoise seas. Unrivalled views.

IONA ABBEY   687   5 F23

HS. Isle of Iona, Argyll. On an island off the south west tip of the Isle of Mull. Car and coach parking at Fionnphort. By ferry from Oban to Craignure, bus from Craignure to Fionnphort, by ferry to Iona. Day tours from Oban in summer. Open all year. Charge £. Group concessions. Explanatory displays. Gift shop. WC. Induction loop for services. Limited wheelchair access. Telephone (01681) 700512. www.historic-scotland.gov.uk

Iona's wealth of historical and religious attractions and artefacts include the abbey church and cloisters, St Columba's shrine, the site of St Columba's writing cell and a superb collection of over 180 medieval carved stones. In the graveyard many early Scottish kings and chiefs are buried alongside monks. Nearby are the remains of the 13th-century nunnery.

ISLAND ENCOUNTER, WILDLIFE/BIRDWATCH SAFARIS   688   5 G22

c/o Arla Beag Cottage, Arle, Aros, Isle of Mull. Ferry from Oban to Craignure; visitors collected from ferry and other locations on Mull by arrangement. Open Mar–Oct, daily 1030–1700. Charge £££. Group concessions. Guided tours. Picnic lunch provided. Limited wheelchair access. Telephone (01680) 300441. www.mullwildlife.co.uk

Island Encounter wildlife/birdwatch safaris offer whole day trips for visitors wishing to see and experience wildlife and birds in areas of the island not usually visited. Binoculars, telescopes and lunch provided. Otters and eagles a priority.

ISLAY NATURAL HISTORY TRUST   689   7 F26

Islay Wildlife Information Centre, Port Charlotte, Isle of Islay. Below the youth hostel in Port Charlotte. Local bus service. Open Easter–Oct, Sun–Fri 1000–1500; Jul–Aug open daily, 1000–1700; Nov–Easter by arrangement. Charge £. Children under 5 free. Tickets valid for 1 week. Group concessions. Explanatory displays. Gift shop. Children's room, activities. WC. Wheelchair access. Disabled WC. Car parking. Telephone (01496) 850288. www.islaywildlife.freeserve.co.uk

The Wildlife Information Centre has displays on all aspects of Islay's wildlife and landscape, as well as an extensive reference library, a children's room and a laboratory where children and adults can try a number of hands-on activities such as dissecting owl pellets and making seaweed pictures. Family activity sessions during July and August.

ISLAY WOOLLEN MILL   690   7 F26

Bridgend, Islay. On the Askaig Road, 1 mile (2km) from Bridgend. Open all year, Mon–Sat 1000–1700. Closed Christmas and New Year. Free. Guided tours. Explanatory displays. Gift shop. Picnic area. WC. Car and coach parking. Telephone (01496) 810563.

An early Victorian mill containing a tweed and woollen factory which produces tartan including all the tartans used in the films *Braveheart* and *Rob Roy*. Also a shop.

ISLE OF BUTE DISCOVERY CENTRE   691   9 J26

Victoria Street, Rothesay, Isle of Bute. On Rothesay seafront, close to ferry and bus terminal. Open Apr–Oct, Mon–Fri 1000–1700 (Jul and Aug closes 1800), Sat–Sun 1000–1700; Nov–Mar, Mon–Fri 1000–1700, Sat and Sun 1000–1600. Free. Explanatory displays. Gift shop. Bistro with panoramic views over Rothesay Bay. WC. Wheelchair access. Disabled WC. Telephone (08707) 200619. www.visitbute.com

Housed in Rothesay's famous 1924 Winter Garden, now fully restored to its former glory, this exciting award-winning centre is a 'must see' for all visitors to the beautiful island of Bute. A unique multi-media exhibition showcases the island's many attractions, and includes fascinating film footage of bygone Bute, and the island today. Genealogy Centre helps visitors trace their local family roots. Discovery Theatre features all the latest film releases. Also comprehensive and friendly Tourist Information Centre.

ISLE OF JURA DISTILLERY   692   7 G25

Craighouse, Isle of Jura, Argyll. By ferry from Islay. Shop open Easter–Oct, daily 1000–1600; Nov –Easter 1200–1500. Tours by arrangement. Charge £. Guided tours. Gift shop. Limited wheelchair access. Disabled WC. Car and coach parking. Telephone (01496) 820240. www.isleofjura.com

A distillery built in 1810 on a site where illegal distillation occurred for almost 300 years.

ISLE OF MULL LANDROVER WILDLIFE EXPEDITIONS   693   5 G22

Torr Buan, Ulva Ferry, Isle of Mull, Argyll. Tours run all year. Charge £££. Charge includes refreshments and lunch. Group concessions. Guided tours. Explanatory displays. No guide dogs. Car parking. Telephone (01688) 500121. www.scotlandwildlife.com

Explore Mull's wildlife and the island's immensely varied habitats, guided by

Hebridean wildlife expert David Woodhouse. Visitors usually see otters, sea eagles, golden eagles, seals, deer, porpoises etc.

ISLE OF MULL MUSEUM   694   5 G22

Main Street, Tobermory, Isle of Mull. Main Street, Tobermory, Isle of Mull. By ferry from Oban to Craignure, bus from Craignure. Open Easter–Oct, Mon–Fri 1000–1600, Sat 1000–1300. Charge £. Explanatory displays. Wheelchair access.

Small museum crammed with information about the history of Mull and its people.

ISLE OF ULVA BOATHOUSE VISITOR CENTRE   695   5 G22

Isle of Ulva. On the north west side of Mull. From Salen take B8035 then B8073 to Ulva Ferry. Post bus service. Open Apr–Oct, Mon–Fri; Jun–Aug also Sun. Charge ££. Charge £ for mountain bikes. Group concessions by arrangement. Explanatory displays. Gift shop. Tearoom/shellfish bar. Waymarked walks. WC. Limited wheelchair access. Car parking. Telephone (01688) 500264. www.ulva.mull.com

Provides information on the history of Ulva and also the local natural history. Five waymarked walking trails. See also 696 Sheila's Cottage.

ISLE OF ULVA, SHEILA'S COTTAGE   696   5 G22

Isle of Ulva. On the north west side of Mull. From Salen take B8035 then B8073 to Ulva Ferry. Post bus service. Open Apr–Oct, Mon–Fri; Jun–Aug also Sun. Charge ££. Limited wheelchair access. Car parking. Telephone (01688) 500264 or 500241. www.ulva.mull.com

A faithful reconstruction of a traditional thatched croft house which was home to Sheila MacFadyen in the early 19th century. Also a display depicting the fascinating history of Ulva, from Mesolithic man to the present day. See also 695 Isle of Ulva Boathouse Visitor Centre.

KEILLS CHAPEL   697   7 H25

HS. 6 miles (9.5km) south west of Tayvallich, Argyll. Bus from Lochgilphead to Tayvallich, then walk or taxi. Access at all reasonable times. Free. Telephone (01786) 431326. www.historic-scotland.gov.uk

A small west Highland chapel housing a collection of grave slabs and Keills Cross.

KILBERRY SCULPTURED STONES   698   7 H26

HS. At Kilberry Castle off the B8024, 17 miles (27km) south south-west of Lochgilphead, on west coast of Knapdale, Argyll. Access at all reasonable times. Free. Telephone 0131 668 8800. www.historic-scotland.gov.uk

A fine collection of late medieval sculptured stones gathered from the Kilberry estate.

KILCHURN CASTLE   699   5 K23

HS. At the north east end of Loch Awe, 2.5 miles (4km) west of Dalmally, Argyll. Nearest railway station Loch Awe, bus to Loch Awe from Oban or Glasgow. Regular sailings to Kilchurn by steamer from Loch Awe Pier in village, contact ferry company (01838) 200400 or 200449. Open in summer at all reasonable times; closed in winter. Free. Charge for boat trip. Telephone 0131 668 8800. www.historic-scotland.gov.uk

A substantial ruin based on a square tower built by Colin Campbell of Glenorchy circa 1550, but much enlarged in 1693 by Ian, Earl of Breadalbane, whose arms are over the gateway with those of his wife. It incorporates the first purpose built barracks in Scotland. Spectacular views down Loch Awe

KILDALTON CROSS   700   7 G26

HS. On the island of Islay, 2 miles (3km) east north-east of Port Ellen, Argyll. Limited post bus service. Access at all reasonable times. Free. Telephone 0131 668 8800. www.historic-scotland.gov.uk

The finest intact High Cross in Scotland, carved in the late 8th century.

KILMAHOG WOOLLEN MILL   701   5 M24

Kilmahog, Callander, Trossachs. 1 mile (2km) north of Callander. Open Apr–Sep, Mon–Sat 0930–1730, Sun 1000–1700; Oct–Mar, Mon–Sat 1000–1700, Sun 1200–1600. Free. Gift shop. Restaurant. WC. Wheelchair access with assistance. Car and coach parking. Telephone (01877) 330268. www.ewm.co.uk

A 250-year-old mill with the original waterwheel. Visitors can trace the history of Scottish clans and tartans. Knitwear, clothing, gifts and a large selection of whisky for sale.

KILMARTIN HOUSE MUSEUM OF ANCIENT CULTURE   702   5 H24

Kilmartin, Argyll. On the A816, 9 miles (14.5km) north of Lochgilphead. Nearest railway station Oban, bus from Oban or Lochgilphead. Open all year, daily 1000–1730 (except Christmas and New Year). Charge ££. Group concessions. Guided tours by arrangement. Audio-visual displays. Gift shop. Café. Garden. WC. Wheelchair access. Disabled WC. Car parking. Telephone (01546) 510278. www.kilmartin.org

Award-winning archaeological museum which examines the relationship between Scotland's richest prehistoric landscape and its people, over 5000 years. Ancient monuments, local artefacts and bookshop.

KILMARTIN SCULPTURED STONES   703   5 H24

HS. In Kilmartin Churchyard, Kilmartin, Argyll. On the A816, 9 miles (14.5km) north of Lochgilphead. Nearest railway station Oban, bus from Oban or Lochgilphead. Access at all reasonable times. Free. Car parking. Telephone 0131 668 8800. www.historic-scotland.gov.uk

Carved west Highland grave slabs housed in a former mausoleum and in the church. One cross dates from the 16th century.

KILMICHAEL GLASSARY CUP AND RING MARKS   704   5 H24

HS. Kilmartin Glen. Near the schoolhouse in village of Kilmichael Glassary, 5 miles north of Lochgilphead, Argyll. Nearest railway station Oban, then bus to Lochgilphead. Access at all reasonable times. Free. Telephone 0131 668 8800. www.historic-scotland.gov.uk

Bronze Age cup and ring carvings on a natural rock outcrop.

KILMODAN SCULPTURED STONES   705   7 J25

HS. At Clachan of Glendaruel, on the A886, 8 miles (13km) north of Colintraive, Argyll. Access at all reasonable times. Free. Telephone (01786) 431326. www.historic-scotland.gov.uk

A group of west Highland carved grave slabs in a churchyard.

KILMORY CASTLE GARDENS   706   7 J25

Kilmory Castle, Lochgilphead, Argyll. On A83, 2 miles from centre of Kilmory, by council buildings. Bus service from Glasgow. Open all year, daily 0900–1800. Free. Guided tours by special arrangement only. Explanatory displays. Picnic area. WC. Wheelchair access. Car parking. Telephone (01546) 602127. www.argyll-bute.gov.uk

The garden was started in the 1770s and included around 100 varieties of rhododendron – it supplied plants for Kew Gardens. Now attached to the local council buildings, the gardens have been restored, with woodland walks, nature trails, herbaceous borders and a sensory trail. The gardens form part of Kilmory Woodland park, which also offers a network of woodland walks linking a lochside picnic area, bird hide, superb viewpoints and archaeological sites with year round programme of events for all the family.

KILMORY KNAP CHAPEL   707   7 H25

HS. On the shore between Loch Sween and Loch Caolisport in South Knapdale. Access at all reasonable times. Free. Telephone (01786) 431326. www.historic-scotland.gov.uk

A small medieval west Highland church with a collection of typical grave slabs. In the church is Macmillan's Cross, a splendid piece of medieval carving.

KILMUN ARBORETUM   708   9 K25

5.6 miles (9km) north of Dunoon in Kilmun village. Access at all times. Free. Limited wheelchair access. Car parking. www.forestry.gov.uk

There are a variety of different walks around this Forest Enterprise arboretum, where a wealth of exotic tree species can be found, including many fine examples of eucalyptus.

KILMUN (ST MUNN'S) CHURCH   709   9 K25

Kilmun, Argyll. 6 miles (10km) from Dunoon on A880. Bus service from Dunoon. Open May–Sep, Tue and Thu 1330–1630; Other dates and times by appointment. Admission by donation. Guided tours. Leaflets available. Gift shop. Tearoom. WC. Wheelchair access with assistance (wheelchair ramps installed). Car and coach parking. Telephone (01369) 840342.

On the site of a 10th-century Celtic monastery. The tower of a 15th-century collegiate church still stands. The present building by Thomas Burns dates from 1841, with the interior re-modelled in 1899. Important stained glass. Water-powered organ. Ancient graveyard including fine 18th-century carved stones. Mausoleum of Dukes of Argyll. Douglas vault. Grave of Elizabeth Blackwell, the first lady doctor.

KING'S KNOT   710   10 N24

HS. Below the Castle Rock in Stirling. Nearest railway station Stirling, buses from Glasgow and Edinburgh. Access at all reasonable times. Free. Telephone (01786) 431326. www.historic-scotland.gov.uk

The earthworks of a splendid formal garden, probably made in 1628 for Charles I.

KINLOCHLAICH GARDENS   711   5 J22

Kinlochlaich House, Appin, Argyll. On the A828, entrance beside the police station at Appin. Bus from Oban or Fort William. Open Apr–Oct, Mon–Sat 0930–1730, Sun 1030–1730; Nov–Mar, Mon–Sat 0930–1730. Christmas and New Year by appointment. Admission by donation £2. WC. Guide dogs by arrangement. Wheelchair access with assistance (gravel paths, slight slope). Disabled WC. Car parking. Telephone (01631) 730342. www.kinlochlaich-house.co.uk

A walled garden behind Kinlochlaich House surrounded by mature trees in outstanding Highland scenery. Built with the house at the end of the 18th century by John Campbell. Garden plant centre offering an extensive range of plants. Dogs not permitted.

KINNEIL HOUSE   712   10 N25

HS. Bo'ness. On the western outskirts of Bo'ness, West Lothian. Bus from Falkirk. View exterior only. Car parking. Telephone (01786) 431326. www.historic-scotland.gov.uk

A 15th-century tower set in a public park. Remodelled by the Earl of Arran between 1546 and 1550 and transformed into a stately home for the Dukes of Hamilton in the 1660s.

KIPPEN PARISH CHURCH   713   5 M24

Fore Road, Kippen, Stirling. Off the A811, 9 miles (14.5km) west of Stirling. Bus from Stirling. Open daily 0930–1700. Free. Explanatory displays. Garden. WC. Limited wheelchair access. Car and coach parking.

A church built in 1824, but modernised in 1924 under the guidance of Sir D. Y. Cameron RA. He and others donated works of art which, with distinguished Webster Windows, make it one of the most beautiful churches in Scotland.

KNAPDALE FOREST   714   7 H25

FE. Near Lochgilphead, Argyll. Access at all times. Free. Explanatory displays. Picnic area. Schedule of events during summer months. Wheelchair access. Car parking. www.forestry.gov.uk

The name Knapdale is derived from Cnap (hill) and Dall (field). The forest is flanked to the north by the Crinan Canal and to the west by the Sound of Jura and Loch Sween. Historical and archaeological sites include ancient Castle Dounie. Waymarked walks and cycle rides, from where seals, otters and porpoises can be seen. See also 598 Barnluasgan Visitor Centre.

KYLES OF BUTE   715   7 J25

Narrow arm of the Firth of Clyde, between Isle of Bute and Argyll. For viewpoint follow A8003 for 2.5 miles (4km) north east of Tighnabruaich. Car parking.

A 16-mile (25.5km) stretch of water which presents a constantly changing view of great beauty. It can perhaps be best appreciated from the A8003, Tighnabruaich to Glendaruel road, where there are two view indicators. The western indicator (Scottish Civic Trust) looks over the West Kyle and identifies many features. The eastern one (NTS) looks over Loch Ridden and the East Kyle.

LAGAVULIN DISTILLERY VISITOR CENTRE   716   7 F26

Port Ellen, Isle of Islay. 3 miles (5km) from ferry on A846. Air to Islay (airport 5 miles). Bus from Port Askaig to Port Ellen, then to Ardbeg passing distillery. Tours all year, Mon–Fri 0930, 1115 and 1430. Telephone for appointment. Charge ££. Guided tours. Gift shop. WC. Wheelchair access to reception centre and pier. Disabled WC. Car and coach parking. Telephone (01496) 302730.

Home of the famous Lagavulin single malt, established in 1816. The distillery is set beside the ruins of Dun Naomhaig Castle, ancient stronghold of the Lords of the Isles. Tours and tastings.

LAMONT MEMORIAL   717   9 K25

In Dunoon's west bay. Access at all times. Free. Car parking.

Stone Celtic cross erected in 1906 to mark the massacre of the Lamonts by the Campbells in 1646.

LAPHROAIG DISTILLERY   718   7 F26

Port Ellen, Isle of Islay. Open all year (except Jul and first two weeks Aug), Mon–Thu. Tours at 1015 and 1415. All visits by arrangement only. Free. Guided tours. Explanatory displays. Gift shop. WC. Limited wheelchair access. Disabled WC. Car and coach parking. Telephone (01496) 302418.

A traditional malt whisky distillery established in 1815.

LETTERSHUNA RIDING CENTRE   719   5 J22

Appin, Argyll. On A828, 25 miles (40km) south of Fort William and 20 miles (32km) north of Oban. Bus from Oban or Fort William. Open easter–Oct, daily. First ride of morning at 1030, first ride of afternoon at 1400, last ride of day at 1630. Charges dependent on length of ride. WC. Wheelchair access. Car parking. Telephone (01631) 730227.

A small family-run riding centre established in 1973. Specialises in small groups, with all rides led by Ride Leader. One and 2 hour rides for experienced riders confident in trotting and cantering. Half-hour or 1 hour ride for all comers, with the pace geared to the slowest member of the group. Nervous riders and the very young will be led if necessary.

LEVENGROVE PARK   720   9 L25

In Dumbarton, follow High Street across old bridge, main entrance in Clydeshore Road. Free. WC.

Beautiful open park stretching to the shores of the River Clyde. Formal flower gardens and magnificent trees. Contains the ruins of an old parish church and the burial place of the Dixon family. Putting green, crazy golf.

LINN BOTANIC GARDENS AND NURSERY   721   9 K25

Cove, Helensburgh, Dunbartonshire. On the B833, 10 miles (16km) from Garelochhead. Nearest railway station Helensburgh, then bus. Garden open all year dawn to dusk; plant sales open daily 1100–1700. Charge ££. Charge for garden £. Children under 5 free. Group concessions by arrangement. Guided tours for groups by arrangement. Plant name labels. Refreshments nearby. Car and coach parking. Telephone (01436) 842242.

A garden developed since 1971 around a listed Clyde coast villa in the style of Greek Thompson. Thousands of unusual, exotic and rare plants, extensive water garden, formal ponds and fountains, herbaceous borders, glen with waterfall, cliff garden and rockery. Signed route of just over half-mile (1km) through garden.

LISMORE HISTORICAL SOCIETY   722   5 H22

The Old School House, Achnacroish, Isle of Lismore, Argyll. Halfway down Lismore, approximately 5 miles (8km) from either ferry terminal. Nearest railway stations at Appin and Oban, then ferry to Lismore. Open Easter–end Sep, daily 1000–1700. Charge £. Guided tours. Explanatory displays. Wheelchair access. Car parking. Telephone (01631) 760346.

A reconstructed thatched croft house circa 1890. Built by the islanders and depicting a way of life long disappeared from Lismore. Heritage centre depicting the local history.

LOCH FAD FISHERY 723   9 J26

Loch Fad, Isle of Bute. On the B878, 0.75 mile (1km) from Rothesay pier. Nearest railway station Wemyss Bay. Open for fly fishing Mar–late Dec and bait fishing mid Mar–early Oct. Charge £££. Group concessions. Explanatory displays. Picnic area. WC. Limited wheelchair access. Disabled WC. Car and coach parking. Telephone (01700) 504871. www.lochfad.com

Fishing for rainbow or brown trout from banks or boats.

LOCH GRUINART RSPB NATURE RESERVE 724   7 F26

Deep inlet on north coast of Islay. Signed from A847 Bridgend to Bruichladdich, 3 miles (5km) from turn off. Reserve open at all times. Visitor centre open Apr–Oct, daily 1000–1700; Nov–Mar, daily 1000–1600 (closed 25–26 Dec and 1–2 Jan). Free. Guided tours. Explanatory displays. Nature trails and birdwatching hide. WC. Wheelchair access. Disabled WC. Car and coach parking. Telephone (01496) 850505. www.rspb.org.uk/scotland

During the spring there are hundreds of breeding wading birds (lapwings, redshanks and snipe) and the nights resound to the call of the corncrake. Hen harriers nest on the moor and hunting golden eagles and peregrines occur all year round. Loch Gruinart is famous for the large numbers of barnacle and white-fronted geese that spend the winter on Islay. The reserve can be seen easily from the road. In the visitor centre, a live video camera lets visitors get even closer views of the grazing geese.

LOCH LOMOND 725   5 L24

Cruises available from a number of operators, including: at Balloch, Sweeney's Cruises (01389) 752376, and Mullens Cruises (01389) 751481 (group booking); at Balmaha, McFarlane and Son (01360) 870214; at Luss, Round the Islands Cruises (Mar-Oct, Luss Pier); at Tarbet, Cruise Loch Lomond (01301) 702356.

Loch Lomond, the largest stretch of inland water in Britain, and framed by lovely mountain scenery, is a popular centre for all watersports. Cruises around the banks and attractive small islands are available. See also 726 Loch Lomond and the Trossachs National Park, 599 Ben Lomond, 729 Lomond Shores and 731 Maid of the Loch.

LOCH LOMOND AND THE TROSSACHS NATIONAL PARK 726   5 L24

Access at all times. Free. Car and coach parking. Telephone (01389) 722600.

Loch Lomond, the Trossachs area and the Argyll Forest Park, renowned for its beauty, comprise Scotland's first National Park. The area offers many activities and opportunities for walking. See 599 Ben Lomond, 725 Loch Lomond, 729 Lomond Shores and 731 Maid of the Loch.

LOCH LOMOND, SWEENEY'S CRUISES 727   9 L25

Riverside, Balloch, Dunbartonshire. At south end of Loch Lomond, 30 minutes from Glasgow. Railway station in Balloch. Cruises around the loch operate daily throughout the year. Telephone for timetable. Charge £££. Children under 4 free. Group concessions. Fully stocked bar. Tea and coffee available. WC. Wheelchair access with assistance. Car and coach parking. Telephone (01389) 752376. www.sweeney.uk.com

Sweeney's Cruises have been operating on Loch Lomond for almost 100 years. Today they sail five passenger boats. Live commentary on all cruises. Private charter available.

LOCH SLOY HYDRO ELECTRIC STATION   728   5 K24

By Inveruglas on the A82, Loch Lomondside. Car and coach parking. Telephone (01796) 484000 to arrange visits.

Opened in 1950, Loch Sloy was the first of the Hydro Electric Boards major generating plants to come into service. Station open to organised parties on application (charge). Interesting walk to Loch Sloy dam across the road.

LOMOND SHORES   729   9 L25

Balloch, Glasgow. At the southern tip of Loch Lomond. Nearest railway station Balloch. Telephone or visit website to confirm opening times. Entry to Lomond Shores free, charge (£££) for attraction only. Guided tours. Explanatory displays. Restaurants, café, bars and picnic areas. Unique retail crescent. Baby changing facilities. Children's play area, beach and events area. WC. Wheelchair access. Disabled WC. Car and coach parking. Telephone (01389) 222406. www.lochlomondshores.com

Loch Lomond Shores is set amidst the breathtaking beauty of Loch Lomond. A mixture of leisure and retail, there is quite literally something for everyone to enjoy. Experience Loch Lomond like never before through the giant screen film *Legend of Loch Lomond,* fly over the loch or travel back in time with our adventurous young otter, Ollie. Discover Scotland's first national park through the interactive exhibition, park rangers and tourist information centre.

MACLEAN'S CROSS   730   5 F23

HS. On the island of Iona, off the west coast of Mull, Argyll. By passenger ferry (no cars) from Fionnphort, Mull. Day tours from Oban in summer. Nearest railway station Oban, bus service from Craignure. Parking in Fionnphort. Access at all reasonable times. Free. Telephone (01786) 431326. www.historic-scotland.gov.uk

A fine 15th-century free-standing cross.

MAID OF THE LOCH   731   9 L25

The Pier, Pier Road, Balloch. Nearest railway station Balloch. Open Easter–Oct, daily 1100–1600; Nov–Mar, Sat–Sun 1100–1600. Free. Explanatory displays. Gift shop. Restaurant and bar. Hire of ship for functions. WC. Wheelchair access to the pier, partial access to the deck at present. Disabled WC. Car and coach parking. Telephone (01389) 711865. www.maidoftheloch.co.uk

Maid of the Loch is the largest UK inland waterways vessel ever built, a paddle steamer originally launched in 1953 and laid up in 1981. Now under restoration, visitors can see an exhibition and watch the restoration underway. New for 2006 is the Steam Slipway Complex offering monthly demonstrations of the steam engine and carriage in action. This is the slip that will take the Maid out of the water. See also 726 Loch Lomond and the Trossachs National Park, 599 Ben Lomond, 725 Loch Lomond, 729 Lomond Shores.

MAR'S WARK   732   10 N24

HS. At the top of Castle Wynd, Stirling. Nearest railway station Stirling, bus from Glasgow and Edinburgh. Open at all reasonable times. Free. Telephone (01786) 431326. www.historic-scotland.gov.uk

A remarkable Renaissance mansion built by the Regent Mar in 1570, of which the façade is the main surviving part.

MCCAIG'S TOWER   733   5 H23

On a hill overlooking Oban. Access at all times. Free.

McCaig was a local banker who tried to curb unemployment by using local craftsmen to build this tower (1897–1900) as a memorial to his family. Its walls are 2 feet (0.5m) thick and from 30–47 feet (9–14m) high. The courtyard within is landscaped and the tower is floodlit at night in summer. An observation platform on the seaward side was added in 1983.

MCCAIG'S WAREHOUSE   734   5 H23

Unit 3/4, The Heritage Centre, Oban, Argyll. On harbour front in Oban. Rail and bus service from Glasgow. Open Jun–Sep, Mon–Fri 0900–1900, Sat 0900–1730, Sun 1000–1700; Apr, May and Oct, Mon–Sat 0900–1730, Sun 1000–1700; Nov–Mar, Mon–Sat 1000–1700, Sun 1100–1600. Free. WC. Wheelchair access. Disabled WC. Telephone (01631) 566335. www.ewm.co.uk

An amazing range of knitwear, clothing, accessories and gifts. The Spirit of Scotland whisky shop offers a large selection of single malts and blended whiskies. Free tasting sessions

MID-ARGYLL SWIMMING POOL   735   7 H25

Oban Road, Lochgilphead, Argyll. On outskirts of Lochgilphead. Bus service from Glasgow. Open all year (except Christmas and New Year), Mon–Fri 0900–2100, Sat–Sun 1000–1500. Charge £. Group concessions. Refreshments available. WC. Wheelchair access. Disabled WC. Car and coach parking. Telephone (01546) 606676. postmaster@midargyllswimming.co.uk

A small community swimming pool. Sauna and sunbed facilties

MILL TRAIL VISITOR CENTRE   736   10 N24

Glentana Mill, West Stirling Street, Alva, Clackmannanshire. On the A91, 8 miles (13km) east of Stirling. Bus from Stirling or Alloa. Open all year (except Christmas and New Year), Jan–Jun and Sep–Dec 1000–1700; Jul–Aug 0900–1700. Free. Explanatory displays. Gift shop. Coffee shop. Baby changing facilities. Children's play area. WC. Portable induction loop. Wheelchair access. Disabled WC. Car and coach parking. Telephone (01259) 769696.

An exhibition telling the story of spinning and weaving in Clackmannan (the Wee County) and highlighting what to do and see in Clackmannanshire. Original weaving and knitting looms. Shop sells wide variety of local craft goods, books and knitwear.

MOINE MHOR NATIONAL NATURE RESERVE   737   5 H24

Car park on B8025, 2 miles (3km) south of Kilmartin and 6 miles (9.5km) north of Lochgilphead via the A816. On Lochgilphead/Kilmartin bus routes. Access at all times. Free. Interpretive panels and leaflets. Picnic area. Trail suitable for less able visitors. Car parking. Telephone 01546 603611 (Scottish Natural Heritage). www.nnr-scotland.org.uk

The best views of this nature reserve are from the Crinan Canal (see 632) near Bellanoch or the ancient hill fort of Dunadd (see 646). From here you can see the waterlogged system of pools and bogs alongside the gentle twists and turns of the River Add. Down at bog level look out for hen harriers and curlews, as well as an impressive range of dragonflies. All visitors should stay on the paths to avoid wet and uneven ground and hidden holes.

MOIRLANICH LONGHOUSE   738   5 L23

NTS. c/o NTS Office, Lynedoch, Main Street, Killin, Perthshire. Off A827, 1 mile (1.5km) north west of Killin. Open Easter Sunday and May–Sep, Wed and Sun 1400–1700. Charge £. Group concessions. Guided tours for groups by prior arrangement. Explanatory displays. Limited wheelchair access. Car parking. Telephone (01567) 820988 Mon-Fri 0900-1500. www.nts.org.uk

An outstanding example of a traditional cruck-frame cottage and byre dating from the mid 19th century. Inhabited until 1968, the house retains many original features and is furnished according to archaeological evidence.

MONUMENT HILL   739   5 K23

Off the old road to Inveraray, 2 miles (3km) south west of Dalmally. Access at all times. Free.

Monument to Duncan Ban Macintyre (1724–1812), the Burns of the Highlands, who was born near Inveroran.

MORAG'S FAIRY GLEN   740   9 K25

In Dunoon at the end of the West Bay, 1 mile (1.5km) from Dunoon Pier.

This delightful glen was gifted to the town by Bailie George Jones.

MOTORING HERITAGE CENTRE   741   9 L25

Main Street, Alexandria, Dunbartonshire. Nearest railway station at Alexandria. Open Fri–Mon 1000–1730 and Sun 1100–1700. Charge £. Group concessions. Guided tours. Explanatory displays. Gift shop. Licensed bar. WC. Wheelchair access. Disabled WC. Car and coach parking. Telephone (01389) 607862.

A motor heritage centre situated in what was once the world's largest motor car works, now Loch Lomond Galleries. Display traces the history of the once-famous Argyll marque and the story of Scottish motoring. Visitors can sit in a Model T Ford, see unique archive film and fascinating cars.

MOUNT STUART   742   9 J26

Mount Stuart, Isle of Bute. 5 miles (8km) south of Rothesay. By ferry from Wemyss Bay to Rothesay, bus from Rothesay. Courtesy shuttle between reception and house. House and gardens open Easter weekend and then May–Sep, Sun–Fri 1100–1700, Sat 1000–1420. Gardens open daily 1000–1800. Charge £££. Group concessions. Guided tours (1230 and 1430). Explanatory displays. Visitor centre. Gift shop. Tearoom and picnic areas. Children's adventure play area. WC. Induction loop. Wheelchair access. Disabled WC. Car and coach parking. Telephone (01700) 503877. www.mountstuart.com

Spectacular Victorian Gothic house, the ancestral home of the Marquess of Bute. Splendid interiors, art collection and architectural detail. Mature Victorian pinetum, arboretum and exotic gardens, waymarked walks. Three hundred acres (121ha) of ground and gardens. Audio-visual presentation.

MULL POTTERY AND CAFÉ/BISTRO   743   5 G22

Baliscate Estate, Salen Road, Tobermory, Isle of Mull. Salen Road is by speed limit sign into Tobermory. Bus service between Craignure and Tobermory will stop. Car parking and parking for small coaches only. Open all year, daily. Studio/workshop

Mon–Sat 0930–1800, Sun 1030–1800; café 1000–1700; bistro from 1800 with last orders 2030. Free. Displays on pottery production. Gift shop. Outdoor seating. Baby changing facilities. Outside tie rings for dogs. WC. Limited wheelchair access. Telephone (01688) 302347. www.mull-pottery.com

The pottery produces distinctive hand thrown pieces from white stoneware porcelain. Visitors will see exhibition pieces and Iona and Seashore tableware as well as Scottish landscapes, woodturning and gifts. The café and bistro serve homebaking, snacks and evening meals.

MULL RAIL   744   5 H22

Old Pier Station, Craignure, Isle of Mull, Argyll. In Craignure, 0.25 mile (0.5km) south east of ferry terminal. By ferry from Oban to Craignure. Open Easter–mid Oct, daily 1100–1700. Charge (single) £, (return) ££. Group concessions. Gift shop. Wheelchair access and adapted coaches. Car and coach parking. Telephone (01680) 812494. www.mullrail.co.uk

Scotland's only (narrow gauge) island passenger railway running between Craignure and Torosay Castle (see 797). Scenic journey lasts 20 minutes. Steam and diesel locomotives.

MULL THEATRE   745   5 G22

Dervaig, Isle of Mull, Argyll. 0.25 mile (0.5km) outside Dervaig on unclassified Salen road. Bus service from Tobermory. Open Apr–Oct (6 nights a week Jul–Sep). Charge £££. Some shows cost less, e.g. children's programmes. Check publicity for details. Group concessions. Refreshments available at interval. WC. Car parking. Telephone (01688) 302828. www.mulltheatre.com

With just 43 seats, Mull Little Theatre is the smallest professional repertory theatre in the country. Its unique performance space is home to the acclaimed Mull Theatre Company whose productions tour throughout Scotland. The venue also plays host to a range of touring shows from the UK and beyond. "The people of Mull and their visitors are luckier than they know to have McCrone and his company around, plugging them into the mainstream of Scottish theatrical life with so little fuss and so much grace." Joyce McMillan, The Scotsman.

NATIONAL WALLACE MONUMENT   746   10 N24

Abbey Craig, Hillfoot Road, Stirling. 2.6 miles (4.2km) north north-east of Stirling city centre. Nearest railway station Stirling, local bus service. Free shuttle bus runs between car park and monument, charge £. Open all year daily; Jan–Feb and Nov–Dec 1030–1600; Mar–May and Oct 1000–1700; June 1000–1800; Sept 0930–1700; Jul–Aug 0930–1800. Closed Christmas and New Year. Last recommended admission 45 minutes prior to closing. Charge ££. Group concessions by prior arrangement. Group concessions. Explanatory displays and audio-visual displays (in 5 languages). Gift shop. Coffee shop and picnic area. WC. (access to grounds, limited access to the monument). Disabled WC. Car and coach parking. Telephone (01786) 472140. www.nationalwallacemonument.com

Re-live Wallace's life and trial. Stunning panoramic views, Wallace's famous battle sword, Hall of Heroes, Building the Monument, woodland walks and nature trail.

NETHER LARGIE CAIRNS   747   5 H24

HS. Kilmartin Glen. Between Kilmartin and Nether Largie, Argyll. Nearest railway station Oban, then bus to Kilmartin. Access at all reasonable times. Free. Telephone (01786) 431326. www.historic-scotland.gov.uk

One Neolithic and two Bronze Age cairns. There is access to the chamber in the north cairn.

NETWORK CARRADALE HERITAGE CENTRE 748   7 H27

Carradale, Argyll. On B842, 22 miles (35km) south of Tarbert and 14 miles (22.5km) north of Campbeltown. Bus service from Campbeltown. Open Easter–Oct, daily 1030–1630. Admission by voluntary contribution. Explanatory displays. Gift shop. Tearoom. WC. Wheelchair access. Disabled WC. Car parking. Telephone (01583) 431296.

The centre contains graphic displays featuring the history of fishing, farming and forestry in the Carradale area. Hands-on activities for children. Forestry walks.

NORTH THIRD TROUT FISHERY 749   5 M24

Greathill House, Stirling. 5 miles (8km) south west of Stirling. Open Mar-Oct daily; Mar–Apr 1000–1700; May–Aug 1000–2300; Sep–Oct 1000–1700. Charge £££. Children free with paying adult. Discounts for OAP and UB40 Mon–Fri. WC. Car and coach parking. Telephone (01786) 471967. www.fishtrout.co.uk/norththird

A rainbow trout fly-only fishery with over 120 acres (48ha) of water set in magnificent surroundings and offering both boat and bank fishing. Float tube allowed. Tackle hire and expert advice available

OBAN DISTILLERY VISITOR CENTRE 750   5 H23

Stafford Street, Oban, Argyll. In centre of Oban. Within walking distance from railway station and bus stops. Open Dec and Feb, Mon–Fri 1230–1600; Mar and Nov, Mon–Fri 1000–1700; Easter–Jun and Oct, Mon–Sat 0930–1700; Jul–Sep, Mon–Fri 0930–1900, Sat 0930–1700, Sun 1200–1700. Last tour one hour before closing. Charge ££. Children free. Guided tours. Explanatory displays leaflet in French, German, Italian , Swedish, Spanish and Japanese. Gift shop. WC. No guide dogs. Limited wheelchair access. Disabled WC. Telephone (01631) 572004.

Take a guided tour and learn about the ancient craft of distilling. Visitor centre with exhibition and audio-visual programme tells the history of Oban. Shop with single malts, gifts and souvenirs.

OBAN HIGHLAND THEATRE 751   5 H23

George Street, Oban, Argyll. In centre of Oban, 0.5 mile (1km) from station. Car and coach parking nearby. Open daily in summer from 1400; in winter Mon–Fri from 1800, Sat 1400. Charge £££. Group concessions. Explanatory displays. Gift shop. WC. Wheelchair access. Disabled WC. Telephone (01631) 562444.

A complex of two cinemas, theatre and exhibition area. Occasional videos focussing on Oban, Lorn and the Isles.

OBAN RARE BREEDS FARM PARK 752   5 H23

Glencruitten, Oban, Argyll. 2 miles (3km) from Oban along the Glencruitten Road. Nearest railway station Oban, bus from Oban. Open late Mar–Oct, 1000–1800 (Jun–Aug closes 1900); Nov–Dec, Sat–Sun 1100–1600. Charge £££. Wheelchair users free. No admission charge to tearoom. Group concessions. Guided tours by prior arrangement. Explanatory displays. Gift shop. Tearoom and picnic areas. Children's parties. WC. Limited wheelchair access. Disabled WC. Car and coach parking. Telephone (01631) 770608. www.obanrarebreeds.com

Displays rare breeds of farm animals – cattle, sheep, pigs, poultry, goats. Pets' corner and pure bred rabbits and guinea pigs. Woodland walk and beautiful views. Souvenir shop.

OCHIL HILLS WOODLAND PARK   753   10 N24

0.5 miles (1km) north of A91 between Alva and Tillicoultry. Bus from Alloa and
Stirling. Access at all times. Free. Explanatory displays. Picnic areas. Play area.
Limited wheelchair access. Car parking. Telephone (01259) 450000.
www.clacksweb.org.uk

The remains of the grounds of Alva House (now demolished). Woodland walks
and children's play area.

OLD BYRE HERITAGE CENTRE   754   5 G22

Dervaig, Isle of Mull, Argyll. 1.5 miles (2.5km) south west of Dervaig (0.6 mile/1km
private road off Torloisk road at Dervaig end). Nearest railway station Oban, then
ferry to Craignure with limited bus service connecting to Dervaig. Open Easter–Oct,
daily 1030–1830, last show at 1730. Charge £. Group concessions. Explanatory
displays and film. Gift shop. Tearoom. Sun terrace. WC. Wheelchair access to
tearoom and gift shop only. Disabled WC. Car and coach parking. Telephone (01688)
400229.

A genuine stone byre which has been converted into a museum, tearoom and gift
shop. Audio-visual show.

OVERTOUN ESTATE   755   9 L25

Via Milton Brae, by Dumbarton. Park open all year, daily. Free. Car parking.
Telephone (01389) 732610. www.overtounhouse.com

Historic gardens, picnic areas, spectacular views, Victorian architecture, and
wildlife. Self-guided walks of grounds.

PORT ELLEN PLAYING FIELDS ASSOCIATION   756   7 F26

Port Ellen Playing Fields Association, Port Ellen, Isle of Islay. In Port Ellen, next to
Ramsay Hall. Local bus service. Open May–Sep, daily 1200–1600 and 1800–2100. No
admission charge. Payment for use of equipment. Café. Disabled WC nearby.
Outside seating. WC. Limited wheelchair access. Car parking. Telephone (07831)
249611.

Facilities and equipment hire for putting, tennis and bowls. Also bicycle
hire.

PUCK'S GLEN FOREST WALKS   757   5 K25

FE. 5.5 miles (9km) north of Dunoon on A880 at foot of Loch Eck. Infrequent bus
service from Dunoon. Open at all times. Free. Limited wheelchair access (access to
one walk). Car parking. www.forestry.gov.uk

Perhaps the finest walk in the Argyll Forest Park, meandering up the burn with
numerous bridge crossings and the sound of cascading water adding to the
charm of this enchanted woodland walk through giant Redwoods. Parents are
advised to keep children under control at all times.

PUFFIN DIVE CENTRE   758   5 H23

Port Gallanach, Oban, Argyll. 1.5 miles (2.5km) south of Oban. Open all year, daily
0800–1830. Charge dependent on activity. Picnic area and snack van. WC. Car and
coach parking. Telephone (01631) 566088. www.puffin.org.uk

A comprehensive dive centre for all, from complete beginners to experienced
divers. Also scenic tours aboard a fast super rib boat.

QUEEN ELIZABETH FOREST PARK VISITOR CENTRE   759   5 L24

FE. Queen Elizabeth Forest Park, Aberfoyle. Open Easter–Oct, daily 1000–1800;
Nov–Dec daily, 1100–1700 for Christmas tree sales. Explanatory displays. Gift shop.
Tearoom and picnic area. Shop. Cycle routes, walks and forest drive. WC. Wheelchair
access. Disabled WC. Car and coach parking. Telephone (01877) 382258.
www.forestry.gov.uk

The Queen Elizabeth Forest Park was first designated a Forest Park by the
Forestry Commission in 1953, to mark the coronation of Queen Elizabeth II. It
encompasses mountain and moorland, forest and woodland, rivers and lochs,
and is home to a rich variety of animal and plant life. The visitor centre is
situated on a hillside above Aberfoyle, with spectacular views in all directions,
and provides information on all aspects of the forest and activities throughout
the year. Resident woodcarver. Orienteering routes.

QUEEN'S VIEW, LOCH LOMOND   760   9 L25

Off A809, 12 miles (19km) north north-west of Glasgow. Access at all times. Free. Car
parking.

From the west side of the road a path leads to a viewpoint where, in 1879, Queen
Victoria had her first view of Loch Lomond.

REST AND BE THANKFUL   761   5 K24

FE. At the head of Glen Croe on A83, 4 miles (6.5km) north west of Ardgarten, 6 miles
(10km) north of Arrochar. Frequent bus services from the south. Access at all times.
Free. Wheelchair access. Car and coach parking.

The well-known viewpoint and landmark at the summit of the old Rest and Be
Thankful road, where cattle drovers enjoyed a break after a tough climb and one
of the military roads built in 1748 by General Wade to provide access to the west
coast of Scotland after the 1745 rebellion.

RI CRUIN CAIRN   762   5 H24

HS. Kilmartin Glen. 1 mile (2km) south west of Kilmartin, Argyll. Nearest railway
station Oban, then bus to Kilmartin. Access at all reasonable times. Free. Car
parking. Telephone (01786) 431326. www.historic-scotland.gov.uk

A Bronze Age burial cairn with the covering removed to reveal three massive
cists. Axe heads are carved on one of the cist slabs.

ROB ROY AND TROSSACHS VISITOR CENTRE   763   5 M24

Ancaster Square, Callander , Perthshire. In Callander, 16 miles (25.5km) north west of
Stirling on the A84. Nearest railway station Stirling, buses from Stirling and
Edinburgh. Open Jan–Feb, Mon–Fri 1100–1500, Sat–Sun 1100–1600; Mar–May and
Oct–Dec, daily 1000–1700; Jun, daily 0930–1800; Sep, daily 1000–1800; Jul–Aug,
daily 0900–1800. Last admission 45 minutes prior to closing. Charge ££. Group
concessions. Guided tours (translations in French, German, Italian and Spanish).
Explanatory displays. Gift shop. Play area. WC. Wheelchair access. Disabled WC. Car
parking. Telephone (01877) 330342.

Rob Roy MacGregor. Hero or villain? Patriot or thief? Learn about the life and
times of Scotland's most famous Highlander. Hear his innermost thoughts,
witness his exploits and decide who was the real Rob Roy. Step back in time and
explore a reconstructed 18th-century farmhouse, just as Rob Roy would have
experienced it.

ROB ROY'S GRAVE   764   5 L23

West end of Balquhidder Churchyard, off A84, 14 miles (22.5km) north north-west of Callander. Access at all reasonable times. Free.

Three flat gravestones enclosed by railings are the graves of Rob Roy, his wife and two of his sons. The church itself contains St Angus' Stone (8th century), a 17th-century bell from the old church, and old Gaelic Bibles.

ROTHESAY CASTLE   765   9 J26

HS. Castlehill Street, Rothesay, Isle of Bute. By ferry from Wemyss Bay on the A78. Nearest railway station and ferry Wemyss Bay, buses from Largs and Glasgow via Greenock. Open Apr–Sep, daily 0930–1830; Oct–Mar, Mon–Sun 0930–1630, closed Thu and Fri. Charge £. Group concessions. Explanatory displays. Gift shop. WC. Limited wheelchair access. Telephone (01700) 502691. www.historic-scotland.gov.uk

A remarkable 13th-century castle of enclosure, circular in plan, with 16th-century forework. Breaches made by Norsemen in 1240 are evident. A favourite residence of the Stewart kings.

ROUGH CASTLE   766   9 N25

HS. Off the B816, 6 miles (9.5km) west of Falkirk. Nearest railway and bus stations Falkirk. Access at all reasonable times. Free. Telephone (01786) 431326. www.historic-scotland.gov.uk

The best preserved length of the Antonine Wall. Consists of a rampart and ditch, together with the earthworks of a fort. Also a short length of military way with quarry pits. See also 573 Antonine Wall.

SADDELL ABBEY   767   7 H27

Saddell Village, by Campbeltown, Argyll. B842, between Campbeltown (8 miles/13km) and Carradale (4 miles/6.5km). Look out for brown sign and then sign for car park at entrance to Saddell village. On bus route between Campbeltown and Carradale. Open all year, during daylight hours (visitors should respectfully remember that the site lies within a consecrated graveyard which is still in use). Free. Explanatory displays. Limited wheelchair access. Car and coach parking. www.saddellabbeytrust.org

Founded in the 13th century by the legendary celtic warrior Somerled, the conserved ruin of what remains of Saddell Abbey gives little indication of the site's historical significance. Apart from Iona itself, Saddell Abbey was once the most important ecclesiastical site in Scotland. In addition to the abbey, an award-winning shelter displays a number of medieval grave slabs and effigies depicting giant green warriors, sympathetically displayed in a stunning setting.

ST BLANE'S CHURCH, KINGARTH   768   9 J26

HS. At the south end of the Isle of Bute, 8.5 miles (13.5km) south of Rothesay. By ferry from Wemyss Bay on the A78. Nearest railway station and ferry Wemyss Bay, buses from Largs and Glasgow via Greenock. Access at all reasonable times. Free. Car parking. Telephone (0131) 5507603. www.historic-scotland.gov.uk

The ruins of a 12th-century Romanesque chapel set within the foundations of a Celtic monastery.

ST COLUMBA CENTRE   769   5 F23

HS. Fionnphort, Isle of Mull, Argyll. 38 miles (61km) from Craignure and situated behind Fionnphort village, near ferry terminal for Iona. Ferry from Oban to

Craignure, then bus to Fionnphort. Open Easter–Sep, daily 1100–1700. Group concessions. Explanatory displays. Gift shop. Tea and coffee available. Wheelchair access. Disabled WC. Car and coach parking. Telephone (01681) 700640. www.historic-scotland.gov.uk

Exhibition on St Columba, Iona and Celtic heritage of interest to all visitors. Opportunities to practise script writing.

ST COLUMBA'S CAVE   770   7 H25

On west shore of Loch Killisport (Caolisport), 1 mile (1.5km) north of Ellary, 10 miles (16km) south west of Ardrishaig. Access at all times. Free.

Traditionally associated with St Columba's arrival in Scotland, the cave contains a rock-shelf with an altar, above which are carved crosses. A large basin, perhaps a Stone Age mortar, may have been used as a font. The cave was occupied from the Middle Stone Age. In front are traces of houses and the ruins of a chapel (possibly 13th century). Another cave is nearby.

ST JOHN'S CHURCH, DUNOON   771   9 K25

Argyll Street, Dunoon. Ferry from Gourock. Open May–Sep, Mon–Fri 1000–1200 and other times by appointment. Free. Guided tours. Refreshments. Garden. WC. Wheelchair access. Car and coach parking. www.stjohnsdunoon.org.uk

A magnificent nave and aisles church by R. A. Bryden (1877) with Gothic spired tower. Galleried concert hall interior, raised choir behind central pulpit, organ 1895. Interesting stained glass windows, including Lauder Memorial.

ST MARY'S CHAPEL, ROTHESAY   772   9 J26

HS. On the A845, 0.5 mile (1km) south of Rothesay on the Isle of Bute. By ferry from Wemyss Bay on the A78. Nearest railway station and ferry Wemyss Bay, buses from Largs and Glasgow via Greenock. Open Apr–Sep, daily 0800–1700; Oct–Mar closed Fri. Free. Telephone (0131) 5507603. www.historic-scotland.gov.uk

The late-medieval remains of the chancel of the parish church of St Mary, with fine tombs.

ST NINIAN'S, ISLE OF BUTE   773   9 J26

South west of Rothesay along B878 for 2.5 miles (4km), joining A844 at Milton then unclassified road to Straad. Access at all times. Free.

The foundations of St Ninian's chapel, dating back to the 6th century, together with its surrounding garth wall are still clearly visible on this remote peninsula.

SANDAIG MUSEUM   774   5 D22

The Thatched Cottage Museum, Sandaig. In Sandaig village, western Tiree. Ferry from Oban or by air from Glasgow. Open Jun–Sep, Mon–Fri 1400–1600. Admission by donation. Guided tours. Explanatory displays, guide booklet supplied. Restaurant adjacent. Wheelchair access with assistance. Car and coach parking. Telephone (01865) 311468. www.hebrideantrust.org

Located in a terrace of traditional thatched buildings, the museum houses a unique collection of items illustrating life in a late 19th-century cottar's home. The adjoining byre and barn display elements of agricultural work at the croft, a testimony to the Hebridean islanders' self-sufficiency.

SCOTTISH SEALIFE SANCTUARY 775   5 J22

Barcaldine, Connel, Oban, Argyll. On the A828, 10 miles (16km) north of Oban. Nearest railway station Oban, bus from Oban. Open all year, daily from 1000; summer closes 1800; telephone or visit website for winter hours. Last admission 1 hour before closing. Charge £££. Group concessions. Explanatory displays, talks and demonstrations. Gift shop. Restaurant, coffee shop and picnic area. Adventure playground and nature trail. WC. Touch pools for blind visitors. Wheelchair access (there is a specific wheelchair route accessing 95 per cent of displays). Disabled WC. Car and coach parking. Telephone (01631) 720386. www.sealsanctuary.co.uk

Scotland's leading marine conservation experience displaying an amazing variety of sea creatures in over 35 fascinating natural marine habitats, from sharks and seahorses to otters and seals. The sanctuary is in a picturesque setting amongst a mature spruce forest on the shores of Loch Creran.

SCOTTISH WOOL CENTRE 776   5 L24

Aberfoyle, Stirlingshire. Off Main Street in Aberfoyle. Nearest railway station Stirling, buses from Stirling or Glasgow. Open daily Apr–Oct, 0930–1800, Nov–Mar 1000–1700. Admission free. Charge ££ live show. Group concessions. Guided tours. Show programmes in European languages and Japanese. Explanatory displays. Gift shop. Coffee shop. WC. Wheelchair access. Disabled WC. Car and coach parking. Telephone (01877) 382850. www.ewm.co.uk

Visitor centre and theatre telling the story of Scottish sheepdog shill, with a live show using Border Collie dogs. There is also a birds of prey aviary. Watch traditional spinners in action and browse through the shops which contain a wide range of top quality woollens, knitwear, gifts and souvenirs.

SEABEGS WOOD 777   9 N25

HS. 1 mile (2km) west of Bonnybridge, Stirlingshire. Nearest railway and bus stations Falkirk. Access at all reasonable times. Free. Telephone (01786) 431326. www.historic-scotland.gov.uk

A stretch of rampart and ditch of the Antonine Wall with military way behind (see 573).

SEA LIFE SURVEYS 778   5 G22

Ledaig, Tobermory, Argyll. Trips depart from Ledaig car park, Tobermory. Local bus service. Open Apr–Oct, daily 0900–2100. Charge £££. Group concessions. Gift shop. Refreshment available. WC. Limited wheelchair access. Disabled WC. Car and coach parking. Telephone (01688) 302916. www.sealifesurveys.com

A range of trips from half-hour thrill rides, exciting adventures to neighbouring islands and even dedicated basking shark watching!

SKIPNESS CASTLE AND CHAPEL 779   7 J26

HS. On the coast at Skipness on the B8001, 10 miles (16km) south of Tarbert, Argyll. Bus from Tarbert to Skipness, then 0.5 mile (1km) walk. Castle and chapel accessible all year round, except tower which is open during normal hours in summer only (opened by keykeeper during the summer). Car parking. Telephone (01786) 431326. www.historic-scotland.gov.uk

A fine 13th-century castle with a 16th-century tower house in one corner. Nearby is an early 14th-century chapel with fine grave slabs.

SMITH ART GALLERY AND MUSEUM   780   10 N24

Dumbarton Road, Stirling. In Stirling, a short walk from the bus and rail stations. On Stirling Heritage Bus route. Open all year, Tue–Sat 1030–1700, Sun 1400–1700. Free. Guided tours for special exhibitions. Explanatory displays. Gift shop. Tearoom. Biodiversity garden and picnic area. WC. Induction loop. Wheelchair access. Disabled WC. Car and coach parking. Telephone (01786) 471917. www.smithartgallery.demon.co.uk

Displays and exhibitions on the history of Stirling. Fine art, natural history, garden. Educational programme (telephone for details).

SPRINGBANK DISTILLERY   781   7 H28

Campbeltown. In the centre of Campbeltown. Local bus service. Open Easter–Sep, tour Mon–Thu 1400 by appointment only. Charge £. Guided tours. WC. Limited wheelchair access. Car parking. Telephone (01586) 552009.

Founded in 1828, the distillery remains under the control of the great-great grandson of the original founder. Springbank Distillery is the only distillery in Scotland to carry out the entire distilling process, from traditional malting through to bottling.

STAFFA   782   5 F22

NTS. Island 6 miles (10km) north east of Iona and 7 miles (11km) west of Mull, Argyll. Boat cruises from Iona, Mull or Oban. Open all year. Landing charge £. Guided tours by boat. Telephone NTS Regional Office (01631) 570000. www.nts.org.uk

Romantic uninhabited island famed for its extraordinary basaltic column formations. The best known of these is Fingal's Cave, inspiration for Mendelssohn's *Hebrides* overture. Visitors can view the cave from a boat, or land on the island if weather conditions permit. A colony of puffins nests on the island.

STIRLING CASTLE   783   10 N24

HS. Castle Wynd, Stirling. At the head of Stirling old town, off the M9. Nearest railway station Stirling, buses from Glasgow and Edinburgh. Open Apr–Sep, daily 0930–1800; Oct–Mar daily 0930–1700. Last entry 45 minutes before closing. Charge £££. Charge includes admission to Argyll's Lodging. Group concessions. Guided tours. Explanatory displays. Gift shop. Café and picnic area. WC. Courtesy vehicle provided by the Bank of Scotland. Limited wheelchair access. Disabled WC. Car and coach parking. Telephone (01786) 450000. www.historic-scotland.gov.uk

Considered by many as Scotland's grandest castle, it is certainly one of the most important. The castle architecture is outstanding and the Great Hall and Chapel Royal are amongst the highlights. Mary, Queen of Scots was crowned here and narrowly escaped death by fire in 1561. Medieval kitchen display and exhibition on life in the royal palace. Tapestry weaving studio and full summer events programme. See also 585 Argyll and Sutherland Highlanders Regimental Museum.

STIRLING OLD BRIDGE   784   10 N24

HS. In Stirling just beside the Customs Roundabout off the A9. Nearest railway station Stirling, buses from Glasgow and Edinburgh. Access at all reasonable times. Free. Telephone (01786) 431326. www.historic-scotland.gov.uk

A handsome bridge built in the 15th or early 16th century. The southern arch was rebuilt in 1749 after it had been blown up during the '45 rebellion to prevent the Stuart army entering the town.

STIRLING OLD TOWN JAIL   785   10 N24

St John Street, Stirling. At the top of the Old Town in Stirling, five minute walk from rail and bus stations. Nearest railway station Stirling, tour bus in summer. Open all year daily, Apr–Sep, 0930–1700; Mar and Oct, 0930–1600; Nov–Feb, 1030–1530 (closed Christmas and New Year). Charge £££. Group concessions. Guided tours (available in French, German, Italian and Spanish). Explanatory displays. Gift shop. Garden and grounds. WC. Scripts for the deaf. Limited wheelchair access (limited access to upper floor). Disabled WC. Car parking. Telephone (01786) 450050. www.oldtownjail.com

Experience life as a prisoner in a Victorian jail where history really comes to life through live performances. Meet Stirling's notorious hangman and look out for a possible jail break! Take a tour of the jail which includes a modern day prison exhibition and find out how crime and punishment is dealt with today in comparison with Victorian times.

STIRLING VISITOR CENTRE   786   10 N24

Castle Esplanade, Stirling. Located at Stirling Castle esplanade. Nearest railway and bus stations Stirling. Open daily, Apr–Jun and Sep–Oct 0930–1800; Jul–Aug 0930–1800; Nov–Mar 0930–1700. Free. Guided tours. Explanatory displays. Gift shop. WC. Wheelchair access with assistance. Car and coach parking. Telephone (01786) 462517. www.visitscottishheartlands.org

The story of Royal Stirling, from the wars of independence and life in the medieval burgh, to the present day. Sound and light exhibition, multi-lingual audio-visual show.

STONEFIELD CASTLE HOTEL AND GARDEN   787   7 H25

Stonefield, Tarbert, Argyll. 2 miles (3km) north of Tarbert on A83. Glasgow to Campbeltown bus stops at hotel entrance. Gardens open all year, dawn–dusk. Free. Guided tours by arrangement. Gift shop. Restaurant, bar and coffee lounges. WC. Limited wheelchair access. Car and coach parking. Telephone (01880) 820836. www.innscotland.com

Stonefield Castle was built in 1837 for the Campbell family. The house is now a 4 star hotel and the gardens, which were planted mainly from seed in the 1830s, are open to the public. Stonefield boasts the second largest collection of Himalayan rhododendrons in the UK, along with other exotic shrubs and trees. With its spectacular location on the shores of Loch Fyne, the gardens are influenced by the Gulf Stream, often producing the first blooms of the season as early as March.

THE STORY OF SKERRYVORE LIGHTHOUSE   788   5 E22

Hynish, Isle of Tiree. At Hynish village, western Tiree. Ferry from Oban, by air from Glasgow. Open May–Sep, daily. Telephone or visit website to confirm times. Admission by donation. Explanatory displays. Teas available Thur and Sun during summer. Wheelchair access (but not to signal tower). Car parking. Telephone (01865) 311468. www.hebrideantrust.org

The exhibition tells the story of the construction of the lighthouse located 11 miles (17.5km) south west of Tiree. Skerryvore lighthouse was constructed on the infamous reef of the same name, by a team led by Alan Stevenson (uncle of Robert Louis Stevenson). The exhibition focuses on the role of Tiree, and Hynish in particular, in this great feat of Victorian engineering. Visitors may also climb the steep steps to the signal tower observation deck look out toward Skerryvore (visible on a clear day).

STRACHUR SMIDDY MUSEUM   789   5 J24

The Clachan, Strachur, Argyll. On the A815 beside Loch Fyne, 20 miles (32km) north of Dunoon and 20 miles (32km) east of Inveraray. Buses from Dunoon or Inveraray. Open Easter–mid Oct, Fri–Mon 1300–1600, and at other times by prior arrangement. Charge £. Group concessions. Guided tours. Explanatory displays. Gift shop. WC. Wheelchair access. Disabled WC. Car and coach parking. Telephone (01369) 860565. www.opraappers.nl/strachursmiddy/museum.htm

Dating from before 1790, now restored to working order. On display are bellows, anvil, boring beam, hammers, tongs and other tools of the blacksmith and the farrier. Occasional demonstrations. Also a craft shop with a selection of modern craftwork.

SWANSWATER FISHERY   790   5 M24

Sauchieburn, Stirling. Exit junction 9 from M9, take A872 and follow signs for Swanswater Fishery. Bus and train stations in Stirling town centre. Open all year (except Christmas and New Year's Day) from 0800, closing times vary according to season. Charges dependent on duration and location of fishing. Group concessions. Fishing lodge supplying complimentary hot drinks. Soup, soft drinks, crisps and sweets for sale. Microwave for anglers' use. Limited selection of flies and nylon on sale. Tackle can be hired.. WC. Wheelchair access to all the ponds. Disabled WC. Car parking. Telephone (01786) 814805. www.swanswater-fishery.co.uk

Fly fishing on three ponds. The main water is approximately 10 acres (4ha) with boats for hire (book in advance). The two smaller ponds are particularly suitable for beginners and children. All waters are stocked daily with rainbow, steelhead, gold, brown, blue and tiger trout. Tuition available by arrangement.

TARBERT GOLF CLUB   791   7 H25

Kilberry Road, Tarbert. On B8024 Kilberry road (1 mile/1.5km off A83 south of Tarbert). Charge £££. Licensed clubhouse open weekends. WC. Limited wheelchair access. Car and coach parking. Telephone (01880) 820565.

Picturesque nine-hole golf course overlooking west Loch Tarbert

TAYNISH NATIONAL NATURE RESERVE   792   7 H25

Small car park 1 mile (1.5km) south of Tayvallich, on partly unmetalled road. Bus from Lochgilphead to Tayvallich. Access at all times. Free. Reserve leaflet. Waymarked routes with all ability access to Taynish Mill picnic area. Car parking. Telephone 01546 603611 (Scottish Natural Heritage). www.nnr-scotland.org.uk

Nature reserve. The ancient deciduous woodland at Taynish is one of the largest in Britain. It lies on a scenic peninsula overlooking Loch Sween and has an atmosphere all of its own. The woodland's dripping ferns and mosses mingle with marshland and grassland to support over 300 plant species and more than 20 kinds of butterfly. Look out, too, for the colourful marine life of the loch shores.

TEMPLE WOOD STONE CIRCLES   793   5 H24

HS. 0.25 mile (0.5km) south west of Nether Largie, Argyll. Access at all reasonable times. Free. Telephone (01786) 431326. www.historic-scotland.gov.uk

A circle of upright stones about 3000 years old, and the remains of an earlier circle.

TIGHNABRUAICH VIEWPOINT   794   7 J25

NTS. North east of Tighnabruaich, Argyll on A8003. Access at all times. Free.
Explanatory displays. www.nts.org.uk

A high vantage point, with explanatory indicators identifying surrounding sites.
Spectacular views over the Kyles of Bute and the islands of the Firth of Clyde.

TOBERMORY DISTILLERY   795   5 G22

Tobermory, Isle of Mull. By ferry from Oban to Craignure, bus from Craignure. Open
Easter–Oct, Mon–Fri 1000–1700. Charge £. Children under 18 free. Guided tours.
Explanatory displays. Gift shop. Limited wheelchair access. Car and coach parking.
Telephone (01688) 302647.

Malt whisky is distilled using traditional methods. Guided tours and a video
presentation reveal the ingredients and distilling process.

THE TOLBOOTH   796   10 N24

Jail Wynd, Stirling. In the centre of Stirling, near the castle. Nearest railway and
coach station, Stirling. Open daily (telephone for times). Charge varies according to
programme. Group concessions by arrangement. Guided tours. Explanatory
displays. Refreshments available. Gift shop selling Scottish crafts and specialist CDs.
WC. Induction loop and infra red system. Wheelchair access. Disabled WC. Car
parking. Telephone (01786) 274002. www.stirling.gov.uk/tolbooth

Close to Stirling Castle, the Tolbooth is a vibrant centre for music and the arts.
Facilities include auditorium, attic studio (with great views) and digital
recording studio.

TOROSAY CASTLE AND GARDENS   797   5 H22

Craignure, Isle of Mull. 1.5 mile (2.5km) south east of Craignure. Local bus service
and Mull Little Railway runs from Craignure to Torosay. Open Apr–Oct, daily
1030–1700; Nov–Easter, daily 1030–sunset, garden only. Charge ££. Group
concessions. Guided tours by arrangement. Explanatory displays. Gift shop. Tearoom
and picnic area. Garden. Holiday cottages. WC. Limited wheelchair access (easy
access to garden). Disabled WC. Car and coach parking. Telephone (01680) 812421.
www.holidaymull.org/members/torosay

This Victorian family home contains furniture, pictures and scrapbooks dating
from Edwardian times. Torosay is surrounded by 12 acres (5ha) of gardens,
including formal terraces and a statue walk, set amidst fuchsia hedges.
Woodland and water gardens, eucalyptus walk and rockery all contain many and
varied plants. The gardens offer extensive views past Duart Castle and the Sound
of Mull to the mountains of Lorne. See also 744 Mull Rail.

TOWARD CASTLE   798   9 K25

2 miles (3km) south of Innellan on A815. Access at all times. Free.

Ruins of the seat of the Clan Lamont, destroyed by the Campbells in 1646.

TRALEE RALLY KARTING   799   5 J22

18 Keil Crofts, Benderloch, by Oban. 8 miles (13km) north of Oban on A828. Local bus
service. Open Easter–mid Sep, weekends, Bank Holidays, Easter school holidays,
Whitsun week and summer school holidays, 1000–1800 weather permiting. No
booking required but telephone in advance if weather is doubtful. Charge £££. Snacks
available. Picnic area. WC. Wheelchair access. Car parking. Telephone (01631) 720297.

Arrive and drive. Off-road rally karting for all the family. Junior and senior karts available. Helmets and overalls provided.

TROSSACHS DISCOVERY CENTRE   800   5 L24

Main Street, Aberfoyle, Stirling. Nearest railway station Stirling, buses from Stirling or Glasgow. Open mid Mar–Jun, daily 1000–1700; Jul–Aug, daily 0930–1800; Sep–Oct, daily 1000–1700; Nov–Mar, Sat–Sun 1000–1600. Free. Explanatory displays. Gift shop. Children's play area. WC. Interactive screen for deaf visitors. Wheelchair access. Disabled WC. Car and coach parking. Telephone (01877) 382352.

The Discovery Centre contains interactive touch screens and interpretive displays describing local geography, geology and famous local characters. Also shop selling local maps, guides and gifts.

TROSSACHS PIER COMPLEX   801   5 L24

Loch Katrine, by Callander, Perthshire. 8 miles (13km) west of Callander on A821. Bus service from Callander in summer months. Open Easter–Oct, daily 0900–1700, Sat 1000–1700. Boat trips at 1100, 1345 and 1515 (charge £). Free. Charge £ for parking. Guided tours. Explanatory displays. Gift shop. Café. WC. Wheelchair access with assistance, disabled parking, lift to café. Disabled WC. Car and coach parking. Telephone (01877) 376316.

Set in the heart of the Trossachs, the complex has extensive lochside walks and cycle routes, and cruises on Loch Katrine on a steam ship first launched in 1899.

TROSSACHS WOOLLEN MILL   802   5 M24

Kilmahog, Callander, Trossachs. 1 mile (2km) north of Callander. Open May–Sep, daily 0900–1730; Oct–Apr, daily 1000–1630. Free. Explanatory displays. Gift shop. Coffee shop. WC. Wheelchair access. Car and coach parking. Telephone (01877) 330178. www.ewm.co.uk

Resident weaver demonstrates skilled weaving techniques to produce the unique Trossachs Woollen Rug, available in the mill shop. Also quality knitwear, outerwear and gifts.

TULLIBARDINE 1488   803   5 N24

Tullibardine Ltd, Stirling Street, Blackford. On A9 between Perth and Stirling. Gleneagles train, Docherty's Midland Coaches or First Edinburgh. Open all year (except Christmas and New Year), Mon–Sat 0900–1800 and Sun 1000–1800. Charge £. Group concessions. Guided tours. Explanatory displays. Gift shop. Cafe. Baby changing. WC. Limited wheelchair access. Disabled WC. Car parking. Telephone (01764) 682252. www.tullibardine.com

Tullibardine Distillery is part of one of the best out of town retail locations in Scotland. As well as unforgettable tours of the distillery by specialist distillery guides and connoisseur tours with the vastly experienced distillery manager, the distillery also includes a 'nosing and tasting' room. Cafe 1488 uses fresh ingredients to create home baking and home-made hot and cold meals.

UNION CANAL   804   10 N25

From Edinburgh Quay, Fountainbridge, Edinburgh, via Ratho and Linlithgow to the Falkirk Wheel. Excellent links along the canal's route. Access at all times to the towpath unless stoppage works prevent access. Free. Fishing (permits available through Lowland Canals Angling Partnership Scotland), canoeing, cycling, boat hire, boat trips, guided walks, picnic spots and charity, British Waterways Scotland and canal society events and activities. Telephone (01324) 671217. www.britishwaterways.co.uk/scotland

The Union Canal, one of Scotland's registered Ancient Monuments, has been beautifully restored and there are many extremely pleasant places along its length to enjoy the canal experience – with or without a boat! Many restaurants, hotels, bed and breakfasts, pubs, boat hire and luxury holiday hire boats are in the towns and villages along the Lowland Canals. The spectacular Falkirk Wheel (see 658) joins the Union Canal to the Forth and Clyde Canal (see 491). The Wheel alone makes visiting the Union Canal a 'not to be missed' experience. See also 324 Edinburgh Canal Centre and 414 Linlithgow Canal Centre.

VERTICAL DESCENTS 805   5 J21

Inchree Falls, Inchree Holiday Centre, Onich. 8 miles (13km) south of Fort William off A82, 1 mile (1.5km) from Onich. Bus services from Fort William, Oban and Glasgow. Open May–Sep. Activities are run daily. Charge dependent on activity. Group concessions. Car and coach parking. Telephone (01855) 821593. www.activities-scotland.com

Exhilarating, active and adventurous activities including canyoning, fun yakking, climbing, mountain biking, paintball, white water rafting, 4x4, and rib rides.

VILLAGE GLASS 806   10 N24

14 Henderson Street, Bridge of Allan, Stirlingshire. 4 miles (6.5km) north of Stirling on A9. Nearest railway station Stirling, bus from Stirling. Open all year, Mon–Fri 1000–1700, Sat 1000–1700. Free. Guided tours and demonstrations. Explanatory displays. Gift shop. Wheelchair access. Car parking. Telephone (01786) 832137. www.villageglass.co.uk

Unique glass studio. A large selection of beautiful glassware made in Bridge of Allan, and elsewhere in Scotland.

WESTQUARTER DOVECOT 807   9 N25

HS. At Westquarter, near Laurieston, West Lothian, 2 miles (3km) east of Falkirk. Bus from Falkirk. Access at all reasonable times. Free. Telephone (01786) 431326. www.historic-scotland.gov.uk

A handsome rectangular dovecot with a heraldic panel dated 1647 over the entrance doorway.

PERTHSHIRE, ANGUS AND DUNDEE, AND THE KINGDOM OF FIFE

ABBOT HOUSE HERITAGE CENTRE 808   10 P25

Maygate, Dunfermline, Fife. 2 miles (3km) from M90 (signposted). Walking distance from Dunfermline railway and bus station. Coach parking nearby. Open all year (except Christmas and New Year's Day), daily 1000–1700. Charge £. Accompanied children free. Garden and ground floor free. Group concessions. Guided tours (French, German, Spanish and Korean available). Explanatory displays. Gift shop. Restaurant with outside seating in garden. Garden. WC. Limited wheelchair access to ground floor (with video display) and gardens. Car parking for disabled. Disabled WC. Car parking. Telephone (01383) 733266. www.abbothouse.co.uk

This award-winning heritage centre is in the restored 15th-century residence of the Abbot of Dunfermline. Learn Scotland's story from Pictish to modern times and find out about King Robert the Bruce, St Margaret and other important figures who played a role in the history of Scotland's ancient capital. Attractive art work by Alasdair Gray and other artists. Enjoy the garden with access to Dunfermline Abbey next door (see 913).

ABERDOUR CASTLE   809   10 P25

HS. Aberdour, Fife. In Aberdour, 5 miles (8km) east of the Forth Bridges on the A921. Nearest railway station Aberdour, bus from Kirkcaldy and Inverkeithing. Open Apr–Sep, daily 0930–1830; Oct–Mar, Mon–Sun 0930–1630 (closed Thu and Fri). Charge £. Group concessions. Explanatory displays. Gift shop. Tearoom. WC. Limited wheelchair access. Disabled WC. Car parking. Telephone (01383) 860519. www.historic-scotland.gov.uk

A 13th-century fortified residence overlooking the harbour. Extended in the 15th, 16th and 17th centuries with splendid residential accommodation and a terraced garden and bowling green. There is a fine circular dovecot.

ABERFELDY WATERMILL   810   5 N22

The Watermill, Mill Street, Aberfeldy. Off A827 in Aberfeldy. Nearest railway station is Pitlochry and there is a bus service from Pitlochry and Aberfeldy to Perth. Open all year, Mon–Sat 0930–1700 and Sun 1200–1700. Free. Gift shop. Coffee shop with lunchtime snacks. Baby changing station. WC. Limited wheelchair access. Disabled WC. Telephone (01887) 822896. www.aberfeldywatermill.com

The largest bookshop in the rural highlands with over 5000 titles. A music department with an outstanding selection of classical, jazz, world and Celtic cd's. The contemporary art gallery shows works by famous names of post-war art as well as work by emerging talent. In the Watermill you can settle into a comfy chair while you browse a book or enjoy looking at a painting.

ABERLEMNO SCULPTURED STONES   811   6 R22

HS. At Aberlemno on the B9134, 6 miles (9.5km) north east of Forfar, Angus. Nearest railway station Arbroath, bus from Arbroath to Forfar. Access at all resonable times. Free. Telephone 0131 668 8800. www.historic-scotland.gov.uk

A magnificent upright cross-slab sculptured with Pictish symbols stands in the churchyard. All are covered from Oct–Mar to protect them from the elements.

ABERNETHY ROUND TOWER   812   6 P23

HS. In Abernethy on the A913, 9 miles (14.5km) south east of Perth. Nearest railway station Perth, bus from Perth to Kintillo. Open summer only, keys available locally . Free. Telephone 0131 668 8800. www.historic-scotland.gov.uk

One of two round towers of the Irish style surviving in Scotland and dating from the end of the 11th century. Beside it is a Pictish stone.

ADVENTURELAND AND BEACHCOMBER AMUSEMENTS   813   10 Q24

Car and coach parking nearby. Open Apr–Oct, daily 1100–2100. Gift shop. Tearoom. WC. Wheelchair access. Disabled WC. Car and coach parking.

Childrens action play centre

AITON FINE ARTS   814   5 N23

63 King Street, Crieff, Perthshire. Nearest railway station Gleneagles. Open all year, Mon–Fri 0900–1700, Sat 0900–1200. Free. WC. Wheelchair access. Car parking. Telephone (01764) 655423.

Family-run art gallery showing contemporary Scottish artists' painting, prints and sculpture.

ALEXANDER III MONUMENT   815   10 Q25

By A921, south of Kinghorn at Pettycur Promontory. Access at all times. Free. Car parking.

On the King's Crag, a monument marks the place where Alexander III was killed in a fall from his horse in 1286.

ALLEAN FOREST   816   5 N21

FE. 7 miles (11km) west of Pitlochry, on B8019. Access at all times. Free. Explanatory displays on archaeological features. WC. Disabled WC. Car parking. Telephone (01350) 727284. www.forestry.gov.uk

Magnificent views of Loch Tummel and surrounding mountains from waymarked walks through this working forest. The trails pass a reconstructed 18th-century farmhouse and the remains of an 8th-century ring fort.

ALYTH MUSEUM   817   6 Q22

Commercial Street, Alyth, Perthshire. In Alyth centre. Bus from Perth or Dundee. Open May–Sep, Wed–Sun 1300–1700. Free. Explanatory displays. Car parking. Telephone (01738) 632488.

Displays of local history relating to Alyth and the surrounding agricultural area.

ANSTRUTHER PLEASURE TRIPS TO THE ISLE OF MAY   818   10 R24

The Harbour, Anstruther, Fife. Nearest railway station Leuchars or Kirkcaldy. Buses from Edinburgh, Glasgow or Kirkcaldy. Open May–Sep, telephone for sailing times. Charge £££. Children under 3 years free. Group concessions midweek only, May–Jun group leader of groups numbering 30+ free. Explanatory displays. Snack bar on board. Visitor centre and picnic area on Isle of May. WC. Limited wheelchair access. Disabled WC on Isle of May. Car and coach parking. Telephone (01333) 310103. www.isleofmayferry.com

Daily boat trips to the Isle of May nature reserve to view large numbers of sea birds, including puffins. Also colony of grey seals, remains of a 12th-century monastery and lighthouses. Five hour trip, including three hours ashore and a cruise around the island. Boat carries 100 passengers.

ARBROATH ABBEY   819   6 R22

HS. Abbey Street, Arbroath, Angus. In Arbroath town centre. Nearest railway station Arbroath, bus services from Dundee and Montrose to Arbroath. Open Apr–Sep, Mon–Sun 0930–1830; Oct–Mar, Sat–Wed 0930–1630 . Charge £. Group concessions. Explanatory displays. Easy wheelchair access to visitor centre. Telephone (01241) 878756. www.historic-scotland.gov.uk

The substantial ruins of a Tironesian monastery founded by William the Lion in 1178 and intended as his own burial place. Parts of the Abbey Church and domestic buildings remain, notably the gatehouse range and the abbot's house. Famous for its association with the Declaration of Arbroath in 1320, which asserted Scotland's independence from England. The visitor centre tells the story of the abbey.

ARBROATH ART GALLERY 820   6 R22

Public Library, Hill Terrace, Arbroath. In the centre of Arbroath. Nearest railway station Arbroath 0.5 mile (1km), bus station 0.5 mile (1km). Open all year, Mon–Sat 1000–1700. Free. Guided tours by arrangement. WC. Loop system. Car parking. Telephone (01241) 872248.

Two galleries feature changing displays from Angus Council's art collections. Also exhibitions from elsewhere and locally generated shows.

ARBROATH MUSEUM 821   6 R22

Signal Tower, Ladyloan, Arbroath. 16 miles (26km) north of Dundee on A92. Six minute walk from Arbroath bus and railway stations. Open all year (except 25–26 Dec and 1–2 Jan), Mon–Sat 1000–1700; Jul–Aug also Sun 1400–1700. Free. Guided tours (booking required). Explanatory displays. Gift shop. Garden. WC. Limited wheelchair access. Car and coach parking. Telephone (01241) 875598.

Housed in the shore station for the Bell Rock lighthouse, the museum features displays devoted to this renowned lighthouse as well as exhibits exploring the fishing community with life-size models which converse in the local dialect. Recreated 1950s schoolroom, Victorian parlour and wash house complete with noises and smells. Displays on Arbroath's linen and engineering industries plus maritime wildlife tableaux.

ARDESTIE AND CARLUNGIE EARTH HOUSES 822   6 R23

HS. Ardestie, about 6 miles (9.5km) east of Dundee and 1.25 miles (2km) north of Monifieth, at junction with B962. Nearest railway station Dundee, bus to Monifieth. Carlungie is 1 mile (1.5km) north on an unclassified road. Open all year. Free. Telephone (01786) 431324. www.historic-scotland.gov.uk

Two examples of large Iron Age earth houses attached to surface dwellings (both now uncovered). At Ardestie the gallery is curved and 80 feet (24m) in length. The Carlungie earth house is 150 feet (45.5m) long and most complex.

ARDUNIE ROMAN SIGNAL STATION 823   5 N23

HS. At Trinity Gask, 4 miles (6.5km) north of Auchterarder, Perthshire. Nearest railway station Perth, bus from Perth to Crieff, then bus to Kinkell Bridge. Access at all reasonable times. Free. Telephone (01786) 431324. www.historic-scotland.gov.uk

The site of a Roman watchtower, one of a series running between Ardoch and the River Tay. First century AD. See 1005 Muir O'Fauld Signal Station.

ATHOLL COUNTRY LIFE MUSEUM 824   5 N21

Blair Atholl, Perthshire. In Blair Atholl on A924. Nearest railway station Blair Atholl. Bus from Pitlochry. Open Easter, then Jun–Sep daily 1330–1700; Jul–Sep, Mon–Fri 1000–1700. Charge £. Group concessions. Guided tours by arrangement. Explanatory displays. Gift shop. Picnic area. WC. Blind visitors may handle artefacts. Wheelchair access. Disabled WC. Car and coach parking. Telephone (01796) 481232. www.blairatholl.org.uk

Folk museum with lively displays showing past life in the village and glen, including blacksmith's smiddy, crofter's stable, byre and living room. Road, rail and postal services, the school, the kirk, the vet and gamekeeper are all featured. Attractions include the Trinafour post office and shop, the Caledonian Challenge Shield for rifle shooting.

ATHOLL ESTATES INFORMATION CENTRE   825   5 N21

Old School Park, Blair Atholl, Perthshire. 5 miles (8km) north of Pitlochry off A9. Railway station and bus stop close by. Open Easter–Oct, daily 0900–1645. Staff available 0900–1000 and 1530–1645. Free. Explanatory displays. Café next door. Picnic area beside River Tilt. Toilets close by. Car parking. Telephone (01796) 481646. www.athollestatesrangerservice.co.uk

Displays on the estates throughout the year, ideas on what to see and do, details of waymarked trails and a children's corner. The rangers will give advice on walks, off-road cycling and wildlife opportunities. A good place to visit before exploring the wider countryside around Blair Atholl.

AUCHINGARRICH WILDLIFE AND HIGHLAND CATTLE CENTRE   826   5 M23

Comrie, Perthshire. 2 miles (3km) south of Comrie on B827. Open all year, daily 1000–dusk. Charge £££. Children under 3 and visitors in wheelchairs free. Group concessions. Guided tours. Explanatory displays. Gift shop. Restaurant, tearoom and picnic/barbecue area. Indoor play barn. WC. Handling facilities for blind visitors. Limited wheelchair access. Disabled WC. Car and coach parking. Telephone (01764) 679469 or 670486.

Wildlife centre set in 100 acres (40ha) of scenic Perthshire countryside. Abundance of animals and birds including foxes, otters, meerkats, deer, Highland cattle, birds of prey and wildcats. Hatchery where visitors can handle newly born chicks. Covered walkway. Falconry centre with flying displays and photo opportunities. The Highland Cattle Centre tells the story of the cow's evolution. See all the different types of Highland cattle, from young calves to hugh bullocks. The cattle can be touched.

AUCHTERARDER HERITAGE   827   5 N23

Auchterarder Tourist Office, 90 High Street, Auchterarder, Perthshire. Nearest railway stations Perth and Gleneagles. Bus from Perth. Open Apr–Oct, Mon–Sat 0930–1700, Jul–Aug also Sun 1100–1600. Free. Explanatory displays. Telephone (01764) 663450.

History of the town and area told in descriptive panels using old photographs. Information on the railway, local history, the territorial army and church history.

AVIATION MUSEUM   828   6 Q22

Bellies Brae, Kirriemuir. Off the A90, near Forfar. Local bus service. Open Apr–Sep, Mon–Thu and Sat 1000–1700, Fri and Sun 1100–1700. Donations welcome. Guided tours. Explanatory displays. Picnic area nearby. Wheelchair access with assistance. Car and coach parking. Telephone (01575) 573233.

Open since 1983, the museum displays a large and varied collection of ephemera associated with flight, from radar and radio equipment, model planes and photographs, to uniforms and operation manuals.

BALBIRNIE CRAFT CENTRE   829   10 Q24

Balbirnie Park, Markinch, Fife. On eastern outskirts of Glenrothes in Markinch. Nearest railway station Markinch, bus service from Glenrothes. Open all year, Mon–Sat 1000–1700, Sun 1400–1700. Individual workshop times may vary. Park open all year round. Free. Guided tours by appointment. Gift shop. Restaurant and WC in park. Limited wheelchair access. Car and coach parking. Telephone (01592) 753743. www.murrayjewellers.co.uk

Independently owned craft workshops producing leather goods, wrought ironwork, paintings and prints, gold and silver jewellery and glass blowing. The craft centre is located in the centre of Balbirnie Park with woodland walks, specimen trees and rhododendrons. Bronze Age stone circle. Hotel, golf course, picnic area and children's play area within park boundaries.

BALVAIRD CASTLE   830   6 P24

HS. About 6 miles (9.5km) south east of Bridge of Earn, Perthshire. Nearest railway station Perth, bus from Perth to Glenfarg. Limited opening; confirm by telephone. Charge £. Limited wheelchair access. Car and coach parking. Telephone (01786) 431324. www.historic-scotland.gov.uk

A late 15th-century tower on an L-plan, extended in 1581 by the addition of a walled courtyard and gatehouse. Refined architectural details.

BARBARAFIELD RIDING SCHOOL   831   6 Q24

Barbarafield Farm, Craigrothie, by Cupar, Fife. 2 miles (3km) south of Cupar on A916 before Craigrothie. Nearest railway station at Cupar. Open all year, daily during daylight hours. Charge £££. Refreshments available nearby. WC. Limited wheelchair access. Car and coach parking. Telephone (01334) 828223. www.barbarafields.co.uk

Hacking and lessons on farmland. Activities for adults and children held throughout the year. Groups and beginners welcome.

J. M. BARRIE'S BIRTHPLACE AND CAMERA OBSCURA   832   6 Q22

NTS. 9 Brechin Road, Kirriemuir, Angus. On A90/A926 in Kirriemuir, 6 miles (10km) north west of Forfar. By bus from Dundee. Open Easter–Jun and Sep, Sat–Wed 1200–1700; Jul–Aug, Mon–Sat 1100–1700 and Sun 1300–1700. Charge ££. Group concessions. Explanatory displays (information in Dutch, German, French, Italian, Spanish, Swedish and Japanese). Tearoom. WC. Induction loop, braille information sheets. Limited wheelchair access. Car and coach parking. Telephone (01575) 572646. www.nts.org.uk

Birthplace of J. M. Barrie, creator of Peter Pan. Exhibition about his work, with his first theatre – an outside wash-house – also on display. Camera Obscura, within the cricket pavillion on Kirrie Hill, presented to Kirriemuir by the author.

BARRY MILL   833   6 R23

NTS. Barry, Carnoustie, Angus. North of Barry village between A92 and A930, 2 miles (3km) west of Carnoustie. By bus from Dundee or Arbroath (stop in Barry 0.5 mile from the Mill). Open Apr–Sep, Thur–Mon 1200–1700 and Sun 1300–1700. Charge ££. Group concessions. Guided tours. Explanatory displays. Picnic area. Waymarked walks. WC. Wheelchair access. Disabled WC. Car and coach parking. Telephone (01241) 856761. www.nts.org.uk

A working 19th-century meal mill. Full demonstrations, usually Sunday afternoons and by prior arrangement. Attractive country walk to mill lade.

BEACON LEISURE CENTRE   834   10 P25

Lammerlaws Road, Burntisland, Fife. 7 miles (11km) west of Kirkcaldy. Nearest railway station Burntisland. Open all year, daily. Charge £. Charges dependent on activities. Café overlooking poolside and Burntisland beach. Picnic area. WC. Wheelchair access. Disabled WC. Car and coach parking. Telephone (01592) 872211. www.thebeaconfife.com

The centre contains a 25m pool with waves. Also classes, fitness suite, health suite, and sunbed and relaxation area.

BEN LAWERS 835   5 M22

NTS. Off A827, 6 miles (9.5km) north east of Killin. Office at Lynedoch, Main Street, Killin, Perthshire. Visitor centre open May–Sep, daily 1000–1700. Charge for audio-visual programme £ (honesty box). Explanatory displays, special audio-visual programme for children. Guided walks by rangers, nature trails. WC. Induction loop. Wheelchair access to visitor centre. Disabled WC. Car and coach parking. Telephone (01567) 820397. www.nts.org.uk

Perthshire's highest mountain (3984 feet/1214m) with views from the Atlantic to the North Sea. Noted for the rich variety of mountain plants and the bird population – birds include raven, ring-ouzel, red grouse, ptarmigan, dipper and curlew. Nature trail. Extensive information on site at the visitor centre. Ranger service.

BEVERIDGE PARK 836   10 Q24

Kirkcaldy, Fife. Close to the town centre off Abbotshall Road. Nearest railway station Kirkcaldy. Open all year. Free. Children's play area. Car and coach parking. www.thebeveridgepark.com

Public park with woodland and formal gardens and extensive leisure facilities. Rowing boat hire, crazy golf, bowling, miniature railway, pets' corner and various football, rugby and hockey pitches.

BIRKS OF ABERFELDY 837   5 N22

Crieff Road, Aberfeldy. Short walk from the centre of Aberfeldy. Access at all reasonable times. Free. Guided tours by arrangement with ranger service. Explanatory displays (on-site panel), leaflet available. Picnic area. WC nearby in Aberfeldy. Limited wheelchair access. Car parking.

Robert Burns wrote *The Birks of Aberfeldy* here in 1878. The birks (Scots for birch trees) still cloak the steep slopes of the Moness gorge, along with oak, ash and elm. A narrow path climbs to a bridge directly above the Falls of Moness, providing spectacular views.

BIRNAM OAK 838   6 P22

Close to the centre of Birnam. Access at all reasonable times. Free.

An ancient tree believed to be the last surviving remnant of Birnam Wood, the great oak forest made famous in Shakespeare's *Macbeth*. The tree's lower branches are supported on crutches and the first 10 feet (3 metres) of its trunk are hollow.

BLACK SPOUT WOOD, PITLOCHRY 839   5 N21

Perth Road, Pitlochry. South of Pitlochry town centre off the A924. Nearest railway station Pitlochry, buses from Perth or Inverness. Access at all reasonable times. Free. Guided tours by arrangement with ranger service. Explanatory displays (on-site panel). Picnic area. WC nearby. Car parking.

Attractive oak woodland deriving its name from the spectacular waterfall, the Black Spout. The wood forms part of the Pitlochry walks system.

BLACK WATCH MONUMENT 840   5 N22

Taybridge Drive, Aberfeldy. In Aberfeldy, 10 miles (16km) west of A9 at Ballinluig. Nearest railway station Pitlochry, local bus service. Free. WC. Wheelchair access. Disabled WC. Car parking.

A cairn surmounted by a statue of Private Farquhar Shaw dressed in the original uniform of the Black Watch Regiment. The monument was unveiled in 1887 by the Marquess of Breadalbane to commemorate the first muster of the regiment in May 1740. The muster took place on the north bank of the Tay, on what is now part of the golf course.

BLACKFRIARS CHAPEL   841   6 R23

HS. In South Street, St Andrews, Fife. Nearest railway station Leuchars 4 miles (6.5km), connecting bus to St Andrews. Buses from Dundee and Edinburgh. Access at all reasonable times. Free. Telephone (01786) 431324. www.historic-scotland.gov.uk

The vaulted side apse of a church of Dominican friars. Rebuilt about 1516.

BLACKHILL ROMAN CAMPS   842   5 N24

HS. Ardoch. 0.5 mile (1km) north of Braco, Perthshire. Nearest railway station Dunblane, bus from Dunblane to Braco (ask driver for Ardoch Roman Fort). Access at all reasonable times. Free. Telephone (01786) 431324. www.historic-scotland.gov.uk

Parts of the defences of two Roman marching camps, probably dating from the early 3rd century AD.

BLAIR ATHOL DISTILLERY   843   5 N21

Perth Road, Pitlochry, Perthshire. 1 mile (1.5km) south of Pitlochry town centre on A924. Pitlochry railway station 1.5 miles (2.5km), bus service. Open Apr–Sep, Mon–Sat 0900–1700, Jun–Sep also Sun 1200–1700; Oct, Mon–Fri 1000–1700; Nov–Mar, Mon–Fri 1100–1600. Last tour 1 hour before closing. Charge ££. Group concessions by arrangement. Guided tours. Explanatory displays. Gift shop. Banqueting suite available for private parties. WC. Wheelchair access to shop only. Disabled WC. Car and coach parking. Telephone (01796) 482003.

Established in 1798 in the popular Highland resort of Pitlochry, Blair Athol distillery is the home of Bell's 8 Year Old Extra Special, the biggest selling blended whisky in the UK. Exhibition.

BLAIR CASTLE   844   5 N21

Blair Atholl, Pitlochry, Perthshire. 7 miles (11km) north of Pitlochry off A9. Railway station 874 yards (800m), bus stop 765 yards (700m). Open 1 Apr or Easter (whichever is earlier) to last Friday in Oct, daily 1000–1730, last entry at 1630. Charge £££. Group concessions. Guided tours for groups. Explanatory displays. Gift shop. Licenced restaurant, tearoom and picnic areas. Children's play area. WC. Wheelchair access to ground floor and facilities only. Disabled WC. Car and coach parking. Telephone (01796) 481207. www.blair-castle.co.uk

A white turreted baronial castle, the ancient seat of the Dukes and Earls of Atholl. The oldest part, Cumming's Tower, dates back to 1269. Visited by Mary, Queen of Scots, Prince Charles Edward Stewart and Queen Victoria. The last castle in Britain to be besieged (1746). The present Duke of Atholl maintains the only private army in Europe – the Atholl Highlanders. Fine collections of furniture, portraits, lace, china, arms, armour, Jacobite relics and Masonic regalia. Deer park, pony trekking, caravan park, woodland, riverside and mountain walks. Admission to grounds allows access to the 18th-century walled garden restoration project.

BOLFRACKS GARDEN   845   5 N22

Aberfeldy, Perthshire. 2 miles (3km) west of Aberfeldy on A827. Nearest railway station Pitlochry, buses to Aberfeldy. Open Apr–Oct, daily 1000–1800. Charge £.

Under 16s free. No dogs please. Guided tours by appointment. WC. Car and coach parking. Telephone (01887) 820207.

A garden overlooking the Tay Valley with spectacular views. A wide range of trees, plants, shrubs, perennials and bulbs. Specialities are rhododendrons, mecanopsis, old and Scottish roses, all contained within a walled garden and a less formal wooded garden with stream and pond.

BONHARD NURSERY   846   6 P23

Murrayshall Road, Scone, Perth. 2 miles (3km) north east of Perth, just off A94. Coach parking by arrangement. Open all year, daily 0900–1700. Free. Coffee shop. WC. Wheelchair access. Disabled WC. Car parking. Telephone (01738) 552791.

The nursery is set within a Victorian walled garden with the original glasshouses still housing productive grape vines. There is a vast range of trees, shrubs, heathers, alpines and herbaceous plants, many of which can be seen in display borders lined with mature box hedging.

BRECHIN BRIDGE   847   6 R21

In Brechin, Angus.

Known locally as the Auld Brig, this is one of the oldest stone bridges in Scotland. Until the 1780s it was the only bridge over the River South Esk.

BRECHIN CASTLE CENTRE   848   6 R21

Haughmuir, Angus. At the southern Brechin junction off A90, 25 miles (40km) north of Dundee. Nearest railway station Montrose (9 miles/14.5km), bus service to Brechin (1 mile/2km). Minibus service runs from Stonehaven to centre daily. Open summer months, Mon–Sat 0900–1800, Sun 1000–1800; winter months, Mon–Sat 0900–1700, Sun 1000–1700; closed Christmas and New Year. Charge £. Group concessions. Guided tours by prior arrangement. Explanatory displays. Gift shop. Restaurant and picnic areas. Play area for under fives and main play area in country park. WC. Wheelchair access. Disabled WC. Car and coach parking. Telephone (01356) 626813. www.brechincastlecentre.co.uk

Brechin Castle Centre is part of the Dalhousie Estates. Scottish breeds of domestic animals, pets' corner and pheasantry, farm buildings and display of traditional agricultural machinery and implements. Garden centre, country park and coffee shop.

BRECHIN CATHEDRAL ROUND TOWER   849   6 R21

HS. In Brechin, Angus. Nearest railway station Montrose, bus to Montrose. View exterior only. Access at all reasonable times. Telephone (01786) 431324. www.historic-scotland.gov.uk

One of the two remaining round towers of the Irish type in Scotland. Built in the late 11th century with a remarkable carved doorway. Capped by a stone roof added in the 15th century. Now attached to the Cathedral. See also 554 Paisley Abbey.

BRECHIN MUSEUM   850   6 R21

Brechin Townhouse Museum, 28 High Street, Brechin. 9 miles (15km) from Montrose on A935, two miles from turn-off on A94. Bus service from Montrose, Caledonian steam railway. Open all year (except Christmas and New Year), Mon–Tue and Thu–Sat 1000–1700, Wed 1000–1300. Free. Explanatory displays. WC. Wheelchair access. Disabled WC. Car parking. Telephone (01356) 625536. www.angus.gov.uk

Local collections tell the story of the development of Brechin from the Celtic church of the 10th century to the last days of the burgh in 1975. There is a small display of some of the works of D. Waterson, etcher and colourist.

BRITISH GOLF MUSEUM   851   6 R23

Bruce Embankment, St Andrews, Fife. Ten minutes walk from town centre, opposite the Royal and Ancient Golf Club. Nearest railway station Leuchars 4 miles (6.5km), connecting bus to St Andrews. Buses from Dundee and Edinburgh. Open Easter–Oct, daily 0930–1730; Nov–Mar, daily 1000–1600. Charge ££. Children under 5 free. Group concessions. Explanatory displays. Gift shop. Braille guide available. Wheelchair access. Disabled WC. Car and coach parking. Telephone (01334) 478880. www.britishgolfmuseum.co.uk

At the British Golf Museum visitors encounter many famous professionals and amateurs of status. Touch screen videos allow visitors to look deeper into the lives of champions and to test their skills and knowledge of the game of golf. An interactive gallery, The 18th Hole, provides visitors with the opportunity to try out old clubs and balls on a mini-putting green.

BROUGHTY CASTLE   852   6 Q23

HS. In Broughty Ferry, east of Dundee. Nearest railway station Dundee, bus service from Dundee. Telephone for opening times. Free. Explanatory displays. Telephone (01382) 436916. www.historic-scotland.gov.uk

A 16th-century tower adapted for changing defence needs during the 19th century. Now houses a branch of Dundee Arts and Heritage Department.

MICHAEL BRUCE'S COTTAGE   853   10 P24

The Cobbles, Kinnesswood, Kinross. 4 miles (6.5km) east of Milnathort. Bus from Kinross. Open Apr–Sep, daily 1000–1800. Keys available from garage, Main Street, Kinnesswood. Donations welcome. Guided tours by appointment. Garden. No guide dogs. Telephone (01592) 840255.

An 18th-century pantiled weaver's cottage and a museum since 1906. Houses collection relating to the life of the poet, and local history including the manufacture of vellum and parchment.

BUCKHAVEN MUSEUM   854   10 Q24

College Street, Buckhaven. 8 miles (13km) east of Kirkcaldy. Bus service stops outside museum. Call 01592 412860 for opening hours. Free. Explanatory displays. Limited wheelchair access. Car and coach parking. Telephone (01592) 412860.

Museum displays Buckhaven's history with a focus on the fishing industry. Stained glass windows made by local people with the help of a community artist. Recreation of a 1920s kitchen.

BURLEIGH CASTLE   855   10 P24

HS. Near Milnathort, off the A911, 2 miles (3km) north east of Kinross, Perthshire. Nearest railway station Perth, bus from Perth to Milnathort. Open Apr–Sep, Mon–Sat 0900–1830, Sun 1400–1830. Keys collected from 16 Burleigh Road, Milnathort, (01577) 862408. Free. Telephone 0131 668 8800. www.historic-scotland.gov.uk

The roofless but otherwise complete ruin of a tower house of about 1500 with a section of defensive barmkin wall and a remarkable corner tower with a square cap-house corbelled out. The seat of the Balfours of Burleigh; much visited by James IV.

BURNTISLAND EDWARDIAN FAIR MUSEUM   856   10 P25

102 High Street, Burntisland, Fife. 7 miles (11km) west of Kirkcaldy. Nearest railway station Burntisland. Coach parking nearby. Call 01592 412860 for opening times. Free. Explanatory displays. WC. Telephone (01592) 412860.

Permanent display about the Edwardian Fair that visited Burntisland every year, plus displays on the local history of Burntisland.

BUTTERCHURN AND SCOTTISH FOOD AND CRAFT CENTRE   857   10 P24

By junction 4 of M90, on B914. Car parking. Coaches by prior arrangement. Open all year, daily (except Christmas and New Year). Seasonal opening hours, telephone or visit website for details.. Free. Explanatory displays. Gift shop. Restaurant (telephone to book). Children's play area. Garden. Farmyard pets. WC. Wheelchair access. Disabled WC. www.kathellan.co.uk

6000 products. Set in 25 acres of scenic farmland with a food hall, delicatessen, kitchenware, jewellery, bookshop, and arts and crafts. Regular cookery demonstrations and events.

THE BYRE THEATRE OF ST ANDREWS   858   6 R23

Abbey Street, St Andrews, Fife. Nearest railway station at Leuchars. Bus service to St Andrews. Open all year, Mon–Sat 1000–2400. Charges vary per production. Group concessions. Explanatory displays. Café-Bar Restaurant. WC. Signed and audio described performances. Wheelchair access. Disabled WC. Telephone 01334 476288; Box Office 01334 475000; Café-Bar Restaurant 01334 468720. www.byretheatre.com

A year-round programme of contemporary and classic drama, dance, concerts, opera, comedy and innovative education and community events.

CAIRN O'MOHR FRUIT WINERY   859   6 Q23

East Inchmichael, Errol, Perth. 8 miles (13km) east of Perth, off A90. Follow brown tourist signs. Nearest railway stations in Perth and Dundee (10 miles/16km). Open all year, Mon–Fri 0900–1800, Sat 1000–1700, Sun 1230–1700. Free. Guided tours, (glass of wine, tour and tastings) by appointment (charge). Explanatory displays. Gift shop. Picnic area. WC. Wheelchair access with assistance. Car and coach parking. Telephone (01821) 642781. www.cairnomohr.co.uk

Visitors can study wine-making displays and sample, for free, the full range of 12 different types of wine, all fermented on the premises from locally grown leaves, fruits and flowers. You are welcome to bring a picnic and sit at tables on the deck overlooking the winery.

CAIRNIE FRUIT FARM AND MEGA MAZE   860   6 Q23

Cairnie Lodge, Cupar, Fife. 2 miles (3km) north of Cupar. Nearest railway station in Cupar. Local bus service. Open Jul–Sep, daily: pick your own 0930–1900; maze 1000–1800 (last entry 1600). Charge for maze and for pick your own fruit. Tearoom and picnic area. Children's play area. Wheelchair access. Car and coach parking. Telephone (01334) 652384. www.cairniefruitfarm.co.uk

Growers of Grade I fruit since 1970. Pick your own strawberries, raspberries, tayberries, gooseberries, red and blackcurrants and brambles. Also ready picked fruit, fresh local produce and Cairnie Fruit Farm jams. 5 acre (2ha) maze, sown in maize. The labyrinth of pathways and blind alleys follow a different theme each year.

CALEDONIAN RAILWAY, BRECHIN   861   6 R21

The Station, 2 Park Road, Brechin, Angus. Near Brechin town centre, follow road
signs. Nearest railway station Montrose, bus or tour bus from Montrose. Open
Easter, May–Sep and Dec, Sun only; telephone to confirm. Charge ££. Higher fares
may apply during special events. Group concessions. Guided tours by prior
arrangement. Explanatory displays. Gift shop. Light refreshments, picnic area at
Bridge of Dun. Baby changing facilities at Brechin. WC. Wheelchair access with
assistance (telephone to request). Disabled WC. Car and coach parking. Telephone
(01561) 377760 publicity, (01356) 622992 station. www.caledonianrailway.co.uk

From the unique Victorian terminus at Brechin, board a steam train and journey
back in time as you travel the falling grade to Bridge of Dun. The station at
Bridge of Dun was a junction on the former Strathmore main line and a
frequent stopping point for Royal Trains. A short distance from the station,
visitors can take interesting walks along both banks of the South Esk and part of
the Montrose Basin bird sanctuary. Static display of model trains. Special events
held throughout the year, particularly Easter, June, July, August and December.

EPPIE CALLUM'S TREE   862   5 N23

Walk from the centre of Crieff. Access at all reasonable times. Free.

A 600-year-old oak tree standing 70 feet (21m) high, named after a local woman.
The tree is said to have once sheltered notorious outlaw Rob Roy Macgregor
from his enemies. Bonnie Prince Charlie is also said to have hidden in the tree.

CAMBO GARDENS   863   6 R24

Cambo Estate, Kingsbarns, St Andrews. 1 mile (1.5km) south of Kingsbarns on A917,
2.5 miles (4km) north of Crail. Nearest railway station Leuchars, hourly bus service
from St Andrews. Open all year, daily 1000–dusk. Charge ££. Children free. Guided
tours by arrangement. Refreshments can be arranged for large groups, picnics
allowed. WC. Limited wheelchair access. Car and coach parking. Telephone (01333)
450313. www.camboestate.com

Walled garden full of romantic charm designed around the Cambo burn, which
is spanned by ornamental bridges and a greenhouse. Carpets of snowdrops and
bulbs in spring, a lilac walk, magnificent herbaceous borders, an extensive rose
collection and ornamental potager are highlights in summer. There is a
September border and a colchicum meadow in autumn. Woodland walks follow
the burn to a secluded sandy beach.

ANDREW CARNEGIE BIRTHPLACE MUSEUM   864   10 P25

Moodie Street, Dunfermline, Fife. 18 miles (29km) from Edinburgh on A823 off M90.
Nearest railway and bus stations Dunfermline. Frequent service all year. Open
Apr–Oct, Mon–Sat 1100–1700, Sun 1400–1700. Charge £. Children free. Guided tours
by arrangement. Explanatory displays. Gift shop. WC. Wheelchair access. Photo
album of cottage (inaccessible) available. Disabled WC. Car and coach parking.
Telephone (01383) 724302. www.carnegiebirthplace.com

Weaver's cottage and the birthplace of Andrew Carnegie who was born here in
1835. The adjoining memorial hall was provided by his widow in 1928. The displays
tell the extraordinary rags to riches story of Andrew Carnegie, the weaver's son
who emigrated to America and forged a fortune from the furnaces of the American
steel industry. He went on to endow a range of trusts which still operate today.
Weaving demonstrations on the first Friday of the month from May to October.

CARNEGIE LEISURE CENTRE   865   10 P25

Pilmuir Street, Dunfermline, Fife. Situated in the centre of Dunfermline near firestation. Railway station less than 1 mile (1.5km), bus station five minute walk. Open all year, Mon–Fri 0700–2200, Sat, Sun and bank holidays 0800–2200. Charges vary dependent on activity. Group concessions. Guided tours by prior arrangement only. Explanatory displays. Café and vending machines. Crèche. WC. Wheelchair access with lift to upper floors and pool hoist. Also lift to basement, chair lift and ramps to other facilities. Disabled WC. Car parking. Telephone (01383) 314200. www.fifeleisure.com

Listed building dating from 1904. Donated by Andrew Carnegie to the town of his birth. The building is now a fully equipped leisure centre with three swimming pools, squash courts, sports hall, gymnastics hall, combat room, health suite, climbing wall. Wide range of classes.

CASTLE MENZIES   866   5 N22

Weem, Aberfeldy, Perthshire. 1.5 miles (2.5km) west of Aberfeldy. Nearest railway station Pitlochry (12 miles/19km). Bus service to Aberfeldy. Coach parking by prior arrangement . Open Apr–Oct, Mon–Sat 1030–1700, Sun 1400–1700. Last entry 1630. Charge ££. Group concessions. Explanatory displays and self-guided leaflet (also available in French and German). Gift shop. Tearoom. Walled garden. WC. Limited wheelchair access. Disabled WC. Car parking. Telephone (01887) 820982.

Imposing 16th-century castle restored by the Menzies Clan Society, a fine example of the transition between a Z-plan clan stronghold and a later mansion house. Seat of the clan chiefs for over 400 years, Castle Menzies was involved in a number of historic occurrences. Bonnie Prince Charlie stayed here on his way to Culloden in 1746. Small clan museum.

CATERTHUNS   867   6 R21

HS. Near the village of Menmuir about 5 miles (8km) north west of Brechin, Angus. Nearest railway station Montrose, bus to Brechin. Open all year. Free. Telephone (01786) 431324. www.historic-scotland.gov.uk

Two spectacular large Iron Age hill forts standing either side of the road from Balrownie to Pitmundie. The Brown Caterthun has four concentric ramparts and ditches; the White Caterthun is a well-preserved fort with a massive stone rampart, defensive ditch and outer earthworks.

CERAMIC EXPERIENCE, CRIEFF   868   5 N23

Bennybeg, Muthill Road, Crieff, Perthshire. One mile (1.5km) from Crieff on the A822. Local bus service. Open all year, Mon–Fri 1000–1700, Sat–Sun 1000–1730. Free. Charge £–£££ to paint ceramics. Explanatory displays. Café and picnic area. Nature trail. WC. Special needs workshops. Wheelchair access. Disabled WC. Car parking. Telephone (01764) 655788. www.ceramicx.biz

Visitors can paint their own designs onto a plate or mug. Holiday classes for children (items can be taken away same day). Also adult evening classes and children's parties. Soft play area. Ceramics for sale.

CHARLESTOWN LIME HERITAGE TRUST   869   10 P25

Granary Building, Rocks Road, Charlestown. Off A985, 4 miles (6.5km) south of Dunfermline. Nearest railway station Dunfermline, local bus service. Open May–Sep, guided walks Sun 1400; groups by arrangement. Charge £. Group concessions.

Guided tours. Explanatory displays. Gift shop. Restaurant and tearoom. WC. Limited wheelchair access. Car and coach parking. Telephone (01383) 872006.

Charlestown is a very early example of a planned village and has a fascinating, unique story to tell. Established in 1756 by Charles Bruce, 5th Earl of Elgin and 9th of Kincardine, the village was a self-sufficient complete industrial complex based on the large deposits of limestone in the surrounding area. Today there are 14 kilns. The works closed in 1956.

CHARLETON FRUIT FARM AND DRIED FLOWER FARM 870   6 S21

Hillside, By Montrose, Angus. On A92, 1 mile (1.5km) north of Montrose. Nearest railway station at Montrose. Local bus service. Open Apr, May and Jun, Tue–Sun 1100–1600; Jul–Aug, daily 0900–1700, Sep, Nov and Dec, Wed–Sun 1100–1600. Free. Gift shop. Tearoom with outdoor seating. Children's play area. WC. Wheelchair access. Disabled WC. Car and coach parking. Telephone (01674) 830226. www.charleton-fruit-farm.co.uk

A good day out for the whole family. Pick your own fruit (raspberries, strawberries, gooseberries, black and redcurrants). Dried flower barn for ready-made dried flower arrangements or made-to-order. Giftshop. Bedding plants in season.

CLAN DONNACHAIDH MUSEUM 871   5 N21

Bruar, by Pitlochry, Perthshire. 4 miles (6.5km) north of Blair Atholl, 328 yards (300m) from A9. Nearest railway station Blair Atholl, local bus service. Open Easter–Oct, Mon–Sat 1000–1730, Sun 1100–1730. Free. Guided tours on request. Explanatory displays. External seating area and garden. Wheelchair access. Car and coach parking. Telephone (01796) 483770. www.donnachaidh.com

Clan Donnachaidh history and artefacts from the 14th century to the present day.

CLAYPOTTS CASTLE 872   6 Q23

HS. South of A92, near Broughty Ferry, Angus. Nearest railway station Dundee, bus service from Dundee. Limited opening hours; telephone to check. Charge £. Group concessions. No guide dogs. Telephone (01786) 431324. www.historic-scotland.gov.uk

An unusually complete tower house with circular towers at diagonally opposite corners corbelled out to form overhanging cap houses. Built in the late 16th century for the Strachan family and later the property of Bonnie Dundee, John Graham of Claverhouse.

CLUNY CLAYS 873   10 P24

Cluny Mains Farm, by Kirkcaldy, Fife. 2 miles (3km) north of Kirkcaldy on B922, also signposted from A92. Nearest railway station Kirkcaldy - 10mins, Edinburgh 40 mins. Visitors can be collected if pre-arranged. Open daily (except Christmas and New Year) 0930–2030. Charges dependent on activity. Concessions negotiable. Gun and shooting accessory shop, archery shop, golf and clothing shop. Licensed restaurant, coffee lounge with daily papers and home baking. Picnic area and outdoor seating. Purpose-built meeting rooms, outdoor seating, parkland areas, woodland and riverside walks. WC. Wheelchair access. Disabled WC. Car and coach parking. Telephone (01592) 720374. www.clunyclays.co.uk

Activity complex with comprehensive clay-pigeon shooting ranges covering all disciplines, indoor and outdoor archery ranges, indoor air-rifle ranges, 27-bay golf driving range and a nine-hole golf course (intermediate standard, full length). Children's play park, putting and trampoline.

CLUNY HOUSE GARDENS   874   5 N22

Aberfeldy, Perthshire. 3.5 miles (5.5km) north east of Aberfeldy on the minor road between Weem and Strathtay. Car parking. Coach parking by arrangement. Nearest railway station Pitlochry (13 miles/21km), occasional bus service from Aberfeldy and Pitlochry. Open Mar–Oct, daily 1000–1800. Charge ££. Under 16s free. Guided tours. Explanatory displays. Picnic area. Plant stall. Telephone (01887) 820795.

Cluny is a Himalayan woodland garden created and planted by the late Mr and Mrs Robert Masterton from 1950 onwards. It is situated on a slope in the Strathtay valley where the climate and soil provide perfect conditions for growing a profusion of primulas, meconopsis, rhododendrons, lilies, trilliums and spring bulbs. Cluny is at its most colourful in spring and autumn, but at all times of the year there is much of interest. Red squirrels virtually guaranteed.

CRAIGLUSCAR ACTIVITIES   875   10 P24

Craigluscar Farm, by Dunfermline, Fife. 3 miles (5km) north of Dunfermline. Nearest railway in Dunfermline. Open all year. Charges dependent on activity. Forest walks. Car parking. Telephone (01383) 738429. www.craigluscar.co.uk

Ride four-wheel quad bikes over rough, hilly ground or pilot a single seat hovercraft around a circuit.

CRAIGTOUN COUNTRY PARK   876   6 R23

St Andrews, Fife. 2.5 miles (4km) south west of St Andrews on the B939. Nearest railway station Leuchars 10 miles (16km), connecting bus to St Andrews. Buses from Dundee and Edinburgh. Infrequent bus service from St Andrews, then 0.5 mile (1km) walk to main entrance. Open Easter–Oct, daily 1045–1730. Apr and Sep open Sat–Sun only. Park open all year for garden, other facilities available in main season only. Telephone to confirm charge. Group concessions. Gift shop. Tearoom and picnic area. Baby changing facilities. WC. Wheelchair access with assistance. Disabled WC. Car and coach parking. Telephone (01334) 473666.

Craigtoun Country Park was formerly the grounds of Mount Melville House. In 1947 the grounds were purchased by Fife Council. The park consists of 50 acres (20ha) including formal gardens, two ponds (with boating pond), landscaped areas, Dutch village and cypress walk. Also putting, crazy golf, trampolines, bouncy castle, bowling green, train, adventure playground, glasshouses and countryside centre.

CRAIGVINEAN   877   5 N22

FE. 1 mile (1.5km) west of Dunkeld, on A9. Nearest railway station and coach stop at Dunkeld. Access at all reasonable times. Free. Car and coach parking. www.forestry.gov.uk

Craigvinean (Gaelic for *crag of the goats*) is one of Scotland's oldest managed forests. A waymarked walk provides superb views over the Hermitage (see 951) and Dunkeld to Craig a Barns and passes a reconstructed Victorian folly at Torryvald.

CRAIL GUIDED WALKS   878   10 R24

Crail Museum & Heritage Centre, Marketgate, Crail. On A917, 4 miles (6.5km) from Anstruther, 10 miles (16km) from St Andrews. Local bus route from Leven to Dundee passes Crail. Guided walks late Jun–late Aug, Sun 1430. Charge £. Group concessions. Guided tours. Limited wheelchair access. Car and coach parking. Telephone (01333) 450869.

Walking tours (lasting 1.5-2 hours) of the oldest parts of Crail, taking in buildings of architectural and historic interest.

CRAIL MUSEUM   879   10 R24

62-64 Marketgate, Crail, Fife. 10 miles (16km) south of St Andrews in the centre of Crail. Nearest railway station Leuchars, bus service from Edinburgh and St Andrews. Open Easter, weekends, bank holidays and Jun–Sep, Mon–Sat 1000–1300 and 1400–1700, Sun 1400–1700. Free. Guided tours on request. Explanatory displays. Gift shop. Limited wheelchair access. Car and coach parking. Telephone (01333) 450869.

The museum provides an insight into the past life of this ancient Royal Burgh. Visitors can learn about the seafaring tradition, 200-year-old golf club and *HMS Jackdaw*, a World War II Fleet Air Arm station and subsequently as *HMS Bruceboys* Training School and Joint Services School for Languages. The Special Exhibition changes annually. Museum also doubles as a Tourist Information Centre.

CRAIL POTTERY   880   10 R24

75 Nethergate, Crail, Fife. In centre of Crail, down Rose Wynd. Nearest railway station Leuchars, connecting bus to St Andrews and Crail. Bus service from St Andrews. Open all year, Mon–Fri 0800–1700, Sat and Sun 1000–1700. Closed Christmas and New Year. Free. Explanatory displays. Showroom. Limited wheelchair access. Car and coach parking. Telephone (01333) 451212. www.crailpottery.com

Tucked away in a flower and pot-filled medieval yard, three generations of potters produce a huge variety of hand-thrown pottery from porcelain to gardenware, sculpture, teapots and jardinières.

CRAIL TOLBOOTH   881   10 R24

Marketgate, Crail. 9 miles (14.5km) south east of St Andrews.

The Tolbooth, now a library and town hall, dates from the early 16th century, displaying a fish weather vane, and a coat of arms dated 1602. In the striking Dutch Tower is a bell dated 1520, cast in Holland. There have been 18th- and 19th-century additions. Elsewhere in this picturesque fishing village see the Collegiate Church dating back to the 13th century, the Mercat Cross topped by a unicorn, the harbour and the crowstepped, red-tiled houses.

CRAWFORD ARTS CENTRE   882   6 R23

93 North Street, St Andrews, Fife. In centre of St Andrews opposite police station. Nearest railway station Leuchars 6 miles (10km), connecting bus to St Andrews. Buses from Dundee, Edinburgh and Glasgow. Open all year, Mon–Sat 1000–1700, Sun 1400–1700. Closed Christmas and New Year. Free. Charge for workshops. Guided tours by prior arrangement. Gift shop. Coffee available. WC. Wheelchair access. Telephone (01334) 474610. www.crawfordarts.free-online.co.uk

Founded in 1977, the centre provides exciting exhibitions of all kinds of visual art from sculpture and painting to photography, craft and design, and architecture. Moving venue in June 2006 - contact us for details

CRIEFF VISITOR CENTRE   883   5 N23

Muthill Road, Crieff. On the A822 Crieff to Stirling road. Bus service from Perth. Open all year, daily 0900–1700. Drover exhibition 1000–1630. Charge £. Admission charged only for Drovers exhibition. Explanatory displays. Gift shop. Licensed restaurant with outside terrace. Baby changing facilities. Children's play area. WC.

Wheelchair access. Disabled WC. Car and coach parking. Telephone (01764) 654014. www.crieff.co.uk

The Story of the Highland Drovers traces their origins and follows their journeys. Also factory showroom, plant centre and experts to give advice. Large children's play area.

CROFT-NA-CABER WATERSPORTS AND ACTIVITY CENTRE   884   5 M22

Kenmore, Perthshire. 6 miles (10km) west of Aberfeldy on A827, 14 miles (22.5km) east of Killin on A827. Nearest railway station Pitlochry, bus services from Pitlochry or Aberfeldy. Open all year, daily 0900–1700. Charge dependent on activity. Group concessions. Restaurant, tearoom and bar with views over the loch. WC. Limited wheelchair access. Car and coach parking. Telephone (01887) 850236. www.croftnacaber.com

On the banks of Loch Tay, offering an unrivalled variety of water sports and other activities for individuals, families and groups. Suitable for all abilities. Power boating, windsurfing, sailing, canoeing, jetbiking, surfbiking, kayaking, aqua-sausage, ringo, quad bike trekking, golf, fishing, archery, clay shooting and mountain biking.

CROMBIE COUNTRY PARK   885   6 R22

Monikie, Broughty Ferry, Angus. Follow A92 dual carriageway to Muirdrum exit, then clearly signposted at crossroads. Nearest railway station Dundee, bus service from Dundee to Monikie then 2.5 mile (4km) walk. Open May–Aug, daily 0900–2100; Sept–Apr, daily 0900–1700. Charge £. Parking £ (disabled free). Guided tours by prior arrangement. Explanatory displays. Vending machine, picnic and barbecue area (two free marquees available Apr-Sep). WC. Wheelchair access. Disabled WC. Car and coach parking. Telephone (01241) 860360. crombiepark@sol.co.uk

A Victorian reservoir with the appearance of a natural loch. Set in 250 acres (101ha). Wildlife hide, trails, displays and interpretation centre, ranger service, guided walks, child play park. Barbecue area. Also angling, telephone Monikie Angling Club (01382) 370300.

ROBINSON CRUSOE STATUE   886   10 Q24

Lower Largo. Bus from Edinburgh or St Andrews. Access at all times. Free.

Bronze statue of Alexander Selkirk, the real life mariner on whom Daniel Defoe based his famous character. The statue has stood on the site of his home for over 100 years.

CULROSS ABBEY   887   10 N25

HS. In Culross, Fife. Off A985, 12 miles (19km) west of Forth Road Bridge. Bus from Dunfermline. Access at all reasonable times. Free. Telephone (01786) 431324. www.historic-scotland.gov.uk

The remains of a Cistercian monastery founded in 1217. The eastern parts of the Abbey Church form the present parish church. There are also ruins of the nave, cellars and other domestic buildings.

CULROSS PALACE   888   10 N25

NTS. Culross, Fife. Off A985, 12 miles (19km) west of Forth Road Bridge, 6 miles (9.5km) west of Dunfermline. Bus from Glasgow or Dunfermline. Palace and Town House open Easter–Sep, daily 1200–1700. Charge £££. Group concessions.

Explanatory displays. Guidebook and video programme in French and German, information sheets in seven languages. Gift shop. Tearoom. Town trail, palace garden. WC. Induction loop and Braille guide. Limited wheelchair access. Disabled WC. Car and coach parking. Telephone (01383) 880359. www.nts.org.uk

Many buildings from the 16th and 17th centuries survive in this ancient royal burgh on the north shore of the River Forth. Most spectacular is the palace, built 1597–1611 for local entrepreneur Sir George Bruce. Visitor reception in Town House, with exhibition and video.

DEEP SEA WORLD   889   10 P25

North Queensferry, Fife. In village of North Queensferry. Nearest railway station North Queensferry, bus services (Fife Scottish). Take junction 1 off M90 and follow signs. Open Mar–Oct, daily 1000–1800, Jul–Aug closes 1800; Nov–Mar, Mon–Fri 1000–1700, Sat–Sun and public holidays 1000–1800. Charge £££. Carers with ID badges go free. Group concessions. Guided tours. Explanatory displays. Gift shop. Café and picnic area. WC. Wheelchair access. Disabled WC. Car and coach parking. www.deepseaworld.co.uk

A triple award-winning aquarium. Visitors can enjoy a spectacular diver's eye view of our marine environment on an underwater safari through the world's longest underwater tunnel; come face to face with Europe's largest collection of sand tiger sharks and watch divers hand feed a spectacular array of sea life; touch the live exhibits in the large rockpools, and visit the stunning Amazonian Experience which features ferocious piranhas and electrifying eels. Other exhibits include the dangerous animals tank, seahorses, octopuses, wolf fish and many many more fascinating creatures. New exhibits include the Amazing Amphibians display featuring the world's most poisonous frog, and animal handling sessions including snakes. Free behind the scenes tours.

DEN OF ALYTH   890   6 P22

Bamff Road, Alyth. 300 yards (300m) west of Alyth on the Bamff Road. Access at all reasonable times. Free. Guided tours by arrangement with ranger service. Explanatory displays, (on-site panel), leaflet available. Picnic area. WC nearby. Limited wheelchair access. Car and coach parking. www.pkc.gov.uk/sport_culture/walks.htm

The Den of Alyth is a broadleaved woodland through which the Alyth Burn flows. Walks of varying length through shady woods in a steep sided valley. There is also a large picnic area with play equipment.

DEWARS WORLD OF WHISKY   891   5 N22

Aberfeldy Distillery, Aberfeldy, Perthshire. 20 miles north of Perth on A827, off A9. Bus service from Pitlochry or Perth. Open Apr–Oct, Mon–Sat 1000–1800, Sun 1200–1600; Nov–Mar, Mon–Sat 1000–1600. Last entry one hour before closing. Charge £££. Group concession or private booking by arrangement. Guided tours (distillery); audio guided tour (visitor centre). Explanatory displays. Gift shop. Tearoom. Garden, forest walk and nature trail. WC. Wheelchair access. Disabled WC. Car and coach parking. Telephone (01887) 822010. www.dewarsworldofwhisky.com

Celebrating the lives of the entrepreneurial Dewar family and the art of blending whisky, visitors will enjoy this interactive, contemporary attraction with a traditional working distillery tour. Fun for all the family.

DOGTON STONE   892   10 P24

HS. Off B922, at Dogton farmhouse, near Cardenden. 5 miles (8km) north west of Kirkcaldy, Fife. 1.5 miles (2.5km) east north-east of Cardenden railway station, bus from Kirkcaldy or Dunfermline. www.historic-scotland.gov.uk

An ancient Celtic cross with traces of animal and figure sculpture.

DRUMMOND CASTLE GARDENS   893   5 N23

Drummond Castle, Muthill, Crieff. 2 miles (3km) south of Crieff. Nearest railway station Gleneagles, bus service from Stirling to Crieff. Open Easter, then May–Oct, daily 1300–1800; last entry 1700. Charge ££. WC. Limited wheelchair access. Disabled WC. Car and coach parking. Telephone (01764) 681433. www.drummondcastlegardens.co.uk

One of Scotland's largest formal gardens with magnificent early Victorian parterre, fountains, terracing and topiary. It is laid out in the form of a St Andrews cross. The multi-faceted sundial by John Mylne, master mason to Charles I, has been the centrepiece since 1630.

DRUMMOND HILL   894   5 M22

FE. At Kenmore, 4.5 miles (7km) west of Aberfeldy, off the A827. Nearest railway station Pitlochry, bus service from Kenmore. Access at all reasonable times. Free. Picnic area and WCs at Dalerb. Wheelchair access at Dalerb. Disabled WC. Car parking. www.forestry.gov.uk

Historically important for both forestry and capercaillie, Drummond Hill has forest walks with stunning views of Loch Tay. Also mountain bike routes. Picnic area at Dalerb beside Loch Tay, one mile west of Kenmore on A827.

DUNDEE, CAIRD HALL   895   6 Q23

City Square, Dundee. Close to rail and bus stations. Opening hours are dependent on programme – telephone (01382) 434451 for further details. Charges vary depending on event. Group concessions. Guided tours on request during the week (subect to programme). Explanatory displays. Gift shop. Refreshments available. WC. Induction loop. Wheelchair access. Disabled WC. Car and coach parking. Telephone (01382) 434030. www.cairdhall.co.uk

A multi-use facility staging an array of events throughout the year, e.g. opera, ballet, pop and classical concerts and exhibitions.

DUNDEE, CAMPERDOWN WILDLIFE CENTRE   896   6 Q23

Camperdown Country Park, Coupar Angus Road, Dundee. 3 miles (4km) north of Dundee on A923. Nearest railway and bus stations Dundee. Open Mar–Sep, daily 1000–1630; Oct–Feb, daily 1000–1530. Charge £. Children under 3 free. Group concessions. Explanatory displays. Gift shop. Picnic area. WC. Special needs play area. Wheelchair access. Disabled WC. Car and coach parking. Telephone (01382) 432661. www.angusanddundee.co.uk

Over 80 species of native Scottish wildlife; brown bears, lynx, arctic foxes and other more unusual species, such as Britain's rarest mammal, the pine martin. Walkabout map and wildlife trail – complete the wildlife trail and you qualify for a free certificate. Special needs play area. Boating pond, kiddies cars, trampolines and golf course.

DUNDEE, CLATTO COUNTRY PARK 897   6 Q23

Dalmahoy Drive, Dundee. Take A932 Dundee to Coupar Angus road and cross the Kingsway. At next roundabout turn right and follow signs. Local bus service. Park and woodland open at all times. Telephone to confirm visitor centre opening hours. Charge for watersports. Picnic area. Children's play area. WC. Limited wheelchair access. Disabled WC. Car and coach parking. Telephone (01382) 436505. www.dundeecity.gov.uk

Parkland surrounding 24 acres (10ha) of water. A variety of watersports are available, with hire and tuition. Visitor centre and woodland walks.

DUNDEE CONTEMPORARY ARTS 898   6 Q23

152 Nethergate, Dundee. In the centre of Dundee, within five minutes walk of railway station and 15 minutes from bus station. Open all year: galleries and shop, Tue–Sat 1030–1730 (Thu closes 2030), Sun 1200–17.30. Free. Charge for cinema. Group concessions. Guided tours. Explanatory displays. Gift shop. Café-bar. Baby changing facilities. WC. Induction loop in cinema. Wheelchair access. Disabled WC. Car and coach parking. Telephone (01382) 909900. www.dca.org.uk

Centre for contemporary art and film with two galleries, two screen cinema, print studio, craft shop, visual research centre and activity room. Courses, workshops, talks and tours are offered.

DUNDEE, DISCOVERY POINT 899   6 Q23

Discovery Quay, Dundee. In Dundee, beside the railway station. Opposite railway station in Dundee, 10 min walk from bus station. Open daily Apr–Oct, 1000–1800; Nov-Mar, 1000–1700 (except Christmas and New Year). Sun open from 1100. Last entry one hour before closing. Charge £££. Children under 5 free. Group concessions. Guided tours by arrangement (available in French and German). Explanatory displays. Gift shop. Café. WC. Induction loop system. Limited wheelchair access (virtual reality tour of below decks available). Disabled WC. Car and coach parking. Telephone (01382) 201245. www.rrsdiscovery.com

Dundee's flagship attraction centred around Royal Research Ship *Discovery*, Captain Scott's famous polar exploration ship. Spectacular exhibits and special effects recreate the historic voyages of *Discovery* – built in Dundee at the turn of the century to take Scott to the ends of the earth – such as the ship's rescue from the ice by Dundee whaler *Terra Nova* and the *Morning*. Visitors can step on board *Discovery* herself, experience life below decks and feel the atmosphere of the ward room where Scott and his officers talked of the perils of a journey to where no man had gone before. Children's interactive games, giant jigsaws and quiz boards add to the fun and enjoyment for the whole family.

DUNDEE, HM FRIGATE UNICORN 900   6 Q23

Victoria Dock, Dundee. Just east of road bridge, 0.5 mile (1km) from rail station. Nearest railway station Dundee, then 15 minute walk; ten minute walk from bus station. Open Apr–Oct, daily 1000–1700; Nov–Mar, Wed–Fri 1000–1600, Sat–Sun 1000–1600. Other times by arrangement (closed over Christmas and New Year). Charge ££. Children under 5 free. Group concessions. Guided tours. Explanatory displays. Gift shop. Tearoom. WC. No guide dogs. Limited wheelchair access. Car and coach parking. Telephone (01382) 200900. www.frigateunicorn.org

Unicorn was launched at Chatham in 1824 and is one of the best preserved wooden-hulled warships in the world. A navy drill ship in Dundee until 1968.

DUNDEE, THE HOWF   901   6 Q23

Meadowside, Dundee. In Dundee city centre.

An historic graveyard which was formerly the garden of Greyfriars Monastery, gifted to the people of Dundee by Mary, Queen of Scots. Until 1778 it was the meeting place of the Nine Trades of Dundee and on the great variety of gravestones are seen the signs and symbols of the old craft guilds.

DUNDEE, JUNGLE KIDS   902   6 Q23

Dronley Road, Birkhill, Dundee. On the Coupar Angus road, 1.5 miles (2.5km) from Camperdown Park entrance. Bus from Dundee centre. Open all year, Mon–Fri 1100–1830, Sat 1000–1830, Sun 1100–1830. Adults free; charge £–££ children. Group concessions. Café. Internet access. WC. Wheelchair access. Disabled WC. Car and coach parking. Telephone (01382) 580540. www.junglekids.co.uk

A large indoor play centre for children up to 12 years, including a selection of slides, ball pools, large climbing frames; soft play area for children under 3. Birthday party rooms. Supervision. Viewing lounge for parents with CCTV monitor.

DUNDEE LAW   903   6 Q23

Access at all reasonable times. Free. Car park at top of hill. Floodlit at night.

The Law is the highest point in the city, and takes its name from the old Scots word for a hill. It is the remains of a volcanic plug and was later the site of an ancient hill fort. Atop the Law is Dundee's War Memorial with a beacon which is lit four times a year. Magnificent panoramic views across Dundee and the surrounding countryside to Fife and the northern mountains.

DUNDEE, MCMANUS GALLERIES   904   6 Q23

Albert Square, Dundee. In Dundee centre, ten minute walk from bus and railway stations. Open all year, Mon–Sat 1030–1700 (Thu closes 1900), Sun 1230–1600. Free. Guided tours by arrangement. Explanatory displays. Gift shop. Café. WC. Induction loop system in selected galleries. Wheelchair access and disabled parking (wheelchair on request). Disabled WC. Telephone (01382) 432084. www.dundeecity.gov.uk

Victorian Gothic building designed by Sir George Gilbert Scott containing collections of national importance. Features local history, costume, natural history, archaeology, decorative arts, a superb Scottish Victorian art collection and a changing exhibition and events programme throughout the year. Also the magnificent Albert Hall, with its fine stained glass window and vaulted roof.

DUNDEE, MERCAT CROSS   905   6 Q23

Nethergate, in Dundee city centre. Access at all times.

Standing on the south side of St Mary's Tower, this is a replica of Dundee's old mercat cross which formerly stood in the Seagate. On top of the shaft is a unicorn sculpted by Scott Sutherland, RSA.

DUNDEE, MILLS OBSERVATORY   906   6 Q23

Balgay Hill, Glamis Road, Dundee. In the heart of Balgay Park, signposted from major routes access via Glamis Road. Buses pass the park. Open Apr–Sep, Tue–Fri 1100–1700, Sat–Sun 1230–1600; Oct–Mar, Mon–Fri 1600–2200, Sat–Sun 1230–1600. Free. Charge for events. Charge for groups (includes presentation). Guided tours for groups by arrangement. Explanatory displays. Gift shop. Refreshments available. WC. Limited wheelchair access. Disabled WC. Car and coach parking. Telephone (01382) 435846. www.mills-observatory.co.uk

Constructed in 1935 for the people of Dundee, the Mills Observatory is today Britain's only full-time public observatory. Located in picturesque wooded surroundings, it houses a 10-inch (25cm) refracting telescope. Panoramic views over the Tay to Fife.

DUNDEE, ST ANDREW'S CHURCH AND THE GLASITE HALL   907   6 Q23

King Street, Dundee. In Dundee city centre.

St Andrew's Church was designed by Samuel Bell and completed in 1772. It was built and paid for entirely by the Nine Trades' Guild of Dundee and there are fine stained glass windows depicting the trades emblems. Immediately to the east is a curious building completed in 1777.

DUNDEE, SENSATION   908   6 Q23

Greenmarket, Dundee. In central Dundee. Nearest railway and bus stations, Dundee. Open all year daily (except Christmas Day, Boxing Day and New Year's Day), summer 1000–1800; winter 1000–1700. Last admission 1630 in summer and 1530 in winter.. Charge £££. Concessions for pre-booked groups. Children under free. Explanatory displays, staff available to help. Gift shop. Café. Soft play area. WC. Wheelchair access. Disabled WC. Car and coach parking. Telephone (01382) 228800. www.sensation.org.uk

At this innovative science centre you can explore the world through the five senses by walking through six zones themed around sound, touch, light, taste and smell, temperature and position, with over 80 fascinating hands-on exhibits.

DUNDEE, TAY RAIL BRIDGE   909   6 Q23

Dundee. Visible on entering the city from the west on A85 or east on A92.

The present bridge, carrying the main railway line from London to Aberdeen, was completed in 1887. It replaced the first Tay Rail Bridge which was blown down by a storm in 1879 with the loss of 75 lives. At 2 miles and 73 yards long (3.28km) it was the world's longest rail bridge when opened.

DUNDEE, UNIVERSITY OF DUNDEE BOTANIC GARDEN   910   6 Q23

Riverside Drive, Dundee. Nearest railway station Dundee, bus from city centre. Open daily, Mar–Oct 1000–1630; Nov–Feb 1000–1530. Charge £. Guided tours. Explanatory displays. Gift shop. Coffee shop and plant sales. WC. Wheelchair access. Disabled WC. Car and coach parking. Telephone (01382) 647190. www.dundee.ac.uk/botanic

Designed and inaugurated in 1971. Botanic and teaching garden with a fine collection of trees and shrubs, landscaped naturalistically. Two large tropical and temperate plant houses. Award-winning visitor centre.

DUNDEE, VERDANT WORKS   911   6 Q23

West Hendersons Wynd, Dundee. Ten minute walk from bus and railway stations. Open daily Apr–Oct, 1000–1700; Nov–Mar 1000–1600 except Christmas and 1–2 Jan. Sun opens 1100. Last entry one hour before closing. Charge £££. Children under 5 free. Group concessions. Explanatory displays and introductory talk. Gift shop. Café. WC. Loop system. Wheelchair access. Disabled WC. Car and coach parking. Telephone (01382) 225282. www.verdantworks.com

European Museum of the Year 1999. A restored 19th-century jute works surrounding a cobbled courtyard. One of the few surviving and complete examples of the industry. Visitors can view the period office (unchanged since the last century), discover why Dundee became the jute capital of the world and see working machinery processing jute to woven cloth. They can also see a reconstructed tenement balcony, outside loo and the contrasting conditions inside the home of a wealthy jute baron.

DUNFALLANDY STONE   912   5 N22

HS. 1 mile (2km) south of Pitlochry, Perthshire. Nearest railway station Pitlochry, bus from Perth to Pitlochry. Access at all reasonable times. Free. Telephone (01786) 431324. www.historic-scotland.gov.uk

A fine Pictish sculptured stone with a cross on one face and figures on both faces.

DUNFERMLINE ABBEY AND PALACE   913   10 P25

HS. St Margaret Street, Dunfermline, Fife. Off the M90. Short walk from Dunfermline railway and bus stations. Open Apr–Sep, Mon–Sun 0930–1830; Oct–Mar, Mon–Sat 0930–1830, Sun 1400–1630, closed Thu pm and Fri. Charge £. Group concessions. Explanatory displays. Gift shop. Telephone (01383) 739026. www.historic-scotland.gov.uk

The remains of the great Benedictine abbey founded by Queen Margaret in the 11th century. The foundations of her church are under the present nave, built in the 12th century in the Romanesque style. At the east end are the remains of St Margaret's shrine, dating from the 13th century. Robert the Bruce is buried in the choir, now the site of the present parish church (closed during the winter). Of the monastic buildings, the ruins of the refectory, pend and guest house remain. The guest house was later reconstructed as a royal palace where Charles I was born.

DUNFERMLINE MUSEUM   914   10 P25

Viewfield Terrace, Dunfermline, Fife. In Dunfermline centre between the rail and bus stations. Telephone for access. Free. Wheelchair access to ground floor. Car and coach parking. Telephone (01383) 313838.

The headquarters for Fife Council's museums in west Fife. Telephone for information on collections, displays and other west Fife venues.

DUNFERMLINE PUBLIC PARK   915   10 P25

Dunfermline Public Park, Dunfermline. In centre of Dunfermline, easily accessed from local car parks, adjacent railway station and Fife Cycle Network. Open at all times. Free. Refreshments available at nearby Carnegie Hall. WC. Wheelchair access. Disabled WC. Car parking.

The park dates back to 1889 when it was purchased by the council. Mature trees surround large open spaces with panoramic views of the south side of the city to the Firth of Forth and beyond. The park is linked to the Music Institute and the refurbished Carnegie Hall, where performances from Scottish National Opera, a Royal Marine Band, small children's theatre groups and local amateur productions can be enjoyed.

DUNKELD   916   6 P22

NTS. The Ell Shop, Dunkeld, Perthshire. Off A9, 15 miles (24km) north of Perth. By rail (station 1 mile/1.5km from village). NTS shop open Apr–Sep, Mon–Sat

1000–1730, and Sun 1330–1730; Oct–Christmas, Mon–Sat 1000–1630. Access to village all year. Explanatory displays. Gift shop. Cafés in village (not NTS). WC. Subtitled video. Wheelchair access. Disabled WC. Car and coach parking. Telephone (01350) 727460. www.nts.org.uk

Attractive village with mostly ruined Gothic cathedral on banks of River Tay. The National Trust for Scotland owns many houses dating from the rebuilding of the town in 1689 after the Battle of Dunkeld. They have been carefully restored. NTS shop in restored Ell House; Atholl Memorial Fountain. Many delightful walks.

DUNKELD BRIDGE   917   6 P22

Over the River Tay at Dunkeld. Parking available. Access at all times. Free. Riverside path not suitable for wheelchairs.

One of Thomas Telford's finest bridges, a seven-arched bridge and tollhouse built in 1809. An attractive riverside path leads from here downstream to the famous Birnam Oak, last relic of Macbeth's Birnam Wood, and then around the village of Birnam. Best view is from riverside garden. Wheelchair users should approach from the square through the archway.

DUNKELD CATHEDRAL   918   6 P22

HS. High Street, Dunkeld, Perthshire. 15 miles (24km) north north-west of Perth. Nearest railway station Birnam, bus from Perth, then 15 minute walk from Birnam. Telephone for opening times. Free. Explanatory displays. Picnic area. Cathedral shop. WC. Wheelchair access. Telephone (01350) 728732. www.historic-scotland.gov.uk

Beautifully situated on the banks of the River Tay. The restored choir is now the parish church. Originally 12th-century, but nave and great north west tower from 15th century.

DUNNINALD   919   6 S22

Dunninald, Montrose, Angus. 2 miles (3km) south of Montrose. Nearest railway station Montrose, then taxi. Open Jul, Tue–Sun 1300–1700 (garden from 1200). Charge ££. Charge for house and garden ££, garden only £. Group concessions. Guided tours. Explanatory displays. Small gift shop. Teas available . Garden (dogs must be kept on lead). WC. Wheelchair access to garden only. Disabled WC. Car and coach parking. Telephone (01674) 674842.

This family home, the third Dunninald to be built on the estate, was designed by James Gillespie Graham in the gothic revival style, and was completed for Peter Arkley in 1824. Set in a planned landscape dating from 1740, there is an attractive walled garden.

DUNSINANE HILL VITRIFIED FORT   920   6 P23

SE of Collace, off A94 Perth/Coupar Angus road. Access at all reasonable times. Free.

Magnificent views from summit, reached by steep footpath beinning on north side of hill.

EARTHQUAKE HOUSE   921   5 M23

The Ross, Comrie. Bus service to Comrie. Open Apr–Oct at all times. Free. Explanatory displays. Car parking. Telephone (01764) 652578 (Crieff Tourist Information Centre).

Situated on the highland boundary fault line, Earthquake House contains replica and modern seismic measuring instruments. Explanatory boards are on the exterior of the building (no access to the interior).

EASSIE SCULPTURED STONE   922   6 Q22

HS. In Eassie churchyard, west of Glamis off the A94. 7 miles (11km) west south-west of Forfar, Angus. Access at all reasonable times. Free. Telephone (01786) 431324. www.historic-scotland.gov.uk

A fine elaborately carved monument with richly decorated Celtic cross on one side and Pictish symbols and processional scenes on the reverse.

EDEN ESTUARY CENTRE   923   6 Q23

Main Street, Guardbridge, Fife. By main entrance for paper mill. Bus from Cupar, Dundee or St Andrews. 1 mile (2km) from Leuchars station. Open daily 0900–1700 (except for Leuchars Air show, Christmas Day and New Year's Day). Free. Guided tours can be arranged via ranger. Explanatory displays. WC. Wheelchair access to centre only. Disabled WC. Car parking. Telephone 01334 473047 or 07939 169291.

A small centrally-heated hide overlooking Eden Estuary local nature reserve, with displays relating to natural and local history of the site and its management.

EDRADOUR DISTILLERY   924   5 N21

Edradour, Pitlochry, Perthshire. On the A294, 2.5 miles (4km) east of Pitlochry. Nearest railway and bus station Pitlochry. Open Mar–Oct, Mon–Sat 0930–1800, Sun 1200–1700; Nov–Feb 1000–1600. Free. Guided tours. Explanatory displays. Gift shop. WC. Limited wheelchair access. Disabled WC. Car and coach parking. Telephone (01796) 472095. www.edradour.co.uk

The smallest distillery in Scotland, established in 1825. Visitors can taste a hand-crafted single malt whisky.

EDZELL CASTLE AND GARDEN   925   6 R21

HS. Edzell, by Brechin, Angus. At Edzell, off B966, 6 miles (9.5km) north of Brechin. Nearest railway station Montrose, bus service from Montrose or Brechin to Edzell. Open Apr–Sep, daily 0930–1830; Oct–Mar, Mon–Sun 0930–1630 (closed Thu and Fri). Charge £. Group concessions. Explanatory displays and visitor centre. Gift shop. Picnic area. WC. Limited wheelchair access. Disabled WC. Car and coach parking. Telephone (01356) 648631. www.historic-scotland.gov.uk

A remarkable and very beautiful complex with a late medieval tower house incorporated into a 16th-century courtyard mansion, and walled garden with a bathhouse and summerhouse laid out by Sir David Lindsay in 1604. The carved decoration of the garden walls is unique in Britain.

ELCHO CASTLE   926   6 P23

HS. Rhynd, Perth. On the River Tay, 3 miles (5km) south east of Perth. Nearest railway station Perth, no bus. Open Apr–Sep, daily 0930–1830. Charge £. Group concessions. Explanatory displays. Gift shop. Picnic area. WC. Limited wheelchair access. Telephone (01738) 639998. www.historic-scotland.gov.uk

A handsome and complete fortified 16th-century mansion. Notable for its tower-like jambs or wings and for the wrought-iron grills protecting its windows. An ancestral seat of the Earls of Wemyss.

ELIE WATERSPORTS   927   10 R24

Harbour, Elie, Fife. 15 miles (24km) east of Kirkcaldy. Local bus service. Open Easter–mid Oct, daily. Charge varies depending on activity. Group concessions. Gift shop. Picnic area. WC. Limited wheelchair access. Disabled WC. Car and coach parking. Telephone (01333) 330962. www.eliewatersports.com

Elie Watersports provides hire and instruction in windsurfing, sailing, kayaking and waterskiing on the sheltered waters of Elie Bay. Sandy beach. RYA training centre. Also inflatable rides and pedal boats and mountain bikes for hire.

EMBROIDERY WORKSHOP   928   10 Q24

Blacketyside Farm, Leven. On A915 coast road to St Andrews, 0.5 mile (1km) north of Leven. Local bus service from Leven to Dundee (via St Andrews), request stop. Open all year, Tue–Sat 1000–1700. Free. Gift shop. Garden. Wheelchair access. Car parking. Telephone (01333) 423985. www.embroideredoriginals.co.uk

A tiny craft workshop and gift shop, housing an extensive range of original handmade designs. Visitors can watch craftspeople at work. Situated on a farm amid beautiful open countryside, with attractive walks and spectacular views.

FALKLAND PALACE AND GARDEN   929   10 Q24

NTS. Falkland, Cupar, Fife. On A912, 10 miles (16km) from junction 8, M90, and 11 miles (17.5km) north of Kirkcaldy. Bus stop in High Street. Open Mar–Oct, Mon–Sat 1000–1800 and Sun 1300–1730. Charge £££. Charge for palace and garden ££, garden only £. Group concessions. Guided tours by arrangement. Explanatory displays. Guidebook in French and German, text in seven languages. Gift shop. Garden. WC. Tape tour for visually impaired. Limited wheelchair access (wheelchair available). Car and coach parking. Telephone (01337) 857397. www.nts.org.uk

Country residence of the Stewart kings and queens. The gardens contain the original royal tennis court, built in 1539 and the oldest in Britain.

FALLS OF ACHARN   930   5 M22

South Loch Tay road, 2 miles (3.2km) south west of Kenmore, by Acharn village. Access at all reasonable times. Free.

Waterfalls on the Acharn burn, nearly 0.5 mile (1km) south of where the burn enters Loch Tay.

FALLS OF BRUAR   931   5 N21

At Bruar, 10 miles (16km) north of Pitlochry, off A9. Car parking.

Robert Burns visited the Bruar gorge in 1787. At that time the steep slopes were bare and Burns wrote *The Humble Petition of Bruar Water*, urging the Duke of Atholl to plant its bleak banks with trees. When Burns died in 1796, the duke created a wild garden in his memory.

THE FAMOUS GROUSE EXPERIENCE   932   5 N23

The Hosh, Crieff, Perthshire. On the A85 towards Comrie, 1.25 miles (2km) from Crieff. Open all year (except 25–26 Dec), Mon–Sat 0930–1800, Sun 1200–1800. Last tour 1630. Charge £££. Children under 5 free. Group concessions. Guided tours (translation sheets in European languages and Japanese). Audio-visual presentation and exhibition. Gift shop. Restaurants and bar. WC. Limited wheelchair access. Disabled WC. Car and coach parking. Telephone (01764) 656565. www.famousgrouse.com

Scotland's oldest distillery and spiritual home of Scotland's favourite whisky. A range of guided tours available, including our Bafta award winning show. A VisitScotland 5 star attraction

FASKALLY FOREST   933   5 N21

FE. 1 mile (1.5km) north of Pitlochry, on B8019. Access at all reasonable times. Free. WC. Wheelchair access on Dunmore Walk. Car parking. www.forestry.gov.uk

Compact, wonderfully mixed woodland beside Loch Faskally. Quite and peaceful at all times but a riot of colour in autumn, especially around Loch Dunmore.

FIFE AIRPORT   934   10 Q24

Goatmilk, Glenrothes, Fife. Off the B921, 2 miles (3km) west of Glenrothes. Nearest railway station Kirkcaldy or Thornton, bus from Glenrothes then short walk or taxi. Open all year, Mon–Sat 0830–2100, Sun 0830–2030 (no circuits allowed until 0930). Charges dependent on activity. Trial flights £££ for half hour. Explanatory displays. Gift shop. Restaurant and bar (meals 1200-1400 and 1830-2100, snacks 1400-1830). Beer garden. WC. Wheelchair access. Disabled WC. Car parking. Telephone (01592) 753792. www.tayviation.co.uk

A regional airport which is also the home of Fife Flying Club, providing all forms of flying training. Includes the Tipsy Nipper Restaurant, with good views of the airfield.

FIFE FOLK MUSEUM   935   6 Q24

The Weigh House, High Street, Ceres, Fife. Bus from Cupar, St Andrews, Dundee or Kirkcaldy. Easter and May–Oct, daily 1130–1630. Charge £. Accompanied children free. Group concessions. Guided tours by arrangement. Explanatory displays. Gift shop. Terraced garden. Limited wheelchair access. Car and coach parking. Telephone (01334) 828180. www.fifefolkmuseum.co.uk

A local museum housed in a 17th-century tollbooth and 18th-century cottages overlooking the Ceres Burn. The collection illustrates the social, economic and cultural history of rural Fife and includes an outdoor display of agricultural implements. There is a heritage trail.

FINAVON DOOCOT   936   6 R21

NTS. Angus. 6 miles (10km) north of Forfar, off A90. Open all year. Free. Explanatory displays. Car and coach parking. Telephone (01738) 631296. www.nts.org.uk

A 16th-century dovecot, the largest in Scotland, Finavon Doocot had 2400 nesting boxes. It is believed to have been built by the Earl of Crawford. Visitors should obtain the key from the Finavon Hotel.

FISHER STUDIO AND GALLERY   937   10 R24

11-13 High Street, Pittenweem, Fife. In Pittenweem town centre, on A917, 9 miles (14.5km) south of St Andrews. Regular bus service from Kirkcaldy and St Andrews. Open all year except during February, daily, summer 1000–1800; winter 1000–1700. Free. Gift shop. Refreshments available nearby. WC. Wheelchair access. Car parking. Telephone (01333) 312255. www.fishergallery.co.uk

The gallery and studio shows work by many Scottish artists, particularly artists living in Fife. It is also the home and studio of artists John and Anna Fisher, whose work is always on display. Pittenweem has a thriving artistic community and holds an annual festival of the arts during the first week in August.

FORRESTER PARK GOLF RESORT   938   10 P25

Pitdinnie Road, Cairneyhill, by Dunfermline, Fife. By junction of A985 and A994, west of Dunfermline. Nearest railway stations at Dunfermline and Inverkeithing. Open all year, daily, summer weekdays from 0800, weekends from 0700; winter weekdays from 0900, weekends from 0800. Entrance free, charge for golf from £££. Group concessions. Gift shop. Restaurants. WC. Wheelchair access. Disabled WC. Car and coach parking. Telephone (01383) 880505. www.forresterparkresort.com

In the heart of the ancient Keavil Estate, this is one of Scotland's finest championship courses. Offering a superb golf shop and driving range. Open to all for pay and play golf.

FORTH BRIDGES EXHIBITION   939   10 P25

Queensferry Lodge Hotel, St Margaret's Head, North Queensferry, Fife. On the B981 off the A90, 8 miles (13km) north of Edinburgh. Bus or train from Edinburgh. Open all year (except Christmas) 0900–2100. Free. Explanatory displays. Gift shop. Restaurant and coffee shop. WC. Wheelchair access with assistance. Disabled WC. Car and coach parking. Telephone (01383) 410000.

An exhibition telling the fascinating story of the rail and road bridges. The bridges can be viewed from a gallery, or travel over the road bridge to South Queensferry for a stunning view of both bridges. See also 336 Edinburgh, Forth Rail Bridge.

FORTINGALL YEW   940   5 M22

Fortingall, 9 miles (14.5km) west of Aberfeldy. Access at all reasonable times. Car parking.

The surviving part of the great yew in an enclosure in the churchyard is reputedly over 3000 years old, perhaps the oldest tree in Europe. The attractive village, which was rebuilt in 1900 with many thatched cottages, is claimed to be the birthplace of Pontius Pilate and has been a religious centre since St Columban times.

FOWLIS WESTER SCULPTURED STONE   941   5 N23

HS. In the church at Fowlis Wester, 6 miles (9.5km) north east of Crieff, Perthshire. Nearest railway station Perth; bus from Perth to Fowlis Wester. Access at all reasonable times. Free. Telephone (01786) 431324. www.historic-scotland.gov.uk

A tall cross-slab carved with Pictish symbols, figure sculpture and Celtic enrichment. A replica stands in the village square.

GLAMIS CASTLE   942   6 Q22

Glamis, Angus. On A94, 6 miles (9.5km) west of Forfar. Bus from Dundee. Open Mar–Oct, daily 1000–1800, Nov–Dec as advertised. Charge £££. Wheelchair users free admission. Group concessions. Guided tours (by arrangement for groups in French, German, Italian, Spanish or Portuguese). Explanatory displays. Gift shop. Restaurant, kiosk and picnic area. Playpark, garden. WC. Disabled WC. Car and coach parking. Telephone (01307) 840393. www.glamis-castle.co.uk

There has been a building on this site from very early times and Malcolm II is said to have died here in 1034. One of the oldest parts is Duncan's Hall, legendary setting for Shakespeare's *Macbeth*. The present castle was modified in the 17th century. Famous for being the childhood home of Queen Elizabeth, The Queen Mother, and birthplace of Princess Margaret. Fine collections of china, painting, tapestries and furniture. Two exhibitions, Coach House and Elizabeth of Glamis. Annual events include the Strathmore Vintage Vehicle Club Extravaganza, Scotland's countryside festival, and a Grand Scottish Proms weekend. Nature trails and pinetum.

GLEN ESK FOLK MUSEUM   943   6 R21

The Retreat, Glenesk, Brechin, Angus. 18 miles (29km) up Glen Esk off the B966.
Open Easter–Jun, Sat–Sun 1200–1800; Jul–Oct, daily 1200–1800. Charge £. Group
concessions. Guided tours for schools and young people's groups only. Explanatory
displays. Gift shop. Restaurant. WC. Wheelchair access. Disabled WC. Car and coach
parking. Telephone (01356) 6748070.

A museum housing antiques, documents and artefacts reflecting the history of
Glen Esk and surrounding area. Records, costumes, photographs and tools
portray the daily life in a close-knit rural community. Shop sells a range of local
craft and gift items. The interpretive centre houses a large relief model of Glen
Esk, a stable in original form and displays on past and present local life.

GLEN LYON GALLERY   944   5 M22

Boltachan, by Aberfeldy, Perthshire. Off the B846, 1 mile (1.5km) north of Aberfeldy.
Nearest railway sation Pitlochry, bus to Aberfeldy. Open Mar–Dec, Thur–Tue
1000–1700. Winter opening may vary. Free. Explanatory displays. Wheelchair access.
Disabled WC. Car and coach parking. Telephone (01887) 820202.

A unique gallery. All works of art are exclusively by renowned artist, Alan B.
Hayman who specialises in wildlife and landscape painting and paints. The
gallery setting is atmospheric and beautifully Scottish.

GLEN QUEY, GLEN SHERUP, AND GEORDIE'S WOOD   945   10 N24

In Glendevon, accessed from A823, 4 miles (6.5km) south of Gleneagles and north of
Muckhart. Access at all times. Free. Telephone (01764) 662554. www.woodland-
trust.org.uk

The Glendevon sites of Glen Quey, Geordies Wood, and Glen Sherup (see 946)
cover more than 3000 acres (1200ha), separated only by a Forestry Commission
plantation. Glen Quey has a long distance footpath running through, which is
utilised by walkers from Dollar and Castle Campbell to Glendevon.

GLEN SHERUP   946   10 N24

In Glendevon, accessed from A823, 4 miles (6.5km) south of Gleneagles and north of
Muckhart. Access at all times. Telephone (01764) 662554. www.woodland-trust.org.uk

The Glendevon sites of Glen Sherup, Geordies Wood, and Glen Quey (see 945)
cover more than 3000 acres (1200ha), separated only by a Forestry Commission
plantation. At Glen Sherup there is a circular hill ridge walk, with spectacular
views, connecting the high tops in Glen Quey via Tarmangie Hill to Cairnmorris
Hill and Ben Shee.

GLENGOULANDIE COUNTRY PARK   947   5 M22

Glengoulandie, Foss, by Pitlochry, Perthshire. On the B846, 8 miles (13km) north west
of Aberfeldy. Open Easter–Oct, daily 0900 to 1 hour before sunset. Charge £. Group
concessions. Gift shop. Café and picnic area. WC. No guide dogs. Disabled WC. Car
and coach parking. Telephone (01887) 830495. www.glengoulandie.co.uk

Situated at the foot of Schiehallion, the 'magic mountain'. The deer park is home
to native animals housed in a natural environment. There are fine herds of red
deer and Highland cattle. Cars can drive through the park, or it can be explored
on foot. Dogs must be kept in car at all times. Caravan park adjacent to Deer
Park, with static caravans to let as well as serviced pitches.

NIEL GOW'S OAK   948   5 N22

FE. Walk from the Hermitage (see 951), near Dunkeld. Nearest railway station
Dunkeld. Access at all reasonable times. Free. Car and coach parking.
www.forestry.gov.uk

Famous fiddle player Niel Gow (1727-1807) lived at nearby Inver and, according to
local folklore, liked to sit here and play.

HAZLEHEAD PARK   949   6 S19

Groats Road, Aberdeen. 4 miles (6.5km) from city centre on west side of Aberdeen on
B9189. Open 0800–1 hour before dusk. Free. Restaurant. WC. Wheelchair access.
Disabled WC. Car and coach parking. Telephone (01224) 522734.
www.aberdeencity.gov.uk

Nature trails and woodland bridle paths. Privet maze, flower gardens, rose walk,
heather garden, fountain and arbours. Children's play areas, crazy golf and table
tennis.

HEATHERGEMS   950   5 N21

22 Atholl Road, Pitlochry, Perthshire. In Pitlochry, behind the Tourist Information
Centre. Open Mar–Oct, daily 0900–1730; winter Mon–Sat 0900–1700. Free.
Explanatory displays. Gift shop. Wheelchair access. Car parking. Telephone (01796)
474391.

A Scottish jewellery factory and visitor centre. Visitors can see products being
made. Seated video area and a large shop.

THE HERMITAGE   951   5 N22

NTS. Off A9, 2 miles (3km) west of Dunkeld, Perthshire. By bus from Perth or
Dunkeld. Open all year. Free. Charge for parking. Explanatory displays. Guided walks
by rangers. Disabled parking near folly. Car and coach parking. Telephone (01796)
473233 or (01350) 728641. www.nts.org.uk

Interesting walks in mixed conifer and deciduous woodland. The focus is a
delightful folly, Ossian's Hall, in a gorge of the River Braan. Ranger service.

HIGHLAND ADVENTURE SAFARIS   952   5 N22

Drumdewan Farmhouse, Dull, Aberfeldy, Perthshire. On B846, 3 miles (5km) west of
Aberfeldy. Open all year, daily 0900–1700. Free entry to centre, charge from ££ for
safari tours. Guided tours. Explanatory displays. Gift shop. Refreshments available.
Audio visual experience and shop overlooking a field with grazing red deer. Gold
panning centre and nature trail. WC. Wheelchair access. Car parking. Telephone
(01887) 820071. www.highlandadventuresafaris.co.uk

The visitor centre is the launch pad for the award-winning Highland safaris. It
also incorporates an exciting gold panning flume, where visitors can pan for
indigenous semi precious gems and 'Scottish gold'.

HIGHLAND HEATHERS   953   5 M23

Muirend, South Crieff Road, Comrie, Perthshire. On road parallel to A85, 6 miles
(9.5km) west of Crieff. Local bus service stops 0.5 mile (1km) away. Open all year,
daily 1000–1800 (closed Nov and Jan–Mar, Mon). Free. Car parking. Telephone
(01764) 670440. www.highlandheathers.co.uk

Visitors can browse through the heather garden and walk around the working
nursery. Horticultural and design advice available. More than 140 different

varieties of heather. Also conifers, shrubs, bedding plants, free range eggs and sundries.

GRISELDA HILL POTTERY   954   6 Q24

Kirkbrae, Ceres, Cupar, Fife. 3 miles (5km) south east of Cupar. Nearest railway station Cupar. Open all year, Mon–Fri 0900–1630, Sat–Sun 1200–1700. Free. Guided tours. Explanatory displays. Gift shop. WC. Limited wheelchair access. Disabled WC. Car parking. Telephone (01334) 828273. www.wemyss-ware.co.uk

Since 1985, the Griselda Hill pottery has revived the production of Wemyss Ware, beautifully hand-painted cats, pigs and other pottery in bright cheerful colours. Visitors are always welcome at the factory showroom where all products are made and hand painted.

HILL OF TARVIT MANSION HOUSE AND GARDEN   955   6 Q24

NTS. Cupar, Fife. Off A916, 2.5 miles (4km) south of Cupar. By bus to Ceres, then 1 mile (1.5km) walk. Open Apr–Sep and weekends in Oct, daily 1300–1700. Charge £££. Charge for house and garden ££, garden only £ (honesty box). Group concessions. Guided tours by arrangement. Explanatory displays. Information sheets in four languages. Gift shop. Tearoom and picnic area. Garden. WC. Limited wheelchair access (wheelchair available). Disabled WC. Car and coach parking. Telephone (01334) 653127. www.nts.org.uk

Fine Edwardian house designed by Sir Robert Lorimer and built in 1906 for a Dundee industrialist to provide a setting for his important collection of French, Chippendale-style and vernacular furniture. Superb paintings, including works by Raeburn and Ramsay. Formal gardens also designed by Lorimer. Restored Edwardian laundry in grounds. Woodland walk.

HOUSE OF BRUAR   956   5 N21

The House of Bruar by Blair Atholl, Perthshire. On A9 11m (18km) north of Pitlochry. Local bus service. Open Easter–Oct, daily 0830–1800; Nov–Easter, daily 1000–1700. Free. Gift shop. Restaurant. Baby changing, dog walking area, and children's playground. WC. No guide dogs. Limited wheelchair access. Car and coach parking. Telephone (01796) 483236. www.houseofbruar.com

The House of Bruar is Scotland's most prestigious store. It comprises of mens and ladies country clothing halls, a shoe and handbag department, Scotland's largest cashmere hall, a 10,000sqft department dedicated to country living, a 500-seater restaurant, foodhall and delicatessen.

HOUSE OF DUN   957   6 R21

NTS. Montrose, Angus. On A935, 3 miles (5km) west of Montrose. By bus from Montrose. Open Apr–Jun, Sep Wed–Sun, daily 1230–1730; Jul–Aug, daily 1130–1730. Garden and grounds open all year, daily 0930–sunset. Charge £££. Charge for house and garden £££, garden only £ (honesty box). Group concessions. Guided tours by arrangement. Explanatory displays. Gift shop. Restaurant. Adventure playground. WC. Braille information sheets, subtitled video programme. Wheelchair access with assistance (wheelchairs available). Car and coach parking. Telephone (01674) 810264. www.nts.org.uk

Beautiful Georgian house overlooking Montrose Basin, designed in 1730 by William Adam and with superb contemporary plasterwork. Home in 19th century to Lady Augusta Kennedy-Erskine, daughter of William IV and the actress Mrs Jordan. Many of her belongings remain, as well as her wool work and embroidery. Restored Victorian walled garden and attractive woodland walks.

HOUSE OF MENZIES   958   5 N22

Castle Menzies Farm, Aberfeldy, Perthshire. 2 miles (3km) out of Aberfeldy on B846.
Nearest railway station Pitlochry, local bus service to Aberfeldy. Open May–Oct,
Mon–Sat 1000–1700, Sun 1100–1700; Nov–Apr, Wed–Sat 1000–1600, Sun
1000–1600. Free. Gift shop. Licensed coffee shop with freshly made light meals and
baking. Baby changing facilities. WC. Wheelchair access. Disabled WC. Car parking.
Telephone (01887) 829666. www.houseofmenzies.com

Situated within an original doocot and cattle court, the House of Menzies
features work by contemporary Scottish artists, potters and silversmiths, over
300 New World wines (tasting and sales area), and a wide range of Scottish
delicatessen products.

HUNTINGTOWER CASTLE   959   6 P23

HS. Huntingtower, Perth. Off the A85, 3 miles (5km) north west of Perth. Nearest
railway and bus stations Perth, bus from Perth. Open Apr–Sep, daily 0930–1830;
Oct–Mar, Mon–Sun 0930–1630 (closed Thu and Fri). Charge £. Group concessions.
Gift shop. Picnic area. Limited wheelchair access. Car and coach parking. Telephone
(01738) 627231. www.historic-scotland.gov.uk

A 15th-century castellated mansion, known as Ruthven Castle until 1600. Two
fine and complete towers, now linked by a 17th-century range. There are fine
painted ceilings.

INCHCOLM ABBEY   960   10 P25

HS. On Inchcolm Island in the Firth of Forth. Nearest railway station Dalmeny, bus
from Edinburgh. Reached by ferry (30 minutes) from South Queensferry. For ferry
times telephone 0131 3314857. Open Apr–Sep, daily 0930–1830. Charge £. Additional
charge for ferry. Group concessions. Explanatory displays. Gift shop. Picnic area.
WC. Limited wheelchair access. Car and coach parking. Telephone (01383) 823332.
www.historic-scotland.gov.uk

The ruins of an Augustinian house founded circa 1123 and including a 13th-
century octagonal chapter house. The best preserved group of monastic
buildings in Scotland. The island is famed for its seals, wildlife and coastal
defences from two world wars.

INNERPEFFRAY CHAPEL   961   5 N23

HS. Innerpeffray, Crieff. 4 miles (6.5km) south east of Crieff. Nearest railway station
Perth, bus from Perth to Crieff, then bus to Innerpeffray. Car parking. Telephone
(01786) 431324. www.historic-scotland.gov.uk

A rectangular collegiate church founded in 1508. Still retains its altar and
evidence of its furnishings. See also 962 Innerpeffray Library.

INNERPEFFRAY LIBRARY   962   5 N23

Innerpeffray, Crieff, Perthshire. On the B8062, 4 miles (6.5km) south east of Crieff.
Open Mar–Oct, Mon–Wed and Fri–Sat 1000–1245 and 1400–1645, Sun 1400–1600;
Nov–Feb by appointment only. Charge £. Group concessions. Guided tours.
Tearoom. WC. Wheelchair access with assistance to chapel; difficult access to library.
Car and coach parking. Telephone (01764) 652819.

The first lending library in Scotland, founded in 1680. A collection of 3000 titles
printed between 1500 and 1800 now housed in a purpose-built library completed
in 1762. Many rare and interesting volumes, including books from the library of

The Great Marquess of Montrose. Adjacent collegiate chapel built in 1508, burial place of the Drummond family. See also 961 Innerpeffray Chapel.

INVERKEITHING MUSEUM   963   10 P25

The Friary, Queen Street, Inverkeithing, Fife. In Inverkeithing, 1 mile (2km) from north end of the Forth Road Bridge. Nearest railway station Inverkeithing, then ten minute walk. Bus from Edinburgh or Dunfermline. Open all year, Thu–Sun 1100–1230 and 1300–1600. Free. Explanatory displays. Car parking. Telephone (01383) 313594.

Local history of Inverkeithing and Rosyth. Small display on Admiral Greig, founder of the Russian navy.

IRON FAIRY AT KELTNEYBURN SMITHY   964   5 M22

Keltneyburn Smithy, by Aberfeldy, Perthshire. 5 miles (8km) west of Aberfeldy. Take B846 and follow signpost for Fortingall. Keltneyburn is 0.25 mile (0.5km) along this road. Open all year, Mon–Fri 0900–1700; Apr–Oct, also Sat–Sun 1000–1600; weekends in winter by arrangement. Free. Gift shop. Wheelchair access. Car and coach parking. Telephone (01887) 830267. www.ironfairy.co.uk

A family-run traditional smithy. As well as traditional blacksmithing, the family produce contemporary sculpture, furniture and gifts. The bothy showroom contains the handcrafted designs. Larger sculptures can be seen outside, around the car park.

ISLE OF MAY NATIONAL NATURE RESERVE   965   10 R24

5 miles (8km) south east of Anstruther inthe East Neuk of Fife. Can only be accessed by boat – boat trips depart from Anstruther and North Berwick. Island open to visitors Apr–Sep. Free entry to nature reserve; charge for boat trip. Easy walking over two main paths. No dogs. WC. Wheelchair access with assistance (limited to visitor centre and road to top of island which is steep and uneven). Disabled WC. Telephone (01334) 654038. www.nnr-scotland.org.uk

The Isle of May is a haven for thousands of nesting sea birds which flourish on the steep sea cliffs and rocky shores and supports one of the largest grey seal colonies in north east Britain. A 7th-century chapel is close to the visitor centre and has its own interpretation boards. Other features include two lighthouses. All visitors met by warden who will give information on what to see and can answer questions. The May Princess sails daily from Anstruther and Aquatrek sails on Wed and Thur from North Berwick.

JERDAN GALLERY   966   10 R24

42 Marketgate South, Crail, Fife. On A917, 4 miles (6.5km) from Anstruther, 10 miles (16km) from St Andrews. Local bus route from Leven to Dundee passes Crail. Telephone to confirm opening times. Free. Limited wheelchair access. Car and coach parking. Telephone (01333) 450797. www.thejerdangallery.co.uk

Regularly changing exhibitions and regular gallery artists. Also jewellery and glass. Attractive gallery garden contains sculptures and works of art.

KARTSTART, KIRKCALDY   967   10 Q24

Unit 1, Merchant Place, Mitchelston Industrial Estate, Kirkcaldy. Just off A92, Dunfermline to Kirkcaldy link road. Nearest railway and bus stations Kirkcaldy. Open all year, daily 1200–1730 and 1830–2200 (Sat and Sun closes at 2100). Closed Christmas and New Year. Admission free. Charge £££ for driving. Group concessions. Explanatory displays. Café. WC. Wheelchair access. Disabled WC. Car and coach parking. Telephone (01592) 650200. www.kartstartscotland.co.uk

The largest indoor kart circuit (350 metres) in Scotland. Offers the opportunity to experience the thrill of real motor sport. All-weather facility. Mini-quads, cadet karts, senior karts, pro-karts. See also 1206 Kartstart, Dyce.

KELLIE CASTLE AND GARDEN   968   10 R24

NTS. Pittenweem, Fife. On B9171, 3 miles (5km) north of Pittemweem. Limited bus service. Easter weekend and May–Sep, daily 1300–1700. Gardens open all year, daily 0930–sunset. Charge £££. Group concessions. Guided tours by arrangement. Explanatory displays in five languages. Gift shop. Tearoom and picnic area. Adventure playground. WC. Induction loop. Limited wheelchair access (wheelchair available). Car and coach parking. Telephone (01333) 720271. www.nts.org.uk

The oldest part of Kellie Castle dates from 1360, and most of the present building was completed around 1606. It was sympathetically restored by the Lorimer family, who lived here in the 1870s. Late Victorian organic walled garden. Lorimer exhibition in the summerhouse.

KILLIECRANKIE   969   5 N21

NTS. Pitlochry, Perthshire. On the B8079, 3 miles (5km) north of Pitlochry. Bus from Pitlochry. Site open all year, daily (free). Visitor centre open Apr–Oct, daily 1000–1730. Car parking £. Explanatory displays. Guidebook in French and German, information sheets in seven languages. Gift shop. Snack bar and picnic area. WC. Braille guidebook. Remote camera in visitor centre allows viewing of wildlife. Wheelchair access with assistance to visitor centre (wheelchair available). Disabled WC. Car and coach parking. Telephone (01796) 473233. www.nts.org.uk

Site of the 1689 battle of Killiecrankie, won by the Highland Jacobites under Bonnie Dundee, this dramatic wooded gorge is now a haven for wildlife. Visitors can see Soldiers Leap, where a fleeing government soldier made a spectacular jump over the River Garry during the battle. The visitor centre exhibition features the battle and natural history of the area.

KILMAGAD WOOD   970   10 P24

Kinnesswood, Loch Leven. Off A911 between Kinnesswood and Scotlandwell, approximately 4 miles (6km) south east of Milnathort. Local parking difficult. Access at all times. Free. Telephone (01764) 662554. www.woodland-trust.org.uk

Kilmagad is a popular place for recreation. The steep nature of the slopes provide excellent viewpoints across the Leven Basin. A number of less formal routes cross the site and connect with longer distance routes. Visitors come to walk the Tetley Trail, a permissive medium-distance route around the villages of Scotlandwelland Kinnesswood. A selection of the trail follows an asserted right of way, which contours around the lower slopes of the site.

KIN KRAFT CENTRE FOR SCOTTISH CRAFTS   971   10 P24

Kinross Services Area, Turfhills, Kinross. Off junction 6 on the M90. Open Mar–Dec, daily 1000–1700; Feb, Sat–Sun 1000–1700. Free. Explanatory displays. Gift shop. Refreshments nearby. WC. Wheelchair access. Car and coach parking. Telephone (01577) 861300.

Gallery displaying traditional and contemporary Scottish crafts

KINNOULL HILL WOODLAND PARK   972   6 P23

FE. c/o Tay Forest District Office, Inverpark, Dunkeld, Perthshire. 1 mile (1.5km) east of Perth. Open at all times. Free. Explanatory displays. Limited wheelchair access. Car parking. Telephone 01350 727284 or council 01738 475000. www.forestry.gov.uk

Comprising five hills (Corsiehill, Deuchny Hill, Barnhill, Binn Hill and Kinnoull Hill). Kinnoull Hill, the highest and most impressive, offers spectacular views over the Ochil and Lomond hills. There are four waymarked forest walks.

KIRKCALDY MUSEUM AND ART GALLERY   973   10 Q24

War Memorial Gardens, Kirkcaldy, Fife. Adjacent to the railway station in Kirkcaldy, ten minute walk from bus station. Open all year except public holidays, Mon–Sat 1030–1700, Sun 1400–1700. Free. Explanatory displays. Gift shop. Café. Garden. WC. Wheelchair access. Disabled WC. Car parking. Telephone (01592) 412860.

A collection of fine and decorative arts of local and national importance. There is an outstanding collection of 18th–20th century Scottish paintings and probably the largest public collection of works (outside the National Galleries of Scotland) by William McTaggart and the Scottish colourist S. J. Peploe. There is also an award-winning permanent museum display, Changing Places, which tells the story of the social, industrial and natural heritage of the area. Lively changing exhibitions programme featuring art, craft, photography, social and natural history.

KIRRIEMUIR GATEWAY TO THE GLENS MUSEUM   974   6 Q22

The Townhouse, 32 High Street, Kirriemuir, Angus. In the centre of Kirriemuir, 6 miles (9.5km) from A94. Nearest railway station Dundee, bus to Kirriemuir from Dundee and Forfar. Open all year, Mon–Wed and Fri–Sat 1000–1700, Thu 1300–1700 (closed Christmas and New Year). Free. Guided tours in the evening by arrangement. Explanatory displays. Small gift area. WC. Induction loop. Limited wheelchair access (touch screen computer duplicates information upstairs). Disabled WC. Telephone (01575) 575479.

Housed in Kirriemuir's oldest building (1604). Exhibitions on Kirriemuir from its earliest days, with a stunning model of the town circa 1604. Also features on the western Angus Glens including a Highland wildlife display full of birds and animals. An interactive computer allows the visitor to discover Kirriemuir and the glens' historical wildlife and geological interest. Details of walks in the area.

KNOCK OF CRIEFF   975   5 N23

Ferntower Road, Crieff. Within a short walk from the centre of Crieff. Access at all reasonable times. Free. Guided tours by arrangement with ranger service. Explanatory displays local walk panels, leaflet available. Refreshments and WC nearby. Car parking. Telephone (01738) 475256.

A mixed woodland site located in beautiful Strathearn. The Knock has been incorporated into the Crieff walks system along with other council countryside properties.

KNOCKHILL RACING CIRCUIT   976   10 P24

Dunfermline, Fife. On the A823, 6 miles (9.5km) north of Dunfermline. Open all year, daily 0900–1700, closed two weeks at Christmas. Charge £££ (some events free). Group concessions. Gift shop. Restaurant, tearoom and picnic area. WC. No guide dogs. Limited wheelchair access. Disabled WC. Car and coach parking. Telephone (01383) 723337. www.knockhill.co.uk

Scotland's National Motor Sports Centre with racing events for motor cars and motor cycles most weekends between April and October. Visitors can watch or participate. Karts, quadbikes, skid pan and on-road defensive driving.

LAING MUSEUM 977   6 P23

High Street, Newburgh, Fife. In Newburgh town centre. Nearest railway, Newburgh, bus service from Cupar, Perth and Dundee. Open Apr–Sep daily 1200–1700; Oct–Mar open by appointment. Free. Guided tours by prior arrangement. Explanatory displays. Gift shop. Refreshments nearby. Car parking. Telephone (01337) 883017 or (01334) 412690. www.fifedirect.org.uk/museums

The museum was gifted to the town by Alexander Laing, a much respected local scholar and historian, and first opened in 1896. One gallery is devoted to Laing and his collections while the other holds temporary exhibitions with a local flavour.

WILLIAM LAMB MEMORIAL STUDIO 978   6 S22

Market Street, Montrose, Angus. Situated in the Trades Close off the High Street in Montrose. By rail or bus from Aberdeen, Dundee, Edinburgh or Glasgow. Open Jul–mid Sep, daily 1400–1700; other times by appointment. Free. Guided tours. Explanatory displays. Gift shop. WC. Limited wheelchair access. Telephone (01674) 673232. www.angus.gov.uk

The working studio of the famous Montrose sculptor includes displays of his sculptures, etchings, paintings and drawings. Also featured are his workroom and tools and his living room with self-styled furniture. See 1003 Montrose Museum and Art Gallery.

LETHAM GLEN 979   10 Q24

Sillerhole Road, Leven, Fife. On the A915, on the outskirts of Leven. Bus from Kirkcaldy or Leven. Glen open daily all year. Nature centre, telephone for opening times. Free. Guided tours by arrangement. Explanatory displays in nature centre. Picnic areas. Pets' corner. WC. Limited wheelchair access. Car parking. Telephone (01333) 429231.

The nature centre displays information and pictures about wildlife. Various exhibits throughout the year. Nature trail through the glen. Booklets and maps, pets' corner. Picturesque surroundings.

LEVENMOUTH SWIMMING POOL AND SPORTS CENTRE 980   10 Q24

Promenade, Leven, Fife. In centre of Leven, 12 miles (19km) east of St Andrews. Nearest railway station in Kirkcaldy. Local bus service. Open all year, Mon–Fri 0800–2200, Tue and Thu open at 0700, Sat–Sun closes 2100. Charge £. Group concessions. Refreshments available. Swimming pool, creche, sports hall, solarium and sauna. WC. Wheelchair access. Disabled WC. Car parking. Telephone (01333) 592500. www.fifedirect.org.uk

One of Fife's leading leisure facilities. Free-form swimming pool with beach entry, spa bath, water cannon, waves and flume slide. Fitness suite with both aerobic and resistance equipment.

LINN OF TUMMEL 981   5 N21

NTS. Walk from Garry Bridge, 2.5 miles (4km) north of Pitlochry on B8019. Access at all reasonable times. Free. Car parking. www.nts.org.uk

Follow a riverside nature trail through mixed woodland to the meeting place of the Rivers Garry and Tummel. The Linn of Tummel (pool of the tumbling stream) comprises a series of rocky rapids in a beautiful setting.

LOCH FITTY TROUT AND COARSE FISHERY   982   10 P24

Kingseat, By Dunfermline, Fife . On B912, 3 miles (4km) west of Cowdenbeath and
north east of Dunfermline. Nearest railway station at Dunfermline. Bus service from
Dunfermline. Open Mar–Nov, daily 0830–dusk. Charge dependent on limit. Tackle
shop. Tearoom and picnic areas. WC. Wheelchair access. Car and coach parking.
Telephone (01383) 620666. www.lochfitty.co.uk

Loch Fitty is a shallow, fertile naturally formed loch of approximately 170 acres
(69ha). It is an attractive beauty spot in a rural setting, giving excellent trout and
coarse fishing. Delightful walks around a young tree plantation. Lots of birds,
including heron, buzzards, greater spotted woodpeckers, tree creepers, jays,
grebes and a host of other more common birds. In the spring, an osprey has
sometimes been seen. There are four separate fishing areas within the loch, each
offering different sport for both boat and shore fishing (boats must be booked in
advance).

LOCH LEVEN NATIONAL NATURE RESERVE   983

See 1097 Vane Farm RSPB Nature Reserve.

LOCH OF KINNORDY RSPB NATURE RESERVE   984   6 Q22

RSPB. By Kirriemuir. Loch of Kinnordy, 0.5 miles (1km) west of Kirriemuir on B951.
Bus service to Kirriemuir. Reserve open daily 0900–dusk (closed Sep and Oct, Sat
only). Charge £. Explanatory displays and occasional guided walks. Limited
wheelchair access. Car parking. Telephone (01738) 630783. www.rspb.org.uk/scotland

The lochs, mires and fens are surrounded by farmland. On the reserve wildfowl,
wading birds and ospreys vist regularly in the spring and summer, when black-
necked grebes may also occur. In winter, the reserve is full of wildfowl. There is
a nature trail of 550 yards (500m) and three bird watching hides, some accessible
to wheelchairs.

LOCH OF THE LOWES VISITOR CENTRE   985   6 P22

Loch of the Lowes, Dunkeld, Perthshire. 2 miles (3km) north east of Dunkeld.
Nearest railway station Dunkeld and Birnam, bus from Perth to Dunkeld. Open
Apr–Sep, 1000–1700. Admission by donation, children free. Explanatory displays.
Gift shop. Selection of fresh rolls, cakes, fruit and juices available daily.. WC.
Limited wheelchair access. Disabled WC. Car and coach parking. Telephone
(01350) 727337.

A visitor centre with wildlife displays and small aquaria, manned by volunteers
and ranger staff. Observation hide at lakeside with fitted binoculars and
telescopes. Live nest camera to osprey eyrie. Birds include breeding ospreys,
great crested grebe, tufted duck, coot, mallard, and occasionally cormorants,
heron and goldeneye duck.

LOCH TAY POTTERY   986   5 M22

Fearnan, Aberfeldy, Perthshire. Off the A827 (Fortingall Road), 3 miles (5km) from
Kenmore. Open all year daily, 1000–1700. Free. Gift shop. Wheelchair access with
assistance. Car parking. Telephone (01887) 830251.

A showroom and workshop in a former croft. Andrew Burt produces a wide
variety of stoneware pots for kitchen and other domestic use and decoration.
Visitors can watch him at work.

LOCHLEVEN CASTLE   987   10 P24

HS. By Kinross, Tayside. On an island in Loch Leven. Accessible by boat from Kinross.
Bus service from Edinburgh to Kinross. Open Apr–Sep, daily 0930–1830. Charge ££.
Charge includes ferry. Group concessions. Gift shop. Picnic area. WC. Limited
wheelchair access. Car parking. Telephone (07778) 040483. www.historic-
scotland.gov.uk

A late 14th- or early 15th-century tower on one side of an irregular courtyard.
The prison of Mary, Queen of Scots in 1567.

LOCHORE MEADOWS COUNTRY PARK   988   10 P24

Crosshill, Lochgelly, Fife. Nearest railway station Lochgelly, bus from Lochgelly or
Edinburgh. Open Apr–Sep, daily 0900–1930; Oct–Mar, daily 0900–1700. Free.
Explanatory displays in visitor centre. Café. WC. Braille maps for woodland trail.
Wheelchair access. Disabled WC. Car and coach parking. Telephone (01592) 414300.
www.lochore-meadows.co.uk

Green and pleasant countryside around a large lake reclaimed from coal mining
waste in the 1960s. A slide show, displays and ranger-guided walks tell the story
of the reclamation. Ancient historical remains. Wildlife study, walks, picnics.
Activities include fishing, sailing, windsurfing, canoeing, golf, riding. Adventure
play area.

MACDUFF CASTLE   989   10 Q24

East Wemyss, Fife, beside the cemetery overlooking the sea.

Reputed to be home of MacDuff of Shakespeare's *Macbeth*; now in ruins.

MAISON DIEU CHAPEL   990   6 R21

HS. In Maison Dieu Lane, Brechin, Angus. Nearest railway station Montrose, bus
from Montrose or Dundee to Brechin. Access at all reasonable times. Free. Telephone
(01786) 431324. www.historic-scotland.gov.uk

Part of the south wall of a chapel belonging to a medieval hospital founded in
the 1260s, with finely-detailed doors and windows.

LADY MARY'S WALK   991   5 N23

Milnab Street, Crieff. Walk from the centre of Crieff. Access at all reasonable times.
Free. Guided tours by arrangment with ranger service. Explanatory displays, walks
panel, leaflet available. Refreshments and WC nearby. Wheelchair access. Car
parking. Telephone (01738) 475256.

A favourite walk of Lady Mary Murray, whose family owned the surrounding
land in the early 19th century. It provides a peaceful stroll beside the
picturesque River Earn, along an avenue of mature oak, beech, lime and sweet
chestnut trees.

THE MEFFAN   992   6 Q22

20 West High Street, Forfar, Angus. In Forfar centre, 3 miles (5km) from A94. Nearest
railway station Dundee, bus from Dundee, Brechin and Aberdeen. Open all year
(except Christmas and New Year), Mon–Sat 1000–1700. Free. Guided tours by
arrangement. Explanatory displays. Gift shop. WC. Wheelchair access with assistance
(ground floor only). Disabled WC. Telephone (01307) 464123.
www.angus.gov.uk/localhistory

Two art galleries with constantly changing exhibitions featuring art from contemporary Scottish artists and Angus collections. *The Forfar Story* features original Pictish stones from Angus, an interactive guide to the stones, a walk through an old Forfar vennel with its shoppies and a witch burning scene.

MEIGLE SCULPTURED STONES   993   6 Q22

HS. Meigle Museum, Dundee Road, Meigle, Perthshire. On the A94 in Meigle, 12 miles (19km) west south-west of Forfar, Angus. Bus service from Dundee or Perth to Meigle. Open Apr–Sep, daily 0930–1830. Charge £. Group concessions. Explanatory displays. Gift shop. WC. Wheelchair access. Disabled WC. Telephone (01828) 640612. www.historic-scotland.gov.uk

One of the most notable collections of Dark Age sculpture in Western Europe. Twenty-five sculptured monuments of the Early Christian period.

MEIKLEOUR BEECH HEDGE   994   6 P22

10 miles (16km) east of Dunkeld, on A93. Access at all times. Free. Car parking.

An incredible living wall of beech trees, 100 feet (30m) high and 1/3 mile (530m) long. The trees were planted in 1745 and are now officially recognised in the *Guinness Book of Records* as the highest hedge in the world.

MELVILLE MONUMENT   995   5 M23

One mile (1.5km) north of Comrie, 6 miles (9.5km) west of Crieff. Access at all times by footpath from parking place on Glen Lednock road. Free. Car parking.

The obelisk in memory of Lord Melville (1742–1811) stands on Dunmore, a hill of 840 feet (256m), with delightful views of the surrounding countryside. The access path is linked to the scenic 4-mile (6.5km) Glen Lednock circular walk, running from Comrie and back through varied woodland (signposted).

METHIL HERITAGE CENTRE   996   10 Q24

272 High Street, Methill, Fife. 8 miles (13km) east of Kirkcaldy on A915 or A955. Coach parking nearby. Bus from Kirkcaldy, Glenrothes or St Andrews. Open all year (except public holidays), Tue–Thu 1100–1630, Sat 1300–1630. Free. Explanatory displays. Gift shop. Tearoom. WC. Wheelchair access. Disabled WC. Telephone (01333) 422100.

A lively community museum, interpreting the social and individual history of the area. Permanent exhibition and a varied programme of temporary displays.

MILTON HAUGH FARM SHOP   997   6 R22

Carmyllie , Arbroath, Angus. On B961, 2 miles (3km) west of Redford, just north of Carnoustie. Local bus service. Open all year. Shop Mon–Sat 0900–1700, Sun 1000–1700; coffee shop, daily 1000–1600. Free. WC. Wheelchair access. Disabled WC. Car and coach parking. Telephone (01241) 860579. www.miltonhaugh.com

Well-established farm shop and coffee shop, offering a wide variety of Scottish and local produce. A country park is being developed, with pond, trees and wildflowers.

MINIATURE RAILWAY   998   6 R22

West Links Park, Arbroath, Angus. By the seafront to the west of Arbroath. Nearest railway station Arbroath 2 miles (3km), local bus service. Open Easter–Sep, Sat and Sun 1400–1700 (Jul–mid Aug daily), weather permitting. Charge £. Group concessions. Explanatory displays, leaflet available (book for sale). Snack bar nearby.

WC. Wheelchair access. Disabled WC. Car and coach parking. Telephone (01241) 879249. www.geocities.com/kmr_scotland

Open since 1935, the small trains run alongside the British Rail Aberdeen to Edinburgh main line from West Links Station, which is complete with platforms, booking office, footbridge, signal box, turntable and locomotive shed. The 0.5 mile (1km) round trip includes a tunnel. There are six locomotives, two of which are coal-fired steam.

MONCREIFFE HILL WOOD   999   6 P23

Bridge of Earn, Perthshire. South of Perth, off M90 at junction 9 or A912 at Bridge of Earn, take minor road to Rhynd following tourist signposting. Access at all times. Free. Car parking. Telephone (01764) 662554. www.woodland-trust.org.uk

The magnificent slopes of Moncreiffe Hill Wood occupy a prominent position about two miles south of Perth. A visit to this spectacular 333 acre (134ha) wood, which is owned and managed by the Woodland Trust Scotland, will allow visitors to enjoy outstanding views along the River Tay and Strathearn and you may also catch a glimpse of some of the wildlife which inhabits the wood, such as deer, red squirrels and birds of prey.

MONIKIE COUNTRY PARK   1000   6 R22

Main Lodge, Monikie, Angus. Off the B962 between Dundee and Arbroath. Bus from Dundee. Open daily, May–Jul 0900–2100, Aug–Nov 0900–1700, Dec–Jan 0900–1600 (closed Christmas and New Year), Feb–Apr 0900–1700. Free. Charge for parking (£) and watersports. Group concessions. Guided tours by ranger. Explanatory displays. Picnic area. Barbecue area (requires booking). WC. Limited wheelchair access. Disabled WC. Car and coach parking. Telephone (01382) 370202.

The country park comprises 185 acres (75ha), with reservoirs, woodland and grassland. Instruction and hire for windsurfing, sailing, canoeing (May–September). Also rowing boats. Play area, orienteering trails and woodland walks. High ropes course.

MONTROSE AIR STATION MUSEUM   1001   6 S22

Waldron Road, Montrose, Angus. At the north end of Montrose on the A92. 15 minute walk from rail station, buses from Aberdeen and Dundee. Open Apr–Sep, Mon–Sat 1000–1600, and all year Sun 1200–1600. Charge £. Group concessions. Guided tours. Explanatory displays. Gift shop. WC. No guide dogs. Limited wheelchair access. Car and coach parking. Telephone (01674) 678222. www.rafmontrose.org.uk

RFC/RAF and wartime artefacts and memorabilia housed in the wartime RAF Montrose HQ. Various aircraft on display outside, also pillbox and Anderson shelter.

MONTROSE BASIN WILDLIFE CENTRE   1002   6 S22

Rossie Braes, Montrose. 1 mile (1.5km) south of Montrose on A92. From Aberdeen, Edinburgh and Glasgow to railway station Montrose, local bus service then short walk. Open mid Mar–mid Nov, daily 1030–1700; mid Nov–mid Mar, Fri–Sun 1030–1600. Charge £. Group concessions. Guided tours. Explanatory displays. Gift shop. Vending machine and picnic area. WC. Touch tables for blind visitors. Limited wheelchair access. Disabled WC. Car and coach parking. Telephone (01674) 676336. www.montrosebasin.org.uk

Television cameras bring the wildlife literally into the centre. Unique displays show how a tidal basin works and the routes of migrating birds. Magnificent views of wildlife on the basin through high powered telescopes and binoculars. Interactive displays.

MONTROSE MUSEUM AND ART GALLERY   1003   6 S22

Panmure Place, Montrose, Angus. On the Mid Links a few minutes walk from the High Street. By rail or bus from Aberdeen, Edinburgh, Dundee or Glasgow. Open all year (except 25–26 Dec and 1–2 Jan), Mon–Sat 1000–1700. Free. Guided tours. Explanatory displays. Gift shop. WC. Wheelchair access with assistance. Car and coach parking. Telephone (01674) 673232. www.angus.gov.uk

Tells the story of Montrose from prehistoric times, including local geology and wildlife. On show are various Pictish stones, pottery, whaling and Napoleonic artefacts. Art gallery. See also 978 William Lamb Memorial Studio.

MONTROSE SEAFRONT SPLASH ADVENTURE PLAY AREA   1004   6 S22

Trail Drive, Montrose. 1 mile (1.5km) south of Montrose town centre. Railway station in Montrose. No direct bus service. Open all year, daily. Telephone for details. Free. Information boards. Café and picnic areas. WC. 24-hour Radar toilet. Disabled parking. Wheelchair access. Car and coach parking.

A play area providing a variety of play opportunities for toddlers and older children, including those with disabilities. Paddling pool and water play during summer. Pitch and putt. Family orientated amusement arcade. Beach changing facilities. Adjacent is a 4 mile (6.5km) area of beach, which has blue flag status, with dog control in the immediate area of Seafront Splash.

MUIR O' FAULD SIGNAL STATION   1005   5 N23

HS. East of Ardunie, Perthshire. Nearest railway station Perth, bus from Perth to Crieff, then Crieff to Kinkell Bridge. Access at all reasonable times. Free. Telephone (01786) 431324. www.historic-scotland.gov.uk

The site of a Roman watch tower. See also 823 Ardunie Roman Signal Station.

MUSEUM OF ABERNETHY   1006   6 P23

School Wynd, Abernethy. In the centre of Abernethy. Car and coach parking nearby. Regular bus service from Perth. Open mid May–Sep, Thu–Sun 1300–1700. Free. Donations welcome. Explanatory displays. Gift shop. WC. Limited wheelchair access. Disabled WC. Telephone (01738) 850889.

An independent museum housed in a restored 18th-century cattle byre and stable in the centre of the historic village of Abernethy. The museum depicts life in the parish of Abernethy from Pictish times to the present day.

MUTHILL CHURCH AND TOWER   1007   5 N23

HS. On the A822 in Muthill. 3 miles (5km) south west of Crieff on A822. Nearest railway station Perth, bus service from Perth to Crieff, then bus to Muthill, also buses from Stirling. Access at all reasonable times. Free. Telephone (01786) 431324. www.historic-scotland.gov.uk

The interesting ruins of an important 15th-century parish church, with a tall Romanesque tower at its west end.

MUTHILL VILLAGE MUSEUM   1008   5 N23

Station Road, Muthill, Perthshire. 5 miles (8km) south of Crieff on A822. Nearest railway station Perth, bus service from Perth to Crieff, then bus to Muthill, also buses from Stirling. Open Jun–Sep, Wed, Sat and Sun 1230–1500. Admission by donation. Explanatory displays. Refreshments nearby. WC. Limited wheelchair access. Car parking.

Collection of local objects from yesteryear – pictures, photographs, implements, kitchenware. Model castle and steam railway display.

OATHLAW POTTERY AND GALLERY   1009

6 Q22

By Forfar, Angus. 1 mile (1.5km) from A90, north of Forfar. Open May–mid Sep and late Nov–Xmas, Tue–Sat 1000–1700. For other times please telephone to check. Free. Car parking. Telephone (01307) 850272. www.oathlawpotteryandgallery.com

A working studio pottery and gallery, set around a delightful small courtyard of 19th-century steading buildings. During the year there are ongoing exhibitions of work designed and made in the studio, featuring ceramics in stoneware and raku. Also summer and winter exhibitions of fine and applied art. Telephone or visit website for information.

PANBRIDE CHURCH   1010

6 R22

Panbride, Carnoustie, Angus. Nearest railway station Carnoustie.

The first mention of Panbride was in 1178 when William I gave the church and parish to Arbroath Abbey. At the church gates is a loupin stane, used to assist church-goers mounting horses. By the loupin stane there is a footpath which heads north to Muirdrum. Follow this footpath for a few hundred yards and you are at the top of the fairy steps. You are supposed to make a wish on the third step.

PARENT LARCH   1011

6 P22

Close to Dunkeld Cathedral (see 918). Access at all reasonable times. Free. www.hilton.com/dunkeld

The sole survivor from a group of larches planted here as seedlings over 250 years ago. The young trees had been collected from the Tyrol mountains in central Europe in 1738. These trees became famous as the seed source for the large-scale larch plantings carried out by the Dukes of Atholl on the hillsides around Dunkeld.

PEEL FARM COFFEE AND CRAFTS   1012

6 Q22

Lintrathen, by Kirriemuir, Angus. Off the B954, 20 miles (32km) north of Dundee, 6 miles (9km) from Alyth; also off B951, 9 miles (14.5km) from Kirriemuir. Nearest railway station Dundee, then bus to Kirriemuir or Alyth, then walk (contact Angus Transport Forum on 01356 665000. Open Mar–Dec, daily 1000–1700. Free. Guided tours. Explanatory displays. Gift shop. Tearoom and picnic area. Play area. WC. Wheelchair access. Disabled WC. Car and coach parking. Telephone (01575) 560718. www.peelfarm.com

A working farm in an unspoilt area of rural Angus close to the majestic Reekie Linn waterfall. Warm country welcome with home baking, prize-winning jam and snack lunches. Craft demonstrations (Sat 1400–1630). Also antiques and crafts, furnishings, patchwork fabrics and gifts for sale. Farm shop.

PERTH, BELL'S CHERRYBANK GARDENS   1013

6 P23

The Bell's Cherrybank Centre, Perth. On western outskirts of Perth. Open Mar–Oct, Mon– Sat 1000–1700, Sun 1200–1700; Nov–Dec, Mon–Sat 1000–1600, Sun 1200–1600; Jan–Feb, Thur–Sat 1000–1600, Sun 1200–1600. Charge ££. Children under 12 years free . Group concessions. Guided tours. Explanatory displays. Gift shop. Tearoom. WC. Wheelchair access. Disabled WC. Car and coach parking. Telephone (01738) 472800. www.thecalyx.co.uk

The gardens contain the Bell's National Heather Collection. This is the largest collection in the UK and has over 900 varieties from all over the world, with plants flowering every month of the year. Other features include a dovecot, aviary, play area and putting green, acoustic pool, hidden pool, pond, the Rocky Island, natural burn, sculpture collection and a fountain, also gift shop and cafe.

PERTH, BLACK WATCH REGIMENTAL MUSEUM   1014   6 P23

Balhousie Castle, Hay Street, Perth. Entrance from Hay Street and North Inch. Public transport by summer city bus tour only. Open May–Sep, Mon–Sat (including public holidays) 1000–1630, (closed last Sat in Jun); Oct–Apr, Mon–Fri 1000–1530. Closed Dec 23–Jan 4 inclusive. Other times by appointment. Free. Explanatory displays and audio tour. Gift shop. WC. Car parking. Telephone 0131 310 8530. www.theblackwatch.co.uk

Balhousie Castle houses the Regimental Headquarters and Museum of the Black Watch Regiment, describing its history from 1740 to the present day. Displays of silver, colours, uniforms and medals.

PERTH, BRANKLYN GARDEN   1015   6 P23

NTS. 116 Dundee Road, Perth. On A85 near Perth city centre, 25 minute walk from Perth railway station. Buses from Perth and Dundee stop near the garden. Open Apr–Oct, daily 1000–1700. Charge ££. Group concessions. Guided tours of the garden. Explanatory displays. Gift shop. WC. Limited wheelchair access. Disabled WC. Car and coach parking. Telephone (01738) 625535. www.nts.org.uk

Started in 1922 on the site of a former orchard, Branklyn is an outstanding 2 acre (0.8ha) garden with rhododendrons, alpines, herbaceous and peat garden plants.

PERTH, CAITHNESS GLASS VISITOR CENTRE   1016   6 P23

Inveralmond Industrial Estate, Perth. On A9 Perth western bypass at the Inveralmond roundabout. Nearest railway and bus stations Perth, bus service to site Mon–Fri. Visitor centre open all year, Mon–Sat 0900–1700 (Sun, Mar–Nov 1000–1700 then Dec–Feb 1200–1700). Glass-making all year, Mon–Fri 0900–1630 (except Christmas and New Year). Free. Explanatory displays and factory viewing. Gift shop. Licenced restaurant. Baby changing facilities. WC. Wheelchair access. Disabled WC. Car and coach parking. Telephone (01738) 492320. www.caithnessglass.co.uk

See the fascinating process of glass-making. Also paperweight collectors' gallery, audio-visual theatre and children's play area. Factory shop.

PERTH CITY SIGHTSEEING OPEN TOP TOUR   1017   6 P23

Perth Railway Station. Pick up point outside bus station. Tours run Jun–Aug, Mon–Sat.. Charge £££. Group concessions. Taped commentary. Wheelchair access with assistance. Telephone (01789) 294466. www.city-sightseeing.com

An open top bus tour encompassing all the highlights of Perth city centre and Scone Palace.

PERTH, DEWARS CENTRE   1018   6 P23

Glover Street, Perth. In centre of Perth. Within walking distance of bus and railway stations. Open all year, daily 0800–midnight; skating at scheduled times, telephone to confirm. Free. Charge by activity, equipment hire. Group concessions. Explanatory displays. Restaurant/coffee shop. WC. Wheelchair access. Disabled WC. Car and coach parking. Telephone (01738) 624188. www.dewarscentre.co.uk

A range of sporting activities is available at the centre: curling, ice skating and indoor bowling are offered in a multi-purpose building housing conference, catering and leisure facilities.

PERTH, DAVID DOUGLAS MEMORIAL   1019   6 P23

In the grounds of the old church at Scone; walk from Quarrymill Woodland Park (see 1023). Access at all reasonable times.

David Douglas was one of the greatest plant hunters and explorers of America's northwest. He introduced over 200 new plants to Britain, including many trees and commonly grown garden plants.

PERTH, FERGUSSON GALLERY   1020   6 P23

Corner of Tay Street and Marshall Place, beside the river Tay. Five–ten minute walk from bus and train station. Open all year (except Christmas and New Year), Mon–Sat 1000–1700. Free. Explanatory displays. Gift shop. WC. Enlarged label text. Limited wheelchair access (wheelchair available). Disabled WC. Car and coach parking. Telephone (01738) 441944. www.pkc.gov.uk/ah/museums_galleries.htm

An art gallery devoted to the work of the Scottish colourist painter, John Duncan Fergusson (1874–1961) and housing the largest collection of his work. Three galleries, two of which are circular, show changing thematic displays of his paintings, drawings, watercolours and sculpture. An extensive archive is available for consultation by appointment.

PERTH MUSEUM AND ART GALLERY   1021   6 P23

George Street, Perth. In central Perth. Local bus route passes door. Walking distance from rail and bus stations. Open all year (except Christmas and New Year), Mon–Sat 1000–1700. Free. Explanatory displays. Gift shop. WC. Wheelchair access. Disabled WC. Car parking. Telephone (01738) 632488. www.pkc.gov.uk/ah/museums_galleries.htm

Collections of local history, fine and applied art, natural history and archaeology allow visitors a fascinating look into life in Perthshire throughout the ages. Permanent and changing exhibitions. Please telephone or visit website for details of current exhibitions and events.

PERTH, NOAH'S ARK ACTIVITY CENTRE   1022   6 P23

Glendevon Farm, Western Edge, Perth. Off the Western Bypass (A9). Nearest railway station Perth, bus from city centre to top of Burghmuir Road, then ten minute walk. Open all year daily (except Christmas and New Year), 1030–1830; please telephone to confirm. Charge children £–££; adults charge for karting only. Group concessions. Explanatory displays. Café and picnic area. WC. Wheelchair access. Disabled WC. Car and coach parking. Telephone (01738) 445568. www.noahs-ark.co.uk

A specially equipped and supervised children's softplay barn for under-12s. Also indoor kart tracks for adults and children, no booking required, ten pin bowling alley, ceramic studio and trampoline (seasonal).

PERTH, QUARRYMILL WOODLAND PARK   1023   6 P23

Isle Road, Perth. On the outskirts of Perth along A93 Blairgowrie road. Access at all times. Car park open May–Oct 0800–1900; Nov–Apr 0800–1630. Free. Explanatory displays. Gift shop. Visitor centre and coffeeshop during summer. Barbecue (can be booked). WC. Limited wheelchair access. Disabled WC. Telephone (01738) 633890.

Twenty-seven acres (11ha) of woodland around the Annety Burn. Paths specially designed for disabled visitors.

PERTH RACECOURSE   1024   6 P23

Scone Palace Park, Perth. Located in the grounds of Scone Palace. Nearest railway station Perth 3 miles (5km), free bus from city centre. Racing from Apr–Sep. Charge £££. Children free (Centre course £7.00 for Adult). Group concessions. Two main restaurants (book in advance), numerous bars, and picnic area. Crèche and children's entertainment on major meetings. WC. Limited wheelchair access. Disabled WC. Car and coach parking. Telephone 01738 551597 (ticket hotline). www.perth-races.co.uk

Horse racing over jumps in a beautiful setting with a fantastic atmosphere.

PERTH, ST JOHN'S KIRK   1025   6 P23

St John's Place, Perth. In Perth centre. Open by appointment. Free. Guided tours by arrangement. Explanatory displays in European languages and Japanese. WC. Induction loop during services. Wheelchair access. Disabled WC. Telephone (01738) 638482. www.perthshire.co.uk

Consecrated in 1242, this fine cruciform church largely dates from the 15th century and was restored 1923–26. Here in 1559 John Knox preached his momentous sermon urging the 'purging of the churches from idolatry'. The town kirk of Perth, it is frequently a venue for musical and dramatic productions. Furnishings include modern commissioned pieces as well as historic items.

PERTH, ST NINIAN'S CATHEDRAL   1026   6 P23

North Methven Street, Perth. Junction of Atholl Street and North Methven in Perth city centre. Nearest bus and railway stations Perth. Open all year, Mon–Fri 0900–1700, Sun 0800–1400. Special arrangements can be made for viewing outwith these times. Free. WC. Wheelchair access. Disabled WC. Car parking. Telephone (01738) 632053. www.perthcathedral.co.uk

St Ninian's Cathedral, Perth, the first cathedral church (except for St Paul's Cathedral, London) built in Britain since the Reformation, was the production of two giants of the 19th century Gothic revival – William Butterfield and J.L. Pearson. As importantly, it is a monument to the faith of the Scottish Episcopal Church. There are ten stained glass windows (the west window shows 12 pictures of the fall and redemption of man), the Baldachhino (made of Cornish granite), war memorial, portable font, pulpit, chapel of St Andrews, the site of Bishop Torry's tomb and the Lady Chapel

PERTH, SCONE PALACE   1027   6 P23

Scone, Perth. On the A93 (to Blairgowrie), 2 miles (3km) north east of Perth. Nearest railway station Perth, limited bus service from Perth. Open Apr–Oct, daily 0930–1645 (closes 1715). Charge £££. Charge for palace and grounds £££, grounds only ££. Group concessions. Explanatory displays. Gift shop. Self sevice coffee shop and picnic area. Adventure playground. Gardens with woodland walks and maze. WC. Wheelchair access. Disabled WC. Car and coach parking. Telephone (01738) 552300. www.scone-palace.co.uk

The crowning site of the Scottish kings on the Stone of Scone and the ancestral home of the Earls of Mansfield. The castellated palace was enlarged and embellished in 1803 and houses a magnificent collection of porcelain, furniture, ivories, and fine art. Surrounded by over 100 acres of woodland gardens and a 19th century pinetop, the grounds of Scone Palace feature Perthshire's only maze.

PERTH SCULPTURE TRAIL   1028   6 P23

The Perthshire Public Art Trust, c/o Perth Museum and Art Gallery, 78 George Street, Perth. Sculpture park in Perth (Norie-Miller Park, Rodney Gardens, Bellwood Riverside Park and Moncrieffe Island) access via Dundee Road. Nearest railway station Perth. Open at all times. Free. Guided tours. Explanatory displays. Leaflet available. Picnic area. Garden. Tactile sculptures. Wheelchair access (except Moncrieffe Island). Car and coach parking. Telephone (01738) 632488.

Perth Sculpture Trail extends through 1 mile (1.5km) of riverside parkland. Permanent public artworks have been specially created by national and international artists. Visitors may drop in to enjoy part of the trail for a few minutes or stay and enjoy the entire site.

PERTH, SOUTAR HOUSE   1029   6 P23

27 Wilson Street, Perth. In Craigie, Perth. Car parking nearby. Within 0.5 mile (1km) of Perth railway and bus station; local bus service. Open by prior arrangement. Free. Guided tours. Explanatory displays. Garden. Limited wheelchair access. Telephone (01738) 643687.

This is the former home of the Perth poet William Soutar. The room where he lay bedridden for 14 years, his father's wood panelling of most of the ground floor of the house and the stained glass have been meticulously preserved. Part of Soutar's library has been restored to his room, together with copies of his work, photographs and settings of some of his poems to music by contemporary composers from Benjamin Britten to James Macmillan.

PERTH THEATRE   1030   6 P23

Perth Theatre, 185 High Street, Perth. In the centre of Perth. Nearest railway station Perth, then five minute walk; coach and bus service to city centre. Open all year, Mon–Sat 1000–1930 (closes 1730 on days with no performances). Charge £££ dependent on show. Group concessions. Guided tours (backstage tours), also tours for the visually impaired by arrangement. Explanatory displays. Restaurant, café and bar. WC. Induction loop, infra-red enhanced hearing, signed performances and audio description for selected performances. Wheelchair access (disabled parking by arrangement). Disabled WC. Car parking. Telephone (01738) 621031. www.horsecross.co.uk

Perth Theatre is open all year and offers a wide variety of events produced by Perth Theatre Company and visiting companies, including comedies, musicals, dramatic theatre and children's and family shows.

PERTH CONCERT HALL   1031   6 P23

Perth Concert Hall, Mill Street, Perth. Perth city centre. Perth bus and rail station a ten minute walk. Open all year round, Mon–Thur 1000–2300, Fri–Sat 1000–0000, and Sun 1200–2300. Prices vary. Contact for details. Guided tours by appointment. Cafe-bar and restaurant. WC. Disabled WC. Car and coach parking. Telephone (01738) 624576. www.horsecross.co.uk

Perth Concert Hall is a new building seating 1200 or 1600 including standing area for concerts. Its Threshhold foyer is Scotland's premier space for digital new media arts. Threshold café-bar and restaurant offers quality food and drink from 1000 until late daily.

PERTH, THE EDINBURGH WOOLLEN MILL   1032   6 P23

Huntingtower Park, Perth. Just off A9 on A85 Perth/Crieff road. Bus service from Perth town centre. Open all year, Mon–Sat 0900–1700, Sun 1000–1700. Free. Explanatory displays. Gift shop. Restaurant. WC. Wheelchair access. Disabled WC. Car and coach parking. Telephone (01738) 474170. www.ewm.co.uk

A large selection of lambswool and Aran knitwear, wax jackets and high street fashions. Also golf clothing and equipment, gifts and souvenirs.

PERTHSHIRE VISITOR CENTRE   1033   6 P22

Bankfoot, Perth. In Bankfoot, off the A9, 7 miles (9.5km) north of Perth. Bus from Perth. Open Apr–Sep, 0900–2000; Oct–Mar, daily 0900–1900. Charge £. Group concessions. Explanatory displays. Gift shop. Restaurant and tearoom. Play area. WC. Wheelchair access. Disabled WC. Car and coach parking. Telephone (01738) 787696. www.macbeth.co.uk

Perthshire visitor centre has a wide range of products spread throughout the sales area. Enjoy browsing through the shops – a unique blend of leisure clothing, exciting gifts, and Scottish food.

PERTH THEATRE   1034

Perth Theatre, 185 High Street, Perth. Perth city centre. Perth bus and rail station a ten minute walk. Open all year round, Mon–Thur 1000–2300 and Fri–Sat 1000–0000. Prices vary. Contact for details. Guided tours by appointment. Café-bar and restaurant. Baby changing. WC. Audio described performances available on last Thur and Sat matinee of each production. Wheelchair access with assistance. Disabled WC. Car and coach parking. Telephone 0845 612 6319. www.horsecross.co.uk

Right in the heart of the city perth Theatre is much-loved and well used. It features an enchanting Edwardian 460 seat auditorium and presents a wide range of classic and contemporary theatre. The theatre is home to the 150-strong Perth Youth Theatre.

PICTAVIA   1035   6 R21

By Brechin Castle Centre, Haughmuir, Brechin, Angus. At the southern Brechin junction off A90, 25 miles (40km) north of Dundee. Nearest railway station Montrose. Bus service from Brechin. Open summer, Mon–Sat 0930–1730, Sun 1030–1730; winter, Sat 0900–1700, Sun 1000–1800. Charge ££. Group concessions. Explanatory displays. Gift shop. Restaurant (within the centre). Garden centre, countryside park, farmyard animals. WC. Wheelchair access. Disabled WC. Car and coach parking. Telephone (01356) 626241. www.pictavia.org.uk

Discover Scotland's ancient past through the legacy of the ancient Picts. Pictavia offers an insight into the culture and heritage of these enigmatic people who were central to the foundation of what is now known as Scotland. Interactive exhibits, replicas and artefacts. An all-weather attraction set in the beautiful countryside park at Brechin Castle Centre (see 848).

PIPERDAM GOLF AND COUNTRY PARK   1036   6 Q23

Fowlis, Dundee, Angus. On A923 Coupar Angus road. Open all year, daily. Charge dependent on activity. Bar and restaurant. Pro shop. Limited wheelchair access. Car parking. Telephone (01382) 581374. www.piperdam.com

Golf and fishing in beautiful surroundings with views. The Osprey course is par 72 and is 6500 yards off the medal tees. Also floodlit driving range

PITLOCHRY BOATING STATION   1037   5 N21

Loch Faskally, Clunie Bridge Road, Pitlochry. At north end of Pitlochry. Nearest railway station Pitlochry, buses from Perth or Inverness. Parking for cars and small coaches. Open Mar–Nov, daily 0830–1730. Rowing boats from ££, fishing boats from £££. Group concessions. Gift shop. Tearoom and picnic area. WC. Wheelchair access. Disabled WC. Telephone (01796) 472919.

Rowing and fishing boats for hire. Also crafts and fishing tackle for sale. Local walks.

PITLOCHRY CHILDREN'S AMUSEMENT PARK   1038   5 N21

Armoury Road, Pitlochry, Perthshire. In the centre of Pitlochry, off the main street on road to dam and fish ladder. 546 yards (500m) from railway station. Open mid Mar–Oct, daily 1030–1700. Admission free. Charge £ per ride. Group concessions. Picnic area and snack bar. WC. Wheelchair access. Car parking. Telephone (01796) 472876. www.childrensamusementpark.co.uk

Have a fun day out for all the family, young and old. Pirate ship, cups and saucers, magic roundabout, bumper cars, boats and orbiter shuttles, water blasters, super trucks, family amusement arcade and much more.

PITLOCHRY FESTIVAL THEATRE   1039   5 N21

Port-Na-Craig, Pitlochry, Perthshire. West of the town between the River Tummel and the bypass. Nearest railway station Pitlochry, buses from Perth or Inverness, short walk from railway station. Open all year round. Free. Charge for performances. Group concessions. Guided tours. Gift shop. Restaurant, café, and foyer bar. Explorers garden. WC. Induction loop. Audio description. Wheelchair access. Disabled WC. Car and coach parking. Telephone 01796 484626 box office. www.pitlochry.org.uk

One of Scotland's most admired repertory theatres with a resident company performing a rolling repertoire throughout the summer season. Beautifully situated overlooking the river. Art gallery. Sunday concerts and literary events. See also 1084 Scottish Plant Collectors' Garden.

PITMUIES GARDENS   1040   6 R22

House of Pitmuies, Guthrie, Forfar. 7 miles (11km) east of Forfar, 1 mile (1.5km) west of Friockheim on A932. Nearest railway station Arbroath, 8 miles (13km); infrequent bus service. Open Apr–Oct, daily 1000–1700. Charge £. Children free. Guided tours. Explanatory displays. Picnic areas. WC. Limited wheelchair access. Car and coach parking. Telephone (01241) 818245.

Adjacent to an 18th-century house and courtyard, two walled gardens lead down to a small river with an informal riverside walk with fine trees and two unusual buildings – a turreted dovecote and a Gothic washhouse. Massed spring bulbs. In summer the gardens are resplendent with old-fashioned roses, herbaceous plants and borders of blue delphiniums.

PITTENCRIEFF HOUSE MUSEUM   1041   10 P25

Pittencrieff Park, Dunfermline, Fife. On the outskirts of West Dunfermline in Pittencrieff Park, ten minute walk from centre . Nearest railway station Dunfermline. Open daily, Apr–Sep 1100–1700, Oct–Mar 1100–1600. Free. Tearoom and picnic area in park. WC. Wheelchair access to ground floor only. Disabled WC. Car and coach parking. Telephone (01383) 722935 or 313838.

Housed in a converted 17th century mansion the exhibition "Magic of the Glen" tells the story of the park, a story which involves dinosaurs, fossils, furry creatures as well as people. Children's activities.

PITTENCRIEFF PARK   1042   10 P25

Dunfermline. Located at the west end of Dunfermline High Street, off A994 Pittencrieff Street. Nearest railway and bus stations Dunfermline. Open all year. Glasshouses, Mon–Fri 0830–1530, Sat–Sun 1300–1600. Free. Explanatory displays. Refreshments available during summer. Baby changing facilities, play areas, formal flower gardens. WC. Limited wheelchair access. Disabled WC. Car and coach parking. Telephone (01383) 313700.

Landscaped park.The glasshouses are planted with a mixture of perennial and seasonal plants.

PORTMOAK MOSS   1043   10 P24

Between Kinnesswood and Scotlandwell, off A911. Access at all times. Free. Wheelchair access. Car parking. Telephone (01764) 662554. www.woodland-trust.org.uk

Once a peat bog, part of common land where local people could dig for peat and obtain turf for roofing. In the early 1960s the land was drained and planted with mixed conifers. Today it is under restoration to encourage regeneration of native trees such as birch, rowan, willow and Scots pine. Circular walk within the wood approximately 1.25 miles (2km) long. Restoration of the peat bog is underway, it is one of the few remaining examples in Central Scotland.

BEATRIX POTTER EXHIBITION   1044   6 P22

Birnam Institute, Station Road, Birnam, by Dunkeld. 15 miles (24km) north of Perth on A9. Nearest railway station and bus stop Birnam and Dunkeld, then five minute walk. Open all year, daily 1000–1700. Free. Explanatory displays. Gift shop. Restaurant/coffee shop, picnic area. Garden. WC. Induction loop system. Wheelchair access. Disabled WC. Car and coach parking. Telephone (01350) 727674. www.birnaminstitute.com

Housed in the Birnam Institute, a Victorian building erected in 1883. Visitors can enjoy the garden, and woodlands where the famous author walked. Changing exhibitions and arts programme.

PRESSMENNAN WOOD   1045   10 R25

1 mile (1.5km) south east of Stenton, off B6370. Access at all times. Free. Car parking. Telephone (01764) 662554. www.woodland-trust.org.uk

Purchased by the Woodland Trust in 1988, the wood comprises 210 acres (85ha) of woodland (under restoration). The wood was formerly part of the Biel and Dirleton Estate. Pressmennan Lake was formed artificially in 1819 by constructing a dam at the eastern end of a narrow, marsh glen. Waymarked walks and forest tracks. A fantastic example of ancient oakwood surrounds the lake

QUEEN'S VIEW VISITOR CENTRE   1046   5 N21

FE. Strathtummel, By Pitlochry, Perthshire. 7 miles (11km) west of Pitlochry on B8019. Open Apr–Oct. Charge for parking £. Explanatory displays, audio-visual show. Educational visits by arrangement. Gift shop. Tearoom. WC. Wheelchair access. Disabled WC. Car and coach parking. Telephone (01350) 727284. www.forestry.gov.uk

The centre, close to the viewpoint, is the focal point of the Tay Forest Park and provides an ideal introduction, describing the history of the people and forests in Highland Perthshire. The view across Loch Tummel to the mountain of Schiehallion and beyond is stunning. The viewpoint is thought to have been visited by Queen Victoria in 1866, but is more likely named after Queen Isabella, wife of Robert the Bruce.

RANNOCH FOREST   1047   5 M22

FE. On south shore of Loch Rannoch, 3 miles (5km) west of Kinloch Rannoch. Access at all reasonable times. Free. Picnic area. WC. Disabled WC. Car parking. www.forestry.gov.uk

There are fine forest walks on the southern shores of Loch Rannoch, offering panoramic views of the loch and distant hills.

RAVENSCRAIG PARK   1048   10 Q24

Dysart Road, Kirkcaldy, Fife. Along Fife coastal path. Access at all times. Free. Picnic area. WC. Car parking.

Woodland park, beach and coastal walks. Also putting course, tennis courts, bowls, children's play area and access to the ruins of 15th-century Ravenscraig Castle.

RED CASTLE   1049   6 R22

Off A92, 7 miles (11km) south of Montrose. Access at all times. Free.

This red stone tower on a steep mound beside the sandhills of Lunan Bay probably dates from the 15th century, when it replaced an earlier fort built for William the Lion by Walter de Berkely. Robert the Bruce gave it to Hugh, 6th Earl of Ross, in 1328.

REEKIE LINN FALLS   1050   6 Q22

South west of Kirriemuir on B954. Picnic area.

Spectacular waterfall in the natural gorged woodland, its spume effects accounting for its smoky description.

RESTENNETH PRIORY   1051   6 Q22

HS. Off the B9113, 1.5 miles (2.5km) east north-east of Forfar, Angus. Nearest railway station Arbroath, bus from Arbroath. Access at all reasonable times. Free. Car parking. Telephone (01786) 431324. www.historic-scotland.gov.uk

The ruins (chancel and tower) of an Augustinian priory church. The lower part of the tower is early Romanesque.

RIVERSIDE GRANARY   1052   6 P22

Lower Mill Street, Blairgowrie, Perthshire. In Blairgowrie centre. Buses from Perth or Dundee. Open Feb–Mar, daily (except Tue) 1000–1700; Apr–Sep, daily 1000–1700; Oct–Dec, daily except Tue 1000–1700. Free. Gift shop. Coffee shop selling homemade soups and cakes. Picnic area. WC. Wheelchair access to ground floor. Disabled WC. Car and coach parking. Telephone (01250) 873032. www.segima-fine-art.co.uk

An art and craft gallery in a converted grain mill.

RUMBLING BRIDGE   1053 · 10 P24

A823 at Rumbling Bridge. Access at all reasonable times. Free. Car parking.

The River Devon is spanned here by two bridges, the lower one dating from 1713, the upper one from 1816. A footpath from the north side gives good access to spectacular and picturesque gorges and falls, one of which is known as the Devil's Mill. Another, Cauldron Linn, is a mile downstream, whilst Vicar's Bridge is a beauty spot a mile beyond this.

ST ANDREWS AQUARIUM   1054 · 6 R23

The Scores, St Andrews, Fife. Nearest railway station Leuchars 4 miles (6.5km), connecting bus to St Andrews. Buses from Dundee and Edinburgh. Open all year (except Christmas and New Year), daily from 1000; please telephone to confirm winter opening times. Charge £££. Free to wheelchair users. Group concessions. Explanatory displays. Gift shop. Restaurant, coffee shop and picnic area. WC. Limited wheelchair access. Disabled WC. Car and coach parking. Telephone (01334) 474786.

Over 30 dramatic displays of native sea creatures. Everything from shrimps and starfish to sharks and conger eels. Graceful rays nose the surface of their display to watch you watching them. Visitors can see the enchanting resident seals and diving ducks. *Magical Kingdom of the Seahorse* exhibition.

ST ANDREW'S BOTANIC GARDEN   1055 · 6 R23

The Canongate, St Andrews. Nearest railway station Leuchars 4 miles (6.5km), connecting bus to St Andrews. Buses from Dundee and Edinburgh. Bus from town centre. Garden open May–Sep, 1000–1900; Oct–Apr, 1000–1600. Glasshouses open all year daily, 1000–1600. Charge £. Reduced admission for disabled visitors and carers. Group concessions. Guided tours by arrangement. Explanatory displays. Gift shop. Tea hut. WC. Limited wheelchair access. Car and coach parking. Telephone (01334) 476452 or 477178. www.st-andrews-botanic.org

Founded in 1887–8 by Dr John Wilson in St Mary's College, South Street, but moved to this site in 1960. Eighteen acres (7ha) of impressively landscaped gardens and glasshouses with a wide range of plants which have won international recognition. Peat, rock, heath and water gardens bounded by the Kinness Burn.

ST ANDREW'S CASTLE   1056 · 6 R23

HS. The Scores, St Andrews, Fife. On the A91 in St Andrews, Fife. Nearest railway station Leuchars 4 miles (6.5km), connecting bus to St Andrews. Buses from Dundee and Edinburgh, ten minute walk from bus station. Open Apr–Sep, daily 0930–1830; Oct–Mar 0930–1630. Charge ££. Joint admission ticket with St Andrew's Cathedral and St Rule's Tower. Group concessions. Explanatory displays in visitor centre. Gift shop. WC. Limited wheelchair access. Disabled WC. Telephone (01334) 477196. www.historic-scotland.gov.uk

The ruins of the castle of the Archbishops of St Andrews, dating in part from the 13th century. Notable features include a bottle dungeon and mine, and counter-mine tunnelling made during the siege that followed the murder of Cardinal Beaton in 1546. These siege works are the finest of their kind in Europe. An exhibition shows the history of the castle and the cathedral.

ST ANDREW'S CATHEDRAL AND ST RULE'S TOWER   1057   6 R23

HS. The Scores, St Andrews, Fife. On the A91 in St Andrews. Nearest railway station Leuchars 4 miles (6.5km), connecting bus to St Andrews. Buses from Dundee and Edinburgh, ten minute walk from bus station. Open Apr–Sep, daily 0930–1830; Oct–Mar, Mon–Sun 0930–1630. Charge £. Joint admission ticket with St Andrews Castle. Group concessions. Explanatory displays in visitor centre. Gift shop. Limited wheelchair access, assistance may be required. Telephone (01334) 472563. www.historic-scotland.gov.uk

The remains of one of the largest cathedrals in Scotland and the associated domestic ranges of the priory. The precinct walls are well preserved. A museum houses an outstanding collection of early Christian and medieval monuments and other *objets trouvés*. St Rule's Tower in the precinct is part of the first church of the Augustinian canons at St Andrews, built early in the 12th century. Splendid views from the top of the tower.

ST ANDREW'S GUIDED WALKS   1058   6 Q23

Nearest railway station Leuchars 4 miles (6.5km), connecting bus to St Andrews. Buses from Dundee and Edinburgh. Tours by appointment. Charge ££. Children under 12 free. Group concessions. Guided tours (available in French and German). Walks can be managed by wheelchair users and visitors with other special needs can be catered for. Telephone (01334) 850638.

Guided walks of St Andrews cover the area around the cathedral, castle, university and golf course. General and specialist tours available. Qualified Blue Badge guides.

ST ANDREWS LINKS   1059   6 R23

Pilmour House, St Andrews, Fife. Eden clubhouse and golf practice centre located off A91 at entrance to St Andrews. Links clubhouse follow A91 into town, turn left into Golf Place and continue to West Sands Road. Nearest railway station at Leuchars, 10 minutes by bus or taxi. St Andrews bus station is five minute walk from first tee of Old Course. In summer courses and clubhouses open daily from 0700. The Old Course opens at 0630 Mon–Sat and is closed Sun. In winter courses are open during daylight hours, clubhouses open at 0800. Charges dependent on course and time of year. Guided walk on Old Course Jun weekends only, Jul–Aug daily. Information boards, bar/lounge and golf shops in both clubhouses. A la carte restaurant in Links Clubhouse. Shops in Links Clubhouse; behind the 18th green of the Old Course; and in Links Road, adjacent to the 18th fairway.. WC. Disabled WC. Car and coach parking. Telephone (01334) 466666. www.standrews.org.uk

St Andrews Links is the largest public golf complex in Europe comprising six public golf courses, including the world famous Old Course, two public clubhouses, a golf practice centre and three shops. St Andrews Links Trust, a charitable organisation set up by an Act of Parliament in 1974, is responsible for the preservation and maintenance of the courses and facilities. Free shuttle bus service between clubhouses (Apr–Oct). Golf club and shoe hire.

ST ANDREWS MUSEUM   1060   6 R23

Kinburn Park , Doubledykes Road, St Andrews, Fife. Nearest railway station Leuchars 4 miles (6.5km), connecting bus to St Andrews. Buses from Dundee and Edinburgh. Open Apr–Sep, daily 1000–1700; Oct–Mar (except Christmas and New Year), daily 1030–1600. Free. Guided tours by arrangement. Explanatory displays. Gift shop.

Restaurant and picnic area. Baby changing facilities. Parkland. WC. Wheelchair access. Disabled WC. Car parking. Telephone (01334) 412690. www.fifedirect.org.uk/museums

Opened in 1991 in Kinburn House, a Victorian mansion set in pleasant parkland. The museum traces the development of the city as a pilgrimage shrine to St Andrew, Scotland's patron saint, and as a power centre for medieval kings and bishops, with Scotland's largest cathedral and first university. Also a changing programme of temporary exhibitions, supported by a range of talks, concerts and children's activities throughout the year.

ST ANDREW'S OPEN TOP BUS TOUR   1061   6 R23

St Andrews Bus Station, City Road, St Andrews. Tour starts from Church Street, stopping at bus station. Tours operate end Jun–end Aug, daily. Charge £££. Wheelchair access with assistance. Telephone (01334) 474238. www.stagecoachbus.com

A one hour tour around St Andrews with stops at the Golf Museum, Aquarium, historic university buildings, St Andrews Cathedral and St Andrews Bay Golf Resort. Commentary is provided.

ST ANDREW'S POTTERY SHOP   1062   6 R23

4 Church Square, St Andrews, Fife. In pedestrian area in town centre next to public toilets. Nearest railway station Leuchars 4 miles (6.5km), bus station five minute walk, service from Edinburgh, Dundee and Perth. Open Jul–Aug, Mon–Sat 0930–1900, Sun 1130–1630; Sep–Jun, Mon–Sat 0930–1730, Sun 1130–1630. Free. Explanatory displays. Gift shop. Wheelchair access. Car parking. Telephone (01334) 477744.

Shop selling full range of pots made locally by well-known potter, George Young. Video of pottery processes. Also exclusive Scottish outlet for Pithoi Greek garden pots.

ST ANDREW'S PRESERVATION TRUST MUSEUM AND GARDEN   1063   6 R23

12 North Street, St Andrews, Fife. Near the cathedral in St Andrews. Nearest railway station Leuchars 4 miles (6.5km), connecting bus to St Andrews. Buses from Dundee and Edinburgh. Open Easter, May–Sep and St Andrew's week (Nov) daily 1400–1700. Free. Guided tours by arrangement. Explanatory displays. Gift shop. Garden. Wheelchair access with assistance. Telephone (01334) 477629.

A charming 16th-century building with a beautiful sheltered garden. Displays include old shops and businesses in the town and some of Scotland's earliest photographs. Changing exhibitions.

ST BRIDGET'S KIRK, DALGETY   1064   10 P25

HS. Off the A92 at Dalgety Bay, 2 miles (3km) south west of Aberdour, Fife. Nearest railway station Aberdour, bus from Kirkcaldy or Dunfermline. Access at all reasonable times. Free. Telephone (01786) 431324. www.historic-scotland.gov.uk

The shell of a medieval church much altered in the 17th century for Protestant worship. At the west end of the building is a burial vault, with a laird's loft above, built for the Earl of Dunfermline.

ST FILLAN'S CAVE   1065   10 R24

Cove Wynd, Pittenweem, Fife. 1 mile (2km) west of Anstruther. Nearest railway station Cupar, bus from Dundee or Edinburgh. Open all year, Easter–Oct, Mon–Sat

0900–1730; Nov–Easter, Tue–Sat 0900–1730, Sun 1200–1700. Charge £. Guided tours by arrangement. Wheelchair access with assistance. Car parking. Telephone (01333) 311495.

A cave associated with St Fillan, a 7th-century missionary to the Picts, who lived in the area. Renovated in 1935 and rededicated for worship and renovated again in 2000 to provide disabled access.

ST MARGARET'S CAVE   1066   10 P25

In Dunfermline, below Bruce Street car park, down 80 steps. By rail or bus from Edinburgh, 20 minute walk from rail station and ten minute walk from bus station. Open Easter–Sep, daily 1100–1600. Free. Guided tours by appointment. Explanatory displays. Gift shop. Car and coach parking. Telephone (01383) 314228 or 313838.

A site of Catholic pilgrimage where Margaret, 11th-century queen and saint, sought refuge for meditation and prayer.

ST MARY'S CHURCH, GRAND TULLY   1067   5 N22

HS. Off the A827 at Pitcairn Farm, 3 miles (5km) east north-east of Aberfeldy, Perthshire. Nearest railway station Pitlochry, bus from Perth to Aberfeldy (request stop for St Mary's Church). Open at all reasonable times. Free. Car parking. Telephone (01786) 431324. www.historic-scotland.gov.uk

A simple 16th-century parish church with a finely painted wooden ceiling illustrating heraldic and symbolic subjects.

ST MARY'S CHURCH, ST ANDREWS   1068   6 R23

HS. Kirkheugh, St Andrews. Behind the cathedral in St Andrews, Fife. Nearest railway station Leuchars 4 miles (6.5km), connecting bus to St Andrews. Buses from Dundee and Edinburgh. Access at all reasonable times. Free. Telephone (01786) 431324. www.historic-scotland.gov.uk

The scanty foundations of a small cruciform church on the edge of a cliff. This was the earliest collegiate church in Scotland and was destroyed in the Reformation.

ST MONANS WINDMILL   1069   10 R24

St Monans, Fife. 1 mile (2km) west of Pittenweem, 0.25 mile (0.5km) from St Monans. Nearest railway station Leuchars 4 miles (6.5km), connecting bus to St Andrews, buses from St Andrews or Leven. Open on request to keyholder (Spar and Post Office in St Monans). Open Jul–Aug, 1200–1600. Free. £5 deposit for key during winter. Explanatory displays. Books for sale. Picnic area. Car and coach parking. Telephone 01333 739043/01334 412690. www.fifedirect.org.uk/museums

A late 18th century windmill on Fife's coastal path, with saltpans close by.

ST ORLAND'S STONE   1070   6 Q22

HS. In a field near Cossans Farm, 4.5 miles (7km) west of Forfar, Angus. Access at all reasonable times. Free. www.historic-scotland.gov.uk

An early Christian sculptured slab with a cross on one side and Pictish symbols and figures on the other.

ST SERF'S CHURCH, DUNNING   1071   6 P23

HS. In Dunning, Perthshire. Nearest railway station Perth, bus from Perth to Dunning. Open Apr–Sep, daily 0930–1830. Telephone (01764) 684497. www.historic-scotland.gov.uk

The parish church of Dunning, with a square Romanesque tower and tower arch. The rest of the church was rebuilt in 1810, but contains some of the original fabric. The church houses the Dupplin Cross, a 9th-century freestanding cross heavily decorated with spiral work, interlacing and figures of men, animals and birds. It is believed to symbolise the uniting of the Picts and Scots into one nation.

ST VIGEANS SCULPTURED STONES   1072   6 R22

HS. 0.5 mile (1km) north of Arbroath, Angus. Nearest railway station Arbroath, bus services from Dundee or Montrose. Open all year (keys available from Arbroath Abbey). Free. Explanatory displays. Telephone (01241) 878756. www.historic-scotland.gov.uk

A fine collection of 32 early Christian and Pictish stones set into cottages in the village of St Vigeans.

SCOTLAND'S SECRET BUNKER   1073   6 R23

Crown Buildings, Troywood, St Andrews, Fife. On the B9131, 5 miles (8km) from St Andrews. Nearest railway station Leuchars 4 miles (6.5km), connecting bus to St Andrews. Open late Mar–Oct, daily 1000–1800. Last admission 1700. Bookings taken throughout the year for parties, weddings and corporate events. Charge £££. Group concessions. Guided tours. Explanatory displays. Gift shop. Café. WC. Car and coach parking. Telephone (01333) 310301. www.secretbunker.co.uk

The amazing labyrinth built 100 feet (30.5m) underground where central government and the military commanders would have run the country in the event of nuclear war. Its existence was only revealed in 1993 and it is now open to the public. Visitors can see the nuclear command centre with its original equipment. Three cinemas show authentic cold war films. There is a display of vehicles in the grounds.

SCOTSTARVIT TOWER   1074   6 Q24

HS. Off the A916, 3 miles (5km) south of Cupar, Fife. Nearest railway station Cupar, bus from Cupar or Ceres. Open during summer; apply to keyholder at Hill of Tarvit House. Free. Car parking. Telephone (01334) 653127. www.historic-scotland.gov.uk

A handsome and well-built 15th-century tower house remodelled in the mid 16th century. Renowned as the home of Sir John Scot, author of *Scot of Scotstarvit's Staggering State of the Scots Statesmen.*

CAPTAIN SCOTT AND DR WILSON CAIRN   1075   6 Q21

In Glen Prosen on unclassified road north west of Dykehead. Access at all times. Free.

The cairn replaces the original fountain which was erected in memory of the Antarctic explorers, Captain Scott and Dr Wilson. Early planning for the expedition took place at Dr Wilson's home in the glen.

SCOTTISH ANTIQUE AND ARTS CENTRE   1076   6 Q23

Abernyte, Perthshire. 1.5 miles (2.5km) from the A90. Bus from Dundee or Perth. Open all year, daily (except Christmas and New Year's Day) 1000–1700. Free. Guided tours. Explanatory displays. Gift shop. Cafe. Delicatessen. WC. Wheelchair access. Disabled WC. Car and coach parking. Telephone (01828) 686401.

A large antique and arts centre with over 100 dealers selling collectables, paintings, new furniture, lighting, cushions, candles, and gifts.

SCOTTISH CRANNOG CENTRE   1077   5 M22

Kenmore, Perthshire. 6 miles (10km) west of Aberfeldy on A827, 14 miles (22.5km) east of Killin on A827. Nearest railway station Pitlochry, bus services from Pitlochry or Aberfeldy. Car and coach parking permitted at nearby hotel. Open daily, Mar–Oct 1000–1730; Nov, Sat–Sun 1000–1600. Last tour 1 hour before closing. Charge ££. Group concessions. Guided tours. Explanatory displays. Gift shop. Refreshments by arrangement. WC. Wheelchair access with assistance. Disabled WC. Car and coach parking. Telephone (01887) 830583. www.crannog.co.uk

A unique recreation of an Iron Age loch dwelling, authentically built from evidence obtained from underwater archaeological excavations of crannogs in the loch. Visitors can walk back in time and experience the life of crannog-dwellers. There are a wide range of ancient craft demonstrations and plenty of hands-on activities. Exhibition with information panels and several short videos. This is an 5-star all-weather attraction.

SCOTTISH DEER CENTRE   1078   6 Q23

Cupar, Fife. On the A91, 3 miles (5km) west of Cupar. Nearest railway station Cupar, bus from Cupar or Kinross. Open all year, daily 1000–1800. Charge ££. Group concessions available (groups must be pre-booked a week in advance and consist of more than 10 people in total). Guided tours. Ranger tours around deer park, wolf wood and falconry display. Explanatory displays. Gift shop. Coffee shop, takeaway service, indoor and outdoor picnic areas. Indoor and outdoor play areas. WC. At certain times of year, depending on breeding cycle, guided tours can contain an opportunity to touch the animals and feel antlers/coat, which blind customers often enjoy (please telephone for details). Wheelchair access. Disabled WC. Car and coach parking. Telephone (01337) 810391. www.ewm.co.uk

The Scottish Deer Centre is set in fifty-five acres (22ha) of beautiful countryside and boasts a 140 head of deer covering 9 different species. Experience the spectacular falconry displays and take the opportunity to see one of Scotland's greatest wild animals, the grey wolf. There is also an aerial walkway, viewing platforms and trailer rides. The Courtyard contains shops offering a wide selection of knitwear, outerwear, gifts, golf clothing and equipment, and specialities such as venison and malt whiskies in the Highland smokehouse.

SCOTTISH FISHERIES MUSEUM   1079   10 R24

Harbourhead, Anstruther, Fife. In Anstruther, 10 miles (16km) south of St Andrews. Nearest railway station Leuchars 4 miles (6.5km), then bus to St Andrews. Bus from St Andrews or Leven. Open all year (except Christmas and New Year), Mon–Sat 1000–1630, Sun 1100–1600. Charge ££. Group concessions. Guided tours for groups by arrangement. Explanatory displays. Gift shop. Tearoom. WC. Wheelchair access. Disabled WC. Car and coach parking. Telephone (01333) 310628. www.scottish-fisheries-museum.org

Housed in 16th- to 19th-century buildings, the award-winning museum displays fishing and ships' gear, model and actual fishing boats (including *Fifie* and *Zulu* in harbour). Interior of a fisherman's cottage and extended reference library.

SCOTTISH HYDRO-ELECTRIC VISITOR CENTRE   1080   5 N21

Pitlochry Power Station, Pitlochry, Perthshire. In Pitlochry on the River Tummel. Nearest railway and bus stations Pitlochry. Open Apr–Oct, Mon–Fri 1000–1730; Jul–Aug and bank holidays also Sat–Sun. Charge £. Salmon viewing and downstairs exhibition is free. Audio-visual displays (French and German). Gift shop. WC.

Limited wheelchair access. Disabled WC. Car and coach parking. Telephone (01796) 473152. www.scottish-southern.co.uk

An exhibition shows how Scottish and Southern Energy's hydro-electric power stations are controlled and operated, and the Salmon Story. Visitors can also observe salmon coming upstream in the fish ladder and see into the station's turbine hall.

SCOTTISH LIQUEUR CENTRE   1081   6 P23

Hilton, Bankfoot, Perthshire. 7 miles (11km) north of Perth at the Bankfoot exit of the A9. Regular bus service from Perth. Open all year (except Christmas and New Year), Mon–Sat 0930–1700. Free. Explanatory displays. Gift shop. Refreshments, coffee shop, and WC on site. Wheelchair access. Car and coach parking. Telephone (01738) 787044. www.scottish-liqueur-centre.co.uk

The family-run company produces original Scottish liqueurs. Free tutored tastings of products are offered, together with a brief presentation on the company's history and development. Quality local crafts and paintings on display.

SCOTTISH NATIONAL GOLF CENTRE   1082   6 Q23

Drumoig, Leuchars, by St Andrews, Fife. 8 miles (13km) from St Andrews. Rail and bus services to St Andrews. Open all year, Mon–Fri 0900–2200, Sat–Sun 0900–1900. Charges dependent on activity. Group concessions. Bistro and bar. WC. Wheelchair access with assistance. Disabled WC. Car and coach parking. Telephone (01382) 541144. www.sngc.scottishgolf.com

Indoor practice area and outdoor driving range/short game area. Also sports halls, fitness suite and treatment room. Various packages and golf schools for all ages and abilities.

SCOTTISH OFF-ROAD DRIVING CENTRE   1083   6 P24

Strathmiglo, Fife. Open daily 0900–1700. Charge £££ per vehicle (holds 4). Group concessions. Self-service tea and coffee. WC. Car and coach parking. Telephone (01337) 860528. www.scotoffroad.co.uk

An off-road driving range covering a 100 acres (40ha) site. Vehicle provided or visitors can bring their own vehicle for a reduced charge.

SCOTTISH PLANT COLLECTORS' GARDEN   1084   5 N21

Pitlochry Festival Theatre, Port-Na-Craig, Pitlochry, Perthshire. Nearest railway station Pitlochry, buses from Perth or Inverness, short walk from railway station. Open Apr–Oct, Mon–Sat 1000–1700; May–Oct also Sun 1100–1700. Guided tours available. Charge £. Group concessions. Explanatory displays. Gift shop. Restaurant, tearoom and picnic area. WC. Wheelchair access. Disabled WC. Car and coach parking. Telephone (01796) 484600. www.scottishplantcollectorsgarden.com

Scotland's newest garden celebrates 300 years of plant collecting by Scotsmen. Art and sculpture are combined with landscape features to provide a unique experience. Also facilities for outdoor performances, both musical and theatrical. See also 1039 Pitlochry Festival Theatre.

SCOTTISH VINTAGE BUS MUSEUM   1085   10 P25

M90 Commerce Park, Lathalmond, Dunfermline, Fife. On the B915, 2 miles (3km) west of junction 4 on the M90 and 2 miles north of Dunfermline. Open Easter–early Oct, Sun 1230–1700. Charge £. Increased charge for special events. Group concessions. Guided tours. Explanatory displays. Gift shop. Refreshments. WC. Wheelchair access (not onto vehicles). Disabled WC. Car and coach parking. Telephone (01383) 623380. www.busweb.co.uk/svbm

A collection of over 150 historic buses from the 1920s, mostly of Scottish origin, which can be seen in all stages of restoration. Also many artefacts depicting Scottish bus history. Visitors can observe restoration work or travel in a vintage bus around the site. Occasional special events.

SHINAFOOT ART STUDIOS   1086   5 N23

Shinafoot, Dunning Road, Auchterarder, Perthshire. 1 mile (1.5km) north of Auchterarder on B8062. Nearest railway station Gleneagles. By appointment only. Free. Car and coach parking. Telephone (01764) 663639. www.shinafoot.co.uk

Year-round art courses and painting holidays for all ages and abilities. Also picture framing, art materials and paintings for sale.

SOUTH LISSENS POTTERY   1087   10 P24

22 Church Street, Milnathort, Kinross. In Milnathort, 2 miles (3km) from Kinross Tourist Information Centre. Nearest railway station Perth, buses from Perth or Edinburgh. Open all year, Mon–Sat (closed Wed) 1000–1800, Sun 1200–1700 (closed Christmas and New Year). Free. Gift shop. WC. Wheelchair access. Car parking. Telephone (01577) 865642.

A pottery workshop located in an old Presbyterian church built in 1769. Traditional country pottery and contemporary pots decorated with unusual lustre effects.

STOCKS STONES AND STORIES, EXHIBITION OF CRIEFF STOCKS
AND CROSSES   1088   5 N23

c/o Crieff Tourist Information Centre, Town Hall, High Street, Crieff. In Crieff town centre. Bus from Perth and Stirling. Open Apr–Jun and Sep–Oct, Mon–Sat 0930–1700, Sun 1100–1500; Jul–Aug, Mon–Sat 0930–1830, Sun 1000–1600; Nov–Mar, Mon–Sat 1000–1600. Free. Explanatory displays. WC nearby in town centre. Wheelchair access. Car and coach parking. Telephone (01764) 652578. www.perthshire.co.uk

A fascinating exhibition in the basement of Crieff Town Hall, housing three of the town's conserved historical monuments: the Crieff Burgh cross (a pictish cross slab of the 9th century); the Drummond or Mercat cross; and the town stocks – unique in design. Panels give historical and conservation information for each object.

STONEHAVEN OPEN AIR POOL   1089   6 S20

Queen Elizabeth Park, Stonehaven, Kincardineshire. 15m south of Aberdeen on the A90. Open Jun and Sep, Mon–Fri 1300–1930 and Sat– Sun 1000–1800; Jul–Aug, Mon–Fri 1000–1930 and Sat–Sun 1000–1800. Midnight swims on Wed, Jul–Aug. Charge £. Refreshments available. WC. No guide dogs. Wheelchair access with assistance. Disabled WC. Car and coach parking. Telephone (01569) 762134. www.stonehavenopenairpool.co.uk

This art deco pool is the only functioning 50 metre, filtered, heated (to 30c), seawater open-air facility known to survive in the United Kingdom. It was earmarked for closure in 1994 but this threat saw the formation of the Friends of the Pool who now jointly run the pool with Aberdeenshire Council.

STRATHEARN RECREATION CENTRE   1090   5 N23

Pittenzie Road, Crieff. Adjacent to Crieff High School. Local bus service. Open all year, Mon–Fri 1000–2200, Sat–Sun 1000–1800 (closed Christmas and New Year). Charge £. Children under 5, carers of disabled and spectators free. Group concessions. Guided tours. Explanatory displays. Vending machines. WC. Wheelchair access. Disabled WC. Car and coach parking. Telephone (01764) 653779. www.perthandkinrossleisure.co.uk

Heated swimming pool, fitness suite and fully equipped sports hall offering table tennis, basketball, indoor bowls, football, volleyball, badminton and many other activities.

JOHN MCDOUALL STUART MUSEUM   1091   10 Q24

Rectory Lane, Dysart, Kirkcaldy, Fife. In Dysart, 2 miles (3km) east of Kirkcaldy. Bus from Kirkcaldy. Open Jun–Aug, daily 1400–1700. Free. Explanatory displays. WC. Telephone (01592) 412860.

An exhibition about the great 19th-century explorer of Australia, located in the house where he was born. There is a small permanent exhibition about Stuart and about the history of Dysart.

TEALING DOVECOT AND EARTH HOUSE   1092   6 Q22

HS. 0.5 mile (1km) down an unclassified road to Tealing, Angus, off the A929, 5 miles (8km) north of Dundee. Access at all reasonable times. Free. Telephone (01786) 431324. www.historic-scotland.gov.uk

The dovecot dates from the late 16th century, and is an elegant little building. The earth house, of Iron Age date, comprises an underground passage, now uncovered.

TENTSMUIR NATIONAL NATURE RESERVE   1093   6 R23

At very north east edge of Fife, where the Tay enters the North Sea, 1.5 miles (2.5km) east of Tayport or north from Forest Enterprise Kinshaldy car park (off B945). Open at all times. Free. £1.00 charge for parking. WC and disabled WC, picnic tables, barbecue for hire and children's adventure trail at Kinshaldy car park. Limited wheelchair access (tracks through forest are typical metal road forest tracks; main paths in the reserve are grass and sand). Car and coach parking. Telephone Scottish Natural Heritage 01382 553704; Forest Enterprise 01350 727284. www.nnr-scotland.org.uk; www.forestry.gov.uk

A large area of sand dunes and beach at the mouth of the Tay estuary, forming an important roosting and feeding area for huge concentrations of seaduck, waders and wildfowl, as well as a haul-out area for over 2000 common and grey seals. The reserve's grassland and dunes are especially favoured by a wide variety of colourful butterflies.

TRINITY ARTS   1094   10 R24

3 Midshore, Pittenweem, Fife. On A917, 10 minutes from St Andrews. Bus service from St Andrews. Open all year, Mon–Sat 1030–1300 and 1400–1800, Sun 1100–1630. Free. Wheelchair access. Car and coach parking. Telephone (01333) 313360. www.trinity4arts.co.uk

Art material shop and art gallery displaying prints and originals of local and abstract art. Framing service.

TULLIBARDINE CHAPEL   1095   5 N23

HS. Off the A823, 6 miles (9.5km) south east of Crieff, Perthshire. Nearest railway station Perth, bus from Perth to Crieff, then bus to Tullibardine. Open Apr–Sep only; keyholder at adjacent farmhouse. Free. Explanatory displays. Telephone 0131 668 8800. www.historic-scotland.gov.uk

One of the most complete and unaltered small medieval churches in Scotland. Founded in 1446 and largely rebuilt circa 1500. Good architectural detail.

VALLEYFIELD WOOD   1096   10 N25

On the north side of A985, High Valleyfield, near Culross, Fife. Open all year. Free. Wheelchair access.

Beautiful woodland walks, originally the gardens of a mansion house, landscaped by Sir Humphrey Repton.

VANE FARM RSPB NATURE RESERVE   1097   10 P24

RSPB. Kinross, Tayside. 1 mile (2km) along the B9097 east of junction 5 off M90. Nearest railway station Lochgelly, bus service from Edinburgh to Kinross (5 miles/8km). No bus to reserve. Reserve open at all times. Visitor centre open all year, daily 1000–1700 (except Christmas and New Year). Charge £. RSPB/Wildlife Explorer members free on production of membership card, group leaders free. Group concessions. Guided tours by arrangement. Explanatory displays. Gift shop. Tearoom and picnic area. Two nature trails, observation room. WC. Wheelchair access to visitor centre. Disabled parking. Disabled WC. Car and coach parking. Telephone (01577) 862355. www.rspb.org.uk/scotland

Vane Farm Visitor Centre overlooks Loch Leven, and is part of a national nature reserve, where thousands of geese and ducks spend the winter. Two trails take visitors to hides overlooking the wetlands and loch and through woodlands to Vane Hill. There is no disabled access to the trails, but there are telescopes in the tearoom enabling visitors to see the whole reserve.

WADE'S BRIDGE   1098   5 N22

On B846, north of Aberfeldy. Access at all times. Free. Car parking.

The bridge across the River Tay was begun in 1733 by General Wade, with William Adam as architect. It is considered to be the finest of all Wade's bridges. The Black Watch Memorial is a large cairn surmounted by a kilted soldier, erected close to the bridge in Queen Victoria's Jubilee Year (1887). Easy access across lawn to river bank.

MAGGIE WALL'S MONUMENT   1099   5 N23

1 mile (1.5km) west of Dunning, Perthshire, on B8062. Access at all times. Free. Wheelchair access with assistance. Car and coach parking. Telephone (01764) 684448.

The monument marks the spot where Maggie Wall was allegedly burned as a witch in 1657. It is constructed from rough field boulders and a plinth stone topped with a cross. Nothing is known of Maggie Wall but as a non-Christian why the cross? One opinion is that those who killed her repented of their actions and tried to make redress by erecting this cairn.

WATER MILL AND TEAROOM   1100   5 N21

Ford Road, Blair Atholl, Pitlochry. 5 miles (8km) north of Pitlochry off A9. Railway station and bus stop 200 yards (182m). Open Apr–Oct, Mon–Sat 1000–1730, Sun

1000–1730. Charge £. Group concessions. Guided tours by arrangement. Explanatory displays. Gift shop. Tearoom. Garden. WC. Limited wheelchair access (easy access to garden, short flight of stairs to tearoom, difficult access to mill). Car and coach parking. Telephone (01796) 481321.

Dating from 1613, this working museum produces oatmeal and flour which is on sale in the tearoom. The stoneground oatmeal flour is an ingredient in a variety of baking on sale at the mill and locally. Also available is honey from local beehives.

WEEM WOOD 1101   5 N22

FE. 1.5 miles (2.5km) west of Aberfeldy, on the B846. Nearest railway station Pitlochry, bus service to Aberfeldy. Access at all reasonable times. Free. Guided tours (occasional – see what's on guide). Picnic area. Wheelchair access to picnic area only. Car parking. www.forestry.gov.uk

A circular path takes walkers across ancient woodland-covered crags to St David's Well, a natural spring named after a 15th-century local laird who lived as a hermit in one of the caves on the hillside. Look out for sculptures.

WEST PORT, ST ANDREWS 1102   6 R23

HS. In South Street, St Andrews, Fife. Nearest railway station Leuchars, 4 miles (6.5km), connecting bus to St Andrews. Buses from Dundee and Edinburgh. Ten minute walk from bus station. Free. www.historic-scotland.gov.uk

One of the few surviving city gates in Scotland, built in 1589, renovated in 1843.

ABERDEEN AND GRAMPIAN HIGHLANDS

ABERDEEN ART GALLERY 1103   6 T19

Schoolhill, Aberdeen. City centre, off Union Street. 15 minute walk from Aberdeen railway and bus stations. Open all year, Mon-Sat 1000–1700, Sun 1400–1700. Free. Guided tours. Explanatory displays. Gift shop. Licensed café. Baby changing facilities. Highchairs and pushchairs available. WC. Wheelchair access. Disabled WC. Telephone (01224) 523700. www.aagm.co.uk

One of the city's most important tourist attractions, Aberdeen's splendid art gallery houses an important fine art collection with particularly good examples of 19th- and 20th-century works, a rich and diverse applied art collection and an exciting programme of special exhibitions.

ABERDEEN ARTS CENTRE 1104   6 T19

33 King Street, Aberdeen. Aberdeen City Centre . Open all year, Mon–Sat 1000–1600. Charges vary for theatre. Gallery free. Guided tours. Cafe and bar. WC. Wheelchair access. Disabled WC. Telephone (01224) 635208.

Theatre staging mainly local amateur performances and touring companies. Small gallery usually local artists

ABERDEEN, BRIDGE OF DEE 1105   6 S20

Access at all times. Free.

Built in the 1520s by Bishop Gavin Dunbar in James V's reign. Seven arches span 400 feet (122m) and it formerly carried the main road south. The medieval solidity of the structure is enlivened by heraldic carvings.

ABERDEEN, BRIG O' BALGOWNIE   1106   6 T19

At Bridge of Don, north of Aberdeen, upstream of main A92 bridge. Access at all times. Free.

Also known as the Auld Brig o'Don, this massive arch, 62 feet (19m) wide, spans the deep pool of the river and is backed by fine woods. It was completed circa 1320 and repaired in 1607. In 1605 Sir Alexander Hay endowed the bridge with a small property. This so increased in value that it built the New Bridge of Don downstream (in 1830 at a cost of £26,000), bore most of the cost of the Victoria Bridge, and contributed to many other public works. Now closed to motor vehicles.

ABERDEEN, CATHEDRAL CHURCH OF ST MACHAR   1107   6 S19

The Chanonry, Old Aberdeen. Bus from city centre. Open all year, daily 0900–1700; Mar–Oct 1000–1600; (note that a weekly Sunday service is held at 1100 and 1600 and the church regularly hosts weddings, funerals and unscheduled special events). Admission by donation (£2 suggested). Guided tours by arrangement. Explanatory displays. Gift shop. WC. Induction loop system during services. Wheelchair access. Disabled WC. Car and coach parking. Telephone (01224) 485988. www.stmachar.com

On an ancient site of worship dating from 580 AD, becoming a cathedral church in 1140, the present building dates from 1350-1520. It is a twin-towered granite building with stone pillars and impressive stained glass windows on three sides. A heraldic ceiling of panelled oak dates from 1520 and depicts notable sovereigns of Europe and the nobles and ecclesiastical households of Scotland. There is also a collection of medieval charters in the Charter Room. Outside is the tomb of Bishop Gavin Dunbar.

ABERDEEN, CRUICKSHANK BOTANIC GARDEN   1108   6 S19

Old Aberdeen Campus, Aberdeen University, Aberdeen. Nearest railway station Aberdeen, bus from city centre. Open all year, Mon–Fri 0900–1630; May–Sep, Sat and Sun 1400–1700. Free. Guided tours. Refreshments available at Kings College, Old Aberdeen. Wheelchair access. Telephone (01224) 272704.

Originally founded in 1898 as the University of Aberdeen's teaching and research garden. The 11 acres (4.5ha) are laid out in an ornamental style. Rock garden and ponds, herbaceous border, rose garden, terrace and arboretum.

ABERDEEN, DOONIES FARM   1109   6 T20

Coast Road, Nigg, Aberdeen. Off A956 to village of Cove, signposted from there (look for golf course). Bus from city centre to Torry or Cove then walk 1 mile (2km). Open all year, daily 1000–1830 summer and 1000–1600 winter. Charge £. Children under 5 free. Group concessions. Guided tours. Explanatory displays. Picnic area. Play area. WC. Wheelchair access. Disabled WC. Car and coach parking. Telephone (01224) 875879. www.aberdeencity.gov.uk

A 182 acre (74ha) working farm populated with rare breeds (animals and birds). Visitors can wander around freely.

ABERDEEN, GLOVER HOUSE   1110   6 T19

79 Balgownie Road, Aberdeen. Bridge of Don, north of Aberdeen. Local bus service passes the entrance. Open all year, Mon–Sat, by arrangement. All visitors are guided

around the house, so please telephone in advance to confirm your arrival time. Charge £. Group concessions. Guided tours, tours available in Japanese, other languages by arrangement. Explanatory displays. Gift shop. Garden. WC. Limited wheelchair access. Disabled WC. Telephone (01224) 709303.

Glover House celebrates the 19th-century Scottish entrepreneur Thomas Blake Glover whose fascinating story unfolds as you are shown through each room of this, his former family home. Apart from texts and photographs associated with the beginnings of Japan's industrial, political, transport, mining and shipping development, there is a full set of samurai armour, several swords, three kites (including a Japanese fighting kite) and many large examples of Japanese art (shodo). These are all displayed in an original Victorian house setting, complete with old-fashioned kitchen, servants' quarters and genuine period furniture. Children have the opportunity to put on a samuri armour helmet, and to handle a sharkskin handled sword.

ABERDEEN, GORDON HIGHLANDERS MUSEUM   1111   6 T19

St Luke's, Viewfield Road, Aberdeen. Aberdeen, off North Anderson Drive and Queens Road roundabout. Bus from city centre. Open Apr–Oct, Tue–Sat 1030–1630, Sun 1330–1630. Other times by arrangement. Charge £. Group concessions by arrangement. Guided tours by appointment. Explanatory displays, both audio-visual and interactive. Temporary exhibitions. Gift shop. Tearoom. Baby changing facilities. Gardens. WC. Induction loop system in audio-visual room, handling facilities for blind visitors. Wheelchair access. Disabled WC. Car parking. Telephone (01224) 311200. www.gordonhighlanders.com

Regimental museum of the Gordon Highlanders. Displays of the regiment's unique collection recalling 200 years of service and gallantry. Housed in the former home and studio of the famous Victorian artist Sir George Reid PRSA.

ABERDEEN, KINGS COLLEGE CENTRE   1112   6 S19

College Bounds, Old Aberdeen, Aberdeen. In the University of Aberdeen campus, 2 miles (3km) from city centre. Open all year (except Christmas and New Year). Free. Explanatory displays. Gift shop. James McKay Hall Coffee shop, Zeste restaurant and cafe. WC. Wheelchair access. Disabled WC. Car parking. Telephone (01224) 273702.

A multi-media centre giving the history of the university.

ABERDEEN, KIRK OF ST NICHOLAS   1113   6 T19

Union Street, Aberdeen. In churchyard bounded by Union Street, Back Wynd, Schoolhill and Correction Wynd, 0.25 mile (0.5km) from bus and rail stations. Open May–Sep (except local holidays) Mon–Fri 1200–1600, Sat 1300–1500. Other times by arrangement. Admission by donation. Guided tours, guide book available in English, French, German, Dutch, Italian, and Spanish. Explanatory displays. Churchyard. WC. Wheelchair access with assistance. Disabled WC. Telephone (01224) 643494.

Aberdeen's original parish church. Twelfth-century transept, refurbished in 1990, 15th-century vaulted lower church (variously used as a chantry chapel, witches' prison, soup kitchen, place of worship for Gaelic and Russian Orthodox services and presently as a Third World centre), 18th-century West Kirk, retaining its characteristic reformed layout, 19th-century East Kirk, medieval effigies, medieval and 17th-century carved woodwork, 17th-century needlework, 48-bell carillon, 20th-century Scottish stained glass.

ABERDEEN, MARISCHAL MUSEUM   1114   6 T19

Marischal College, Broad Street, Aberdeen. In city centre, next to Town House.
Nearest railway station Aberdeen, then ten minute walk. Local buses stop
outside. Open all year, Mon-Fri 1000–1700, Sun 1400–1700. Free. Explanatory
displays. WC. Disabled WC. Telephone (01224) 274301. www.abdn.ac.uk/diss/historic/
museum

Lying inside a spectacular granite building, Marischal Museum displays the
collections of graduates and friends of Aberdeen University over 500 years.
Exhibitions include the Encyclopedia of the North East, containing objects from
all periods and parts of the region, exploring its character; and Collecting the
World, which includes objects from Africa, Australia, America, India and the
Pacific, ancient Egyptian mummies and much more.

ABERDEEN, MARITIME MUSEUM   1115   6 T19

Shiprow, Aberdeen. City centre, off Union Street. 15 minute walk from Aberdeen
railway and bus stations. Open all year, Mon-Sat 1000–1700, Sun 1200–1500. Free.
Explanatory displays. Gift shop. Restaurant. WC. Induction loop system in
auditorium. Wheelchair access. Disabled WC. Telephone (01224) 337700.

Aberdeen Maritime Museum tells the story of the city's long and fascinating
relationship with the sea through a unique collection of ship models, paintings,
artefacts, computer interaction and set-piece exhibitions. A major display about
the offshore oil industry features a 28 foot (8.5m) high model of the Murchison
oil platform. Situated on four floors and incorporating the 16th-century Provost
Ross's House, the complex is linked by a modern glass structure to Trinity
Church.

ABERDEEN, PROVOST SKENE'S HOUSE   1116   6 T19

Guestrow, Aberdeen. City centre, off Broad Street. 15 minute walk from Aberdeen
railway and bus stations. Open all year, Mon–Sat 1000–1700, Sun 1300–1600. Free.
Explanatory displays. Coffee shop serving snacks and light meals. WC. Telephone
(01224) 641086.

One of Aberdeen's few remaining examples of early burgh architecture. Splendid
room settings including a suite of Georgian rooms, an Edwardian nursery,
magnificent 17th-century ceilings and wood panelling. The painted gallery
houses the most important cycle of religious painting in north east Scotland.
Archaeological and social history displays. Costume gallery with changing
displays of fashion and dress.

ABERDEEN, ST ANDREW'S CATHEDRAL   1117   6 T19

28 King Street, Aberdeen. At the junction of Union Street and King Street. Railway
and bus stations close by. Open May–Sep, Tue–Fri 1100–1600. Free. Explanatory
displays. Gift shop. Tearoom Fri am only. WC. Induction loop, large print
information. Wheelchair access. Disabled WC. Car parking. Telephone (01224)
640290. www.cathedral.aberdeen.anglican.org

Birthplace of the Anglican Communion overseas. The first Anglican Bishop
outside of the UK, Bishop Samuel Seabury of Connecticut, was consecrated in
Aberdeen in 1784. He sought consecration in England but was refused. Three
Scottish Bishops agreed to act as consecrators to form a link with the American
Episcopal Church, strongly maintained to this day.

ABERDEEN, ST MACHAR'S CATHEDRAL TRANSEPTS   1118   6 S19

HS. In Old Aberdeen. Nearest railway station Aberdeen, bus from city centre. Access at all reasonable times. Free. Telephone (01667) 460232. www.historic-scotland.gov.uk

The nave and towers of the cathedral remain in use as a church, and the ruined transepts are in care. The fine tomb of Bishop Dunbar is in the south transept.

ABERDEEN, SATROSPHERE   1119   6 T19

The Tram Sheds, Constitution Street, Aberdeen. In Aberdeen, 0.5 miles (1km) from the railway and bus stations. Open daily (except Christmas and New Year) Mon–Sat 1000–1700, Sun 1130–1700. Charge ££. Group concessions. Explanatory displays. Gift shop. Restaurant. Baby changing facilities. WC. Wheelchair access. Disabled WC. Car parking. Telephone (01224) 640340. www.satrosphere.net

An interactive science centre with more than 70 exciting exhibits covering all aspects of science and technology. Science gifts, kits and books on sale.

ABERDEEN, DAVID WELCH WINTER GARDENS AND RESTAURANT   1120   6 T19

Duthie Park, Polmuir road, Aberdeen. By bus from city centre. Open daily, Apr 0930–1730; May–Aug 0930–1930; Nov–Mar, 0930–1630. Free. Guided tours (charge £). Explanatory displays. Gift shop. Restaurant. WC. Wheelchair access. Disabled WC. Car and coach parking. Telephone (01224) 585310. www.aberdeencity.gov.uk

One of Britain's most popular attractions. Two acres (1ha) of covered gardens displaying plants from around the world. Features entrance hall and Bromeliad house, cacti and succulent hall, Victorian corridor and outside gardens, floral hall, corridor of perfumes and fern house.

ABERDEENSHIRE FARMING MUSEUM   1121   6 T18

Aden Country Park, Mintlaw, Peterhead. 10 miles (16km) west of Peterhead on A950. Bus from Aberdeen to Mintlaw. Open May–Sep, daily 1100–1630; Apr and Oct, Sat–Sun and school holidays 1200–1630. Free. Guided tours. Explanatory displays. Gift shop. Tearoom and picnic area. WC. Limited wheelchair access. Disabled WC. Car and coach parking. Telephone (01771) 622807. www.aberdeenshire.gov.uk/heritage

Visitors can relive the story of north east Scotland's famous farming past. Unique semi-circular home farm steading where visitors can explore the *Aden Estate Story* and the *Weel Vrocht Grun* exhibitions, and visit Hareshowe, a working farm set in the 1950s. Features award-winning displays and audio-visual show, guided tours and costumed guides. Temporary exhibitions. See also 1122 Aden Country Park.

ADEN COUNTRY PARK   1122   6 T18

Mintlaw, Aberdeenshire. 10 miles (16km) east of Peterhead on A92. Bus to Mintlaw, 1.5 mile (2.5 km) walk to Park. Open daily Apr–Oct, 0700–2200; Nov–Mar 0700–1900. Free. Gift shop. Restaurant, picnic and barbecue area. WC. Sensory garden. Limited wheelchair access. Disabled WC. Car and coach parking. Telephone Ranger Service (01771) 622857; Heritage Service (01771) 622906; for picnics and barbecues (07770) 314634.

A 230 acre (93 ha) country park containing Wildlife Discovery Centre (open for groups only on request), woodland walks, nature trails and tree trail, orienteering course, sensory garden, adventure play area, lake and caravan park. Ranger service with special events run throughout the year. Aden is also the home of the award-winning Aberdeenshire Farming Museum (see 1121).

ALFORD HERITAGE CENTRE   1123   6 R19

Mart Road, Alford, Aberdeenshire. 25 miles (40km) west of Aberdeen on A944
Highland Tourist Route. Local bus from Aberdeen. Open Apr–Oct, Mon–Sat
1000–1700, Sun 1300–1700. Charge £. Group concessions. Guided tours for parties
by arrangement. Explanatory displays. Gallery and shop featuring work by local
crafts people. WC. Wheelchair access. Disabled WC. Car and coach parking.
Telephone (019755) 62906.

The centre is located in the old cattle mart, a unique building preserved in its
original state, and holds a huge collection of items (from tractors to teaspoons)
illustrating a century of rural life. There is a room dedicated to local poet
Charles Murray. Special events programme and an opportunity to hear the local
dialect (the Doric).

ALFORD VALLEY RAILWAY   1124   6 R19

Alford Station, Station Yard, Alford, Aberdeenshire. At Alford Station. Alford is 25
miles (40km) west of Aberdeen on the A944 Highland Tourist Route. Nearest railway
station Insch 11 miles (18km), bus service to Alford from Aberdeen (Stagecoach).
Open Apr, May and Sep, Sat and Sun; Jun, Jul and Aug daily. 30 minute service from
1300, last train at 1630. Charge £. Explanatory displays. Gift shop. Picnic area. Play
area. WC. Wheelchair access. Disabled WC. Car and coach parking. Telephone
(019755) 62811.

Narrow gauge railway running a 30 minute trip from the restored Alford Station
to Haughton Caravan Park, which is approximately 1 mile (1.5 km) away. Train
collection includes a former Aberdeen suburban tram, three diesel Simplex
locomotives and a diesel hydraulic locomotive.

ARBUTHNOT MUSEUM   1125   6 T18

St Peter Street, Peterhead. In Peterhead town centre. Bus from Aberdeen. Car and
coach parking nearby. Open Mon–Tue, Thu–Sat 1100–1300 and 1400–1630; Wed
1100–1300. Closed public holidays. Free. Guided tours. Explanatory displays. Gift
shop. Telephone (01771) 622807. www.aberdeenshire.gov.uk/heritage

One of Aberdeenshire's oldest museums, once privately owned. Features
Peterhead's maritime history, Inuit art, Arctic whaling and animals, and one of
the largest coin collections in northern Scotland. Temporary exhibitions and
changing programme.

ARCHAEOLINK PREHISTORY PARK   1126   6 R19

Berryhill, Oyne village, Insch, Aberdeenshire. At Oyne village, 1 mile (1.5km) off the A96
Aberdeen to Inverness road, 25 miles (40km) west of Aberdeen. Railway station Insch
(2.5 miles/4km), bus service to Insch from Aberdeen. Open Apr–Oct, daily 1000–1700.
Charge ££. Group concessions. Guided tours. Explanatory displays. Gift shop.
Restaurant. Children's play area. WC. Induction loop. Wheelchair access. Disabled WC.
Car and coach parking. Telephone (01464) 851500. www.archaeolink.co.uk

Discover Scotland's prehistoric past – from Stone Age to Iron Age. Indoor and
outdoor displays make it a unique living history experience for all ages.

BALLINDALLOCH CASTLE AND GOLF COURSE   1127   6 P18

Near Aberlour, Banffshire. On the A95, 13 miles (20km) north east of Grantown-on-
Spey. Open Easter–Sep, Sun–Fri 1000–1700. Charge for castle and grounds £££
(children under 6 free), grounds only £. Group concessions. Guided tours and self-

guided tours. Explanatory displays in French, German, Italian and Spanish. Gift shop. Tearoom and picnic area. Audio-visual display, pitch and putt, dog-walking area, golf course. WC. Limited wheelchair access. Disabled WC. Car and coach parking. Telephone (01807) 500206. www.ballindallochcastle.co.uk

One of the few privately owned castles to be lived in continuously by its original family, the Macpherson-Grants, since 1546. Ballindalloch exemplifies the transition from the stark tower house, necessary for survival in 16th-century Scotland, to the elegant and comfortable country house so beloved of Victorians in the Highlands. Ballindalloch is also the home of the famous Aberdeen Angus herd of cattle founded by Sir George Macpherson-Grant in 1860, and now the oldest herd in continuous existence.

BALMORAL CASTLE   1128   6 Q20

Balmoral, Ballater, Aberdeenshire. 8 miles (13km) west of Ballater off A93. Nearest railway station Aberdeen, bus service from Aberdeen to Ballater (some buses to Braemar) stop at Crathie for Balmoral. Open daily Apr–Jul, 1000–1700. Last admission 1630. Charge £££. Explanatory displays. Gift shop. Cafeteria. WC. Wheelchairs and battricars available free of charge from estates office. Wheelchair access. Disabled WC. Car and coach parking. Telephone (013397) 42354. www.balmoralcastle.com

The Highland holiday home of the Royal Family since 1852. Queen Victoria visited the earlier castle in 1848 and Prince Albert bought the estate in 1852. The new castle was designed by Prince Albert and William Smith of Aberdeen and was completed in 1855. Exhibition of paintings and works of art in the castle ballroom. Wildlife. Grounds and garden with country walks.

BALVENIE CASTLE   1129   6 Q18

HS. Dufftown, Banffshire. At Dufftown on the A941, 16 miles (25.5km) south south-east of Elgin. Nearest railway stations Elgin or Keith, then bus to Dufftown. Open Apr–Sep, daily 0930–1830. Charge £. Group concessions. Gift shop. Picnic area. WC. Car parking. Telephone (01340) 820121. www.historic-scotland.gov.uk

Picturesque ruins of a 13th-century moated stronghold originally owned by the Comyns. Additions in the 15th and 16th centuries. Visited by Edward I in 1304 and Mary, Queen of Scots in 1562. Occupied by Cumberland in 1746.

BANCHORY MUSEUM   1130   6 S20

Bridge Street, Banchory. In the centre of Banchory. Car and coach parking nearby. Bus service from Aberdeen. Open May–Sep, Mon–Sat 1100–1300 and 1400–1630; Jul–Aug also Sun 1400–1630; Apr and Oct telephone for details. Free. Guided tours. Explanatory displays. Gift shop. Wheelchair access. Telephone (01771) 622807. www.aberdeenshire.gov.uk/heritage

Features the life of Banchory-born musician and composer J. Scott Skinner, the 'Strathspey King', royal commemorative china, 19th-century tartans, Deeside natural history.

BANCHORY WOOLLEN MILL   1131   6 S20

North Deeside Road, Banchory. Just before village of Banchory, on A93. Bus service from Aberdeen. Open all year, Mon–Sat 0930–1730, Sun 1200–1600. Free. No refreshments at mill but Banchory has several excellent restaurants. WC. Wheelchair access. Car and coach parking. Telephone (01330) 823231. www.ewm.co.uk

The Mill Shop has a superb selection of gifts, woollens and outdoor clothing.

BANFF MUSEUM   1132   6 R17

High Street, Banff. In the centre of Banff. Car and coach parking nearby. Bus service from Aberdeen. Open Jun–Sep, Mon–Sat 1400–1630. Free. Guided tours. Explanatory displays. Gift shop. Limited wheelchair access. Telephone (01771) 622807. www.aberdeenshire.gov.uk/heritage

One of Scotland's oldest museums, founded in 1828. Features an electrotype copy of the Deskford Carnyx, a unique 2000-year-old Iron Age war trumpet, award-winning natural history display, local geology, nationally-important collections of Banff silver, arms and armour.

BAXTERS HIGHLAND VILLAGE   1133   6 Q17

Fochabers, Moray, Speyside. 1 mile (1.5km) west of Fochabers on the A96. Nearest railway stations Keith and Elgin. Local bus service. Open daily Jan–Mar, 1000–1700; Apr–Dec, 0900–1730. Free. Explanatory displays and audio-visual presentation, cooking demonstrations and tastings. Gift shop. Restaurant. Children's play area. WC. Wheelchair access (visitor centre only). Disabled WC. Car and coach parking. Telephone (01343) 820393. www.baxters.com/village

The Baxter family has been producing fine foods in the heart of Speyside since 1868. Baxters Highland Village allows the visitor to take a walk through history to see how the company has developed into the success it is today. Visitors can also browse through the range of shops and enjoy refreshment in the Spey Restaurant.

BELWADE FARM   1134   6 R20

Aboyne, Aberdeenshire. Between Kincardine O'Neil and Aboyne. Follow brown tourist signs on A93. Open all year, Wed, Sat, Sun and Bank Holidays 1100–1400. Free. Guided tours. Explanatory displays. Gift shop. Picnic area. WC. Limited wheelchair access. Car and coach parking. Telephone (01339) 887176. www.ilph.org

A recovery and rehabilitation centre for rescued horses and ponies, set in stunning Deeside. Meet the horses during a guided tour of the stables and close paddocks. For the more adventurous, there are longer walks through woodland and over the hills. Bring a picnic and enjoy the views.

BEN AIGAN CYCLE TRAILS   1135   6 Q18

FE. Off A95, 1.5 miles (2km) south of Mulben to eastern end (car park); or from north of Craigellachie, follow the Speyside Way via Arndilly to western end (no car park). Open all year except when timber harvesting – contact District Office. Free. Explanatory displays at car park. Leaflet available. Car parking. Telephone (01343) 820223. www.forestry.gov.uk

Two forest mountain bike trails giving excellent views over the winding River Spey. Colour-coded routes: the red trail of 4.5 miles (7km) follows part of the Speyside Way, the blue trail of 6 miles (10km) covers demanding terrain.

BENNACHIE CENTRE   1136   6 S19

FE. Esson's Car Park, Chapel of Garioch, Inverurie. On a minor road, approx 2 miles (3km) south of Chapel of Garioch off A96. Nearest bus and railway stations Inverurie. Open Apr–Sep, Tue–Sun 1030–1700; Oct–Mar, Tue–Sun 0930–1600 (closed every Mon except public holidays). Free. Explanatory displays and leaflets. Gift shop. Snacks available. Picnic area. WC. Wheelchair access. Disabled WC. Car and coach parking. Telephone (01467) 681470. www.forestry.gov.uk

The centre describes the local social and natural history through visual displays, CD-Rom presentations and video. A wide range of activities take place throughout the year, including guided walks, bat and bird box building, fungal forays and classes for beginners on painting, bodging, drystone dyke building and other countryside skills. Plenty of walks up and around the Bennachie Hills.

BENROMACH DISTILLERY   1137 6 P17

Benromach Distillery, Invererne Road, Forres, Moray. Off A96, 0.33 mile (0.5km) on north side of Forres bypass. Nearest railway station Forres. Open May–Sep, Mon–Sat 0930–1700, also Jun–Aug, Sun 1200–1600; Oct–Apr, Mon–Fri 1000–1600. Closed Christmas and Jan. Charge £. Children free. Group concessions. Guided tours. Last tour 1 hour before closing. Leaflets available in French, German, Spanish, Italian and Japanese. Explanatory displays. Gift shop. Picnic area. Children's toys. WC. Limited wheelchair access. Disabled WC. Car and coach parking. Telephone (01309) 675968. www.benromach.com

Benromach Distillery and Malt Whisky Centre is Moray's smallest distillery, reopened by Prince Charles in 1998. The attractive wood panelled malt whisky centre, sited in the former drier house, describes 100 years of history and tradition in whisky making.

BIBLICAL GARDEN   1138 6 P17

King Street, Elgin, Moray. At Cooper Park in Elgin by the cathedral. Bus and railway station in Elgin. Open daily, May–Sep 1000–1930. Free. Explanatory displays. Wheelchair access. Car and coach parking.

A 3 acre (1.2ha) garden created using the Bible as a reference. A desert area depicts Mount Sinai and the cave of resurrection and there is an area of marsh contained with the garden. An impressive central walkway is laid in the shape of a Celtic cross. Planted with every species of plant mentioned in the Bible. Also life-size statues depicting various parables.

THE BLAIRS MUSEUM   1139 6 S20

South Deeside Road, Aberdeenshire. 5 miles (8km) south west of Aberdeen on B9077. Open Apr–Sep, Sat 1000–1700 and Sun 1200–1700. Other times by appointment. Charge £. Group concessions. Guided tours by prior arrangement. Limited wheelchair access. Car parking. Telephone (01224) 863767. www.blairsmuseum.com

Roman Catholic school and seminary founded in 1829. The school closed in 1986 but is still home to an internationally renowned collection of fine and decorative art, embroidered vestments and church plate. Also objects and paintings relating to the Stewarts and Mary, Queen of Scots and the newly restored St Mary's Chapel.

BRAEMAR HIGHLAND HERITAGE CENTRE   1140 6 P20

Mar Road, Braemar, Ballater. In centre of Braemar. Bus service from Aberdeen. Open Apr–Sep, daily 0900–1730; and Oct–Apr, dailt 0900–1700. Free. Explanatory displays (with French and German translations). Gift shop. WC. Wheelchair access. Disabled WC. Car and coach parking. Telephone (013397) 41944.

A 15 minute audio-visual presentation about Braemar: its history, heritage and royal connections. There are also displays of Highland dress and the famous Braemar Highland Gathering, together with storyboards to give a more in-depth view.

BRANDER MUSEUM   1141   6 R18

The Square, Huntly. In centre of Huntly. Nearest railway station and bus services
Huntly. Car and coach parking nearby. Open all year (closed public holidays),
Tue–Sat 1400–1630. Free. Explanatory displays. Gift shop. Wheelchair access with
assistance. Telephone (01771) 622807. www.aberdeenshire.gov.uk/heritage

A display about Huntly-born author George Macdonald. Also extensive
collection of communion tokens, finds from archaeological excavations at
Huntly Castle, and arms and armour from 19th-century Sudan.

BRANDSBUTT SYMBOL STONE   1142   6 S19

HS. About 1 mile (2km) north west of Inverurie, Aberdeenshire. Bus from Aberdeen
to Inverurie then 1 mile (2km) walk. Access at all reasonable times. Free. Telephone
(01667) 460232. www.historic-scotland.gov.uk

An early Pictish symbol stone with an ogham inscription.

BURGHEAD WELL   1143   6 P17

HS. In King Street, Burghead, Moray. Nearest railway station Elgin, bus from Elgin
to Burghead. Access at all reasonable times. Free. Telephone (01667) 460232.
www.historic-scotland.gov.uk

A rock-cut well, identified by some as an early Christian baptistry associated
with the local cult of St Ethan.

BURN O VAT   1144   6 Q20

On A93 and A97, immediately to the north and west of Dinnet village. Nature reserve
open at all times. Visitor centre. Free. Picnic area. WC . Car parking.

Situated within the Muir of Dinnet National Nature Reserve. Extensive
birchwood, wetlands and heather moor surrounding two lochs. To the west is
the Vat, a spectacular geological feature. Many fine circular walks. The visitor
centre has displays on natural history, geology and archaeology.

BUTTERWORTH GALLERY   1145   6 R20

Ballogie Shop, Ballogie, Aboyne, Aberdeenshire. 4 miles (6km) south east of Aboyne.
Nearest railway station at Aberdeen. Bus service to Aboyne. Open all year, May–Oct,
Thu–Sun 1100–1600; Nov–Apr, Sat–Sun 1100–1600. Free. Guided tours by
arrangement in advance. Explanatory displays. Gift shop. Coffee and soft drinks
available. WC. Limited wheelchair access. Car and coach parking. Telephone (013398)
86104. www.butterworthpaintings.co.uk

A permanent exhibition of publications and prints by Royal Deeside's artist,
Howard Butterworth. The range includes originals, prints, cards and jigsaws.
Howard Butterworth has painted full time for over 30 years and has a well-
established following.

CAMBUS O' MAY FOREST   1146   6 Q20

FE. 2.5 miles (4km) east of Ballater on A93. Bus stops on main road, 655 feet (200m)
downhill from forest entrance. Access at all times unless timber harvesting in
progress. Free. Charge for ranger guided walks/events. Explanatory displays.
Information board at viewpoint. Leaflet available. Picnic area. Orienteering course, 4
waymarked walks, wheelchair accessible paths. Car parking. www.forestry.gov.uk

A wonderful forest with four waymarked walks (some with surfaced paths, some
leading through rough and natural terrain), a permanent orienteering course,

and a dog walkers car park and dog loop. One of the car parks has wheelchair accessible paths leading to a viewpoint and to two forest lochans. Novel interpretive posts note points of interest, and map boards, a leaflet and waymarking keep people on the right route. No cycling or horseriding permitted.

CARDHU DISTILLERY VISITOR CENTRE   1147   6 P18

Knockando, Aberlour. From Elgin take the A941 south to Rothes, continue for 3 miles (5km) then travel west on the B9102 for approximately 7 miles (11km). From Grantown-on-Spey take the B9102 north east for approximately 17 miles (27km). Tours Jan–Easter, Mon–Fri 1100, 1300, 1400; Oct–Dec, Mon–Fri 1100, 1300, 1400. Open Easter–Jun, Mon–Fri 1000–1700; Jul–Sep, Mon–Sat 1000–1700, Sun 1200–1600 (last tour one hour before closing). Charge ££. Charge £ (includes voucher). Guided tours. Explanatory displays. Gift shop. Picnic area. WC. Limited wheelchair access. Disabled WC. Car parking. Telephone (01340) 872555.

The origins of Cardhu go back to the heyday of illicit distilling, when farmers made use of their own barley and local water. Licensed since 1824, the Cumming family expanded and improved the distillery over many years. Now a major element in the Johnnie Walker brand. Visitor centre, shop with gifts and souvenirs.

CARNEGIE MUSEUM   1148   6 S19

Town Hall, The Square, Inverurie. In Inverurie. Nearest railway and bus service Inverurie. Car and coach parking nearby. Open all year (closed public holidays), Mon and Wed–Fri 1400–1630, Sat 1000–1300 and 1400–1600. Free. Explanatory displays. Gift shop. Telephone (01771) 622807. www.aberdeenshire.gov.uk/heritage

Local archaeology including Beaker folk and Pictish carved stones and transportation.

CASTLE FRASER   1149   6 S19

NTS. Sauchen, Inverurie. Off A944, 16 miles (25.5km) west of Aberdeen. Bus from Aberdeen. Open Easter–Jun and Sep, daily (except Fri and Mon) 1200–1700; Jul–Aug, daily 1100–1700. Charge £££. Group concessions. Guided tours by arrangement. Explanatory displays (information sheets in six languages). Gift shop. Tearoom and picnic area. Adventure playground. WC. Limited wheelchair access. Disabled WC. Car and coach parking. Telephone (01330) 833463. www.nts.org.uk

Magnificent castle completed in 1636 and one of the most sophisticated Scottish buildings of the period, with a particularly fine Great Hall. Notable paintings and furnishings. Peaceful walled garden and interesting woodland walks.

CORGARFF CASTLE   1150   6 P19

HS. Corgarff, Strathdon, Aberdeenshire. Off A939, 15 miles (24km) north west of Ballater, Aberdeenshire. Bus from Aberdeen to Strathdon only, then 9 mile (14.5km) walk. Open Apr–Sep, daily 0930–1830; Oct–Mar, Sat–Sun 0930–1630. Charge £. Group concessions. Explanatory displays. Gift shop. Limited wheelchair access. Car and coach parking. Telephone (01975) 651460. www.historic-scotland.gov.uk

A 16th-century tower house converted into a barracks for government troops in 1748 by being enclosed within a star-shaped loopholed wall. The castle was burned in 1571 by Edom o' Gordon, killing the family and household of Alexander Forbes, the owner.

COVESEA GOLF COURSE   1151   6 P17

Duffus, Elgin. On the B9040, 2 miles (3km) west of Lossiemouth. Open Mar–Oct or Nov, daily 0900–2000; telephone to confirm times. Charge £££. Cold drinks available. WC. Limited wheelchair access. Disabled WC. Car and coach parking. Telephone (01343) 814124.

A links course, 12-hole 3-par short course, set on the spectacular Moray Firth coast. Equipment for hire.

CRAIGELLACHIE BRIDGE   1152   6 Q18

Near A941, just north of Craigellachie, 12 miles (19km) south south-east of Elgin. Access at all times. Car parking.

One of Thomas Telford's most beautiful bridges. Opened in 1814, it carried the main road until 1973 when a new bridge was built alongside. It has a 152 feet (46m) main span of iron, cast in Wales, and two ornamental stone towers at each end.

CRAIGIEVAR CASTLE   1153   6 R19

NTS. Alford, Aberdeenshire. On A980, 26 miles (42km) west of Aberdeen. Open Easter–Jun, Fri–Tue 1200–1730; Jul–Aug, daily 1200–1730. Charge £££. Explanatory displays. Information sheets in four languages. Gift shop. Picnic area. Woodland walk. Car parking. Telephone (013398) 83635. www.nts.org.uk

A 'fairytale' castle, a masterpiece of Scottish Baronial architecture, which seems to grow out of the hillside. Much of the building is still as it was when completed in 1626. Fine collection of family portraits and 17th- and 18th-century furniture.

CRAIGSTON CASTLE   1154   6 S17

Turriff, Aberdeenshire. 5 miles (8km) from Turriff on the B9105. Nearest bus station Turriff. Open end Jul–early Sep, telephone to confirm exact dates. Wed–Sun 1000–1600 (last tour 1500). Other times by appointment. Charge ££. Guided tours. Explanatory displays. Picnic area. Garden. WC. Car and coach parking. Telephone (01888) 551228.

Craigston Castle was built between 1604 and 1607 and is still owned by the original family. Few changes have been made to the castle's exterior in 400 years. The main exterior feature is a sculpted balcony unique in Scottish architecture. It depicts a piper, two grinning knights, and David and Goliath. The interior decoration dates mainly from the early 19th century. Remarkable carved wood panels. Library. Beautiful mixed woodland.

CRATHES CASTLE   1155   6 S20

NTS. Banchory. On A93, 3 miles (5km) east of Banchory and 15 miles (24km) west of Aberdeen. Bus from Aberdeen. Open Apr–Sep, daily 1030–1730; Oct 1030–1630. Garden and grounds open all year, daily 0900–sunset. Charge £££. Group concessions. Guided tours by arrangement. Explanatory displays. Information sheets in 12 languages. Gift shop. Restaurant and picnic area. Plant sales, garden and adventure playground. WC. Leaflet lists facilities available to disabled visitors. Audio guide for blind visitors. Limited wheelchair access (wheelchairs available). Disabled WC. Car and coach parking. Telephone (01330) 844525. www.nts.org.uk

Sixteenth-century castle built on lands granted to the Burnett family in 1323 by King Robert the Bruce. Remarkable original painted ceilings and a collection of Scottish furniture; some of it contemporary with the castle building.

Famous walled garden contains eight separate gardens designed for colour combinations.

CULBIN FOREST 1156   2 N17

FE. Moray. A96 from Nairn to Brodie, then unclassified road to Cloddymoss; or A96 from Forres to Findhorn bridge then Kintessack road for 3 miles (5km) to Wellhill car park. Nearest bus at Nairn, 1 mile (2km) to Kingsteps (western end of forest); or Brodie on A96, 1.5 miles (3km) to Cloddymoss (centre of forest); nearest railway stations Nairn and Forres. Open daily all year. Free. Guided tours by appointment through Moray Forest District Office (01343) 820223. Explanatory displays. Leaflet available. Picnic areas. WC at Cloddy Moss (closed in winter). Guided walks and events. Limited wheelchair access (Easy blue trail from Wellhill car park). Car parking. Telephone (01343) 820223. www.forestry.gov.uk

An extensive pine forest, from Nairn to Findhorn Bay. Planted from the 1920s to stabilise the drifting sands. Unique natural history. Botanical trail. Five waymarked low level walks, from 1 to 3.5 miles (1.5 to 5.5km) from Wellhill car park. One walk of 3 miles (5km) and cycle trails of 9 and 11 miles (14.5 and 17.5km) from Nairn east beach (western forest). Informal walks throughout the forest. Ranger service.

CULLERLIE FARM PARK 1157   6 S19

Cullerlie, Echt, Aberdeenshire. On the B9125, 12 miles (19km) west of Aberdeen and 5.5 miles (9km) from Banchory. Nearest railway station Aberdeen. Local bus service. Open daily, Apr–May and Sep–Oct 1030–1700; Jun–Aug 1000–1730. Other times by appointment. Charge £. Group concessions. Explanatory displays. Gift shop. Tearoom with home baking. Baby changing facilities. WC. Wheelchair access. Disabled WC. Car and coach parking. Telephone (01330) 860549.

A family-run park with one of the largest privately owned collections of farming memorabilia. Lots of farm animals, including Clydesdale horses.

CULSH EARTH HOUSE 1158   6 R19

HS. On B919 at Culsh, 1 mile (2km) east of Tarland, Aberdeenshire. Nearest railway station Aberdeen, bus from Aberdeen. Access by Culsh Farmhouse at all reasonable times. Free. Telephone (01667) 460232. www.historic-scotland.gov.uk

A well-preserved underground passage with roofing slabs intact over the large chamber and entrance. About 2000 years old.

DALLAS DHU HISTORIC DISTILLERY 1159   6 P17

HS. Mannachie Road, Forres, Morayshire. Off the A940, 1 miles (1.5km) south of Forres, Moray. Nearest railway station Forres, bus from Inverness or Aberdeen, then 2 mile (3km) walk. Open Apr–Sep, daily 0930–1830; Oct–Mar, Mon–Sun 0930–1630, (closed Thu and Fri). Charge ££. Explanatory displays. Visitor centre. Audio-visual presentation in several languages. Gift shop. Picnic area. WC. Limited wheelchair access. Disabled WC. Car and coach parking. Telephone (01309) 676548. www.historic-scotland.gov.uk

A picturesque small distillery built in 1898 to supply malt whisky for Wright and Greig's Roderick Dhu blend. Video on the history of Scotch whisky. Visitors may sample whisky.

DEE VALLEY CONFECTIONERS 1160   6 Q20

Station Square, Ballater, Aberdeenshire. 44 miles (70km) west of Aberdeen. Bus service from Aberdeen. Shop open Apr–Oct, Mon–Thu 0900–2000; factory open to visitors Apr–Oct, Mon–Thu 0900–1200 and 1400–1630. Free. Gift shop. Wheelchair access. Car and coach parking. Telephone (01339) 755499.

The visitor can observe sweets being made from a viewing area. Watch the process of colours and flavours being added to the candy, followed by the stretch and pull methods for stripes and lettering. The old-fashioned machines form the sweets and cool the candy. Free samples.

DEER ABBEY 1161   6 T18

HS. Off A950 at Old Deer, 10 miles (16km) west of Peterhead, Aberdeenshire. Bus to Mintlaw then 1.5 mile (2.5km) walk. Access at all reasonable times. Free. Car parking. Telephone (01667) 460232. www.historic-scotland.gov.uk

Scant remains of a Cistercian monastery founded in 1218.

DELGATIE CASTLE 1162   6 S17

Delgatie, Turriff, Aberdeenshire. Off the A947, on the B9170. 3 miles (5km) north east of Turriff. Nearest railway and bus station Aberdeen. Open Apr–Oct, daily 1000–1700; Nov–Mar, daily 1000–1600 (not Christmas and New Year weeks). Charge ££. Group concessions. Guided tours. Explanatory displays. Gift shop. Tearoom and picnic area. WC. Wheelchair access to ground floor and tearoom. Disabled WC. Car and coach parking. Telephone (01888) 563479 or 562750. www.delgatiecastle.com

An 11th-century tower house, home of the late Captain Hay of Delgatie who restored it over the last 50 years. The castle contains displays of Victorian clothes, late 16th-century painted ceilings and has the widest turnpike stair in Scotland. Mary, Queen of Scots stayed here after the Battle of Corrichie.

DEN WOOD 1163   6 S18

4 miles (6.5km) north east of Inverurie, close to Old Meldrum. Access at all times. Free. Car parking. Telephone (01764) 662554. www.woodland-trust.org.uk

Formerly part of the Meldrum Estate, Den Wood is situated in a rich agricultural landscape. There are a range of woodland habitats and clearings, supporting badgers, roe deer and native plants and insects. Four circular trails, including one to the summit of the wood, offering panoramic views.

DESKFORD CHURCH 1164   6 R17

HS. On B9018 to Keith, 4 miles south of Cullen, Banffshire. Nearest railway station Elgin, bus from Elgin then 0.5 mile (1km) walk. Access at all reasonable times. Free. Telephone (01667) 460232. www.historic-scotland.gov.uk

Ruin of a small, late medieval church with a richly carved sacrament house characteristic of north east Scotland.

DRUM CASTLE AND GARDENS 1165   6 S20

NTS. Drumoak, Banchory, Aberdeenshire. Off A93, 10 miles (16km) west of Aberdeen. By bus from Aberdeen. Open Easter–May, Sep, daily 1230–1730; Jun–Aug, daily 1000–1730. Grounds open all year, daily 0930–sunset. Charge £££. Charge for house and gardens £££, gardens only £. Group concessions. Guided tours by arrangement. Explanatory displays. Information sheets in five languages. Gift shop. Tearoom. Garden and play area. WC. Wheelchair access with assistance (wheelchair available). Disabled WC. Car and coach parking. Telephone (01330) 811204. www.nts.org.uk

The 13th-century tower of Drum is one of the three oldest tower houses in Scotland and was the work of Richard Cementarius, first Provost of Aberdeen and King's Master Mason. Jacobean and Victorian extensions make this a fine mansion house with notable portraits and furniture, much from the 18th century. The grounds contain a 16th-century chapel and a unique garden of historic roses.

DRUMTOCHTY FOREST   1166   6 S21

FE. Drumtochty, Aberdeenshire. Between Auchenblae and the Cairn o'Mount road, B974. Access at all times unless timber harvesting in progress. Free. Charge for ranger guided walks/events. Explanatory displays. Leaflet available. Picnic area. WC (summer only). Ranger guided walks. Disabled WC. Car and coach parking. www.forestry.gov.uk

Two waymarked walks along an old mill lade leading through a beautiful small gorge. A third waymarked walk leads along fairly level ground to a bench, before climbing steps to return through an oak wood. Waymarked cycle trails can be used as a loop to start and return to the car park, or as a link to miles and miles of waymarked cycle trails in adjacent Fetteresso Forest. A peaceful and beautiful forest.

DUFF HOUSE COUNTRY GALLERY   1167   6 R17

Banff, Aberdeenshire. Between Banff and Macduff, 47 miles (75km) north of Aberdeen. Nearest railway station Huntly, bus from Elgin or Aberdeen to Banff, then five minute walk. Open all year, telephone for details. Charge £££. Group concessions. Guided tours by arrangement. Explanatory displays. Gift shop. Tearoom. Children's play area and action playground. WC. Audio guides and induction loops. Wheelchair access. Disabled WC. Car and coach parking. Telephone (01261) 818181. www.duffhouse.com

Constructed between 1735 and 1740 by William Adam for William Duff of Braco, the house has been in turn a ducal residence, a hotel, a sanatorium, a prisoner of war camp, and is now a country house gallery of the National Galleries of Scotland. It is one of the finest examples of Georgian baroque architecture in Britain. It contains a fine collection of paintings, furniture, tapestries and artefacts drawn from the National Galleries, the Erskine of Torrie Institute and several private lenders.

DUFFUS CASTLE   1168   6 P17

HS. Off B9012, 5 miles (8km) north west of Elgin, Moray. Nearest railway station Elgin, bus from Elgin then ten minute walk. Open at all reasonable times. Free. Car parking. Telephone (01667) 460232. www.historic-scotland.gov.uk

Massive ruins of a fine motte and bailey castle surrounded by a moat, still complete and filled with water. A fine 14th-century tower crowns the Norman motte, the original seat of the de Moravia family, the Murrays, now represented by the dukedoms of Atholl and Sutherland.

DUNNOTTAR CASTLE   1169   6 S20

Dunnottar Castle Lodge, Stonehaven. On A92, 2.5 miles (4km) south of Stonehaven. Bus from Stonehaven or Montrose. Open Easter Mon–second week of Oct, Mon–Sat 0900–1800, Sun 1400–1700; third week of Oct–Easter Sun, Fri–Mon 0930–sunset. Charge ££. Children under 5 free. Group concessions. Guidebook. Picnics welcome. WC. Free entry for blind visitors and companion. Car and coach parking. Telephone (01569) 762173.

A spectacular ruin 160 feet (48.5m) above the sea. An impregnable fortress to the Earls Marischals of Scotland. The site for the successful protection of the Scottish crown jewels against the might of Oliver Cromwell's army.

DYCE SYMBOL STONES   1170   6 S19

HS. At Dyce Old Church, 5 miles (8km) north west of Aberdeen. Bus from Aberdeen to Dyce then 1.5 mile (2.5km) walk to Dyce Old Kirk. Access at all reasonable times. Free. Car parking. Telephone (01667) 460232. www.historic-scotland.gov.uk

Two fine examples of Pictish symbol stones in the ruined parish church, one with the older type of incised symbols, and the other with symbols accompanied by a Celtic cross and decoration.

EASTER AQUHORTHIES STONE CIRCLE   1171   6 S19

HS. Approximately 1 mile (2km) west of Inverurie, Aberdeenshire. Nearest railway station Inverurie. Bus from Aberdeen to Inverurie then 2.5 mile (4km) walk. Access at all reasonable times. Free. Car parking. Telephone (01667) 460232. www.historic-scotland.gov.uk

A recumbent stone circle about 4000 years old.

ELGIN CATHEDRAL   1172   6 P17

HS. Elgin, Morayshire. In Elgin on the A96. Nearest railway station Elgin, bus from Aberdeen or Inverness. Open Apr–Sep, daily 0930–1830; Oct–Mar, Mon–Sat 0930–1630, (closed Thu pm and Fri). Charge £. Group concessions. Explanatory displays. Gift shop. Limited wheelchair access. Car and coach parking. Telephone (01343) 547171. www.historic-scotland.gov.uk

The superb ruin of what was perhaps the most beautiful cathedral in Scotland. It was known as the Lantern of the North. Founded in 1224 but burned in 1390 by the Wolf of Badenoch, after which it was modified. It fell into ruin after the Reformation. The octagonal chapter house is the finest in Scotland. A Pictish slab lies in the choir.

ELGIN MUSEUM   1173   6 P17

1 High Street, Elgin, Moray. On the A96, 35.5 miles (57km) east of Inverness. Bus or train from Inverness or Aberdeen. Open Apr–Oct, Mon–Fri 1000–1700, Sat 1100–1600, Sun 1400–1700; in winter by appointment. Charge £. Group concessions. Guided tours occasionally. Explanatory displays. Gift shop. WC. Mini induction loop. Virtual tour access to upper floor. Limited wheelchair access. Disabled WC. Car parking. Telephone (01343) 543675. www.elginmuseum.org.uk

An independent museum interpreting the natural and human heritage of Moray. Internationally known for its fossils and Pictish stones.

FALCONER MUSEUM   1174   6 P17

Tolbooth Street, Forres, Moray. On the A96, 11 miles (17.5km) west of Elgin. Nearest railway station Forres. Bus service from Aberdeen and Inverness. Open Apr–Oct, Mon–Sat 1000–1700; Nov–Mar, Mon–Thu 1100–1230 and 1300–1530. Free. Guided tours. Explanatory displays. Gift shop. Induction loop. Limited wheelchair access. Car and coach parking. Telephone (01309) 673701. www.moray.org/museums

Founded in 1871, Falconer Museum contains a wealth of Moray heritage. From social history and the early history of Moray to the story of the Corries Folk Group.

FARAWAY RIDING AND RECREATION CENTRE   1175   6 R18

Faraway Riding & Recreation Centre, South Baloon, Forgue, Huntly, Aberdeenshire. On B9024 8 miles (12.6km) from Huntly and Turriff. Nearest Train 8m. Nearest bus 8m. Open all year, riding school Tue–Sat 0900–2100, riding centre Tue–Sun

0900–2100, restaurant and shop Tue–Sun 1000–1600. Free. Explanatory displays. Gift shop. Restaurant. WC. Limited wheelchair access. Car and coach parking. Telephone (01466) 730358.

Faraway Riding and Recreation Centre is a superb equestrian centre offering riding lessons, trekking and competitions. Faraway offers quality instructon on well-schooled, quiet, horses and ponies, for complete beginners to advanced riders, in private or group sessions – they cater for your needs. For the equestrian enthusiast there is wonderful countryside to explore on horseback. The centre is STB (4 stars), BHS, ABRS and TRSS approved and includes indoor and outdoor arenas and a x-country course. Sunday is show day, ideal for riders and spectators.

Quad biking is also available.

FASQUE   1176   6 R21

Fettercairn, Laurencekirk. On the B974, 0.5 mile (1km) north of Fettercairn village. Bus from Brechin or Laurencekirk. Open for groups and tour bookings only, all year, by prior arrangement. Charge £££. Guided tours. Explanatory displays. Gift shop. Refreshments can be pre-booked. WC. Limited wheelchair access. Car and coach parking. Telephone (01561) 340569.

A spectacular example of a Victorian 'upstairs-downstairs' stately home bought by Sir John Gladstone in 1829. Home to Prime Minister William Ewart Gladstone for much of his life. An unspoiled old family home where little has changed. Exhibition of William Gladstone memorabilia. Family church nearby welcomes visitors. Beautiful grounds with deer park.

FETTERCAIRN ARCH   1177   6 R21

In Fettercairn. On B9120, 4 miles (6.5km) west of Laurencekirk, Kincardineshire. Access at all times. Free.

Stone arch built to commemorate the visit to Fettercairn by Queen Victoria and the Prince Consort in 1861.

FETTERCAIRN DISTILLERY VISITOR CENTRE   1178   6 R21

Distillery Road, Fettercairn, Laurencekirk. 0.5 mile (1km) west of Fettercairn. Bus from Brechin or Laurencekirk. Open Easter–Sep, Mon–Sat 1000–1630 (last tour 1600), Sun 1200–1630 (last tour 1530). Free. Guided tours. Explanatory displays with information sheets in foreign languages. Gift shop. WC. Limited wheelchair access. Disabled WC. Car and coach parking. Telephone (01561) 340205.

A distillery visitor centre with tours which describe the processes of whisky making. Audio-visual presentation. Includes a free dram of Old Fettercairn (12-year-old malt whisky).

FINDHORN FOUNDATION   1179   6 P17

The Park, Findhorn, Forres. Off the A96, 25 miles (40km) east of Inverness. Nearest railway station and coach stop Forres, local bus from Forres. Visitor Centre open Apr–Oct, Mon–Fri 0900–1230 and 1400–1700, Sat and Sun 1400–1700; Oct–Mar, daily 1400–1700. Charge £. Children free. Group concessions. Guided tours (by arrangement in Dutch, French, German, Italian, Portuguese and Spanish). Explanatory displays. Gift shop. Café. WC. Wheelchair access. Disabled WC. Car and coach parking. Telephone (01309) 690311. www.findhorn.org

The Findhorn Foundation Community was established in 1962 and has grown from a handful of people to more than 400 living in harmony with spirit and with nature. Visitors can see ecological barrel houses, turf roofs, innovative architecture, renewable energy sources such as a wind turbine and solar panels, and a Living Machine natural sewage treatment system.

FINDHORN HERITAGE CENTRE AND ICE HOUSE   1180   6 P17

Northshore, Findhorn, Forres. 5 miles (8km) north east of Forres, from Kinloss take B9011 to Findhorn. Nearest railway station Forres; local bus service from Forres to Findhorn. Open May and Sep, Sat–Sun 1400–1700; Jun–Aug, Daily 1400–1700. Admission by donation. Group concessions. Guided tours. Explanatory displays. Gift shop. Children's activity area. WC. Wheelchair access. Disabled WC. Car and coach parking. Telephone (01309) 690659.

Discover the intriguing history and ecology of Findhorn village in the heritage centre. Explore the unique historical undergound icehouse, an ancient monument.

FORDYCE JOINER'S WORKSHOP VISITOR CENTRE   1181   6 R17

Church Street, Fordyce, Banffshire. In Fordyce 4 miles (6.5km) south west of Portsoy. Car and coach parking nearby. Open summer, Thu–Mon 1000–1800; winter Fri–Mon 1300–1800. Free. Explanatory displays. Garden. WC. Wheelchair access. Disabled WC. Telephone (01771) 622807. www.aberdeenshire.gov.uk/heritage

Visitors can learn about the importance of the rural carpenter/joiner to the local community over the last century and a half, in the days before mass-produced goods. Displays of early tools and machinery, photographs, and an audio-visual presentation. Demonstration by wood craftsman. Victorian style garden. Fordyce is one of Scotland's best conserved small villages and largely traffic-free. It is built around a 16th-century castle and an early church containing splendid canopied tombs.

FORVIE NATIONAL NATURE RESERVE   1182   6 T18

11 miles (17.5km) north of Aberdeen. Take A92 then A975 for 2.5 miles (4km) through village of Newburgh. Aberdeen to Peterhead buses stop by request at Collieston road, then 20 minute walk. Visitor centre open Nov–Mar, Mon–Fri. Reserve open at all times. Free. Displays, video presentation and large print information boards. WC (open Apr–Oct only). Jigsaws and feely boxes. Hide. Wheelchair access with assistance. Car parking. Telephone (01358) 751330. www.nnr-scotland.org.uk

The reserve is a huge area of sand dunes and coastal heath lying next to the Ythan Estuary. Sea cliffs, the estuary and the riverside combine to make this a particularly rich area for a variety of plants and other wildlife (including the largest colony of breeding eider duck in Britain and four species of terns). The estuary is also home to geese and waders in winter. The visitor centre includes information on the history of the reserve. Waymarked walks on well-defined tracks.

FRASERBURGH HERITAGE CENTRE   1183   6 T17

Quarry Road, Fraserburgh, Aberdeenshire. In Fraserburgh town centre, adjacent to the Museum of Scottish Lighthouses (see 1237) which is well signposted. Open Apr–Oct, Mon–Sat 1100–1700, Sun 1300–1700. Charge £. Children under 5 free. Group concessions. Guided tours, group and school visits are welcome during the closed season by prior arrangement. Please telephone (01346) 513802 to book. Explanatory displays. Gift shop. Activities for children. WC. Wheelchair access. Car and coach parking. Telephone (01346) 512888.

The Centre describes the history of Fraserburgh and its community over the past 400 years, from the bustling quayside in the age of sail to the haute couture of dress designer Bill Gibb.

FYVIE CASTLE   1184   6 S18

NTS. Fyvie, Turriff, Aberdeenshire. Off A947, 8 miles (12.5km) south east of Turriff and 25 miles (40km) north west of Aberdeen. Bus from Aberdeen bus station to Fyvie village (1 mile/1.5km). Open Easter–Jun and Sep, Sat–Wed 1200–1700; Jul–Aug, daily 1100–1700. Charge £££. Group concessions. Guided tours by arrangement. Explanatory displays. Information sheets in six languages. Gift shop. Tearoom and picnic area. WC. Braille sheet and guidebook. Limited wheelchair access (wheelchair available). Disabled WC. Car and coach parking. Telephone (01651) 891266. www.nts.org.uk

The castle is probably the grandest example of Scottish baronial architecture. The five towers of Fyvie Castle enshrine five centuries of Scottish history, each named after one of the five families who owned the castle. The oldest part dates from the 13th century. Contemporary decoration, important collection of portraits, arms and armour, and 17th-century tapestries. The grounds and Fyvie Loch were designed around the beginning of the 18th century. Castles of Mar exhibition, restored racquets court, ice house, bird hide, restored patent earth closet, lakeside walks.

MAUD RAILWAY   1185   6 S19

Maud Railway Station, Maud, Peterhead, Aberdeenshire. 14 miles (22km) west of Peterhead on the B9029. Nearest railway station Aberdeen, bus from Aberdeen and Peterhead. Telephone for details of opening times. Free. Explanatory displays. Gift shop. Picnic area. Wheelchair access. Car and coach parking. Telephone (01771) 622807. www.aberdeenshire.gov.uk/heritage

Relive the great days of steam trains at the former Maud Railway Station. Sound effects add to the nostalgia of varied displays of railway memorabilia from GNSR, LNER, and British Rail.

GLEN GRANT DISTILLERY AND GARDEN   1186   6 Q17

Rothes, Aberlour, Banff. At the north end of Rothes, about 10 miles (16km) south of Elgin on the A941. Bus from Elgin. Open Apr–Oct, Mon–Sat 1000–1600, Sun 1230–1600. Free. Under 8s not allowed into production area. Group concessions. Guided tours. Explanatory displays. Gift shop. Garden. WC. Limited wheelchair access. Car and coach parking. Telephone (01340) 832118.

At Glen Grant Distillery fine single malt whisky has been produced since 1840. Founded by brothers John and James Grant, it was inherited by Major James Grant in 1872, whose study has been recreated. Celebrated for his journeys in India and South Africa, he created a romantic woodland garden which has now been restored. Visitors can tour the distillery, sample a dram in the study or heather-thatched pavilion and explore the garden.

GLEN MORAY DISTILLERY   1187   6 P17

Bruceland Road, Elgin. Off the A96 to Inverness, at the western outskirts of Elgin. Nearest railway station Elgin, local bus stops at Grays Hospital then 0.4 mile (0.5km) walk. Open all year except Christmas and New Year, Mon–Fri. Tours at 0930, 1030, 1130, 1330, 1430 and 1530. Charge £. Guided tours. Explanatory displays. Gift shop. WC. Limited wheelchair access. Car parking. Telephone (01343) 542577. www.glenmoray.com

Originally built as a brewery and converted to a distillery in 1987. Constructed in the classic square layout of a Scottish farm, the distillery features an attractive courtyard surrounded by the buildings where the whisky is produced.

GLENBUCHAT CASTLE   1188   6 Q19

HS. Bridge of Buchat. 14 miles (22.5km) west of Alford, Aberdeenshire. Bus from Aberdeen or Alford to Strathdon. Access at all reasonable times. Free. Car parking. Telephone (01677) 460232. www.historic-scotland.gov.uk

A fine example of a Z-plan tower house, built in 1590.

GLENDRONACH DISTILLERY   1189   6 R18

Forgue, Huntly, Aberdeenshire. On junction of B9001 and B9024 between Huntly and Inverurie. Open all year, Mon–Fri, tours at 1000 and 1400. Other times by arrangement. Closed Christmas and New Year. Free. Guided tours. Audio-visual displays. Gift shop. Picnic areas. Woodland. WC. Limited wheelchair access. Disabled WC. Car and coach parking. Telephone (01466) 730202.

A traditional malt whisky distillery established in 1825. The grounds contain The Gordon Wood in commemoration of the Gordon Highlanders. Highland cattle in the grounds.

GLENFARCLAS DISTILLERY   1190   6 P18

Glenfarclas, Ballindalloch, Banffshire. On the A95, 4 miles (6.5km) west of Aberlour. Open all year: Apr–Sep, Mon–Fri 1000–1700; Oct–Mar 1000–1600; Jul–Sep, also Sat 1000–1600. Charge ££. Uber 18's free. Group concessions. Guided tours, last tour leaves approximately 90 mins before closing time. Explanatory displays. Gift shop. WC. Wheelchair access to visitor centre only. Disabled WC. Car and coach parking. Telephone (01807) 500257. www.glenfarclas.co.uk

Established in 1836 and family owned since 1865 we invite you to visit out truly independent distillery and discover our renowned Single Highland Malt Whisky.

GLENFIDDICH DISTILLERY   1191   6 Q18

Dufftown, Banffshire. On the A941, 0.3 mile (0.5km) north of Dufftown. Bus from Keith or Elgin stations. Open all year (except Christmas and New Year), Mon–Fri 0930–1630; Easter–Oct, also Sat 0930–1630 and Sun 1200–1630. Free. Guided tours (in summer in European languages). Connoisseurs tour – an in-depth tour followed by tutored nosing and tasting. Cost £12 per person. Booking strongly recommended. Takes approx 2 to 2.5 hours. Explanatory displays. Gift shop. Picnic area. Bar and coffee shop. WC. Wheelchair access. Disabled WC. Car and coach parking. Telephone (01340) 820373. www.glenfiddich.com

A distillery, opened in 1887, producing the only Highland single malt whisky that is distilled, matured and bottled at its own distillery. Visitors can tour the distillery and bottling hall after an audio-visual introduction. Free sample.

GLEN GARIOCH DISTILLERY   1192   6 S18

Distillery Road, Old Meldrum, Aberdeenshire. 18m (29km) from Aberdeen off the A947. Nearest train station is Inverurie which is 5m (8km), Bus number 305 from Aberdeen bus depot. Open all year, Mon–Fri 0900–1600. Charge ££. Guided tours. Gift shop. All visitors receive a dram of Glen Garioch single malt Scotch whisky. WC. Disabled WC. Car and coach parking. Telephone (01651) 873450. www.glengarioch.com

Established in 1797, Glen Garioch (pronounced 'Geery") is Scotland's most easterly distillery and is situated in the Aberdeenshire village of Old Meldrum.

This small distillery takes its name from the valley of the Garioch, traditionally the finest barley growing area in Scotland. For over 200 years Glen Garioch has been handcrafting a beautiful range of single malt Scottish whiskies.

GLENLIVET DISTILLERY   1193   6 P18

Ballindalloch, Banff. About 10 miles (16km) north of Tomintoul. Nearest railway and bus stations Elgin. Open Apr–Oct, Mon–Sat 1000–1600, Sun 1230–1600. Free. Under 8s not allowed into production area. Group concessions. Guided tours. Visitor centre with audio-visual programme and exhibition. Gift shop. Cafeteria. WC. Wheelchair access with assistance to visitor centre. Disabled WC. Car and coach parking. Telephone (01340) 821720. www.theglenlivet.com

High in the foothills of the Cairngorm Mountains, the Glenlivet Distillery is situated in one of the most scenic and romantic glens in the Scottish Highlands. The Glenlivet has a rich cultural and historical heritage and the visitor centre presents the story of its history and that of the surrounding area. The guided distillery tour also includes the chance to see inside a vast bonded warehouse and to sample a dram.

GLENLIVET ESTATE   1194   6 P19

Glenlivet Estate Office, Main Street, Tomintoul, Ballindalloch. On the A939, 14 miles (22km) south east of Grantown-on-Spey. Estate walks and trails open all year. Information centre open weekdays; Mon–Fri 0900–1700. Free. Guided tours. Explanatory displays. Picnic areas. Waymarked walks and cycle trails. Ranger service. WC. Audio guide to estate. Hearing loop. Wheelchair access with assistance to visitor centre. Disabled WC. Car and coach parking. Telephone (01807) 580283. www.glenlivetestate.co.uk

A large Highland estate in the Cairngorms National Park, encompassing some of the finest landscapes of the Grampian Highlands. A network of over 60 miles of waymarked trails provides access for walkers, mountain bikers and Nordic skiers along forest roads and farm and estate tracks. A variety of ranger services enable visitors to learn about the history, countryside, wildlife and management of the local area. An estate information centre (in Tomintoul) is open (free) throughout the year. Free maps/guides to the walking/cycling trails are available.

GRAMPIAN TRANSPORT MUSEUM   1195   6 R19

Alford, Aberdeenshire. On the A944, 25 miles (40km) west of Aberdeen. Bus from Aberdeen. Open daily, Apr–Sep 1000–1700; Oct 1000–1600. Charge ££. Reduced admission for educational groups. Group concessions. Guided tours for schools by arrangement. Explanatory displays. Gift shop. Tearoom (open Sun Apr–Oct; daily Jul and Aug) and picnic area. Adventure playground. WC. Wheelchair access with assistance. Disabled WC. Car and coach parking. Telephone (019755) 62292. www.gtm.org.uk

Dramatic displays, working exhibits and video presentations trace the history of travel and transport. Many of the exhibits are changed every year. Lots to see and do for all the family.

GRASSIC GIBBON CENTRE   1196   6 S21

Arbuthnott, Laurencekirk, Kincardineshire. On B967, 3 miles (5km) from Inverbervie (A92) or Fordoun (A90). Nearest railway station Montrose or Stonehaven, limited bus service from Stonehaven and school buses. Open Apr–Oct, daily 1000–1630. Groups at other times by arrangement. Charge £. Group concessions. Explanatory displays and video presentation. Gift shop. Restaurant, tearoom and picnic area. Children's play area. WC. Wheelchair access. Disabled WC. Car and coach parking. Telephone (01561) 361668. www.grassicgibbon.com

Visitor centre dedicated to the life and times of the novelist Lewis Grassic Gibbon (James Leslie Mitchell).

GREEN HALL GALLERY   1197   6 Q18

The Green Hall Gallery, 2 Victoria Street, Craigellachie, Aberlour. 12 miles (19km) south of Elgin on A95. Nearest railway station Elgin, bus to Craigellachie. Open all year, Mon–Sat 0900–1300 and 1400–1730, Sun 1400–1730. Free. Gift shop. Wheelchair access. Car parking. Telephone (01340) 871010. www.aboutscotland.com/greenhall

Situated in the old Gospel Hall built circa 1890. Featuring over 100 prints and a selection of handmade cards. Original oils and watercolours also on display, featuring local scenes, animals, birds, flowers and fish. Commissions undertaken.

HADDO HOUSE   1198   6 S18

NTS. Ellon, Aberdeenshire. Off B999, 4 miles (6.5km) north of Pitmedden, 19 miles (30km) north of Aberdeen. By bus from Aberdeen. Open Easter weekend 1100–1630; May–Jun, Sat–Sun 1100–16.30; Jul–Aug, daily 1100–16.30; Sep, Sat–Sun 100–16.30. Charge £££. Group concessions. Guided tours every 45 mins. Explanatory displays. Information sheets in four languages. Gift shop. Restaurant. Garden and country park. WC. Limited wheelchair access (wheelchairs available). Disabled WC. Car and coach parking. Telephone (01651) 851440. www.nts.org.uk

Elegant house designed by William Adam in 1731 for the 2nd Earl of Aberdeen. Much of the interior is Adam Revival, dating from the 1880s. Beautiful library; permanent exhibition of James Giles' paintings. Adjacent country park is run by Aberdeenshire County Council.

HEUGHHEAD FISHINGS   1199   6 R20

Strachan, Banchory, Aberdeenshire. On B9033, 3 miles (5km) south of Banchory . Nearest railway station at Aberdeen (20 miles/32km). Bus service to Banchory. Open Apr–Sep, Mon–Sat during daylight hours. Other times by arrangement with ghillie. Charge £££. Hire of rods, etc extra. Group concessions. Full cooking and washroom facilities available in fishing hut. Wheelchair access with assistance. Car parking. Telephone (07968) 861537. www.heughhead.co.uk

Heughhead Fishings extends to one mile (1.5km) of left bank fishing on the River Feugh. Fishing is separated into an upper and lower beat, consisting of five and four named pools respectively. Species of fish include salmon, sea trout and brown trout. The brown trout and salmon seasons run from May to September, with the months of July, August and September seeing the most salmon. Sea trout can be expected from early June onwards. A purpose-built fishing hut provides full facilities whilst retaining a character in harmony with the surrounding environment.

HIGHLAND GLIDING CLUB   1200   6 P17

Easterton Airfield, Birnie, Elgin. 4 miles (6.5km) south of Elgin. Birnie is signposted off A941. The airfield is signposted from the Birnie Inn. Nearest railway station at Elgin. Local bus service. Weather permitting, flying takes place all year, Sat and Sun; May–Aug also Wed evenings. No flying takes place in rain, poor visibility or strong crosswinds. No charge for admission or parking. Trial lesson from £££. Guided tours, groups of 6–12 persons can arrange exclusive use of facilities by appointment.

No catering facilities but plenty of space for picnics. WC for members and visitors only. WC. Deaf and blind people welcome. Wheelchair access (grass surfaces, no footpaths). Disabled WC. Car and coach parking. Telephone (01343) 860272. www.highglide.co.uk

The Highland Gliding Club welcomes visitors at all times when flying is taking place. Trial lessons with a qualified instructor in modern two-seater gliders are offered subject to availability. During a trial lesson, the student will have the opportunity to take control of the glider, but is not obliged to do so. All visitors must comply with safety instructions given by club members.

HIGHLAND HORSEBACK 1201   6 Q18

East Bodylair, Glass, Huntly. 7 miles (12.6km) from Huntly on A920. From Huntly by railway and bus. 10 day ride £1550, 5 day ride £850. Group concessions. Car parking. Telephone (01466) 700304. www.highlandhorseback.co.uk

5 or 10 day rides across Scotland on horseback.

HUNTLY NORDIC AND OUTDOOR CENTRE 1202   6 R18

Hill of Haugh, Huntly, Aberdeenshire. On the outskirts of Huntly by Huntly Castle. Nearest railway station Huntly, bus from Aberdeen or Inverness. Open winter, Mon–Tue and Thu–Fri 1100–1600, Sat–Sun 0930–1700; telephone for summer hours. Charge £££. Group concessions. Guided tours (booking essential). Explanatory displays. Shop. Refreshments available. WC. Wheelchair access. Disabled WC. Car and coach parking. Telephone (01466) 794428. www.huntly.net/hnoc

Cross-country ski centre with year-round artificial ski track suitable for all the family. From December to April a fully serviced ski centre offers ski hire and lessons for all abilities. Fifteen miles (25km) of machine-prepared ski trails in Clashindarroch Forest, Rhynie. Current conditions available on website or answerphone. Also hire of mountain bikes and rollerskis. Self-guided or accompanied cycle tours, cycling skills courses.

HUNTLY PEREGRINE WILDWATCH 1203   6 Q17

Forestry Commission Scotland, Ordiquhill, Portsoy Road, Huntly, Aberdeenshire. 2.5m (4km) west of Huntly off A96. Nearest train station Huntly. Bus stops within 200m of site. Open early Apr–Aug, daily 0930–1730. Free. Guided tours. Explanatory displays. Gift shop. Picnic area. WC. Wheelchair access. Disabled WC. Car and coach parking. Telephone (01466) 07880780431.

Wardens and information displays provide details about peregrines and other regularly seen wildlife. Live TV pictures in centre. Please note access to top hide is now possible with warden.

THE INSCH CONNECTION MUSEUM 1204   6 R18

Railway Station, Insch, Aberdeenshire. Open Apr–Oct, Wed and Sun 1330–1700. Opening at other times by appointment. Admission free but donations welcome. WC. Wheelchair access (entry from station platform). Telephone (01464) 821354.

A volunteer-run museum encompassing both railway and local Insch history, including a scale model of the railway, photographs, artefacts, archive material and everyday stories of how life used to be in Insch.

JOHNSTON'S CASHMERE VISITOR CENTRE 1205   6 P17

Johnstons of Elgin, Newmill, Elgin, Moray. 35 miles (56km) east of Inverness on A96 near Elgin Cathedral. Rail and bus service to Elgin from Inverness and Aberdeen.

Open all year, Mon–Sat 0900–1730; Jul–Sep, Mon–Fri closes at 1800; Apr–Dec, Sun 1100–1700. Free. Guided tours (information available in French, German, Italian, Spanish and Japanese). Explanatory displays. Audio-visual in European languages and Japanese. Gift shop. Licenced coffee shop. WC. Wheelchair access. Disabled WC. Car and coach parking. Telephone (01343) 554099. www.johnstonsofelgin.com

This five star attraction provides a unique insight into the Scottish Textile industry through the mill's colourful 200 year history. Coffee shop serving the finest traditional Scottish food and drink. Mill shop offering an extensive collection of clothing, accessories and homeware crafted from the world's finest fibres.

KARTSTART, DYCE   1206 6 S19

Unit 7A, Stoneywood Business Centre, Stoneywood Road, Dyce, Aberdeen. Off A947 Aberdeen to Dyce road. Open all year, Mon–Fri 1200–2200, Sat–Sun 1200–2100 (track closed 1730–1830 daily). Charge £££. Explanatory displays. Refreshments available. WC. Wheelchair access. Disabled WC. Telephone (01224) 772727. www.kartstartscotland.co.uk

The opportunity to experience the thrill of real motor sport. All weather facility. Cub Kart (3–8 year olds), Cadet Karts (8 years and upwards), Senior and V-Twin pro-karts. All equipment provided. See also 967 Kartstart, Kirkcaldy.

KEITH AND DUFFTOWN RAILWAY   1207 6 Q18

Dufftown Station, Dufftown, Banffshire. 50 miles (80km) west of Aberdeen on the A96, on B9014 from Keith. Coach parking by arrangement. Keith Scotrail Station is 15 minute walk from Keith Town Station. Bus service from Elgin to Dufftown. Open Easter–end May and Sep, Sat–Sun; Jun–Aug, Fri–Sun. Telephone or visit website for details. Charge ££–£££ for return journey. Group concessions. Guided tours can be arranged, please telephone or visit website for information. Explanatory displays, audio-visual presentation and exhibition. Gift shop. Licenced static restaurant car at Dufftown serving morning coffee, light lunches and afternoon tea. WC. Wheelchair access (but telephone in advance as not all trains have access). Disabled WC. Car parking. Telephone (01340) 821181 (Tue, Thu and Sat–Sun during operating season). www.keith-dufftown.org.uk

Explore an area where the climate and geology are perfect for malt whisky distilling – fifty per cent of Scotland's whisky distillers are here. Sit back, relax and be prepared for enchantment as the train meanders through an every-changing landscape of colour, with tiny rivers coiling their way through a gentle patchwork of hamlets, rich fertile farm land and dark green forest, with an abundance of wildlife. A delightful round trip of 22 miles (35km).

KILDRUMMY CASTLE   1208 6 R19

HS. Kildrummy, by Alford, Aberdeenshire. 10 miles (16km) south west of Alford on the A97. Nearest railway station Huntly or Aberdeen, local bus service. Open Apr–Sep, daily 0930–1830. Charge £. Group concessions. Explanatory displays. Gift shop. WC. Limited wheelchair access. Disabled WC. Car and coach parking. Telephone (01975) 571331. www.historic-scotland.gov.uk

Called the Queen of Highland castles, this was the stronghold of the Earls of Mar and headquarters for organising the 1715 Jacobite rising. Scotland's most complete 13th-century castle.

KILDRUMMY CASTLE GARDENS   1209   6 Q19

Kildrummy, Alford, Aberdeenshire. Off the A97, 10 miles (16km) west of Alford (via A944). Nearest railway station Aberdeen, bus service to Strathdon. Open Apr–Oct, daily 1000–1700. Charge £. Children free. Guided tours. Explanatory displays. Gift shop. Tearoom and picnic areas. Play area and video room. WC. Wheelchair access with assistance. Disabled WC. Car and coach parking. Telephone 019755 71277 or 71203. www.kildrummy-castle-gardens.co.uk

The shrub and alpine garden in an ancient quarry are of interest to botanists for their great variety. The water gardens lie below the ruins of the 13th-century castle of Kildrummy. Specimen trees are planted below in the Back Den. Interesting old stones. Museum and art exhibition.

KINKELL CHURCH   1210   6 S19

HS. On the east bank of the River Don, off the B993, 2 miles (3km) south of Inverurie, Aberdeenshire. Nearest railway station Inverurie, bus from Aberdeen. Access at all reasonable times. Free. Telephone (01667) 460232. www.historic-scotland.gov.uk

The ruins of a 16th-century parish church with a fine sacrament house dated 1524 and the grave slab of Gilbert of Greenlaw, killed in battle in 1411.

KINNAIRD HEAD LIGHTHOUSE   1211   6 T17

HS. On a promontory in Fraserburgh, Aberdeenshire. Nearest railway station Aberdeen, then bus to Fraserburgh. Open all year, daily, telephone for details. Charge £. Joint ticket with Museum of Scottish Lighthouses (see 1237). Explanatory displays in visitor centre. Gift shop. Tearoom. WC. Limited wheelchair access. Disabled WC. Car and coach parking. Telephone (01346) 511022. www.historic-scotland.gov.uk

A fine 16th-century castle built for the Fraser family but altered to take the first lighthouse built by the Commissioners of the Northern Lighthouses in 1787. The light is still in working order but has been replaced by a small unmanned light nearby. Managed by the Kinnaird Head Trust.

KIRKHILL FOREST   1212   6 S19

FE. Near Aberdeen, on the north side of the A96 between Blackburn and Dyce roundabouts. Access at all times unless timber harvesting in progress. Free. Explanatory displays. Leaflet available. Car and coach parking. www.forestry.gov.uk/aberdeenwoods

This forest has something for everyone: two waymarked walks, one of which takes you to Tappie Tower with good views north west over Bennachie; a waymarked cycle trail; and Trail Quest cycle orienteering. Waymarked horse trail (permit required) and a permanent orienteering course for those who want to explore the forest further.

LANTERN GALLERY OF FINE ART   1213   6 P17

18 South Guildry Street, Elgin, Morayshire. 400m from Elgin railway station. Limited car parking. Open all year, Tue–Sat 1100–1700. Free. Wheelchair access with assistance. Telephone (01343) 546864. lantern-gallery.co.uk

Paintings for sale by Roy and Anne Munn and local artists. Local scenes and landscapes, boats, birds, flowers, still life and craft work.

LEITH HALL AND GARDEN   1214   6 R18

NTS. Huntly, Aberdeenshire. On B9002, 34 miles (54km) north west of Aberdeen. By bus from Aberdeen. Open Easter weekend 1200–1700; May–Sep, Fri–Tue 1200–1700.

Grounds and garden open all year, daily. Charge £££. Group concessions. Guided tours by arrangement. Explanatory displays. Information sheets in five languages. Tearoom and picnic area. Garden. WC. Limited wheelchair access (wheelchair available). Disabled WC. Car and coach parking. Telephone (01464) 831216. www.nts.org.uk

Mansion house which was home to the Leith family for 300 years. Exhibition on family's military history. The house is set in a 286-acre (116-ha) estate with ponds, trails and a bird hide. Formal and informal gardens noted for colour and diversity.

LITTLE TREASURES DOLLS HOUSE AND TOY MUSEUM   1215   6 S19

Petersfield, Kemnay, Aberdeenshire. On B993 14 miles (22.5km) north of Aberdeen, between Inverurie and Kemnay. Nearest railway station at Inverurie. Limited bus service from Inverurie and Kemnay. Open all year, Fri–Sat and Mon 1000–1700, Sun 1300–1700; Jul, Aug and Dec open daily. Open at other times by appointment. Charge £. Free entry to shop. Group concessions. Guided tours by arrangement. Explanatory displays. Gift shop. Picnic area. WC. All exhibits labelled. Wheelchair access. Car and coach parking. Telephone (01467) 642332. www.littletreasures.uk.com

A delightful private collection of dolls houses, miniature displays and antique and collectable toys, attractively arranged for visitors' enjoyment. The adjoining shop stocks dolls houses, furniture and accessories, gifts, crafts and collectables. Something for all ages.

LOANHEAD STONE CIRCLE   1216   6 S18

HS. Near Daviot, off B9001, 5 miles (8km) north west of Inverurie, Aberdeenshire. Nearest railway station Inverurie, bus from Inverurie, then 1 mile (2km) walk. Access at all reasonable times. Free. Car parking. Telephone (01677) 460232. www.historic-scotland.gov.uk

The best known of a group of recumbent stone circles about 4000 to 4500 years old. Encloses a ring cairn and is beside a small burial enclosure.

LOCH OF STRATHBEG RSPB NATURE RESERVE   1217   6 T17

RSPB. Crimond, Fraserburgh, Aberdeenshire. Starnafin visitor centre is 1 mile (1.5km) from Crimond village on A90, between Peterhead and Fraserburgh. Public transport is infrequent. Access to all hides is difficult without a vehicle. Reserve open at all times. Charge £. RSPB members free. Explanatory displays. Events programme (leaflet available from visitor centre). WC. Limited wheelchair access. Disabled WC. Car and coach parking. Telephone (01346) 532017. www.rspb.org.uk/scotland

The loch covers 544 acres (220ha) and is the largest dune loch in Britain, surrounded by marshes, reedbeds, grassland and dunes. Visitors can see many different species of birds including large flocks of wintering geese and swans, and summer breeding waders including lapwing and redshank, from the four hides and trails. A visitor centre provides panoramic views and detailed information.

LOCHTER FISHERY   1218   6 S18

Oldmeldrum, Inverurie, Aberdeenshire. West of Oldmeldrum (4miles/7km north east of Inverurie). Nearest bus stop 1 mile (1.5km). Open all year, daily, fishery 0800–dusk; gift shop 0900–1700; restaurant 0900–1600; activities 0900–dusk (advance booking required). Charge £££ for fishing and activities. Group concessions. Tours by appointment. Explanatory displays. Gift shop. Restaurant overlooks main fly fishing loch. Picnic and barbecue areas. WC. Wheelchair access with assistance. Disabled WC. Car and coach parking. Telephone (01651) 872000. www.lochter.net

Set in a beautiful valley with spectacular views of the surrounding hills. Four fishing lochs for fly and bait fishing. Activites offered include clay pigeon shooting, grass rally karting, off-road driving, archery, target golf, obstacle driving, paint jousting and mini digger challenge. Also putting green, nature walks, fish feeding, falconry displays, children's play area and bouncy castle.

LOGIE STEADING 1219 2 N17

Forres, Moray. 6 miles (10km) south of Forres on A940. Nearest railway station and bus service Forres. Open Easter–Christmas, daily 1030–1700. Free. Charge for gardens £ (children free). Explanatory displays. Cafe. WC. Wheelchair access with assistance. Disabled WC. Car and coach parking. Telephone (01309) 611378. www.logie.co.uk

Originally built as a model farm in the 1920s, the steading has been converted to house an unusual visitor centre. Art gallery (contemporary Scottish art), secondhand books, antique country furniture, furniture restoration including cane and rush seating, glass engraving, dress making, plant shop. River Findhorn Heritage Centre, walk and playground. Walled garden.

LOSSIEMOUTH FISHERIES AND COMMUNITY MUSEUM 1220 6 P17

2 Pitgaveny Quay, Lossiemouth, Moray. Bus from Elgin. Open Easter–Sep, Mon–Sat 1000–1700. Charge £. Group concessions. Guided tours (leaflets in French and German). Explanatory displays. Gift shop. WC. Wheelchair access to ground floor only. Disabled WC. Car and coach parking. Telephone (01343) 813772.

Exhibits on the history of fishing and the local community. Features a study of Ramsay McDonald, the first Labour Prime Minister, born in Lossiemouth.

LOST GALLERY 1221 6 Q19

Strathdon, Aberdeenshire. On A97 in Cairngorms National Park, 48 miles (77km) west of Aberdeen. Open all year, Wed–Mon 1100–1700. Free. WC. Limited wheelchair access. Disabled WC. Car parking. Telephone (01975) 51287. www.lostgallery.co.uk

Contemporary art in an idyllic setting. The gallery is set deep in the tranquility of Glen Nochty, a delightful drive through the woodland that surrounds Strathdon in Upper Donside. It is housed in a 19th-century farmhouse on Moss Hill. Over 60 paintings, oil, watercolours, mixed media and photography, and over 60 indoor and outdoor sculptures.

MACALLAN DISTILLERY 1222 6 Q18

Craigellachie, Banffshire, . On B9102 opposite Craigellachie, 15 miles (24km) south of Elgin. Nearest railway station at Elgin. Limited bus service to Craigellachie. Open Easter–Oct, Mon–Sat 0930–1630 (last tour at 1530); Nov–Easter, 1100-1500 Mon–Fri only, telephone for tour times and availability. Closed Christmas and New Year. Distillery 'silent season' where there is no production or tours, end Jun–early Aug. Regular tour free of charge. Special interest tours chargeable and booking in advance essential. Gift shop. WC. Tours for deaf visitors can be organised. Limited wheelchair access. Disabled WC. Car parking. Telephone (01340) 872280.

A working distillery with tours for small groups (up to ten people) from the visitor centre. The shop sells the full range of Maccallan whiskies, artefacts and handcrafted gifts.

MACDUFF MARINE AQUARIUM   1223   6 S17

11 High Shore, Macduff, Banff. In Macduff close to the harbour. Bus service from
Aberdeen and Elgin to Macduff. Open daily all year except Christmas and New Year,
1000–1700. Charge ££. Children under 3 free with paying adult. All day tickets.
Group concessions. Guided tours (available in French and German). Explanatory
displays. Gift shop. Picnic area. WC. Limited sign language, audio tour. Wheelchair
access. Disabled WC. Car and coach parking. Telephone (01261) 833369. www.marine-
aquarium.com

Exciting displays feature the sea life of the Moray Firth. The central exhibit,
unique in Britain, holds a living kelp reef. Divers feed the fish in this tank.
Other displays include an estuary exhibit, splash tank, rock pools, deep reef tank
and ray pool. Young visitors especially enjoy the touch pools. Talks, video
presentations and feeding shows throughout the week.

MAGGIE'S HOOSIE   1224   6 T17

26 Shore Street, Inverallochy, Fraserburgh, Aberdeenshire. At the east end of
Fraserburgh Bay. Open Jun–Sep, Mon–Thur 1400–1600. Charge £. Children free.

A preserved but and ben fisher cottage with earth floor, box beds and original
furnishings.

MAIDEN STONE   1225   6 S19

HS. Near Chapel of Garioch, 4.5 miles (7km) north west of Inverurie, Aberdeenshire.
Bus from Aberdeen, 1.5 mile (2.5km) walk from Oyne fork. Access at all reasonable
times. Free. Telephone (01667) 460232. www.historic-scotland.gov.uk

A 9th-century Pictish cross-slab bearing a Celtic cross on one side and a variety
of Pictish symbols on the other.

MAR LODGE ESTATE   1226   6 P20

NTS. Braemar, Aberdeenshire. Access from the A93 on unclassified road, 5 miles
(8km) west of Braemar. Bus to Braemar. Estate open all year. Mar Lodge open on
special days, telephone for details. Free. Car parking. Telephone (013397) 41433.
www.nts.org.uk

Part of the core area of the Cairngorms, internationally recognised as the most
important nature conservation landscape in Britain. The estate contains four of
the five highest mountains in the UK. Outstanding wildlife, short- and long-
distance walks. Ranger service.

MEMSIE CAIRN   1227   6 T17

HS. Near Rathen, 3.5 miles (5.5km) south of Fraserburgh, Aberdeenshire. Nearest
railway station Aberdeen, bus from Fraserburgh to Memsie. Access at all reasonable
times. Free. Telephone (01677) 460232. www.historic-scotland.gov.uk

A large stone-built cairn, possibly Bronze Age, but enlarged during field
clearance in the last two centuries.

MILL OF ELRICK FISH FARM   1228   6 T18

Auchnagatt, Ellon, Aberdeenshire. 7 miles (11km) north of Ellon. Bus service via
Ellon. Open all year, Thu–Tue 0800–2000 or dusk if earlier. Charges vary according
to type of fishing and fish caught. Additional charge for equipment hire. Group
concessions. Fishing hut. WC. Limited wheelchair access (ramp access to WC but
must walk a few steps to lochside). Disabled WC. Car and coach parking. Telephone
(01358) 701628. www.elrickfishfarm.co.uk

Two lochs – the Any Method Loch, set up especially for beginners and suitable for fly, spool or bait fishing; the Fly Only Loch, for more advanced fishers.

MILLBUIES LOCHS   1229   6 P17

Longmorn, 5 miles (7.5km) south of Elgin on A941 to Rothes. Open Jan–Dec (fishing Mar–Oct) daily. Free. Car parking.

The lochs are in a wooded setting with numerous walks where wildlife and flora can be seen. Four boats are available for anglers.

THE MILLERS   1230   6 S19

North Lurg, Midmar, Aberdeenshire. On B9119 Aberdeen/Tarland road, 3 miles (5km) west of Echt. Open all year (except Christmas and New year). Shop Mon–Fri 0900–1730, Sat 0900–1700, Sun 0930–1700. Restaurant Mon–Sat 0930–1630, Sun 0930–1700. Free. Explanatory displays. Gift shop. WC. Wheelchair access (wheelchair for customers' use). Disabled WC. Car and coach parking. Telephone (01330) 833462. www.millersmidmar.info

A unique visitor and retail centre with restaurant, food shop, gift department, book room and country and casual clothing department. Local history and food exhibition.

MONYMUSK ARTS CENTRE   1231   6 R19

Monymusk, Inverurie. 18 miles (29km) west of Aberdeen, 3 miles (5km) south west of Kemnay on the B993. By rail to Aberdeen or Inverurie, then bus to Monymusk. Open May–Sep, daily 1000–1600; telephone for other times. Free. Guided tours. Explanatory displays. Gift shop. Small garden. WC. Wheelchair access. Disabled WC. Car and coach parking. Telephone (01467) 651220 or 651213.

Located in an 18th-century stone-polishing mill converted to a church in 1801. Wide selection of local crafts during summer months. Art exhibition every two weeks and small educational resource centre of 18th century local social history and geography, featuring some early maps. Craft-worker often in residence.

MORAY FIRTH WILDLIFE CENTRE   1232   6 Q17

Tugnet, Spey Bay, Buckie, Moray. At the end of the B9104, 5 miles (8km) north of Fochabers on the A96. Nearest railway station Keith (12 miles/19km). Bus to Fochabers. Open daily Easter–Oct 1030–1700; telephone to confirm times during winter. Group concessions. Explanatory displays. Gift shop. Tearoom, picnic area and wildlife garden. WC. Wheelchair access. Disabled WC. Car and coach parking. Telephone (01343) 820339. www.mfwc.co.uk

Housed in a former salmon fishing station built in 1768 and providing an ideal place to watch ospreys hunting, seals, dolphins, otters and many birds. An exhibition describes the Moray Firth dolphins and the marine environment. Hands-on activities for children. A base for research projects studying the dolphins. Environmental resource room.

MORAY LEISURE CENTRE   1233   6 P17

Borough Briggs Road, Elgin, Moray. In Elgin, behind Tesco supermarket. Elgin rail station 0.75 miles (2km), bus station 0.5 mile (0.7km). Open all year, daily 0700–2200. Various admission charges. Group concessions. Guided tours by arrangement. Explanatory displays. Café bar, vending machines and picnic area. Crèche. WC. Wheelchair access. Disabled WC. Car and coach parking. Telephone (01343) 550033. www.moray-leisure-centre.co.uk

A leisure centre providing for many different activities. Ice rink, swimming and leisure pools, health and fitness suite, relaxation suite (sauna, steam room, spa pool and solarium), squash courts, child care, complimentary practice suite and soft play area.

MORAY MOTOR MUSEUM   1234   6 P17

Bridge Street, Elgin, Moray. 30 miles (48km) west of Inverness. Open Apr–Oct, daily 1100–1700. Charge ££. Group concessions. Explanatory displays. Gift shop. WC. Wheelchair access. Disabled WC. Car and coach parking. Telephone (01343) 541120.

Unique collection of high quality cars and motorbikes housed in an old mill building.

MOSSAT TROUT FISHERY   1235   6 R19

Mossat Trout Fishery, Little Bridgend Farm, Mossat, near Alford, Aberdeenshire. On A97, 14 miles (22.5km) south of Huntly and 34 miles (54.5km) east of Aberdeen. Clearly signposted from the main road (A97) as you approach. Nearest railway station at Huntly. Bus service from Huntly, Alford and Aberdeen. Open all year, daily 0800–dusk (early morning fishing by arrangement). Prices vary depending on number of fish limit. Reduction for children 12 and under. Additional charge for tackle hire and tuition. Group concessions. Free friendly guided tours of the fishery at any time. Refreshments available in fishing bothy. Picnic area. WC. Wheelchair access (the lochs are surrounded by easy access grass banks but no wheelchair access to the fishing bothy). Car and coach parking. Telephone (01464) 861000. www.mossattroutfishery.co.uk

Situated in a peaceful location, amid beautiful scenery and lots of wildlife. Fly fishing is offered over three naturally fed lochs and a stretch of the Mossat Burn for rainbow trout, American brook trout, brown, blue and golden trout. Fish of up to 14lb available to catch. Suitable for beginner or expert. Tuition and tackle hire available.

MOSSATBURN WATER GARDEN CENTRE   1236   6 R19

Mossat, Alford, Aberdeenshire. On A944, 7 miles (11km) west of Alford. Bus service to Lumsden (1.5 miles/2.5km). Open Mar–Sep, daily 0930–1800; Oct–Dec and Feb, Wed–Mon 1000–1600 (closed from Christmas to end of Jan). Refreshments available nearby. WC. Wheelchair access with assistance. Car and coach parking. Telephone (019755) 71235.

A 0.75 acre (0.3ha) site of mature gardens and ponds, established in 1986. Shop sells water features, pumps, filters, statues, water and nursery plants, coldwater fish and Koi, gifts.

MUSEUM OF SCOTTISH LIGHTHOUSES   1237   6 T17

Kinnaird Head, Fraserburgh, Aberdeenshire. In Fraserburgh. Bus from Aberdeen. Open Apr–Oct, Mon–Sat 1000–1800, Sun 1200–1800; Nov–Mar, Mon–Sat 1000–1600, Sun 1200–1600. Charge ££. Children under 6 free. Joint ticket with Kinnaird Head Lighthouse (see 1211). Group concessions. Guided tours. Explanatory displays including multi-screen projector show and touch screens. Gift shop. Café. WC. Limited wheelchair access. Disabled WC. Car and coach parking. Telephone (01346) 511022.

A museum housed in a former castle which became the first lighthouse built by the Northern Lighthouse Board in 1787, now a monument to Scotland's lighthouse service. Shows the skill and dedication, the science and romance of Scotland's lighthouses. Tour to the top of the lighthouse. Special events and children's holiday activities.

NELSON TOWER   1238   6 P17

Grant Park, Forres. On A96, 11 miles (17.5km) west of Elgin in Forres. Nearest railway station Forres. Bus service from Aberdeen and Inverness. Open May–Sep, Tue–Sun 1400–1600. Free. Guided tours. Explanatory displays. Gift shop. Picnic area. Car and coach parking. Telephone (01309) 673701. www.moray.org/museums

Nelson Tower was built by the Trafalgar Club to commemorate Nelson's victory at Trafalgar. Displays on Lord Nelson and views of old Forres. There are also spectacular views of the Moray Firth from the tower.

NOAH'S ARK   1239   6 R19

Old Schoolhouse Croft, Craigievar, Alford, Aberdeenshire. On A980 between Lumphanan and Alford, 0.5 mile (1km) past Crossroads Hotel (signposted O'Neil Corse). Local bus service passes Crossroads Hotel. Open by appointment only, May–Sep 1000–1700. Charge £. Children under 3 free. Groups by advance booking. Group concessions. Guided tours. Explanatory displays. Gift shop. Refreshments available in shop, picnic area. Play area and pets' corner. WC. No guide dogs. Wheelchair access with assistance. Car and coach parking. Telephone (013398) 83670.

A unique experience for visitors of all ages on a working farm. Guided tours let visitors feed and tend to the animals. The information centre is packed full of facts on farming and farm animals. Farm shop. Beautiful surroundings.

OLD MANSE GALLERY   1240   6 R21

Old Manse, Western Road, Insch, Aberdeenshire. In Insch, 25 miles (40km) north west of Aberdeen. Nearest railway station Insch, bus from Inverurie or Huntly. Open by appointment, please telephone. Free. Gift shop. WC. Wheelchair access. Car and coach parking. Telephone (01464) 820392. www.celticcarpetsscotland.com

Sales display of oriental and Celtic carpets (Celtic designs can be made to customers' requirements). Permanent exhibition of work from the Royal Society of Miniature Painters, the Society of Limners and the Russian Fedoskino School. Also many local scenes in mixed media. Commissions accepted for portraits and landscapes.

OLD ROYAL STATION, BALLATER   1241   6 Q20

Old Royal Station, Station Square, Ballater. Nearest railway station Aberdeen, bus service from Aberdeen to Ballater. Open daily, Oct–May 1000–1700; Jun–Sep 0900–1800; Jul–Aug 0930–1900; also Easter weekend 1000–1800. Free. Explanatory displays. Gift shop. Restaurant. WC. Induction loop. Wheelchair access. Disabled WC. Car and coach parking. Telephone (013397) 55306. www.aberdeen-grampian.com

Restored Victorian railway station containing displays on the 100 year history of royal use. Unique royal waiting room built for Queen Victoria. Also Tourist Information Centre. Covered extension over former railway line showing life-size replica of royal carriage.

RON PARKER SCULPTURE   1242   2 N18

Beachens Two, Dunphail, Forres, Moray. 9.5 miles (15km) south of Forres on A940. Nearest railway and bus stations Forres. Open all year (except Christmas and New Year), daily 0900–1800. Free. Guided tours. Explanatory displays, sale of exhibited work. WC. Wheelchair access. Car parking. Telephone (01309) 611273.

Wood sculpture workshop where each piece is individually handmade from managed local hardwoods. No two sculptures are the same. A wide range of large and small work is available for sale. Visitors are always welcome at the workshop and may bring their own wood to be worked to their own design.

PEACOCK VISUAL ARTS   1243   6 T19

21 Castle Street, Aberdeen. Aberdeen City Centre. 10 min walk from Aberdeen bus/railway station. Open all year round, Tue–Sat 0930–1730. Free. Gift shop. WC. Limited wheelchair access. Telephone (01224) 639539. www.peacockvisualarts.co.uk

Peacock Visual Arts is the north east's main contemporary visual arts organisation and is supported by Aberdeen City Council and the Scottish Arts Council. It was established in 1974 as a printmaking workshop, and the facilty has gradually developed into a centre for the promotion of art and visual media.

PEEL RING OF LUMPHANAN   1244   6 R20

HS. 0.5 mile (1km) south west of Lumphanan, Aberdeenshire. Nearest railway station Aberdeen, bus from Aberdeen. Access at all reasonable times. Free. Car parking. Telephone (01677) 460232. www.historic-scotland.gov.uk

A major early medieval earthwork 120 feet (36.5m) in diameter and 18 feet (5.5m) high. The site of a fortified residence. Links with Shakespeare's *Macbeth*.

PETERHEAD MARITIME HERITAGE   1245   6 T18

The Lido, South Road, Peterhead. On the south side of Peterhead. Bus from Aberdeen. Open Jun–Aug, Mon–Sat 1030–1700, Sun 1130–1700. Free. Group concessions. Guided tours. Explanatory displays. Gift shop. Tearoom. Children's playground. WC. Wheelchair access. Disabled WC. Car and coach parking. Telephone (01771) 622807. www.aberdeenshire.gov.uk/heritage

Tells the story of Peterhead maritime life in sound and vision. Features audio-visual display on marine life, interactive display on fishing, whaling, navigation and the oil industry, observation box with telescope views across Peterhead Bay.

PICARDY SYMBOL STONE   1246   6 R18

HS. Near Mireton, Insch, Aberdeenshire. Nearest railway station Inverurie, bus from Huntly or Inverurie. Access at all reasonable times. Free. Telephone (01677) 460232. www.historic-scotland.gov.uk

One of the oldest and simplest Pictish symbol stones, possibly 7th century.

PITFOUR SPORTING ESTATES   1247   6 T18

Old Deer, Mintlaw, Aberdeenshire. 10 miles (16km) east of Peterhead. Bus service to Mintlaw. Open mid Mar–end Oct, daily 0900–2200. Charge £££. Additional charges for boat and engine hire. Group concessions. Tea and coffee available. Barbecue facilities. Car parking. Telephone (01771) 624448. www.assf.net/subpages/pitfour.htm

Fly fishing for rainbow and brown trout on a 33 acre (13ha) lake, surrounded by mature forest. Bank and boat fishing. Troutmasters and ASSF water. Tuition available.

PITMEDDEN GARDEN   1248   6 S18

NTS. Pitmedden village. On A920, 14 miles (22km) north of Aberdeen near Ellon. By bus from Aberdeen. Open May–Sep, daily 1000–1730. Charge ££. Group concessions. Explanatory displays. Information sheets in four languages. Gift shop. Tearoom and picnic area. WC. Tactile map. Limited wheelchair access (wheelchairs available). Disabled WC. Car and coach parking. Telephone (01651) 842352. www.nts.org.uk

Pitmedden's centrepiece is the Great Garden, originally laid out in 1675 by Sir Alexander Seton. Estate also includes the Museum of Farming Life, herb garden, wildlife garden and woodland walk.

PLUSCARDEN ABBEY   1249   6 P17

Elgin, Moray. By the B9010, 6 miles (9.5km) south west of Elgin. School bus only from Elgin. Open daily 0430–2030. Free. Guided tours on request (French and other languages by prior arrangement). Explanatory displays. Gift shop. Baby changing facilities. Garden. WC. Induction loop. Wheelchair access. Disabled WC. Car and coach parking. Telephone (01343) 890257. www.pluscardenabbey.org

Originally a Valliscaulian house, the monastery was founded in 1230. In 1390 the church was burned, probably by the Wolf of Badenoch who burned Elgin about the same time. It became a dependent priory of the Benedictine Abbey of Dunfermline in 1454 until the suppression of monastic life in Scotland in 1560. Thereafter the buildings fell into ruin, until 1948 when a group of Benedictine monks from Prinknash Abbey returned to restore it. Monastic church services open to the public. Visitor centre, retreats and garden.

QUARRELWOOD   1250   6 P17

FE. West of Elgin, from 8-Acres Hotel to Spynie Kirk Road. Car park 0.5 mile (1km) along this road from A96. Bus from Elgin to Forres along A96. Open all year. Free. Explanatory displays. Leaflet available. Picnic area. Guided walks and events. Limited wheelchair access (easy trail opposite Spynie Hospital, east of wood). Car parking. www.forestry.gov.uk

Oakwood and pine forest. Part owned by Moray Council and managed by Quarrelwood Woodland Park Association. Two waymarked trails lead from modern to ancient henge monuments and to Cuties Hillock, the site of ancient reptile finds.

RAEMOIR TROUT FISHERY   1251   6 R20

Raemoir Road, Banchory. 1 mile (1.5km) north of Banchory on the A980. Nearest railway station Aberdeen (16 miles/25.5km), nearest bus service Banchory. Open all year (subject to weather), daily 0830–dusk. On application. Group concessions. Picnic area. Tea, coffee, soft drinks and snacks available. Barbecue for use of patrons. Wheelchair access. Car and coach parking. Telephone (01330) 820092. www.raemoirtroutfishery.co.uk

The fishery has three fly only lochans and a small bait pond for beginners and children, set in a superb natural setting with a large variety of wildlife inhabiting both the waters and the surrounding land. Notable sightings include otters and osprey.

RANDOLPH'S LEAP   1252   2 N17

Off B9007, 7 miles (11km) south west of Forres. Access at all times. Free. Car parking.

The River Findhorn winds through a deep gorge in the sandstone, and from a path above are impressive views of the clear brown water swirling over rocks or in still dark pools. Randolph's Leap is the most striking part of this valley.

ROB ROY'S STATUE   1253   6 S20

West end of Peterculter by the A93. Access at all times. Free.

Statue of Rob Roy standing above the Leuchar Burn. It can be seen from the bridge on the main road.

ROSEISLE FOREST   1254   6 P17

FE. Moray Forest District Office, Balnacoul, Fochabers, Moray. A96 west from Elgin,
then B9013 Burghead road. Turn left at College of Roseisle then entrance is 2 miles
(3km) . Bus route from Kinloss to Burghead then 0.5 mile (1km) walk. Open all year.
Charge for parking (season ticket available). Picnic and barbecue area. WC (closed in
winter). Guided walks and events. Limited wheelchair access. Disabled WC. Car and
coach parking. Telephone (01343) 820223. www.forestry.gov.uk

Pine forest giving access to the beach. Picnic tables, barbecues and play area make
this site ideal for a family picnic. Waymarked low level walks. Ranger service.

ROYAL LOCHNAGER DISTILLERY   1255   6 Q20

Crathie, Ballater. 9 miles (14.5km) from Braemar on A93, situated near Balmoral
Castle. Nearest bus service stops within 1 mile (1.5km). Open Jan–Mar, Mon–Fri
1100–1600; Apr, Mon–Fri 1000–1700; May–Sep, Mon–Sat 1000–1700 and Sun
1200–1700; Oct, Mon–Fri 1000–1700; Nov–Dec, Mon–Fri 1100–1600. Charge ££.
Under 18s free, children under 8 not permitted to take tour. Guided tours.
Explanatory displays, exhibition area. Whisky shop. WC. Limited wheelchair access.
Disabled WC. Car parking. Telephone (012297) 42700.

Guided tours of a traditional working distillery, with sample dram. The
distillery shop has a range of rare and unusual malt whiskies.

ST CYRUS NATIONAL NATURE RESERVE   1256   6 S21

Off A92, 6 miles (9.5km) north of Montrose. At end of Beach Road, past church, a
steep path leads down to the reserve. Bus service from Aberdeen and Montrose to St
Cyrus village. Access to reserve at all times (no access to tern breeding area
Apr–Aug). Visitor centre open Apr–Oct, daily; Nov–March, Mon–Fri. Free. Please
keep dogs under close control at all times. Car parking. Telephone 01674 830736
(Scottish Natural Heritage). www.nnr-scotland.org.uk

Nature reserve. The cliffs and dunes of St Cyrus support a distinctive range of
plants, including many southern species. The reserve is also noted for its variety
of insects, particularly butterflies and over 200 kinds of moth. Breeding birds
include stonechats and whinchats, and visitors are likely to see fulmars nesting
on the cliffs. Excellent views from cliff top at village end.

ST MARY'S CHURCH, AUCHINDOIR   1257   6 R18

HS. Near Lumsden, 3 miles (5km) north of Kildrummy, Aberdeenshire. Bus from
Huntly. Access at all reasonable times. Free. Telephone (01667) 460232. www.historic-
scotland.gov.uk

The ruins of one of the finest medieval parish churches in Scotland, roofless,
but otherwise complete. There is a rich early Romanesque doorway and a
beautiful early 14th-century sacrament house.

ST NINIAN'S CHAPEL, TYNET   1258   6 Q17

Tynet, Fochabers, Moray. On the A98, 3 miles (5km) east of Fochabers. Nearest
railway station Elgin, bus from Buckie or Elgin. Open all year, dawn to dusk. Mass at
0830 on Sun. Free. Explanatory displays. Picnic area. Wheelchair access with
assistance. Car parking. Telephone (01542) 832196.

Built in 1755 by the Laird of Tynet, ostensibly as a sheepcote, but secretly as a
Catholic chapel (extensively altered since). The oldest post-Reformation
Catholic church still in use.

ST PETER'S KIRK AND PARISH CROSS   1259   6 P17

HS. In Duffus Churchyard in Duffus, Moray. Bus from Elgin. Access at all reasonable times (keys available locally). Free. Telephone (01667) 460232. www.historic-scotland.gov.uk

The roofless remains of the church include the base of a 14th-century western tower, a 16th-century vaulted porch and some interesting tombstones. There is also a 14th-century cross.

SANDHAVEN MEAL MILL   1260   6 T17

Sandhaven, Fraserburgh, Aberdeenshire. On the B9031, 2.5 miles (4km) west of Fraserburgh. Telephone for details of opening times. Free. Guided tours. Explanatory displays. Limited wheelchair access. Car and coach parking. Telephone (01771) 622906. www.aberdeenshire.gov.uk/heritage

Visitors can see how oatmeal used to be ground in this typical 19th-century Scottish meal mill. Working demonstrations.

SCOTTISH TARTANS MUSEUM   1261   6 Q17

The Institute, Mid Street, Keith. In Keith Institute Hall. Nearest railway station Keith, local bus service. Open May, Mon–Sat 1100–1500; Jun–Sep, Mon–Sat 1100–1600. Charge £. Group concessions. Explanatory displays. Refreshments nearby. WC. Wheelchair access. Car parking. Telephone (01542) 888419. www.keithcommunity.co.uk

The museum contains accounts of famous Scotsmen and explains the developments of tartans and the kilt. Over 700 tartans on display.

SPEYSIDE COOPERAGE VISITOR CENTRE   1262   6 Q18

Dufftown Road, Craigellachie, Banffshire. On the A941, 1 mile (2km) south of Craigellachie. Buses from Dufftown or Elgin. Open all year, Mon–Fri 0930–1630. Charge ££. Group concessions. Guided tours. Explanatory displays (in French, German, Italian, Spanish and Japanese). Gift shop. Light refreshments and picnic area (open Mar–Oct). Baby changing facilities. WC. Limited wheelchair access. Disabled WC. Car and coach parking. Telephone (01340) 871108.

Award-winning working cooperage with unique visitor centre. Visitors can watch skilled coopers and apprentices repairing oak casks for the whisky industry. An exhibition traces the history and development of the cooperage industry. Shop specialises in quality wooden items. Highland cattle can be seen.

SPEYSIDE POTTERY   1263   6 P18

Ballindalloch, Banffshire. 5 miles (8km) west of Aberlour, on the A95 near the Glenfarclas Distillery. Open Apr–Oct, daily 1000–1700. Free. Explanatory displays. Wheelchair access with assistance. Car parking. Telephone (01807) 500338. www.speysidepottery.co.uk

Workshop and showroom for onsite production of wood fired, functional stoneware pottery. Production can be viewed.

SPYNIE PALACE   1264   6 Q17

HS. Elgin, Morayshire. Off the A941, 2 miles (3km) north of Elgin. Nearest railway station Elgin, buses from Aberdeen or Inverness, then bus to Spynie. Open Apr–Sep, daily 0930–1830; Oct–Mar Sat–Sun 0930–1630. Charge £. Group concessions. Gift shop. Picnic area. WC. Limited wheelchair access. Disabled WC. Car and coach parking. Telephone (01343) 546358. www.historic-scotland.gov.uk

The residence of the bishops of Moray from the 14th century to 1686. Dominated by the massive tower built by Bishop David Stewart in the 15th century. Spectacular views of Spynie Loch.

ST MARY'S CATHEDRAL   1265   6 T19

Cathedral Clergy House, 20 Huntly Street , Aberdeen. Central Aberdeen. Aberdeen bus depot. Open daily, summer 0800–1900; winter 0800–1800. Free. Guided tours by arrangement only. Gift shop. Wheelchair access. Telephone (01224) 640160.

St Mary's Cathedral was built in 1860 and is the seat of the Roman Catholic bishop of the Diocese of Aberdeen, which stretches from South Aberdeenshire to Shetland. Although the gothic architecture remains, the interior was altered in the late 1960s according to liturgical reforms. The cathedral also has a lady/chapel, where the statue of Our Lady of Aberdeen – or Our Lady of good success – is situated. Devotion to the title of Mary stretches back in the Diocese for centuries. Our church is open every day. You are most welcome to pay a visit, to look round, pray quietly or join in the services.

STORYBOOK GLEN   1266   6 S20

Maryculter, Aberdeen. On the B9077, 6 miles (9.5km) west of Aberdeen. Nearest railway station Aberdeen, bus from Aberdeen to Peterculter, then 1 mile (2km) walk. Open all year, daily 1000–1800. Charge ££. Group concessions. Explanatory displays. Gift shop. Restaurant and picnic area. WC. Wheelchair access. Disabled WC. Car and coach parking. Telephone (01224) 732941. www.storybookglenaberdeen.com

A 28 acre (11.5ha) spectacular theme park with over 100 models of nursery rhymes, old and new, set in beautiful scenic gardens. McDonald farm with all the usual animals. Restaurant and new gift and garden centre.

STRATHISLA DISTILLERY   1267   6 Q17

Seafield Avenue, Keith, Banffshire. In Keith. Nearest railway station Keith, then five minute walk. Bus from Aberdeen or Elgin. Open Apr–Oct, Mon–Sat 1000–1600, Sun 1230–1600. Charge ££. Charge ££ (includes shop voucher). Under 18s free; children under 8 not admitted to production areas. Group concessions. Guided tours. Explanatory displays, reception centre with video presentation. Self-guided tours with coffee and shortbread (and sample whisky). Handbook. Gift shop. WC. Limited wheelchair access. Disabled WC. Car and coach parking. Telephone (01542) 783044. www.chivas.com

The oldest working distillery in the Highlands, established in 1786, and home to Chivas Regal blended Scotch whisky. Guided tour of distillery and traditional warehouse. Tasting of Chivas Regal 12 year old on arrival. Dram of Chivas Regal 18 year old after guided tour.

SUENO'S STONE   1268   6 P17

HS. At the east end of Forres, Moray. Nearest railway station Elgin, bus from Elgin. Access at all reasonable times. Free. Car parking. Telephone (01667) 460232. www.historic-scotland.gov.uk

The most remarkable sculptured monument in Britain, standing over 20 feet (6m) high (now enclosed in glass). Probably a cenotaph dating from the end of the first Millennium AD.

SYLLAVETHY GALLERY   1269   6 R19

Syllavethy , Alford, Aberdeenshire. 25m west of Aberdeen. Bus to Alford–1m from the gallery. Open Wed–Mon 1100–1800. May be closed at other times during the winter months. Free. Explanatory displays. Wheelchair access. Car and coach parking. Telephone (01975) 562278.

This gallery is a converted granite steading, housing three exhibition areas, with wall space for 100 paintings and floor space for 20 sculptures. Outside of the main gallery there is a sculpture garden where visitors can relax on sunny days. Syllavethy exhibits fine art created by locals, as well as international artists and features portraits by Chan Yan Ning, who has been commissioned to paint HM the Queen, Prince Philip, Princess Anne, Sir Richard Branson, Aung San Suu Kyi of Burma, and many others.

TARVES HERITAGE CENTRE   1270   6 S18

The Heritage Centre, The Square, Tarves, Ellon, Aberdeenshire. 18m north-west of Aberdeen on B999. Hourly bus service from Aberdeen Bus Station. Open Easter–Nov, Thur–Sun 1400–1630. Appointments may be arranged outwith public opening hours. Free. Donations are encouraged. Guided tours arranged by prior notice. Explanatory displays. Gift shop. WC. Wheelchair access. Disabled WC. Car parking. Telephone (01651) 851883.

Centrally located in a conservation village, building is a Victorian school housing a heritage museum and Victorian schoolroom. Along with ever-changing displays, there is an extensive archive of photographs, which can be viewed on the computer. Exhibits include items of local interest – farming and domestic life, shops and trades, the school, the kirk, and the history of the area. A very important item, which has pride of place, is a Bronze Age sword that was found locally.

The Victorian schoolroom has been restored to its former glory with reproduction school desks, slates and chalks. School parties visit with their teacher to experience a typical Victorian school day.

Internet access is available to the public during opening hours within a computer suite.

TARVES MEDIEVAL TOMB   1271   6 S18

HS. In Tarves churchyard, 15 miles (24km) north west of Aberdeen. Nearest railway station Aberdeen, bus from Aberdeen. Access at all reasonable times. Free. Telephone (01667) 460232. www.historic-scotland.gov.uk

The fine altar tomb of William Forbes, the laird who enlarged Tolquhon Castle. Remarkable carving.

THE MILTON ART GALLERY   1272   6 S20

Milton of Crathes, Banchory. 11m east of Aberdeen on A93. 201 Aberdeen to Braemar bus. Open Mon–Sat 1000–1700, Sun 1100–1700. Free. Gift shop. Restaurant/tearoom. Baby changing facility. WC. Limited wheelchair access. Disabled WC. Car and coach parking. www.miltonart.com

The Milton Art Gallery is one of six businesses in a converted courtyard/steading. On site is also the Royal Deeside Railway, which hopes to run from the Milton to Banchory when finished. The ethos of the gallery is to support and promote local artists and there is a wide selection of styles and prices.

The gallery shows paintings, prints, sculpture, ceramics, turned wood, stained glass, designer jewellery and much more. Regular exhibitions are held throughout the year.

TOLBOOTH MUSEUM   1273   6 S20

The Harbour, Stonehaven. In Stonehaven centre. By rail or bus to Stonehaven. Open May–Oct, Wed–Mon 1330–1630. Free. Guided tours. Explanatory displays. Gift shop. Limited wheelchair access. Car parking. Telephone (01771) 622807. www.aberdeenshire.gov.uk/heritage

Stonehaven's oldest building, the Earl Marischal's 16th-century storehouse which served as Kincardineshire's Tolbooth from 1600–1767. Features imprisoned priests, links with the sea and local bygones.

TOLQUHON CASTLE   1274   6 S18

HS. Tarves, By Ellon, Aberdeenshire. North of A920, 7 miles (11km) east north-east of Oldmeldrum, Aberdeenshire. Bus from Aberdeen to Tarves then 1 mile (2km) walk. Open Apr–Sep, daily 0930–1830; Oct–Mar, Sat–Sun 0930–1630. Charge £. Group concessions. Gift shop. Picnic area. WC. Limited wheelchair access. Disabled WC. Car and coach parking. Telephone (01651) 851286. www.historic-scotland.gov.uk

Built for the Forbes family, the castle has an early 15th-century tower which was enlarged in the mid 16th century with a large mansion around a courtyard. Noted for its highly ornamented gatehouse, set within a barmkin with adjacent pleasance.

TOMINTOUL MUSEUM   1275   6 P19

The Square, Tomintoul, Moray. The Square, Tomintoul. Open Apr–May and Oct, Mon–Fri 0930–1200 and 1400–1600; Jun–Aug, Mon–Sat 0930–1200 and 1400–1630; Sep, Mon–Sat 0930–1200 and 1400–1600. Free. Guided tours. Explanatory displays. Gift shop. Car and coach parking. Telephone (01309) 673701. www.moray.org/museums

Located in the square of one of the highest villages in Britain, Tomintoul Museum features a reconstructed crofter's kitchen and smiddy, and displays on local wildlife.

TOMNAVERIE STONE CIRCLE   1276   6 R20

HS. Near Mill of Wester Coull, about 3 miles (5km) north west of Aboyne, Aberdeenshire. Nearest railway station Aberdeen, bus to Aboyne, then walk. Access at all reasonable times. Free. Telephone (01667) 460232. www.historic-scotland.gov.uk

A recumbent stone circle about 4000 years old.

TORRIESTON FOREST WALKS   1277   6 P17

FE. From Elgin take the B9010 Dallas road, then the Pluscarden minor road. Torrieston car park is 1 mile (1.5km) beyond Miltonduff. Open at all times. Free. Explanatory displays, leaflet available. Picnic area. WC (closed in winter). Guided walks and events. Limited wheelchair access (wheelchair accessible trail on south side of road). Disabled WC. Car parking. Telephone (01343) 820223. www.forestry.gov.uk

Three varied walks of 1–2 miles (1.5–3km) on the forested hillside above Pluscarden Abbey (see 1249). Ranger service.

TULLICH FISHERY   1278   6 Q20

Braehead House, Tullich, by Ballater, Aberdeenshire. 2 miles (3km) east of Ballater on A93. Bus service from Ballater. Open all year, daily dawn–dusk. Charges vary. Group concessions. Explanatory displays. Picnic area. WC. Wheelchair access. Car and coach parking. Telephone (013397) 55648.

Fly fishing on a 6 acre (2.5ha) loch and a bait loch set in the heart of Royal Deeside. Both lochs are well stocked with high quality rainbow trout.

TYREBAGGER FOREST   1279   6 S19

FE. Take the A96 from Aberdeen, turning left between Blackburn and Dyce roundabouts onto the B979, then 0.3 miles (0.5km). Access at all times unless timber harvesting in progress. Free. Explanatory displays. Leaflet available. Car parking. www.forestry.gov.uk

Two waymarked walks and a wider walks network. There are nine sculptures placed in the forest, each designed by an international artist, many with small information panels. Map boards, a leaflet and waymarking posts keep the visitor on the right paths. No cycling or horseriding permitted.

WHITEASH AND ORDIEQUISH CYCLE TRAILS   1280   6 Q17

FE. Entrance 1 mile (1.5km) east of Fochabers village. Open all year except when timber harvesting – contact District Office. Free. Picnic area at Winding Walks. Car parking. Telephone (01343) 820223. www.forestry.gov.uk

Three medium grade mountain bike trails through mixed forest, suitable for either a family outing or a more adventurous cycle ride. Uphill climbs are rewarded by spectacular views of Moray. Colour-coded routes. Also adventurous downhill trails off-track. See also 1281 Winding Walks Forest Walks.

WINDING WALKS FOREST WALKS   1281   6 Q17

FE. Entrance 1 mile (1.5km) east of Fochabers village. Nearest bus at Fochabers. Open at all times. Free. Explanatory displays. Picnic area. Guided walks and events. Wheelchair access with assistance. Car parking. Telephone (01343) 820223. www.forestry.gov.uk

A maze of paths winds through the magnificent trees of a dramatic steep-sided gully – choose to explore the narrow winding walks' paths or try one of the more sedate waymarked walks. Four walks from 1.5 miles (3km) to 3 miles (6km) with magnificent views over the Moray countryside. Ranger service.

THE HIGHLANDS AND SKYE

ABERLOUR VISITOR CENTRE   1282   6 Q18

Aberlour Distillery, Aberlour, Banffshire. On A95 at the West End of Dunbar. Nearest train station is Elgin. Limited bus service from Elgin to Aberlour. Tours Mar–Oct, Mon–Sat 1030 and 1400, Sun 1130 and 1500; Nov–mid Dec, Mon–Fri 1030. Shop open Mon–Fri 0930–1600. Guided tours. Gift shop. WC. Limited wheelchair access. Disabled WC. Car parking. Telephone (01340) 832157. www.aberlour.com

This exclusive, fascinating and in-depth distillery tour provides a memorable experience. Relaxed and informal, you can nose and taste new distillate and five of our best single malts. For many the highlight of the tour is the chance to hand-fill and purchase your own personalised bottle of single cask selection.

ABRIACHAN FOREST   1283   2 L18

Tyeantore, Abriachan, Inverness. On the shores of Loch Ness, 9 miles (14.5km) south of Inverness on A82 between Abriachan Garden Nursery (see 1284) and the Clansman Hotel. Nearest railway station Inverness. Hourly bus service from Inverness passes wood. Access at all times. Free. Guided tours on request (donations appreciated). Explanatory displays. Picnic areas. Rain shelters, Bronze Age round house, tree house, wildlife viewing hide. WC. Sound signs along boardwalks. Wheelchair access. Disabled WC. Car parking. Telephone (01463) 861259. www.abriachan.org

This community woodland is situated in the hills overlooking Loch Ness and connects with footpaths which rise from the lochside, up and over Carn na Leitise (435m). Visitors can enjoy panoramic views by climbing or discover surprising rainshelters and interpretation boards along the easy access paths. Something for all the family to enjoy.

ABRIACHAN GARDEN NURSERY   1284   2 L18

Loch Ness side, Inverness. North shore of Loch Ness, 9 miles (14.5 km) south west of Inverness on the A82. Bus services from Inverness, Fort William and Fort Augustus. Open Feb–Nov, daily 0900–1900 (or dusk if earlier). Charge £. Group concessions on application. Guided tours. Explanatory displays. Reading room with drinks vending machine, picnic area. Limited wheelchair access. Car and coach parking. Telephone (01463) 861232. www.lochnessgarden.com

Exciting garden on Loch Ness side. A combination of native and exotic plants in a beautiful woodland setting. Hardy perennial plantings are a speciality. The adjacent nursery sells many unusual plants. Catalogue available.

ACHAVANICH STANDING STONES   1285   3 P13

Caithness. Situated approximately 5 miles (8km) from Latheron on the A895 to Thurso.

The stones are set in an unusual U shape and are thought to date from the Bronze Age. Today 36 stones survive out of a possible 54.

ACHILTIBUIE SMOKEHOUSE   1286   4 J15

The Smokehouse, Achiltibuie, Ullapool, Ross and Cromarty. At Altandhu, 5 miles (8km) north west of Achiltibuie village, 25 miles (40km) north west of Ullapool. Open Easter–Oct, Mon–Fri 0930–1700, also Sat during summer. Free. Explanatory displays. No guide dogs. Car parking. Telephone (01854) 622353.

A smokehouse where visitors can view the work areas and see fish being prepared for smoking and other processes.

AIGAS DAM   1287   2 L18

Inverness-shire. By A831, between Beauly and Struy.

This dam, part of the River Beauly Hydro scheme, is by-passed by a fish lift which allows the salmon to migrate upstream.

THE ALUMINIUM STORY LIBRARY AND VISITOR CENTRE   1288   5 K21

Linnhe Road, Kinlochleven. 7 miles (11km) from Glencoe and 21 miles (34km) from Fort William at the head of Loch Leven. Bus service from Fort William. Open Apr–Oct, Mon–Fri 1000–1300 and 1400–1700. Free. Explanatory displays. Gift shop. WC. Induction loop system. Wheelchair access. Disabled WC. Car and coach parking. Telephone (01855) 831663.

The Aluminium Story uses audio-visual displays and a video presentation system to tell the story of the British Aluminium Company which opened a smelter here in 1908. Visitors can learn how the industry and the company's hydro scheme altered the life of the area.

ALVIE ESTATE   1289   5 N19

Kincraig, Kingussie, Inverness-shire. On the B9152, 5 miles (8km) south of Aviemore. Citylink bus from Glasgow to Inverness stops at Kincraig. Open daily (except Christmas Day and New Year's Day) 0900–1700. Entrance to estate free, charges for activities. Guided tours. Gift shop. Picnic area and children's play area in holiday park. WC. Limited wheelchair access. Car and coach parking. Telephone (01540) 651255.

A traditional Highland sporting estate which has been in the same family since 1927. Now diversified into tourism – self catering cottages and chalets, static and touring caravans and tent field. Activities include clay pigeon shooting, fishing, horse riding, quad bike treks, archery, estate tours and corporate entertainment. Spectacular views across the Spey Valley to the Cairngorms.

AN TUIREANN ARTS CENTRE   1290   4 G18

Struan Road, Portree, Isle of Skye. On the B885, 0.5 mile (1km) from Portree centre. Galleries open daily Mon–Sat 1000–1700; cafe Tue–Sat 1000–1630. Free. Guided tours on request. Explanatory displays. Gift shop. Restaurant/café. WC. Induction loop system. Wheelchair access. Disabled WC. Car parking. Telephone (01478) 613306. www.antuireann.org.uk

Exhibition galleries for the visual arts and crafts and related educational events.

ANTA SCOTLAND   1291   2 N16

Fearn, Tain, Ross-shire. Off the A9, 35 miles (56km) north of Inverness. Nearest railway station at Fearn. Bus service from Tain. Open spring and summer, Mon–Sat 0930–1800, Sun 1100–1700; winter Mon–Sat 0930–1800. Free. Guided tours by appointment. Gift shop. WC. Wheelchair access with assistance. Car and coach parking. Telephone (01862) 832477. www.anta.co.uk

A pottery and textile design and manufacturing workshop and factory shop.

ARDCLACH BELL TOWER   1292   2 N18

HS. Off A939, 9 miles (13.5km) south east of Nairn. Nearest railway station Nairn, then post bus to Ardclach (no bus for return). Access at all reasonable times (for access apply to keyholder). Free. Telephone (01667) 460232. www.historic-scotland.gov.uk

A remarkable little two-storey fortified bell tower built in 1655 on the hill above the parish church of Ardclach. It summoned worshippers to the church and warned in case of alarm.

ARDESSIE FALLS   1293   4 J16

Beside the A832 at Dundonnell, Ross and Cromarty.

Waterfalls and impressive views of Little Loch Broom.

ARDNAMURCHAN POINT VISITOR CENTRE   1294   5 F21

Kilchoan, Acharacle, Argyll. On B8007, 6 miles (10km) west of Kilchoan. Ferry terminal at Kilchoan. Open Apr–May to Oct, daily 1000–1700. Charge £. Group concessions. Guided tours tours of Lighthouse Tower. Hourly 11.00–16.00. Explanatory displays. Gift shop. Picnic area. WC. Wheelchair access. Disabled WC. Car parking. Telephone (01972) 510210. www.ardnamurchan.net

Ardnamurchan lighthouse is set amongst spectacular scenery on mainland Britain's most westerly point, embracing world-class views of the Hebrides and the Small Isles. Listen to the keepers' radio conversations, learn how the light tower was built, join in the centre's Whale Watch, visit the beautifully restored original room and trace the history of Ardnamurchan through anecdotes of people past and present.

ARDTORNISH ESTATE   1295   5 H22

Morvern, by Oban, Argyll. 40 miles (64km) south west of Fort William via the Corran Ferry. Gardens open Apr–Oct, daily 0900–1800. Charge £. Market garden free. Leaflet available. Picnic area. Garden. WC. Car and coach parking. Telephone (01967) 421288. www.ardtornish.co.uk

Ardtornish estate is a 35,000 acre (14,164ha) Highland estate with 24 acres (10ha) of established gardens around the Grade A listed Ardtornish House. Fly-fishing for brown trout, sea trout and salmon on three rivers and 16 hill lochs. Free loch fishing to residents of estate's self catering properties.

ARDVRECK CASTLE   1296   2 K14

A837, 11 miles (18km) east of Lochinver, on Loch Assynt. Access at all reasonable times. Free.

Built by the MacLeods, who in the mid-13th century obtained Assynt through marriage, the three-storeyed ruins stand on the shores of Loch Assynt. After his defeat at Culrain, near Bonar Bridge, in 1650, the Marquess of Montrose fled to Assynt but was soon captured and confined here before being sent to Edinburgh and executed.

ARISAIG – THE LAND, SEA AND ISLANDS CENTRE   1297   5 H20

Arisaig, Inverness-shire. On the A830 34 miles (54.5km) west of Fort William and 8 miles (13km) south of Mallaig. Rail and bus service to Arisaig. Open Apr–Oct, Mon–Fri 1000–1500, Sun 1200–1600. Charge £. Children under 10 free and season ticket £5.00. Explanatory displays. Gift shop. Picnic table. Baby changing table. WC. Wheelchair access. Disabled WC. Car parking. Telephone (07973) 252923. www.arisaigcentre.co.uk

The visitor centre is located on the site of a derelict smiddy in a stunning situation in the heart of Arisaig village. A community project, it houses an exhibition that celebrates the social and natural history of the area with photographic displays and artefacts. Subjects include crofting, fishing, church history, marine life, Second World War Special Operations Executive's training grounds and films made in the area. The old forge has been renovated and forms a focal part of the display.

ARIUNDLE OAKWOOD NATIONAL NATURE RESERVE   1298   5 H21

North of Strontian village (on north shore of Loch Sunart). Follow signs for Forestry Commission Airigh Fhionndail car park 2 miles (3km) north of Strontian. Access nature reserve via a track, which also forms part of the Forestry Commission Strontian River Trail, leading to the reserve's nature trail. Access at all times. Free. Car parking. Telephone 01397 704716 (Scottish Natural Heritage); 01397 702184 (Forestry Commission). www.nnr-scotland.org.uk; www.snh.org.uk

Nature reserve. Ancient mossy oakwoods like this one were once widespread along the Atlantic coast. The trees are covered in a lush growth of mosses, ferns, liverworts and lichens, which thrive in this damp west coast climate. The woodland is also home to a wide variety of woodland birds. Nature trail and interpretation boards.

ARMADALE CASTLE GARDENS AND MUSEUM OF THE ISLES   1299   4 G19

Armadale Castle, Sleat, Isle of Skye. 0.5 mile (1km) north of Armadale ferry terminal, 21 miles (34km) south of the Skye Bridge at Kyle of Lochalsh on A851. Car and passenger ferry from Mallaig to Armadale. Bus from Kyle of Lochalsh. Open Apr–Oct, daily 0930–1730 (last entry 1700). Charge ££. Carers of disabled visitors free. Group concessions. Guided tours. Also tour of gardens or small groups. Gift shop. Restaurant and tearoom. Children's play area. WC. Wheelchair access (wheelchairs available for use). Disabled WC. Car and coach parking. Telephone (01471) 844305. www.clandonald.com

A 40 acre (16ha) garden set within the 20,000 (8094ha) Armadale Estate where some of the flora otherwise associated with warmer climes can be grown because of the gulf stream passing close to these shores. Woodland walks and meadows ablaze with wild flowers, seascapes around every corner. Museum explaining the sometimes complex story of Highland history. See also 1599 West Highland Heavy Horses.

AROS EXPERIENCE   1300   4 G18

Viewfield Road, Portree, Isle of Skye. On A850 south of Portree. Bus service from Portree. Open daily, Apr–Sep 0900–2100; Oct–Mar 1000–1700. Charge ££. Children under 12 free. Group concessions. Guided tours. Explanatory displays. Gift shop. Restaurant and café. Crèche and play area. WC. Wheelchair access. Disabled WC. Car and coach parking. Telephone (01478) 613649. www.aros.co.uk

The 'Skye the Island' exhibition is divided into three sections. Initially a small area gives an introduction to Skye including some historical details. Followed by an area where live pictures of sea-eagles are introduced by a warden from the RSPB. Finally, an audio-visual on the scenery of Skye is set to haunting Gaelic melodies.

ASSYNT VISITOR CENTRE   1301   4 J14

Main Street, Lochinver, Sutherland. 98 miles (157km) north of Inverness. Bus service from Inverness. Open Easter–Oct, Mon–Sat 1000–1700; Jun–Sep also Sun. Free. Explanatory displays. Gift shop. WC. Wheelchair access. Disabled WC. Car and coach parking. Telephone (01571) 844373. www.visithighlands.com

Tourist information, wildlife ranger service and informative displays on the Assynt area, for example, live action and recorded highlights from a heronry nest site.

ATTADALE GARDEN AND WOODLAND WALKS   1302   4 J18

Strathcarron, Ross and Cromarty. On south shore of Loch Carron, 2 miles (3km) south of Strathcarron on A890. Nearest railway station Attadale on main Inverness to Kyle of Lochalsh line, then walk 0.5 mile (1km). Open Apr–Oct, Mon–Sat 1000–1730. Charge £. Disabled person and helper are free. Group concessions. Guided tours by arrangement. Explanatory displays. Restaurant close by. Nursery sells unusual plants. WC. Limited wheelchair access. Disabled WC. Car and coach parking. Telephone 01520 722217 or 01520 722603. www.attadale.com

Attadale House was built in 1755 by Donald Matheson. The gardens and woodlands were started in 1890 by Baron Schroder and planted with rhododendrons, azaleas and specimen trees. Since the storms of the 1980s, more old paths have been revealed, bridges have been built and water gardens have been planted with candelabra primulas, gunnera, iris and bamboo. Restored sunken garden, vegetable and herb gardens, Japanese garden. Tree list. Sculpture. Visitors are advised to wear waterproof shoes.

AUCHGOURISH GARDENS   1303   5 N19

Auchgourish Gardens, Street of Kincardine, Boat of Garten, Inverness-shire. On B970 between Boat of Garten and Aviemore. Open Apr–Sep, daily 1000–1700;

Oct–Mar, Sat–Sun 1000–1500. Opening subject to weather. Charge ££. Children free but must be accompanied by an adult. Group concessions. Guided tours by special arrangement. Plant sales. Picnic area. Wheelchair access. Car and coach parking. Telephone (01479) 831464. www.auchgourishgardens.com

A botanic garden laid out in bio-geographic regions. Includes a large Japanese garden (the largest open to the public in the north of Scotland) and features plants from Korea, the Himalayas, China, Asia and Europe. Also rockeries containing Scottish alpine plants. Further areas are being developed including a St Andrew's Garden and rare white Highland cattle.

AULTBEA WOODCRAFT AND HARDWOOD CAFÉ 1304   4 H16

Drumchork, Aultbea, Achnasheen, Ross and Cromarty. Off the A832, 6 miles (9.5km) north of Inverewe Garden (see 1454). Bus from Inverness. Open all year Mon–Sat 0930–1800. Free. Gift shop. Tearoom. Garden. WC. Wheelchair access. Disabled WC. Car parking. Telephone (01445) 731394. www.eweview.com

A wood-turning workshop, craft shop and tearoom with superb views over loch and mountains. Large display of wood-turning in native and exotic woods. Wood-turning tuition available.

AURORA CRAFTS 1305   4 F18

2 Ose, Struan, Isle of Skye. In Ose, 0.25 mile (0.5km) off the A863, 6 miles (9.5km) south of Dunvegan. Open Apr–Oct, daily 0900–1900. Free. Gift shop. Wheelchair access. Car parking. Telephone (01470) 572208.

A craft shop where visitors can see demonstrations of lace-making on most days. Lace, embroidery, knitwear, spinning, wood-turned articles and other articles made on the premises.

BADBEA OLD VILLAGE 1306   3 P14

Caithness. North of Ousdale on A9. Footpath leads from the lay-by to groups of ruined crofthouses perched above cliffs.

Tenants evicted from inland straths during the infamous Clearances founded this lonely settlement. The site is very exposed – tradition has it that children and livestock had to be tethered to prevent them being blown over the cliffs. Many of the inhabitants emigrated to America or New Zealand, as the monument, erected in 1911, testifies.

BAILLE AN OR, GOLDRUSH TOWN 1869 1307   3 N14

Sutherland. 4 miles (6.5km) north west of Helmsdale, on A897 Strath of Kildonan road.

Gold panning still takes place and you can get all the necessary equipment from the craft shop in Helmsdale.

BALMACAAN WOOD 1308   2 L18

Lewiston, Drumnadrochit. 0.5 mile (1km) off A82. Nearest car park in Drumnadrochit, 15 minutes walk from wood. Access at all times. Free. Information boards. Public toilets (including disabled toilets) in car park at Drumnadrochit. Telephone (01764) 662554. www.woodland-trust.org.uk

Balmacaan Wood provides a great place to visit, with diverse and interesting walks for all. Since ancient times native trees such as oak, birch, alder, rowan and hazel have been widespread in Glen Urquhart (in Gaelic Gleann Urchadainn meaning wooded glen). The laird encouraged the protection and planting of the

woods, including exotic trees such as giant redwood, Douglas fir and
rhododendron. Visitors can still see these trees today, with one grand fir
measuring 180 feet (55m) in height and 25 feet (7.5m) in girth – one of the largest
grand firs in Scotland.

BALMACARA ESTATE AND LOCHALSH WOODLAND GARDEN   1309   4 H18

NTS. Lochalsh House, Balmacara, Ross and Cromarty. On A87, 3 miles (4.8km) east of
Kyle of Lochalsh. By bus from Inverness and Glasgow. Open all year, daily
0900–sunset; information kiosk (unstaffed) open Apr–Sep, daily 0900–1700. Charge
£ (honesty box). Explanatory displays. Car parking. Telephone (01599) 566325.
www.nts.org.uk

A beautiful Highland estate where traditional crofting is still carried out.
Includes the village of Plockton, an outstanding conservation area and location
for the television series *Hamish Macbeth*. The garden provides sheltered lochside
walks among pine, ferns, fuchsias, hydrangeas and rhododendrons.

BALNACRA POTTERY   1310   4 J18

The Smithy, Lochcarron, Wester Ross. On the A896, 1 mile (2km) east of Lochcarron.
Nearest railway station Strathcarron, then 1.5 mile (2.5km) walk. Open all year,
Mon–Fri 1030–1700, Sat by appointment. Free. Car and coach parking. Telephone
(01520) 722722. www.balnacra.com

Pottery inspired by animals, archeology, history, anthropology and ancient art,
created and fired in custom-built workshop. See also 1562 Smithy Heritage
Centre.

BALNAKEIL CRAFT VILLAGE   1311   2 L12

Balnakeil, Durness, Sutherland. 1 mile (1.5km) west of Durness, off the single track
road to Balnakeil Bay. Nearest railway station Lairg, post bus from Lairg to Durness.
Bookshop & restaurant: Easter–end of Sep Mon–Sat 1000–1700, and Sun 1000–1600;
Oct–end of Dec Tue–Sat 1000–1630, Sun 1000–1600, Mon closed; Jan–Easter
Wed–Sun 1000–1600, closed Mon,Tue. Craft shop open Easter–Oct, opening times
vary. Free. Gift shop. Licensed restaurants and picnic area. Baby changing facilities.
WC. Wheelchair access. Disabled WC. Car and coach parking. Telephone (01971)
511277 or (01971) 511777 for bookshop. www.scottish-books.net

Craft village including print and painting galleries, pottery and ceramic
sculpture, weaving, spinning and feltwork, clothes, enamelwork, basketry,
woodwork and bookshop. Stone polishing and geology display. The bookshop
stocks a wide range of general titles and has a restaurant on site serving
everything from a pot of tea to a three-course lunch. Theme nights, occasional
live music and other events.

BEAULY PRIORY   1312   2 L18

HS. The Square, Beauly, Inverness-shire. On A9 in Beauly, 12 miles (19km) west of
Inverness. Nearest railway and bus station Inverness, bus to Beauly. Open daily mid
Jun–Sep, 0930–1830. Charge £. Group concessions. Guided tours. Gift shop. WC.
Limited wheelchair access. Car parking. Telephone (01667) 460232. www.historic-
scotland.gov.uk

Ruins of a Valliscaulian priory founded in about 1230, although much of the
building was later reconstructed. Notable windows and window-arcading.

BEINN EIGHE NATIONAL NATURE RESERVE   1313   4 J17

South of Loch Maree near Kinlochewe, Ross and Cromarty. Visitor centre on A832, 1mile (1.5km) north west of Kinlochewe. Nearest railway station at Achnasheen. Limited bus service from Inverness. Nature reserve open at all times. Visitor centre open Easter–Oct, daily 1000–1700. Free. Picnic area. Limited wheelchair access (easy access to visitor centre, three trails suitable for wheelchairs). Car parking. Telephone (01445) 760254. www.nnr-scotland.org.uk

Britain's oldest National Nature Reserve, set up in 1951, and long renowed as one of Scotland's most attractive mountain areas. The reserve includes a huge cluster of rugged peaks, ridges and scree-covered slopes between Loch Maree and Glen Torridon, and the ancient pinewood west of Kinlochewe. The trails from the visitor centre include poetry, artworks and interpretation.

BELLA JANE BOAT TRIPS   1314   4 G19

Elgol, Isle of Skye. 15 miles (24km) from Broadford on B8083. Post bus from Broadford twice a day, Mon-Fri. Sailings Apr–mid Oct daily. Nov–Mar by arrangement. Booking essential, telephone between 0730–1000 or visit website. Group concessions. Guided tours. Refreshments on trip. Binoculars and water capes provided. WC. Wheelchair access with assistance (by prior arrangement). Car and coach parking. Telephone (0800) 7313089. www.bellajane.co.uk

Bella Jane run a three-hour trip from Elgol which sails to Loch Coruisk in the Cuillin Mountains, pausing to see a seal colony then landing ashore. Hot drinks and shortbread on the return journey. Knowledgeable skipper and crew. Award-winning. Also day excursions aboard *AquaXplorer* to the small Isles of Rum, Canna, and Soay as well as west coast trips.

BEN NEVIS   1315   5 K21

2 miles (3km) from Fort William.

Britain's highest (4406 feet/1344m) and most popular mountain for both rock climber and hill walker. It is best seen from the north approach to Fort William, or from the Gairlochy Road, across the Caledonian Canal (see 1456).

BEN NEVIS DISTILLERY VISITOR CENTRE   1316   5 K21

Lochy Bridge, Fort William. On the A82, 2 miles (3km) north of Fort William. Nearest railway station Fort William, bus from Fort William. Open all year Mon–Fri 0900–1700; Jul and Aug closes at 1930, also open Sun 1200–1600. Easter–Oct, Sat 1000–1600; large groups book in advance. Charge £. Admission refunded upon certain whisky purchases. Guided tours (leaflets in French, German and Italian). Explanatory displays. Gift shop. Tearoom. WC. Guide dogs welcome in visitor centre. Limited wheelchair access. Disabled WC. Car and coach parking. Telephone (01397) 702476. www.bennevis.co.uk

Visitors can tour distillery and taste the famous whisky, the Dew of Ben Nevis. Exhibition and video programme. Award-winning whiskies available.

BEN NEVIS WOOLLEN MILL   1317   5 K21

Belford Road, Fort William, Inverness-shire. 0.5 mile (1km) outside Fort William town centre at entrance to Glen Nevis. Railway station in town centre, regular bus service. Apr–Oct, daily 0900–1730; Nov–Mar, daily 1000–1600. Free. Gift shop. Restaurant. WC. Wheelchair access. Disabled WC. Car and coach parking. Telephone (01397) 704244. www.ewm.co.uk

At the end of the West Highland Way, Ben Nevis Woollen Mill stocks fleeces, waterproofs and accessories. Also knitwear, tweeds and Scottish gifts. Whisky shop and daily tastings.

BEN WYVIS NATIONAL NATURE RESERVE 1318   2 L17

Off A835, 15 miles (24km) west of Inverness. Nearest railway station at Garve (4 miles/6.5km). On bus route between Inverness and Ullapool. Car park on A835. Access at all times. Free. Telephone 01349 865333 (Scottish Natural Heritage). www.nnr-scotland.org.uk

Nature reserve. The great whaleback of Ben Wyvis, covered in a carpet of woolly hair moss, is one of the highest mountains in Easter Ross. It is home to many interesting plants and animals, including red and roe deer, pine marten and golden eagle. The lower slopes support dwarf shrub heath and boglands with plants like dwarf birch, cloudberry and dwarf cornel. A footpath through the forest onto the reserve is signposted from the car park.

BIG BURN WALK 1319   2 N15

Start point of walk in Golspie, Sutherland.

One of the finest woodland walks in Sutherland. The extensive and well-maintained paths cross the burn by a series of bridges and allow access up to a waterfall.

BLACK ISLE WILDLIFE AND COUNTRY PARK 1320   2 M17

Drumsmittal, North Kessock, by Inverness. North of Inverness off A9, take first junction right after Kessock bridge to Drumsmittal, park is 1.5 miles (2.5 km) on left. Nearest railway station Inverness; bus from Inverness to North Kessock. Open Apr–Oct, Mon–Sun 1000–1800. Last admission 1700. Charge £. Group concessions. Gift shop. Tearoom. WC. Wheelchair access with assistance. Disabled WC. Car and coach parking. Telephone (01463) 731656.

Ducks, geese, swans, goats, rabbits, pigs, llamas, wallabies, zebras, lemurs, meerkats, racoons, snakes, deer, sheep and cattle. Train rides and children's play area.

BOATH DOOCOT 1321   2 N17

NTS. Auldearn, Nairn, Highland. 2 miles (3km) east of Nairn, off A96. Nearest railway station Nairn. Open all year. Charge £ (honesty box). Explanatory displays. www.nts.org.uk

A 17th-century doocot on the site of an ancient motte. Montrose defeated the Covenanters nearby in 1645; battle-plan on display.

BORRERAIG PARK 1322   4 E17

Dunvegan, Isle of Skye. 8 miles (13km) north west of Dunvegan on the Glendale Visitor Route. Open all year, daily 1000–1800. Charge £. Group concessions. Guided tours. Explanatory displays. Gift shop. WC. Wheelchair access. Disabled WC. Car and coach parking. Telephone (01470) 511311.

A local history museum incorporating the history of the McCrimmon Pipers and bagpiping in general. Craft shop selling the work of many local artisans, local wool and knitwear; also bagpipes and accessories, music and CDs.

BRAHAN SEER PLAQUE, CHANONRY POINT 1323   2 M17

On the shore near Chanonry Lighthouse, Fortrose, Black Isle.

Commemorating the burning at the stake of Kenneth MacKenzie (Coinneach Odhar) – the Brahan Seer. This cruel act was instigated by the Countess of Seaforth when the Brahan Seer, on the insistence of the Countess, told of the 'goings on' of her husband who was on state business in Paris and was away longer than his wife thought necessary. The famous Brahan Seer, who lived in the first half of the 17th century, made many prophecies about the Highlands, some of which are still coming true.

BRIDGE OF CARR   1324   5 N19

Carrbridge. Access at all times. Free.

High and narrow single-arch bridge. Built by John Niccelsone, mason, in summer 1717, for Sir James Grant.

BRIDGE OF OICH   1325   5 L19

HS. On the A82, 4 miles (6.5km) south of Fort Augustus, Inverness-shire. Bus service from Inverness or Fort William. Telephone (01667) 460232. www.historic-scotland.gov.uk

A splendid suspension bridge designed by James Dredge in 1854. It employs a patented design of double cantilevered chains with massive granite pylon arches at each end.

BRIGHT WATER VISITOR CENTRE   1326   4 H18

The Pier, Kyleakin, Isle of Skye. Approximately 1 mile (1.5km) left of Skye Bridge on the Isle of Skye. Nearest railway station Kyle of Lochalsh then bus to Kyleakin; or coach to Kyleakin/Skye. Open Apr–Oct, Mon–Fri 1000–1800. Donation box, charge for walking tour of island. Group concessions. Guided tours. Explanatory displays. Gift shop. Wheelchair access. Car and coach parking. Telephone (01599) 530040. www.eileanban.org

Set in idyllic surroundings on the pier in Kyleakin, the Bright Water Visitor Centre makes the ideal, all weather activity. This unique experience unfolds the secrets of the area's dramatic history and celebrates the wealth of wildlife in the local environment. Also exclusive tours of the nature reserve on the lighthouse island where there is a museum dedicated to the author Gavin Maxwell in the building which was his last home.

BRIN HERB NURSERY   1327   2 M18

The Old School, Flichity, Farr, Inverness. 7 miles (11km) from A9 on Daviot-Fort Augustus road. Infrequent local bus service from Inverness. Open Mar–Sep, Mon–Sat 1000–1800; May–Aug also Sun 1230–1700. Free. Guided tours (small groups by arrangement). Explanatory displays. Gift shop. Tearoom. Garden. WC. Wheelchair access with assistance. Disabled WC. Car parking. Telephone (01808) 521288. www.brinherbnursery.co.uk

Over 300 varieties of herb and wild flower plants are grown on the nursery at 700 feet (213m) above sea level. Display gardens give planting ideas. Shop sells fine foods from the Highlands, Scotland, UK and beyond as well as books, cards and gifts.

LAURENCE BRODERICK SCULPTURE EXHIBITION   1328   4 H19

Gallery An Talla Dearg, Eilean Iarmain, Isle Ornsay, Isle of Skye. On the A851 between Broadford and Armadale, 8 miles (13km) from Broadford . Nearest railway station Kyle of Lochalsh or Mallaig; bus from Broadford or Armadale. Open Aug and Sep,

Mon–Fri 0900–1700, Sat 0900–1300. Free. Guided tours on request. WC. Wheelchair access with assistance. Disabled WC. Car and coach parking. Telephone (01767) 650444. www.laurencebroderick.co.uk

A gallery displaying the work of the sculptor, especially carvings of otters and turtles. Work in various stones, including Skye marble, and in bronze. Sculptor usually available to discuss his work and to give demonstrations.

BRODIE CASTLE   1329   2 N17

NTS. Brodie, Forres, Moray. Off A96, 4.5 miles (7km) west of Forres. By bus from Inverness. Open Easter–Apr and Jul–Aug, daily 1200–1600; May–Jun and Sep, Sun–Thur 1200–1600. Charge £££. Group concessions. Guided tours (with information sheets in six languages). Explanatory displays. Gift shop. Tearoom and picnic area. Garden and adventure playground. WC. Braille guides and personal audiotape for blind visitors. Limited wheelchair access (wheelchair available). Disabled WC. Car and coach parking. Telephone (01309) 641371. www.nts.org.uk

The oldest parts of the castle are 16th century, with 17th- and 19th-century additions. Fine collections of furniture and porcelain and a major art collection. Woodland walk, 4 acre (1.6ha) pond with wildlife observation hides. Famous daffodil collection in spring.

BRORA HERITAGE CENTRE   1330   2 N15

Fascally, Brora, Sutherland. Signposted from centre of Brora. Open May–Sep, Mon–Sat 1030–1730. Free. Guided tours on request. Explanatory displays. Tea and coffee machine, picnic area. Baby changing facilities. WC. Wheelchair access. Disabled WC. Car parking. Telephone (01408) 622024. www.highland.gov.uk/cl/publicservices/visitorcentres/broraheritage.htm

Hands-on exhibition illustrating the history of Brora with historical photographs and local artefacts. The story of the area is told from stone age times to the present day, including exhibits on the local whisky, coal and woollen industry, and genealogy. Dinosaur play area. Fantastic views.

BUCHOLIE CASTLE   1331   3 Q12

Caithness. South of Freswick on the A9 John O' Groats to Wick road.

The 12th-century stronghold of Sweyn Asliefson, the Norse pirate. The Mowats brought the present name of Bucholie with them from their estates in Aberdeenshire.

CAIRN O' GET   1332   3 Q13

HS. 5 miles (8km) north east of Lybster, Caithness. Dunnet's buses to Ulbster (request stop for Cairn o' Get), then 2 mile (3km) walk. Access at all reasonable times. Free. Telephone (01667) 460232. www.historic-scotland.gov.uk

A horned and chambered burial cairn.

CAIRNGORM GLIDING CLUB   1333   5 N19

Feshie Airstrip, Feshiebridge, Kincraig, Inverness-shire. 2 miles (3km) east of Kincraig. Nearest railway stations Kingussie and Aviemore, bus to Kincraig or taxi. Open all year, weekends, bank holidays and midweek at certain periods, dependent on weather. Telephone to confirm. Charge £££. Group concessions. Snacks available. WC. Wheelchair access. Disabled WC. Car and coach parking. Telephone (01540) 651317. www.gliding.org

Founded in 1966 by a group of ten pilots and would-be pilots, this members club offers trial lessons and week (5 day) courses.

CAIRNGORM MOUNTAIN RAILWAY   1334   5 N19

Cairngorm Mountain, Aviemore, Inverness-shire. 9 miles (14.5km) east of Aviemore, 30 minute drive from Inverness. Nearest railway station Aviemore, local bus service. Open May–Oct, daily 1000–1730 (last train up 1630); Nov–Apr opening times vary. Charge £££. Group concessions. Explanatory displays. Ranger guided walks May-Sep. Gift shop. Restaurant (evening dining Jul and Aug). Mountain walking trails, one suitable for wheelchair use. WC. Wheelchair access. Disabled WC. Car and coach parking. Telephone (01479) 861261. www.cairngormmountain.com

Scotland's only mountain railway, taking visitors on a spectacular journey to Cairngorm Mountain – the United Kingdom's fifth highest mountain. A safe and comfortable adventure for all ages and abilities. Interactive mountain exhibition.

CAIRNGORM REINDEER CENTRE   1335   5 N19

Reindeer House, Glenmore, Aviemore, Inverness-shire. 6 miles (10km) east of Aviemore on B970. Nearest railway station Aviemore, bus service to Glenmore. Open Feb half-term holiday–New Year (closed Christmas Day and New Year's Day). Tours to the reindeer May–Sep 1100 and 1430; Oct–Apr 1100 only. Centre open daily, 1000–1700. Charge £££. Group concessions. Guided tours. Explanatory displays. Gift shop. Refreshments available nearby. No guide dogs. Limited wheelchair access. Car and coach parking. Telephone (01479) 861228. www.reindeer-company.demon.co.uk

Britain's only free-ranging herd of reindeer. Visitors join the guide for a walk to the reindeer's hillside grazing (weather permitting – stout footwear and suitable outdoor clothing advisable, Wellington boot hire available). For visitors unable to make the walk, reindeer can also be seen at the centre from Easter until New Year. Exhibition and gift shop. Opportunity to adopt your own reindeer.

CAIRNGORM SLEDDOG ADVENTURE CENTRE   1336   5 N19

Moormore Cottage, Rothiemurchus Estate, Aviemore. 3 miles (5km) from centre of Aviemore. Nearest railway station in Aviemore. Local bus service. Open all year. Daily tours at 1400. Trips and courses held Oct–Apr. Charge £££. Group concessions. Guided tours. Explanatory displays. WC. No dogs other than guide dogs. Wheelchair access with assistance. Car and coach parking. Telephone (07767) 270526. www.sled-dogs.co.uk

The first and only sleddog centre in Britain. Meet the musher and his sleddogs. The dogs live in whisky barrels at the foot of the Cairngorms. Visitors can experience the thrill of a sleddog ride through the spectacular scenery of Rothiemurchus Estate, having helped to water and harness a 12-dog team. Museum cabin dedicated to Alex 'Scotty' Allan, the Scotsman who organised the very first sleddog race in Alaska in 1908. Lots of wildlife in this beautiful area. All visitors must book in advance.

CAIRNGORMS NATIONAL PARK   1337   6 P18

Cairngorms National Park Authority, 14 The Square, Grantown-on-Spey, Moray. Telephone (01479) 873535. www.cairngorms.co.uk

The Cairngorms National Park is Scotland's second, and Britain's largest, national park, an area of outstanding natural beauty. Many sports are available within the park, including downhill skiing, snowboarding, mountain biking, gliding, golfing, salmon fishing, pony trekking and walking. Contact the national park authority for more information.

CAITHNESS NATURAL HISTORY DISPLAY   1338   3 P12

Dunnet Pavilion, Dunnet, Castletown, Caithness. On the A836, 7 miles (11km) east of Thurso, next to caravan site. Nearest railway station Thurso, bus from Thurso. Open Jun–Sep, Sun–Fri 1400–1700 (closed Sat). Free. Explanatory displays and guided walks. Picnic area. WC. Limited wheelchair access. Car and coach parking. Telephone (01847) 821531.

A display illustrating the natural history of Caithness

CAMUS A CHARRAIG   1339   4 J15

Ross and Cromarty. On the main road to Mellon Udrigle, north of Gairloch on A832.

A beautiful white sand beach which borders a broad sandy bay of sparkling blue-green waters surrounded by mountains.

CANAL HERITAGE VISITOR CENTRE   1340   5 L19

Ardchattan House, Canalside, Fort Augustus. On the Inverness to Fort William bus route. Open Apr–Oct, daily 0930–1730. Free. Explanatory displays. Gift shop. Wheelchair access. Disabled WC. Telephone (01320) 366493. www.scottishcanals.co.uk

The centre describes the fascinating history of the Caledonian Canal, from its conception to its present day refurbishment. Visitors can see the dramatic lock flight in operation. See also 1456 Caledonian Canal and 1519 Neptune's Staircase.

CANNA   1341   5 F19

NTS. Inner Hebrides. Access by ferry (no cars) from Mallaig. Open all year. Free. Telephone (01687) 462466. www.nts.org.uk

This beautiful Hebridean island offers spectacular views, interesting archaeological remains and fascinating birdlife. The small farming population still uses traditional crofting systems. There is a post office, but no shops, pubs or roads. For details of work camps and holiday accommodation, contact the NTS Head Office in Edinburgh on 0131 243 9300.

CAPE WRATH   1342   4 K12

12 miles (19.5km) north west of Durness. Ferry telephone (01971) 511376. Minibus telephone (01971) 511287 or 511343.

The most northerly point of Scotland's north west seaboard. A passenger ferry (summer only) connects with a minibus service to the cape. Also mainland Britain's highest sea cliffs at Clo Mor which stand 920 feet (280.5m) high.

CARN LIATH   1343   2 N15

HS. By the A9, 3 miles (5km) east north-east of Golspie, Sutherland. Nearest railway station Dunrobin. Bus service from Inverness, alight past Dunrobin Castle. Access at all reasonable times. Free. Car parking. Telephone (01667) 460232. www.historic-scotland.gov.uk

A typical broch, surviving to first-floor level, with associated settlement.

CARRON POTTERY, CRAFT SHOP AND ART GALLERY   1344   4 J18

Cam-Allt, Strathcarron, Ross and Cromarty. 1 mile (1.5km) south of Strathcarron railway station on A890. Open Mar–Dec, Mon–Sat 0900–1800. Closed Sun. Free. Gift shop. Restaurant next door. WC. Wheelchair access. Disabled WC. Car and coach parking. Telephone (01520) 722321.

Well-established craft shop selling a wide range of Scottish and local crafts. Visitors can view the pottery attached to the shop. Art Gallery with work by local and professional artists. Occasional solo exhibitions. Sculptures and ceramics.

CASSLEY FALLS   1345   2 L15

At Invercassley, Sutherland, on A837.

Attractive falls and walkway by Rosehall. Salmon can be seen leaping during the summer months.

THE CASTLE AND GARDENS OF MEY   1346   3 Q12

Mey, Thurso, Caithness. 14 miles (22.5km) east of Thurso on A836. Nearest railway station at Thurso. Local bus and taxi service. Open mid May–Jul and early Aug–Sep, Sat–Thur 1030–1600. Charge ££. Group concessions. Gift shop. WC. Limited wheelchair access. Disabled WC. Car and coach parking. Telephone (01847) 851473. www.castleofmey.org.uk

The Caithness home of the late Queen Mother and the only property that she ever owned. The gardens and the principal rooms of the castle are open to the public.

CASTLE CRUISES ON LOCH NESS   1347   2 L18

The Art Gallery, The Green, Drumnadrochit. 14.5 miles (23km) west of Inverness on A82. Regular bus service from Inverness. Sailings Mar–Oct, daily at 1000, 1100, 1200, 1400, 1500, 1600, 1700 and 1800 (dependent on passenger numbers and local weather conditions, maximum of 12 passengers per cruise). Charge £££. No charge for babies. Commentary available in Spanish. Explanatory displays. Gift shop in the art gallery. WC. Wheelchair access with assistance. Disabled WC. Car and coach parking. Telephone (01456) 450695. www.lochnesscruises.com

Loch-side born and raised skipper gives personal commentary on the loch and its legendary resident – discover the facts, legends and history. The skipper has been personally involved in research on the loch for over 50 years. Colour echo sounder and audio-visual presentation.

CASTLE KEEP   1348   4 G18

The Steadings, Strathaird, Isle of Skye. On the road from Broadford to Elgol, four miles before reaching Elgol. Open all year, Mon–Fri 1000–1630. Free. Explanatory displays. Gift shop. WC. Car parking. Telephone (01471) 866376. www.castlekeep.co.uk

Bladesmith making hand-forged swords, knives, dirks and traditional Scottish weaponry.

CASTLE OF OLD WICK   1349   3 Q13

HS. 1 mile (2km) south of Wick, Caithness. Nearest railway station Wick, bus service from Wick. Free. Telephone (01667) 460232. www.historic-scotland.gov.uk

The ruin of an early Norse tower house on a spectacular site on a spine of rock, known as the Brig O' Trams, projecting into the sea between two deep narrow gulleys. Great care required when visiting site.

CASTLE VARRICH   1350   2 M13

Tongue, Sutherland. Ruin located above Kyle of Tongue on a promontory. Steep path to castle accessible from the gate beside the Royal Bank of Scotland.

A 14th-century MacKay stronghold. Beautiful views along Kyle of Tongue

CAWDOR CASTLE   1351   2 N17

Nairn. 5 miles (8km) south west of Nairn on B9090 off the A96. Bus service from Inverness and Nairn. Open May–mid Oct, daily 1000–1730, last admission 1700. Charge £££. Free to blind visitors. Group concessions. Explanatory displays. Gift shop. Licensed restaurant, snack bar and picnic area. WC. Limited wheelchair access. Disabled WC. Car and coach parking. Telephone (01667) 404401. www.cawdorcastle.com

Cawdor Castle is the name romantically associated by Shakespeare with *Macbeth*. The medieval tower and drawbridge are still intact and generations of art lovers and scholars are responsible for the eclectic collection of paintings, books and porcelain to be found in the castle. There are beautiful gardens, five nature trails, a nine-hole golf course and putting green, gift, book and wool shops with a wide range of Scottish knitwear and children's clothes.

CHAPEL OF SAND   1352   4 J16

In Laide, north of Gairloch, Ross and Cromarty.

Said to have been constructed by St Columba in the 6th century. Parts of the intricately carved windows of the chapel are still intact and a large remnant of an arch can be seen.

CLAN CAMERON MUSEUM   1353   5 K20

Achnacarry, Spean Bridge, Inverness-shire. 5 miles (8km) from the Commando Memorial on B8005. Signposted. Open Apr–mid Oct, daily 1330–1700; Jul–Aug, daily 1100–1700. Charge £. Children free. Concessions and groups £1.5. Group concessions. Guided tours if requested. Explanatory displays. Gift shop. Garden. WC. Wheelchair access. Car and coach parking. Telephone (01397) 712090. www.clan-cameron.org

The history of the Cameron Clan, its involvement in the Jacobite Risings and the subsequent resurgence of the clan. Visitors can also learn about the story of Achnacarry and its wildlife. There are sections on the Queen's Own Cameron Highlanders and the Commandos who trained at Achnacarry during World War II. The building is on the site of a croft burned by Cumberland's soldiers in 1746.

CLAN GUNN HERITAGE CENTRE AND MUSEUM   1354   3 P14

Latheron, Caithness. On A99, 200m north of intersection with A9, 16 miles (25.5km) from Wick. Nearest railway station at Wick. On Wick bus route. Open Jun–Sep, Mon–Sat 1100–1300 and 1400–1600. Charge £. Group concessions. Audio-visual introduction. Explanatory displays. Gift shop. WC. Limited wheelchair access. Disabled WC. Car and coach parking. Telephone (01593) 741700.

The Clan Gunn Heritage Centre tells the story of one of Scotland's oldest clans from its Norse origins to the present day, set against the background of the history of the north of Scotland. Descended from the Norse Earls of Orkney and Sweyn Asleifs' son, the hero of the Orkneyenga Saga and the Celtic Mormaers of Caithness, the can has played a major role in the turbulent history of Caithness and Sutherland. An early chief of the clan is reputed to have been part of an expedition to America 90 years before Columbus. The evidence is in the centre! One of the best clan archives covering the Clan Gunn and its many septs.

CLAN MACPHERSON MUSEUM   1355   5 M20

Clan House, Main Street, Newtonmore. 15 miles (24km) south of Aviemore on A86. Nearest railway station 0.5 mile (1km), Citylink bus service stops outside. Open Apr–Oct, Mon–Sat 1000–1700; Jul–Aug also Sun 1400–1700. Admission by donation.

Guided tours. Explanatory displays. Gift shop. WC. Wheelchair access. Disabled WC. Car parking. Telephone (01540) 673332. www.clan-macpherson.org

Museum depicting the history of the Clan Macpherson with portraits, photographs and other Macpherson memorabilia.

CLANSMAN CENTRE   1356   5 L19

Canalside, Fort Augustus, Inverness-shire. On A82, 38 miles (61km) west of Inverness at the southern end of Loch Ness. Bus service from Inverness and Fort William. Open Apr–Oct, daily 1000–1800. Charge £. Group concessions. Guided tours (also available in Dutch, French and German). Explanatory displays. Gift shop. Picnic area. WC. Wheelchair access with assistance. Car and coach parking. Telephone (01320) 366444. www.scottish-swords.com

See how the 17th-century Highland clans lived, ate and survived inside a reconstructed turf house. Hear a live presentation by an authentically dressed clansman, including clothing and weapons demonstration. Craft shop and scottish armoury.

CLAVA CAIRNS   58   2 M18

HS. Near Culloden, Inverness-shire, off B9006, 6 miles (10km) east of Inverness. Nearest railway station Inverness, bus from Inverness to Culloden Battlefield, then 2 mile (3km) walk. Access at all reasonable times. Free. Car and coach parking. Telephone (01667) 460232. www.historic-scotland.gov.uk

Two chambered cairns and a ring cairn in a row, each surrounded by a circle of stones. Of late Neolithic or early Bronze Age date. An extensive and well-preserved site in a beautiful setting.

CLOOTIE WELL   1357   2 M17

Munlochy, south of Fortrose, Black Isle.

Wishing well dedicated to St Boniface (or Curidan). Although no trace of it can now be found there is said to have been a chapel on this site. The trees and fence around the well are draped with thousands of rags. To have your wish granted you must spill a small amount of water three times on the ground, tie a rag on a nearby tree, make the sign of the cross and then drink from the well. Tradition states that anyone removing a rag will succumb to the misfortunes of the original owner.

CLYNELISH DISTILLERY   1358   2 N15

Brora, Sutherland. 58 miles (93km) north of Inverness on A9. Rail and bus service to Brora. Open Apr–Oct, Mon–Fri 0930–1600; Nov–Mar by appointment. Charge ££. Children free. Guided tours. Gift shop. Garden. WC. No guide dogs. Wheelchair access to shop and visitor centre only. Disabled WC. Car and coach parking. Telephone (01408) 623000. www.malts.com

The original Clynelish Distillery was built in 1819 by the Marquis of Stafford, later to become Duke of Sutherland. The superb quality of Clynelish whisky was so much in demand that only private customers at home and abroad could be supplied. Trade orders were refused. The distillery was extended in 1896 by the Leith Whisky blenders, Ainslie and Co. In 1967 the new Clynelish Distillery was built alongside the original building with three times the production capacity. Clynelish is available as a 14-year old single malt and is the heart of Johnnie Walker's Gold Label blend.

CNOC FREICEADAIN LONG CAIRNS   1359   3 N12

HS. 6 miles (9.5km) west south-west of Thurso, Caithness. Nearest railway and bus stations Thurso. Access at all reasonable times. Free. Telephone (01667) 460232. www.historic-scotland.gov.uk

Two unexcavated Neolithic long-horned burial cairns, set at right-angles to each other.

COBB MEMORIAL   1360   2 L19

Between Invermoriston and Drumnadrochit by A82. Access at all times. Free.

A cairn commemorates John Cobb, the racing driver, who lost his life near here in 1952 when attempting to beat the water speed record, with his jet speedboat, on Loch Ness.

COMMANDO MEMORIAL   1361   5 K20

Off A82, 11 miles (17.5km) north east of Fort William. Access at all times. Free. Car parking.

An impressive sculpture by Scott Sutherland, erected in 1952 to commemorate the commandos of World War II who trained in this area. Fine views of Ben Nevis and Lochaber.

CONFECTIONARY FACTORY VISITOR CENTRE   1362   5 J21

Old Ferry Road, North Ballachulish, Fort William. On the A82, 13 miles (20km) south of Fort William. Local bus service from Fort William to Oban, Glasgow or Kinlochleven. Open all year. Free. , video viewing room (video on chocolate production). Explanatory displays. Gift shop. Tea and coffee available. Picnic area. WC. Limited wheelchair access. Car and coach parking. Telephone (01855) 821277.

Displays of products and an explanation of the history of Islay tablet, its origins on Islay and reason for the use of goats' milk. Also speciality Scottish food shop. Scenic views of Loch Leven and Ballachulish Bridge.

CORRIMONY CAIRN   1363   2 L18

HS. In Glen Urquhart, 8.5 miles (13.5km) west of Drumnadrochit, Inverness-shire. Bus service from Inverness to Cannich, then walk from Cannich. Open all year. Free. Telephone (01667) 460232. www.historic-scotland.gov.uk

A chambered burial cairn surrounded by a kerb of stone slabs, outside of which is a circle of standing stones.

CORRIMONY RSPB NATURE RESERVE   1364   2 L18

RSPB. By Cannich, Inverness-shire. 22 miles (35km) south west of Inverness off A831 between Cannich and Glen Urquhart. Request bus stop 1.5 miles (2.5km) from reserve. Reserve open at all times. Free. Nature trail way-marked to Loch Comhnard. Car and coach parking. Telephone (01467) 715000. www.rspb.org.uk/scotland

Set in one of the most superb landscapes in Britain, Corrimony has moorland, conifer plantations and native woodland. A nature trail is way-marked to guide visitors to Loch Comhnard, which in summer attracts common sandpipers, green shanks and curlews, along with occasional red-throated divers and ospreys. In winter, look for golden eyes and whooper swans. Black grouse are often seen in the birchwood and spotted flycatchers, bullfinches and wood warblers nest in the pinewoods.

COTTON MILL, SPINNINGDALE   1365   2 M16

In Spinningdale, between Dornoch and Bonar Bridge, Sutherland.

The ruins of an 18th-century cotton mill destroyed by fire in 1808.

CRAGGAN FISHERY AND GOLF COURSE   1366   6 P18

Craggan, Grantown-on-Spey, Moray. 1 mile (2km) south of Grantown-on-Spey on
A95. Bus service from Grantown, Aviemore and Carrbridge. Fishery open Apr–Oct,
daily 0800–1800. Golf course open all year, daylight hours, weather permitting.
Charges dependant on activity. Group concessions. Tearoom and picnic area. WC.
Limited wheelchair access. Disabled WC. Car and coach parking. Telephone (01479)
873283. www.cragganforleisure.co.uk

An 18-hole 3-par golf course suitable for individuals and families of all levels.
Fly fishing and bait fishing for adults and children.

CRAGGAN MILL RESTAURANT, CRAFTS AND ART GALLERY   1367   6 P18

Grantown-on-Spey, Moray. 1 mile (1.5km) south of Grantown-on-Spey on A95. Bus
service from Grantown, Aviemore and Carrbridge. Open all year, summer daily
1030–2200; winter, Mon–Sat 1830–2200, telephone to check. Closed for two weeks in
Oct. Free. Gift shop. Restaurant and beer garden. WC. Limited wheelchair access.
Car and coach parking. Telephone (01479) 872288.

Old converted water mill displays local crafts and paintings, wooden sculptures,
dried flowers and wrought iron work in art gallery. Restaurant.

CRAIG HIGHLAND FARM   1368   4 H18

Plockton, Ross-shire. Situated between Plockton and Achmore on shore road.
Nearest railway station Duncraig, request stop. Postbus from Kyle of Lochalsh. Open
Easter–Oct, daily 1000–dusk. Charge £. Group concessions. Explanatory displays.
Picnics or barbecues welcome on beach. WC. Car parking. Telephone (01599) 544205.

Rare breeds farm and animal sanctuary situated in bay on shore of Loch Carron.
Visitors can feed the llamas, ponies, donkeys, goats and poultry and observe the
owls, pigs and rabbits. Low tide gives access to Scottish Wildlife Trust island via
Coral Beach heronry.

CRAIGELLACHIE NATIONAL NATURE RESERVE   1369   5 N19

Park at Aviemore Tourist Information Centre and take track between youth hostel
and caravan park. Access the reserve via the subway under A9. Nearest railway station
in Aviemore. Access at all times. Free. Car parking. Telephone (01349) 865333.
www.nnr-scotland.org.uk

Directly to the west of Aviemore is the hill and nature reserve of Craigellachie,
the lower slopes of which are cloaked in mature birch woodland. Scenic trails
through the birchwood provide fine views across Aviemore and Strathspey to the
Cairngorms. Visitors may even spot peregrine falcons, which regularly nest on
the cliff here. Woodland trails.

CREAG MEAGAIDH NATIONAL NATURE RESERVE   1370   5 L20

On A86 between Newtonmore and Spean Bridge, 10 miles (16km) west of Laggan.
Nearest railway stations at Newtonmore and Tulloch. Access at all times. Free. No
dogs please. Car parking. Telephone (01528) 544265 (Scottish Natural Heritage).
www.nnr-scotland.org.uk

Creag Meagaidh is 3706 feet (1130m) high and the magnificent ice-carved crags of Coire Ardair are just one of the attractions of this varied wildlife reserve, stretching from lochside shore to mountain top. The area provides a vivid demonstration of how readily native woodland of birch, alder, willow, rowan and oak recovers when the number of grazing animals is controlled. Path to Coire Lochan from car park.

CROICK CHURCH   1371   2 L16

At Croick, Sutherland, 9 miles (14.5km) west of Ardgay.

Made famous in 1845, during the Highland clearances, when many of the tenants of nearby Glencalvie were evicted to make way for sheep. They took refuge in the churchyard and even now names scratched on the east window bear witness to their distress.

CROMARTY COURTHOUSE MUSEUM   1372   2 M17

Chruch Street, Cromarty. 25 miles (40km) north of Inverness on A832. Bus service from Inverness. Open Apr–Oct, daily 1000–1700. Telephone to check winter opening hours. Charge ££. Group concessions. Guided tours, digital tour in English, French, and German. Explanatory displays. Gift shop. Induction loop. Car and coach parking. Telephone (01381) 600418. www.cromarty-courthouse.org.uk

The courthouse, which dates from 1773, has been converted into an award-winning museum interpreting the history of the well-preserved town of Cromarty. Displays include a reconstructed trial in the courtroom, prison cells, animated figures and costumes. A personal tape tour of the town is included in the admission price.

CULBIN SANDS RSPB NATURE RESERVE   1373   2 N17

RSPB. By Nairn. On the coastline between Nairn and Findhorn Bay. Car and coach parking in Nairn (East Beach car park). Nearest railway and bus stations in Nairn, then 1 mile (1.5km) walk.

Reserve open at all times. Free. Explanatory displays. Refreshments and facilities in Nairn. Limited wheelchair access. Disabled WC. Telephone (01463) 715000. www.rspb.org.uk/scotland

Overlooking the Moray Firth. The reserve has sandy beaches, saltmarsh, mudflats and shingle ridges. Thousands of ducks and waders winter here and in the summer you can see butterflies, dragonflies and wild flowers. Much of the reserve is remote and undisturbed.

CULLODEN   1374   2 M18

NTS. Visitor Centre, Culloden Moor, Inverness. On B9006 5 miles (8km) east of Inverness. Bus from Inverness. Visitor Centre open Feb and Nov–Dec, daily 1100–1600; early Mar–mid Mar, daily 1000–1600; late Mar–May and Sep–Oct, daily 0900–1730; Jul–Aug, daily 0900–1800. Charge ££. Group concessions. Guided tours in summer. Explanatory displays, audio-visual programme in five languages. Guidebook in French and German. Gift shop. Restaurant. WC. Braille guide, raised maps and audio tape for blind visitors. Induction loop, subtitled audio-visual programme and special audio-visual channel for hard of hearing. Wheelchair access (wheelchairs available). Disabled WC. Car and coach parking. Telephone (01463) 790607. www.nts.org.uk

Site of the battle on 16 April 1746, when the forces of Bonnie Prince Charlie were defeated by the Hanoverian army, so ending the Forty-Five Jacobite uprising.

Visitor centre with Jacobite exhibition, displays, audio-visual programme and bookshop.

DALDON BORDER COLLIES 1375   4 F17

Daldon, Bernisdale, Portree, Isle of Skye. On A850 between Portree and Dunvegan. Demonstrations Jun–Oct, daily at 1000 and 1600. Charge ££. No charge for children. Group concessions. Car and coach parking. Telephone (01470) 532331.

A new venture to show the public the abilities of the Border Collie working in his natural surroundings. The shepherd, a Scottish and International Sheep Dog Brace Champion, demonstrates with both sheep and ducks in a relaxed atmosphere where visitors are encouraged to participate. Also guided tours through the croft museum, with a detailed history of Skye over the past 400 years and lots of photographs.

DALWHINNIE DISTILLERY VISITOR CENTRE 1376   5 M20

Dalwhinnie, Inverness-shire. Off the A9, 50 miles (80km) north of Perth. Nearest railway station Dalwhinnie, bus from Inverness or Perth stops 2 miles (3km) on A9. Open Easter–Sep, Mon–Fri 0930–1700; Jun–Sep also Sat 0930–1700; Jul and Aug also Sun 1230–1700; Oct Mon–Fri 1100–1600; Nov–Easter 1300–1600 (appointments advised). Charge ££. Groups of students under 18 £. Children under 8 not allowed into production area. Group concessions. Guided tours. Explanatory displays. Leaflets available in Dutch, French, German, Italian, Japanese and Spanish. Gift shop. WC. Guide dogs to visitor centre only. Limited wheelchair access. Disabled WC. Car and coach parking. Telephone (01540) 672219.

The highest distillery in Scotland, opened in 1898. Tour guides explain the secrets of distilling. The exhibition features the history and geography of the area, and the classic malts.

DANDELION DESIGNS AND IMAGES GALLERY 1377   4 F17

The Captain's House, Stein, Waternish, Isle of Skye. On the B886, Waternish Road, betwen Edinbane and Dunvegan. By bus from Portree or Dunvegan (limited service). Open Mar–Oct, daily 1100–1700. Nov–Feb by arrangement. Free. Gift shop. Refreshments nearby. Wheelchair access. Car and coach parking. Telephone (01470) 592218 or 592223. www.dandelion-designs.co.uk

A craft workshop and gallery. A local artist demonstrates craft work and painting techniques. Situated in a fine listed building on the shore of Loch Bay with spectacular views.

DINGWALL MUSEUM 1378   2 L17

Town House, High Street, Dingwall, Ross and Cromarty. 11 miles (18km) north of Inverness via A9 and A835. Nearest railway station Dingwall; bus service from Inverness, Strathpeffer and the north. Mid May–Sep, Mon–Fri 1000–1630. Free. Group concessions. Guided tours. Explanatory displays. Gift shop. Picnic area. Garden and outdoor display area. Amplified hearing units available. Personal guides for blind visitors. Limited wheelchair access. Car and coach parking. Telephone (01349) 865366.

The award-winning museum contains a reconstructed smiddy and kitchen; military room and artefacts relating to the history of the ancient burgh. Special attractions including giant jigsaws for children. Changing exhibitions and activities such as spinning and blanket stamping.

DIVACH FALLS   1379   2 L18

A82 from Inverness through Drumnadrochit, turning right at Lewiston onto
Balmacaan road (Falls signposted). Car park at top.

A 100 foot (30.5m) fall above the village of Drumnadrochit. The falls are
overlooked by Divach Lodge where J. M. Barrie once stayed.

DOLPHINS AND SEALS OF THE MORAY FIRTH   1380   2 M18

Tourist Information Centre, North Kessock, by Inverness. Off the A9, just north of
the Kessock Bridge. Bus from Inverness. Open Jun–Sep, daily 0930–1630. Free.
Explanatory displays and group talks. Gift shop. Picnic area. WC. Wheelchair access
with assistance. Disabled WC. Car and coach parking. Telephone (01463) 731866.

An exhibition about the local bottle-nosed dolphin population. Video display.
Children's activities. Reference corner and interpretive staff. Visitors may watch
the dolphins and hear them through underwater microphones.

DORNOCH CATHEDRAL   1381   2 N16

Dornoch, Sutherland. On A9, 40 miles (64km) north of Inverness. Bus from Inverness
or Tain (station). Open all year 0900–dusk. Free. Guided tours after Sun eve service
in summer; other times with advance notice. Explanatory displays. Small gift shop
(summer, Mon-Fri 1000-1600). Crèche during Sunday church service. WC. Induction
loop and personal radio receivers available on request. Wheelchair access. Car and
coach parking. Telephone (01862) 810357.

A small well-maintained cathedral founded in 1224 by Gilbert, Archdeacon of
Moray and Bishop of Caithness. Partially destroyed by fire in 1570 and restored
1835-37, and again in 1924. The fine 13th-century stonework is still visible.

DORNOCH LOCHANS   1382   2 N16

Davochfin Farm, Dornoch, Sutherland. 1 mile (2km) west of Dornoch on Cuthill Road.
Bus from Dornoch. Open Apr–Nov, Mon–Sat 1000–2200, Sun 1400–1800. Charges
vary. Picnic and barbecue area. WC. Wheelchair access with assistance. Disabled WC.
Car and coach parking. Telephone (01862) 810600. www.dornochlochans.co.uk

A trout fishery with four ponds. Also pitch and putt, croquet and boule and golf
driving range.

DOUNREAY VISITOR CENTRE   1383   3 N12

Dounreay, Thurso, Caithness. On A836, 9 miles (14.5km) west of Thurso. Bus service
from Thurso. Open Easter–Oct, daily 1000–1600. Free. Explanatory displays.
Tearoom and picnic area. WC. Limited wheelchair access. Car and coach parking.
Telephone (01847) 802572.

The Dounreay Visitor Centre tells the story of the pioneering work carried out at
the site over the last fifty years and how UKAEA is working with the community
to establish Caithness as a global centre of excellence in nuclear
decommissioning. The exhibition can be enjoyed by the whole family.

JACK DRAKE'S ALPINE NURSERY   1384   5 N19

Aviemore, Inverness-shire. On the B970, 4 miles (6.5km) south of Aviemore. Nearest
railway station Aviemore. Open Mar–Oct, daily 1000–1700. Free. Large groups by
appointment only. Tearoom serving homebaked cakes and tea and coffee. WC.
Limited wheelchair access. Car and coach parking. Telephone (01540) 651287.
www.drakesalpines.com

Informal garden and hardy plant nursery with a wide range of hardy plants in idyllic woodland. Viewing room overlooking red squirrel/bird feeders.

DULSIE BRIDGE   1385   2 N18

Inverness-shire. Off the A939 from Ferness, take the B9007 south, turn right onto an unclassified road to Dulsie.

An old stone bridge dating from 1764 spans the spectacular Findhorn Gorge at this well-known beauty spot.

DUN BEAG BROCH   1386   4 F18

HS. 0.25 miles (0.4km) west of Bracadale, Skye. Bus service from Kyle of Lochalsh to Sligachan or Portree, bus from there past Struan, then short walk. Access at all reasonable times. Free. Car parking. Telephone (01667) 460232. www.historic-scotland.gov.uk

A fine example of a Hebridean broch, apparently occupied until the 18th century.

DUN CANNA   1387   2 K15

Ardmair, north of Ullapool, Ross and Cromarty.

The site of a Viking Fort. Also a flat pebble beach with good swimming.

DUN DORNAIGIL BROCH   1388   2 L13

HS. 10 miles (16km) south of Hope, Sutherland. Post bus from Lairg via Altnahara to Hope, alight before Alltnacaillich. Access at all reasonable times. Free. Car parking. Telephone (01667) 460232. www.historic-scotland.gov.uk

A well-preserved broch standing to a height of 22 feet (6.5m) above the entrance passage.

DUNBEATH HERITAGE CENTRE   1389   3 P14

Old School, Dunbeath, Caithness. Bus from Inverness, Wick or Thurso. Open Apr–Oct, daily 1000–1700; Nov–Mar, Mon–Fri 1100–1500. Charge £. Children free. Group concessions. Guided tours. Interpretive display. Gift shop. Picnic area. WC. Wheelchair access. Disabled WC. Car and coach parking. Telephone (01593) 731233. www.dunbeath-heritage.org.uk

Landscape interpretation centre, Neil Gunn's Highland River, local history, archaeology and specialist bookshop.

DUNCANSBY HEAD   1390   3 Q12

The north east point of mainland Scotland, 18 miles (29km) north of Wick. Access at all times. Free.

The lighthouse on Duncansby Head commands a fine view of Orkney, the Pentland Skerries and the headlands of the east coast. A little to the south are the three Duncansby Stacks, huge stone needles in the sea. The sandstone cliffs are severed by great deep gashes (geos) running into the land. One of these is bridged by a natural arch.

DUNNET HEAD   1391   3 P12

B855, 12 miles (19km) north east of Thurso. Access at all times. Free. Car parking.

This bold promontory of sandstone rising to 417 feet (127m) is the northernmost point of the Scottish mainland. There are magnificent views across the Pentland

Firth to Orkney and a great part of the north coast to Ben Loyal and Ben Hope. The windows of the lighthouse are sometimes broken by stones hurled up by the winter seas.

DUNROBIN CASTLE AND GARDEN   1392   2 N15

Golspie, Sutherland. Off A9, 1 mile (2km) north of Golspie. Nearest railway station at foot of Castle Drive, bus service from Inverness. Open Apr–May and Oct, Mon–Sat 1030–1630, Sun 1230–1630; Jun–Aug, Mon–Sat 1030–1730, Sun 1230–1730. Charge £££. Group concessions. Guided tours (available in German, pre-booking essential). Explanatory displays. Gift shop. Tearoom. Garden. WC. Car and coach parking. Telephone (01408) 633177.

Set in a great park with magnificent formal garden overlooking the sea. Dunrobin Castle was originally a square keep, built circa 1275 by Robert, Earl of Sutherland, after whom it was named Dun Robin. For centuries this has been the seat of the Earls and Dukes of Sutherland. The present outward appearance results from extensive changes made 1845–50. Fine paintings, furniture and a steam-powered fire engine. Falconry displays and museum.

DUNVEGAN CASTLE   1393   4 F17

Dunvegan, Isle of Skye. On A850, 1 mile (2km) north of Dunvegan village. By train to Kyle of Lochalsh or bus from Portree. Open Mar–Oct, daily 1000–1730; in winter 1100–1600. Charge £££. Children under 5 free. Group concessions. Explanatory displays. Gift shop. Restaurant, tearoom and picnic area. WC. Limited wheelchair access. Disabled WC. Car and coach parking. Telephone (01470) 521206. www.dunvegancastle.com

Historic stronghold of the Clan Macleod, set on the sea loch of Dunvegan, the home of the chiefs of Macleod for 800 years. Possessions on view include books, pictures, arms and treasured relics. Trace the history of the family and clan from the days of their Norse ancestry through 30 generations to the present day. Boat trips from the castle jetty to the seal colony. Extensive gardens and grounds. Audio-visual room. Clan exhibition with items belonging to Bonnie Prince Charlie.

EAS COUL AULIN FALLS   1394   2 K14

At the head of Loch Glencoul, 3 miles (4.5km) west of A894 near Unapool. For boat trips to waterfall telephone Statesman cruises (01571) 844446.

The tallest waterfall in Britain, dropping 658 feet (200m). Seals and the occasional elusive otter may be seen on the loch.

EATHIE BURN   1395   2 M17

Rosemarkie, north of Fortrose, Black Isle.

Fossils may be found on the foreshore.

EDINBANE POTTERY   1396   4 F17

Edinbane, Isle of Skye. Just off the A850, 14 miles (22.5km) from Portree, 8 miles (13km) from Dunvegan, 48 miles (77km) from Skye bridge. Buses from Portree or Dunvegan. Open Easter–Oct, daily 0900–1800; winter Mon–Fri only. Free. Explanatory displays. Gift shop. Children's play area. Wheelchair access. Car and coach parking. Telephone (01470) 582234. www.edinbane-pottery.co.uk

Workshop and gallery, specialising in both wood-fired and saltglaze handmade functional pottery. Work in progress may be seen.

EILEAN DONAN CASTLE   1397   4 J19

Dornie, by Kyle of Lochalsh, Ross and Cromarty. On the A87, 8 miles (13km) east of Kyle of Lochalsh. Nearest railway station Kyle, bus from Glasgow, Inverness and Kyle. Also taxi from Kyle. Open Apr–Oct, daily 1000–1730; Mar and Nov, daily 1000–1530. Charge ££. Group concessions for larger groups. Registered disabled free. Guided tours (translations available in Dutch, French, German, Italian and Spanish). Explanatory displays. Gift shop. Coffee shop. Baby changing facilities. WC. Wheelchair access to visitor centre. Disabled WC. Car and coach parking. Telephone (01599) 555202. www.eileandonancastle.com

On an islet (now connected by a causeway) in Loch Duich, this picturesque and inhabited castle dates back to 1214. It passed into the hands of the Mackenzies of Kintail who became the Earls of Seaforth. In 1719 it was garrisoned by Spanish Jacobite troops and was blown up by an English man o' war. Now completely restored and the home of the MacRaes.

EMBO BEACH, ANCHOR   1398   2 N16

Embo, north of Dornoch, Sutherland.

The anchor probably came from the Prussian barque *Vesta* which was wrecked in 1876. It came ashore 300 yards (275m) north of the village and Embo fishermen rescued all 11 crew.

FAIRY GLEN RSPB NATURE RESERVE   1399   2 M17

RSPB. Rosemarkie, Black Isle, Ross-shire. 16 miles (25.5km) from Inverness, 0.25 miles (0.5km) from Rosemarkie on A832. Regular bus service from Inverness stops in Rosemarkie. Reserve open at all times. Free. Explanatory displays. Refreshments and facilities in Rosemarkie. Car and coach parking. Telephone (01463) 715000. www.rspb.org.uk/scotland

One mile (1.5km) of attractive woodland glen with a stream and two waterfalls, on the edge of a coastal village. Lots of woodland plants to see, and breeding dippers and grey wagtails. The glen has many tales and legends connected with it and is reputed to be the home of a black witch.

FALLS OF FOYERS   1400   2 L19

Foyers, on the eastern shore of Loch Ness. Car park in village, then walk.

These falls, which are particularly spectacular in spate, are surrounded by woodland trails. The falls were visited and written about by Robert Burns.

FALLS OF GLOMACH   1401   4 J18

NTS. Highland. 18 miles (28km) east of Kyle of Lochalsh, north east off A87. Open all year. Free. Car and coach parking. www.nts.org.uk

At 370 feet (112m), this is one of the highest waterfalls in Britain, set in a steep narrow cleft in remote countryside. The falls are a 5 mile (8km) walk from the car park at Dorusduain.

FALLS OF ROGIE   1402   2 L17

FE. Car park on east side of A835, 2 miles (3km) west of Contin. Nearest railway station at Garvie. Access at all times. Free. Explanatory displays. Picnic area. WC. Car and coach parking. Telephone (01463) 791575. www.forestry.gov.uk

The word Rogie comes from the Norse language and means splashing foaming river. The car park is the starting point for three trails leading to a larch-decked suspension bridge which crosses the Blackwater River. Impressive views of the falls which, although not particularly high, are greatly enhaced by their beautiful woodland setting. Leaping salmon may be viewed from the bridge.

FALLS OF SHIN   1403   2 M15

Lairg, Sutherland. Off the A836, 5 miles (8km) north of Bonar Bridge. Bus from Inverness or Lairg. Salmon leap and waterfall open all year. Visitor centre open all year, daily 1000–1800. Free. Gift shop. Restaurant. WC. Wheelchair access. Disabled WC. Car and coach parking. Telephone (01549) 402231. www.fallsofshin.com

Waterfalls in a beautiful wooded section of the Achany Glen. Popular for watching salmon leaping as they migrate upstream. The visitor centre is a popular stop.

FARAID HEAD AND BALNAKEIL BAY   1404   2 L12

North of Durness, Sutherland.

The Balnakeil area is of outstanding nature conservation interest for its outcrops of Durness limestone and the associated plant communities. Faraid Head, behind the beautiful Balnakeil beach, is a narrow headland with dunes, coastal grasslands and steep cliffs. During the summer months a ranger service is operated from the Tourist Information Centre where advice on guided walks and areas of wildlife interest can be obtained.

FARIGAIG   1405   2 L19

FE. By Inverfarigaig on south side of Loch Ness, 18 miles (29km) south west of Inverness. Open daily all year. Free. By arrangement. Forest exhibition. Public toilets open Easter-Sep. WC. Wheelchair access. Car parking. Telephone (01320) 366322. www.forestry.gov.uk

Farigaig Forest offers excellent views over Loch Ness and across Inverfarigaig to Dum Dearduil, the site of a vitrified Iron Age fort dating from around 500 BC. The forest comprises large specimen conifers, introduced from America during the last century, and a mixture of native trees including birch, rowan, alder, ash, willow, hazel, elm and oak.

FERRYCROFT COUNTRYSIDE CENTRE   1406   2 M15

Lairg, Sutherland. Nearest railway station Lairg. Bus service from Inverness. Open Apr–Oct, daily 1000–1700. Free. Explanatory displays. Gift shop. Tea and coffee available. Picnic area. Garden with play equipment. WC. Wheelchair access (excluding archaeological trail). Disabled WC. Car and coach parking. Telephone (01549) 402160.

A Tourist Information Centre where visitors can learn about Sutherland. The audio-visual displays show the many changes to Sutherland's landscape from the Ice Age to the present day. Themes include forest cover, inhabitants, hydro-electric schemes, wildlife, conservation and archaeology. There are indoor puzzles and a play area for children. Visitors can also book accommodation, buy maps and books, exchange currency and obtain angling permits. Archaeological trail and forest walks.

FLOW COUNTRY   1407   3 P13

Caithness. At Golticlay, just north of Rumster Forest on the Lybster to Achavanich road.

A view of the open peatlands of central Caithness. To the west, beyond Loch Rangag and Loch Ruard, these ancient peatlands have remained unchanged for thousands of years. Blar nam Faoileag National Nature Reserve is visible and is part of the largest single expanse of actively growing blanket bog remaining in Britain. These peatlands, with their extraordinary surface patterns of pools and ridges, collectively form what is commonly known as the Flow Country.

FORSINARD RSPB NATURE RESERVE   1408
3 N13

RSPB. Forsinard, Sutherland. On the A897, 24miles (38km) inland from Helmsdale. Nearest railway station Forsinard (no bus). Reserve open at all times, visitor centre open Apr–Oct, daily 0900–1800. Free. Donations welcome. Guided tours. Explanatory displays. WC. Wheelchair access to Visitor Centre. Disabled WC. Car and coach parking. Telephone (01641) 571225. www.rspb.org.uk/scotland

Lying at the heart of the internationally important Flow Country of Caithness and Sutherland, Forsinard nature reserve is one of the most unspoilt peatlands in the world. Birds including golden plovers, dunlins and merlins breed on the reserve. The RSPB are conserving the bogs while encouraging limited access via the visitor centre at Forsinard railway station, a bog pool tail, regular guided walks and road-side viewing.

FORT GEORGE   1409
2 M17

HS. Visitor Centre, Ardersier, Inverness. Off the A96, by Ardersier, 11 miles (17.5km) east of Inverness. Nearest railway station Inverness, bus service from Inverness. Tour bus from Inverness. Open Apr–Sep, daily 0930–1830; Oct–Mar, Mon–Sun 0930–1630. Charge £££. Group concessions. Explanatory displays and visitor centre. Gift shop. Tearoom and picnic area. WC. Wheelchair access with assistance. Disabled WC. Car and coach parking. Telephone (01667) 462777. www.historic-scotland.gov.uk

A vast site of one of the most outstanding artillery fortifications in Europe. It was planned in 1747 as a base for George II's army and was completed in 1769. Since then it has served as a barracks. It is virtually unaltered and presents a complete view of the defensive system. There is a reconstruction of barrack rooms in different periods and a display of muskets and pikes. Includes The Highlanders Regimental Museum (see 1447).

FORTROSE CATHEDRAL   1410
2 M17

HS. In Fortrose, Ross and Cromarty, 8 miles (13km) south south-west of Cromarty. Nearest railway and bus stations Inverness, bus to Fortrose. Open at all reasonable times. Free. Car parking. Telephone (01667) 460232. www.historic-scotland.gov.uk

The surviving fragments consist of the 13th-century vaulted undercroft of the chapter house and the south aisle of the nave, a 14th-century vaulted structure, both finely worked, with two canopied monuments and other memorials.

THE FUN HOUSE   1411
5 N19

Hilton Coylumbridge, Aviemore. On B970, 2.5 miles (4km) from Aviemore. Nearest railway station at Aviemore. Open all year, daily 1000–1800. Charges dependent on age and activity, from £. Group concessions. American themed diner. Fully registered creche open all year, daily 0800–2100. WC. Wheelchair access. Disabled WC. Car and coach parking. Telephone (01479) 813081. www.aviemorefunhouse.co.uk

A large indoor facility for all the family, with Cyril the Squirrel's softplay tree house, adventure mini golf (indoors and out) and ten pin bowling.

FYRISH MONUMENT   1412

2 M17

Above village of Evanton on Fyrish Hill, off A9. Access at all times. Free.

Curious monument erected in 1782 by Sir Hector Munro who rose from the ranks and distinguished himself at the relief of Seringapatam. The monument is a replica of the Indian gateway and was built to provide work at a time of poverty and unemployment in the Evanton area.

GAELIC WHISKIES – WHISKY EXHIBITION   1413

4 H19

An Oifig, Eilean Iarmain, Sleat, Isle of Skye. On the A851, 8 miles (13km) south of Broadford. Bus from Armadale or Broadford. Open all year, Mon–Fri 0900–1730; Jun–Sep, Sat 1030–1400. Free. Explanatory displays and short talk (English or Gaelic). Gift shop. Meals available in Hotel Eilean Iarmain next door. Art gallery open in summer. WC. Wheelchair access. Disabled WC in hotel. Car and coach parking. Telephone (01471) 833266. www.gaelic-whiskies.co.uk

The only whisky company with its headquarters in the Hebrides. An exhibition about whisky is located in historic buildings, once the Isle Ornsay harbour shop.

GAIRLOCH HERITAGE MUSEUM   1414

4 H16

Achtercairn, Gairloch, Ross-shire. In Gairloch, on A832 70 miles (112km) north west of Inverness. Bus from Inverness or Achnasheen (station). Open Apr–Sep, Mon–Sat 1000–1700; Oct, Mon–Fri 1000–1330. Winter by prior arrangement. Charge £. Group concessions. Explanatory displays. Gift shop. Restaurant. Hands-on activities for children, demonstrations and talks. WC. Wheelchair access. Car and coach parking. Telephone (01445) 712287. www.gairlochheritagemuseum.org.uk

A museum displaying all aspects of life in a typical west Highland parish from the Stone Age to the present day, including archaeology, fishing, agriculture and domestic arts. Reconstructed croft house room, schoolroom, dairy and shop. The lens from the local lighthouse and preserved fishing boats are also on display. Archive and library.

GAIRLOCH MARINE LIFE CENTRE AND CRUISES   1415

4 H16

Pier Road, Gairloch, Ross-shire. At Gairloch harbour on A832. Infrequent bus service from Inverness. Open Easter–Oct, daily 0900–1700. Telephone to confirm. Free. Charge £££ for cruises (duration 2 hours minimum). Group concessions. Guided tours. Explanatory displays. Gift shop. WC. Wheelchair access. Disabled WC. Car parking. Telephone (01445) 712636. www.porpoise-gairloch.co.uk

Established in1989 this is the areas longest running cruise operator. Owned and operated by a marine biologist specialising in cetacean research. The visitor centre has interpretive displays and film of local wildlife including whales, dolphins, porpoises, white tailed and golden eagle plus many other sea birds. There is also daily marine wildlife cruises with expert marine biologist on-board throughout the cruise.

GARVAMORE BRIDGE   1416

5 M20

6 miles (9.5km) west of Laggan Bridge, 17 miles (27km) south west of Newtonmore. Access at all times. Free.

This two-arched bridge at the south side of the Corrieyairick Pass was built by General Wade in 1735.

GEMINI EXPLORER MARINE WILDLIFE TOURS   1417

6 P17

Buckie Harbour, Buckie. Midway between Inverness and Aberdeen on the A96. Nearest train station is Keith and nearest bus station is Buckie. Open all year round, dependent on weather. Please contact for times. Charge £££. Family and group prices negotiable. Group concessions. Guided tours. Explanatory displays. Gift shop. Tea, coffee, and biscuits during the trip. WC. No guide dogs. Wheelchair access with assistance. Car and coach parking. Telephone 07747626280. peter@geminiexplorer.co.uk

Gemini Explorer Marine Tours offer an outstanding wildlife watching opportunity aboard a very stable and safe Ex 72Ft lifeboat. The crew on board, which includes a marine biologist, are dedicated to ensuring that passengers have a very rewarding and educational time whilst on board, cruising within the Moray Firth's resident dolphin habitat. Photographic opportunities are second to none.

GLASS CREATIONS   1418   3 P12

Thurso Glass Studio, Riverside Road, Thurso, Caithness. First right on entry over bridge to Thurso. Nearest railway station Thurso. Open all year, Mon–Sat 1000–1700. Free. Explanatory displays. Gift shop. Wheelchair access. Car parking. Telephone (01847) 894017. www.glasscreations.ukf.net

On the banks of the River Thurso with uninterrupted views of salmon, seals and otters. The studio uses the lampworking method to create glass items and sculptures. Demonstrations in glass blowing on request. Small orders completed for visitors on holiday.

GLEN AFFRIC NATIONAL NATURE RESERVE   1419   2 K19

31 miles (50km) south west of Inverness. From A831 at Cannich take the unclassified road south beyond Cannich village to Loch Affric. Reserve open at all times. Free. Picnic tables and interpretation boards. Waymarked walks. Programme of ranger-led guided walks during summer. WC (seasonal) at Dog Falls and River Affric car parks. Disabled WC (seasonal) at River Affric car park. Wheelchair access with assistance (three main car parks are fairly flat and each one has accessible picnic tables, parts of the forest road at River Affric car park are less steep). Car parking. Telephone (01320) 366322. www.forestry.gov.uk/glenaffric

Known as one of the most beautiful glens in Scotland, Glen Affric is a mix of high mountains, lochs, rivers and part of the ancient Caledonian Pine forest. Main features include Dog Falls in the lower Glen, Loch Affric and the wilder West Affric owned by the National Trust for Scotland.

GLEN NEVIS VISITOR CENTRE (IONAD NIBHEIS)   1420   5 K21

Glen Nevis, Fort William. 1.25 miles (2km) up Glen Nevis, located 2 miles (3km) east of Fort William. Nearest railway station Fort William, hourly local bus service to Glen Nevis. Open May–early Sep, daily 0900–1700. Free. Explanatory displays. Gift shop. Refreshments and picnic area. WC. Wheelchair access. Disabled WC. Car parking. Telephone (01397) 705922.

Information on the history, geology, flora and fauna of Ben Nevis and Glen Nevis. Ranger guided walks during June, July and August.

GLEN ORD DISTILLERY VISITOR CENTRE   1421   2 L17

Muir of Ord, Ross-shire. Just off the A832 on the outskirts of Muir of Ord, 15 miles (24km) west of Inverness. Bus from Inverness or Dingwall, or rail to Muir of Ord. Open Jan–Feb, Mon–Fri 1130–1500; Mar–June, Mon–Fri 1000–1700; Jul–Sep, Mon–Sat 1000–1700, Sun 1200–1600; Oct, Mon–Fri 1100–1600; Nov–Dec, Mon–Fri 1130–1500 (last guided tour 1 hour before closing). Charge ££. Children under 8 are not permitted into production areas. Guided tours. Explanatory displays. Gift shop. Picnic area. WC. Wheelchair access. Disabled WC. Car and coach parking. Telephone (01463) 872004.

The sole survivor of nine distilleries which once operated around Glen Ord. Licensed in 1838. The tour and exhibition show the history of the Black Isle and the main processes of distilling. Complimentary tasting.

GLENCOE   1422   5 J21

NTS. Visitor Centre, Glencoe, Ballachulish, Argyll. On A82, 17 miles (27km) south of Fort William. Bus from Edinburgh, Glasgow or Fort William. Open Mar, daily 1000–1600; Apr–Aug, daily 0930–1730; Sep–Oct, daily 1000–1700; Nov–Feb, Thur–Sun 1000–1600. Charge ££. Group concessions. Explanatory displays. Guided walks in glen. Gift shop. Snack bar and picnic area. WC. Induction loop. Wheelchair access to visitor centre. Disabled WC. Car and coach parking. Telephone (01855) 811307. www.nts.org.uk

Dramatic and historic glen, scene of the 1692 massacre of part of the MacDonald clan by soldiers of King William. Its steep sided mountains offer superb walking and climbing. Red deer, wild cat, golden eagle and rare arctic plants can be seen among the breathtaking peaks and spectacular waterfalls. Ranger service. Learn more about the area in the new eco-friendly visitor centre with exciting interactive exhibits for the whole family.

GLENCOE MOUNTAIN RESORT   1423   5 K22

Kingshouse, Glencoe, Argyll. On the A82, 30 miles (48km) south of Fort William, 12 miles (19km) from station at Bridge of Orchy. Nearest railway station Bridge of Orchy, bus from Glasgow. Open for skiing Christmas–Apr; chairlift and restaurant open Jun–Aug. Charge ££. Telephone for winter skiing charges. Group concessions. Explanatory displays. Gift shop. Restaurant (café on plateau). WC. Limited wheelchair access. Disabled WC. Car and coach parking. Telephone (01855) 851226. www.glencoemountain.com

Scotland's original ski centre, Glencoe is renowned for its exhilarating skiing and friendly atmosphere. For skiers and boarders of all standards, Glencoe provides on-site facilities including ski and snowboard school and hire departments. The chairlift and restaurant are open in summer. During the summer the chairlift is open offering superb views over Glencoe.

GLENCOE AND NORTH LORN FOLK MUSEUM   1424   5 K22

Glencoe, Argyll. Off the A82 in Glencoe village. Bus from Glasgow, Inverness, Oban and Fort William. Open Easter and May–Sep, Mon–Sat 1000–1730. Charge £. Children free. Group concessions. Explanatory displays. Gift area. Wheelchair access. Car and coach parking. Telephone (01855) 811664.

A local museum in four heather-thatched buildings and two outbuildings. Many exhibits reflect Highland rural life, history, geology and wildlife.

GLENELG BROCHS   1425   4 H19

HS. About 8 miles (13km) south east of Kyle of Lochalsh, Ross and Cromarty. Nearest railway station Kyle of Lochalsh, limited post bus service to Glenelg. Access at all reasonable times. Free. Telephone (01667) 460232. www.historic-scotland.gov.uk

Two Iron Age broch towers standing over 30 feet (9m) high, with well-preserved structural features.

GLENELG CANDLES ARTS AND CRAFTS CENTRE   1426   4 H19

Glenelg, Rosshire. In Glenelg, 2 miles (3km) from car ferry to Skye and 7 miles (11km) from Shiel Bridge on the A87. By post bus from Kyle of Lochalsh (nearest railway station). Open Mar–Oct daily, 0930–1700; Nov–Feb, Mon–Fri 1000–1600 workshop only open, telephone to confirm. Free. Demonstrations. Gift shop. Licensed coffee shop selling all-day light lunches and home baking (organic and local produce used). Picnic area. Garden. WC. Wheelchair access. Disabled WC. Car and coach parking. Telephone (01599) 522313. www.glenelgcandles.co.uk

A candle workshop where visitors can see demonstrations of handmade Highland landscape candles, or browse among paintings by local artists, books and gifts.

GLENFINNAN MONUMENT   1427   5 J20

NTS. Information Centre, Glenfinnan, Inverness-shire. On A830, 18.5 miles (30km) west of Fort William. By rail to Glenfinnan Station (1 mile/1.5km). Site open all year. Visitor centre open Apr–Oct, daily 1000–1700; Jul–Aug, daily 0930–1730. Charge £. Group concessions. Explanatory displays. Audio programme in French, Gaelic and German. Gift shop. Snack bar and picnic area. WC. Audio tour. Wheelchair access to information centre (wheelchair available). Disabled WC. Car and coach parking. Telephone (01397) 722250. www.nts.org.uk

Set amid superb Highland scenery at the head of Loch Shiel, the monument was erected in 1815 in tribute to the clansmen who died for the Jacobite cause. It is on the site where Bonnie Prince Charlie raised his standard in 1745. Displays and audio-visual programme in information centre.

GLENFINNAN VIADUCT   1428   5 J20

At Glenfinnan, near Loch Shiel.

Spectacular railway viaduct.

GLENMORANGIE DISTILLERY VISITOR CENTRE   1429   2 M16

Tain, Ross and Cromarty. On the A9, 0.5 mile (1km) north of Tain. Bus or train from Tain or Inverness. Open all year, Mon–Fri 0900–1700; Jun–Oct, Sat–Sun (restricted hours). Charge £. Guided tours (translations in French, German, Italian or Spanish). Explanatory displays. Gift shop. WC. Limited wheelchair access. Disabled WC. Car and coach parking. Telephone (01862) 892477. www.glenmorangie.com

Describes 150 years of the distillery's history. Personal and informative tours, and free sample.

GLENMORE VISITOR CENTRE   1430   5 N19

FE. Ski Road, Glenmore, Aviemore, Inverness-shire. 7 miles (11km) along Ski Road from Aviemore. Bus from Aviemore. Open all year (except Christmas Day, Boxing Day and New Year) daily, 0900–1700. Free. Guided tours by prior arrangement. Explanatory displays. Gift shop. Forest café and picnic area. Water sports facilities. WC. Wheelchair access to visitor centre. Disabled WC. Car and coach parking. Telephone (01479) 861220. www.forestry.gov.uk

The Glen More Forest Park is situated in the foothills of the Cairngorm National Nature Reserve. Caravan and camping site, visitor centre, car parks and picnic areas. Waymarked walks, off-road cycle routes, lochside activities, bird watching. Ranger services. Guided walks and tours.

GRANTOWN MUSEUM AND HERITAGE TRUST   1431   6 P18

Burnfield House, Burnfield Avenue, Grantown-on-Spey. Open Mar–Dec, Mon–Fri 1000–1600. Charge £. Children under 10 free. Group concessions. Explanatory displays.

Gift shop. Picnic area. Garden. WC. Induction loop. Wheelchair access. Disabled WC. Car and coach parking. Telephone (01479) 872478. www.grantownmuseum.co.uk

Located at Burnfield House, a refurbished school originally built in 1865. The permanent exhibition tells the story of Sir James Grant's Town – a fine example of a planned town – bringing the history of Grantown-on-Spey to life through audio-visual and traditional displays.

GREY CAIRNS OF CAMSTER   1432   3 Q13

HS. Off the A9, on the Watten Road, 5 miles (8km) north of Lybster, Caithness. Nearest railway station Wick, bus from Wick to Lybster, request stop at road end for cairns, then 8 mile (13km) walk. Access at all reasonable times. Free. Car parking. Telephone (01667) 460232. www.historic-scotland.gov.uk

Two Neolithic chambered burial cairns – one long with two chambers and projecting 'horns'; one round with a single chamber.

GROAM HOUSE MUSEUM   1433   2 M17

High Street, Rosemarkie, Ross and Cromarty. In Rosemarkie on the A832, 15 miles (24km) north east of Inverness. Bus from Inverness. Open Easter week, daily 1400–1630; May–Oct, Mon–Sat 1000–1700, Sun 1400–1630; Nov–Apr, weekends 1400–1600. Free. Guided tours by prior arrangement. Explanatory displays and videos. Gift shop. Limited wheelchair access. Car and coach parking. Telephone (01381) 620961.

Award-winning Pictish museum. The centre-piece in a stunning display of locally-found stones is the magnificent 8th-century Rosemarkie cross-slab. Part of the nationally important collection of original work by George Bain, the artist responsible for the revival of Celtic art, is also exhibited. Temporary exhibitions of local history or Pictish interest.

NEIL M. GUNN MEMORIAL VIEWPOINT   1434   2 L17

Heights of Brae, Strathpeffer. Access at all reasonable times. Free. Car parking.

Memorial viewpoint for the author Neil M. Gunn, who lived nearby.

HALISTRA POTTERY   1435   4 F17

7 Halistra, Waternish, Isle of Skye. 2 miles (3km) after Stein turn left down Carnach Road, pottery is the third building on the right. Open Apr–Oct, daily 1000–1800; Nov–Mar, Mon–Thu 1000–1800. Free. Explanatory displays, demonstrations and explanation by resident potter. Wheelchair access. Car parking. Telephone (01470) 592347. www.halistra-pottery.co.uk

Situated on Waternish peninsula, one of the craft centres of Skye, this is a purpose built gallery and open plan workshop allowing visitors to see the pottery being made. Wonderful views across Loch Dunvegan to the outer isles.

HANDA ISLAND FERRY TRIPS   1436   4 K13

Handa Island is 6 miles (10km) north of Scourie. Passenger ferry leaves from Tarbet, off A894, 2 miles (3km) north of Scourie. Nearest railway station Lairg, post bus from Lairg stops on request at Tarbet junction. Open Apr–Sep, Mon–Sat. First ferry 0930. Crossings on demand and weather dependent. Last outbound journey usually at 1400, last return journey at 1700. Charge £££. Visitors are asked to make small contribution towards cost of managing the island. Guided tours by arrangement. Explanatory displays. Restaurant and WC (including disabled) at Tarbet. No guide dogs. Car and coach parking. Telephone 01463 714746 (Scottish Wildlife Trust). www.swt.org.uk

Handa Island is internationally famous for its sea bird colonies including the largest breeding colony of guillemots in Britain. The island is also renowned for its magnificent Torridonian Sandstone cliffs, which rise to a height of 400 feet (122m) along the dramatic northern edge of the island. From this viewpoint you may also see many of the area's marine wildlife such as dolphins, porpoises, seals and the occasional whale. A footpath circles the island. Visitors are asked to stay on the path or boardwalk at all times for safety and to avoid disturbing the wildlife. No dogs allowed.

HARTMOUNT WOODTURNING AND CABINET MAKING STUDIO 1437   2 M16

Tigh an Fhraoich, Hartmount, Tain, Ross-shire. Off minor road to Scotsburn, 3 miles (5km) south of Tain. Bus and rail services to Tain. Transport from Tain if required. Open all year, including evenings (on request). Free. Guided tours. Explanatory displays. Gift shop. Two acre (1ha) garden. Wheelchair access. Car parking. Telephone (01862) 842511.

Family business with over 35 years experience. Custom-built woodworking shop and display area. Work produced to client's requirements. Mainly local hardwoods used. Various exotic hardwoods used in small quantities.

HEBRIDEAN CRUISES 1438   5 H20

Arisaig Harbour, Inverness-shire. On A830, 7 miles (11km) south of Mallaig. Railway station at Arisaig, 10 minute walk from harbour. Bus stop five minute walk from harbour. Open Easter–end Sep, Mon–Sat 0900–1730, Sun 0900–1300. Charge £££. Group concessions. Snacks available on all islands, hot drinks can be purchased on board. WC on all islands. Limited wheelchair access. Car and coach parking. Telephone (01687) 450224. www.arisaig.co.uk

Cruise to the idyllic islands of Eigg, Muck and Rum, with time ashore to explore. Regular close sightings of whales, dolphins, seals, otters, puffins, eagles and much more. Visit Kinloch Castle on Rum, climb the Sgurr or stroll along the 'Singing Sands' on Eigg, or explore the beauty of Muck. Something for all ages.

HIGHLAND AND RARE BREEDS CROFT 1439   5 L19

Auchterawe Road, Fort Augustus. Footpath walk begins beside the local Tourist Information Centre. Open Mar–Oct, daily 1000–1800. Charge £. Group concessions. Guided tours. Explanatory displays. Picnic areas. WC. Wheelchair access. Disabled WC. Car and coach parking. Telephone (01320) 366433.

Footpath walk around enclosed fields containing red deer, highland cattle, various breeds of sheep, goats, pigs, hens and pheasants, ducks and Shetland ponies.

HIGHLAND AND RARE BREEDS FARM 1440   2 K15

Elphin, Sutherland. On the A835, 15 miles (24km) north of Ullapool. Bus from Ullapool. Open May–Sep, 1000–1700. Charge ££. Children under 3 free. Group concessions. Guided tours (leaflets in five foreign languages). Explanatory displays. Gift shop. Picnic area. WC. Limited wheelchair access. Car and coach parking. Telephone (01854) 666204.

The Scottish Farm Animal Centre which has over 36 breeds of animals, ancient and modern, in 15 acres (6ha) of farmland, river and mountain scenery. A croft has been adapted for education and conservation. A working organic farm has an exhibition of farm tools, farming demonstrations, guided tours and information sheets.

HIGHLAND FOLK MUSEUM, KINGUSSIE   1441   5 M20

Duke Street, Kingussie, Inverness-shire. In Kingussie, 12 miles (19km) south west of Aviemore off the A9. Nearest railway station Kingussie. Buses from Inverness, Perth or Edinburgh. Open Apr–Oct, telephone to confirm times. Charge £. Guided tours (Nov–Mar). Explanatory displays. Gift shop. Picnic area. Garden. WC. Wheelchair access. Disabled WC. Car and coach parking. Telephone (01540) 661307.

An open air museum, partly housed in an 18th-century shooting lodge. Features a Black House from Lewis, a clack mill and exhibits of farming equipment. Indoors, a fine display of barn, dairy, stable and an exhibition on Highland tinkers. Special features on costume, musical instruments and Highland furniture.

HIGHLAND FOLK MUSEUM, NEWTONMORE   1442   5 M20

Aultlarie, Newtonmore, Inverness-shire. In Newtonmore off the A9, 15 miles (24km) south west of Aviemore; 65 miles (104km) north of Perth. Nearest railway station Newtonmore. Buses from Inverness, Perth or Edinburgh. Open Apr–Oct, telephone to confirm times. Charge ££. Group concessions. Explanatory displays and costumed guides. Gift shop. Café and picnic area. Children's play area. WC. Limited wheelchair access. Disabled WC. Car and coach parking.

A fascinating glimpse into 300 years of social history in the Highlands – an 18th-century farming township with turf houses authentically furnished with box beds and cruisie lamps; an early 20th-century school complete with many of its original fittings; a clockmakers workshop; curling hut and pond; and working croft.

HIGHLAND MUSEUM OF CHILDHOOD   1443   2 L17

The Old Station, Strathpeffer, Ross and Cromarty. On the A834, 5 miles (8km) west of Dingwall. Nearest railway station Dingwall, bus from Dingwall. Open Apr–Oct, Mon–Sat 1000–1700, Sun 1400–1700; Jul and Aug, closes 1900 Mon–Fri. Charge £. Group concessions. Guided tours by appointment. Explanatory displays. Gift shop. Tearoom and picnic area. WC. Tape tour for partially sighted. Wheelchair access. Car and coach parking. Telephone (01997) 421031. www.highlandmuseumofchildhood.org.uk

Located in part of the old station, the museum tells the story of childhood in the Highlands over the last century through a fascinating doll and toy collection. Audio-visual displays and hands-on activities for children.

HIGHLAND STONEWARE   1444   4 J14

Lochinver, Assynt, Sutherland. 98 miles (157km) north of Inverness. Bus service from Inverness. Open all year (except Christmas), Mon–Fri 0900–1800; Easter–Oct also Sat 0900–1700. Free. Explanatory displays (visitors can also walk around factory and speak to artists at work). Gift shop. Children's play area nearby. Wheelchair access with assistance. Car and coach parking. Telephone (01571) 844376. www.highlandstoneware.com

Highland Stoneware was formed in 1974, and has built an international reputation for quality and innovation. Visitors can watch the craftspeople at work to see the full range of making and decorating skills used in creating our unusual and distinctive pottery.

HIGHLAND WILDLIFE PARK   1445   5 N19

Kincraig, Kingussie, Inverness-shire. On the B9152, 7 miles (11km) south of Aviemore. Nearest railway station Kingussie. Bus from Inverness, Perth and Edinburgh. Open daily all year (weather permitting): Apr–Oct 1000–1800; Jun–Aug

1000–1900; Nov–Mar 1000–1600. Last entry two hours before closing. Charge £££ per person (reduced rates in winter). Group concessions. Guided tours. Explanatory displays. Gift shop. Coffee shop and picnic area. Baby changing facilities. Children's play area. Kennels for pets. WC. No guide dogs. Wheelchair access to visitor centre. Disabled WC. Car and coach parking. Telephone (01540) 651270. www.highlandwildlifepark.org

Visitors can discover Scottish wildlife, from native species to those creatures long extinct, and explore themed habitats on foot. Cars can be driven around the main reserve (those without a car will be driven by staff). Wolves, otters, bison, beaver, lynx, capercaillie and more. Themed special events at weekends. Managed by the Royal Zoological Society of Scotland. Warden-led talk every day

HIGHLAND WINERIES   1446   2 L18

Moniack Castle, By Inverness. Off the A862, 7 miles (11km) west of Inverness. Nearest railway station Inverness, bus from Inverness to Inchmore then 1 mile (2km) walk. Open Mar–Oct, daily (except Sun) 1000–1700; Nov–Apr 1100–1600. Charge £. Children free. Group concessions. Guided tours. Gift shop. Picnic area. WC. Limited wheelchair access. Car and coach parking. Telephone (01463) 831283.

A family business in a 16th-century castle producing country wines, liqueurs, meat and game preserves, all made by hand. Tour, tastings, video and talk by tour guide.

THE HIGHLANDERS REGIMENTAL MUSEUM
(QUEEN'S OWN HIGHLANDERS COLLECTION)   1447   2 M17

Fort George, Ardersier, Inverness. At Fort George (see 1409), 14 miles (22.5km) east of Inverness. Nearest railway station Inverness, bus service from Inverness. Tour bus from Inverness. Open Apr–Sep daily, 1000–1800; Oct–Mar, Mon–Fri 1000–1600. Free. Explanatory displays. Gift shop. Refreshments nearby. WC. Limited wheelchair access. Disabled WC. Car and coach parking. Telephone (01463) 224380.

A regimental museum with collections of medals, uniforms and other items showing the history of the Queen's Own Highlanders, Seaforth Highlanders, The Queen's Own Cameron Highlanders, and Lovat Scouts.

HILL O' MANY STANES   1448   3 Q14

HS. At Mid Clyth, 4 miles (6.5km) north east of Lybster, Caithness. Nearest railway and bus stations Wick, bus from Inverness or Wick to Mid Clyth road end, then 1 mile (2km) walk. Access at all reasonable times. Free. Telephone (01667) 460232. www.historic-scotland.gov.uk

More than 22 rows of low slabs arranged in a slightly fan-shaped pattern, which may have formed a prehistoric astronomical observatory.

HILTON OF CADBOLL CHAPEL   1449   2 N16

HS. At Hilton of Cadboll, 12 miles (19km) north east of Invergordon, Ross and Cromarty. Nearest railway station Fearn (request stop), bus service from Inverness. Access at all reasonable times. Free. Telephone (01667) 460232. www.historic-scotland.gov.uk

The foundation remains of a small rectangular chapel.

HISTORYLINKS MUSEUM   1450   2 N16

The Meadows, Dornoch, Sutherland. On A9, 40 miles (64km) north of Inverness. Bus from Inverness or Tain (station). Open May–Sep, Mon–Sat 1000–1600. Charge £. Group concessions. Explanatory displays. Gift shop. WC. Wheelchair access. Disabled WC. Car parking. Telephone (01862) 811275. www.historylinks.org.uk

Historylinks is dedicated to the history and development of the Royal Burgh of Dornoch. Interpretive displays, historic objects and local tales give visitors a precious insight into Dornoch's past. Learn about the treachery of Picts and Vikings, feuding clans and witchcraft. See the golf professional's workshop where Dornoch's Donald Ross honed his skills before designing 500 American courses. Follow the fortunes of the Dornoch railway and learn how Andrew Carnegie, the world's richest man, came to live at Skibo. Children can have fun dressing up, being 'locked' in the stocks or completing quizzes and puzzles.

THE HYDROPONICUM, GARDEN OF THE FUTURE 1451   4 J15

Achiltibuie, Ross-shire. North of Ullapool in the Coigach Peninsula. Open Easter–Sep, daily 1000–1800; also tours in Oct, Mon–Fri 1200 and 1400. Charge ££. Group concessions. Guided tours. Gift shop. Café and picnic area. Children's activities. Access to shore. WC. Wheelchair access to lower level (wheelchair provided if required). Disabled WC. Car and coach parking. Telephone (01854) 622202. www.thehydroponicum.com

A pioneering indoor garden created for the 21st century, overlooking the beautiful Summer Isles. Guided tours take visitors around modern growing houses, each with different climatic zones. Here lush, sub-tropical fruit trees, exotic flowers, scented plants, vegetables and herbs all grow without soil or pesticides.

ICEBERG GLASSBLOWING STUDIO 1452   2 L18

Victoria Buildings, Drumnadrochit, Inverness-shire. In Fort Augustus on the A82. Bus from Inverness or Fort William. Open daily summer, 1000–2100; winter, 1000–1600 (closed Mon). Free. Explanatory talk given on request. Gift shop. Wheelchair access. Car parking. Telephone (01456) 450601. www.iceberg-glass.co.uk

A glass-blowing studio manufacturing both solid and hollow glassware, mostly small delicate pieces including vases, Christmas decorations, animals, and modern jewellery. Visitors can see the manufacturing process.

INSH MARSHES RSPB NATURE RESERVE 1453   5 N20

RSPB. Insh, Kingussie, Inverness-shire. On the B970, 2 miles (3km) south of Kingussie. Nearest railway station and bus stop Kingussie. Reserve open at all times. Free, but donations welcome. Guided tours. Explanatory displays. Picnic area. Bird-watching hides and nature trails. Car and coach parking. Telephone (01540) 661518. www.rspb.org.uk/scotland

Insh Marshes is a national nature reserve and one of the most important wetlands in Europe. The best time to visit this reserve is between Nov and Jun. In spring lapwings, redshanks and curlews nest here and in winter the marshes flood, providing roosting and feeding for flocks of whooper swans and greylag geese. There are three nature trails with good views of the reserve from the B970, but due to the rocky terrain none are accessible for wheelchairs or pushchairs. There are also two birdwatching hides.

INVEREWE GARDEN 1454   4 H16

NTS. Poolewe, Ross and Cromarty. On A832, 6 miles (10km) north east of Gairloch. Infrequent bus from Inverness. Garden open all year, daily 0930–1600; visitor centre Easter–Sep, daily 0930–1700; Oct, daily 0930–1600. Charge £££. Group concessions. Explanatory displays. Guidebook in French and German, text in four languages. Gift shop. Restaurant. Guided garden walks mid Apr-mid Sep, Mon-Fri 1330. Plant sales. WC. Guide dogs only. Wheelchair access (wheelchairs available). Disabled WC. Car and coach parking. Telephone (01445) 781200. www.nts.org.uk

A world-famous garden created from a once-barren peninsula on the shore of Loch Ewe by Victorian gardener Osgood Mackenzie. Exotic plants from many countries flourish here in the mild climate created by the North Atlantic Drift. Spectacular lochside setting among pinewoods, with superb views.

INVERLOCHY CASTLE   1455   5 K21

HS. 2 miles (3km) north east of Fort William, Inverness-shire. Nearest railway and bus stations Fort William, bus from Fort William, request stop. Telephone for opening times. Car parking. Telephone (01667) 460232. www.historic-scotland.gov.uk

A fine well-preserved 13th-century castle of the Comyn family in the form of a square with round towers at the corners. The largest tower was the donjon or keep.

INVERNESS, CALEDONIAN CANAL OFFICE   1456   2 M18

Canal Office, Seaport Marina, Muirtown Wharf, Inverness. Access at all times. Free. Limited wheelchair access – contact office for details. Car parking. Telephone (01463) 233140. www.scottishcanals.co.uk

Designed by Thomas Telford and completed in 1822, the Caledonian Canal links the lochs of the Great Glen (Loch Lochy, Loch Oich and Loch Ness). It provides a coast to coast shortcut between Corpach near Fort William and Clachnaharry at Inverness. The canal has been described as the most beautiful in Europe – the spectacular Highland scenery of lochs, mountains and glens is unusual for a canal. A wide variety of craft use the canal throughout the year and can usually be seen at close quarters as they pass through locks and bridges. There are a number of pleasure cruises available on the canal and small boats are available for hire. See also 1340 Canal Heritage Visitor Centre, 1462 Jacobite Cruises and 1519 Neptune's Staircase.

INVERNESS CATHEDRAL   1457   2 M18

11 Kenneth Street, Inverness. On the west bank of the River Ness, below Ness Bridge, ten minute walk from railway and bus stations. Open daily 0730–1800. Explanatory displays and guide books. Gift shop. Tearoom (and other facilities) open May-Sep, Mon-Sat 1030-1530. WC. Induction loop. Car parking. Telephone 01463 225553/07080 651456. www.invernesscathedral.net

The cathedral church of the Diocese of Moray, Ross and Caithness, the first new cathedral to be completed in Britain since the Reformation. Built 1866–69 in the Gothic style to the design of Alexander Ross. Features twin towers with a ring of ten bells, octagonal chapter house, monolithic pillars of polished Peterhead granite, stained glass, sculpture, carved reredos, angel font after Thorvaldsen (Copenhagen), founder's memorial, icons presented by the Tsar of Russia. In beautiful riverside setting.

INVERNESS, CHISHOLMS HIGHLAND DRESS   1458   2 M18

47-51 Castle Street, Inverness. Inverness town centre. Ten minute walk from railway and bus stations. Open all year, Mon–Sat 0900–1730 and 0700–2100 during summer. Free. Guided tours by request. Explanatory displays. Gift shop. Limited wheelchair access. Telephone (01463) 234599.

Display of kilt-making and of Scottish Highland dress. There are also models in Highland dress and uniforms from 1745 to the present day. Tartans, swords and other weapons on show.

INVERNESS CITY SIGHTSEEING OPEN TOP TOUR   1459   2 M18

Inverness Sightseeing Ltd, 1 Russell Place, Nairn. Tour pickup point outside Inverness Tourist Information Centre. Tours run end May–end Sep, daily. Charges from ££. Group concessions. Taped commentary around Inverness. Fully-guided tours of other attractions. Wheelchair access with assistance. Telephone 07808713959.

Open top bus tours around the city of Inverness, Culloden battlefield, Cawdor Castle and Fort George – explore Inverness or visit all of these attractions.

INVERNESS, DISCOVER LOCH NESS   1460   2 M18

Trips depart from Inverness Tourist Information Centre, Castle Wynd, Inverness. Train and bus stations nearby. Trips run all year, daily, departing at 0930 (summer additional trip at 1400, winter 1200). Half day trip returns at 1400, all day trip returns 1800. Telephone to confirm. Booking advisable. Charges vary according to trip. Group concessions. Guides have expert knowledge of local history, heritage and natural history. Short video shown on bus. Gift shop. Refreshments available at attractions visited. WC at visitor attractions and on boats. No guide dogs. Car parking. Telephone freephone 0800 7315565. www.discoverlochness.com

Various tours of Loch Ness and the surrounding area, featuring a boat trip on the loch and visits to Urquhart Castle and Loch Ness 2000. As well as information on the Loch Ness mystery, the trips give visitors an insight into the natural history, culture and people of the area.

INVERNESS, FLORAL HALL AND COFFEE SHOP   1461   2 M18

Bught Lane, Inverness. In Bught Park, off the A82, 1.5 miles (2.5km) from city centre. Open Apr–Oct, Mon–Sun 1000–1700; Nov–Mar, daily 1000–1600 (closed Christmas–New Year). Charge £. Children 12 and under free. Guided tours. Explanatory displays. Coffee shop with home baking. WC. Gardening feature containing sensory and tactile plant material. Wheelchair access. Disabled WC. Car and coach parking. Telephone (01463) 713553. www.invernessfloralhall.com

An award-winning subtropical indoor oasis landscaped with a wonderful array of exotic plants and cacti. Children will be fascinated by the friendly koi carp which swim in the pond below the cascading waterfall. Attractive outdoor display garden.

INVERNESS, JACOBITE CRUISES   1462   2 M18

Jacobite–Experience Loch Ness, Glenurquhart Road, Inverness. 1 mile (1.5km) west of Inverness town centre on the A82. On local bus route. Tours and cruises all year round at various times. Please telephone or visit website. Charge £££. Group concessions. Explanatory displays. Commentary in Dutch, French, Swedish, German, Italian, Japanese and Spanish. Gift shop. Licensed snack bar on board. WC. Wheelchair access for round trip cruises (toilets down eight steps); difficult access for combined cruise and coach tours. Car and coach parking. Telephone (01463) 233999. www.jacobite.co.uk

4-star cruises and coach/cruise tours on the mysterious waters of Loch Ness. Visits to Urquhart Castle and Loch Ness 2000 Exhibition can be included. Choose from one-hour cruises to 6-hour cruises

INVERNESS LEISURE   1463   2 M18

Bught Park, Inverness. 1 mile (1.5km) west of Inverness town centre off the A82. Nearest railway and bus stations Inverness. Open all year except 25–26 Dec and 1–2 Jan. Charge ££. Children under 18 months free, reduced rates for under 4s. Group concessions. Guided tours. Cafés. WC. Wheelchair access. Disabled WC. Car and coach parking. Telephone (01463) 5. www.invernessleisure.co.uk

Inverness Leisure has a wide variety of activities from high-tech fitness gym, dance studio and classes, basketball to badminton, trampoline, children's camps, coaching and athletics stadium, indoor climbing wall, 8-lane (25m) competition pool, leisure waters with wave lagoon, flumes, outdoor pool, river and splash pool with play equipment. Also beauty salon, sun beds, steam room, sauna, spa bath and relaxation area.

INVERNESS, MORAY FIRTH DOLPHIN CRUISES   1464   2 M18

Shore Street Quay, Shore Street, Inverness. Ten minute walk from town centre at harbour. Free bus service from Tourist Information Centre departs 15 minutes before each cruise. Open Mar–Oct, 0900–1800, telephone for times of cruises. Charge £££. Children under 3 free. Group concessions on application. Guided tours. Explanatory displays. Gift shop. Refreshments. WC. Telephone re disabled access. Car and coach parking. Telephone (01463) 717900. www.netmedia.co.uk/users/dolphins

The Moray Firth dolphins are the largest resident population in Britain. Moray Firth Dolphin Cruises operate the *M.V. Miss Serenity*, which will carry 90 passengers in comfort. The company participates in the International Dolphin Watch programme. A good opportunity to see common and grey seals, porpoise, minke whales, terns, gannets, razor bills, kittiwakes and ospreys.

INVERNESS MUSEUM AND ART GALLERY   1465   2 M18

Castle Wynd, Inverness. In Inverness centre. Inverness railway and bus stations five minute walk. Local bus stops nearby. Open all year (except public holidays), Mon–Sat 0900–1700. Free. Gift shop. WC. Limited wheelchair access. Telephone (01463) 237114.

Displays of natural and human history of Inverness and the Highlands. Features exhibition of Highland and Inverness silver, weapons and musical instruments. Temporary exhibitions and events.

INVERNESS, JAMES PRINGLE WEAVERS   1466   2 M18

Holm Mills, Dores Road, Inverness. On the B862, 1.5 miles (2.5km) south west of Inverness. Nearest railway station Inverness, bus from Inverness. Open daily, Jan–Feb 1000–1700; Mar–Oct 0900–1730; Nov–Dec 0900–1700. Free. Guided tours of weaving factory. Explanatory displays. Gift shop. Restaurant. WC. Wheelchair access with assistance. Disabled WC. Car and coach parking. Telephone (01463) 223311. www.ewm.co.uk

Tartan is woven in an original mill dating back to 1798. Weave your own piece of tartan. Also cashmere, lambswool, tweeds, whisky and golf equipment.

INVERNESS, RIVERSIDE GALLERY   1467   2 M18

11 Bank Street, Inverness. In Inverness town centre by the River Ness. Open all year, Mon–Fri 0930–1730, Sat 0930–1500. Free. Limited wheelchair access. Car parking. Telephone (01463) 224781. www.riversidegallery.info

Original paintings, prints, etchings, etc. from the best of Scottish Artists. Work from 19th century through to the latest contemporary images, including small select range of sculptures and ceramics.

INVERNESS, SCOTTISH KILTMAKER VISITOR CENTRE   1468   2 M18

Hector Russell Kiltmaker, 4-9 Huntly Street, Inverness. In the centre of Inverness. Open May–Sep, Mon–Sat 0900–2100, Sun 0900–2100; Oct–May, Mon–Sat 0900–1700.

Charge £. Group concessions. Guided tours (leaflet in French). Explanatory displays. Gift shop. Coach parking. Telephone (01463) 222781. www.hectorrussell.com

Scotland's only visitor attraction devoted to the kilt. You can learn all about its history and development, its tradition and culture, as well as how it is worn today. Audio-visual, costume and tartan displays create a colourful, authentic and memorable experience. You can also see kilts being made in the world's largest kiltmaking workshop.

INVERNESS, SCOTTISH SHOWTIME   1469   2 M18

Ramada Hotel, Church Street, Inverness. In city centre beside bus station, close to railway station. Jun–Jul, Mon–Thu and Aug–Sep, Mon–Fri 2030–2215. Charge £££. Group concessions. Guided tours. Refreshments available. WC. Priority seating for deaf and blind. Wheelchair access. Disabled WC. Car parking. Telephone (01349) 830930. www.scottishshowtime.com

An award-winning show for the whole family. This professional production which has been delighting audiences for the past 33 years. The fast moving colourful spectacle includes traditional song, music, dance, and much more. Performed by the cast with passion, from the heart.

ISLE OF SKYE FALCONRY   1470   4 F17

Kirklee, Kensaleyre, Portree, Isle of Skye. On A87, 5 miles (8km) north of Portree. Nearest railway station at Kyle of Lochalsh, bus station at Portree. Open all year (except Christmas Day), daily. Booking essential. Charges vary. Telephone or visit website for details. Car parking. Telephone (01470) 532489. www.isleofskye-falconry.co.uk

Award-winning falconry. Visitors can see and handle birds from around the world in a closely supervised environment. Bird of prey displays, hawk walks, bird of prey introduction, management and children's courses. Also hunting days (Oct–Mar only).

JOHN O' GROATS   1471   3 Q12

Caithness. Bus from Wick or Thurso. Tourist office. Gift shop. Refreshments. WC. Car and coach parking.

John O' Groats claims to be the most northerly point of mainland Scotland, but in fact Dunnet Head, to the west, is. Named after Jan de Groot, a Dutch ferryman who settled there in the 16th century. A few miles further east is Duncansby Head (see 1390).

JOHN O' GROATS FERRIES   1472   3 Q12

Ferry Office, John O'Groats, Caithness. Bus from Wick or Thurso. Office open all year, daily 0800–1800. Wildlife cruises Jun–Aug, daily at 1430. Day trips to Orkney, May–Sep, daily at 0900. Charges vary depending on tour. Group concessions. Refreshments availabe in John O' Groats and on Orkney. WC. Wheelchair access with assistance. Car and coach parking. Telephone (01955) 611353. www.jogferry.co.uk

Wildlife cruises in a comfortable 250-passenger boat with easy gangway access. Visitors can see gannets, skuas, fulmars, seals, porpoises and even the occasional whale. Also puffins, razorbills, kittiwakes and guillemots. Day trips to Orkney give visitors a full tour of the island in the company of a local driver.

JOHN O' GROATS KNITWEAR   1473   3 Q12

County Road, John O'Groats, Caithness. Bus from Wick or Thurso. Open all year, daily, Jan–Mar and Oct–Dec 1000–1630; Apr–May 1000–1700; Jun–Sep 0900–1800.

Free. Gift shop. WC. Wheelchair access. Car and coach parking. Telephone (01955) 611326. www.ewm.co.uk

A superb selection of quality knitwear, clothing, accessories and souvenirs in the unique location of mainland Britain's most northerly village.

KERRACHAR GARDENS   1474   4 K14

Kerrachar, Kylesku, Sutherland. On the south shore of Loch a' Chairn Bhain. Sea access only, from Kylesku slipway. Bus service from Ullapool to Kylesku. Open mid May–mid Sep, Tue, Thu and Sun. Boat departs Kylesku slipway 1300. Additional visits can be arranged for large parties (max 40) during season, telephone or visit website for details. Charge £££. Children under 12 free. Ticket includes return boat trip. Guided tours. Picnic area. Car and coach parking. Telephone (01571) 833288. www.kerrachar.co.uk

Situated in an extremely remote and beautiful location, Kerrachar is only accessible by a 30 minute boat trip from Kylesku. The gardens contain a wide range of shrubs and perennials, including many unusual species, many of which are for sale.

KILDONAN CHURCH   1475   3 N14

10 miles (16km) north of Helmsdale on A897 Strath of Kildonan road. Walk up track from Kildonan Farm.

The present church, completed in 1896, contains the old pulpit with the foot marking of Alexander Sage, minister from 1787–1824, a man of 'great bodily weight'. His son, the Rev Donald Sage wrote *Memorabilia Domestica*, an interesting account of Highland life in the 18th and 19th centuries.

KILMORACK GALLERY   1476   2 L17

Old Kilmorack Church, by Beauly. 2 miles (3km) west of Beauly along the Cannich road. Local bus service. Open Apr–Nov and during Christmas, daily 1100–1730; other times by arrangement. Free. Guided tours. WC. Wheelchair access. Car parking. Telephone (01463) 783230. www.kilmorackgallery.co.uk

Kilmorack Gallery is the largest private art gallery in the Highlands, specialising in work by leading Scottish artists. The gallery is housed in a spectacular 18th-century church which remains largely unchanged since it was re-cast in 1835.

KILRAVOCK CASTLE   1477   2 N17

Croy, Inverness-shire. 6 miles (10km) west of Nairn on B9101. Nearest railway station Nairn. Telephone or visit website for details of castle tours.. Charge for castle tours ££, gardens £. Group concessions. Guided tours for groups by prior arrangement. Gift shop. Restaurant and picnic area. Garden. WC. No guide dogs. Limited wheelchair access. Car and coach parking. Telephone (01667) 493258. www.kilravockcastle.com

Presently undergoing redevelopment, the extensive grounds and garden of this 15th-century castle are noted for the large variety of beautiful trees, some centuries old. There are sports facilities and a tree garden, nature trails and river host an abundance of wildlife.

KILT ROCK   1478   4 G17

Off A855, 17 miles (27km) north of Portree, Skye. Can be seen from the road. Care should be taken not to go too near the edge of the cliff. Car parking.

The top rock is composed of columnar basalt, the lower portion of horizontal beds, giving the impression of the pleats in the kilt. There is a waterfall nearby.

KINLOCH FOREST AND LEITIR FURA WALK   1479   4 H19

FE. On the Isle of Skye (Sleat) 4 miles (6.5km) south of Skulamus along A851at Kinloch car park. Access at all times. Free. Explanatory displays. Car parking. www.forestry.gov.uk

Leitir Fura is a ruined township located in Kinloch Forest, a fine example of native woodland. The 4 mile (6.5km) walk overlooks the Sound of Sleat providing fine views and good opportunities to see wildlife.

KINTAIL AND MORVICH   1480   4 J19

NTS. Highland. 16 miles (26km) east of Kyle of Lochalsh, north off A87. Bus from Inverness and Glasgow. Open all year. Countryside Centre at Morvich, May–Sep, daily 0900–2200. Charge £ (honesty box). Explanatory displays. WC. Wheelchair access with assistance. Car and coach parking. Telephone (01599) 511231. www.nts.org.uk

A west Highland estate which includes the Falls of Glomach and the Five Sisters of Kintail, four of which are over 3000 feet (914.5m). The site of the Battle of Glen Shiel, which took place in 1719, is within this area, 5 miles (8km) from Morvich. The best access to the mountains is from the Countryside Centre at Morvich.

KIRKAIG FALLS   1481   4 J14

Inverkirkaig, south of Lochinver, Caithness.

Popular beauty spot and walk.

KNOCKNAGAEL BOAR STONE   1482   2 M18

HS. In Highland Council Offices, Glenurquhart Road, Inverness. On ground floor of council chambers. Nearest railway and bus stations Inverness. Access during council office opening hours of (except public holidays), Mon–Fri, 0930–1630. Free. Telephone (01667) 460232. www.historic-scotland.gov.uk

A rough slab incised with the Pictish symbols of a mirror-case and a wild boar. Can be viewed at any time through window.

KYLERHEA OTTER HAVEN   1483   4 H19

FE. Kylerhea, Isle of Skye. Open daily all year round. Free. Explanatory displays. Summer warden. Public toilets Easter-Sep. Wheelchair access. Car parking. www.forestry.gov.uk

Kylerhea is a superb place for otters – and from the hide you may be lucky enough to see them. Specially constructed paths are designed to protect the habitat and the wildlife, and visitors should keep to the designated paths and leave the shoreline undisturbed. Success in seeing an otter will be mostly down to your own skills in field craft, an element of luck, and patience. As well as otters, there are falcons, waders, sea birds and seals in the area.

LAEL FOREST GARDEN   1484   2 K16

6 miles (9.5km) south of Ullapool on A835 to Inverness.

Extending to 17 acres (7ha), the garden was set aside in 1933 for interesting and ornamental trees of native and foreign origin. The oldest specimen trees were planted around 1870 and there are now some 150 different trees and shrubs.

LAIDHAY CROFT MUSEUM   1485   3 P14

Laidhay, Dunbeath, Caithness. On the A9, 1 mile (2km) north of Dunbeath. Nearest railway station Wick, bus from Wick. Open two weeks Mar and Nov; Apr–Oct, daily 1000–1800. Charge £. Group concessions. Guided tours on request. Tearoom and picnic area. WC. Wheelchair access. Disabled WC. Car and coach parking. Telephone (01593) 731244.

An early 18th-century croft complex with stable, dwelling house and byre under one rush-thatched roof. Separate cruck barn with winnowing doors. Completely furnished in period style. Crofting hand tools, machinery and harness on view.

LANDMARK FOREST THEME PARK   1486   5 N19

Carrbridge, Inverness-shire. On the B9153 (old A9), 7 miles (11km) north of Aviemore. Nearest railway station Carrbridge, bus from Edinburgh, Inverness or local bus/taxi from Aviemore. Open all year (except Christmas Day), 1000–1800 (closes 1700 in winter, 1900 mid Jul–late Aug). Charge £££. Group concessions. Large information display. Gift shop. Restaurant and snack bar. Dogs welcome on leads, owners must clean up. WC. Limited wheelchair access. Disabled WC. Car and coach parking. Telephone 0800 731 3446. www.landmark-centre.co.uk

Scotland's most exciting heritage park with wild watercoaster ride, nature trail, treetop trail, Clydesdale horse, steam-powered sawmill demonstrations, forestry skill area, viewing tower, maze, adventure play area, microworld exhibition, minielectric cars and remote-controlled trucks, aerial rope course and 'parachute jump'.

LAST HOUSE MUSEUM   1487   3 Q12

John O'Groats, Caithness. Bus service to John O'Groats. Open all year, Jun–Aug, daily 0800–1930; Sep, daily 0830–1800; Oct, Tue–Sat 0900–1630; Nov–Feb, Tue–Fri 1000–1530; Mar–Easter, Tue– Sat 0800–1730; and May daily 080–1730. Free. Explanatory displays. Picnic area. Wheelchair access. Car and coach parking. Telephone (01955) 611250.

A local history museum featuring photographs and a collection of artefacts. Also photographs of shipwrecks in the Pentland Firth, Scapa Flow and views of Stroma. All postcards purchased are stamped with the Last House in Scotland and John O' Groats' postmark.

LEDMORE AND MIGDALE WOOD   1488   2 M16

Spinningdale, between Dornoch and Bonar Bridge on A949. Nearest railway station Ardgay 2.5 miles (4km). Bus from Ardgay to Spinningdale (twice daily). Access at all times. Free. Explanatory displays. Picnic area. Wheelchair access with assistance. Car parking. Telephone (01764) 662554. www.woodland-trust.org.uk

One of the largest oakwoods and colony of juniper bushes in the north of Scotland. Also Scots pine, birch, hazel, willow and ash trees. An area of great archaeological interest – to-date 28 different features have been recorded, including several chambered cairns dating from over four thousand years ago. Waymarked trails. A spectacular site to visit - teeming with wildlife

J. F. LINDSAY TARGEMAKER   1489   2 M18

Balquhidder, Main Street, North Kessock, by Inverness. 4 miles (6.5km) north of Inverness off A9, take first junction left after Kessock bridge. Bus from Inverness to North Kessock. Open all year, 0900–1900. Telephone to confirm as space is limited. Free. Explanatory displays. Gift shop. Wheelchair access. Car parking. Telephone (01463) 731577. www.targemaker.co.uk

Small workshop making high quality hand-crafted reproductions of original Jacobite targes (shields). The targemaker is happy to answer questions. Photos may be taken holding targe and sword. Targes, swords and other items for sale.

LITTLE GALLERY   1490   4 F18

7 Portnalong, Isle of Skye. 3 miles (5km) west of Talisker distillery on the B8009. Open Easter–Oct, daily 1000–1800; Nov–Easter by arrangement. Free. Wheelchair access. Car parking. Telephone (01478) 640254. www.the-little-gallery.co.uk

Overlooking Loch Harport, the gallery displays etchings, prints and watercolours depicting the Cuillin, Skye landscapes and the native flora and fauna.

LOCH ERIBOLL   1491   2 L13

Situated between Tongue and Durness in the north of Sutherland.

Reputedly the deepest sea loch or inlet in Britain. Both the loch itself and its shores are steeped in history. Despite the inhospitable landscape of today, archaeological remains indicate that people have lived here for at least the last 4000 years.

LOCH FLEET NATIONAL NATURE RESERVE   1492   2 M15

Off A9 between Dornoch and Golspie (3 miles/5km). Bus services connect Dornoch and Golspie with Inverness and Thurso/ Wick. In addition Golspie has a train station connecting with Inverness and Thurso/ Wick. Access at all times. Free. Summer walks by ranger service. Information panels on both south and north shores. Car parking. Telephone 01408 633602 (Scottish Natural Heritage). www.nnr-scotland.org.uk

This nature reserve occupies a stunning coastal location where a river flows through a tidal basin. Common seals regularly haul out on the mudflats at low tide and visitors can enjoy great views of wildfowl and waders. Sand dunes and coastal heath are rich in wild flowers and the attractive pinewood plantations provide a home for flowers more usually seen in ancient native pinewoods.

LOCH GARTEN RSPB OSPREY CENTRE   1493   5 N19

RSPB. By Nethybridge, Inverness-shire. Off the B970, 8 miles (13km) north east of Aviemore. Bus from Aviemore then 2 mile (3km) walk, or Strathspey steam railway from Aviemore to Boat of Garten, then 4 mile (6.5km) walk. Open Apr–Aug, daily 1000–1800. Caperwatch daily, Apr–mid May 0530–0830 (telephone to confirm). Charge £. RSPB/Wildlife Explorer members free on production of membership card. Explanatory displays in visitor centre. Gift shop. WC. Wheelchair access to centre. Disabled WC. Car and coach parking. Telephone (01479) 821409. www.rspb.org.uk/scotland

A public viewing facility overlooking the famous Loch Garten osprey tree-top nest. Direct viewing with telescopes or binoculars; CCTV transmits pictures of the nest to the centre. To avoid disturbance, view capercaillie from the centre. Nature trails through rare Caledonian pine forest offer views of crested tits, Scottish crossbills and red squirrels.

LOCH INSH WATERSPORTS   1494   5 N19

Kincraig, Inverness-shire. 7 miles (11km) south of Aviemore. Nearest railway and bus stations Aviemore. Watersports from Apr–Oct, daily 0830–1730; Skiing, Dec–Apr. Charge per activity. Group concessions. Explanatory displays and audio-visual room. Gift shop. Restaurant, bar and open balcony, picnic area. Children's adventure area. Beach. WC. Wheelchair access (including showers for beach). Disabled WC. Car and coach parking. Telephone (01540) 651272. www.lochinsh.com

Watersports include sailing, windsurfing, canoeing, salmon/trout fishing and rowing. Dry ski slope skiing, mountain biking, archery. Hire and instruction. The 2 mile (3km) interpretation/fun trail and stocked fishing lochan were especially designed with wheelchair users in mind. Three children's adventure areas.

LOCH MORAR   1495   5 H20

South east of Mallaig. Rail, bus and ferry from Fort William. Car parking.

Said to be the deepest freshwater loch in Britain and the home of Morag, a monster with a strong resemblance to the Loch Ness Monster.

LOCH NAM UAMH CAIRN   1496   5 H20

Off A830, south of Arisaig. Car parking.

The loch is famous for its association with Bonnie Prince Charlie. The memorial cairn on the shore marks the spot from where Prince Charles Edward Stewart sailed for France on 20 September 1746, after having wandered round the Highlands as a fugitive with a price of £30,000 on his head.

LOCH NESS   1497   2 M18

Between Inverness and Fort William.

This striking 24-mile (38.5-km) long loch in the Great Glen forms part of the Caledonian Canal which links Inverness with Fort William. Up to 700 feet (213m) deep, the loch contains the largest volume of freshwater of any lake in the British Isles. Famous worldwide for its mysterious inhabitant, the Loch Ness Monster, it is also ideal for cruising and sailing.

LOCH NESS 2000   1498   2 L18

The Official Loch Ness Exhibition Centre, The Drumnadrochit Hotel, Drumnadrochit, Inverness. In Drumnadrochit on the A82, 15 miles (24km) south of Inverness. Bus from Inverness or Fort William. Open Easter–May 0930–1730; Jun–Sep 0930–1830; Jul–Aug 0900–2030; Oct 0930–1800; winter 1000–1600. Charge £££. Disabled visitors free. Group concessions. Explanatory displays. Gift shop. Restaurants. Garden, pets' corner, boat trips on Loch Ness. WC. Wheelchair access. Disabled WC. Car and coach parking. Telephone (01456) 450573. www.loch-ness-scotland.com

A fully automated multi-room presentation takes visitors through themed areas describing Loch Ness from the pre-history of Scotland, exploring the cultural roots of the story in Highland folklore; and into the present controversy and all the phases of investigation and exploration. Includes the world's largest inflatable and one of the world's smallest submersibles. Also Loch Ness boat trips aboard the famous *Deepscan*, and themed shops.

LOCH NESS CLAYWORKS   1499   2 L19

Bunloit, Drumnadrochit. Leave A82 Lewiston Bridge, drive to the end of Bunloit Road. Open all year, daily 1000–1800. Free. Gift shop. Wheelchair access with assistance. Car parking. Telephone (01456) 450402.

Situated in a beautiful area with stunning views, this is a small and prolific pottery producing a wide range of colourful artistic and domestic pieces including mugs, bowls, plates, jugs, vases, oil lamps, night lights and more. Items can be purchased.

LOCH NESS, ORIGINAL VISITOR CENTRE   1500   2 L18

Drumnadrochit. Bus from Inverness or Fort William. Open all year, Mar–May 0900–1900; Jun–Aug; 0900–2200; Sep–Oct 0900–2000; Nov–Feb 0900–1700.

Charge ££. Teachers and guides free. Group concessions. Explanatory displays.
Cinema exhibition (in Dutch, French, German, Italian, Japanese, Spanish and
Swedish). Gift shop. WC. Wheelchair access. Disabled WC. Car and coach parking.
Telephone (01456) 450342. www.lochness-centre.com

The story of Loch Ness, the monster, and other mysteries of the area is
presented in a wide-screen cinema. Exhibition, various gift shops.

LOCH NESS TRAVEL CO   1501 · 2 L18

Bases in West Lewiston, by Drumnadrochit, Loch Ness. On A82, 16 miles (25.5km)
south west of Inverness. Some tours start from Inverness. Bus from Inverness or Fort
William. Tours take place all year. Charge dependent on tour. Car parking. Telephone
(01456) 450550. www.lochnesstravel.com

Personalised car/minicoach day tours around Loch Ness, the Highlands and
specialist Whisky, Castle and Wildlife tours. Also guided 2–3 day minibus tours
around the Highlands and Islands. Coach available for larger groups.

LOCH SHIEL CRUISES   1502 · 5 J20

c/o Glenfinnan House Hotel, Glenfinnan, Fort William. On the A830, 15 miles (24km)
north west of Fort William. Bus or rail from Fort William. Open Easter–Oct, daily
0900–1700 and special evening cruises. Charge ££–£££. Group concessions. Guided
tours (in French or German by request). Explanatory displays. Refreshments and bar
on boat. WC. Telephone for disabled access. Car and coach parking. Telephone
(01687) 470322. www.highlandcruises.co.uk

Eagle-Watch wildlife cruises on stunning Loch Shiel. See golden eagles, black-
throated divers and red deer at home in one of Scotland's last wilderness areas

LOCH-AN-EILEIN POTTERY   1503 · 5 N19

Rothiemurchas, Aviemore, Highland. 2 miles (3km) south west of Aviemore on the
Loch-An-Eilein road. Open all year, Tue–Sun 1000–1700. Free. Gift shop. Picnic area.
WC. Pot-making sessions suitable for blind visitors. Wheelchair access with
assistance. Car parking. Telephone (01479) 810837. www.penspots.co.uk

Small rural craft pottery making terracotta domestic wares, glazed in blues and
greens. The pottery is situated on the Rothiemurchus estate near Aviemore.
Hands-on make your own pot activity on Tuesday and Thursday mornings.

LOCHINDORB   1504 · 2 N18

Unclassified road off A939, 10 miles (16km) north west of Grantown-on-Spey.

On an island in this lonely loch stand the ruins of a 13th-century castle, once a
seat of the Comyns. It was occupied in person by Edward I in 1303 and greatly
strengthened. In 1336 Edward III raised the siege in which the Countess of
Atholl was beleaguered by the Regent Moray's troops. In 1371 the castle became
the stronghold of the Wolf of Badenoch, the vicious Earl of Buchan who
terrorised the area. The castle was dismantled in 1456.

LOGIE FARM RIDING CENTRE   1505 · 2 N18

Logie Farm, Glenferness, Nairn. On the A939, 10 miles (16km) from Nairn. Open all
year, daily 1000–1700. Charge for riding £££ (per hour). Group concessions.
Explanatory displays. WC. No guide dogs. Car parking. Telephone (01309) 651226.
www.angelfire.com/fm/logiefarm

A riding centre with quality horses and ponies. Traffic-free riding, stunning
scenery, an extensive cross-country course, show jumping and dressage areas,

outdoor arena and first class instruction. Riding holidays for adults or unaccompanied children. Livery yard and approved student training centre.

LYTH ARTS CENTRE   1506   3 Q12

Lyth, Wick, Caithness. 4 miles (6.5km) off the A99 between Wick and John o' Groats. Nearest railway station at Wick. Exhibitions open Jul–Aug, daily 1200–1700. Open Apr–Dec for evening performances as advertised locally. Exhibitions free. Performances £££. Explanatory displays. Gift shop. Snack bar. Garden. WC. Loop induction system. No guide dogs. Wheelchair access. Disabled WC. Car and coach parking. Telephone (01955) 641270. www.lytharts.org.uk

Up to ten new exhibitions of contemporary fine art shown simultaneously each season, ranging from local landscapes to the work of established British and foreign artists. Regular performances by touring drama, music and dance companies. Fully refurbished and re-opened in 2004, now has comfortable foyer and veranda

SIR HECTOR MACDONALD MONUMENT   1507   2 L17

Overlooking the town of Dingwall from the Mitchell Hill Cemetery.

This monument was erected in memory of General Sir Hector MacDonald (1853–1903) who became an outstanding soldier, starting his career in the Gordon Highlanders. Known as Fighting Mac, he was born in the nearby Parish of Ferintosh.

MADE IN SCOTLAND   1508   2 L17

The Made in Scotland Shop and Restaurant, Station Road, Beauly, Inverness-shire. 12 miles (19km) north west of Inverness on the A862. Regular bus from Inverness to Beauly. Open all year, Mon–Sat 0930–1730, Sun 1000–1700. Free. Gift shop. Restaurant and tearoom. WC. Wheelchair access. Disabled WC. Car and coach parking. Telephone (01463) 782821.

One of Scotland's largest craft centres, housing the cream of Scottish designer and handmade products.

MALLAIG HERITAGE CENTRE   1509   5 H20

Station Road, Mallaig, Inverness-shire. In Mallaig centre between railway station and Marine Hotel, off A830. By rail or bus from Fort William or by ferry. Open Jul–Sep, Mon–Sat 1000–1700, Sun 1300–1600; Apr–Jun and Oct, Mon–Sat 1100–1600; Nov–Mar telephone for details. Charge £. Free admission for carers accompanying disabled. Group concessions. Guided tours by appointment. Explanatory displays. Video film show and multimedia access point. Gift shop. Garden. WC. Large print guides for partially sighted. Wheelchair access. Disabled WC. Telephone (01687) 462085. www.mallaigheritage.org.uk

Exhibits and displays all aspects of the history of Mallaig and West Lochaber – social history, crofting, fishing, railway archaeology, maritime history, and the Knoydart clearances. Children's quizzes and play area

MALLAIG MARINE WORLD   1510   5 H20

The Harbour, Mallaig, Inverness-shire. In Mallaig 100 yards (91m) from the station. By rail or bus from Fort William or by ferry from Skye. Open Jun–Sep, Mon–Sat 0900–2100, Sun 1000–1800; Oct–May, Mon–Sat 0900–1700, Sun 1000–1700 (Nov–Mar, closed Sun). Charge £. Children under 5 free. Group concessions. Guided tours on request. Explanatory displays. Leaflets available in eleven European languages. Gift shop. Marine scientist on site. WC. Wheelchair access. Disabled WC. Car and coach parking. Telephone (01687) 462292.

Aquarium and exhibition featuring local marine species. A fishing display features the Mallaig fishing fleet and a video illustrates boats at work.

MARY-ANN'S COTTAGE 1511   3 P12

Westside, Dunnet, Caithness. At Dunnet, 10 miles (16km) east of Thurso. Open Jun–mid Sep, Tue–Sun 1400–1630. Charge £. Guided tours. Explanatory displays. WC. Wheelchair access with assistance. Car parking. Telephone (01847) 851765.

A cottage built in 1850 by John Young. The croft was succesively worked by three generations of the family, ending with Mary-Ann and James Calder. All the furniture, fittings and artefacts are original, the way of life and working practices changing little over the generations.

MARYCK MEMORIES OF CHILDHOOD 1512   4 K14

Unapool, Kylesku, Sutherland. On A874, 0.5 mile (1km) south of Kylesku bridge, midway between Ullapool and Durness. Open Easter–Oct, daily 1300–1730. Charge £. Children under 5 free. Explanatory displays. Gift shop. WC. Wheelchair access. Disabled WC. Car parking. Telephone (01971) 502341.

The exhibition includes dolls, doll's houses, teddy bears and toys from between 1880 and the present day. The craft shop has a range of items for sale, most made in Scotland and some handmade locally. Toys and dressing up opportunities for the under-8s (parental supervision required).

MEADOW WELL 1513   3 P12

In Thurso, Caithness.

Once a major source of the local water supply and where the local fishwives gathered to sell fresh fish.

HUGH MILLER'S MUSEUM AND BIRTHPLACE COTTAGE 1514   2 M17

NTS. Church Street, Cromarty, Ross and Cromarty. Off A832 in Cromarty, 22 miles (35km) northeast of Inverness. By bus from Inverness. Open Easter–Sep, daily 1200–1700; Oct, Sun–Wed 1200–1700. Charge ££. Group concessions. Explanatory displays. Information sheets in five languages. Braille guide sheets and captioned video. Limited wheelchair access. Car and coach parking. Telephone (01381) 600245. www.nts.org.uk

Birthplace of Hugh Miller (1802–56), famous stonemason, geologist, writer and church reformer. Thatched cottage, built circa 1698, with restored cottage garden. Many of Miller's belongings, including fine fossil collection now a display in the new museum.

MONSTER ACTIVITIES 1515   5 K20

Great Glen Water Park, South Laggan, By Spean Bridge, Inverness-shire. On A82, 25 miles (40km) north of Fort William and 35 miles (56km) south of Inverness. Nearest railway station at South Spean Bridge . Bus stop on main road. Open all year, daily 0930–1730. Charge varies depending on activity. Group concessions. Guided tours. Explanatory displays. Restaurant, tearoom and picnic area. WC. Wheelchair access with assistance. Car and coach parking. Telephone (01809) 501340. www.monsteractivities.com

Established since 1997 to provide the widest range of outdoor activities in Scotland. Visitors are offered a comprehensive programme of tailor-made activities, specialising in the best of the outdoor world, including white water rafting, clay pigeon shooting, waterskiing, quad biking and many more. Fun for all ages and abilities.

MORAY FLY FISHING AND GLEN OF ROTHES TROUT FISHERY   1516   6 Q18

Moray Fly Fishing and Glen of Rothes Trout Fishery, Rothes, Moray. 6m south of
Elgin on main Elgin to Rothes road. Open all year apart from Christmas day and New
Year's day. Contact the fishery for details of prices. Group concessions. Explanatory
displays. Gift shop. Tackle shop onsite, qualified instruction available, and there is a
fishing lodge. WC. Limited wheelchair access. Disabled WC. Car and coach parking.
Telephone (01340) 831888. www.morayflyfishing.co.uk

Trout fishery with superb fighting fish to 20lbs on two lochans of six acres with
two separate lochs for bait fishing. There are hot and cold snacks and free tea
and coffee. Resident osprey in summer with plenty of wildlife to see.

NAIRN LEISURE PARK AND SWIMMING POOL   1517   2 N17

Marine Road, Nairn. On the A96, 15 miles (24km) east of Inverness. Nairn station, bus
from Nairn to within 0.5 mile (2km). Swimming pool open all year, Mon–Fri 0800–2100;
weekends 0900–1700. Leisure park games complex open Easter–May and Sep,
1400–1700; Jun–Aug 1100–1800. Charge £. Explanatory displays. Vending machines.
WC. Wheelchair access. Disabled WC. Car parking. Telephone (01667) 452061.

Leisure park with aerial runway, adventure play trails, trim trail, adventure fort,
outdoor giant board games, woodland suspension bridge, toddlers' playground,
swimming pool and steam room, woodland walks, outdoor games complex.
Beside Nairn beaches.

NAIRN MUSEUM   1518   2 N17

Viewfield House, Viewfield Drive, Nairn. Just off A96 Inverness to Aberdeen road.
Open end Mar–end Oct, Mon–Sat 1000–1630; Nov Sat–Sun only. Charge £. School
groups free. Group concessions. Guided tours. Explanatory displays. Gift shop.
Picnic area. WC. Wheelchair access. Car and coach parking. Telephone (01667) 456791.
www.nairnmuseum.co.uk

A local history museum with five rooms of displays and a changing exhibition
each month. Local and family history research room and children's area.

NEPTUNE'S STAIRCASE   1519   5 K21

Off A830 at Banavie, 3 miles (4.5km) north west of Fort William. Car parking.

A series of eight locks, built between 1805 and 1822, which raises Telford's
Caledonian Canal (see 1456) 64 feet (19.5 metres). See also 1340 Canal Heritage
Visitor Centre.

NIGG BAY BIRD RESERVE   1520   2 M17

Cromarty Firth, north of Invergordon, Ross and Cromarty.

Bird reserve. The best access is along the shore from Barbaraville.

NORTH SHORE POTTERY   1521   3 P14

Mill of Forse, Latheron, Caithness. South east Caithness. Nearest railway station
Helmsdale or Wick, bus service from Wick stops at entrance. Open all year, Tue–Sat
1000–1700; Jul–Aug, daily 1000–1700. Free. Guided tours and demonstrations,
special events days. Explanatory displays. Gift shop. Picnic area. Garden. Wheelchair
access. Disabled WC. Car parking. Telephone (01593) 741777.

Studio and showroom located in a restored oatmeal mill. Visitors can see the
potter at work, creating hand thrown pots, salt-glazed and reflecting the local
landscape.

NORTHERN NATURAL HISTORY   1522   2 N15

Greenhill, Brora, Sutherland. On the A9, 1.5 miles (2.5km) north of Brora. Nearest railway station Brora, bus from Inverness to Brora. Open all year (except bank holidays), Mon–Fri 0900–1700. Free. Explanatory displays. WC. Limited wheelchair access. Car parking. Telephone (01408) 621500. www.nnh.co.uk/taxidermy

Taxidermy workshop with work for sale.

NORTHLANDS VIKING CENTRE   1523   3 Q13

Auckengill, Keiss, Wick, Caithness. On the A99, 10 miles (16km) north of Wick. Nearest railway station Wick, bus from Wick. Open Jun–Sep, daily 1000–1600. Charge £. Group concessions. Explanatory displays. Gift shop. Picnic area. WC. Wheelchair access with assistance. Car and coach parking. Telephone (01955) 607771.

A display explaining the heritage of Caithness including the pre-Viking kingdom of the Catti and the Norse settlers. Features models of the Viking settlement at Freswick, a Viking longship and currency.

OLD MAN OF STOER   1524   4 J14

2 mile (3km) walk from Stoer Lighthouse, north of Lochinver, Sutherland.

This is the most westerly point of Sutherland and on a clear day it is possible to see the Hebridean Island of Lewis.

ON THE ROCKS   1525   4 J14

114 Achmelvich, Lochinver, Sutherland. 98 miles (157km) north of Inverness and 3 miles (5km) north of Lochinver. Bus service from Inverness. Open all year, daily 1000–1700. Free. Explanatory displays. Gift shop. Wheelchair access with assistance. Car parking. Telephone (01571) 844312.

Silk painting, original watercolours and handmade jewellery

ORBOST GALLERY   1526   4 F18

Dunvegan, Isle of Skye. 4 miles (6.5km) south of Dunvegan off the A863. Open Apr–Oct, daily 1000–1800; other times by appointment. Free. Explanatory displays. WC. Wheelchair access. Car and coach parking. Telephone (01470) 521207. www.orbostgallery.co.uk

Paintings and prints of the landscape of Skye and adjacent highlands. Also calligraphy, wood engravings and a selection of antique prints. Picture framing service available and artists' materials on sale.

ORCADIAN STONE COMPANY   1527   2 N15

Main Street, Golspie, Sutherland. 60 miles (96.5km) north of Inverness on A9. Nearest railway station Golspie, bus from Inverness stops nearby. Open Easter–end Oct, Mon–Sat 0900–1730. Charge £. Charge £ (museum); students free. Group concessions. Explanatory displays. Gift shop. Picnic area. Garden. WC. Limited wheelchair access. Car and coach parking. Telephone (01408) 633483. www.orcadianstone.co.uk

A high quality geological exhibition featuring: worldwide fossils; a comprehensive collection of Highland rocks, minerals and fossils, with geological relief model and diorama; worldwide minerals chosen for beauty and rarity. The gift shop sells mineral specimens, stone clocks, vases and other items, jewellery and geological books and maps.

PLODDA FALLS

ORD OF CAITHNESS   1528   3 P14

At the hairpin bends on the A9, north of Helmsdale, Sutherland.

From here there are spectacular views of the Caithness coastline. In the early
morning or late evening, herds of red deer can often be seen.

ORD SUMMIT   1529   2 L15

West of Lairg village, Sutherland.

Dotted with burial mounds, hut circles, a burnt mound (a type of ancient
barbecue) and topped by two chambered cairns dating back 5000 years. The view
from the summit of the Ord is stunning.

OTTERSHOP   1530   4 G19

Wildlife and Tourist Information Centre, Central Car Park, Broadford, Isle of Skye.
Nearest railway station Kyle of Lochalsh, bus from Kyle of Lochalsh. Open all year,
Mon–Fri 0930–1700; summer also Sat–Sun 1000–1600. Free. Guided tours can be
arranged with the International Otter Survival Fund (IOSF). Displays on otters and
wildlife. Gift shop. WC nearby. Wheelchair access with assistance. Car and coach
parking. Telephone (01471) 822713. www.otter.org

The Ottershop provides general tourist information and information on
the wildlife and environment of Skye to make the most of your visit to the
island. Find out where and how to watch for animals such as otters and seals,
and also the best places to walk without disturbing these creatures. It is also
the local biological recording centre with a wide database. The Ottershop
has a unique selection of gifts and books for that extra special something
to take home. Run by the IOSF and all profits are used to conserve otters
worldwide.

PARALLEL ROADS   1531   5 K20

Glen Roy, unclassified road off A86, 18 miles (29km) north east of Fort William. Free.

These parallel roads are hillside terraces marking levels of lakes dammed by
glaciers during the Ice Age.

PHOENIX BOAT TRIPS   1532   2 N17

Nairn Harbour. 12 miles (19km) east of Inverness. Railway station at Nairn. Local bus
service. Open Apr–Sep. One 2 hour trip per day. Telephone or visit website for
information. Charge £££. Group concessions. Tea and coffee available. Boat WC.
Limited wheelchair access. Car and coach parking. Telephone (01667) 456078.
www.greentourism.org.uk/phoenix.html

Enjoy a 2 hour boat trip to see the beauty of the Moray Firth. Visit the local seal
colony sunning themselves on the sand banks of Ardersier. Further down the
coast, visitors will see the ramparts of Fort George. There is also the possibility
of a visit from the bottlenose dolphins of Rosemarkie Bay. Skipper provides
local information. Member of Dolphin Space Watch Programme.

PLODDA FALLS   1533   2 K18

From Drumnadrochit take the A831, turning left before Cannich onto the
unclassified road to Tomich.

Waterfalls 100 foot (30.5m) high, south of the village of Tomich. They are
particularly impressive when in spate.

PORT NA CON SOUTERRAIN   1534   2 L12

0.5 miles (1km) north of Port na Con pier, near Durness, Sutherland.

Marked by two cairns at the east side of the road, this is a well preserved souterrain (Iron Age store room). Take extreme care and enter at your own risk.

PULTENEY DISTILLERY   1535   3 Q13

Huddart Street, Wick, Caithness. Railway and bus station in Wick. Tours Apr–Sep, daily at 1030, 1230, 1330 and 1530; Oct–Mar by arrangement. Telephone to confirm. Free. Refreshments available. Wheelchair access with assistance. Car parking. Telephone (01955) 602371. www.oldpulteney.com

The visitor centre offers a tour of the distillery and a historical journey of the whisky making process and the seafaring history of Wick.

QUIRANG   1536   4 G17

Off unclassified Staffin to Uig road, 19 miles (30.5km) north of Portree, Isle of Skye. Access at all times. Free. Limited car parking.

An extraordinary mass of towers and pinnacles into which cattle were driven during forays. A rough track (not suitable for the elderly or infirm) zigzags up to the Needle, an imposing obelisk 120 feet (36.5m) high. Beyond the Needle, in a large amphitheatre, stands the Table, a huge grass-covered rock mass. Impressive views.

RAVENS ROCK FOREST WALK   1537   2 L15

Sutherland. At Linsidemore on the A837. Explanatory displays, leaflet available from Forest Enterprise and Tourist Information Centres.

A delightful and under-frequented walk alongside the deep gorge of the Allt Mor Burn, through old mixed woods of mature conifers and beech trees. The paths are easy and there is plenty to keep children interested. The partially suspended path leads you upward to magnificent views over the burn towards Strathoykel.

RED KITE VIEWING   1538   2 M18

North Kessock Tourist Information Centre, North Kessock, by Inverness. On the Black Isle at the north end of Kessock Bridge, Inverness, off the A9 northbound. Nearest railway station Inverness 3 miles (5km); local bus service stops at the centre. Open late Apr–Jun, Mon–Sat 1000–1700, Sun 1200–1700; Jul–Aug, Mon–Sat 1000–1730, Sun 1100–1730; late Sep–late Oct, Mon–Sat 1000–1600. Free. Explanatory displays. Gift shop. Picnic area. Seal and Dolphin Centre, walks. WC. Wheelchair access. Car and coach parking. Telephone (01463) 731505.

The red kite is one of the most beautiful birds of prey in Europe. Using a closed-circuit television camera system, live pictures are beamed back to a monitor in the North Kessock Tourist Information Centre. From the comfort of the Tourist Information Centre, and safe in the knowledge that these rare birds are not being disturbed, you may have the chance to see close-up pictures of wild red kites nesting in the Highlands. Please confirm with the Tourist Information Centre before visiting.

RED SMIDDY   1539   4 H16

Poolewe, north east of Gairloch on A832.

Poolewe was an important centre for early ironworking and the remains of Scotland's earliest blast furnace – the Red Smiddy – lies close to the village on the banks of the River Ewe.

REELIG GLEN   1540   2 L18

FE. At Moniack, 8 miles from Inverness. 1 mile (0.5km) south of A862 Inverness to
Beauly road. Bus service between Inverness and Beauly. Open at all times. Free.
Explanatory displays. Picnic area. Limited wheelchair access. Car parking. Telephone
(01463) 791575. www.forestry.gov.uk

Woodland walk with viewpoint and picnic place. A feature is the number of
specimen trees on the walk, with some of the tallest trees in Britain. Leaflet
available from Forest Enterprise, Smithton.

REVACK GARDENS   1541   6 P18

Revack Lodge, Revack Estate, Grantown-on-Spey, Moray. On the B970, 1 mile (2km)
south of Grantown-on-Spey. Nearest railway station Aviemore, bus from Grantown-
on-Spey (request stop). Coaches by appointment only. Open all year (except
Christmas and New Year), daily 1000–1730. Free. Gift shop. Restaurant and tearoom.
WC. Wheelchair access. Disabled WC. Car and coach parking. Telephone (01479)
872234.

Walled garden, ornamental lakes, garden centre, adventure playground and gift
shop.

RHUE BEACH   1542   2 J15

West of Ullapool.

A good family beach, with safe swimming and also the possibility of catching a
glimpse of seals and various sea birds.

ROSSAL INTERPRETIVE TRAIL   1543   2 M13

1 mile (1.5km) from the car park at Syre, on B873 Altnaharra to Bettyhill road,
Sutherland.

A pre-clearance village of great historic interest. Several displays and
explanations.

ROTHIEMURCHUS ESTATE   1544   5 N19

Rothiemurchus, Aviemore, Inverness-shire. On the B970, 1.5 miles (2.5km) from
Aviemore . Nearest railway station Aviemore, bus from Aviemore. Open all year, daily
0930–1730 (except Christmas Day). Charge dependent on activity. Guided tours.
Explanatory displays. Gift shop. Farm shop. Picnic area. WC. Wheelchair access to
limited areas. Disabled WC. Car and coach parking. Telephone (01479) 812345.
www.rothiemurchus.net

Rothiemurchus combines the tranquility of the lochs and forests of the new
Cairngorm National Park with activities for all the family. With guided walks,
way marked walks, clay shooting, 4x4 driving, quad trekking, mountain biking,
pony trekking, wildlife watching, fishing on loch and river and Land Rover
Estate Tours for a behind the scenes visit to view points, red deer & Highland
cattle, there is something for everyone to enjoy. Visitor Centre is at the heart of
the estate where you can get all the information about what's going on.

RUM NATIONAL NATURE RESERVE   1545   5 F20

Island 16.5 miles (25km) from mainland Scotland, between Isle of Skye and
Ardnamurchan peninsula. Ferry service from Mallaig (telephone 01687 462403 or
visit www.calmac.co.uk), boat trips from Arisaig (telephone 01687 450224 or visit
www.arisaig.co.uk). Charge for boat trip. Fast boats can also be chartered from Skye
and Mallaig. Simple nature trails from Kinloch village. Special events and guided

walks during the summer, including tours of Kinloch Castle. Shop and café in Kinloch. Telephone (01687) 462026. www.nnr-scotland.org.uk

The largest of the Small Isles and a spectacular sight when approaching from sea. The Rum Cuillin mountains are the remains of an extinct volcano and attract geologists from all over the world. The island is home to a magnificent array of birds, animals and wild plants, and also possesses some of the best preserved pre-Clearance villages and landscapes in the Highlands. Waymarked and rough walks.

RUTHVEN BARRACKS   1546   5 M20

HS. On the B970, 0.5 mile (2km) south of Kingussie, Inverness-shire. Nearest railway station Kingussie, bus service from Aviemore then 15 minute walk. Access at all reasonable times. Free. Car parking. Telephone (01667) 460232. www.historic-scotland.gov.uk

The ruins of an infantry barracks erected in 1719 with two ranges of quarters and a stable block. Captured and burned by Bonnie Prince Charlie's army in 1746.

ST DUTHAC'S CHAPEL   1547   2 M16

Tain, Ross and Cromarty.

Built in the 11th or 12th century and now in ruins. Robert the Bruce's wife and daughter were captured here in 1306. James IV made an annual pilgrimage to this chapel. See also 1576 Tain Through Time.

ST FERGUS ART GALLERY   1548   3 Q13

Wick Library, Sinclair Terrace, Wick, Caithness. Nearest railway station Wick, then 0.25 mile (0.5km) walk. Open all year, Mon–Thu 1330–1800, Wed 1000–1230, Fri 1330–2000, Sat 1030–1300. Free. Explanatory displays. Gift shop. Car and coach parking. Telephone (01955) 603489.

The gallery is situated in an attractive 19th-century building that also houses the town's library and county archives. Exhibitions change regularly and include a touring exhibition and work by artists in the Highlands. All mediums are catered for from sculpture, painting and ceramics to jewellery and handmade paper.

ST MARY'S CHAPEL, CROSSKIRK   1549   3 P12

HS. Off the A836, 6 miles (9.5km) west of Thurso, Caithness. Nearest bus and railway stations Thurso, bus from Thurso. Access at all reasonable times. Free. Car parking. Telephone (01667) 460232. www.historic-scotland.gov.uk

A simple dry-stone chapel, probably 12th century.

SANDWOOD BAY   1550   4 K13

4 miles (6.5km) walk north from Kinlochbervie, north west Sutherland.

A relatively undisturbed bay with great views. The beach is said to be haunted.

SEA EAGLE VIEWING   1551   4 G18

RSPB. Aros Experience, Viewfield Road, Portree, Isle of Skye. On A850 south of Portree. Bus service from Portree. Centre open all year daily, May–Sep 0900–2300; Oct–Apr 0900–1800. Sea eagle viewing mid May–end Aug, daily 0900–1800. Charge £. Free to RSPB members. Explanatory displays. Gift shop. Refreshments available. WC. Limited wheelchair access. Disabled WC. Car and coach parking. Telephone (01478) 613649. www.rspb.org.uk/scotland

Located in the Aros Experience. Displays and camera offer live footage of sea eagle and grey heron nest sites. RSPB staff are present May–Aug. See also 1300 Aros Experience.

SEAL ISLAND CRUISES   1552   5 K21

Town Pier, Fort William. In Fort William next to the Crannog Restaurant, just off Fort William bypass on the shore of Loch Linnhe. Nearest railway and bus station Fort William. Sailing times: history cruise, 1000 and 1400; Seal Island cruise, 1100 and 1500; evening buffet cruise (buffet optional), 1830. Charge from ££–£££ dependent on cruise. Group concessions. Explanatory displays. Gift shop. Picnic area by pier, bar on board. Car and coach parking. Telephone (01374) 705589. www.crannog.net

A variety of boat trips. See a working salmon farm and a colony of grey and common seals on Seal Island (90 minutes), learn the history of Fort William on a cruise around the bay (50 minutes) or indulge in an evening buffet cruise with a full meal provided (90 minutes).

SEAPROBE ATLANTIS GLASS BOTTOM BOAT TRIPS   1553   4 H18

Old Ferry Slipway, Kyle of Lochalsh. 75 miles (120km) west of Inverness and north of Fort William on A87. Bus and railway station in Kyle. Boat trips available Easter–end Oct, daily 1030–1630. Charge £££. Children under 1 free. Group concessions. Guided tours. Explanatory displays. Gift shop. Refreshments available. Underwater viewing gallery. WC. Wheelchair access with assistance. Car and coach parking. Telephone Freephone 0800 980 4846. www.seaprobeatlantis.com

Seaprobe Atlantis is the only semi-submersible glass bottom boat in the UK, offering everyone the opportunity to explore the underwater world in comfort and safety. Operating from the Marine Special Area of Conservation at Kyle of Lochalsh, the *Atlantis* offers regular daily trips to explore all the scenery and wildlife above and below the waves. Underwater viewing gallery. Remote operated underwater vehicle filming images onto plasma screens. See spectacular scenery, beautiful underwater kelp forests, fish, jellyfish, seals, seabirds, otters, porpoise and the World War II *Port Napier* shipwreck.

SHIELDAIG ISLAND   1554   4 H17

NTS. Highland. Situated in Loch Torridon, off Shieldaig village, A896. Open all year. Free. Car and coach parking. Telephone (01445) 791368. www.nts.org.uk

This 32 acre (13ha) island is almost entirely covered in Scots pine, which once formed vast forests covering much of the Scottish Highlands.

SHILASDAIR   1555   4 F17

Carnach, Waternish, Isle of Skye. 22 miles (35km) north west of Portree on A850, then B886. Open Apr–Oct, daily 1000–1800; other times by appointment. Free. Guided tours. Explanatory displays. Gift shop. Coffee (free). WC. Wheelchair access. Disabled WC. Car and coach parking. Telephone (01470) 592297. www.shilasdair-yarns.co.uk

Fleece from the owner's flock of fine woolled sheep, plus exotic fibres are dyed with natural dyes in a unique and expansive range of colours. Hand and commercially spun yarns, knitkits and designer garments available. Dye garden, dyehouse and spinning workshop.

SINCLAIR AND GIRNIGOE CASTLE   1556   3 Q13

Caithness. Noss Head, near Wick.

Built by Earl William Sinclair in the 1470s. The older part of the castle, Girnigoe, dates from between 1476 and 1486. The new wing, locally known as Castle

Sinclair, was built in 1607. The castle was largely destroyed during a siege in 1690.

SKELBO CASTLE   1557   2 N15

Located north of Dornoch at Skelbo, Sutherland.

This site was probably chosen by invading Norsemen for the protection of the ships, beached on the shores of Loch Fleet, in the 9th century. The ruins can be seen from the roadside.

SKYE MUSEUM OF ISLAND LIFE   1558   4 F16

Kilmuir, Isle of Skye. On the A855, 5 miles (8km) north of Uig. Bus from Portree to Kilmuir, ask driver for museum stop. Open Apr–Oct, Mon–Sat 0930–1700. Charge £. Group concessions. Guided tours. Explanatory displays. Gift shop. WC. Wheelchair access. Disabled WC. Car and coach parking. Telephone (01470) 552206.

An interesting museum of rural life housed within a group of thatched cottages. It depicts the lifestyle of the crofting community of the island a century or so ago and displays a wide range of agricultural tools and implements. One house is furnished with period furniture.

SKYE SERPENTARIUM   1559   4 G19

The Old Mill, Harrapool, Broadford, Isle of Skye. On the A850, 8 miles (13km) north of Kyleakin. Nearest railway station Kyle of Lochalsh, buses from Kyle, Kyleakin or Armadale. Open Easter–Oct, Mon–Fri 1000–1700; Jul–Aug also Sun; and bank holidays. Charge £. Group concessions. Guided tours for groups by arrangement. Explanatory displays. Gift shop. Coffee shop. WC. Wheelchair access. Car and coach parking. Telephone (01471) 822209. www.skyeserpentarium.org.uk

A unique award-winning reptile exhibition and breeding centre in a converted water mill. Visitors can watch a world of snakes, lizards, frogs and tortoises in bright natural surroundings. Also a refuge for neglected and illegally imported reptiles. Frequent informative snake handling sessions. Baby snakes for sale.

SKYELINE CERAMICS   1560   4 H19

Grianach, Harrapool, Broadford, Isle of Skye. At Heaste Road junction in Broadford. Railway stations on mainland at Kyle (8 miles/13km) and Mallaig (15 miles/24km) plus ferry trip. Open all year, Easter–Oct, Mon–Sat 1000–1300 and 1400–1800 with some late nights (ocassionally closed on Mon or Sat); Oct–Easter times vary, telephone to confirm. Free. Visitors are welcome to watch the work in progress. Gift shop. Wheelchair access. Car parking. Telephone (01471) 822023. www.skyelineceramics.co.uk

A small working studio with a shop. There are book ends, sheep with character, porcelain pictures, delicate shell-like bowls, pebble people and more. The work is inspired by Skye's mountains, hills and their inhabitants and each piece is individually made by hand using stone and porcelain clays.

SKYESKYNS   1561   4 F17

17 Lochbay, Waternish, Isle of Skye. On the B886, 4.5 miles (7km) from the A850, 19 miles (30km) north of Portree. Kyle of Lochalsh station, bus from Portree or Kyle. Open all year, daily 1000–1800. Free. Guided tours (available in French). Explanatory displays. Gift shop. WC. Limited wheelchair access. Disabled WC. Car and coach parking. Telephone (01470) 592237. www.skyeskyns.co.uk

Showroom visitors are offered free guided tours of the tanning workshop, the only one of its kind in Scotland. They can see the traditional tools of the trade in use – the beam, paddles, drum, buffing wheel, combs and iron. Demonstrations of rare tanning skills and hand-finishing of finest lambswool rugs. Wide range of leather goods.

SMITHY HERITAGE CENTRE   1562   4 J18

Lochcarron, Strathcarron, Ross and Cromarty. On the A896, 1 mile (2km) east of Lochcarron. Nearest railway station Strathcarron, then 1.5 mile (2.5km) walk. Open Easter–Oct, Mon–Sat 1000–1700. Free. Guided tours by arrangement (available in Gaelic). Explanatory displays with video. Picnic area. Limited wheelchair access. Car and coach parking. Telephone (01520) 722246.

A restored smithy with information on the history of the building, the business and the blacksmith who worked in it. Walk through a plantation of native trees. Speakers, demonstrations and crafts at advertised times.

SMOO CAVES   1563   2 L12

In Durness, Sutherland.

This impressive limestone cave has formed at the head of a narrow coastal inlet. An easy and safe access path has been made from the road above leading into the cave. With its entrance at least 100 feet (30m) wide this is arguably one of the largest cave entrances in Britain. A wooden pathway extends into the cave and allows viewing of the second inner chamber where the Allt Smoo falls from an opening in the roof above. In the outer cave there is an ancient midden which would indicate that Stone Age man once lived here.

SPEAN BRIDGE WOOLLEN MILL   1564   5 K20

Spean Bridge, Inverness-shire. On the bridge at Spean Bridge next to Spean Bridge railway station. Bus from Fort William. Open Apr–Sep, Mon–Sat 0900–1730, Sun 1000–1500; Oct–Mar, daily 1000–1600. Free. Explanatory displays. Gift shop. Restaurant. Garden. WC. Wheelchair access. Disabled WC. Car and coach parking. Telephone (01397) 712260. www.ewm.co.uk

A picturesque weaving mill in a former farm steading. Clan tartan centre, whisky tasting, knitwear and gifts.

SPEY VALLEY SMOKEHOUSE   1565   6 P18

Achnagonalin, Grantown-on-Spey. On the outskirts of Grantown-on-Spey on the B970. Open all year, Mon–Fri 0900–1700; also Apr–Sep, Sat 1000–1400. Free. Explanatory displays and audio-visual presentation. Gift shop. Picnic area. Children's play area. WC. Wheelchair access. Disabled WC. Car and coach parking. Telephone (01479) 873078. www.speyvalleysmokedsalmon.co.uk

With a history of salmon smoking since 1888, the Spey Valley Smokehouse offers visitors the opportunity to experience the traditional smoking process in the most modern facilities. Gourmet salmon products available for purchase.

SPEYSIDE HEATHER CENTRE   1566   5 N19

Skye of Curr, Dulnain Bridge, Inverness-shire. Off the A95, 9 miles (14.5km) from Aviemore, 6 miles (9.5km) from Grantown-on-Spey. Nearest railway station Aviemore, nearest bus stop Dulnain Bridge. Open all year daily, 0900–1730 (reduced opening hours Jan–Feb). Admission free. Charge £ for exhibition. Group concessions. Guided tours (text in twelve languages). Explanatory displays. Gift shop. Tearoom/restaurant and picnic area. Play area and show garden. WC. Wheelchair access. Disabled WC. Car and coach parking. Telephone (01479) 851359. www.heathercentre.com

An exhibition, craft shop, garden centre and show garden, with heather as a speciality. Includes the famous Clootie Dumpling Restaurant and a gallery and antiques shop.

SPLIT STONE, MELVICH   1567   3 N12

1 mile (1.5km) east of Melvich in the north of Sutherland.

Local history says that an old woman was returning from a shopping trip and was chased by the devil. She ran round and round the stone and the devil in his temper split it. The woman escaped.

STOREHOUSE OF FOULIS   1568   2 M17

Foulis Ferry, Evanton, Ross and Cromarty. 16 miles (26km) north of Inverness on A9, 1 mile (1.5km) north of Cromarty Bridge. Nearest railway station and bus service Inverness. Open all year daily, 0930–1730; closed Christmas and New Year's Day. Charge ££. Group concessions. Explanatory displays. Gift shop. Restaurant and picnic area. WC. Wheelchair access. Disabled WC. Car and coach parking. Telephone (01349) 830000. www.storehouseoffoulis.co.uk

Discover the secret of the Munro clan and explore the stories of seven centuries of land and people brought to life in the rogue's gallery. *Son et lumière* shows. Also information on the behaviour of seals, which visitors might see from the shore.

STORR   1569   4 G17

Two miles (3km) from A855, 8 miles (12.5km) north of Portree, Isle of Skye. Free. Car parking.

A series of pinnacles and crags rising to 2360 feet (719m). No access, but can be seen from the road. The Old Man of Storr, at the east end of the mountain, is a black obelisk, (160 feet/49m) high, first climbed in 1955. Visitors can see Storr from the main road; due to erosion it is now closed to walkers.

STRATHNAVER MUSEUM   1570   2 M13

Clachan, Bettyhill, by Thurso, Sutherland. 12 miles (19km) east of Tongue. Bus from Thurso. Open Apr–Oct, Mon–Sat 1000–1300 and 1400–1700; telephone to arrange admission during winter. Charge £. Group concessions. Guided tours. Explanatory displays. Books available for sale. Leaflets available. Limited wheelchair access. Car and coach parking. Telephone (01641) 521418. www.strathnaver.com

A local museum housed in the former parish church of Farr. Shows the story of the Strathnaver Clearances and the Clan Mackay. Collection of local artefacts, including prehistoric and Pictish items.

STRATHSPEY STEAM RAILWAY   1571   5 N19

Aviemore Station, Dalfaber Road, Aviemore. 35 miles (56km) south of Inverness. Nearest railway station Aviemore, buses from Edinburgh, Inverness and Perth. Daily service Jun–Sep, see timetable for service outwith these months. Charge £££. NB: prices for complete round trip. Other fares available between any two stations. Group concessions. Explanatory displays. Gift shop. Refreshments on train. WC. Wheelchair access with assistance. Disabled WC. Car and coach parking. Telephone (01479) 810725. www.strathspeyrailway.co.uk

A steam railway, re-opened in 1978, and running between Aviemore, Boat of Garten and Broomhill (10 miles/16km).

STRUIE VIEWPOINT   1572 2 M16

South of Dornoch Firth on B9176.

Overlooking the picturesque Dornoch Firth. The Sutherland mountains are marked on an indicator board.

STUDIO JEWELLERY WORKSHOP AND GALLERY   1573 2 K17

Achnasheen, Ross and Cromarty. At railway station in Achnasheen. Open all year, daily 0900–1730. Free. Explanatory displays. Gift shop. Café and picnic area. Children's play area. WC. Wheelchair access. Disabled WC. Car and coach parking. Telephone (01445) 720227.

Craft centre incorporating jewellery/silversmithing workshop. Viewing windows allow visitors to watch work going on, but demonstrations are not given. Silver and gold jewellery and small silverware are on sale, together with other craft items.

SUMMER QUEEN CRUISES   1574 4 J15

1 Royal Park, Ullapool, Ross-shire. 55 miles (88km) north west of Inverness on A835. Bus from Inverness. Open Apr–Oct; four-hour trip, Mon–Sat 1000; two-hour trip, daily 1415 also Sun 1100. Group concessions. Refreshments available. WC. Limited wheelchair access. Telephone (01854) 612472. www.summerqueen.co.uk

An attractive group of islands, the largest of which is Tanera Mhor. Pleasure cruises give views of seals, birdlife and extraordinary rock formations. A four-hour cruise takes in all the Summer Isles and lands on Tanera Mhor where visitors can purchase the unique Summer Isles stamp. Also a two-hour cruise around the Isle of Martin.

SWANSON ART GALLERY   1575 3 P12

Davidsons Lane, Thurso, Caithness. Bus service from Inverness. Car and coach parking nearby. Open all year, Mon–Wed 1300–1700, Fri 1300–2000, Sat 1000–1300 (closed Thu and Sun). Free. Explanatory displays. Gift shop. WC. Wheelchair access. Telephone (01847) 896357.

The gallery displays regularly changing exhibitions of a wide range of contemporary art and crafts such as ceramics, jewellery and textiles.

TAIN THROUGH TIME   1576 2 M16

Tower Street, Tain, Ross and Cromarty. 1 mile (2km) off A9. Railway station and bus stations Tain. Open Apr–Oct, Mon–Sat 1000–1700; Jul–Aug 1000–1800, other times by appointment. Charge ££. Carers/group leaders free. Group concessions. Guided tours. Explanatory displays. Gift shop. Churchyard with seats. WC. Limited wheelchair access. Disabled WC. Car and coach parking. Telephone (01862) 894089. www.tainmuseum.org.uk

Comprises St Duthuc's Chapel and Collegiate Church, which was an important medieval pilgrimage site (see 1547); the Pilgrimage visitor centre with an audio-visual interpretation of the history of Tain; and Tain and District Museum offering an insight into the local history.

TALISKER DISTILLERY VISITOR CENTRE   1577 4 F18

Carbost, Isle of Skye. On the B8009, just off the A863 where it joins the A87 at Sligachan. Bus from Portree. Open Apr–Jun and Oct, Mon–Fri 0900–1630; Jul–Sep, Mon–Sat 0900–1630; Nov–Mar, Mon–Fri 1400–1630. Last tour 1630. Charge ££. Guided tours. Explanatory displays. Gift shop. Picnic area. WC. Limited wheelchair access. Disabled WC. Car parking. Telephone (01478) 614308. www.malts.com

The only distillery on Skye. An exhibition tells the history of the distillery and its place in the community.

TARBAT DISCOVERY CENTRE   1578   2 N16

Tarbatness Road, Portmahomack, Tain, Ross-shire. Approximately 45m (72km) northeast of Inverness. From Inverness take the A9, turning towards Portmahomack. Open Mar–Apr and Oct, daily 1400–1700; May–Sep, daily 1000–1700; Nov, Fri–Sat 1400–1600. Charge ££. Children under 12 free, children 12–18 £. Group concessions on application. Explanatory displays, activity room with touch screen displays, audiovisual presentation. Gift shop. WC. Wheelchair access (except to crypt). Disabled WC. Telephone (01862) 871351. www.tarbat-discovery.co.uk

The Museum is housed in the beautifully restored 18th century (and last of six icarnations dating back to the Picts in the 8th century) Tarbat Old Church. Archaeological excavations of the site next to the church have revealed the remains of a wealthy and very sophisticated Pictish monastic community with leather, metal and glass making workshops. Intricately carved stones discovered inside and outside the church are displayed within the Treasury.
Interpretations of the church and the settlement can be viewed throughout the Centre. The more recent history and development of the local community is also on permanent display.

THREE FOLLIES AT AUCKENGILL   1579   3 Q12

Auckengill, Caithness on the A9 Wick to John O' Groats road, 6 miles (9.5km) south of John O' Groats.

The first folly on the left was a boat's lantern; the second held a barometer, a log book and weather information; the third is known as Mervin's tower, built for a small boy who spent all his time with the workmen. The motto means hasten slowly.

THURSO HERITAGE MUSEUM   1580   3 P12

Town Hall, High Street, Thurso. Open Jun–Sep, Mon–Sat 1000–1300, 1400–1700. Charge £. Group concessions. Guided tours on request. Explanatory displays. Wheelchair access with assistance. Disabled WC. Car and coach parking. Telephone (01847) 892692.

A varied collection which includes historical Pictish stones, fossils, relics of the flagstone industry, local military memorabilia, and reconstructions of granny's kitchen and living room. Historical perspective of local figures in the community, and photographic history of the area.

TIMESPAN HERITAGE CENTRE AND ART GALLERY   1581   3 P15

Dunrobin Street, Helmsdale, Sutherland. 70 miles (112.5km) north of Inverness, on A9 to John O'Groats. Nearest railway station Helmsdale, buses from Inverness and Wick. Open Apr–Oct, Mon–Sat 1000–1700, Sun 1200–1700. Charge ££. Group concessions. Guided tours by prior arrangement. Explanatory displays. Gift shop. Café. Art gallery. WC. Wheelchair access. Disabled WC. Car and coach parking. Telephone (01431) 821327. www.timespan.org.uk

Timespan museum features the dramatic history of Helmsdale. The gallery has an extensive program of contemporary exhibitions and the riverside café serves home baking daily. The shop complements the centre with interesting gifts and souvenirs. Outside is a picturesque herb garden beside the river Helmsdale.

TOMATIN DISTILLERY 1582   2 N18

Tomatin, Inverness-shire. Just off the A9, 15 miles (24km) south of Inverness, buses
from Inverness or Aviemore. Nearest bus stop 0.5 mile (1km) away. Open all year,
Mon–Fri 0900–1700, Sat 0900–1200; last tour 1530. Free. Advance notice required
for large groups. Guided tours. Explanatory displays and video. Gift shop. WC.
Wheelchair access. Disabled WC. Car and coach parking. Telephone (01808) 511444.
www.tomatin.com

One of Scotland's largest malt whisky distilleries and over one hundred years
old.

TORRIDON 1583   4 J17

NTS. Visitor Centre, Torridon, Achnasheen, Ross-shire. Off A896, 9 miles (14.5km)
south west of Kinlochewe. Estate, deer park and deer museum open all year. Visitor
centre open Apr–late Sep, daily 1000–1800. Charge £. Explanatory displays. Guided
walks by rangers. WC. Wheelchair access to visitor centre and deer museum only.
Disabled WC. Car parking. Telephone (01445) 791221. www.nts.org.uk

Around 16,000 acres (6475ha) of some of Scotland's finest mountain scenery
whose peaks rise over 3000 feet (914m). Of major interest to geologists, Liathach
and Beinn Alligin are of red sandstone, some 750 million years old. The visitor
centre at the junction of A896 and Diabaig road has an audio-visual presentation
on the local wildlife. Deer museum (unmanned) and deer park open all year.
Ranger led walks in season.

TOUCHSTONE MAZE 1584   2 L17

Strathpeffer, west of Dingwall.

A large-scale labyrinth pathway amongst standing stones and turf walls. The
maze has been built to incorporate alignments with sun and moon positions.

TOY MUSEUM 1585   4 F18

Holmisdale House, Glendale, Isle of Skye. 7 miles (11km) west of Dunvegan. Post bus
from Dunvegan. Open all year, Mon–Sat 1000–1800. Charge £. Group concessions.
Guided tours. Explanatory displays. Gift shop. Garden with waterfall. WC. Artefacts
can be handled by blind visitors on a guided tour. Wheelchair access. Car parking.
Telephone (01470) 511240. www.toy-museum.co.uk

Award-winning toy museum, with a unique display of toys, games and dolls from
Bisque to Barbie, Victorian to Star Wars. Also on display are early examples of
Pinball.

TREASURES OF THE EARTH 1586   5 J21

Corpach, Fort William. 4 miles (6.5km) from Fort William, on A830. Bus from Fort
William. Open all year (except Christmas and Jan), daily 1000–1700; Jul–Sep
0930–1900. Charge ££. Group concessions. Guided tours for groups by
arrangement. Explanatory displays. Leaflet in French, German, Italian and Spanish.
Gift shop. WC. Wheelchair access. Disabled WC. Car and coach parking. Telephone
(01397) 772283.

This is a large collection of gemstones and crystals, displayed in recreated
caverns and mines, just as they were found beneath the earth. Nuggets of gold
and silver, aquamarines, red garnets, rubies, opals and diamonds are amongst
many other gemstones and crystals on display, some weighing hundreds of kilos.

TROTTERNISH ART GALLERY   1587   4 G16

Kilmaluag, Duntulm, Isle of Skye. 25 miles (40km) north of Portree on the A855. Bus
service from Portree. Open Apr–Sep, daily, 0900–1900; Oct–Mar, daily 0900–1730
(closed Christmas). Free. Retail gallery. Limited wheelchair access. Car parking.
Telephone (01470) 552302.

Working landscape gallery set in a beautiful part of Skye with magnificent and
spectacular pinnacles and cliffs. Wide selection of originals, and mounted
photographic work. All artwork exclusive to gallery.

PETER TYLER – WOODTURNER   1588   2 M18

Milton of Tordarroch, Dunlichity, by Farr, Inverness-shire. 9 miles (14.5km) south of
Inverness, 5 miles (8km) west of A9. Open Apr–Dec, Mon–Sat 1000–1730; Apr and
Oct–Dec closed Mon. Free. Explanatory displays. Gift shop. Picnic area. Wheelchair
access with assistance (gravel path). Car parking. Telephone (01808) 521414.
www.petertyler.fsbusiness.co.uk

Producing a wide range of turned domestic woodware using local Scottish
hardwoods. Visitors can watch the craftsman at work. Locally handmade
craftwork available. The shop and workshop are in a scenic valley with abundant
birdlife and views over moorland.

UDALE BAY RSPB NATURE RESERVE   1589   2 M17

RSPB. By Jemmimaville, Black Isle. 0.5 mile (1km) west of Jemimaville on B9163. Bus
service from Inverness. Reserve open at all times. Free. Explanatory displays.
Wheelchair access. Car parking. Telephone (01463) 715000. www.rspb.org.uk/scotland

The vast area of sand and mud deposits is a National Nature Reserve. Udale Bay
is a mecca for birdwatchers. Herons, greylag, geese, widgeon, teal, mallard,
goldeneye and shelduck can all be found here in good numbers. The hide has
full disabled access and can comfortably accommodate ten people. Best visited
within two hours of high tide, the reserve can offer spectacular views of flocks of
birds.

UIG POTTERY   1590   4 F17

Uig, Isle of Skye. Bus from Portree. Open Apr–Oct, Mon–Sat 0900–1800, Sun
1100–1600; Nov–Mar, Mon–Sat 0900–1700. Free. Gift shop. WC. Wheelchair access.
Disabled WC. Car and coach parking. Telephone (01470) 542421.
www.uigpottery.co.uk

A pottery making unique and functional pieces.

ULLAPOOL MUSEUM AND VISITOR CENTRE   1591   2 K15

7-8 West Argyle Street, Ullapool. In Ullapool centre. Bus from Inverness. Open
Apr–Oct, Mon–Sat 1000–1700; Nov–Mar open by arrangement. Charge £. Group
concessions. Explanatory displays. Gift shop. WC. Induction loop for audio-visual
presentation. Large print text. Alternative methods of accessing upstairs displays.
Limited wheelchair access (disabled set down point outside building). Disabled WC.
Telephone (01854) 612987. www.ullapoolmuseum.co.uk

Housed in an A-listed historic building, a former Telford Parliamentary Church.
The award-winning museum interprets the natural and human history of the
Lochbroom and Coigach area. This includes the establishment of Ullapool by
the British Fisheries Society in 1788 and the voyage of the *Hector* in 1773, the first
emigrant ship to sail direct from Scotland to Nova Scotia. The museum displays

artefacts, photographs, community tapestries and quilts, and uses audio-visual and computer technology. Maps and records are available for study. There is also a genealogy enquiry service.

VICTORIA FALLS 1592   4 J17

Off A832, 12 miles (19km) north west of Kinlochewe, near Slattadale. Access at all times. Free. Car parking.

Waterfall named after Queen Victoria who visited Loch Maree and the surrounding area in 1877.

WALTZING WATERS 1593   5 M20

Balvail Brae, Newtonmore, Inverness-shire. On the main street in the village of Newtonmore. Bus service from Inverness or Perth, bus stop at entrance. Open Feb–early Jan, daily. 45 minute show on hour, every hour, 1000–1600. End Mar–end Oct, additional shows at 1700 and 2030. Charge ££. Group concessions. Gift shop. Coffee shop. Play park. WC. Wheelchair access (except coffee shop). Disabled WC. Car and coach parking. Telephone (01540) 673752.

Indoor water, light and music spectacular in theatrical setting.

WATER SAMPLING PAVILION, STRATHPEFFER 1594   2 L17

Strathpeffer, west of Dingwall.

An opportunity for visitors to sample the sulphur waters, which made Strathpeffer Spa renowned as a destination for Victorians.

WATERLINES 1595   3 Q14

Lybster Harbour, Lybster, Caithness. 13 miles (21km) south of Wick on main A99. Bus service to Lybster stops within 0.5 mile (1km). Open May–Sep, daily 1100–1700. Charge £. Group concessions by arrangement. Guided tours. Explanatory displays. Coffee shop and picnic area. Terrace. WC. Wheelchair access. Disabled WC. Car and coach parking. Telephone (01593) 721520.

The visitor centre explains the natural heritage of the east Caithness coast and the history of Lybster harbour, once the third most important herring port in Scotland. Live CCTV on bird cliffs, also wooden boatbuilding display. Shower and laundry facilities for yachts.

WELL OF SEVEN HEADS 1596   5 K20

Off A82 on the west shore of Loch Oich. Access at all times. Free. Car parking.

A curious monument inscribed in English, Gaelic, French and Latin and surmounted by seven men's heads. It stands above a spring and recalls the grim story of the execution of seven brothers for the murder of the two sons of a 17th-century chief of Keppoch.

WEST AFFRIC 1597   2 K18

NTS. Highland. 22 miles (35.5km) east of Kyle of Lochalsh, off A87. Open all year. Free. Guided walks by rangers. Telephone (01599) 511231. www.nts.org.uk

Stretching over 9000 acres (3642ha), this important wild and rugged landscape adjoins the NTS property at Kintail. West Affric is magnificent and challenging walking country, and includes one of the most popular east–west Highland paths. This was once the old drove road taking cattle across Scotland from the Isle of Skye to market at Dingwall.

WEST HIGHLAND DAIRY   1598   4 H18

Achmore, Stromeferry, Kyle. 0.3 mile (0.5km) down lane towards Fernaig and Portnacullin from Achmore village. Nearest railway station Stromeferry. Parking available for small coaches only. Open Mar–Dec, daily 1000–1800. Free. Dairy shop and picnic area. Wheelchair access with assistance. Car and coach parking. Telephone (01599) 577203. www.westhighlanddairy.co.uk

Small commercial dairy producing a range of cheeses, some award-winning. The dairy also makes ice cream, yogurt and traditional dairy desserts. Once a month, courses of three days duration are offered covering all aspects of dairying.

WEST HIGHLAND HEAVY HORSES   1599   4 G19

Riding with Heavy Horses at Armadale Home Farm, Isle of Skye. 0.5 mile (1km) north of Armadale ferry terminal, 21 miles (34km) south west after the Skye Bridge at Kyle of Lochalsh, on A851. Car and passenger ferry from Mallaig to Armadale. Bus from Kyle of Lochalsh. Riding offered all year. Telephone or visit website for details. Charge dependent on tour taken (from ££–£££). Group concessions. Guided tours. All facilities available at Armadale Castle Gardens. WC. Wheelchair access with assistance (every effort taken to accommodate all visitors). Car and coach parking. Telephone 01471 844759; mobile 07769 588565. www.westhighlandheavyhorses.com

Based at Armadale Home Farm on the beautiful Sleat Penninsula, Isle of Skye. Heavy horse riding using Clydesdales and Shires. Amidst spectacular scenery, rides to suit all (although specialising in experienced riders) from a half-hour or 2-hour ride, to several days in the saddle on our wonderful, well-schooled, responsive Clydesdales. Plus short breaks and holidays at which guests enjoy a hands-on experience to learn harnessing, driving, horse riding and horse management skills.

WEST HIGHLAND WOOLLEN COMPANY   1600   2 K15

5 Shore Street, Ullapool, Wester Ross. On harbour front in Ullapool. Open all year, Mon–Sat 0900–1800, Sun 1100–1600; Jul and Aug late night opening Mon–Sat untill 2200. Free. Car and coach parking. Telephone (01854) 612399. www.ewm.co.uk

This superb store situated on the beautiful harbour front has a large selection of Scottish knitwear, clothing, accessories and gifts.

WHALIGOE STEPS   1601   3 Q13

At Ulbster, Caithness.

Three hundred flagstone steps descend the steep cliffs to a small quay below, built in the 18th century during the herring boom. Care should be taken in wet or windy conditions – the steps are not suitable for the young or infirm.

WITCH'S STONE   1602   2 N16

In the Littletown area of Dornoch, Sutherland.

An upright slab bearing the date 1722, marking the place where the last witch in Scotland was burned.

WOLFSTONE   1603   3 N15

Sutherland. Situated in a lay-by, 6 miles (9.5km) south of Helmsdale at Loth.

The stone marks the spot where, in 1700, the last wolf in Scotland was killed.

WORKING SHEEP DOGS   1604   5 N19

Leault Farm, Kincraig, Kingussie, Inverness-shire. 6 miles (10km) south of Aviemore
on B9152. Nearest railway station Kingussie, local bus service. Demonstrations
May–Nov daily except Sat, May and Oct times by arrangement; Jun and Sep, 1200
and 1600; Jul–Aug, 1000, 1200, 1400 and 1600. Charge ££. Group concessions.
Explanatory displays and demonstrations. Gift shop. Wheelchair access. Car and
coach parking. Telephone (01540) 651310.

Displays of up to eight border collies and their skilful handlers. Traditional
hand-shearing displays – visitors can participate. Also ducks, puppies and
orphan lambs. Visitors can learn about the working day of a Highland shepherd.

THE OUTER ISLANDS

AN LANNTAIR   1605   4 G14

Town Hall, South Beach, Stornoway, Isle of Lewis. On the seafront in Stornoway
adjacent to ferry and bus station. Open all year, Mon–Sat 1000–1730. Free. Gift shop.
Tearoom. WC. Wheelchair access. Car and coach parking. Telephone (01851) 703307.
www.lanntair.com

Main public arts facility in the Western Isles. A forum for local, national and
international arts, promoting a year-round programme of exhibitions and events.

BALFOUR CASTLE   1606   3 R10

Shapinsay Island, Orkney. 25 minute car ferry journey from Kirkwall. Open all year for
resident guests, May–Sep for guided tours Sun only, 1415 from Kirkwall. Book with
Balfour Castle. Charge £££. Guided tours. Gift shop. Picnic area. Garden. WC. No
guide dogs. Car and coach parking. Telephone (01856) 711282. www.balfourcastle.com

Personally guided tours by member of family around this Victorian castle with
original furnishings and 2 acre walled garden. One of the tour highlights is a
traditional Orkney tea with home produce from the island, inclusive in tour price.

BALRANALD RSPB NATURE RESERVE   1607   4 C17

RSPB. North Uist, Western Isles. 3 miles (5km) north of Bayhead. Turn for Hougharry
off A865. Post bus service only. Reserve open at all times. Visitor centre open
Apr–Aug, daily 0900–1800. Free. WC. Limited wheelchair access. Disabled WC. Car
and coach parking. Telephone (01870) 560287. www.rspb.org.uk/scotland

Sandy beaches and a rocky foreshore, separated from the machair and marshes
by sand dunes; also shallow lochs. Visitor centre explains the importance of
traditional crofting agriculture for the now rare corncrake and other wildlife.
Many species of wading birds nest on the flower-rich machair and the croftland.

BAYANNE HOUSE   1608   1 V2

Sellafirth, Yell. On A968, 1.5 miles (2.5km) south of Gutcher ferry terminal. Open all
year, daily 0900–2100. Free. Guided tours. Explanatory displays. Gift shop. Coffee
and biscuits available. Picnic area. WC. Wheelchair access. Car and coach parking.
Telephone (01957) 744219. www.bayanne.co.uk

A purpose built workshop, on the beach at Basta Voe, providing facilities for
visitors including internet micro-café, Shetland genealogy research, textile
design, archaeological site and access to a working croft. Otters, seals, wading
birds and wild flowers.

BERNERA MUSEUM 1609   4 H19

Bernera, Lewis. On B8059, 2 miles (3km) from Bernera Bridge. Bus on request to local operator (01851) 612224 or 612350. Open Jun–early Sep, Tue–Sat 1200–1600. Charge £. Group concessions. Explanatory displays. Café. Children's play area. WC. Wheelchair access. Disabled WC. Car and coach parking. Telephone (01851) 612331.

Opened in 1995 as part of a community centre, the museum displays information on genealogy, archaeology and historical sites, also archives, old photographs and a lobster fishing exhibition in summer.

BISHOP'S AND EARL'S PALACES 1610   3 Q10

HS. Watergate, Kirkwall, Orkney. In Kirkwall. Open Apr–Oct, daily 0930–1830. Charge £. Group concessions. Guided tours. Explanatory displays. Gift shop. Telephone (01856) 871918. www.historic-scotland.gov.uk

The Bishop's Palace is a 12th-century hall house, later much altered with a round tower built by Bishop Reid between 1541 and 1548. A later addition was made by the notorious Patrick Stewart, Earl of Orkney, who built the adjacent Earl's Palace between 1600 and 1607 in a splendid Renaissance style.

BLACK HOUSE 1611   4 F13

HS. 42 Arnol, Barvas, Isle of Lewis. At Arnol, on the A858. 15 miles (24km) north west of Stornoway. Ferry from Ullapool to Stornoway, bus from Stornoway. Open Apr–Sep, Mon–Sat 0930–1830; Oct–Mar, Mon–Sat 0930–1630. Charge £. Group concessions. Guided tours. Explanatory displays. Gift shop. WC. Limited wheelchair access. Car and coach parking. Telephone (01851) 710395. www.historic-scotland.gov.uk

A traditional Hebridean thatched house with byre, attached barn and stackyard, complete and furnished.

BLACKHAMMER CAIRN 1612   3 Q10

HS. North of the B9064 on the south coast of the island of Rousay, Orkney. Bus from Kirkwall to Tingwall then ferry to Rousay. Access all year. Free. Telephone (01856) 751360. www.historic-scotland.gov.uk

A long Neolithic cairn bounded by a retaining wall with a megalithic burial chamber divided into seven compartments.

BÖD OF GREMISTA 1613   1 V5

Gremista, Lerwick, Shetland. 1.5 miles (2.5km) north of Lerwick town centre. Open Jun–Sep, Wed–Sun 1000–1300 and 1400–1700. Free. Guided tours. Explanatory displays. WC. Limited wheelchair access. Car and coach parking. Telephone (01595) 694386.

A restored 18th-century fishing booth, the birthplace of local shipowner and politician Arthur Anderson. Displays tell the story of Anderson's life and service to Shetland, and of the fisheries 200 years ago. Also recreated room interiors of the kitchen and bedroom, including many original objects such as furniture, models, utensils, fishing gear and paintings.

BONHOGA GALLERY 1614   1 V4

Weisdale, Shetland. 12 miles (19km) west of Lerwick. Bus service from Lerwick and Westside. Open all year, Tue–Sat 1030–1630, Sun 1200–1630. Free. Guided tours. Gift shop. Café. WC. Wheelchair access. Disabled WC. Car and coach parking. Telephone (01595) 830400.

Bonhoga Gallery displays local, national and international art and craft exhibitions. Plus the Shetland Textile Working Museum. Café in conservatory overlooking the Weisdale Burn.

BORGH POTTERY   1615   4 F13

Fivepenny House, Borgh, Isle of Lewis. On A857 to Ness, 18 miles (29km) from Stornoway. Local bus service. Open all year, Mon–Sat 0930–1800. Free. Guided tours by request. Gift shop. Wheelchair access with assistance. Car and coach parking. Telephone (01851) 850345. www.borghpottery.com

Established in 1974, for the production of hand thrown stoneware. The glazes are mixed from raw materials, ensuring the individuality of each piece. As well as pottery, the showroom displays a range of gifts, including Celtic patterned knitwear, jewellery, cards and wallhangings, candles and soaps. The pottery is set in an attractive garden and visitors are welcome to walk around (fishpond – children must be supervised at all times).

BROCH OF GURNESS   1616   3 Q10

HS. Evie, Orkney. Off the A966 at Aikerness, about 14 miles (22.5km) north west of Kirkwall. Tour bus from Kirkwall. Open Apr–Sep, daily 0930–1830. Charge £. Group concessions. Explanatory displays. Gift shop. Wheelchair access with assistance. Car and coach parking. Telephone (01856) 751414. www.historic-scotland.gov.uk

An Iron Age broch over 10 feet (3m) high, surrounded by stone huts, deep ditches and ramparts.

BROUGH OF BIRSAY   1617   3 P10

HS. On the island of Birsay, at the north end of mainland Orkney. 20 miles (32km) north west of Kirkwall. Tourist bus from Kirkwall to Birsay. Telephone to confirm opening times. Charge £. Group concessions. Explanatory displays. Telephone (01856) 841815. www.historic-scotland.gov.uk

The remains of a Romanesque church and a Norse settlement.

CALANAIS (CALLANISH) STANDING STONES   1618   4 F14

HS. At Calanais, off A859, 12 miles west of Stornoway, Isle of Lewis (Western Isles). Bus service from Stornoway. Site open all year. Free. Charge for visitor centre. Explanatory displays. Gift shop. Tearoom. WC. Wheelchair access with assistance. Disabled WC. Car and coach parking. Telephone (01851) 621422. www.historic-scotland.gov.uk

A unique cruciform setting of megaliths second in importance only to Stonehenge. Erected about 3000 BC. An avenue of 19 monoliths leads north from a circle of 13 stones, with rows of more stones fanning out to the south, east and west. Inside the circle is a small chambered tomb. See also 1619 Callanish – The Scottish Stonehenge.

CALLANISH – THE SCOTTISH STONEHENGE   1619   4 F14

Olcote, New Park, Callanish, Isle of Lewis. On A858, 1 mile (1.5km) north of Callanish. Bus service from Stornoway. Tours available all year, Mon–Sat by arrangement. £££ per hour per group of 1–10 people. Larger groups by arrangement. Visitors must provide their own transport for tour, with seat for Margaret Curtis. Limited wheelchair access. Car and coach parking. Telephone (01851) 621277.

The tours are led by archaeologist Margaret Curtis (Ponting). She has lived locally, excavated and researched the standing stones for 30 years, giving her intimate professional knowledge of Callanish. The tours give an insight into how and why prehistoric people set up and used the Callanish stones. The connection between the Callanish Stones, the moon and the 'sacred' landscape culminates in a special lunar event every 18.6 years, as in 2006. The basic tour visits four of the 20 sites, uses explanatory diagrams, and can be modified to suit individual interests. See also 1618 Calanais (Callanish) Standing Stones.

CARRICK HOUSE   1620   3 R9

Eday, Orkney Islands. At the end of a private road. 20 miles (32km) north of Kirkwall by ferry. Ferry runs twice daily, air service from Kirkwall on Wed. Taxis and bicycles available from pier, 7 miles (11km) to house. Open end Jun–mid Sep (by appointment only). Free-donations to charity. Guided tours (available in French and German). Explanatory displays. Postcards for sale. Picnic area. Garden. WC. Limited wheelchair access. Car parking. Telephone (01857) 622260.

Historic private house dating from the 17th century, built by John Stewart, Earl of Carrick, younger brother of Patrick Stewart, Earl of Orkney. The house was the scene of the capture of Pirate Gow in 1725. It was renovated into a larger house incorporating earlier buildings in the mid 19th century. It is built of local sandstone and is harled and crow-stepped in the traditional Orkney style. The guided tours take in the house, garden and other parts of the island. Spectacular views.

ST MAGNUS CHURCH   1621   3 Q10

HS. On the Isle of Egilsay, Orkney. Bus from Kirkwall to Tingwall, ferry from Tingwall to Egilsay. Access at all reasonable times. Free. Telephone (01856) 841815. www.historic-scotland.gov.uk

The complete, but roofless, ruin of a 12th-century church with a remarkable round tower of the Irish type. Dramatically sited.

CILLE BHARRA   1622   4 C19

At Eolaigearraidh (Eoligarry), at the north end of Isle of Barra. Access at all times. Free. Telephone (01871) 810336 (Castlebay Tourist Office).

The ruined church of St Barr, who gave his name to the island, and the restored chapel of St Mary formed part of the medieval monastery. Among the gravestones preserved there was a unique stone carved with a Celtic cross on one side and Norse runes on the other. A replica of this stone now stands in Cille Bharra.

CLICK MILL   1623   3 Q10

HS. At Dounby, on mainland Orkney. Bus from Kirkwall. Access at all reasonable times. Free. Telephone (01856) 841815. www.historic-scotland.gov.uk

The last surviving and working horizontal water mill in Orkney, a type well represented in Shetland and Lewis.

CLICKIMIN BROCH   1624   1 V5

HS. About 1 mile (2km) south west of Lerwick, Shetland. Bus from Lerwick. Access at all reasonable times. Free. Telephone (01856) 841815. www.historic-scotland.gov.uk

A good example of a broch tower with associated secondary buildings of Iron Age date.

COLL POTTERY   1625   4 G13

Coll Pottery, Back, Isle of Lewis, Western Isles. In township of Coll on the B895, 6 miles (9.5km) north east of Stornoway. Bus from Stornoway. Open Apr–Sep, Mon–Sat

0900–1730; Oct–Mar, Mon–Sat 0900–1700. Free. Explanatory displays. Gift shop.
Tearoom. WC. Wheelchair access. Disabled WC. Car and coach parking. Telephone
(01851) 820219. www.broadbayceramics.co.uk

A working pottery making a wide range of items, from the unique marbled ware
of the Hebridean range and the figurines of the Highlands and Islands, to
traditional thistleware and Highbank Porcelain dolphins and seabirds. Craft
shop and tearoom.

CORRIGALL FARM MUSEUM 1626   3 Q10

Harray, Orkney. Off A986, south east of Mirbister. Open Mar–Oct, Mon–Sat
1030–1300 and 1400–1700, Sun 1400–1700. Free. Explanatory displays. WC.
Wheelchair access with assistance. Car parking. Telephone (01856) 771411.
www.orkney.org/museums

A working museum set on an ancient farmstead, originally dating from the 18th
century. Visitors can get a vivid insight into the lives of the typical Orcadian
farmer. Working barn with grain kiln. Traditional crafts and livestock. Horse
drawn implements and machines. See also 1659 Kirbuster Farm Museum.

COTTASCARTH AND RENDALL MOSS RSPB RESERVE 1627   3 Q10

RSPB. By Finstown, Orkney. 3.5 miles (5.5km) north of Finstown, off A966. Linked to
Mainland by North Link Ferries. Reserve open at all times. Free. Car and coach
parking. Telephone (01856) 850176. www.rspb.org.uk/scotland

Cottascarth and Rendall Moss is a wonderful place to see hen harriers, merlins
and short-eared owls. Rendal Moss has one of the highest densities of breeding
curlews in Europe.

CUBBIE ROW'S CASTLE 1628   3 Q10

HS. On the island of Wyre, Orkney. Bus from Kirkwall to Tingwall and ferry from
Tingwall to Wyre. Access at all reasonable times. Free. Telephone (01856) 841815.
www.historic-scotland.gov.uk

Probably the earliest stone castle authenticated in Scotland. Built circa 1145 by
Norseman Kolbein Hruga, it consists of a small rectangular tower enclosed in a
circular ditch. Nearby are the ruins of St Mary's Chapel, late 12th century in the
Romanesque style.

CUWEEN HILL CAIRN 1629   3 Q10

HS. On A965, 0.5 mile (1km) south of Finstown, Orkney. Bus service from Kirkwall or
Stromness then 1 mile (2km) walk. Access at all reasonable times. Free. Car parking.
Telephone (01856) 841815. www.historic-scotland.gov.uk

A low mound covering a Neolithic chambered tomb with four cells. When
discovered, it contained the bones of men, dogs and oxen.

CYCHARTERS LTD 1630   1 V5

Muckle Yard, Scalloway Harbour, Shetland, (bookings can be made through Shetland
Tourist Office). 7 miles (11km) west of Lerwick. Local bus service. Regular sailings
Jun–Sep. Telephone to confirm times. Charges vary. Group concessions. Toilet
facilities onboard. Wheelchair access with assistance. Car and coach parking.
Telephone (01595) 696598. www.cycharters.co.uk

Cycharters take visitors to the island of Foula, 25 miles (40km) west of the
Shetland Mainland, for sightseeing. This unique island has the second highest
cliffs in the UK, and thousands of seabirds. Whales are often spotted around the

coast. Also boat trips through the Scalloway Isles and evening trips to Hildasay, Oxna, Papa or South Havra. The *MV Cyfish* is available for private hire and sea angling trips.

DIM RIV NORSE LONGSHIP BOAT TRIPS   1631   1 V5

Lerwick, Shetland. Open May–mid Sep, Mon only unless hired privately. Book at Tourist Information Centre. Charge ££. Group concessions. Car and coach parking. Telephone (01595) 693097.

Harbour tours on a working replica of a Norse longship.

DOUNE BROCH CENTRE   1632   4 F13

Carloway, Isle of Lewis. On A858, 22 miles (35km) from Stornoway. Local bus service. Open Jun–Sep, Mon–Sat 1000–1630. Free. Explanatory displays. Gift shop. WC and disabled WC open all year. Wheelchair access. Car and coach parking. Telephone (01851) 643338.

The visitor centre is down the hill from the Doune Broch and is built into the hillside with a turf roof. There is a reconstruction of how the broch might have been lived in.

DUN CARLOWAY   1633   4 E13

HS. On the A858, 1.5 miles (2.5km) south of Carloway and 16 miles (25.5km) north-west of Stornoway, Isle of Lewis (Western Isles). Ferry from Ullapool to Stornoway, bus service from Stornoway to Carloway road end. Access at all reasonable times. Free. Car and coach parking. Telephone (01667) 460232. www.historic-scotland.gov.uk

One of the best preserved Iron Age brochs in Scotland.

DWARFIE STANE   1634   3 Q11

HS. Towards the north end of the island of Hoy, Orkney. Ferry from Stromness to Linkness then 3 mile (5km) walk. Access at all reasonable times. Free. Car parking. Telephone (01856) 811397. www.historic-scotland.gov.uk

A huge block of sandstone in which a Neolithic burial chamber has been cut. No other known example in the British Isles. See also 1652 Hoy RSPB Nature Reserve and 1679 Old Man of Hoy.

EYNHALLOW CHURCH   1635   3 Q10

HS. On the island of Eynhallow, Orkney. Enquire at Kirkwall Tourist Information Centre for private hire to Eynhallow. Access at all reasonable times. Free. Telephone (01856) 841815. www.historic-scotland.gov.uk

The ruins of a 12th-century church and a group of domestic buildings.

FAIR ISLE   1636   1 U8

NTS. Between Orkney and Shetland. Flights from Shetland, ferry from Grutness, Shetland. Open all year. Free. Gift shop. Telephone (01463) 232034. www.nts.org.uk

One of Britain's most isolated inhabited islands. It is perhaps most famous for the intricately patterned knitwear which bears its name, a traditional craft which continues today. Fair Isle is important for birdlife, and offers many opportunities for ornithological study. The island also has much of archaeological interest, and traditional crofting is still in evidence. Accommodation is available at the bird observatory (01595 760258) or in bed and breakfast houses.

FETLAR INTERPRETIVE CENTRE   1637   1 W2

Beach of Houbie, Fetlar, Shetland. On the island of Fetlar, 4 miles (6.5km) from the car ferry. Bus service to Gutcher (Yell) then ferry to Fetlar. Open May–Sep, Tue–Sun 1230–1730. Free. Guided tours (available in French, German and Italian). Explanatory displays. Gift shop. Tea and coffee machine. Picnic area. WC. Wheelchair access. Disabled WC. Car and coach parking. Telephone (01957) 207. www.fetlar.com

Museum and visitor information centre with interpretive and interactive display on Fetlar's history, folklore, flora, fauna and geology. Extensive archive of photographs, audio recordings and historic local film. Award-winning exhibition on the history of antiseptic surgery (school packs available).

FORT CHARLOTTE   1638   1 V5

HS. Lerwick, Shetland. In centre of town. Telephone for opening times. Free. Telephone (01466) 793191. www.historic-scotland.gov.uk

A pentagonal artillery fort, with bastions projecting from each corner and massive and high walls. Built in 1665 to protect the Sound of Bressay from the Dutch, but taken by them and burned in 1673. Rebuilt in 1781.

GEARRANNAN BLACKHOUSE VILLAGE   1639   4 E13

Gearrannan Blackhouse Village, Gearrannan, Carloway, Isle of Lewis. Bus service to village during summer. Open Apr–Sep, Mon–Sat 0930–1730. Charge £. Additional charge for guided tours and special events. Group concessions. Guided tours. Explanatory displays. Gift shop. Tearoom and picnic area. WC. Wheelchair access. Disabled WC. Car and coach parking. Telephone (01851) 643416. www.gearrannan.com

On the exposed Atlantic coast of the Isle of Lewis, a traditional blackhouse village restored to recreate 1955, when it was alive and bustling with activity. Innovative touch screen presentation of the history of the village with text and audio commentary.

GLASDRUM WOOD NATIONAL NATURE RESERVE   1640   5 J22

Car park on north side of Loch Creran, 2 miles (3km) east of the new Creagan Bridge and A828 Oban/Fort William road. On Oban/Fort William bus route. Access at all times. Free. Parking and picnic area suitable for less able visitors. Car parking. Telephone 01546 603611 (Scottish Natural Heritage). www.nnr-scotland.org.uk

Nature reserve. This wild woodland climbs from the seashore near the head of Loch Creran up the slopes of Ben Churalain. The changes in altitude and the presence of both acid and lime-rich rocks make for a rich variety of trees, plants and insects. The reserve is also notable for a range of butterfly species, including the rare chequered skipper. Steep woodland trail.

GRAIN EARTH HOUSE   1641   3 Q10

HS. At Hatson, about 1 mile (2km) north west of Kirkwall, Orkney. Open at all reasonable times. Key held by Ortak Visitor Centre (see 1684) in Kirkwall. Free. Telephone (01856) 841815. www.historic-scotland.gov.uk

A well-built Iron Age earth house with an underground chamber supported on stone pillars.

HACKNESS, MARTELLO TOWER   1642   3 Q11

HS. At Hackness, at the south east end of the Island of Hoy, Orkney. Ferry from Stromness to Lyness on Hoy, then 10 mile (16km) walk or passenger ferry to

Longhope and a 3 mile (5km) walk. For access see keyholder. Free. Charge £.
Telephone (01856) 811397. www.historic-scotland.gov.uk

An impressive tower (one of a pair) built between 1813 and 1815 to provide
defence against the French and American privateers for the British convoys
assembling in the Sound of Longhope. Renovated in 1866 and used again in
World War I.

HARBOUR VIEW GALLERY 1643   4 G12

Harbour View Gallery, Port of Ness, Isle of Lewis. Near Butt of Lewis, 28 miles (45km)
north of Stornoway on A857. Daily bus service from Stornoway. Open Mar–Oct,
Mon–Sat 1000–1800; Nov–Feb by appointment. Free. Wheelchair access with
assistance. Car parking. Telephone (01851) 810735. www.abarber.co.uk

Artist's studio gallery in a scenic location at the northern tip of the Isle of Lewis,
situated above the old harbour and beach at Port of Ness. Contemporary, original
paintings by island based artist Anthony J. Barber. Also prints and cards.

HARRIS TWEED WEAVING AND KNITTING 1644   4 E15

4 Plockropool, Isle of Harris, Western Isles. On Golden Road, 5 miles (8km) south of
Tarbert. Bus from Tarbert. Open all year, Mon–Sat 0900–1900. Free. Gift shop. WC.
Wheelchair access. Car and coach parking. Telephone (01859) 511217.
www.harristweedproducts.com

Visitors can see Harris tweed being woven. Also demonstrations of warping,
bobbin winding and wool plying.

HEBRIDEAN BREWING COMPANY 1645   4 F14

18A Bells Road, Stornoway, Isle of Lewis. Short walk from ferry terminal, bus station
and town centre. Open Easter–Oct, daily 0900–1700. Free. Guided tours available by
arrangement. Gift shop. WC. Wheelchair access. Disabled WC. Telephone (01851)
700123. www.hebridean-brewery.co.uk

The only brewery in the Outer Hebrides, producing cask and bottled real ales.
All brewing and bottling takes place on site.

HEBRIDEAN JEWELLERY 1646   4 D18

Iochdar, South Uist, Western Isles. Located at the north end of South Uist near
Benbecula. Bus service from ferry terminals. Open all year, Mon–Fri 0900–1730, Sat
0930–1730, closed Sun. Free. Gift shop. WC. Wheelchair access with assistance. Car
and coach parking. Telephone (01870) 610288.

Celtic jewellery shop and workshop. Visitors can see five jewellers working with
silver, gold and gemstones. Commissions undertaken.

HERMANESS NATIONAL NATURE RESERVE AND VISITOR CENTRE 1647   1 V1

Shorestation, Burrafirth, Unst, Shetland. On the B9086, 3 miles (5km) north west of
Haroldswick. Bus from Lerwick to Haroldswick, Unst. Nature reserve open year
round daily. Visitor centre open Apr–Sep, daily 0900–1700. Free. Explanatory
displays. WC. Wheelchair access with assistance. Disabled WC. Car parking.
Telephone (01957) 711278 when open, otherwise (01595) 693345. www.nnr-
scotland.org.uk

Hermaness is home to over 100,000 seabirds during the summer. Displays in the
visitor centre simulate the sights and sounds of seabirdcliffs and moors for
those unable to visit the reserve

HIGHLAND PARK DISTILLERY   1648   3 Q10

Holm Road, Kirkwall, Orkney. 1 mile (2km) outside Kirkwall. Taxi from Kirkwall. On
local bus route. Open Apr–Oct, Mon–Fri 1000–1700 (tours every half hour, last tour
1600); May–Aug also open Sat 1000–1700 and –Sun 1200–1700; Nov–Mar, Mon–Fri
tour at 1400, shop open 1300–1700. Closed Christmas and New Year. Charge ££.
Children under 12 free. Group concessions. Guided tours (translations in French,
German and Norwegian). Explanatory displays (and audio-visual in English, French,
German, Italian, and Japanese). Gift shop. Coffee shop. Evening use of function suite
for meetings, functions or tastings. WC. Wheelchair access. Disabled WC. Car and
coach parking. Telephone (01856) 874619. www.highlandpark.co.uk

A 200-year-old distillery. Visitors can tour the distillery and traditional floor
maltings (still in use). Most days there is also a kiln burning. Visitor centre.

HOLM OF PAPA WESTRAY CHAMBERED CAIRN   1649   3 R9

HS. On the island of Holm of Papa Westray, Orkney. Ferry from Kirkwall to Westray,
then Papa Westray, then to Holm of Papa. Access at all reasonable times. Free.
Telephone (01856) 841815. www.historic-scotland.gov.uk

A massive tomb with a long narrow chamber divided into three, with 14 beehive
cells opening into the walls. There are engravings on the walls.

HOSWICK VISITOR CENTRE   1650   1 V5

Hoswick, Sandwick, Shetland. 14 miles (22.5km) south of Lerwick. Regular bus
service. Open May–Sep, Mon–Sat 1000–1700, Sun 1200–1700. Free. Explanatory
displays. Presentations on request. Gift shop. Tearoom. WC. Wheelchair access.
Disabled WC. Car and coach parking. Telephone (01950) 431405. www.sandwick-
community.co.uk

Previously a weaving shed and now an exhibition of old weaving looms and radios.
The history of the area is illustrated with photographs of mining, crofting, fishing
and knitting. Variety of documents on the social history of Shetland.

HOXA TAPESTRY GALLERY   1651   3 Q11

Neviholm, Hoxa, St Margaret's Hope, Orkney. On mainland 3 miles (5km) from St
Margaret's Hope and 18 miles (29km) south of Kirkwall. Open Apr–Sep, Mon–Fri
1000–1730, Sat and Sun 1400–1800. Oct–Mar by appointment. Charge £. Studio free.
Group concessions. Guided tours. Explanatory displays. Gift shop. No guide dogs.
Wheelchair access with assistance. Car and coach parking. Telephone (01856) 831395.
www.hoxatapestrygallery.co.uk

The gallery houses an exhibition of large, handwoven tapestries by Leila
Thomson, evoking the rhythm of the landscape of Orkney. Work in progress be
seen in the studio where you can also purchase cards and prints of the
tapestries.

HOY RSPB NATURE RESERVE   1652   3 P11

RSPB. Hoy, Orkney. On north west side of Hoy, opposite Dwarfie Stane footpath
entrance (car and coach parking at Rackwick). Ferry from Stromness to Moness Pier
(Linksness), or Houton to Lyness. Reserve open at all times. Free. Explanatory displays
(interpretation boards) and leaflets. Hoy ranger provides free guided walks. WC at
ferry terminal and Rackwick. Telephone (01856) 791298. www.rspb.org.uk/scotland

RSPB reserve includes the Old Man of Hoy sea stack. Visitors will see and hear a
wide range of birds, including skylarks, sea birds, peregrines and golden

plovers. The site contains the highest hill in Orkney (1571 feet/479m), natural field landscapes, lochans and a healthy population of mountain hares. Also Racknier Crofting Museum, the remains of a Bronze Age settlement and Berriedale, the remnants of Britain's most northerly native woodlands. See also 1634 Dwarfie Stane and 1679 Old Man of Hoy.

ISLESBURGH EXHIBITION   1653   1 V5

King Harald Street, Lerwick, Shetland. In Lerwick town centre, within walking distance from harbour and bus station. late May–early Sep, Mon and Wed 1900–2130. Charge £. Tea and coffee and Shetland bannocks with home made jam sold for supper. Car and coach parking. Telephone (01595) 692114. www.islesburgh.org.uk

A popular annual exhibition that has been held since 1947 to preserve and promote the traditional and contemporary arts and culture of Shetland. Locally produced knitwear and the work of local artists and craftspeople is for sale and on display. Also a reconstruction of a 1920s crofthouse, occasional film shows, fiddle music and Shetland dancing displays and archive and present-day photographs.

ITALIAN CHAPEL   1654   3 R11

Lambholm, Orkney. On mainland at St Mary's, 7 miles (11km) south of Kirkwall. Bus from Kirkwall. Open daily all year in daylight. Admission by donation. Booklets in English and Italian. Wheelchair access. Car and coach parking. Telephone (01856) 781268.

Two Nissen huts transformed into a chapel by Italian prisoners of war.

JARLSHOF PREHISTORIC AND NORSE SETTLEMENT   1655   1 V6

HS. Sumburgh, Shetland. On the A970 at Sumburgh Head, 22 miles (35km) south of Lerwick. Bus from Lerwick. Open Apr–Sep, daily 0930–1830. Charge £. Group concessions. Guided tours, audio guides available in English. Explanatory displays and visitor centre. Gift shop. WC. Limited wheelchair access. Car and coach parking. Telephone (01950) 460112. www.historic-scotland.gov.uk

An extraordinarily important site with a complex of ancient settlements within 3 acres (1.2ha). The oldest is a Bronze Age village of oval stone huts. Above this there is an Iron Age broch and wheelhouses, and even higher still an entire Viking settlement. On the crest of the mount is a house built around 1600. The displays explain Iron Age life and the history of the site.

ELMA JOHNSON'S ISLAND TRAILS   1656   1 V5

Island Trails, Seaview, Brake, Bigton, Shetland Islands. Regular tours at various times between May and September. Charge £££. Guided tours. Car parking. Telephone (01950) 422408. www.island-trails.co.uk

Guided tours offering peoples' stories, rather than architectural tours, including Shetland's oldest streets, smugglers and press gangs, a Shetland croft and traditional Shetland entertainment. Customised tours also offered.

KEEN OF HAMAR NATIONAL NATURE RESERVE   1657   1 W2

Keen of Hamar, Baltasound, Unst, Shetland. On the A968, 1 mile (1.5km) east of Baltasound. Bus from Lerwick. Open daily all year. Free. Guided tours on advertised days. No guide dogs. Car parking. Telephone (01595) 693335. www.nnr-scotland.org.uk

An important botanical site with unique habitat and landscape. A number of specialist plants grow on the serpentine soil.

KINLOCH MUSEUM   1658   4 F14

Laxay (Lacasaigh), Lochs, Isle of Lewis. On A859, 12 miles (19km) south of Stornoway.
Bus service between Stornoway and Tarbert. Open on request. Admission free but
donations welcome. Explanatory displays. WC. Wheelchair access. Disabled WC. Car
parking. Telephone (01851) 830778. www.lochs.net

A small museum and working base for Kinloch Historical Society, dealing with
the genealogy and history of the locality.

KIRBUSTER FARM MUSEUM   1659   3 Q10

Birsay, Orkney. At north end of mainland Orkney, 11 miles (17.5km) north of
Stromness. Open Mar–Oct, Mon–Sat 1030–1300 and 1400–1700, Sun 1400–1700.
Free. WC. Limited wheelchair access. Car parking. Telephone (01856) 771268.
www.orkney.org/museums

Museum housed in an Orkney farm, unusual in that it was of a higher standard
than the average Orkney farm of the time. Larger and better lit than its
contemporaries (see 1626 Corrigall Farm Museum), it was also unusual in that
the animals were housed in separate buildings. Collection of farm implements
and machinery, cottage garden.

KISIMUL CASTLE   1660   4 C20

HS. Castlebay, Isle of Barra, Western Isles. On a tiny island in the bay of Castlebay,
Isle of Barra. By air to Barra. Ferry to Castlebay from Oban and Lochboisdale. Ferry
to island. Open daily Apr–Sep, 0930–1830. Charge ££. Gift shop. Guide dogs
welcome if they can use a small boat. Telephone (01871) 810313. www.historic-
scotland.gov.uk

The only significant surviving medieval castle in the Western Isles, Kisimul
Castle is the seat of the Chiefs of Clan MacNeil. Explore the great hall, kitchen,
chapel, dungeon and tower.

KNAP OF HOWAR   1661   3 R9

HS. On the west side of the island of Papa Westray, Orkney. Ferry from Kirkwall to
Westray then to Papa Westray. Access at all reasonable times. Free. Telephone (01856)
872044. www.historic-scotland.gov.uk

Probably the oldest standing stone houses in north west Europe. Two Neolithic
dwellings, approximately rectangular with stone cupboards and stalls.

KNOWE OF YARSO CHAMBERED CAIRN   1662   3 Q10

HS. On the island of Rousay, Orkney. Bus from Kirkwall to Tingwall then ferry to
Rousay. Access at all reasonable times. Free. Telephone (01856) 751360. www.historic-
scotland.gov.uk

An oval cairn with concentric walls enclosing a chambered tomb divided into
three compartments. Neolithic.

LERWICK TOWN HALL   1663   1 V5

Lerwick, Shetland. In Lerwick town centre, within walking distance from harbour and
bus station. Open all year, Mon–Thur 0900–1700. Free. Guided tours. WC. Wheelchair
access. Disabled WC. Car and coach parking. Telephone (01595) 744502 or 744508.

Lerwick Town Hall stands on a commanding site on the ridge in the older part
of the town known as Hillhead. Built between autumn 1881 and summer 1883,

the chief attraction of the hall is the series of stained glass windows, gifted at the time of construction. These represent leading personalities in the early history of the islands, from Norwegian inhabitation in the 9th century to the pledging of the islands to Scotland in 1469.

LEWIS LOOM CENTRE   1664 — 4 F14

3 Bayhead, Stornoway, Lewis. In Stornoway town centre. Bus station within 0.25 miles (0.5km). Open all year, daily 0900–1800; other times by arrangement. Charge £. Craft shop free. Group concessions. Guided tours. Explanatory displays. Gift shop. WC. Wheelchair access. Car and coach parking. Telephone (01851) 704500 (work) or (01851) 703117 (home).

An enjoyable introduction to the history of Harris tweed. Information on sheep breeds and plant dyes, and demonstrations of hand spinning, looms and all aspects of producing finished cloth. Craft shop selling mostly local produce, tweeds and knitwear.

MAESHOWE   1665 — 3 Q10

HS. Stenness, Orkney. Off A965, 9 miles (14.5km) west of Kirkwall, Orkney. Bus from Kirkwall or Stromness, tour bus from Kirkwall. Open Apr–Sep, daily 0930–1830; Oct–Mar, Mon–Sat 0930–1630, Sun 1400–1630, . Charge £. Group concessions. Guided tours, telephone to arrange a tour time. Explanatory displays. Gift shop. Tearoom. WC. Limited wheelchair access. Car and coach parking. Telephone (01856) 761606. www.historic-scotland.gov.uk

The finest megalithic (Neolithic) tomb in the British Isles, consisting of a large mound covering a stone-built passage and a large burial chamber with cells in the walls. Runic inscriptions were carved in the walls by Vikings and Norse crusaders. Admission, shop and tearoom are at the nearby 19th-century Tormiston Mill (see 1722).

MIDHOWE BROCH AND CAIRNS   1666 — 3 Q9

HS. On the west coast of the island of Rousay, Orkney. Bus from Kirkwall to Tingwall, then ferry to Rousay. Access at all reasonable times. Free. Telephone (01856) 841815 (for ferry telephone (01856) 751360). www.historic-scotland.gov.uk

An Iron Age broch and walled enclosure situated on a promontory cut off by a deep rock ditch. Adjacent is Midhowe Stalled Cairn, a huge and impressive Neolithic chambered tomb in an oval mound with 25 stalls. Now protected by a modern building.

MINE HOWE   1667 — 3 R10

Mine Howe, Veltitigar Farmhouse, Tankerness, Orkney. Off the Kirkwall to Durness road. Open May and late Sep, Weds and Sun 1100–1400; Jun–Aug daily, 1100–1700; early Sep daily, 1100–1600. Telephone to confirm opening which may be extended. Charge £. Children under 5 free. Large groups by arrangement. Explanatory displays, leaflet available. Small gift shop. No guide dogs. Car and coach parking. Telephone (01856) 861234, out of season (01856) 861209.

Unique to Europe, this mysterious Iron Age archaeological site was re-discovered in 1999 and further excavated by television's *Time Team* in 2000. Twenty-six feet (8m) underground, down steep steps, there is a small chamber with two side chambers. Related to the site there is a broch, round howe and long howe.

MORVEN GALLERY 1668   4 F13

Upper Barvas, Isle of Lewis. 12 miles (19km) west of Stornoway. Bus from Stornoway. Open Mar–Oct, Mon–Sat 1030–1730. Free. Guided tours on request. Explanatory displays. Gift shop. Tearoom. WC. Wheelchair access. Car and coach parking. Telephone (01851) 840216. www.morvengallery.com

Fine art by local painters and sculptors. Ceramics, tapestry, carvings and contemporary designer knitwear. Talks, slide shows and conference facility. Workshops and children's activities.

MOUSA BOAT TRIPS 1669   1 V5

Leebitton, Sandwick, Shetland. Departure point for Mousa ferry is Sandwick, 15 miles (24km) south of Lerwick on A970. Bus service from Lerwick and Sumburgh to Sandwick. The ferry runs early Apr–mid Sep, daily (weather permitting). Charge £££. Group concessions. Guided tours, available on specific dates (telephone or visit website for details). Explanatory displays, map of island and general information given to all ferry passengers. Complimentary hot drinks and homebakes served on board. Tearoom in Sandwick. WC. Wheelchair access to ferry but island terrain unsuitable for wheelchairs. Disabled WC. Car and coach parking. Telephone (01950) 431367. www.mousaboattrips.co.uk

Short ferry journey to the tranquil and picturesque island of Mousa, location of Mousa Broch. Abundant wildlife, including common and grey seals, otters, porpoises and, occasionally, killer whales. Mousa is a RSPB Nature Reserve and famous for the breeding seabirds, including arctic terns, arctic skuas and great skuas, and over 6000 pairs of tiny, noctural storm petrels. The ferry has been fitted with a specially designed hydrophone, to allow passengers to listen to the animals. Also local history cruises – the ferry journey includes a description of the local history, illustrated with old photographs.

MOUSA BROCH 1670   1 V5

HS. On the island of Mousa, Shetland. Telephone for details of opening hours. Free. Telephone 01856 841815 (for ferry contact 01950 431367). www.historic-scotland.gov.uk

The finest surviving Iron Age broch tower, standing over 40 feet (12m) high. The stair can be climbed to the parapet.

MUCKLE FLUGGA AND OUT STACK 1671   1 V1

Unst Island, Shetland. At the northern tip of Shetland. Depart from the pier, Mid Yell. Minibus to departure point, booking essential. Open May–Sep, Wed 1000–1700 (weather permitting). Charge £££. Group concessions. Guided tours (available in French). Explanatory displays. Fare includes picnic lunch and tea, and hot drinks on boat. WC. Car parking. Telephone (01950) 422493.

All-day guided tour by motor boat to the seal islands of Yell Sound, the sensational cliffs of the west coast of Unst, around Muckle Flugga lighthouse and Out Stack and on to the Scottish Natural Heritage Centre at Hermaness National Nature Reserve (see 1647) at Burrafirth. See also 1709 Shetland Wildlife Tours and 1676 Noss National Nature Reserve.

MUNESS CASTLE 1672   1 W2

HS. At the south east corner of the island of Unst, Shetland. Bus from Lerwick. Open at all times (apply to keyholder). Free. Explanatory displays. Limited wheelchair access. Car and coach parking. Telephone (01856) 841815. www.historic-scotland.gov.uk

A late 16th-century tower house with fine detail and circular towers at diagonally opposite corners. The most northerly castle in the British Isles.

NESS HERITAGE CENTRE 1673   4 G12

Habost (Tabost), Ness, Lewis. Towards the Butt of Lewis, 28 miles (45km) from Stornoway on the A857. Bus service from Stornoway or taxi. Open Jun–Sep, Mon–Sat 1000–1730; Oct–May, Mon–Fri 1000–1730. Charge £. Guided tours (French and German by arrangement). Explanatory displays. Gift shop. Tea and coffee available, lunch can be arranged with advance notice. Genealogy archive and desk top publishing facilities. WC. Wheelchair access. Disabled WC. Car and coach parking. Telephone (01851) 810377.

The Heritage Centre (Comunn Eachdraidh Nis), a registered museum, provides a unique insight into the social and cultural heritage of the Western Isles. Over 500 artefacts and 7000 photographs illustrate the lifestyle of a people carving out an existence on the very edge of Europe. Genealogical information spanning 250 years proves an invaluable resource to visitors tracing their family histories and the adjoining tele-centre offers technological support and DTP services. Books, maps, videos and tapes for sale.

NESS OF BURGI 1674   1 U6

HS. At the south eastern point of Scatness, Shetland, about 1 mile (2km) south west of Jarlshof. Bus from Lerwick. Access at all reasonable times. Free. Telephone (01856) 841815. www.historic-scotland.gov.uk

A defensive stone blockhouse, probably from the Iron Age, with some features resembling a broch.

NOLTLAND CASTLE 1675   3 Q9

HS. On the island of Westray, Orkney. Ferry from Kirkwall to Westray. Open mid Jun–Sep, daily 0930–1630. Charge £. Telephone (01856) 841815. www.historic-scotland.gov.uk

A fine ruined Z-plan tower built between 1560 and 1573, but never completed. Remarkable for the large number of gun loops and the impressive winding staircase.

NOSS NATIONAL NATURE RESERVE 1676   1 V5

Noss Island, Shetland. Managed by Scottish Natural Heritage (01595) 693345. On an island off the east coast of Bressay by Lerwick. By boat (7 miles/11km) from Victoria Pier, Lerwick in M.V. Dunter II. May–Sep, Tue–Sun 1000 sailing. Charge £££. Group concessions. Guided tours (available in French). Explanatory leaflet. WC on board. Car parking. Telephone Shetland Wildlife Tours (01950) 422483.

A unique three-hour tour of some of Europe's finest scenery and wildlife habitats. Visitors can see up to 100,000 sea birds and dozens of seals at close range. Spectacular caves, sea statues and rock arches. Entertaining commentary on geology, local history and folklore of Bressay and Noss islands. Puffins visible before second week in August. See also 1671 Muckle Flugga and Out Stack, and 1709 Shetland Wildlife Tours.

OISEVAL GALLERY 1677   4 F13

James Smith Photography, Brue, Isle of Lewis. Bus from Stornoway. Open all year, Mon–Sat 1000–1730. Free. Explanatory displays. Limited wheelchair access. Car and coach parking. Telephone (01851) 840240. www.oiseval.co.uk

An exclusive collection of photographic landscapes and seascapes of the Outer Hebrides, including images of St Kilda.

OLD HAA VISITOR CENTRE 1678   1 V3

Burravoe, Yell, Shetland. On the island of Yell. Public transport limited. Open
Apr–Sep, Tue–Thu and Sat 1000–1600, Sun 1400–1700. Admission by donation.
Guided tours. Explanatory displays. Gift shop. Tearoom. Garden. WC. Car and coach
parking. Telephone (01957) 722339.

The oldest building on Yell, with exhibitions on local flora and fauna, arts and
crafts, and local themes of historic interest. Photographs, video and sound
recordings of local musicians, story telling. Genealogical information by
arrangement. Craft shop and art gallery.

OLD MAN OF HOY 1679   3 P11

North west coast of Isle of Hoy, Orkney.

A 450-feet (137m) high isolated stack (pillar) standing off the magnificent cliffs of
north west Hoy. The Old Man of Hoy can also be seen from the Scrabster to
Stromness Ferry. A challenge to experienced climbers. See also 1634 Dwarfie
Stane and 1652 Hoy RSPB Nature Reserve.

OLD SCATNESS IRON AGE VILLAGE 1680   1 V6

A970 Virkie, Sumburgh, Shetland. On the A970, 22 miles (35km) south of Lerwick,
turning right after airport traffic lights. Airport bus passes the gate. Open from Jul
2002, telephone for details. Charge £. Guided tours during excavation. Explanatory
displays. Gift shop Jul-Aug. Snacks available. WC. Limited wheelchair access.
Disabled WC. Car and coach parking. Telephone (01595) 694688. www.shetland-
heritage.co.uk/amenitytrust/

Iron Age Broch and village with excavations in progress. Village stands up to
head height. Visitor centre. Replicas of some buildings. During excavations
(Jul–Aug) living history and displays. Further facilities under development.

ORKNEY CHAIR 1681   3 Q10

Orkney Chair Maker, Rosegarth House, St Ola, Kirkwall, Orkney. In Orphir Road
(A964), 1.5 miles (2.5km) from town centre. Open all year, Mon–Fri 0900–1200 and
1400–1600. Free. Explanatory displays. Gift shop. Car parking. Telephone (01856)
873521. www.orkney-chair.co.uk

See craftspeople at work making traditional Orkney chairs.

ORKNEY MUSEUM 1682   3 Q10

The Orkney Museum, Broad Street, Kirkwall, Orkney. Central Kirkwall, opposite St
Magnus Cathedral. Open May–Sep, Mon–Sat 1000–1700, Sun 1400–1700; Oct–Apr,
Mon–Sat 1030–1230 and 1330–1700. Free. Guided tours by prior arrangement.
Explanatory displays. Gift shop. Garden. WC. Wheelchair access. Disabled WC.
Telephone (01856) 873535 or (01856) 872323.

The museum describes island life through 6000 years, with additional special
exhibitions. It is housed in a merchant-laird's mansion, with courtyard and
gardens, dating from 1574.

ORPHIR CHURCH AND THE EARL'S BU 1683   3 Q11

HS. By the A964, 8 miles (13km) west south-west of Kirkwall, Orkney. Bus from
Kirkwall to Houton. Access at all reasonable times. Free. Car and coach parking.
Telephone (01856) 841815. www.historic-scotland.gov.uk

Earl's Bu are the foundation remains of what may have been a Viking palace.
Nearby are the remains of Scotland's only 12th-century circular medieval church.

ORTAK VISITOR CENTRE   1684   3 Q10

Hatson Industrial Estate, Kirkwall, Orkney. Ten minute walk from centre of Kirkwall. Open Easter–Dec, Mon– Sat 0900–1700 (closed Sat from Jan–Easter). Free. Explanatory displays. Gift shop. Complimentary refreshments. WC. Limited wheelchair access. Disabled WC. Car and coach parking. Telephone (01856) 872224.

The Ortak Visitor Centre houses a permanent exhibition with a video presentation describing how modern jewellery is made and telling the story of Ortak.

OUR LADY OF THE ISLES   1685   4 D17

North of South Uist, Western Isles. Access at all reasonable times. Free.

On Reuval Hill – the Hill of Miracles – is the statue of the Madonna and Child, erected in 1957 by the Catholic community with contributions from all over the world. The work of Hew Lorimer, it is 30 feet (9m) high.

OUR LADY OF THE SEA   1686   4 C20

Heaval, on the Isle of Barra, Western Isles.

Heaval is the highest point in Barra at 1257 feet (383m), and on the slopes of the hill is erected an attractive statue of the Madonna and Child, symbol of the islanders' faith.

PAIRC MUSEUM   1687   4 F15

Old School, Gravir, South Lochs, Isle of Lewis. 25 miles (40km) from Stornoway. Bus service from Stornoway. Open Jul–Sep, daily 1400–1700. Admission by donation. Guided tours. Explanatory displays. Gift shop. Wheelchair access with assistance. Car and coach parking. Telephone (01851) 880225. www.lochs.net

Run by the Pairc Historical Society, most of the artefacts, such as photographs, certificates and a working loom, were given to the museum by local people. Booklets on individual villages, compiled by the society, are on sale, together with information on local points of interest, legends and characters.

PICKAQUOY CENTRE   1688   3 Q10

Muddisdale Road, Kirkwall, Orkney. Open all year, Mon–Fri 1000–2200, Sat–Sun 1000–2000 (many activities must be booked in advance). Creche open all year, Mon and Fri 1000–1200. Charge dependent on activity. Wheelchair access and changing facilities. Disabled WC. Telephone (01856) 879900. www.pickaquoy.com

Sports and events hall, health and fitness suite, floodlit athletics track and outdoor playing fields, print studio and darkroom, adventure play areas for under 10s and toddlers, football and hockey pitch, cinema with video and sound recording studios. Caravan and camping park within the centre complex

PIER ARTS CENTRE   1689   3 Q10

Victoria Street, Stromness, Orkney. Bus from Kirkwall. By ferry from Scrabster in Caithness. Open all year (except Christmas and New Year), Tue–Sat 1030–1230 and 1330–1700. Free. Explanatory displays. Gift shop. Picnic area. WC. Limited wheelchair access. Car and coach parking. Telephone (01856) 850209. www.pierartscentre.com

Former merchant's house (circa 1800), coal store and fishermen's sheds which have been converted into a gallery. Permanent collection of 20th-century paintings and sculpture as well as changing exhibitions.

PIEROWALL CHURCH   1690   3 Q9

HS. At Pierowall on the island of Westray, Orkney. Ferry from Kirkwall to Westray.
Access at all reasonable times. Free. Car parking. Telephone (01856) 841815.
www.historic-scotland.gov.uk

The ruins of a medieval church with some finely lettered tombstones.

QUENDALE WATER MILL   1691   1 U6

Quendale, Shetland. 4 miles (6.5km) from Sumburgh Airport. Open mid Apr–mid
Oct, daily 1000–1700. Charge £. Group concessions. Guided tours. Explanatory
displays and video programme. Gift shop. Hot and cold drinks available. WC.
Wheelchair access. Disabled WC. Car and coach parking. Telephone (01950) 460969
(during working hours). www.quendalemill.shetland.co.uk

A restored 19th-century over-shot water mill with displays of old croft
implements, photographs and family history. Souvenirs and local crafts in
reception area.

QUOYNESS CHAMBERED TOMB   1692   3 R9

HS. On the east side of Els Ness on the south coast of the island of Sanday, Orkney.
Ferry from Kirkwall to Sanday. Access at all reasonable times. Free. Telephone (01856)
841815. www.historic-scotland.gov.uk

A megalithic tomb with triple retaining walls containing a passage with a main
chamber and six secondary cells. Neolithic.

RENNIBISTER EARTH HOUSE   1693   3 Q10

HS. On the A965 about 4.5 miles (7km) west north-west of Kirkwall, Orkney. Bus
service from Kirkwall or Stromness. Access at all reasonable times. Free. Telephone
(01856) 841815. www.historic-scotland.gov.uk

A good example of an Orkney earth house, consisting of a passage and
underground chamber with supporting roof pillars.

RING OF BRODGAR STONE CIRCLE AND HENGE   1694   3 Q10

HS. Between Loch of Harray and Loch of Stenness, 5 miles (8km) north east of
Stromness, Orkney. Bus service from Kirkwall or Stromness. Access at all reasonable
times. Free. Car and coach parking. Telephone (01856) 841815. www.historic-
scotland.gov.uk

A magnificent circle of upright stones with an enclosing ditch spanned by
causeways. Neolithic. See also 1714 Stones of Stenness.

ROVING EYE   1695   3 Q11

Houton Pier, Mainland, Orkney. Houton is on the south coast of Mainland Orkney.
Subject to weather conditions, boat trips leave Houton Pier daily at 1320. Telephone
(01856) 811309 for up-to-date information. Charge £££. Not suitable for children
under 4. Group concessions available, please arrange in advance. Car parking.
Telephone (01856) 811360. www.rovingeye.co.uk

Trips aboard MV Guide to view images of the sunken German fleet in Scapa
Flow via a remote equipped underwater vehicle. The trip includes a video giving
the background to the scuttling of the fleet. The return journey passes colonies
of seals and a variety of seabirds.

ST CLEMENT'S CHURCH, RODEL 1696   4 E16

HS. At Rodel, at the south end of the Isle of Harris (Western Isles). Ferry to Tarbert, Stornoway or Leverburgh. Bus from Stornoway to Tarbert then on to Rodel. Access at all reasonable times. Free. Telephone (01667) 460232. www.historic-scotland.gov.uk

A fine 16th-century church built by Alexander MacLeod of Dunvegan and Harris. Contains his richly-carved tomb.

ST KILDA 1697   4 A15

NTS. Western Isles. 60 miles (96.5km) west of the Isle of Harris. For details of access contact NTS Regional Office on telephone number below. Access by arrangement. Telephone (01631) 570000. www.nts.org.uk

Evacuated in 1930, these remote islands are now a World Heritage Site, unrivalled for their sea bird colonies and rich in archaeological remains. Each year NTS work parties carry out conservation work.

ST MAGNUS CATHEDRAL, KIRKWALL 1698   3 Q10

Broad Street, Kirkwall, Orkney. In the centre of Kirkwall. Car and coach parking nearby, and disabled parking. Bus from ferries or taxi from airport. Open Apr–Sep, Mon–Sat 0900–1800, Sun 1400–1800; Oct–Mar, Mon–Sat 0900–1300 and 1400–1700. Graveyard open all year. Free. Guided tours by arrangement. Explanatory displays. Bookstall. Braille guide. Wheelchair access to half the building. Telephone (01856) 874894.

Founded by Jarl Rognvald and dedicated to his uncle, St Magnus. The remains of both men are in the massive east choir piers. The original building dates from 1137–1200, but sporadic additional work went on until the late 14th century. It contains some of the finest examples of Norman architecture in Scotland, with small additions in transitional styles and some early Gothic work. In regular use as a church. See also 1699 St Magnus Centre.

ST MAGNUS CENTRE 1699   3 Q10

Palace Road, Kirkwall, Orkney. East of St Magnus Cathedral cemetery. Bus station in Kirkwall, tour buses stop near centre. Open Apr–Sep, Mon–Sat 0930–1730, Sun 1330–1730; Oct–Mar, Mon–Sat 1230–1400. Free. Guided tours and audio guide. Explanatory displays. Gift shop. Tea and coffee available. WC. Wheelchair access. Disabled WC. Car parking. Telephone (01856) 878326.

A source of information on St Magnus and his cathedral. A 17 minute video, Saga of Saint Magnus, tells the story of St Magnus in six languages. Study library. Spectacular views of the east end of St Magnus Cathedral (see 1698).

SAWMILL WOODLANDS CENTRE 1700   4 F14

Castle Grounds, Stornoway, Isle of Lewis. Overlooking Stornoway harbour. Open all year, Mon–Sat 1000–1700. Free. Guided walks. Displays on natural heritage and local history. Shop selling gifts and local crafts. Café. Picnic area. WC. Wheelchair access. Disabled WC. Car and coach parking. Telephone (01851) 706916.

A woodland resource centre located in the grounds of Lews Castle. The centre is the starting point for walks throughout the grounds.

SCALLOWAY CASTLE 1701   1 V5

HS. In Scalloway, 6 miles (9.5km) west of Lerwick, Shetland. Bus from Lerwick. Telephone for opening times. Free. Explanatory displays. Car parking. Telephone (01856) 841815. www.historic-scotland.gov.uk

A fine castellated mansion built in 1600 in medieval style by Patrick Stewart, Earl of Orkney. Fell into disuse in 1615.

SCALLOWAY MUSEUM 1702   1 V5

Main Street, Scalloway, Shetland. 7 miles (11km) west of Lerwick. Bus stop at the Public Hall. Open May–Sep, Mon 0930–1130 and 1400–1630, Tue–Fri 1000–1200 and 1400–1630, Sat 1000–1230 and 1400–1630. Sun by arrangement. Admission by donation. Guided tours. Explanatory displays. Gift shop. WC. Wheelchair access. Disabled WC nearby. Car and coach parking. Telephone (01595) 880783 or 880666.

Artefacts and photographs cover the history of Scalloway over the past 100 years, including its involvement with the fishing industry. A major section is devoted to Scalloway's unique role in World War II, when it was a secret base for Norwegian freedom fighters, as 16 Norwegian fishing boats ran a shuttle service to Norway carrying in weapons, ammunition and radio sets, returning with refugees. Realising the importance of this operation, the US Government donated three submarine chasers which operated between 1942 and 1945. Books on the shuttle service available.

SCAPA FLOW VISITOR CENTRE 1703   3 Q11

Lyness, Stromness, Orkney. A few minutes' walk from Lyness ferry terminal. Open all year Mon–Fri 0900–1630; mid May–Oct also Sat and Sun 1030–1530. Free. Guided tours. Explanatory displays. Gift shop. Restaurant. WC. Custodian trained in sign language. Limited wheelchair access (easy access to part of the site). Disabled WC. Car and coach parking. Telephone (01856) 791300.

Scapa Flow was a major naval anchorage in both wars and the scene of the surrender of the German High Seas Fleet in 1919. Today a centre of marine activity as Flotta is a pipeline landfall and tanker terminal for North Sea Oil. The visitor centre is housed in the old pumphouse which was used to feed fuel to ships. See also 1695 Roving Eye.

SEALLAM! EXHIBITION AND GENEALOGY CENTRE 1704   4 E16

Seallam! Visitor Centre, Northton, Isle of Harris. 17 miles (27km) south of Tarbert on A859. Ferry service from Uig and North Uist, bus service from Stornoway or Tarbert. Open all year, Mon–Sat 1000–1700 and by appointment for evenings. Charge £. Group concessions. Guided tours (also available in Gaelic). Explanatory displays. Gift and book shop. Refreshments and picnic area. Baby changing facilities. WC. Wheelchair access. Disabled WC. Car and coach parking. Telephone (01859) 520258. www.seallam.com

A major exhibition on the Hebrides and a genealogical resource.

SHAWBOST SCHOOL MUSEUM 1705   4 F13

Shawbost, Isle of Lewis. 19 miles (31km) north west of Stornoway. Bus from Stornoway. Open Apr–Sep, Mon–Sat 0930–1630. Admission by donation. Explanatory displays. WC. Wheelchair access with assistance. Disabled WC. Car and coach parking. Telephone (01851) 710212.

Created under the Highland Village Competition of 1970, the museum illustrates the old way of life in Lewis.

SHETLAND CROFT HOUSE MUSEUM 1706   1 V6

South Voe, Boddam, Dunrossness, Shetland. On an unclassified road, east of the A970, 25 miles (40km) south of Lerwick. Bus from Lerwick to Boddam. Open

May–Sep, daily 1000–1300 and 1400–1700. Admission free but donations welcome. Guided tours. WC. Car and coach parking. Telephone (01950) 460557.

A 19th-century drystone and thatched croft, consisting of inter-connected house, barn, byre, kiln and stable with watermill nearby. Furnished throughout with period implements, fixtures and furniture. Exhibits include box beds, sea chests, working mill and quern.

SHETLAND MUSEUM   1707   1 V5

Lower Hillhead, Lerwick, Shetland. In the town centre near the Town Hall. Open Mon, Wed and Fri 1000–1900, Tue, Thu and Sat 1000–1700. Free. Explanatory displays. Gift shop. WC. Wheelchair access with assistance. Disabled WC. Car and coach parking. Telephone (01595) 695057. shetland.museum@zetnet.co.uk

A museum covering all aspects of Shetland's history and prehistory. Archaeology from neolithic to medieval times including early Christian sculpture, Viking grave finds, medieval domestic and fishing items. Maritime displays cover fisheries, merchant marine and shipwrecks. Models, fishing gear, maritime trades. Agriculture and domestic life collection, including basketwork, peat cutting, 19th-century social history. Costume display and textiles. Temporary art exhibitions.

SHETLAND TEXTILE WORKING MUSEUM   1708   1 V4

Weisdale Mill, Weisdale, Shetland. 7 miles (11km) west of Lerwick, take A971 and turn right on B9075 for 0.6 mile (1km). Local bus from Lerwick (not Sun) then 0.5 mile (1km) walk. Open mid Mar–Sep, Tue–Sat 1030–1630, Sun 1200–1630. Charge £. Children admitted free. Group concessions. Guided tours, staff available to talk about exhibits. Explanatory displays. Café. WC. Wheelchair access. Disabled WC. Car parking. Telephone (01595) 830419.

A unique collection of Shetland textiles illustrating the history of spinning, knitting and weaving in the islands from their earliest development to the present day. Augmented by a fine collection of artefacts used in the production of these items. Workshops in spinning and knitting arranged and visitors have the opportunity to see demonstrations of local craft skills.

SHETLAND WILDLIFE TOURS   1709   1 V6

Longhill, Maywick, Shetland. Pick-up/drop-off service available on all tours, booking essential. Telephone for details of tours. Charge £££ (dependent on tour). Group concessions. Guided tours. Explanatory displays. Telephone (01950) 422493.

Half-day to seven-day wildlife tours throughout the Shetland Islands with expert naturalist guides. See also 1671 Muckle Flugga and Out Stack, and 1676 Noss National Nature Reserve.

SKAILL HOUSE   1710   3 P10

Breckness Estate, Sandwick, Orkney. Beside Skara Brae, 5 miles (8km) north of Stromness. Public transport from Stromness to Skara Brae during the summer. Open Apr–Sep, Mon–Sat 0930–1830, Sun 0930–1830. Charge £££. Joint ticket with Skara Brae (see 1711) available from visitor centre. Group concessions. Guided tours. Explanatory displays. Gift shop. Garden. WC. Wheelchair access to ground floor. Disabled WC. Car and coach parking. Telephone (01856) 841501. www.skaillhouse.com

The most complete 17th-century mansion house in Orkney. Built for Bishop George Graham in the 1620s, it has been inhabited by successive lairds, who have added to the house over the centuries. On show – Captain Cook's dinner service from his ship the *Resolution*, and gunroom with sporting and military memorabilia. Surrounded by spacious gardens.

SKARA BRAE PREHISTORIC VILLAGE   1711   3 P10

HS. Sandwick, Orkney. On the B9056, 19 miles (30km) north west of Kirkwall. Bus from Stromness, tour bus from Kirkwall. Open Apr–Sep, daily 0930–1830; Oct–Mar, Mon–Sat 0930–1630, Sun 1400–1630. Charge ££. During summer joint ticket with Skaill House (see 1710). Group concessions. Explanatory displays. Gift shop. Restaurant, tearoom and picnic area. Wheelchair access with assistance. Disabled WC. Car and coach parking. Telephone (01856) 841815. www.historic-scotland.gov.uk

The best preserved group of Stone Age houses in Western Europe. The houses are joined by covered passages and contain stone furniture, heaths and drains. They give a remarkable picture of life in Neolithic times.

STANYDALE TEMPLE   1712   1 U4

HS. 3.5 miles (5.5km) east north-east of Walls, Shetland. Bus from Lerwick to Bridge of Walls. Access at all reasonable times. Free. Telephone (01856) 841815. www.historic-scotland.gov.uk

A Neolithic hall, heel-shaped externally and containing a large oval chamber. Surrounded by the ruins of houses, walls and cairns of the same period.

STEINACLEIT CAIRN AND STONE CIRCLE   1713   4 F13

HS. At the south end of Loch an Duin, Shader, 12 miles (19km) north of Stornoway, Isle of Lewis (Western Isles). Ferry from Ullapool to Stornoway, then bus service from Stornoway to Saidar Larach. Access at all reasonable times. Free. Telephone (01667) 460232. www.historic-scotland.gov.uk

The remains of an enigmatic building of early prehistoric date.

STONES OF STENNESS   1714   3 Q10

HS. Between Loch of Harray and Loch of Stenness, about 5 miles (8km) north east of Stromness, Orkney. Buses from Kirkwall or Stromness. Access at all reasonable times. Free. Car and coach parking. Telephone (01856) 841815. www.historic-scotland.gov.uk

The remains of a stone circle surrounded by traces of a circular earthwork. See also 1694 Ring of Brodgar Stone Circle and Henge.

SUMBURGH HEAD RSPB NATURE RESERVE   1715   1 V6

RSPB. Sumburgh, Shetland. Southern-most tip of Mainland Shetland, 2 miles (3km) from Sumburgh airport. Reserve open at all times. Free. Guided tours. Limited wheelchair access. Car and coach parking. Telephone (01950) 460800. www.rspb.org.uk/scotland

The cliffs around Sumburgh Head attract thousands of breeding seabirds, including puffins, guillemots, shags and fulmars. Gannets are regularly seen off-shore and sometimes whales and dolphins.

TAIGH CHEARSABHAGH MUSEUM AND ARTS CENTRE   1716   4 D17

Lochmaddy, North Uist, Western Isles. 109 yards (100m) from Lochmaddy Pier. Open all year, Mon–Sat 1000–1700. Admission to museum by donation. Galleries free. Group concessions. Explanatory displays. Gift shop. Tearoom. WC. Wheelchair access. Disabled WC. Car and coach parking. Telephone (01876) 500293. www.taigh-chearesabhagh.org

Local museum and art gallery with over 3000 archive photos of North Uist. Also sculpture trail. Winner of Highlands and Islands Community Business award.

TAIGH DHONNCHAIDH ARTS AND MUSIC CENTRE   1717   4 G12

44 Habost, Ness, Isle of Lewis. 28 miles (45km) north west of Stornoway at the northerly tip of Lewis. Bus service from Stornoway or taxi. Opening times vary. Please telephone or visit website for information. Charges dependent upon event. Information boards and leaflets. Refreshments available nearby. WC. Wheelchair access. Disabled WC. Car parking. Telephone (01851) 810166. www.taighdhonnchaidh.com

Taigh Dhonnchaidh – Gaelic for Duncan's House – is an arts and music centre located in Ness, the most northerly community in the Hebridean chain. The centre runs weekly classes in traditional music, song, dance and art, also hosting a series of festivals, a summer school, concerts, lectures and ceilidhs presented by local and touring artists.

TANGWICK HAA MUSEUM   1718   1 U3

Eshaness, Shetland. About 40 miles (64km) north of Lerwick via A970 and B9078. Open May–Sep, Mon–Fri 1300–1700, Sat–Sun 1100–1900. Free. Explanatory displays. Gift shop. WC. Limited wheelchair access. Disabled WC. Car and coach parking. Telephone (01806) 503389.

A museum in a restored 17th-century house built by the Cheyne family. Shows various aspects of life (agriculture, fishing, spinning and knitting) in Northmavine through the ages, using photographs and artefacts. Exhibition changes annually.

TAVERSOE TUICK CHAMBERED CAIRN   1719   3 Q9

HS. On the island of Rousay, Orkney. Bus from Kirkwall to Tingwall and then ferry to Rousay. Access to chambers at all reasonable times. Free. Telephone (01856) 841815. www.historic-scotland.gov.uk

A Neolithic chambered mound with two burial chambers, one above the other.

TEAMPULL NA TRIONAID   1720   4 D17

Cairinis (Carinish), close to A865, North Uist.

Ruined remains of an important ecclesiastical site, founded by Beatrice, daughter of Somerled, Lord of the Isles, in about 1203 on the foundations of an earlier place of worship. A major centre of learning in medieval times.

TOMB OF THE EAGLES   1721   3 Q11

Liddle, South Ronaldsay, Orkney. On South Ronaldsay, 20 miles (32km) south of Kirkwall. Ferry, then bus to Burwick in summer (to St Margaret's Hope in winter). Open Apr–Oct 0930–1800; Nov–Feb by arrangement; Mar 1000–1200. Charge ££. Group concessions. Guided tours with some bad weather clothing provided. Explanatory displays. Gift shop. Baby changing facilities. WC. Personal guide for blind visitors in hands-on museum. Limited wheelchair access (easy access in visitor centre). Disabled WC. Car and coach parking. Telephone (01856) 831339. www.tomboftheeagles.co.uk

Tour starts at museum, which contains original artefacts, and proceeds to 5000-year-old tomb. Also a Bronze Age house. Cliff walk and wildlife to see en route.

TORMISTON MILL   1722   3 Q10

HS. On the A965 about 9 miles (14.5km) west of Kirkwall, Orkney. Open Apr–Sep, Mon–Sun 0930–1830; Oct–Mar, Mon–Sat 0930–1830, Sun 1400–1630. Explanatory displays. Gift shop. Tearoom. WC. Car and coach parking. Telephone (01856) 761606. www.historic-scotland.gov.uk

An excellent late example of a Scottish water mill, probably built in the 1880s. The water wheel and most of the machinery have been retained. Now forms a reception centre for visitors to Maeshowe (1665).

UI CHURCH   1723   4 G14

At Aiginis, off A866, 2 miles (3km) east of Stornoway, Isle of Lewis. Access at all reasonable times. Free. Car parking.

Ruined church (pronounced eye) containing some finely carved ancient tombs of the Macleods of Lewis.

UNST   1724   1 V2

NTS. Shetland. At the northern tip of Shetland. Ferry from Aberdeen to Lerwick, then two further ferries. Open all year. Free. Car parking. Telephone (01463) 232034. www.nts.org.uk

Four-thousand-acre (1619ha) estate at the northernmost tip of Britain, interesting for its geology, botany and bird life. The west coast areas are especially beautiful. The land is mostly farmed and there is an excellent Shetland Pony stud.

UNST BOAT HAVEN   1725   1 W1

Haroldswick, Unst, Shetland. At the north end of Unst. Ferry from Mainland Shetland. Open May–Sep, daily 1400–1700. Charge £. Explanatory displays. Gift shop. Adjacent tearoom. Wheelchair access. Disabled WC. Car and coach parking. Telephone (01957) 711528.

The main museum floor area represents a Shetland beach scene, with various traditional boats drawn up and 'afloat'. Around the walls are sections relating to particular aspects of Shetland's maritime heritage – herring fishing, line fishing and boat building, and written information, old photographs and models. One end of the building is covered by a mural of a Shetland beach scene in the 1880s, and the other by a large wall mirror. Also a fine collection of Unst seashell, a bottle message from America and a selection of poems.

UNST HERITAGE CENTRE   1726   1 W1

Haroldswick, Unst, Shetland. At the north end of Unst. Ferry from Mainland Shetland. Open May–Sep, daily 1400–1700. Charge £. Children free. Explanatory displays. Sales area. WC. Wheelchair access. Disabled WC. Car and coach parking. Telephone (01957) 711528.

Local history and family trees of Unst.

UNSTAN CHAMBERED CAIRN   1727   3 Q10

HS. About 3.5 miles (5.5km) north north-east of Stromness, Orkney. Bus from Kirkwall or Stromness. Access to chamber at all reasonable times. Free. Telephone (01856) 841815. www.historic-scotland.gov.uk

A mound covering a Neolithic stone burial chamber, divided by slabs into five compartments.

UP HELLY AA EXHIBITION   1728   1 V5

St Sunniva Street, Lerwick, Shetland. In Lerwick. Open May–Sep, Sat and Tue 1400–1600, Fri 1900–2100. Charge £. Children under 6 free. Group concessions. Explanatory displays. WC. Wheelchair access. Car and coach parking.

An exhibition of artefacts, photographs, costumes and a replica galley from the annual fire festival of *Up Helly Aa*. Audio-visual show.

URQUHART CASTLE   1729   2 L18

HS. Drumnadrochit, Inverness. An the A82 beside Loch Ness, 2 miles (3km) south east of Drumnadrochit. Nearest railway station Inverness, bus service from Inverness. Open Apr–Sep, daily 0930–1830; Oct–Mar, daily 0930–1630. Charge £££. Group concessions. Audio-visual displays. Café and shop selling local products. WC. Disability buggies available. Wheelchair access. Disabled WC. Car and coach parking. Telephone (01456) 450551. www.historic-scotland.gov.uk

The ruins of one of the largest castles in Scotland, which fell into decay after 1689 and was blown up in 1692 to prevent it being occupied by Jacobites. Most of the existing remains date from the 16th century and include a tower. The visitor centre tells the story of the castle.

WESTRAY HERITAGE CENTRE   1730   3 Q9

Pierowall, Westray, Orkney. 7 miles (11km) from ferry terminal, minibus to Pierowall village during summer. Open Sun and Mon, 1130–1700, Tue–Sat, 1000–1200 and 1400–1700. Charge £. Children under 5, youth and school groups free. Group concessions. Explanatory displays. Gift shop. Tearoom and picnic area. WC. Wheelchair access. Disabled WC. Car and coach parking.

A display on the natural heritage of Westray. Many children's hands-on activities. Large collection of black and white photos. Information on local cemeteries. Local memories of wartimes, schooldays, Noup Head lighthouse, sports, kirks, fishing and crafts, and sea transport.

WESTSIDE CHURCH   1731   3 Q9

HS. At Bay of Tuquoy on the south coast of the island of Westray, Orkney. Ferry from Kirkwall to Westray. Access at all reasonable times. Free. Telephone (01856) 841815. www.historic-scotland.gov.uk

A roofless 12th-century Romanesque church.

WHALEBONE ARCH   1732   4 F13

Bragar, on the western side of the Isle of Lewis.

This arch is made from the huge jawbone of a blue whale that came ashore in 1920.

WIDEFORD HILL CHAMBERED CAIRN   1733   3 Q10

HS. On the west slope of Wideford Hill, 2 miles (3km) west of Kirkwall, Orkney. Access to chamber, 0.5m hillwalk, at all times. Free. Telephone (01856) 841815. www.historic-scotland.gov.uk

A fine Neolithic chambered cairn with three concentric walls and a burial chamber with three large cells.

INDEX

Visitor attractions are indexed under the following subjects: